MARK

MARK
A Theological Commentary for Preachers

Cascade Books
An Imprint of Wipf and Stock Publishers
199 W. 8th Ave., Suite 3
Eugene, OR 97401

www.wipfandstock.com

ISBN 13: 978-1-61097-419-6

Cataloging-in-Publication data:

Kuruvilla, Abraham

    Mark : a theological commentary for preachers / Abraham Kuruvilla

    xxviii + 398 p. ; 23 cm. Includes bibliographical references and indexes.

    ISBN 13: 978-1-61097-419-6

    1. Bible. N.T. Mark—Commentaries. I. Title.

BS2585.53 K85 2012

Manufactured in the U.S.A.

To my colleagues
in the
Department of Pastoral Ministries
Dallas Theological Seminary

who teach their students
ἵνα ὦσιν μετ᾽ [Ἰησοῦ]
καὶ ἵνα ἀποστέλλῃ αὐτοὺς κηρύσσειν

(*that they may be with [Jesus],*
and that He may send them to preach)
Mark 3:14

CONTENTS

Contents

ACKNOWLEDGMENTS

". . . brothers and sisters and mothers and children . . ."

Mark 10:30

Those who promoted this venture, particularly by encouraging me with developing the underlying philosophy of this commentary, are many. They go back several years, having cheered me on in my studying, my preaching, my "dissertating," my teaching, and now in my writing. I am grateful to all of them and to God for bringing them into (and keeping them in) my life.

Particularly, in this regard, I continue to be blessed by my father, and my brother and his family, who have borne with my idiosyncrasies for the longest time with patience and goodwill.

For the last two years, every time I saw them, the Morgans would ask me how this project was coming along. There were times when I attacked my scribing task with gusto, just to be able to tell them that, yes, it was moving along fine. Well, folks, it is done! Your love and prayers (and food) helped. Thank you!

Timothy Warren, erstwhile teacher of mine, now colleague and neighbor, would drop into my dwellings on his way to a local park, waving portions of the drafts of the manuscript drenched in his trademark purple ink, to tell me what I could have done better. I took his advice. I always have!

Several generations of students in Dallas Theological Seminary's narrative preaching class, PM104 (which considers the preaching of the Gospel of Mark), suffered through earlier iterations of this work. Those classes were (and still are) delightful laboratories, and those eager seminarians—as well as a number of able graduate teaching assistants—were willing subjects for my hermeneutical "experiments." Hopefully they learned something in the process. In all likelihood, though, I learned more from them than they did from me. I am grateful to God for these who have blessed me in more ways than one, not the least of which was by affording me the privilege of hearing them preach through this magnificent work by Mark each semester that I taught the course.

I am thankful for my colleagues in the Department of Pastoral Ministries at Dallas Seminary for the decades of careful attention they have given to the pedagogy of all matters homiletical, particularly the preaching of the Second Gospel. They have persevered in this endeavor with the fervent hope that their students would not only learn how to preach a narrative text, but also take the lessons of this marvelous piece of inspired Scripture to heart, and "accept the demands of following 'the way of God' in faithful, sacrificial service" (from the *PM104 Expository Preaching II Syllabus*, Spring 2011). To these worthy ones, who labor hard both in the classroom and outside for God's glory, this commentary is dedicated. I am proud to be a part of that team.

A number of friends and fellow seminarians over the years have engaged me in numerous discussions about this Gospel, chiasms, Mark's *doing* with what he was *saying*, the "world in front of the text," etc. Several of them also took on the burden of scrutinizing preliminary versions of the manuscript of this commentary. I am grateful to all who have been game to joust about these issues, and for the feedback they provided and the wisdom I have absorbed from them ἐν τῇ ὁδῷ ("on the way"). In addition to those already mentioned, thanks are especially due to Tommy and Caroline Buie, John Hilber, Rick and Jenny DiMuzio, Juan Eclarin, and A. K. Kuruvilla.

Going through Mark in the process of writing this commentary was a unique blessing in itself, reminding me of the need to reassess and reevaluate my own "Trip of Discipleship." It has been a healthy spiritual undertaking for me personally, and I have come away with a renewed sense of vigor and a deeper faith in, and a greater love for, the Lord Jesus Christ, the one who *did not come to be served, but to serve and to give his life a ransom for* me.

Abraham Kuruvilla
Dallas, Texas
Easter 2011

PREFACE

Rationale, Goal, Assumptions, Structure, and Use

THE AMERICAN SCHOLAR AND philosopher Richard Weaver (1910–1963) once asserted: "The honest rhetorician therefore has two things in mind: a vision of how matters should go ideally and ethically and a consideration of the special circumstances of his auditors. Toward both of these he has a responsibility."[1] One might apply the same sentiment towards homileticians: they have a responsibility to the text of Scripture ("how matters should go ideally and ethically") and to the world of their listeners ("the special circumstances of auditors"). In fact, this is the crux of the preaching endeavor—to bring to bear divine guidelines for life from the biblical text upon the situations of the congregation, to align the community of God to the will of God, for the glory of God. In other words, the ancient text is to be applied to the modern audience. Crucial to the undertaking of homiletics is that such application be both faithful to the textual intention (i.e., authoritative) and fitting for the listening audience (i.e., relevant). This is the preacher's burden—the translation from the *then* of the text to the *now* of listeners. This commentary is part of a larger attempt to help the preacher move from text to praxis.

RATIONALE OF THE COMMENTARY[2]

Particularly pertinent is how this translation from text to praxis may be conducted with respect to the "bite-sized" portion or quantum of the scriptural text that is employed weekly in the corporate gathering of the body of Christ—the preaching unit, the pericope.[3] The pericope is the basic textual unit of Scripture handled in such assemblies, and it is the foundational element of the weekly address from the Word of

---

1. Weaver, *Language Is Sermonic*, 211.

2. For those not particularly inclined towards some of these more academic recitals, they may be skipped without undue loss. The later section "How to Use the Commentary" will, however, be profitable for the reader.

3. While acknowledging its more common connotation of a portion of the Gospels, "pericope" is employed here to demarcate a segment of Scripture, irrespective of genre or length, that forms the textual basis for an individual sermon.

God. What in this slice of Scripture is intended to be carried over into the life of the Christian? What exactly is the author of the text saying that needs to be heard by the listeners of the sermon?[4]

Pericopal Theology

Elsewhere it was proposed that the critical component of the ancient text to be borne into the lives of the modern audience by way of application is the *theology of the pericope.* Pericopal theology is the ideological vehicle through which divine priorities, principles, and practices are propounded for appropriation by readers.[5] This species of theology presents to the Christian "how matters should go ideally and ethically." A biblical pericope is thus a literary instrument inviting men and women to organize their lives in congruence with the theology revealed in that pericope. The goal of any homiletical transaction, thus, is the gradual alignment of the people of God, week by week, to the theology of the biblical pericopes that are preached. Thus it is pericope by pericope that the various aspects of Christian life, individual as well as corporate, are progressively and gradually brought into accord with God's design for his creation—the goal of preaching: faith nourished, hope animated, confidence made steadfast, good habits confirmed, dispositions created, character molded, Christlikeness established.[6]

All such discrete units of pericopal theology together compose a plenary, canonical understanding of God and his relationship to his people, with each individual quantum of pericopal theology forming the weekly ground of life transformation. The interpretation of a pericope at the periodic gathering of the church, then, must portray the particular pericopal portion of the larger canonical vision of the whole. In other words, each homiletical undertaking must delineate the theology of the pericope under consideration, elucidating what that specific text affirms about God and his relationship to mankind. Then, and only then, can valid application be proposed in the sermon, as the people of God are urged by the preacher to align their lives, in specific ways relevant to them, to the theology of that particular text—God's idea of "how matters should go ideally and ethically." It is in the performance of such specific application that that text becomes praxis in the believer and in the church.

The thrust of this commentary, therefore, is essentially this: to develop the theology of each pericope for preachers (the essence of which is to be captured in a sentence—the Theological Focus), so that they may be able to proceed from that crucial intermediary to a sermon that provides valid application, i.e., application that is both authoritative and relevant. Application derived from the Theological Focus becomes *authoritative* because of the integral link of the theology to the text: the theology of the pericope is derived from a close reading of the text and is specific for any given text.

4. For the purposes of this commentary, no particular distinction will be made between divine and human authors of the biblical text. Whenever "Mark" is used to denote the author, it is understood to indicate "Mark/Holy Spirit."

5. See Kuruvilla, *Text to Praxis*, 142–90, for an extended account of the hermeneutic underlying this commentary. Also see idem, "Pericopal Theology."

6. Adapted from Tertullian, *Apol.* 39.

Application derived from this focus becomes *relevant* when the homileticians, keenly aware of the circumstances of listeners in their pastoral capacity, specify application in terms that are pertinent to their situation. There is, thus, a twofold aspect to the sermonic transaction: the exposition of the theological focus of the pericope, and the delineation of how the latter may be applied in real life.

The first move, from text to theology, draws meaning *from* the biblical text with authority; the second, from theology to praxis, directs meaning *to* the situations of listeners with relevance.[7] The advantage of employing theology as the intermediary between text and praxis is that its specificity for (or proximity to) the chosen text makes possible a weekly movement from pericope to pericope, without the tedium of repetition of theological themes, but with a clear progression and development of theological ideas as one traverses the length of a biblical book. This commentary will be particularly helpful, it is hoped, for those who seek to preach in that fashion. To the goal of aiding the preacher with discovering the theological focus of each pericope, this entire work is dedicated. Analysis of the text of Mark's Gospel will therefore be sharply focused upon arriving at the Theological Focus of the pericope. From this locus, the preacher may discover valid application for a sermon.

Pericopal Theology and Mark's Gospel

Mark, in the creation of his gospel story, is not only *saying* something therein, he is also *doing* something with what he is saying.[8] While no doubt a faithful depiction of what actually happened—there is no reason to question the veracity of his account—the narrative of characters and events are to be primarily interpreted as furthering the theological purpose of the writer.[9] The narrative is the "gospel writer's theological perspective through the medium of story."[10] In and through each pericope, a theological idea is being conveyed; pericopal theology (crystallized in this commentary as the

---

7. This commentary expends most of its energy in helping the preacher with this first move, from text to theology (Theological Focus). The latter move, from theology to sermon and application, will not take up as much space in this work for obvious reasons: beyond a few general guidelines (which the commentary does provide, including two possible sermon outlines for each pericope), it is nigh impossible for a third party to determine how exactly specific application is to be provided for a particular audience. That task is between the preacher, the Holy Spirit, and the congregation.

8. Such a view of a "speech" act (which includes written "text" acts as well) is at the core of the field of pragmatics, and forms the ground for discovering the theology of pericopes. See Kuruvilla, *Text to Praxis*, 30–35; and idem, "Pericopal Theology."

9. "The Gospel was written to do something, to persuade or move people to action. All the characters in the Gospel are fashioned to promote that goal, and all of them, regardless of their traditional or historical roots, are also subordinated to that goal, for such an understanding of character-building forms the horizon of writing, reading, and hearing in which the author and first audiences of the Gospel lived" (Tolbert, "How the Gospel of Mark Builds Character," 349).

10. Marshall, *Faith as a Theme*, 29.

Theological Focus) is the goal of the analysis of each pericope in this commentary. Historical material is employed by the Evangelist with a theological purpose in mind, a purpose that Ernest Best is convinced is pastoral: Mark's goal is "to build up his readers as Christians and show them what true discipleship is."[11] Thus, the narrative—its arrangement and organization, its wording and emphases, its style and character—is the product of a narrator with an agenda.[12] "This does not mean that historical elements are excluded from the story, even crucial ones on which the tale turns, but rather that the coherence, meaning, and direction of the events are acknowledged to be the expression of the narrator's vision."[13] Therefore, Mark must be read as story, rather than primarily as history. It is not a *plain-glass window* through which we only see what happened; it is a *stained-glass window* that, in addition, tells a story itself—the theology of the text.[14] The text is not simply a window to be looked *through*; it is one that must be looked *at*.

By that same token, Mark must be read independently from the other Gospels, for to do otherwise would change the story as Mark wants it told, and flatten his unique theological landscape. For the theological thrusts of the author to be respected and discerned, each Gospel story must be considered, for the most part, as being self-contained.[15] This commentary affirms the principle of "intratextuality" as asserted by Donahue and Harrington:

> By 'intratextuality' we mean reading Mark as Mark and by Mark. In reading Mark as Mark we express our interest in the final form of the gospel (not its sources or literary history) and in its words and images, literary devices, literary forms, structures, characterization, and plot. In reading Mark by Mark we want to give particular attention to the distinctive vocabulary and themes that run throughout the gospel and serve to hold it together as a unified literary production.[16]

An example of the problems that arise with "synopticizing" is the interpretation of Mark 14:65: "And some began to spit at Him, and to cover His face, and to beat Him with their fists, and to say to Him, 'Prophesy!'" Whereas Matthew and Luke (Matt

---

11. Best, *Following Jesus*, 11–12. Also see the Introduction, below, for further details on Mark's purpose. The last words of Jesus' didactic discourse in this Gospel reinforce this understanding: "And what I say to you, to *all* I say, 'Be on the alert!'" (13:37). They are addressed not only to the Twelve, or even to the larger body of historical disciples in the narrative; instead, they are addressed to *all* who would follow Jesus, then and always (ibid., 246).

12. Rhoads et al., *Mark as Story*, 5. Needless to say, this is true of every text in the biblical canon; each of its authors has a theological agenda, propounded in and through what they say/write. In other words, writers always *do* something with what they *say*.

13. Fackre, "Narrative Theology," 341.

14. This metaphor is borrowed from Greidanus, *Modern Preacher*, 196.

15. Rhoads et al., *Mark as Story*, 5–6. This is not to deny the unity of the canon or its divine authorship. See Kuruvilla, *Text to Praxis*, 100–141, for "rules of reading" that address this aspect of canonical unity, and how the breadth of the canon influences the reading of any of its individual parts. For the purposes of this commentary, which seeks to identify and follow the specific theological thrust of Mark's Gospel, primary focus will be upon *this* text, construing it as being integral and whole, consistent and coherent in itself, capable of successfully achieving the theological purpose for which it was composed.

16. Donahue and Harrington, *Gospel of Mark*, 1.

26:68; Luke 22:64) inform us of the intention of the mockers—they were taunting Jesus to identify who had hit him—Mark is silent about this malicious goal. Instead, with this omission his account moves in a different direction, focusing immediately upon a prophecy by the derided prophet that comes to pass (Mark 14:66–72).[17] Harmonization of the Gospel accounts disturbs Mark's (pericopal) theological intent and the thrust of his narrative.

In sum, the theology of the pericope (a.k.a. the Theological Focus in this commentary) functions as the bridge between text and praxis, between the circumstances of the text and those of the reading community, enabling the move from *then* to *now*, from canonical inscription to sermonic application that is both authoritative and relevant. The resultant transformation of lives, in the weekly application of pericopal theology, reflects a gradual and increasing alignment to the values of God's kingdom, as pericopes are sequentially preached. In this regular preaching of pericopes, the exposition of their theology thus facilitates the alignment of God's people to his demands—"how matters should go ideally and ethically." Thus, a pericope, as a quantum of the biblical text, is more than *informing*; it is *transforming*, for as the people of God adopt its theological values, they are becoming rightly oriented to God's will. Text will then have become praxis.

GOAL OF THE COMMENTARY

As was noted, this commentary seeks to aid the preacher in arriving at the theology of the pericope by means of a close reading of the text. In all of the interpretive work herein, a concentrated focus on preaching the pericope will be maintained. While there might be many types of sermons possible from the Gospel, this work will seek to help the homiletician preach pericope by pericope, by isolating the theology of each pericope and discerning the momentum and development of Mark's discipleship theme from text to text. Suggestions for preaching the text will also be provided, including a couple of sermon outlines for each pericope. It is assumed that the preacher using this commentary plans to go through the Gospel week by week, taking, perhaps, thirty to forty minutes per sermon. Larger chunks of text are apportioned as preaching units in order to break up the entire narrative into a reasonable number of discrete sections; twenty-five pericopes are demarcated in this commentary—enough to keep a weekly preaching series going for about six months without breaks.[18]

This work does not intend to lead preachers all the way to a fully developed sermon on each pericope; rather, it seeks to take them through the *hermeneutical* aspect of interpretation (i.e., from text to theology). While that is the primary focus of the commentary, it does provide "Possible Preaching Outlines" to advance homileticians

---

17. See under Mark 14:12–52 later in this commentary.

18. One could, of course, create more than twenty-five sermons from Mark, splitting up the pericopes that are delineated here; attention to the theological foci will be of help in dividing the pericopes into smaller units. However, it is likely that that might result in repetition of theological thrusts from one week to the next.

a few more steps closer to a sermon—this is the move from pericopal theology to sermon, the *rhetorical* part of interpretation. Preachers, however, are left to work out the remainder of the sermon on their own, providing moves-to-relevance, specific application, illustrations, etc.—none of which can be done by anyone else but the shepherd who knows the flock well. Therefore, this is not exactly a "preaching" commentary in the usual sense. Rather it is a "theology-for-preaching" commentary, i.e., a work that seeks to undertake an extremely focused interpretation of the text, one that moves the preacher from text to theology, en route to a sermon. In that sense, this is a "theological" commentary, with theology defined as *pericopal theology*, and demarcated here as the Theological Focus of the pericope. Because of its focused destination, this commentary will avoid discussing issues that do not particularly impact the preaching of a particular pericope.[19]

Audience

The work is primarily geared for those interested in preaching through the Gospel of Mark, engaging in a multipart sermonic series on the book, with an emphasis on application. Interested laypersons will also, it is hoped, find the commentary helpful. For that matter, if application is the ultimate goal of Bible study of any kind and at any level, a work such as this could conceivably be useful for small-group leaders, or even those working their own way through Mark devotionally. A working knowledge of Greek will be handy for the reader; however, for those not as facile with the original biblical languages as they might wish to be, every Greek (and the occasional Hebrew) term/phrase employed in the commentary has been both transliterated and translated.

ASSUMPTIONS OF THE COMMENTARY

Personal Stance of the Author

This commentary reflects the conservative Protestant and evangelical tradition of the author, who approaches the text as Scripture and reads Scripture as a Christian, seeking direction from it for both life and beliefs. The assumptions held in this work, while broadly evangelical, are shared with other Christian traditions as well: that the Scriptures are prescriptive for the faith and practice of the Christian and the church; that its relevance to readers is perennial, spanning time and space; and that there is a plurality of application possibilities from any given text.[20]

This perspectival description from a Protestant and evangelical angle is not necessarily for that reason alone rendered unviable; the fact that a description is motivated

---

19. Neither will this work track any major textual or theological controversy in great detail, particularly as these are usually covered exhaustively in other easily accessible interpretive tomes on Mark, should the preacher need recourse to further information. For instance, the question of Gospel priority is not particularly pertinent to the preaching of any given pericope in Mark; this issue will not figure at all in this commentary.

20. See Kuruvilla, *Text to Praxis*, 42–45.

does not disqualify it, "since an unmotivated description independent of any interpretative frame or purpose is impossible to imagine."[21] Indeed, an explicitly confessed frame of reference enables one "to see the events considered from one's own . . . perspective as capable of a different, but not necessarily inaccurate and usually complementary portrayal"—complementary, that is, to the equally perspectival observations of others.[22] No single frame of reference can capture every aspect of the text being interpreted; the contribution of this commentary is therefore from a particular vantage point and will, hopefully, complement those offerings of other interpreters from a variety of traditions.

Final Form of the Text

The commentary will engage the final form of the canonical text, affirming that this form is sufficient as the object of interpretation for preaching purposes. It is the integrated function of the text in its relatively stable final shape, rather than discrete functions in hypothetical precursors, that is to be accorded precedence.[23] Such a reading of the text takes the judgment of the process of canonization as authoritative and as perpetuating this authority in the final disposition of the text, fixing the profile of each individual book of the Bible. This is, of course, not to deny the imprecision of what exactly constitutes the final form, but simply to see the fixity of text form as bearing the most utility for the community that recognizes the text as canonical. As the plethora of modern translations of the Bible and their widespread utilization amply attest, the final form, as far as it is attainable, is *adequate* for the faith and practice of the church, as it has indeed been for over two millennia. A certain degree of inexactness and blurring of the boundaries of the final form is acceptable, and does not render application of biblical texts to daily life impossible. It behooves readers to align themselves to the text after the fashion of the community that calls the canonical Scriptures its own, a community that has continued to use the final form of the canonical text, considering that form alone as having utility for homiletical purposes. Therefore, rather than burden the preacher with text-critical issues, this commentary will assume the sufficiency of the final form.[24]

---

21. Watson, *Text, Church, and World*, 37.

22. Ratner, "Presupposition and Objectivity," 504.

23. Watson criticizes those who are insensitive to the complex unity that is the text's final form, for "dissipating . . . energies on speculative reconstructions that serve only to distract attention from the texts themselves" (*Text, Church and World*, 16–17, 35).

24. The commentary also recognizes the Gospel as ending at verse 16:8 (the "shorter" ending); the majority of scholars appear to hold this view. While a sermon might not be the best place for a discussion of the various extant options of the Gospel's closures, this is a topic that probably should be addressed in a public setting at some point, as one commences preaching through Mark, not least for the reason that most Bibles do not conclude the Gospel at 16:8. Perhaps a Sunday School class, a Bible study, or an evening service could be utilized for that purpose; a crash course on what exactly textual criticism is all about and why it is important for the Christian will, no doubt, be interesting as well as helpful. For comprehensive summaries on Markan endings see, in addition to standard commentaries, Wallace, "Mark 16:8 as the Conclusion"; Magness, *Sense and Absence*; Holmes, "To Be Continued," 12–23, 48–49; Spencer, "Denial of the Good News"; and Stein, "Ending of Mark."

Unity of the Gospel of Mark

This commentary will also assume the unity of the Markan text as an integral whole, intrinsically related in all its parts—it is one language game.[25] Broad coherence and consistency among the pericopes of the text will also be assumed, for it is a unified discourse (just as the canon, as a whole, is construed as unified), and "charitable" reading impels readers of any work to assume so as their first reflex.[26] Such an assumption of integrity—indeed, integrity of a high quality—has already been granted to Mark's Gospel by scholars. Sandmel declared, "I regard Mark as an inordinately skillful writer. . . . To my mind Mark is replete with nuances and overtones, carefully put there by the author. Whoever wrote Mark was neither simple writer, nor a simpleton, but an artful writer usually in full control of his pen."[27] Rhoads, Dewey, and Michie likewise assert:

> Our study reveals Mark's narrative to be of remarkably whole cloth. The narrator's point of view is consistent. The plot is coherent. . . . The characters are consistent from one scene to the next. Literary techniques of storytelling, recurring designs, overlapping patterns, and interwoven motifs interconnect the narrative throughout. There is also a consistent thematic depiction of the human condition, faith, God's rule, ethical choices, and the possibilities for human change. The unity of this Gospel is apparent in the integrity of the story it tells, which gives a powerful overall rhetorical impact.[28]

To these evaluations, this author assents, convinced of Mark's careful and deliberate selection of events and their arrangement for "clear discernible theological reasons," under the inspiration of the Holy Spirit.[29]

Theological Purpose of Mark, the Narrator

Mark's Gospel is a "well-crafted, cohesive narrative" that seeks to persuade the reader to move in a certain direction. It is decidedly not neutral or dispassionate journalistic reportage. Thus, the characters in the story are "creations," i.e., they are both real autonomous beings *and* narrative constructs: "the people presented in the Gospels are not 'real' in the fullest sense of the term. The characters are constructs presented by a narrator within the story," in that an authorially determined selectivity operates in their depiction in the text, a selectivity dependent on the author's agenda.[30] Todorov observed that "[n]o narrative is natural; a choice and a construction will always preside

---

25. See Kuruvilla, *Text to Praxis*, 15–19, for an employment of this Wittgensteinian image for textual hermeneutics.

26. To begin with doubt, Booth warns, "is to destroy the datum"—the material and subject of interpretation; a primary act of assent and surrender is the essential first step in approaching a text (*Company We Keep*, 32).

27. Sandmel, "Prolegomena, " 299.

28. Rhoads et al., *Mark as Story*, 3. Placher proposes that Mark was "a literary genius" (*Mark*, 9).

29. Bailey, "Fall of Jerusalem," 103. Likewise, Geddert: "Perhaps our most important assumption is that Mark's Gospel . . . is not the work of a bungling, inept, careless tradition-compiler, but of a careful, intelligent, and subtle communicator of truth" (*Watchwords*, 27).

30. Iverson, *Gentiles in Mark*, 4, 7–8.

over its appearance; narrative is a discourse, not a series of events."[31] Not everything about each character is portrayed; not everything that was said or done on any particular occasion is described; not everything that happened is revealed. The author's theological agenda determined the choice of what was included in the narrative. It is that theological agenda—for each preaching unit of the text, this agenda is the pericopal theology (Theological Focus in this commentary), portrayed in and through the text—that must be discovered by those who would preach the text for life change. Mark seeks "to do something to the hearer or reader," rather than merely saying something about Jesus or the disciples, and he uses all of his literary and narrative skill to induce "a profound and lasting significance for the reader's life" that persists "long after the initial encounter with the story." In other words, "the Gospel is designed to seduce us permanently."[32] Such a theological agenda that permeates the narrative calls upon interpreters to determine not only what Mark is *saying*, but also what he is *doing* with what he is saying.[33] And, for the most part, what the author is *doing* with what he is saying is recoverable from the text itself. Thus, the discernment of what Mark is *doing* with what he is saying ought to be squarely focused upon the concrete elements of the text, something this commentary attempts to do.

Application Potential of Pericopes

This commentary assumes that every pericope in the canonical Scriptures may be employed for application by the church universal. All the biblical writings are to be utilized in the life of the Christian community for the determination of its faith and the direction of its practices. The divine discourse that the canon is renders it efficacious for the transformation of the individual and community into the will of God, and it asserts the right of every one of its constituent parts to be heard—*all* Scripture is profitable for application (2 Tim 3:16).[34] Neither did Paul hesitate to confirm, in Romans 15:4, that "whatever was written" in earlier times was written for the instruction of the contemporary reader. The canon mandates application of all Scripture because all Scripture is efficacious, and all Scripture is efficacious because it is divinely empowered. Thus, the hermeneutic of this commentary asserts that no pericope of Mark may be disregarded for the purposes of sermons and their applications: every pericope of Scripture must be attended to for the discernment of its theology, and thus utilized for the appropriation of God's will for the faith and practice of the church.

Along with such an assumption of applicability comes the assumption of universal relevance. The consolidation of heterogeneous writings into a single normative

31. Todorov, *Poetics of Prose*, 55.

32. Fowler, *Let the Reader Understand*, 10, 79.

33. As was mentioned, this is the approach taken by the field of pragmatics. Much of the interpretive analysis in this commentary will, therefore, include a close reading of the text and its literary properties. "Mark is a writer of considerable literary skill if not of elegant Greek; it is only by paying attention to the literary structure he created that we can hope to interpret his gospel properly" (Dewey, "Literary Structure," 401).

34. Kelsey, "Bible and Christian Theology," 395.

canon, construed as the Word of God by the people of God, indicates the perennial significance of its texts and enables their application in the individual circumstances of its many and varied readers and hearers (or, as is more pertinent to this current work, to the individual circumstances of the various congregations that hear these texts preached). Thus the canon is rendered potentially relevant for every believer in every era. Chrysostom declared that what was written in the Bible was written "for us" and, therefore, worthy of diligent attention. In like manner, asserting the universality of the canon's relevance and readership, Gregory the Great asked rhetorically: "For what is sacred Scripture but a kind of epistle of Almighty God to His creature?"[35] The Talmud, citing Exodus 13:8, also declared the relevance of the Scriptures for all: "It is therefore incumbent on every person, in all ages, that he should consider it as though he had personally gone forth from Egypt" (*m. Pesaḥ.* 10.5). Expositional application was a fixture of synagogue worship as well. Philo observed that on the Sabbath, a day of learning for all, Scripture is read and "some of those who are very learned explain to them what is of great importance and use, lessons by which the whole of their lives may be improved."[36] This Jewish orientation of reading for application was retained in the hermeneutics of the church. Justin Martyr's description of a second-century worship service in Rome noted that after the reading of the Gospels, "the presider verbally instructs, and exhorts to the imitation of these good things" (*1 Apol.* 67). Such an acceptance of the universal relevance of the historic text emphasizes the momentous significance of the divine discourse that is the Bible.

For the preacher, the offering of application to the congregation is of crucial importance. Augustine wrote that the aim to be pursued by an expositor of the Scriptures is "to be listened to with understanding, with pleasure, and *with obedience*." This church father also borrowed from Cicero on the goal of the orator: "instructing is a matter of necessity, delighting a matter of charm, and *moving them* [i.e., the listeners] a matter of conquest."[37] Application of Scripture was to be the culmination of the move from text to praxis.[38] The application of Scripture in the lives of its readers (and in the

---

35. Chrysostom, *Hom. Gen.* 2:2; Gregory the Great, *Ep. ad Theodorum medicum*. The Bible itself consistently affirms the relevance of its message for future generations. The words of the Mosaic Law, for instance, were expressly intended to transcend the immediate audience: in Deut 29:14–15, Yahweh explicitly establishes his covenant not only with those Israelites present, but also with "those who are not with us here today." Also see Deut 6:6–25; 31:9–13; 2 Kgs 22–23; Neh 7:73b—8:18; Ps 78:5–6; Matt 28:19; Rom 15:4; 1 Cor 9:10; 10:6, 11; 2 Tim 3:16–17; etc.

36. *Spec. Laws* 2.15.62. Also see *Hypoth.* 7.13.

37. *Doctr. chr.* 1.36.40; 4.15.32; and 4.12.27 (from Cicero, *Or. Brut.* 21) (italics added). Augustine decried the futility of persuading hearers of the truth, or delighting them with style, if the learning process does not result in action (*Doctr. chr.* 4.13.29).

38. Classical rhetoric knows of three directions of audience responses sought by a rhetor: a *judicial* assessment of past events, a *deliberative* resolve with regard to future actions of the audience, or an *epideictic* appreciation of particular beliefs or values in the present. See Quintilian, *Inst.* 3.7–9; Anaximenes, *Rhet. Alex.* 1421b; also see Black, "Rhetorical Criticism," 261. Sermonic application, in parallel to this threefold shape of rhetorical purpose, may also be considered broadly as responses culminating in a change of mind (a response of cognition), a change of action (a response of volition), or a change of feeling (a response of emotion). For reasons of clarity and utility, applications in sermons are best conveyed

lives of hearers of sermons based upon Scripture) is a fertile endeavor, the undertaking of those who, like the good soil, "hear the word and accept it and bear fruit" (Mark 4:20). The employment of the Bible as the foundation of the existence, beliefs, and activities of the church, as well as the means of edification for individual and community, assumes that biblical interpretation *will* culminate in application—life change for the glory of God. Divine discourse always demands a response.

Translation of the Greek Text of Mark's Gospel

The translation of the text is the author's own, following the UBS Greek New Testament (4th edition).[39] Necessity has demanded a translation that attempts to show the word plays and Mark's literary artistry, particularly for those less than facile in the Greek. That goal, of course, makes the product rather wooden, often to the detriment of smooth reading. This translation has even opted to retain Mark's polysyndetons, the staccato of conjunctions, in agreement with Sternberg as he complained, "How can one prevail on translators to leave the Bible's art of parataxis alone?"[40] While there are a variety of excellent English translations that easily meet the criteria of readability and aesthetic appeal and may be profitably employed for devotional reading (*lectio divina*), the translation in this commentary is geared for the purpose of study and analysis, to enable the interpreter to appreciate *how* the story is being told—a key step in determining what the author is *doing* with what he is saying.

The Role of the Holy Spirit in Interpretation

The task of the preacher, the "theologian-homiletician,"[41] then, is to unpack, for the purposes of application, the manifold implications of the divine discourse of Scripture, so that thereby God's Word may govern the life of God's people. A sermon is not merely the product of a strategic employment of rules: homiletics, to be sure, cannot be reduced to following recipes. While facility in hermeneutics and skill in rhetoric are essential for the making of an effective preacher, they are not sufficient. The role of the Holy Spirit in the pastor's preaching and spiritual formation can be ignored only with great loss to the preacher, the preaching endeavor, and those at the receiving end of that enterprise. It is hoped that homileticians will undertake this august task of preaching recognizing the importance of the operation of the Spirit, the divine Author of the Word, in their own lives and in the lives of God's people to whom they minister.

---

as imperatives (as the examples in the preaching outlines of this commentary indicate). Such imperatives may, of course, depending on the preacher, be explicit or implicit in the actual sermon.

39. Aland et al., *Greek New Testament*. In order to minimize confusion, divine pronouns are capitalized in the translation.

40. Sternberg, *Poetics of Biblical Narrative*, 525n8.

41. "Theologian-homiletician" is my pedantic term for those preachers who have both a keen hermeneutical perception of the theology of the preaching text, and a vibrant pastoral and sermonic sensibility.

STRUCTURE OF THE COMMENTARY

The structure of each chapter ("Pericope") follows the layout below ("X" designates the number of the particular pericope under consideration)[42]:

REVIEW, SUMMARY, PREVIEW

Review of Pericope X−1: A brief review of the *preceding* pericope.

Summary of Pericope X: A brief summary of the *current* pericope.

Preview of Pericope X+1: A brief review of the *following* pericope

---

THEOLOGICAL FOCUS OF PERICOPE X

X **The comprehensive theological focus of the pericope encompassing all of the textual elements**

   X.1   Theological Focus of a section of Pericope X

       X.1.1   Theological Focus of subsection

       X.1.2   Theological Focus of a subsection

   X.2   Theological Focus of a section of Pericope X

       X.2.1   Theological Focus of a subsection

       X.2.2   Theological Focus of subsection

OVERVIEW

TRANSLATION

NOTES[43]

SERMON FOCUS AND OUTLINES

THEOLOGICAL FOCUS OF PERICOPE X FOR PREACHING

X **A homiletically workable condensation of the more comprehensive Theological Focus of Pericope X.**

---

42. Each chapter is taken up with the details of a single pericope.

43. The Notes are essentially interpretive comments unpacking the Theological Focus of the given section of a pericope. These comments are grouped into subsections that deal, not with every linguistic and literary facet of the text, but with *major concepts* essential for the discovery of the Theological Focus. *Caveat:* There will be far more information presented in the Notes than is necessary for, or can be delivered in, a sermon. This excess results from an attempt to demonstrate how every major textual element contributes to the Theological Focus of the respective section and to the larger, comprehensive Theological Focus of the particular pericope. The preacher will need to decide on what needs to be presented to the congregation in order to validate the derivation of the Theological Focus.

POSSIBLE PREACHING OUTLINES FOR PERICOPE X[44]

    I.   SUGGESTED OUTLINE Point I

           Suggested elements for Point I

    II.   SUGGESTED OUTLINE Point II

           Suggested elements for Point II

    III. *Suggested homiletical imperative!*

Use of the Commentary

It is recommended that one work slowly and reflectively through the material on each pericope with an open Bible.

- Read Mark's text of the entire pericope at least ten times, prayerfully, in a translation of your choice, simply letting it sink in.

- Read this commentary's Translation of the first section of the pericope several times, make notations as you go along.

- Scan the Theological Focus of that section.

- Study the Notes for that section, annotating those elements that might possibly be included in the sermon.[45]

- Come back to the Theological Focus of that section, seeing how it was derived.

- Move to the second section and repeat the previous steps.

- At the end of the pericope, return to the beginning of the chapter and look at the comprehensive Theological Focus that consolidates each section's Theological Focus. Get a feel for the entire pericope.[46]

- Turn to the Sermon Focus and Outlines and look at the Theological Focus of the Pericope for Preaching.

- Scan the comments there.

44. Two such outlines are provided for each pericope in Mark. One must see the points in these outlines as "moves," rather than static chunks of information dumped on the unwary listener. In this regard, preachers would do well to familiarize themselves—discriminatingly—with the "new homiletic" as espoused by Craddock, *Preaching*; idem, *As One without Authority*; Lowry, *Homiletical Plot*; and Buttrick, *Homiletic*. A helpful summary can be found in Eslinger, *Web of Preaching*.

45. Admittedly—and this was noted before, but is worth the repeated warning—the preacher will find far more interpretive material in each preaching unit than can (or should) be employed in a sermon. A good deal of preacherly discretion must therefore be employed in deciding what will be heard by the audience and what will not. Suggestions along these lines are provided with the outlines. Another option would be to utilize one session of the corporate gathering (say, a Sunday or mid-week evening service) to "teach" through the textual details of the pericope, and another session (preferably a Sunday morning service the following weekend) to "preach" the sermon on that pericope, demonstrating its theology, and packing it with a powerful homiletical imperative geared to change lives for the glory of God. On another note, the commentary is rather free with the use of footnotes both for discursive purposes and for providing trails for further study for those who might care to follow potentially interesting rabbits.

46. The Theological Focus of the particular pericope (the essence of the "pericopal theology") is, in effect, what the author (here, Mark) is *doing* with what he is *saying* in his text.

- Look at the Possible Preaching Outlines (including the homiletical imperative[47]) and see if that is something you might want to use.

- Based on your annotations, and working off the suggestions given, create a preaching outline for yourself (or adopt what is provided), including a specific homiletical imperative that you can employ for your particular listening audience.

- Now you are on your own (the Holy Spirit notwithstanding). It will help to man-uscript the sermon to get a concrete sense of what you will say under each main point (and any subpoint). I see the essential task of the preacher as to present the text so that its Theological Focus is brought out in such a way as to be grasped (seen?) by the listeners. Moves-to-relevance at each level are essential (some sug-gestions for these are also found with each of the Possible Preaching Outlines). Manuscripting should include support material (illustrations, quotes, statistics, etc.) and appropriate transitions between points/moves. In your sermon, before you hit the main point of the homiletical imperative, you will, hopefully, have disclosed the Theological Focus from the text.[48]

- Get down to a level of specificity for the homiletical imperative that you are com-fortable with, and that your audience needs, in order that their lives may begin to be changed with this text for the glory of God.

- Internalize the entire sermon, using whatever notes you need (but don't forget to engage your listeners), and deliver the sermon.

Soli Deo gloria!

---

47. The application point in italics in the Possible Preaching Outlines is always given as an imperative.

48. This does not mean that you have to state the Theological Focus (your own or what is offered in the commentary) explicitly. While that is, perhaps, the most perspicuous way of doing things, an implicit presentation of the Theological Focus, unveiled throughout the sermon, is certainly possible. In any case, before one arrives at the homiletical imperative, the Theological Focus of the text must be clear in listeners' minds.

ABBREVIATIONS

ANCIENT TEXTS

1 Apol.	Justin Martyr, *First Apology*
1 Clem.	*First Clement*
Ag. Ap.	Josephus, *Against Apion*
Ann.	Tacitus, *Annales*
Ant.	Josephus, *Antiquities*
Apol.	Tertullian, *Apology*
Bapt.	Tertullian, *Baptism*
Cels.	Origen, *Against Celsus*
Comm. Matt.	Chrysostom, *Commentariorum in Matthaeum libri IV*
Comm. Matt.	Origen, *Commentarium in evangelium Matthaei*
Dial.	Justin Martyr, *Dialogue with Trypho*
Did.	*Didache*
Doctr. chr.	Augustine, *De doctrina christiana*
Enn.	Plotinus, *Enneades*
Ep. ad Theodorum medicum	Gregory the Great, *Epistula ad Theodorum medicum*
Epon.	Livy, *Eponymous*
Haer.	Ireneaus, *Adversus haereses*
Hist. eccl.	Eusebius, *Historia ecclesiastica*
Hom. Gen.	Chrysostom, *Homiliæ in Genesim*
Hypoth.	Philo, *Hypothetica*
Idol.	Tertullian, *De idolatria*
Inst.	Quintilian, *Institutio oratoria*
J.W.	Josephus, *Jewish War*
Lig.	Cicero, *Pro Ligario*
LXX	Septuagint
Marc.	Tertullian, *Adversus Marcionem*
Mart. Pol.	*Martyrdom of Polycarp*
Mor.	Plutarch, *Moralia*
MT	Masoretic Text

Nat.	Pliny the Elder, *Naturalis historia*
Oct.	Minucius Felix, *Octavius*
Or. Brut.	Cicero, *Orator ad M. Brutum*
Peregr.	Lucian, *The Passing of Peregrinus*
Prot.	Plato, *Protagoras*
Quis div.	Clement of Alexandria, *Quis dives salvetur*
Rab. Perd.	Cicero, *Pro Rabirio Perduellionis Reo*
Resp.	Plato, *Republic*
Rhet. Alex.	Anaximenes, *Rhetorica ad Alexandrum*
Sat.	Juvenal, *Saturnalia*
Sera	Plutarch, *De sera numinis vindicta*
Spec. Laws	Philo, *On the Special Laws*
Tract. Ev. Jo.	Augustine, *Tractates on the Gospel of John*
Verr.	Cicero, *In Verrem*

RABBINIC AND TARGUMIC LITERATURE

'Abod. Zar.	*'Abodah Zarah*
b.	Babylonian Talmud
B. Meṣiʿa	*Baba Meṣiʿa*
B. Qam.	*Baba Qamma*
Bek.	*Bekorot*
Ber.	*Berakot*
'Ed.	*'Eduyyot*
Gen. Rab.	*Genesis Rabbah*
Giṭ.	*Giṭṭin*
Ḥag.	*Ḥagigah*
Ketub.	*Ketubbot*
m.	Mishnah
Mak.	*Makkot*
Mek.	*Mekilta*
Mid.	*Middot*
Naz.	*Nazir*
Ned.	*Nedarim*
Nid.	*Niddah*
Num. Rab.	*Numbers Rabbah*
'Ohal.	*'Ohalot*
Pesaḥ.	*Pesaḥim*
Pirqe R. El.	*Pirqe Rabbi Eliezer*
Šabb.	*Šabbat*
Sanh.	*Sanhedrin*
Šeqal.	*Šeqalim*
t.	Tosefta
Taʿan.	*Taʿanit*

Ṭehar.	*Ṭeharot*
Tg. Neb.	*Targum of the Prophets*
Tg. Ps.-J.	*Targum Pseudo-Jonathan*
Yad.	*Yadayim*
Yebam.	*Yebamot*

OLD TESTAMENT APOCRYPHA AND PSEUDIEPIGRAPHA

2 Esd	2 Esdras
1/2/3/4 Macc	1/2/3/4 Maccabees
1 En.	*1 Enoch* (Ethiopic Apocalypse)
2 En.	*2 Enoch* (Slavonic Apocalypse)
3 En.	*3 Enoch* (Hebrew Apocalypse)
2 Bar.	*2 Baruch* (Syriac Apocalypse)
Apoc. Ab.	*Apocalypse of Abraham*
As. Mos.	*Assumption of Moses*
Barn.	*Barnabas*
Gos. Thom.	*Gospel of Thomas*
Herm. *Vis.*	Shepherd of Hermas, *Vision*
Jdt	Judith
Jub.	*Jubilees*
Let. Aris.	*Letter of Aristeas*
Mart. Ascen. Isa.	*Martyrdom and Ascension of Isaiah*
Pss. Sol.	*Psalms of Solomon*
Sir	Sirach/Ecclesiasticus
T. Benj.	*Testament of Benjamin*
T. Dan	*Testament of Dan*
T. Iss.	*Testament of Issachar*
T. Levi	*Testament of Levi*
T. Naph.	*Testament of Naphtali*
Ṭob	Tobit
Wis	Wisdom of Solomon

DEAD SEA SCROLLS

1QH	*Hodayot (Thanksgiving) Hymns* from Qumran Cave 1
1QM	*Milḥamah* or *War Scroll* from Qumran Cave 1
1QS	*Serek hayyahad* (*Rule of the Community*) from Qumran Cave 1
1QSa	Appendix to *Serek hayyahad* (*Rule of the Community*) from Qumran Cave 1
1QpHab	*Pesher Habakkuk* from Qumran Cave 1
4QFlor	*Florilegium* from Qumran Cave 4
11QTemple	*Temple Scroll* from Qumran Cave 11

OTHER ABBREVIATIONS

BBR	*Bulletin for Biblical Research*
BECNT	Baker Exegetical Commentary on the New Testament
Bib	*Biblica*
BibInt	*Biblical Interpretation*
BJRL	*Bulletin of the John Rylands University Library of Manchester*
BR	*Bible Review*
BT	*The Bible Translator*
BTB	*Biblical Theology Bulletin*
BZ	*Biblische Zeitschrift*
CBQ	*Catholic Biblical Quarterly*
ChrCent	*Christian Century*
CTJ	*Concordia Theological Journal*
EncJud	*Encyclopedia Judaica*
EQ	*Evangelical Quarterly*
ExpTim	*Expository Times*
GOTR	*Greek Orthodox Theological Review*
Int	*Interpretation*
JAAR	*Journal of the American Academy of Religion*
JBL	*Journal of Biblical Literature*
JBR	*Journal of Bible and Religion*
JETS	*Journal of the Evangelical Theological Society*
JSNT	*Journal for the Study of the New Testament*
JSNTSup	Journal for the Study of the New Testament: Supplement Series
LB	*Linguistica Biblica*
LNTS	Library of New Testament Studies
NIGTC	New International Greek Testament Commentary
NovT	*Novum Testamentum*
NTS	*New Testament Studies*
Phil. Sci.	*Philosophy of Science*
RB	*Revue biblique*
SBLDS	Society for Biblical Literature Dissertation Series
SNTSMS	Society for New Testament Studies Monograph Series
SP	Sacra pagina
TDNT	*Theological Dictionary of the New Testament*
TrinJ	*Trinity Journal*
WBC	Word Biblical Commentary
WUNT	Wissenschaftliche Untersuchungen zum Neuen Testament

INTRODUCTION

Genre, Authorship, Audience, Style, Structure

Mark 1:1–16:8

*"If anyone wishes to follow behind Me, let him deny himself
and take up his cross and follow Me!"*

Mark 8:34

GENRE

QUITE APPROPRIATELY, THIS GOSPEL is titled τό εὐαγγέλιον κατὰ Μάρκον (*to euangelion kata Markon*, "The Gospel According to Mark," or "The [One] Gospel in Mark's Version").[1] The four remarkable iterations of the life of the protagonist of the NT, Jesus Christ, are all subsumed under a single heading of "the gospel." Each individual version is designated as the Gospel "according to" (κατά, *kata*) its author, demonstrating a unity of subject between the four texts, but with a diversity of theological thrusts—a single, *fourfold* gospel.[2] The early church, therefore, resisted both an exclusive use of one Gospel (e.g., the exclusive use of Luke by Marcion [ca. 85–160 CE]) as well as a harmonizing approach (e.g., the amalgam of all four Gospels, the *Diatessaron*, by Tatian [ca. 120–180 CE]), maintaining that the goal of each individual account was to tell the story of this particular person, Jesus Christ, in this particular way, to further its author's particular theological goal. In other words, the very acceptance of the fourfold gospel by the early church attested to its consideration of these works as not merely histories, but also as crucial theological treatises.[3] That understanding will guide this commentary.[4]

---

1. France, *Gospel of Mark*, 5.

2. 𝔓[66] and 𝔓[75] (from the second and early third centuries) provide these superscriptions to the Gospels.

3. Stanton, "Fourfold Gospel," 343–44.

4. On the other hand, the issue of what specific genre of literature Mark's Gospel is will not receive much attention. "Because of the wide range of purposes such ancient biographies could serve (e.g.,

1

AUTHORSHIP, PROVENANCE, AND DATING

For the best part of the last two millennia, the church has accepted the Second Gospel as having been written by Mark, with input from the apostle Peter. Papias, Bishop of Hierapolis (ca. 70?–155? CE), quotes "the Elder" (John?) as saying that Mark was Peter's "interpreter" (ἑρμηνευτής, *hermēneutēs*) "and wrote accurately, though not in order," for Peter "delivered his teachings as occasion required ["in anecdotal form," πρὸς τὰς χρείας, *pros tas chreias*] rather than compiling a sort of orderly presentation."[5] Conceivably, a pastoral and theological agenda governed Peter's instruction and Mark's inscription.

Early church tradition and considerable evidence, both internal and external, affirm a Roman provenance for this Gospel, perhaps when Peter was still living (no later than 65 CE).[6] The Roman origin is supported by Mark's Latinisms and his translations of Aramaic terms into Greek (12:42; 15:16).[7] The writer assumed the audience's knowledge of titles of Jesus (Christ, Son of God, Son of David, Lord, Son of Man); terms like "the word," "disciples," "baptism," are never explained; and presumably the audience knew the characters and places—all named without explanation or prologue (e.g., John, Pilate, sons of Simon of Cyrene, Jesus' unnamed hometown, other locales, a variety of OT characters, the Sanhedrin, and various Jewish groups and traditions; even Jesus himself bursts upon the scene in Mark without much preamble).[8]

While the exact date is debated, it is likely that the Gospel was completed before the destruction of the Jerusalem temple (70 CE): there is no mention or even allusion in Mark to that catastrophe as having already taken place.[9] Moreover, if written *post factum*, the fact that the temple's destruction occurred in the summer makes the plea that it not happen in the winter (13:18) difficult to comprehend. Boring pictures the situation well:

---

polemical, apologetic, ethical, panegyrical, philosophical), identifying the gospel's genre brings us no closer to understanding the evangelist's purpose for writing" (Winn, *Purpose of Mark's Gospel*, 4).

5. Eusebius, *Hist. eccl.* 3.39.15, citing Papias's five-volume work, *The Interpretation of the Lord's Sayings* (ca. 120/130 CE). Other witnesses from the second to the fourth centuries agreeing with Markan authorship of the Gospel include: Irenaeus (*Haer.* 3.1.1), the Anti-Marcionite Prologue (that calls Mark the "stump-fingered" one), the Muratorian canon, Clement of Alexandria (cited in Eusebius, *Hist. eccl.* 2.15; 6.14.5–7), Origen (cited in Eusebius, *Hist. eccl.* 6.25.5), Tertullian (*Marc.* 4.5.3), and Jerome (*Lives of Illustrious Men: Simon Peter* 1.1).

6. France, *Gospel of Mark*, 38; Winn, *Purpose of Mark's Gospel*, 91. First Peter 5:13 mentions Mark as being with Peter in "Babylon"—Rome. If Peter died around 64/65 CE under Nero, this would place Mark's Gospel in the mid-60s.

7. See Gundry, *Mark*, 1043–45; Witherington, *Gospel of Mark*, 20–21; France, *Gospel of Mark*, 40–41. These idiosyncrasies include Greek transcriptions of Latin words (δηνάριον, *dēnarion*, for *denarius*, Mark 6:37; 12:15; 14:5; κράβαττος, *krabattos*, for *grabatus*, 2:4, 9, 11, 12; 6:55; συμβούλιον, *symboulion*, for *consilium*, 3:6; σπεκουλάτωρ, *spekoulatōr*, for *speculator*, 6:27; etc.) and literal renditions in Greek of Latin idioms (e.g., τὸ ἱκανὸν ποιέω, *to hikanon poieō*, of *satisfacere*, 15:15). See van Iersel, *Mark*, 33–35; and Stein, *Mark*, 11–12.

8. Stein, *Mark*, 9–10.

9. van Iersel, *Mark*, 46.

By any reckoning [whether before or after destruction of Jerusalem], this was a tumultuous time for the empire, for Judaism, and for the new Christian community. Serious earthquakes occurred in 60 and 63 (Tacitus, *Annals* 15.44). The Roman army suffered defeat at the hands of the Parthians on the eastern border of the empire in 62 (Tacitus, *Annals* 15.13–17). In 64, Roman Christians became scapegoats for the disastrous fire that destroyed much of the inner city of Rome: they were rounded up and put to death in the most cruel ways [under Nero]. Both Peter and Paul probably died in this purge. Other Christian leaders had been martyred by the time Mark was written. Nero committed suicide in 68, and struggles for the emperor's throne ensued, with three emperors in one year. Meanwhile, the Roman army put down a revolt in Palestine in a bloody war that devastated the region and destroyed Jerusalem and its temple. During the siege, the commanding general became emperor, and his son completed the war, burned the temple, and carried its sacred objects through the streets of Rome in a triumphal procession. At some point in this chaotic time Mark was written.[10]

In any case, uncertainties about authorship, provenance, or date do not significantly alter the theological interpretation of the Gospel.[11]

AUDIENCE AND PURPOSE

Bauckham, considering the wide networks between Christian communities of the first century, sees the audience for the Gospels as quite indefinite and general—the larger Christian movement of the first century. He takes the Gospel texts to be deliberately open, rather than closed, thereby rendering the specific situations of audiences and occasions rather irrelevant for interpretation. Witherington agrees that while the writers of these texts did have specific audiences in mind, "the Gospels are indeed written with one eye on the larger Christian public, even in places far removed from where the author is."[12]

It is quite likely, however, that in the tumultuous situation in Rome in the late 60s CE, followers of Jesus Christ were sorely shaken and filled with doubt.[13] Was all the suffering they were going through "normal"? How should they respond? Would it not be better to just give up? What exactly does it mean to follow Jesus? Follow him where? How will all this end? In all probability, Mark was writing to provide answers to such troubling questions.

The rather facile way in which characters and themes, institutions and locales, and groups and terms are introduced (as noted above) seems to suggest that providing information was not Mark's primary goal.[14] While Jesus, the protagonist, is present in

---

10. Boring, *Mark*, 14–15.

11. Guelich, *Mark*, xxx, xxxii.

12. Witherington, *Gospel of Mark*, 30 (also see 28–29); Bauckham, "For Whom Were Gospels Written?"

13. The mention of Jesus with wild animals (Mark 1:13), "salting with fire" (9:49), the "reward" of persecution (10:30), as well as the entire discourse in Mark 13 suggests an audience intimate with suffering and oppression, or at least expecting it (Healy, *Gospel of Mark*, 20).

14. "Mark's gospel was not written to provide biographical information about the life of Jesus but was designed to speak to the needs of Mark's church" (Stock, *Method and Message*, 229). That this Gospel was intended for a Christian audience in the first place is incontrovertible. See Bauckham, "For Whom Were Gospels Written?," 9–12.

every episode and pericope, so are the disciples, for the most part. The constant association of Jesus with the disciples suggests the focus of the Gospel is not exclusively christological. That, of course, is not to suggest that discipleship and Christology are separable: "discipleship is the proper outcome of a healthy Christology."[15] One flows out of the other; understanding Jesus' person and accepting his mission results in discipleship. At the same time, the Gospel is not only about the twelve close associates of Jesus, either. Frequently, Mark drops clues that the label "disciples" includes more than those who were historically around Jesus: the usage of the term in 3:20–35 and 4:10, for example, the disappearance of the names of most of the Twelve after their appointment, the employment of "disciples" even before the calling of the Twelve (2:15, 16, 18, 23; 3:7, 9; etc.). "[I]t is not the individuals that Mark wants his readers to notice so much as the group and what they represent."[16] In symbolically representing the reestablishment of the whole people of Israel, Mark is hinting at a reconstitution of God's people, a creation anew. Thus, "disciples" extends beyond the historic space-time frame of the Gospel. Rather, it is about how ordinary men and women of all ages and all places can, like those early followers, embark on the "Trip of Discipleship" with Jesus, and be a part of God's kingdom that he is consummating.[17]

STYLE

It was likely that Mark's Gospel was intended for aural apprehension, considering "his more expansive storytelling manner and his well-known penchant for repetition or for dual expressions where one would do," not to mention the "sandwich" technique he employed—"a well-tried device of the popular raconteur in order to hold the audience's attention."[18] In addition to the "sandwich" story, Mark frequently employs chiasms (or concentric structures/segmentations), a compositional device commonly used in the semiliterate Greco-Roman world of the first century.[19] Many of these will

15. France, *Gospel of Mark*, 28.

16. Ibid., 27. Other subtle hints in Mark that "discipleship" is applicable to those outside the circle of the Twelve are found in 1:31; 2:15; 3:35; 5:20; 7:29; 8:34–38; 9:40; 10:29–31, 52; 11:23; 12:44; 13:13, 37; 14:9; 15:41, 43–46.

17. See Placher, *Mark*, 56. The relationship between Jesus and his disciples (μαθηταί, *mathētai* is, surprisingly, not expressed by the related verb μανθάνειν or its cognates, but rather by the phrase "to follow." It is this concrete and specific action that is in focus in this Gospel: What does it mean to follow Jesus? See Kuthirakkattel, *Beginning of Jesus' Ministry*, 112. Winn doubts if Mark's purpose was to convey the theme of discipleship: he feels the medium of a "gospel" is too indirect for that purpose, as compared to an epistle (*Purpose of Mark's Gospel*, 27). This commentary, it is hoped, will counter that argument, demonstrating how appropriate a catena of narrative pericopes is, to convey the powerful thrust of Mark's argument for the kind of discipleship that he advocates.

18. France, *Gospel of Mark*, 9–10. See also Best, "Mark's Narrative Technique"; and Dewey, "Oral Methods." The frequent use of the historic present tense (at least 150 times) and periphrastic verb forms (especially ἦν, *ēn*, with a present participle) has also been recognized as colloquial style (France, *Gospel of Mark*, 16–17). On "sandwich" stories—literary structures with two halves of an outer story "sandwiching" an inner one—see the appropriate sections on Mark 3:20–35; 5:20–43; 6:7–32; 11:12–25; 14:1–11; and 14:53–72.

19. Students not only learned the Greek alphabet forwards and backwards, but also in chiastic pairs

be encountered in the appropriate sections of the Gospel, beginning with the overall chiastic structure of Mark's work (see below). Nonetheless, one must confess that the Gospel is a written text; as such, it shows signs of textuality and careful, deliberate composition. Literary connections between sections of the text at a distance from each other indicate that the author was not merely writing for the ear, but also for the eye. It is likely that the public reader (the pastor?) was supposed to discern these links and develop their significances for their listening audiences. Mark 13:14 is an obvious example, with its directive to the "reader" to "understand." For the determination of Mark's pericopal theologies, this commentary will take into consideration that aspect of the Gospel's textuality.

STRUCTURE

Mark's Gospel may be conveniently structured on a geographical and topological basis (desert, Galilee, on the way, Jerusalem, and tomb); a subsidiary thematic structure that hinges the main elements can also be noted (blindness to sight, and "on the way" as a figurative phrase for the journey of discipleship).

Title (1:1)	Themes of Discipleship
A **In the desert** (1:2–13) [*topological*]	ACT I: DISCERNMENT of Jesus' PERSON
B **In Galilee** (1:16—8:21) [*geographical*]	
blindness to sight (8:22–26) [*thematic*]	
C **On the way** (8:27—10:45) [*geographical/ thematic*]	ACT II: ACCEPTANCE of Jesus' MISSION
blindness to sight (10:46–52) [*thematic*]	
B′ **In Jerusalem** (11:1—15:39) [*geographical*]	ACT III: FAITHFULNESS to Jesus
A′ **At the tomb** (15:42—16:8) [*topological*]*	

  * van Iersel, *Reading Mark*, 20; idem, "Locality," 49.

Deserts and tombs are places of temptation and demonic habitation and corpses (1:13; 5:2; 15:46), but at either end of Mark they also denote places of new life: baptism in one, resurrection in the other. Both locales have an eschatological messenger (1:6–8; 16:5–7) whose clothing is described; one of them witnesses to the coming of Jesus, the other to his going. Both mark the local movements of Jesus—his coming "after" John (ὀπίσω, *opisō*, 1:7) and his going "ahead" of the disciples (the suffix προ- [*pro-*]

---

beginning with the first and last letters (Α–Ω), the second and penultimate letters (Β–Ψ), the third and prepenultimate letters (Γ–Χ), and so on. "It is therefore probable that the concentric structures found in much ancient literature were originally a structuring and mnemonic device, which had the function of helping reciters structure the text for their listeners" (van Iersel, *Mark*, 70–71). For more on chiasms in antiquity, see Breck, *Shape of Biblical Language*; Lund, *Chiasmus*; Welch, *Chiasmus in Antiquity*; Dart, "Scriptural Schemes," 22–25; Parunak, "Oral Typesetting"; Stock, "Chiastic Awareness"; and van Iersel, "Concentric Structures," 78–81.

in προάγω, *proagō*, 16:8); in each case a response is expected of the listeners/readers (1:15; 16:7).[20]

The two sight-giving miracles (the only two such miracles in the Gospel) book-end the central section of Mark (8:22–26 and 10:46–52, bracketing 8:27—10:45): in the first is a blind man who is healed gradually, and in the second another blind man sees instantly and follows Jesus on the way.[21] In the center, between these two heal-ings, is the journey from Galilee to Jerusalem (8:27—10:45); it is here that Jesus, en route to Jerusalem with his disciples, makes his three Passion Predictions (8:31; 9:31; 10:33–34) as he attempts to unfold his mission to them.

The three acts of the Gospel may thus broadly be classified as the Galilee sec-tion (1:1—8:21), the "on the way" section (8:22—10:52), and the Jerusalem section (11:1—16:8). Van Iersel suggests a further detailed structure within those geographi-cal arenas of Galilee and Jerusalem: a series of controversy dialogues dealing with the issue of Jesus' authority is located in each of these two broad divisions.

Act I: Galilee (1:1–8:21)
- Controversy over authority (1:21—3:6)
    Parabolic extended discourse (4:1–34) (Jesus sitting down, 4:1)
        Lack of discernment of Jesus' person by the disciples emphasized (4:35—8:21)

[Act II: On the Way (8:22—10:52)]

Act III: Jerusalem (11:1—16:8)
- Controversy over authority (11:12—12:40)
    Apocalyptic extended discourse (13:3–27) (Jesus sitting down, 13:3)
        Lack of faithfulness to Jesus by the disciples emphasized (14:1—16:8)

The word ἐξουσία (*exousia*, "authority") occurs in these sections several times (1:22, 27; 2:10; 3:15; and 11:28 [×2], 29, 33), and sizable discursive sections are located after these controversies—parable discourse after 1:21—3:35, and apocalyptic discourse after 11:1—13:2.[22] The two extended discourses take central positions in each of their own sections, standing almost equidistant from the beginning and end of the Gospel respectively. Both are entirely made up of speech; both emphasize the importance of Jesus' words for the readers (4:3, 9, 21–25; and 13:5, 14, 30–31, 37).[23] These are fol-lowed, in Act I (Galilee), by a sequence of events portraying the failure of discern-ment of Jesus' person on the part of the disciples, and in Act III (Jerusalem), by Jesus'

---

20. van Iersel, *Reading Mark*, 20–24.

21. More later about the positioning of these elements.

22. Nonetheless, aspects of one are included in the other—apocalyptic motifs in the first extended discourse (special instruction to "insiders," 4:9–13; light/darkness dualism, 4:22; "harvest," 4:29), and parabolic motifs in the second (the fig tree, 13:28; watchfulness, 13:34–37) (Myers, *Binding the Strong Man*, 170).

23. van Iersel, *Reading Mark*, 110. Also, strikingly, the verb κάθημαι (*kathēmai*, "sit") is used eleven times in Mark but only twice with regard to Jesus, namely in 4:1 and 13:3 (ibid., 112).

Passion; both emphasize their lack of faithfulness to him. While there are similarities in patterning, the Galilee and Jerusalem portions are differentiated as follows[24]:

Act I: GALILEE (Mark 1:1—8:21)	Act III: JERUSALEM (Mark 11:1—16:8)
Calling and sending disciples	No calling or sending disciples
Miraculous ministry (including exorcisms)	Non-miraculous ministry*
Discipleship motif: *Discernment of Jesus' Person*	Discipleship motif: *Faithfulness to Jesus*
Major central discourse: parables	Major central discourse: apocalyptic Temple
Purity, Sabbath, synagogue	
Imposition of silence . . . but preaching continues	No imposition of silence . . . but no preaching occurs†
Fast paced (31/41 occurrences of ϵὐθύς, *euthys*, "immediately")	Slower and chronological (6/41 occurrences of ϵὐθύς)
	(last week of Jesus forms one-third of Mark)
	(last 24 hours of Jesus forms one-sixth of Mark)‡

* Except for the cursing and withering of the fig tree and, of course, the resurrection.

† Κηρύσσω, *kēryssō*, in the first half of Mark is found in 1:4, 7, 14, 38, 39, 45; 3:14; 5:20; 6:12; 7:36; the only two occurrences in the second half of the Gospel are in 13:10 and 14:9, and both of these uses are proleptic, dealing with preaching that will take place in the future (the word does not occur at all in Act II).

‡ In fact, there are only ten other uses of ϵὐθύς in the rest of the NT.

On the Way

Act II (On the Way, 8:22—10:52) is formally launched with Jesus' notification of his intent to go to Jerusalem (8:31). Thus begins the journey "on the way" from Caesarea Philippi in the north to Jerusalem in the south. The section is bracketed on either end with a blind-healing miracle (8:22–26 and 10:46–52).

The word ὁδός (*hodos*, "way") occurs sixteen times in Mark: 1:2, 3; 2:23; 4:4, 15; 6:8; 8:3, 27; 9:33, 34; 10:17, 32, 46, 52; 11:8; 12:14. This Gospel begins by announcing that Jesus, himself, has a *way* (1:2), one that will be seen later to end at the cross. The context of its first use as a theological concept in 1:2, rather than as a literal route, lends primacy to such a use throughout the Gospel.[25] There is no doubt that Jesus traveled to Jerusalem more than once (as John's Gospel recounts), but for Mark there appears to be only a single journey; this Evangelist chooses to structure his Gospel with one simple, non-duplicated, linear movement.[26] The entire life of Jesus is portrayed by this author as one passage with three movements—from Galilee, On the Way, and to Jerusalem (Acts I, II, and III, respectively). This "on the way" theme, then, is Mark's

24. Modified from Boring, *Mark*, 4–5.

25. Danove, *Rhetoric of the Characterization*, 9.

26. The rather artificial structure suggests its employment as a literary device, as France notes: "even as a purely geographical datum it looks like a structure deliberately imposed on the story" (*Gospel of Mark*, 12).

inspired, literary "creation," to be understood theologically, as even Jesus' opponents themselves seem to have discerned (12:14).[27]

The specific phrase ἐν τῇ ὁδῷ (*en tē hodō*, "on the way") is found often in Act II (8:3, 27; 9:33, 34; 10:32, 52); of note is the employment of the term in each of the three Passion Predictions of Jesus (8:27; 9:33; 10:32). The concept of following Jesus "on the way" is, of course, not foreign to the NT. The picture of the Christian life as a pilgrimage is widely utilized therein: Acts 9:2; 19:9, 23; 22:4; 24:14, 22 (where Christians are said to belong to "the Way"); Jesus himself is the "way" (John 14:6); and "walking" (περιπατέω, *peripateō*) is virtually a synonym for conduct of life (Rom 6:4; 13:13; 14:15; Gal 5:16; Phil 3:17; 1 Thess 2:12; etc.). In the OT, the call and journey of Abraham, the Exodus, the exile and the return of the Israelites, etc., are templates for the journey motif. Other allusions to the Christian life as a journey are found in Heb 2:10; 3:7—4:16; 12:1–2; *Barn.* 18–20; *Did.* 1.1–2; 5.1; 6.1; *1 Clem.* 35.5; 1QS 3.17—4.26; etc. A long section in Luke (9:51—19:44) is also set as a journey to Jerusalem. The theological notion of "way" is inherent in the Hebrew word דֶּרֶךְ, *derek,* and is amply supported in the prophetic corpus: Isa 48:17; Jer 2:23; 4:18; Ezek 7:3–9; 9:10; 11:21; 16:43; 22:31; 36:17–19, 31–32; Mal 3:1. Likewise employed with an ethical thrust, as in Isa 40:3, are the phrases דֶּרֶךְ יְהוָה (*derek yhwh,* "the way of Yahweh") and דֶּרֶךְ אֲדֹנָי (*derek 'adonay,* "the way of the Lord"): Gen 18:19; Jdg 2:22; 2 Kgs 21:22; Prov 10:29; Jer 5:4, 5; Ezek 18:25, 29; 33:17, 20.[28]

The Three Facets of Discipleship

The three acts of Mark correspond to three broader themes of discipleship in the Gospel:

- Act I: Discernment of Jesus' Person
- Act II: Acceptance of Jesus' Mission
- Act III: Faithfulness to Jesus

Mark 1:1—8:21 (Act I) consistently brings the focus to bear upon the disciples' lack of discernment of Jesus' person: they do not appear to be following him for the right reasons (1:21–45); they are accused of not "understanding" (4:13; 7:18), of not having faith (4:40); they are skeptical of Jesus' ability to provide food for thousands (6:37; 8:4); they fail to recognize Jesus walking on water (6:49); and they are unable to make sense of Jesus' feeding miracles (8:16–21). Mark 8:22—10:52 (Act II) keeps the spotlight on Jesus' Passion Predictions—the announcement of his mission, which the disciples do not seem to be able to accept (8:32; 9:5–6, 32–50; 10:35–45). Mark 11:1—16:8 (Act III), dealing with Jesus' Passion, shows the disciples to be unfaithful to their Master

---

27. This "way," is, for Mark—as he will depict throughout his Gospel—the way through suffering, to glory.

28. See Hatina, *In Search of a Context,* 174–75. Also see 1QS 8.13–14 for the ethical/theological use of Isa 40:3 in Qumran. The same biblical author may switch between the literal and theological uses of "way," as does Isaiah with דֶּרֶךְ (*derek*). Literal uses include: Isa 9:1; 15:5; 37:29, 34; 42:16; 43:16, 19; 49:9, 11; 51:10; 57:10, 14 [×2]; 62:10; theological uses include: Isa 2:3; 8:11; 10:24, 26; 30:11, 21; 35:8; 40:3, 14, 27; 42:24; 45:13; 48:15, 17; 53:6; 55:7, 8 [×2], 9 [×2]; 56:11; 57:17, 18; 58:2, 13; 59:8; 63:17; 64:5; 65:2; 66:3.

(14:10–11, 18–21, 27–52, 66–72, etc.). In all of these negative depictions, Mark seeks to inspire the follower of Jesus to discern his person, accept his mission, and be faithful to him till the end.[29] Thus, this commentary sees the broader theological idea for the whole Gospel as being: *The disciple is one who follows Jesus, discerning his person, accepting his mission, and being faithful to him, on the way to glory . . . through suffering.*[30]

It should be noted how the Jerusalem section (Act III) ends with Jesus' promise to "go ahead" of the disciples, whom he would meet in Galilee (16:7; see 14:28). A fresh start to the journey of discipleship seems to be in view, with the end pointing back to the beginning, and disciples regathering for a reprise of the expedition. The Gospel, therefore, appears to be ready to undertake another iteration—it is cyclical! And no wonder, for with each new generation of disciples bidden to join the journey, the Trip of Discipleship begins anew. Will the reader follow?

29. See appropriate sections of this commentary. Weeden, *Mark*, 26–51, somewhat along the same lines, sees three stages in the disciples' relationship to Jesus: unperceptiveness, misconception, and rejection.

30. Rhoads et al. assert that *"the story of Mark seeks to create ideal readers who will receive the rule of God with faith and have the courage to follow Jesus whatever the consequences"* (*Mark as Story*, 138, emphasis original).

ACT I: IN GALILEE

Discernment of Jesus' Person

PERICOPE 1

Ready to Follow?

Mark 1:1–20

[John the Baptist; Jesus' Baptism; Call of Disciples]

SUMMARY, PREVIEW[1]

Summary of Pericope 1: In this first pericope of Mark (1:1–20), the author introduces the theme of discipleship—following Jesus on the "way." In broaching this issue through narrative, the motif of call-and-response is laid out: John's divine call and his response; Jesus' divine call and his response; the disciples' divine call and their response. The consequences for John and Jesus as they respond to their respective calls are also spelled out (or strongly hinted at). Striking is the absence of any mention of consequences for the disciples, either in this pericope, or in the rest of the book. But the way the story is structured and presented, the "fate" of the disciples becomes quite obvious to the reader—suffering! Will *you* embark on this way of discipleship, with its call to suffer?

> **Preview of Pericope 2:** The next pericope (Mark 1:21–45) demonstrates that following Jesus in discipleship is not a self-satisfying undertaking, but a self-giving one.

---

1. In a "deductive" fashion, the Summary of the current pericope will state what the author is *doing* with what he is *saying*. What is asserted in these summaries will be elucidated in an "inductive" process from the text in the Notes that follow. How this preaching unit connects with those that precede and follow will also be stated briefly (the Review and Preview, respectively; of course, there is no Review in this first chapter).

1 Mark 1:1–20

THEOLOGICAL FOCUS OF PERICOPE 1*

1 **The life-journey of discipleship, the beginning of the establishment of the king-dom of God introduced by Jesus Christ, the Son of God—the only one whose way is worth following after—calls for sacrifice and suffering, including spiritual warfare, but also promises the disciple the power of the Holy Spirit (1:1–20).**

1.1 The journey of discipleship is a new beginning introduced by Jesus Christ, the Son of God—the good news both *about* him and proclaimed *by* him—the authoritative one above all else, whose way alone is worthy of being followed (1:1–3).

  1.1.1 The beginning of the Gospel, a new way of life, is both about Jesus Christ and announced by Him.

  1.1.2 The only one worth following is Jesus, the authoritative Son of God.

  1.1.3 The presence of the Holy Spirit enables discipleship.

1.2 The journey of discipleship, involving radical life change, is one of sacrifice and suffering, undertaken in the power of the Holy Spirit (1:4–8).

  1.2.1 Discipleship involves a radical change of life.

  1.2.2 Sacrifice and suffering are integral to discipleship.

  1.2.3 The presence of the Holy Spirit enables discipleship.

1.3 The journey of discipleship, following Jesus—the divine one faithful to his mission and pleasing to the Father—on a way that involves testing (spiritual warfare), is the beginning of the establishment of the kingdom of God (1:9–15).

  1.3.1 The one worth following in discipleship is a divine One, endowed by the Holy Spirit, pleasing to the Father.

  1.3.2 Supernatural testing of, and supernatural aid for, followers of the divine One, himself successful in such testing, is to be expected in discipleship.

  1.3.3 The inauguration of the kingdom of God begins with the recruitment of disciples to follow Jesus Christ.

1.4 The journey of discipleship, following obediently after Jesus, who calls and commissions his followers, involves a life of sacrifice and suffering (1:16–20).

  1.4.1 Followers' call and commissioning by Jesus commences their journey of discipleship.

  1.4.2 Following obediently after Jesus involves sacrifice and suffering.

  1.4.3 The sequence of call, commissioning, and consequence adumbrates the nature of the journey of discipleship.

* As was noted in the Introduction, with the intent to be as comprehensive as possible—to deal with every major element of the text—each Theological Focus is necessarily long and pedantic. An abridged version, certainly more useful when one begins to craft the sermon, is located towards the end of each chapter, in the Sermon Focus and Outline. That version of the Theological Focus (the "Theological Focus of Pericope 1 for Preaching") is a condensed one.

OVERVIEW

MARK 1:1–13 LIKELY FORMS a discrete literary section. However, as a preach-ing pericope, 1:1–20 is best taken as a single unit that combines the disciples' call with the formal literary introduction of the Gospel. As will be detailed below, there appears to be a definite "call-and-response" structure in this pericope—those of John and Jesus in 1:1–15, and that of the disciples in 1:16–20. The parallel between Peter's account of the "beginning" in Acts 10:37–39 and Mark's own presentation here is notable—both follow the same sequence: John, then Jesus, then "we," the witnesses/disciples.[2] Thus the calls of John, Jesus, and the disciples may be considered together as an integral preaching unit.

1.1 Mark 1:1–3

THEOLOGICAL FOCUS 1.1

1.1 The journey of discipleship is a new beginning introduced by Jesus Christ, the Son of God—the good news both *about* him and proclaimed *by* him—the authoritative one above all else, whose way alone is worthy of being followed (1:1–3).

    1.1.1 The beginning of the Gospel, a new way of life, is both about Jesus Christ and announced by Him.

    1.1.2 The only one worth following is Jesus, the authoritative Son of God.

    1.1.3 The presence of the Holy Spirit enables discipleship.

Section Summary 1.1: The Son of God, Jesus Christ, introduces the good news of his "way"—symbolic, in Mark, of the journey of discipleship. Jesus' authority and uniqueness are established at the very outset, making him the only one worthy of allegiance. John's call to prepare the way of the Lord is an invitation to all who would follow to get ready to walk along with him on the Trip of Discipleship.

TRANSLATION 1.1

1:1   *The beginning of the gospel of Jesus Christ, Son of God.*

1:2   *Just as it has been written in Isaiah the prophet: "Behold I send My messenger before You, who will make ready Your way;*

1:3   *the voice of one crying, 'In the wilderness prepare the way of the Lord, make straight His paths.'"*

NOTES 1.1

1.1.1   The beginning of the Gospel, a new way of life, is both about Jesus Christ and is announced by him.[3]

There appears to be an allusion here to the "beginning" (רֵאשִׁית, *re'shith*, of Gen 1:1, making it an epochal new start, a re-creation of sorts. The location of action in the wilderness (Mark 1:3) alludes to the calling of the Israelites out of Egypt, and suggests here the calling of a new people—a "regeneration of salvation history," "a new begin-

---

2. As was discussed in the Introduction, it is possible that much of Mark's account is drawn from the memories of the apostle Peter.

3. These subsections (italicized sentences) deal with major textual concepts and are components of the larger Theological Focus of each section. As was noted in the Preface, not every textual element will be dissected; neither will every historical allusion or reference be pursued. The Notes will deal only with those concepts and elements of the text that contribute to the Theological Focus of that section and, ultimately, to the Theological Focus of the pericope.

ning of the discipleship adventure."[4] Once Israel had gone into the Jordan to gain their inheritance; here they are again ("*all* the country of Judea" and "*all* the Jerusalemites," 1:5) returning to that same river for a fresh start, this time with John the Baptist heralding another "Joshua" (יְהוֹשֻׁעַ, *Yehoshuaʻ*, or "Jesus"). Such a new beginning may be intended as a reprise of the history of God's people, albeit new in kind and more momentous in consequence; it involves Gentiles as well, as this Gospel will make clear later. It was a beginning alright, a new start, a new "way" of life with God as directed by Jesus.[5]

Mark's narrative concludes in chapter 16 with a renewed call to the disciples (16:7), bidding them to regather in Galilee, where it all began and where Jesus would now go before them, for a fresh start in the second round of the discipleship expedition. Thus Mark has created a cyclical account of what it means to follow Christ—it begins again at the end. Indeed such an account has to be rewritten for every individual disciple that joins a new iteration of the Trip of Discipleship, generation after generation.[6]

The word εὐαγγελιον (*euangelion*, "gospel/good news") is very "Isaianic" in tone and color (the verb, εὐαγγελίζω [*euangelizō*, "to announce the gospel/good news"], occurs in Isa 40:9 [×2]; 52:7 [×2]; 60:6; 61:1 LXX). For this prophet, it indicates the proclamation of the good news of God's Messiah, who will be victorious over his enemies and establish God's reign.[7] Isaiah 61:1 (and its NT citations, Matt 11:5; Luke 4:18; 7:22) recognizes the Messiah as the one bearing good news about himself, thus rendering the genitive in Mark 1:1 ("gospel *of* Jesus Christ") both subjective and objective: the good news is *about* Jesus Christ, and the good news is also that proclaimed *by* Jesus Christ (1:14).[8] The good news proclaimed through Isaiah to Israel is now being announced to the rest of the world (ultimately through Jesus' disciples, commissioned to "fish" for men, 1:17). God's reign is at hand—this is the good news—and the call to discipleship is the beginning of the establishment of that kingdom. With their co-optation into the company of Jesus' disciples (see below), they would be both citizens of that kingdom and agents of its proclamation and expansion.

1.1.2 The only one worth following is Jesus, the authoritative Son of God.

The title "Son of God" is quite likely intended to be understood both in a divine as well as regal sense (as in the messianic prophecies in Ps 2:7; 2 Sam 7:14; etc.). The mention of God's kingdom in Mark 1:15 reinforces this idea.[9] There are evident allusions here to contemporary Greco-Roman use of the term, particularly its employment in the Roman imperial cult. Julius Caesar was called *divus Iulius* (the "divine Julius") and his son, Octavian, *divi filius* ("son of the divine"); θεοῦ υἱός (*theou huios*, "son of god")

---

4. Myers, *Binding the Strong Man*, 122.

5. Drury, "Mark 1:1–15," 31.

6. For the concept of discipleship as going on the "way" with Jesus, see the Introduction and below.

7. Winn, *Purpose of Mark's Gospel*, 96.

8. This, Wallace's "plenary genitive," is also found in Rev 1:1 (*Greek Grammar*, 120–21). Also see Henderson, *Christology*, 42.

9. Collins, *Mark*, 135.

was often used of Augustus, as well as of Tiberius, Nero, and other Roman regents. And εὐαγγελίζω (*euangelizō*) was frequently associated with the birth, political ascent and accession to the throne, and military successes of the Roman emperors.[10] All of this would have been familiar to Mark's readers, and so the Evangelist appears to be categorizing Jesus as among the greatest of the rulers of that world. Not only is he God's appointed king and Israel's Messiah, but he is also the one who rivals all others who claim divine sonship or regency. Such an introductory statement by Mark is nothing other than a "subversion of the Roman cultural code," almost a "declaration of war." Here is one who was worth following and owing allegiance to, far more than any of the great Roman imperators. "The incipit, therefore, is not only defensive—claiming Jesus . . . as the fulfillment of Jewish messianic prophecy—but also offensive—claiming Jesus' superiority to the Roman emperor."[11]

The application of the epithet "Son of God" to Jesus is not echoed much in the rest of the Gospel by any human voice, until the end (15:39, when the mission of Jesus is accomplished upon his death).[12] The story's circular nature—the regathering in Galilee exhorted in 16:7 (also see 14:28), indicating a new start—strengthens Mark's narrative strategy in the use of "Son of God": the title is asserted here at the "beginning" and again at the end—there, for the first time, by a human voice. In the second iteration of the story, *after* one has been through Round One of the journey of discipleship, this introduction will, no doubt, be understood better, for in the rereading one now has already seen who Jesus is and what exactly his mission was.[13] It is only as disciples apprehend Mark's account of the first round will they grasp the significance of the title, and only then will the second round be anticipated not as bad news, but good (despite the sacrifice and suffering called for), for now they recognize that the one they follow is verily the Son of God, the one who himself suffered on his way to glory.[14]

1.1.3   The way of discipleship is the disciple's journey following Jesus.

The use of ὁδός (*hodos*, "way") twice, in 1:2–3, and the employment of "path" (τρίβος, *tribos*) in 1:3, calls attention to this important Markan motif of the "way." This is Jesus' way, the way he would walk, the way he would call his disciples to follow. As was noted

10. Winn, *Purpose of Mark's Gospel*, 96. Of note is the Priene Calendar Inscription in honor of Caesar Augustus (ca. 9 BCE) that contains the phrase ". . . birthday of the *god* [θεοῦ, *theou*] Augustus was the *beginning* [ἦρξεν, *ērxen*, from the verbal form, ἄρχομαι, *archomai*, "to begin," used in Mark 1:1] of the *good tidings* [εὐαγγελίων, *euangeliōn*] for the world that came by reason of him." The inscription also labels this emperor "savior" (σωτήρ, *sōtēr*). See Evans, "Mark's Incipit." Upon Vespasian's accession to the throne, Josephus notes that every city celebrated the "good news [εὐαγγέλια, *euangelia*]" (*J.W.* 4.10.6).

11. Winn, *Purpose of Mark's Gospel*, 101–2, 179; Myers, *Binding the Strong Man*, 123–24. If the Gospel, as is likely, was written in the reign of Emperor Vespasian (69–79 CE)—who not only claimed to be divinely appointed, but also appropriated Jewish messianic prophecy, entitling himself to be its fulfillment—Mark's first verse is almost polemical in its call to follow this Jesus, who is greater than the current Roman emperor (Winn, *Purpose of Mark's Gospel*, 178).

12. However, God, Jesus himself, and even demons reiterate that title: Mark 1:1, 11; 3:11; 5:7; 9:7 (as also does the high priest, albeit incredulously, in 14:61).

13. Myers, *Binding the Strong Man*, 123.

14. Witherington, *Gospel of Mark*, 69–70.

in the Introduction, this motif is theological, rather than literal, and is used as such in the Gospel (even Jesus' antagonists in 12:14 utilize the word with its theological import). Indeed, the "way" is paradigmatic of the Christian life, the journey of the disciple following Jesus.

Thus this introductory section lays out the key elements of the good news: the identity of the one proclaiming the Gospel, and the way (*his* way) upon which disciples will be called to travel. Those who would follow the way of God are to "prepare" and make ready for it (by repentance, as indicated in 1:3–4, 14). In other words, "[w]hen the Baptist, as the 'voice,' proclaims that the people are to prepare for the 'way of the Lord,' he is . . . focusing on preparing the people to travel along a road that the 'Mightier One' will ask them to travel"—the way of discipleship.[15] This pericope, as will become evident, is a call to follow the way of Jesus. The rest of the Gospel explains what it means to embark on this "way"—the key discipleship motif in Mark.

1.2   Mark 1:4–8

THEOLOGICAL FOCUS 1.2

1.2   The journey of discipleship, involving radical life change, is one of sacrifice and suffering, undertaken in the power of the Holy Spirit (1:4–8).

   1.2.1   Discipleship involves a radical change of life.

   1.2.2   Sacrifice and suffering are integral to discipleship.

   1.2.3   The presence of the Holy Spirit enables discipleship.

Section Summary 1.2: The entry into this way of the Lord involves a drastic life change. It involves the sacrifice of worldly priorities and, potentially, suffering. The promised Holy Spirit strengthens disciples in this (sacrificial/suffering) journey of discipleship.

TRANSLATION 1.2

1:4   *It came about that John the Baptist [was] in the wilderness preaching a baptism of repentance for the forgiveness of sins.*

1:5   *And all the country of Judea was going out to him and all the Jerusalemites, and they were being baptized by him in the Jordan River, as they confessed their sins.*

1:6   *And John was clothed with camel hair and a leather belt around his waist, and he ate locusts and wild honey.*

1:7   *And he was preaching saying, "One who is mightier than I is coming after me, of whom I am not worthy to bend down and untie the strap of his sandals.*

1:8   *I baptized you in water, but he will baptize you with the Holy Spirit."*

---

15. Hatina, *In Search of a Context*, 181–82.

NOTES 1.2

1.2.1 *Discipleship involves a radical change of life.*

Μετάνοια (*metanoia*, "repentance") points to the call for "a reorientation to the para-doxical values of the kingdom of God," a mindset that is not assimilated in the instant of the initial commitment of faith but, rather, through a lifetime of following Christ.[16] This is a radical call—forgiveness outside of the temple confines, remission of sins without sacerdotal involvement, and that with a baptism of (characterized by) repen-tance. This is a call to a new life, a life of discipleship involving drastic life change. John announces to his listeners that they are to prepare the way of the Lord in repentance and baptism (Mark 1:3–4), readying themselves to travel along a road after Jesus.[17] This is how one should begin the Trip of Discipleship.

The element of baptism as a beginning is, in retrospect, ecclesial in concept, marking as it does an initiation into the life journey of following the way of Jesus Christ. The juxtaposition of "Jordan" and "wilderness" (1:3, 4, 5) also repairs to a "New Exodus"—God's leading his people again through the wilderness, where he had once demonstrated his care for them, and into the Promised Land (Isa 48:20–21; Jer 2:6–7; Ezek 20:35; Hos 2:14–20). This is "a new trek with God at the head," and it would take a life-change to embark on this journey.[18]

1.2.2 *Sacrifice and suffering are integral to discipleship.*

The description of John's clothing (Mark 1:6) is almost an exact quote of 2 Kings 1:8, listing the garb of Elijah, the one who did not die (2 Kgs 2:9–12), and who was ex-pected to return before the Day of the Lord as the Messiah's herald (Mal 3:1; 4:5–6). The ruggedness of the Baptist's clothing and the sparseness of his diet, both pointedly noted in the text, suggest this prophet's otherworldliness. It hints at the sacrifices that are involved when one answers the call to follow Jesus on the Trip of Discipleship as a participant in the kingdom of God and as a proclaimer of that rule. The wilderness location also emphasizes denial of things worldly. Following after God's way into God's kingdom calls for a devaluation of the world and its ways. For disciples this is always a sacrifice, and the life change demanded of them ("repentance") assumes that sacrifice.

The fact that this following on Jesus' way involves trying circumstances and pres-ages difficult times is not only implicit in John's location and clothing (Mark 1:3, 4, 6), but also in Jesus' own location and temptation (1:12, 13; and later, in 1:35, 45). The disciples who give up their connections to worldly security to follow Jesus also end up later in the same wilderness location (6:31, 32, 35). These are strong hints as to what may be expected by the follower of Jesus. Indeed, the whole narrative of the Trip of

---

16. France, *Gospel of Mark*, 66–67. Issues of justification are not particularly of interest to Mark. Rather, his work is about what it means to follow Jesus (which, of course, begins with the placing of one's trust in Christ as Savior), and what it means to be aligned to those "paradoxical values," the elaboration of all of which takes up the remaining fifteen chapters of Mark.

17. Moyise, "Wilderness Quotation," 84.

18. Wright, "Spirit and Wilderness," 273, 291. Baptism as a parallel to the experiences of the Exodus generation is also mentioned in 1 Cor 10:2.

Discipleship is set in some rather unwholesome locales: it begins in the wilderness where Satan lurks (1:13) and ends in a tomb (16:1–8), a locus of demonic habitation (5:2). But in Mark these dangerous places also designate the beginning of new life: the baptism of Jesus in one, and the resurrection of Jesus in the other; the call of the disciples in one, and the "recall" of the disciples in the other; the announcement of the kingdom of God in one, and the crux (pun intended!) of the establishment of God's kingdom—the resurrection—in the other. That being said, in the location and description of John the Baptist (1:3, 4, 6) there is a hint that this journey of discipleship is to be one of self-denial and sacrifice.

Outside of Act I (1:1—8:21), "wilderness" does not appear in Mark's Gospel. The wilderness is a place of new beginnings (Jer 2:2; Hos 2:14; 9:10), the locus of covenant entry and of identification as God's people (Deut 29:12), and the place where the kingdom of God begins—indeed, a staging ground for God's deliverance (Isa 40:3; 41:18; 42:11; 43:19; 44:26; 51:3).[19] Not only is John the Baptist intimately associated with the wilderness (Mark 1:3, 4), it is "into the wilderness" that the Spirit drives Jesus to be tempted for forty days (1:13–14). Mark goes to extraordinary lengths, belaboring the point that all of these opening scenes are set in the wilderness. He seems to be at pains to emphasize that this was akin to the exodus (see Ezek 20:35–38), a new beginning loaded with hope.[20] At the same time, one cannot deny the bleakness of the location, compounded by the satanic warfare Jesus faced in that station (Mark 1:13). This journey of discipleship is clearly not going to be an easy trip. Sacrifice and suffering are to be anticipated.

1.2.3   *The presence of the Holy Spirit enables discipleship.*

The allusion to Elijah[21] indicates that John, like his "predecessor," was likely to have had the Holy Spirit's anointing (2 Kgs 2:9, 15; also note Luke 1:17, where the connection between John and Elijah, grounded upon the Spirit's presence and power, is clearly expressed). If this is the case, then what Elijah possessed is being offered to all who would follow Jesus: God will pour out his Spirit upon those who choose to follow the way of his Son (Mark 1:8). Thus the pattern is completed: John, it is implied, in his association with Elijah, has a portion of the Spirit; Jesus has the Spirit descend upon him (1:10); the disciples (those who follow Jesus), it is promised, will be baptized by Jesus in the Spirit (1:8). From what has been disclosed thus far in the Gospel, going on Jesus' way appears to need supernatural help; and this unit assures the follower that the requisite help will be provided!

---

19. Boring, *Mark*, 39.

20. Indeed, those in Qumran expected the appearance of God in the wilderness (1QS 8.13–14; 9.18–21). See France, *Gospel of Mark*, 56–57.

21. The allusions are found both in the description of John's clothing and in the citation of Mal 3:1 in Mark 1:2 (Mal 4:5 mentions Elijah); Jesus explicitly links John and Elijah in Matt 17:11–13.

1.3   Mark 1:9–15

THEOLOGICAL FOCUS 1.3

1.3   The journey of discipleship, following Jesus—the divine one faithful to his mission and pleasing to the Father—on a way that involves testing (spiritual warfare), is the beginning of the establishment of the kingdom of God (1:9–15).

　1.3.1   The one worth following in discipleship is a divine One, endowed by the Holy Spirit, pleasing to the Father.

　1.3.2   Supernatural testing of, and supernatural aid for, followers of the divine One, himself successful in such testing, is to be expected in discipleship.

　1.3.3   The inauguration of the kingdom of God begins with the recruitment of disciples to follow Jesus Christ.

Section Summary 1.3: The unique announcement of Jesus' divine "call" and the manner of his investment with the Holy Spirit, further underscore his worthy leadership as the one whom disciples must follow. His way, however, is fraught with danger, as John the Baptist could have attested. Jesus' model of taking up the baton after the removal of John the Baptist presages a time of his own removal. Who, then, will carry the baton and take up the charge of extending God's kingdom?

TRANSLATION 1.3

1:9   *It came about in those days that Jesus came from Nazareth of Galilee and was baptized in the Jordan by John.*

1:10   *And immediately coming up out of the water, He saw the rending of the heavens and the Spirit as a dove coming down upon Him;*

1:11   *and a voice came about, out of the heavens: "You are my beloved Son, in you I am well-pleased."*

1:12   *And immediately the Spirit drove Him into the wilderness,*

1:13   *and He was in the wilderness forty days being tempted by Satan, and He was with the wild beasts, and the angels were ministering to Him.*

1:14   *Now after John had been given over, Jesus came into Galilee preaching the gospel of God,*

1:15   *and saying, "The time is fulfilled and the kingdom of God has come near; repent and believe in the gospel.*

NOTES 1.3

1.3.1   The one worth following in discipleship is a divine One, endowed by the Holy Spirit, pleasing to the Father.

The baptism of Jesus marks the beginning of his ministry as leader of his followers, the commencement of the journey of discipleship. The reaction of God the Father (and indeed, the presence of the Holy Spirit) demonstrates the Trinitarian credentialing of this divine One who is qualified to lead.

Mark 1:5 and 1:9 are similar, but with significant differences:

	MARK 1:5	**MARK 1:9**
Baptizer	John	John
Location	In the Jordan River	In the Jordan
Baptizee(s)	All Judaea /Jerusalemites	Jesus
Verb of motion	ἐξεπορεύετο (*exoporeueto*, "they went")	ἦλθεν (*ēlthen*, "He came") [same root]
Action	They were being baptized	He was baptized
Size of group	All	One
Manner of baptism	Confessing sins	[No confession of sins]

This deliberate structuring and the contrasts in size of the group and manner of baptism suggest to France that "the one takes the place of the many."[22] At the very least, in light of his introduction as the Son of God, there is an emphasis on the uniqueness of this one who is baptized singly, with a numinous acknowledgment of his person by both God the Father and God the Spirit. Needless to say, he who undergoes baptism without any confession of sin must himself be divine—the Son of God (1:11). In this baptism, unique for this individual, the Son of God motif is stressed again, with its messianic overtones of deity and kingship.[23]

1.3.2   Supernatural testing of, and supernatural aid for, followers of the divine One— himself successful in such testing—is to be expected in discipleship.

In his subsequent wilderness experience (1:12–13), Jesus is depicted as being almost passive, receiving the actions of the Spirit, Satan, and the angels; he himself merely "was" (ἦν, *ēn*) in the wilderness and with the wild beasts. France calls this a "wilderness tableau," with two opposing camps: the Spirit and the angels vs. Satan and the wild beasts.[24]

A   καὶ . . . τὸ πνεῦμα (*kai . . . to pneuma*, "and . . . the Spirit"): Jesus—recipient of the action of the Spirit (1:12)

  B   καὶ ἦν (*kai ēn*, "and he was"): Jesus is the subject (1:13a)   [*wilderness*]

    C   πειραζόμενος (*peirazomenos*, "being tempted"): Jesus—recipient   [*Satanic* of Satan's action (1:13b)   *temptation*]

  B¹   καὶ ἦν ("and he was"): Jesus is the subject (1:13c)   [*wild animals*]

22. France, *Gospel of Mark*, 76. This is perhaps cryptic. But why not intentional? It is likely that the first readers of the Gospel (Roman Christians?) knew about the person and work of Jesus already. The fact that Jesus is not introduced upon his appearance in this Gospel clearly assumes that readers were acquainted with his person, at least by hearsay—another reason to hold that Mark's account is not necessarily, or primarily, an apologetic for Christology.

23. The significance of the "rending" of heaven in Mark 1:10 (Matthew and Luke have "opening") will be discussed with another "rending" at the end of the Gospel (see on 15:39), where, also, there is a mention of the "spirit," as well as a voice acknowledging the Son. This parallel is best dealt with in a sermon on Mark 15. With constraints of time squeezing each sermon, the preacher must carefully define what exactly needs be addressed in each homiletical event to move listeners to application (i.e., specific change of life for the glory of God).

24. France, *Gospel of Mark*, 83. Wild beasts are associated with Satan and demons in *T. Benj.* 5.2; *T. Iss.* 7.7; *T. Naph.* 8.4. The wilderness, Gundry notes wryly, "seems well stocked with a population drawn from heaven, hell, and the zoo" (*Mark*, 61).

A' καὶ οἱ ἄγγελοι (*kai hoi angeloi*, "and the angels"): Jesus—recipient of
the action of the angels (1:13d)*

* From Heil, "Jesus with the Wild Animals," 65. The parallelism also suggests that the sojourn with the
wild beasts was not a benevolent situation, but rather a malevolent one linked with temptation from Satan.

This structuring is a strong hint as to the supernatural forces and conflict behind the
earthly scenes. It is set in a foreboding locale—the wilderness, a place of beginning,
and also by virtue of its historical setting in the exodus, a locus of probationary testing
in preparation for the establishment of God's kingdom. The word πειράζω (*peirazō*,
"tempt") and its cognates, a fixture in the vocabulary of early Christianity, denotes
"being probed and proved, often through hardship and adversity, in order to determine the extent of one's worthiness to be entrusted with, or the degree of one's loyalty
or devotion to, a given commission and its constraints."[25] The forty days of testing
would correspond, then, to the sojourn of the prototypical wilderness generation of
the Exodus (Deut 8:2–4; note ἐκπειράζω [*ekpeirazō*, "test"] in 8:2, 16).

Jesus successfully passes the test. This divinely appointed Son of God, uniquely
qualified and faithful in testing, pleasing to the Father and superior to every other
ruler, is proven to be worthy of being followed. Yet the note of supernatural conflict
is one of warning as well. Not only is John the Baptist and Jesus said to be in the
wilderness, the disciples land there as well. The follower of Jesus, it is implied, will
also have to face such testing and attacks. Those who follow the Son of God are sure
to undergo the kind of opposition that he experienced. Yet it is to be remembered that
the proximity in the description between satanic attack and angelic ministration (1:13)
once again attests to the presence of supernatural help for those disciples so besieged
by demonic elements. The follower of Jesus, though tested exceedingly, can be assured
of help from above.

1.3.3 The inauguration of the kingdom of God begins with the recruitment of disciples to follow Jesus Christ.

The content of the good news is the nearness of the kingdom of God (1:15).[26] Into this
new reign under a new King, listeners (and readers) are exhorted to place themselves,
by repentance and belief. A new age is dawning. The kingdom is near—a regency that
is "both eternal and eschatological, both fulfilled and awaited, both present and imminent," both already and not yet.[27] God's plan to establish his kingdom through his
"beloved Son" has commenced. And for that kingdom, God is creating a people—
Christ-followers, those who by their very act of following their Lord begin to constitute the kingdom and the fulfillment of God's ultimate purposes. The embarkation of

25. Gibson, "Jesus' Wilderness Temptation," 12. In fact, in the first century CE, "it was conventional
to regard ἔρημος [*erēmos*, "wilderness"] as synonymous with being subjected to a 'trial of faithfulness'"
(ibid., 16). Psalm 91:11–13 depicts the angels protecting the Messiah against wild animals.

26. Πεπλήρωται (*peplērōtai*, "is fulfilled") and ἤγγικεν (*ēngiken*, "has come near"), both in the
perfect tense, strongly indicate that the state of fulfillment has already begun; that, however, does not
mean the fulfillment has been completed; final consummation awaits.

27. France, *Gospel of Mark*, 93.

Jesus' followers on this journey of discipleship is the beginning of the establishment of this new reign. The consummation of the kingdom of God will, of necessity, follow a divine eschatological plan and will coincide with the Second Advent of the Son of God. In the meantime, the repentance called for here, as noted earlier, is a "redirection of the entire manner of life, both individually and corporately."[28] What specifically such commitment to Jesus and his way entails as the disciple steps out to walk with Jesus remains to be spelled out in the rest of the Gospel. But the response intended of readers at this juncture is clear: Get ready to follow Jesus on the Trip of Discipleship—the kingdom is nigh!

John had been preaching (1:4); now Jesus begins to preach (1:14–15; also 1:38, 39) after John is "handed over." There is thus a sequential development of the narrative, the relay of a baton: John, then Jesus. Who but the disciples will carry the charge when Jesus himself is "handed over"? Over the next fifteen chapters of the Gospel, one finds the training of the disciples, the next set of recipients of the baton when Jesus finishes his earthly work.[29] Their growth and development—in fits and starts, punctuated by victories and failures—is the lesson of discipleship for all subsequent generations of disciples, who continue to carry and pass on the baton of their Lord faithfully. In other words, this sequential development is Mark's way of implicitly raising the question: Who will carry the baton after Jesus? Will readers be ready and willing to embark upon the next iteration of the Trip of Discipleship?[30]

1.4   Mark 1:16–20

THEOLOGICAL FOCUS 1.4

1.4   The journey of discipleship, following obediently after Jesus, who calls and commissions his followers, involves a life of sacrifice and suffering (1:16–20).

　　1.4.1   Followers' call and commissioning by Jesus commences their journey of discipleship.

　　1.4.2   Following obediently after Jesus involves sacrifice and suffering.

　　1.4.3   The sequence of call, commissioning, and consequence adumbrates the nature of the journey of discipleship.

Section Summary 1.4: The explicit call and commission of Jesus to his disciples bids them follow after him. This "following after" Jesus involves sacrifice and suffering. Indeed, the tripartite call-and-response structure of the pericope, along with the lethal consequences to John and Jesus, suggests to disciples what they, too, can expect as a consequence of embarking on the journey of discipleship.

28. Marshall, *Faith as a Theme*, 48, 51.

29. "Mark's theology of the advancing kingdom is much more like a relay race in which persecution for the sake of the Gospel is the baton passed on from each runner to the next as they take their round on the track . . . or (to stick closer to Mark's imagery), it is the cross passed on from shoulder to shoulder as new recruits travel the 'way' from Galilee to Jerusalem" (Geddert, *Watchwords*, 150).

30. See below on the utilization of this sequential unveiling in 1:1–20 (John/Jesus/disciples) for preaching.

TRANSLATION 1.4

1:16 *And passing by the Sea of Galilee, He saw Simon and Andrew, the brother of Simon, casting a net in the sea; for they were fishermen.*

1:17 *And He said to them, "Come after me, and I will make you become fishers of people."*

1:18 *And immediately they left the nets and followed Him.*

1:19 *And going on a little further, He saw James the son of Zebedee and John his brother; they were also in the boat mending nets.*

1:20 *And immediately He called them; and they left their father Zebedee in the boat with the hired men and they went away after Him.*

NOTES 1.4

1.4.1   Followers' call and commissioning by Jesus commences their journey of discipleship.

The careful structuring of this section is telling:

He saw Andrew and Simon (1:16a)

A   casting a net in the sea, for they were fishermen (1:16b)

    B   "Come after Me" (1:17)

A′   left nets (1:18a)

they followed Him (1:18b)

He saw James and John (1:19a)

A   in the boat mending nets (1:19b)

    B   He called them (1:20a)

A′   left father in boat (1:20b)

they went away after Him (1:20c)[*]

    * Kuthirakkattel, Beginning *of Jesus' Ministry*, 105–6.

In each parallel instance, elements A and A′ repeat the location of these fishermen where Jesus found them—on the water; prominence is given to the brothers' location (1:16, 18, 19, 20). Is this an indirect reference to a "baptism" of sorts? After all, both John and Jesus are baptized. Should not the disciples be? Both pairs of siblings are specifically noted to be on water (1:16, 19); these fishermen "on water" are called by Jesus to be fishermen out of water. In figuratively being "fished" out of water, Jesus promises that they, in turn, will be made "fishers of people." Others will also follow Jesus through these disciples and their example; in turn, these others too are commissioned to share Jesus' ministry as they undertake the Trip of Discipleship. The cycle undergoes a fresh iteration with a new call and commission for every new generation of disciples. The four addressed in this unit responded to Jesus' call. Will the reader of the Gospel?[31]

1.4.2   Following obediently after Jesus involves sacrifice and suffering.

The call to follow involves a sacrifice, a giving up, as modeled by the two sets of siblings in this section: they abandon vocation, family ties, and hopes for the future to follow obediently after Jesus (element A′, in both structures above; 1:18a, 20b). This Trip of Discipleship is characterized by self-denial (and suffering); it demands much of the one following Jesus. A total dedication to the cause of Jesus (and the authority of Jesus) for the establishment of his kingdom is in view here. "By 'follow' he meant not so much the movement of the feet as of the heart, the carrying out of a way of life" (Bede, *Homilies on the Gospels* 1.21).[32] What such dedication entails will be revealed in the rest of the narrative.[33] The preposition ὀπίσω (*opisō*, "after/behind," 1:17, 20), defining "spatial" location in relation to Jesus, occurs four times in the Gospel: 1:17, 20; 8:33, 34. The first two are found here in relation to the initial following after Jesus (1:17–20, at the beginning of Act I: Galilee); the last two occur in relation to the expectation of suffering for disciples as they follow "after" Jesus (8:33, 34, at the beginning of Act II: On the Way). The parallels between the two sections, shown below, hint at the consequences of following "after" Jesus. Discipleship is a call to suffer with Jesus.

MARK 1:16–20 (First Call of Disciples)	MARK 8:33–34 (First Prediction of Passion)
names of four disciples (1:16, 19)	"His disciples" (8:33)
"He said to them" (1:17)	"He said to them" (8:34)
"Come after [ὀπίσω, *opisō*] Me" (1:17)	"Go behind [ὀπίσω] Me" (8:33)
"they went away after [ὀπίσω] Him" (1:20)	"If anyone wishes to follow after [ὀπίσω] Me" (8:34)
"followed Him" (1:18)	"follow Me" (8:34; also 8:33)
καλέω (*kaleō*, "call," 1:20)	προσκαλέω (*proskaleō*, "summon," 8:34)*

* From Kuthirakkattel, *Beginning of Jesus' Ministry*, 109n127.

An adumbration of what is to come is thus signaled to the reader in this pericope. Be warned!

---

31. That Jesus is mentioned as "passing by" (Mark 1:16) suggests that Jesus is already on the way! It only remains for disciples to join him in his ongoing mission.

32. Cited in Oden and Hall, *Mark*, 28.

33. The degree of abandonment is obviously not total: the fishermen retain some degree of control over their boats and homes (1:29; 3:9, 20; etc.); however, the willingness to give all for the walk with Jesus is what is expected of the disciple (10:28–30). The entire Gospel narrative is geared to towards the disciples' training and development, and indirectly, to the training and development of the readers who, hopefully, are themselves committing to "follow after" Jesus. In the successes and failures of the disciples in Mark's narrative, Mark's readers will find the foundation for their own walk of discipleship, by both positive and negative example. See France, *Gospel of Mark*, 94.

1.4.3 The sequence of call, commissioning, and consequence adumbrates the nature of the journey of discipleship.

In this pericope, a tripartite series of calls, commissions, and consequences can be envisaged, with deliberate patterning between these elements relating respectively to John, Jesus, and the disciples.

JOHN	JESUS	DISCIPLES
Call divine voice: Spirit (1:2–3)* sent (1:2) baptism (1:4, 8)	*Call* divine voice: Father (1:11) sent (1:12) [also 9:37; 12:6] baptism (1:8–11)	*Call* divine voice: Son (1:17, 20) called (1:17, 20) [will be sent (3:14; 6:7)] "baptism"? (1:16–20)†
Commission preparing the Lord's way (1:2) wilderness (1:3, 4) preached repentance (1:4, 7)	*Commission* preaching the Gospel (1:14) wilderness (1:12, 13) preached repentance (1:14–15)	*Commission* fishing for men (1:17) [will be in the wilderness (6:31, 32, 35)] [will preach repentance (3:14; 6:12)]
Consequence "betrayed/given over" (1:14)	*Consequence* [will be "betrayed/given over"]‡	*Consequence* ?

* This voice in the citation of Scripture is rightly that of God the Spirit.

† The suggestive allusion to baptism in the disciples' call from on water—a point emphasized by Mark—was noted earlier.

‡ See references below for occurrences in this Gospel of παραδίδωμι (*paradidōmi*, "betray/hand over").

Notice the sequential movement: John comes before Jesus (Mark 1:2), Jesus goes after John (1:7), and the disciples are commanded to follow Jesus who goes before them (1:17, 20).[34] John's call, commission, and consequence ("handed over/betrayed," 1:14) are indicated in the pericope. Jesus' call and commission are likewise indicated, but the consequence ("handed over/betrayed") will be unveiled only as the narrative progresses.[35] The disciples' call and commission are mentioned in the pericope; what will not be found in the Gospel is the consequence of their following Jesus in discipleship.[36] What will their end be? And what will be the fate of *any* disciple who proceeds on this journey? The open-endedness in the narrative regarding the fate of the Twelve enables the author to depict the passing of the baton to disciples of succeeding generations beyond that of the Twelve, and the ongoing pattern of call, commission, and conse-

34. The parallel between Peter's account of the "beginning" (Acts 10:37–39) and that of Mark was noted before; both follow the same sequence: John, then Jesus, then the disciples.

35. Παραδίδωμι (1:14) had a settled semantic field in the tradition of Mark's audience; later in his Gospel, Mark will depict Jesus being betrayed/handed over, even as John was: 3:19; 9:31; 10:33 [×2]; 14:10, 11, 18, 21, 41, 42, 44; 15:1, 10, 15 (the fates of John and Jesus will be further linked in 6:7–32 and 9:12–13).

36. For hints on what the fate of the disciples might be, see on Mark 6:7–30, and also the use of παραδίδωμι in 13:9, 11, 12.

quence set up initially by John and Jesus. It is clearly not a rosy picture of discipleship that is being painted, if what happened to John, and what will happen to Jesus, is any indication. Mark leaves readers hanging with a poignant question: "Will you follow, knowing what might happen as a consequence?"

SERMON FOCUS AND OUTLINES

THEOLOGICAL FOCUS OF PERICOPE 1 FOR PREACHING[*]

1 **The life-journey of discipleship, the beginning of the establishment of God's kingdom, involves suffering (1:1–20).**

* The Theological Focus is the key idea to be proposed in the sermon. In the view of preaching espoused in this commentary, the exposition of this Theological Focus is the critical task of the homiletician. Needless to say, the preacher must also provide the congregation with specifics on how the theological concept of each pericope may be put into practice so that lives are changed for the glory of God.

While the nuances of the broad Theological Focus of this pericope (the expectation of sacrifice and suffering in discipleship) are spelled out in succeeding portions of the Gospel, the sermon on this pericope, as the introduction to a preaching series on Mark, would do best to stay at the general level of the call to discipleship, with overtones of sacrifice and suffering hinted at, as well as the promise of supernatural aid. In fact, the sermon series is itself a journey through the Gospel, taking twenty-five weeks (if one follows the divisions in this commentary), a mini trek of discipleship. Hopefully, that expedition will be simultaneously integrated with other parallel pastoral initiatives in worship, small groups, children's ministries, etc.—all with a thrust on discipleship.

The sequential movements of the episodes, from John to Jesus to the disciples, are probably the best way to grasp what Mark is *doing* in this pericope. The table below, a modified form of the previous table, will clarify this issue.

	Call	Commission	Consequence
JOHN	+	+	+
JESUS	+	+	+
DISCIPLES	+	+	?

There is a pattern of call-commission-consequence for each of the three protagonists. However, the reader is left hanging—the consequence of the disciples' response to the divine call and commission is unstated. The consequences that John faces and that Jesus will face later in the Gospel do not leave much to the reader's imagination as to what the consequences for discipleship might be for all who choose to follow Jesus. John and Jesus were handed over/betrayed to death. What will happen to disciples?

Suffering is surely part of the Trip of Discipleship. The sermon on the first pericope of the book could therefore serve as the beginning of the series, the invitation to contemporary would-be (and those who already are) disciples to follow after Jesus, being willing to suffer, expecting the worst. What are we *not* willing to give up for the cause of Christ? Discipleship is costly! Learn what it costs, the preacher exhorts, by going through the Gospel of Mark.

The positives hinted at in the account are the promise of the Holy Spirit, the strength he provides for the journey, and, of course, the final consummation, one day—hopefully soon!—of the kingdom of God.[37] An important theme of the Gospel is that glory is coming . . . but not before suffering. The glory to come will make all the sacrifice and suffering worthwhile.

It is to be admitted that the intensity of suffering faced by Christians—i.e., from opponents and persecutors—varies in the different parts of the world. One must also note that even the historical disciples in the Markan account did not encounter the vehemence of inimical sentiment faced by many followers of Jesus since that time.[38] In any case, not all suffering necessarily originates from anti-Christian factions. Some of it, to be sure, comes from our living in a broken world. Thus the concept of "suffering" in the sermon may be addressed in different ways. To be willing to suffer, however, is an integral attitude that becomes a disciple.

The two pericopes at the commencement of the Gospel (this one and the next, 1:21–45) outline in general terms what a lifetime of discipleship will be like—suffering (1:1–20) and service (1:21–45). Right at the start of this Trip of Discipleship, these essential mindsets are laid out for the disciple to adopt. While nuances of these themes reappear later in Mark's account, exhorting believers to be willing to suffer and serve for the Gospel in general terms will be adequate in sermons on these two pericopes; pertinent specifics on how such a pattern of life might be commenced will, of course, be helpful and appropriate.

The invitation to follow has been extended. Will the reader join, aware of what the consequences might be? This sermon would therefore introduce the book with a challenge to the congregation to count the cost of discipleship carefully. Suffering first, glory later. The Trip of Discipleship is a way of suffering . . . to glory.

POSSIBLE PREACHING OUTLINES FOR PERICOPE 1[39]

I. CALL: John's, Jesus', the disciples'
   Depict the sequence of calls: 1:2; 1:10–11; 1:16, 20
   Move-to-Relevance: the nature of our call

II. COMMISSION: John's, Jesus', the disciples'
   Depict the sequence of commissions: 1:3–8; 1:14–15; 1:17
   Move-to-Relevance: the nature of our commission parallels that of the disciples

37. The role of the Holy Spirit in helping disciples following Jesus on this arduous way is not particularly emphasized in the entire Gospel; hints of supernatural aid are found in the acknowledgment of angelic ministry to Jesus coincident upon, or immediately following, his temptation by Satan (1:13.)

38. That most of the Twelve did suffer persecution and were martyred is generally accepted; however, Mark does not tell us that.

39. These outlines are deliberately skimpy; they are intended merely to be suggestions for further thought—rough-hewn stones to be polished by the preacher. It is nigh impossible to prescribe an outline without knowing the particular audience it is to be used for, and therefore this commentary will refrain from micromanaging homiletics for the preacher. Some equally abbreviated suggestions for development are provided below each main point.

    III.   CONSEQUENCE: John's, Jesus', (the disciples'?)
Depict the sequence of consequences (and hints of suffering; see Notes): 1:14;
9:31; 10:33 (×2)

    IV.   *Count the cost!* *
Specifically, how can we prepare, how can we count the cost?

* Outlines in this commentary will have an imperative of some sort as a major outline point. The specificity and direction of that imperative is between the Holy Spirit, the text, the preacher, and the audience. A potential application that might be suggested from the pulpit for this pericope might be the encouragement of the congregation to commit to twenty-five weeks of going on Jesus' "way" corporately, as the whole body engages intensely with the text of Mark's Gospel. This would serve as a fitting prologue for the series.

Another option is given below, one that might be more textual in sequence[40]:

    I.   John's Call, Commission, and Consequence

    II.   Jesus' Call, Commission, and Consequence

    III.   Disciples' Call, Commission, and . . . [Consequence?]

    IV.   *Count the cost!*

40. There is nothing magical about having a sermonic outline that parallels the structure of the text. Spoken sermons are a different form of media than scripted Gospels. The former do not necessarily have to follow the sequence of argument or parallel the narration of the latter. The kind of outline appropriate for the audience in the pew, in a sermon uttered by the preacher in the pulpit, must be decided preaching event by preaching event. On the other hand, there may be something to be said for ease of following along (from a congregant's point of view) with a sermon whose structure closely parallels the structure of the biblical text that lies open in the hearer's lap. Parallelism of structure between text and sermon means fewer ungainly leaps around the text by the preacher. The fewer these leaps, the greater the clarity, and thus, hopefully, the firmer the assimilation of truth in the hearts, minds, and lives of listeners.

PERICOPE 2

Following to Serve

Mark 1:21–45

[Exorcism; Healing of Simon's mother-in-law and a Leper]

REVIEW, SUMMARY, PREVIEW

Review of Pericope 1: In 1:1–20, the author, using a call-and-response structure, portrayed Jesus' invitation to all who will follow him to embark on the journey, with all that it entails, including its potential consequences—sacrifice and suffering.

Summary of Pericope 2: The second pericope of Mark (1:21–45) focuses upon the attitude disciples must have as they follow Jesus. The antagonism Jesus faces signals the disciples about the seriousness of Jesus' mission. However, without comprehending the gravity of Jesus' work, many follow him for tangible self-gain, with no thought of self-giving—the kind of selflessness demonstrated by Simon's mother-in-law. The way her story is told points to a positive model of service. Disciples, then, are called to exhibit such an attitude of service, as they embark upon the journey of discipleship, following Jesus' mission of extending the boundaries of God's kingdom.

Preview of Pericope 3: The next pericope (2:1—3:6), with its incrementally increasing antagonism to Jesus, dwells upon the opposition disciples can expect, and how it may be faced—with boldness and persistence.

2 Mark 1:21–45

THEOLOGICAL FOCUS OF PERICOPE 2

2   **Following after Jesus, the authoritative one who confronts opposition to extend the boundaries of God's realm, is not a self-serving enterprise that misunderstands Jesus and his mission, but one of selfless service that embraces the greater cause of the kingdom (1:21–45).**

2.1   Following after Jesus, the authoritative one who confronts demonic forces to further the kingdom of God, is an undertaking of the disciple that invites antagonism (1:21–29).

     2.1.1   The recognition of Jesus as the authoritative One is the right attitude of disciples.

     2.1.2   Supernatural antagonism is what a disciple can expect as one follows Jesus.

2.2   Following Jesus on the way is to join Jesus in his momentous mission for the greater cause of the kingdom of God, seeking to serve selflessly, rather than to secure existential, temporal benefits for oneself (1:28–39).

     2.2.1   Misunderstanding the nature of Jesus' mission can cause the disciple to follow out of self-interest.

     2.2.2   A clear understanding of Jesus' mission is critical for those who would follow him as disciples.

     2.2.3   Self-giving service for the mission of Jesus is the call of the disciple.

     2.2.4   Temporal relief from the ills of life is not the goal of following Jesus in discipleship.

     2.2.5   Kingdom establishment, the mission of Jesus, involves more than deliverance from existential woes.

2.3   The focus of Jesus' mission, while not neglecting the narrower scope of existential human need, is primarily upon the extension of the boundaries of God's realm against opposition (1:40–45).

     2.3.1   Jesus' kingdom mission involves the greater goal of establishing the realm of God, not merely the alleviation of temporal scourges.

     2.3.2   Following Jesus in the establishment of God's kingdom, the disciple can expect antagonism.

OVERVIEW

MARK 1:21–45 IS A fast-paced description of the spreading of Jesus' fame. The section has four exorcism or healing sections: 1:21–28; 1:29–31; 1:32–39; and 1:40–45. In contrast, the following section, 2:1—3:6, is slower paced and moves away from Jesus' popularity; the focus there is on opposition towards him and those who follow him.

This particular pericope, 1:21–45, is set in and around Capernaum, in the space of two twenty-four hour periods (1:32, 35). It contains all the aspects of Jesus' Galilean ministry: teaching (1:21–22, 27), exorcism (1:23–26, 32, 34, 39), healing (1:30–31, 32–34), and preaching (1:38–39)—an overview, perhaps indicating what the newly-called disciples, too, will engage in as they participate in Jesus' mission. In this regard, in this pericope Jesus is constantly shown to be associated with his disciples in his various ministry activities: the transitioning verbs in 1:21 ("went") and in 1:29 ("came," "went") are all plural, and in 1:38 Jesus exhorts his disciples, "Let *us* go . . ." Their training has begun! With what attitude should they undertake to follow Jesus?

2.1   Mark 1:21–29

THEOLOGICAL FOCUS 2.1

2.1   Following after Jesus, the authoritative one who confronts demonic forces to further the kingdom of God, is an undertaking of the disciple that invites antagonism (1:21–29).

   2.1.1   The recognition of Jesus as the authoritative One is the right attitude of disciples.

   2.1.2   Supernatural antagonism is what a disciple can expect as one follows Jesus.

Section Summary 2.1: The depiction of the first action of Jesus and his disciples, after the calling and commissioning of the latter, as a confrontation, is a warning to those who would follow Jesus—this journey of discipleship is not exactly a pleasurable stroll! This is an appropriate cautionary note, for many are prone to follow Jesus for the wrong reasons (see next section of this pericope), misunderstanding the seriousness of his mission to establish and extend the kingdom of God.

TRANSLATION 2.1

1:21   *And they went into Capernaum; and immediately on the Sabbath, He entered into the synagogue and began to teach.*

1:22   *And they were amazed at His teaching; for He was teaching them as one having authority and not as the scribes.*

1:23   *And immediately there was, in their synagogue, a man with an unclean spirit, and he cried out,*

1:24   *saying, "What [is it] with us and You, Jesus the Nazarene? Have You come to destroy us? I know who You are—the Holy One of God."*

1:25   *And Jesus rebuked him, saying, "Be quiet and come out of him."*

1:26   *And the unclean spirit convulsed him, and calling out with a loud call, came out of him.*

1:27   *And they were all astounded, so that they discussed among themselves saying, "What is this? A new teaching with authority; He commands even the unclean spirits, and they obey Him."*

1:28   *And the news about Him immediately went out everywhere, into the whole region of Galilee.*

1:29   *And immediately after they came out from the synagogue, they went into the house of Simon and Andrew, with James and John.*

NOTES 2.1

2.1.1   The recognition of Jesus as the authoritative One is the right attitude of disciples.

The larger section, 1:21—3:30, is centered around the question of Jesus' authority: the word ἐξουσία ("authority") occurs in 1:22, 27; 2:10; and 3:15, but Jesus' authority is also implied in the healings he performs (1:31, 42).[1] In this episode, with Jesus' exorcism the boundaries of the kingdom of God are being extended as the divine authority of Jesus is manifested. Strikingly different from contemporary exorcisms, Jesus' supernatural acts are accomplished without mechanical devices (incense, amulets, herbs, etc.) or "proofs" to demonstrate success, and without incantations or invocations of transcendental authorities—all indicating his own great authority, which, rightly, the crowd acknowledges in this section (1:27).[2]

The first episode opens with a surprising development: the demon-possessed man has supernatural insight about Jesus, calling him "the Holy One of God," a new descriptor in Mark's narrative. Indeed, while most afflicted persons in the Gospel address Jesus with non-specific terms ("teacher," 9:17; "Son of David," 10:47–48; "Rabboni" ["Master"], 10:51), the demons are quite precise in their ascriptions of divine character to Jesus (1:24; 3:11; 5:7).[3] It is ironic, then, that while the humans in this pericope see Jesus as some sort of a cosmic vending-machine as they jostle for proximity to gain his attention to obtain what material benefits he might have to offer (see below), the demons recognize him for who he actually is and seek to separate themselves from him.[4]

2.1.2   Supernatural antagonism is what a disciple can expect as one follows Jesus.

The sequencing of the elements of this first episode (1:21–29) is deliberate[5]:

A   Jesus goes into (εἰσέρχομαι, *eiserchomai*) the synagogue immediately (1:21)

    B   Jesus' teaching with authority (ἐξουσία, *exousia*, and διδαχῇ, *didache*, 1:21–22*); crowd amazed

        C   Man with an unclean spirit (1:23)

            D   Man cries out, saying . . . ". . . Have You come . . .?" (ἦλθες, *ēlthes*, 1:24)

            D′   Jesus rebukes, saying . . . ". . . come out . . ." (ἔξελθε, *exelthe*, 1:26)

        C′   "He commands even the unclean spirits" (1:27)

    B′   Jesus' teaching with authority (ἐξουσία and διδαχὴ, 1:27); crowd astounded

A′   Jesus goes out of (ἐξέρχομαι, *exerchomai*) the synagogue immediately (1:29)

   * Verb forms of διδάσκω (*didaskō*, "teach") also occur in 1:21–22.

Jesus' first "official" action in the company of his disciples is to set foot on the turf of the scribes (1:22)—the synagogue, their symbolic space and domain. There Jesus

---

1. The authority here in 1:21–45 is demonstrated to the crowds; in 2:1—3:6, Jesus' authority is depicted as catching the attention of the hierarchy of Jewish religious leaders. Mark 1:22 is the only place in the Gospels where a miracle is called a "teaching." Of note is that διδάσκειν (*didaskein*, "to teach") is used seventeen times in Mark, sixteen of which have Jesus as subject (the exception is in 6:30, where the apostles teach). Clearly the establishment of the kingdom of God is intimately linked to "teaching," the broad conception of which includes actions such as exorcism and healing.

2. Osborne, "Structure and Christology," 152–53; also see Winn, *Purpose of Mark's Gospel*, 111.

3. Witherington, *Gospel of Mark*, 91.

4. This episode is almost paradigmatic for two other scenes in a later pericope: 4:35–41 and 5:12–20, for which 1:21–29 serves as a "model." See on Pericope 6 below.

5. Myers, *Binding the Strong Man*, 142; Kuthirakkattel, *Beginning of Jesus' Ministry*, 125.

performs his first recorded miracle, an exorcism, and opposition is immediate: the struggle of authority between Jesus and the demon stands at the center of the literary structure (elements D and D' above).[6] Coming soon after the description of a forty-day temptation by Satan and struggles of some sort with wild beasts, such a reading of 1:21–29, seeing hostility in the synagogue in connection with an unclean spirit, makes sense. That this pericope is bookended with mentions of religious leaders (scribes here in 1:21–29, and the healing in 1:40–45 an indictment of the priests; see below) is a subtle hint of opposition from these quarters as well. Indeed, in the next pericope (2:1—3:6) the caucuses and cliques of religious leaders vehemently oppose Jesus and his disciples.

All of this, including the interplay of Jesus' authority and demonic resistance, is a signal to the disciples: this is what they too may expect when following Jesus on the way, extending the kingdom of God—namely, antagonism.[7] In other words, the calling out of disciples, their commission to be fishers of men, and their setting forth after Jesus is one big leap into dangerous territory. Far be it from the disciples to assume that following Jesus in discipleship is a tame affair. Going after this authoritative one leads the disciple directly into opposition, adumbrated in 1:21–29 (and 1:40–45) and expanded upon in 2:1—3:6. "Be warned," Mark seems to be exhorting. In light of the subsequent episodes of the current pericope, which show both crowds and disciples following Jesus for the tangible goods and betterments of life that he might dole out, this episode and the corresponding parallel one at the other end (1:40–45) serve as foils. Discipleship is not a facile, undemanding, follow-for-gain affair. The Trip of Discipleship is decidedly not a walk in the park. On the contrary . . .

2.2   Mark 1:28–39

THEOLOGICAL FOCUS 2.2

2.2   Following Jesus on the way is to join Jesus in his momentous mission for the greater cause of the kingdom of God, seeking to serve selflessly, rather than to secure existential, temporal benefits for oneself (1:28–39).

  2.2.1   Misunderstanding the nature of Jesus' mission can cause the disciple to follow out of self-interest.

  2.2.2   A clear understanding of Jesus' mission is critical for those who would follow him as disciples.

  2.2.3   Self-giving service for the mission of Jesus is the call of the disciple.

  2.2.4   Temporal relief from the ills of life is not the goal of following Jesus in discipleship.

  2.2.5   Kingdom establishment, the mission of Jesus, involves more than deliverance from existential woes.

---

6. Notable is the first-person plural in the mouth of the man with the unclean spirit (singular): "What [is it] with *us* and you . . . ?" (1:24). Is the "us" a subtle hint to refer to the scribes, the nearest plural antecedent (1:22), with those eminent ones being equated to the man with the unclean spirit?

7. The kinds of antagonism that they can expect to face will be spelled out in the following pericope, 2:1—3:6, where escalating opposition to Jesus and his disciples is depicted.

Section Summary 2.2: Following Jesus for the wrong reasons is deprecated in this section. Misunderstanding Jesus' mission of extending the kingdom of God, many assume that coming to Jesus is a painless strategy for self-gain. Rather, this unit compels disciples to adopt an attitude of selfless service for the greater cause of the kingdom of God.

TRANSLATION 2.2

1:28   And the news about Him immediately went out everywhere, into the whole region of Galilee.

1:29   And immediately after they came out from the synagogue, they went into the house of Simon and Andrew, with James and John.[8]

1:30   Now Simon's mother-in-law was lying down, suffering with a fever, and immediately they told Him about her.

1:31   And He came and raised her up, holding her hand; and the fever left her, and she served them.

1:32   When it was evening, when the sun had set, they were bringing to him all who were ill and those demon-possessed.

1:33   And the whole city had gathered at the door.

1:34   And He healed many who were ill with various diseases, and many demons he cast out, and he was not permitting the demons to speak, because they knew Him.

1:35   And early in the morning, while it was still very dark, arising, He went out and went away into a wilderness place, [and] there He was praying.

1:36   And Simon and those with him searched for Him.

1:37   And they found Him and said to Him, "All are seeking you."

1:38   And He said to them, "Let us go elsewhere into the neighboring towns, so that I may preach there also; for I came out for this [purpose]."

1:39   And He went into their synagogues preaching in all Galilee and casting out demons.

NOTES 2.2

2.2.1   Misunderstanding the nature of Jesus' mission can cause the disciple to follow out of self-interest.

With obvious authority, Jesus casts out a demon, and his fame spreads (1:28).

A   Exorcism (demon comes out, ἐξέρχομαι, *exerchomai*, 1:26); unclean; imposition of silence; scribes (1:21–27)

  B   Jesus' fame spreads to the whole (ὅλος, *holos*) region of Galilee (1:28)

    C   Private: in a house, Simon's mother-in-law is cured, after the intervention of the four (1:29–31)

      D   Public: the whole (ὅλος) city; healing/exorcism and imposition of silence (1:32–34)

8. Mark 1:28–29 forms a link between the previous section and this one.

> C′   Private: in a deserted place, Jesus is found, and Simon and those with him intervene (1:35–38)
>
> B′   Jesus goes to all (ὅλος) of Galilee (1:39)
>
> A′   Healing (leprosy goes away, ἀπέρχομαι, *aperchomai*, 1:42); clean/cleansing; imposition of silence; priests (1:40–45)*

* Modified from Kuthirakkattel, *Beginning of Jesus' Ministry*, 66; and Dowd, *Reading Mark*, 18.

The center of the pericope (element D) is the statement that everyone was clamoring for Jesus' presence. This is a key point of this pericope. The crowds were seeking their own liberation from disease; entire regions and whole cities were coming to Jesus, the miracle worker *par excellence*. Following upon an episode that demonstrated the seriousness of Jesus' mission as he authoritatively exorcised an antagonistic demon, these scenes seem to show that the masses around Jesus simply have not understood the nature of his mission. Sadly, the disciples too are caught up in the shallow excitement of Jesus' miracles. The narrator shows them as not being any wiser than the crowd in this regard. Twice they intervene, seeking to have *their* needs met (telling Jesus about the plight of a family member, 1:29–31; executing their own plans for Jesus to meet the needs of the crowds, 1:35–38—the parallel elements C and C′). Uncomprehending, both crowds and disciples are following Jesus for the wrong reasons.[9] The kingdom of God is not merely about providing mankind utilitarian improvements to make existence easy and comfortable. While the disciples follow Jesus, the one who has authority over demons and diseases, the meeting of such existential needs ought not to be the reason for following him. Disciples follow him because he calls with divine authority—an authority that extends far and wide, over domains physical and spiritual—and promises something far greater and longer lasting than any temporal convenience or enrichment: the kingdom of God. Discipleship is a call to be involved in something more magnificent than the securing of one's own temporal comforts and consolations.

2.2.2   *A clear understanding of Jesus' mission is critical for those who would follow him as disciples.*

In light of Jesus' increasing popularity for the wrong reasons, it is no wonder that he imposes silence over and over again (1:25, 34, 44 in the elements A, D, A′; see above). Preaching (i.e., the proclamation and thus, extension, of God's kingdom, the new way of life, 1:14–15) is what Jesus has come to do, not merely to heal, exorcise, and meet the physical needs of his associates and audiences.[10] Despite these exhortations to secrecy,

---

9. None of those of interventions are explicitly wrong; in fact, Jesus assents to the desires of his disciples. Nevertheless, Mark's point here is that disciples ought to be motivated by service, not gain; following Jesus merely for what tangible benefits he might offer is not what discipleship is about.

10. These impositions of silence may have simply served as a means (futile, to be sure) to diminish the spread of his fame as a thaumaturge or magician. From a rhetorical standpoint, however, the author is implying, by Jesus' insistence on concealment, that what disciples must attend to and focus upon is *not* Jesus' capability to improve the quality of their earthly existence. Rather, Jesus seeks a holistic restoration for his people, attainable only by membership in the kingdom of God—the future glory to be attained . . . by way of suffering.

Jesus' popularity keeps growing dramatically: the repetition of ὅλος (*holos*, "whole") in 1:28, 33, and 39 makes this clear (elements A, D, A', above). Throughout the Gospel, such impositions to silence are made upon demons (1:34; 3:12), upon those healed from afflictions (1:43; 5:43; 7:36), and even upon the disciples (8:30; 9:9). It appears that Jesus would rather not have anyone follow him who does not clearly understand the nature of his mission. Therefore, he enjoins silence upon all those who see him as only a wonder-worker; until they are able to grasp his mission and understand him as the suffering one (9:9; 15:39), publicity is proscribed. In 1:25, 34, it is the demons who are so restricted. Jesus does not want their premature acknowledgement of his divine powers to be broadcast, unless accompanied by a disclosure of his suffering ministry. While joy and light are, no doubt, spread by Jesus, the way of God that he proclaims is one that involves pain and darkness in this life, for God's way goes against the way of the world and will meet with opposition. Until that crucial aspect of suffering has been taught and understood, silence is commanded in order to preclude "misdirected popular adulation."[11] After all, the theme of the Gospel is "the way of suffering . . . to glory," the way of/to the kingdom of God. Osborne observes: "The reality of who Jesus is can never be understood merely on the basis of wondrous deeds; this demands supernatural revelation of God himself, primarily in the passion and resurrection of Jesus."[12] Despite all Jesus' efforts, the impositions of silence would be to no avail; Jesus' reputation as a healer and exorcist spreads rapidly, unfortunately for the wrong reasons (1:33, 37, 45; 2:1–2; 3:7–9).

2.2.3   *Self-giving service for the mission of Jesus is the call of the disciple.*

In all of these accounts of Jesus' increasing popularity, only this woman, Simon's mother-in-law, is said to minister to ("serve," 1:31) Jesus—an act of self-giving. Indeed, her story (C, in the structure above) is bounded on either side (B and D) by statements attesting to Jesus' incredible popularity. Nobody in that idolizing crowd is mentioned as giving to Jesus, not even the disciples. Everyone is out to get, except for this anonymous woman. Amidst all who are seeking only to *get* from Jesus, here is one who was willing to *give*, because she herself had been given. It is no doubt significant that there are only two instances of διακονέω (*diakoneō*, "serve") with humans as subjects in Mark's Gospel (1:31 and 15:41), and both times the subjects are women. A subtle jab! The narrator is pointing an appreciative finger at the example of this mother-in-law, a woman who does the male disciples one better![13] She is already doing what Jesus himself will later model for his disciples. The same verb διακονέω is found in the statement on the essence of Jesus' mission: the Son of man did not come to be served, but to *serve* (10:45). The narrator is implying that this woman is a true disciple, serving after the

---

11. France, *Gospel of Mark*, 105. Also see Placher, *Mark*, 56.

12. Osborne, "Structure and Christology," 156.

13. Indeed, the women in this Gospel shine far brighter than the Twelve men. See on the woman with the hemorrhage (5:25–34), the Syrophoenician woman (7:25–30), the widow and her coins (12:38–44), and the woman who anoints Jesus (14:1–11)—all positive models of discipleship.

fashion of her Lord. Simon's mother-in-law is thus a foil to both crowds and disciples, indeed, to all who might follow Jesus for the wrong reasons.

2.2.4 *Temporal relief from the ills of life is not the goal of following Jesus in discipleship.*

Mark seems to be painting a less than wholesome picture of the crowds with the description of their "seeking" him (1:37): all of the uses of ζητέω (*zēteō*, "seek") in Mark have a negative connotation, with implications of hostility and opposition (see 3:32 with 21; also 8:11, 12; 11:18; 12:12; 14:1, 11, 55; and perhaps 16:6 as well). The crowds are simply out to get what they can from this worker of wonders. But temporary alleviation of earthly bane and burden is not the essence of Jesus' mission. He is there to preach the kingdom of God and to call people to follow him (1:15, 38); yet the hordes are only interested in relief from the concrete ailments produced by demonic affliction and pathological abnormality. In the orderly arrangement of the elements in 1:34 (in the Greek), the exorcism of demons and the healing of physical ailments (in italics, below) are neatly equated.[14]

> He healed
>> many
>>> *who were ill with various diseases,*
>>> *and demons*
>> many
> He cast out.

In Markan theology (and perhaps in the rest of the Gospels, as well), both demonic and physical afflictions are *illnesses*, the result of God's way being subverted by satanic influence and human sinfulness. To the crowds, however, both are *diseases*, concrete manifestations that merely affect function, wage-earning capacity, lifespan, and personal comfort. For the reparation of these deficits and the alleviation of these symptoms, they seek Jesus, the miracle man. "The reader may be meant to think that the crowds did not see the exorcisms and healings as Jesus did—as victories in the conflict with Satan, and as examples that the dominion was breaking in. The crowds may have seen them as only a temporary respite from their woes."[15] In other words, the crowds (and the disciples) are following him for the wrong reasons, without comprehending Jesus' mission—the extension of the kingdom of God against all antagonism.

2.2.5 *Kingdom establishment, the mission of Jesus, involves more than deliverance from existential woes.*

As was noted earlier, the intervention of the disciples appears to be intended to "correct" Jesus' ideas of ministry—they, like the crowds, want him engaged in meeting existential needs (their own included; 1:30, 36–37). In the second instance of their intervention (1:35–38), when they attempt to persuade him to return from his solitude,

---

14. As was mentioned, the parallel placement of 1:21–29 (an exorcism) and 1:40–45 (a healing) in this pericope (see the structural layout above) also substantiates this equation of demonic affliction and physiological dysfunction.

15. Witherington, *Gospel of Mark*, 101.

presumably to continue to meet the physical needs of the crowds "seeking" him, Jesus corrects *them:* he has come to preach, to proclaim the kingdom of God—that is his primary aim, not the temporary staving off of physical maladies, demonic visitations, and the like (1:38). However, the fact that he then proceeds to do both—preach *and* exorcise/heal—denotes that Jesus' goal of proclaiming God's kingdom *does* involve the destruction of Satan's strongholds and the relief of human anguish. However, Jesus saw such afflictions as spiritual illnesses, not just physical diseases. Therefore, exorcisms and healings continue to be part of the *modus operandi* of Jesus' proclamation, but not for the ephemeral goals sought by the crowds. Deliverance from woes temporal is not primarily what Jesus' mission is all about; it is about the establishment of a kingdom divine. Only inclusion within such a kingdom—marked by an attitude of service—will give those who follow Jesus what they are truly searching for and what they really need—holistic restoration under the reign of God forever.

2.3 Mark 1:40–45

> **THEOLOGICAL FOCUS 2.3**
>
> 2.3   The focus of Jesus' mission, while not neglecting the narrower scope of existential human need, is primarily upon the extension of the boundaries of God's realm against opposition (1:40–45).
>
> 2.3.1   Jesus' kingdom mission involves the greater goal of establishing the realm of God, not merely the alleviation of temporal scourges.
>
> 2.3.2   Following Jesus in the establishment of God's kingdom, the disciple can expect antagonism.

Section Summary 2.3: The parallels between the story of the leper's cleansing and the earlier one of the exorcism, further specify the nature of Jesus' mission—to expand the boundaries of God's kingdom, in the face of opposition of all kinds from all quarters. Yet the fact that Jesus is not averse to caring for the needs of people is reassuring; indeed, the extension of God's kingdom subsumes the removal of all woes, the satisfaction of every need, and the alleviation of all hurts.

TRANSLATION 2.3

1:40   *And a leper came to him beseeching Him, and falling on his knees, and saying to Him, "If You are willing, You can make me clean."*

1:41   *And moved with compassion, stretching out His hand, He touched and said to him, "I am willing, be clean."*

1:42   *And immediately the leprosy went away from him, and he was cleansed.*

1:43   *And sternly warning him, immediately He sent him out.*

1:44   *And He said to him, "See that you say nothing to anyone, but go, show yourself to the priest and offer for your cleansing what Moses commanded, for a testimony against them."*

1:45 *But as he went out, he began to preach much and spread the word widely, so that He was no longer able to go publicly into a town, but was in wilderness places; and they were coming to Him from everywhere.*

NOTES 2.3

2.3.1 Jesus' kingdom mission involves the greater goal of establishing the realm of God, not merely the alleviation of temporal scourges.

The approach of the man with "leprosy" brings the issue of disease vs. illness to the fore again.[16] One cannot but notice the parallels between the first and last episodes of this pericope (1:21–29 and 40–45):

- Similarity of terms in both episodes:
  ἀκάθαρτος, *akathartos*, "unclean" (1:23, 26, 27)
  καθαρίζω, *katharizō*, "clean" (1:40, 41, 42); καθαρισμός, *katharismos*, "cleansing" (1:44)
- Mention of members of the religious hierarchy in both sections: scribes (1:22) and priest(s) (1:44)
- Jesus' imposition of silence (1:25; 1:44)
- Depiction of the affliction as "departing" in both cases—almost making the healing of leprosy an exorcism
  ἐξέρχομαι, *exerchomai*, the unclean spirit "coming out" (1:25, 26)
  ἀπέρχομαι, *aperchomai*, the leprosy "going away" (1:42)

Such a parallel depiction equates, again, exorcism with leprosy, framing both as "illnesses." Both demon possession and the contagion of leprosy render the sufferer unclean. The elimination of this uncleanness ("illness") is an integral part of Jesus' mission to extend and establish the realm of God, not merely the alleviation of human sufferings and temporal scourges ("diseases"). Nonetheless, the description of Jesus' compassion and the redundant phrasing employed by Mark to depict Jesus freely touching the unclean man ("stretching out His hand, He touched," 1:41) signifies Jesus' care and concern for the existential plight of the victims of disease/illness. Indeed, it is only in the establishment of the kingdom of God that the eradication of all earthly adversity, travail, and ruin will one day be realized—at the consummation of that grand kingdom.

2.3.2 Following Jesus in the establishment of God's kingdom, the disciple can expect antagonism.

Jesus' final instruction is that the leper's healing be an "indictment" against the priests ("for a testimony against them," 1:44). Other instances of this phrase in this Gospel (6:11; 13:9) sound a negative tone, and are found in the context of opposition. While

---

16. "Leprosy" is unlikely to be Hansen's disease: the biblical descriptions of its symptoms differ substantially from those produced by an infection of *Mycobacterium lepra*.

in the first encounter in the synagogue (1:21–29) the scribes are contrasted with Jesus (his authority was greater than theirs), in this last incident (1:40–45), it is the priests who are so compared (Jesus' ability to heal far surpasses their capacity merely to ratify a healing). In both bookends of this pericope, there is a hint of antagonism from religious quarters. This final episode of the chapter therefore prepares the way for 2:1—3:6, where a wave of increasing opposition to Jesus and his disciples is described, coming exclusively from the ecclesiastics of the day.

The healed leper begins preaching the word (1:45). Mark appears to be contrasting this man's "preaching" with that of Jesus, which was just mentioned in 1:38–39. The ex-leper's proclamation of the "word" brought only more popularity to Jesus (1:45—perhaps this was an incomplete proclamation?); on the other hand, the "word" of Jesus (in 2:2; etc.) brought virulent opposition to him and his followers. Again, the reader is being primed for 2:1—3:6, where opposition increases exponentially to the words and works of Jesus. Needless to say, opposition is going to be part and parcel of the Trip of Discipleship—a stark contrast to the expectation of the crowds and the disciples, who anticipate mitigation of woes and palliation of pain. Instead, Mark warns of hostility and enmity as one follows Jesus' way—the way to glory . . . through suffering.

Several "hook words" also serve the function of linking this section (1:21–45) with the following one (2:1—3:6).

> he went out (ἐξέρχομαι, *exerchomai*) (1:45a)
>   the word (1:45b)
>   no longer (1:45c)
>   they were coming (εἰσελθεῖν, *eiselthein*) (1:45d)
>   when He came (εἰσελθών, *eiselthōn*) (2:1a)
>   no longer (2:2b)
>   the word (2:2c)
> they came (ἔρχομαι, *erchomai*) (2:3a)

SERMON FOCUS AND OUTLINES

THEOLOGICAL FOCUS OF PERICOPE 2 FOR PREACHING

2 **Following Jesus is not a self-serving enterprise stemming from a misunderstanding of Jesus and his mission, but one of selfless service (1:21–45).**

In this particular pericope, needs are being met and diseases are being cured—the crowds' narrow point of view. From God's point of view, however, his kingdom is being established as Jesus extends its boundaries, exorcising, healing, preaching. Evil is being pushed back and the kingdom of God presses onward. These are dangerous actions on the part of Jesus, promising antagonism and opposition (which are more specifically encountered in 2:1—3:6); of course, the death of Jesus is itself the culmination of that hostility. However, the crowds and disciples are oblivious to all of these subtleties, as they focus only upon their own needs and Jesus' capacity to meet them. Consequently, Jesus' popularity increases considerably (just as opposition to him mounts in the next pericope).

A misunderstanding of what following Jesus is all about is deprecated in this pericope. While willingness to follow is creditable (1:1–20), the disciple must be aware of what he or she is getting into. This journey of discipleship does not necessarily guarantee earthly returns in terms of tangible goods, relief from affliction, or freedom from pain. At best, such an attitude is naïve; at worst, mercenary. Disciples must be aware of what they are getting into, taking care not to be following Jesus for the wrong reasons. As depicted in this pericope, those wrong reasons include the satisfaction of temporal felt needs and the alleviation of existential difficulties. The journey of discipleship into which one enters by divine call is not primarily intended to make one feel good, comfortable, or happy, at least not in this life. On the contrary, Jesus' mission, which his disciples follow after, is a magnificent and noble undertaking that must be entered into with the primary attitude of selfless service—to give, not to get. In fact, there may be a hint in the pericope that it will only be with the establishment of God's kingdom that all of mankind's existential blights will be remedied; only in that divine realm will such woes be forever banished.

The first two pericopes of the Gospel have outlined in general terms what a lifetime of discipleship will be like—suffering (1:1–20) and service (1:21–45). Fine-tuning of these elements will continue to occur throughout Mark's account, for they are recurrent themes. In these pericopes, exhorting disciples to welcome a lifelong engagement in service to God's people (or with suffering—in the previous pericope) will be sufficient, with appropriate specifics on how one might begin such a pattern of life right away.

POSSIBLE PREACHING OUTLINES FOR PERICOPE 2[17]

I. Following to get: Crowds' response to Jesus; disciples' interventions upon Jesus

    Depict the crowds' and the disciples' negative reactions to Jesus: 1:28, 32–34, 45; 29–31, 35–37

    Move-to-Relevance: Our wrong responses

II. [But . . .] Jesus' program: To extend God's kingdom, not necessarily to satisfy temporal needs

    The exorcism and its significance: What disciples can expect: 1:21–27

    Move-to-Relevance: What the Trip of Discipleship is really like and all about (reprise from 1:1–20?)

III. Following to give: The mother-in-law

    Simon's mother-in-law, the paragon: 1:30–31

IV. [So . . .] *Giving, not getting, is the proper attitude of the disciple!*[*]

    Specifics: How can we demonstrate that proper attitude?

---

[*] There is nothing magical about four-point outlines (as suggested for this pericope and the previous one)! One may have as many points as text, time, expediency, audience, and persuasiveness demand. Neither is there anything sacrosanct about stating the demand of the text in an imperative. While that is helpful for clarity, an implicit imperative, as in this case, will work quite well. The theme of service as integral to discipleship might profitably be addressed in the application.

17. "Self-serving" and "self-giving" in the Theological Focus of the Pericope for Preaching are simplified to "getting" and "giving" in the Possible Preaching Outlines.

ACT I: IN GALILEE

Another option:

I.   Jesus' program: To extend God's kingdom against opposition, not necessarily to satisfy temporal needs

II.   The negative models: Following to get—crowds and disciples

III. The positive model: Following to give—the mother-in-law

IV.   *Giving, not getting, is the proper attitude of the disciple!*

PERICOPE 3

Responding to Antagonism

Mark 2:1—3:6

[Five Controversy Dialogues]

REVIEW, SUMMARY, PREVIEW

Review of Pericope 2: Mark 1:21–45 demonstrates that following Jesus in discipleship is not a self-satisfying undertaking, but a self-giving one.

Summary of Pericope 3: The current pericope (2:1—3:6) indicates the kind of opposition those who follow Jesus might expect to face: antagonism to their claims of following a leader with the divine authority to forgive, to the calling of sinners to join the band of disciples (an implicit labeling of mankind as being in need of a Savior), to their new lifestyle as disciples, and to their critique of traditional practices in light of the new kingdom Jesus is establishing. The model of Jesus' bold persistence in fulfilling his divine mission, as he extends the kingdom of God, is one that disciples must follow, despite opposition of any kind.

Preview of Pericope 4: The next pericope (3:7–35) identifies the disciple as one who does the will of God—the "insider" who is with Jesus.

3   Mark 2:1—3:6

> **THEOLOGICAL FOCUS OF PERICOPE 3**
>
> **3   Following Jesus in discipleship entails facing opposition—to the claim of forgiveness, to disciples' association with sinners, to the newness of their lifestyle, and to their critique of traditional practices—with boldness and persistence, without being deterred from their divine calling (2:1—3:6).**
>
> 3.1   Following Jesus, the divine one with the authority to forgive sin, will engender opposition for the disciple (2:1–12).
>
> 3.2   The call of sinners to join the company of disciples, a message integral to the mission of Jesus to extend the kingdom of God, attracts opposition from self-righteous ones, for it implies they are sinners, as well (2:13–17).
>
> 3.3   The change in the lifestyle of the disciples—their abandonment of old patterns of conduct in light of their new membership in the kingdom of God—raises doubt and opposition (2:18–22).
>
> 3.4   The changed lifestyle of the disciples, as they follow Jesus under his authority, critiques the ways of the world, attracting antagonism (2:23–28).
>
> 3.5   Jesus' boldness and persistence in the fulfillment of his divine call, though he was grieved and angered by his hardhearted antagonists, is the pattern for disciples to follow, not letting opposition deter them from their own divine call to follow Jesus on his mission to establish the kingdom of God (3:1–6).

OVERVIEW

THE PLOT MOVES ON from Jesus' increasing popularity (for misguided reasons) in 1:21–45 to escalating opposition in 2:1—3:6 (also for wrong reasons). The indictment of the religious hierarchy in 1:44, as well as the negative thrusts in, and the contrasts between, the first and last scenes of the previous pericope (1:21–29 and 1:40–45; see above on Pericope 2), prepare the ground for the confrontations in this pericope. While the focus remains on Jesus, the disciples are constantly associated with him in this text; by virtue of this association, they too face the same opposition Jesus faces. Mark 1:21–45 hinted at antagonism towards those engaged in God's kingdom mission; those hints become reality here. All is not promising to be rosy for disciples.

That 2:1—3:6 is a separate unit is evident from its deliberate symmetrical patterning (see below), the programmatic escalation of conflict, the absence of any imposition of silence in this pericope (as was found in 1:21–45), the conclusion of each story with an aphoristic utterance from Jesus, and the staging of action entirely in Capernaum. Moreover, 1:45 could conceivably move seamlessly to 3:7, demarcating 2:1—3:6 as a discrete pericope.[1]

Of the five controversy units in this pericope, the disciples are found only in the three central units (2:13–17, 18–22, and 23–27; see below). Yet Mark makes it clear in his telling that what Jesus faces is what his followers will face. Immediately after a

---

1. Boring, *Mark*, 73. At the same time, the connection between 1:45 and 2:1–2 is undeniable; the chiastic structure of these connections was noted earlier (see under 1:45). Conceivably, this pericope could be split into five separate units, resulting in five separate sermons. However, the thematic similarities between the discrete episodes of 2:1—3:6 make it more practicable to treat it as a single pericope. Interestingly, these five controversies are paralleled by five controversy dialogues later in Jerusalem (see on 11:1—13:2).

disciple is called (Levi, in 2:14), the whole company is corporately involved in Jesus' activities; opposition to him overflows to them. In fact, in two of the episodes (2:18–22 and 23–28), it is the activities of the disciples, rather than those of Jesus, that provoke hostility—the opponents actually complain to Jesus about his disciples! The increased involvement of the disciples in Jesus' mission and their greater identification with the one they follow results in a "fluid oscillation between the individual figure [Jesus] and his collective representatives [disciples]."[2] What happens to the leader will inevitably happen to his followers; the disciples are closely identified with their Master.

The table below depicts the structural organization of the five episodes.[3]

SECTION	OPPONENTS	LITERARY ELEMENTS			
A 2:1–12	Scribes	*healing*	death (2:7)*	hearts (2:6, 8)	raising (2:9, 11, 12)
B 2:13–17	Scribes/ Pharisees	eating (disciples)	"have need" (2:17)		
C 2:18–22	"them"	fasting (disciples)	death (2:20)		
B′ 2:23–28	Pharisees	eating (disciples)	"have need" (2:25)		
A′ 3:1–6	Pharisees/ Herodians	*healing*	death (3:6)	hearts (3:5)	raising (3:3)

* "Death" indicates allusions to the death of Jesus: blasphemy as the cause of his execution (2:7), his "removal" (2:20), and the plotting to kill him (3:6). Sections A, C, and A′ also begin similarly: with εἰσελθὼν πάλιν (eiselthon palin, "he entered again," 2:1), ἐξῆλθεν πάλιν (exēlthen palin, "he went out again," 2:13), and εἰσελθὼν πάλιν (3:1), respectively. Each of the narratives of sections B and B′ begins outdoors and moves indoors (in the latter, at least David the protagonist does), and each closes with quasi-proverbial, christological sayings.

The trajectory of the section builds upon the escalation and increasing antipathy towards Jesus and the disciples, culminating in the plot of their enemies to destroy Jesus (3:6). The crescendo is patently audible, and the accusations become progressively more serious; the silent reasoning of the adversaries in the first episode escalates into outright plotting to assassinate Jesus in the last (see below). The historical issues in question that create all the animus and the waxing hostility of the opponents are summarized below.

SECTION	ISSUE	OPPONENTS' RESPONSE
A 2:1–12	Authority of the forgiver	Scribes, in their hearts, accuse Jesus of blasphemy
B 2:13–17	Association with sinners	Scribes/Pharisees question disciples about Jesus' practice
C 2:18–22	Newness of practice	"They" question Jesus about his disciples' non-conformity
B′ 2:23–27	Oldness reinterpreted	Pharisees question Jesus about disciples' "lawbreaking"
A′ 3:1–6	Response to opposition	Pharisees/Herodians plot to kill Jesus

2. Henderson, *Christology*, 73.

3. From Parrott, "Conflict and Rhetoric," 120; van Iersel, "Concentric Structures," 77, 91; idem, *Mark*, 118; and Byrne, *Costly Freedom*, 54–55.

The inbreaking of God's reign under Jesus is a challenge to every other claim to power. Combined with the general refusal of people to submit to this reign, the result of the nearness of this new regime is a dramatic power struggle.[4] There will be antagonism and virulent hostility directed towards Jesus and those who follow him. The kinds of opposition the disciple can expect are described in this pericope.

As one goes through the theological themes of the sections in this pericope, a line of thought may be discerned. The first two episodes are linked: they deal, respectively, with Jesus' divine authority to forgive sin, and with the fact that all of humankind (self-righteous ones included!) is lost in sin, needing the cure of a Savior. In other words, *everyone* needs the forgiveness Jesus alone has the authority to extend; but the opponents reject both Jesus' authority and their own neediness. The next two episodes are linked as well: they deal, respectively, with antagonism directed towards the changed lifestyles of those who follow Jesus, and with the implicit critiques those changed lifestyles offer to the mores of the world. In other words, ways of life have changed for the disciples and those new ways silently condemn the old ways of the world. But opponents question the validity and spirituality of these changed lifestyles and reject the critique that such lifestyles offer to their own practices. The final episode, as will be seen, concludes the pericope, addressing how the disciple may handle such opposition.

3.1 Mark 2:1–12

THEOLOGICAL FOCUS 3.1

3.1 Following Jesus, the divine one with the authority to forgive sin, will engender opposition for the disciple (2:1–12).

Section Summary 3.1: The structure of this episode, with the accusation of blasphemy in the center, focuses the antagonism of opponents upon Jesus' appropriation of divine prerogatives. In light of the corporate solidarity between leader and led that is exemplified in the entire pericope, disciples, too, can expect to face opposition, as they follow the divine Son of Man who has the authority to forgive sins. The exercise of this authority is a means by which the kingdom of God is extended.

TRANSLATION 3.1

2:1 *And when He entered again into Capernaum after some days, it was heard that He was in the house.*

2:2 *And many were gathered together so that no longer was there room, not even by the door, and He was speaking the word to them.*

2:3 *And they came bringing to Him a paralytic, carried by four men.*

2:4 *And being unable to bring [him] to Him because of the crowd, they unroofed the roof where He was, and digging it out, they let down the pallet on which the paralytic was lying.*

---

4. Witherington, *Gospel of Mark*, 110–11.

2:5   And Jesus, seeing their faith, said to the paralytic, "Son, your sins are forgiven."

2:6   But some of the scribes were sitting there and reasoning in their hearts,

2:7   "Why does this one speak thus? He blasphemes. Who is able to forgive sins but God alone?"

2:8   And immediately Jesus, knowing in His spirit that they were reasoning thus within themselves, said to them, "Why are you reasoning about these things in your hearts?

2:9   Which is easier, to say to the paralytic, 'Your sins are forgiven,' or to say, 'Rise and carry your pallet and walk'?

2:10 But in order that you may know that the Son of Man has authority to forgive sins upon the earth"—He said to the paralytic—

2:11 "I say to you, rise, carry your pallet and go into your home."

2:12 And he rose and immediately carried the pallet and went out before all, so that all were astounded and glorifying God saying, "We have never seen [anything] like this."

NOTES 3.1

3.1   *Following Jesus, the divine one with the authority to forgive sin, will engender opposition for the disciple.*

This section is also chiastically structured, denoting the central element of the accusation of blasphemy[5]:

Narrative introduction (2:1–2)

A   They came (ἔρχομαι, *erchomai*); paralytic carried (αἴρω, *airō*); presence of crowd; pallet let down (2:3–4)

   B   He said to the paralytic, ". . . your sins are forgiven" (2:5)

      C   Scribes reasoning in their hearts (2:6)

         D   Accusation of blasphemy (2:7)

      C′   Scribes reasoning within themselves; reasoning in their hearts (2:8)

   B′   "Your sins are forgiven"; authority to forgive sins; He said to the paralytic (2:9–10)

A′   "Carry [αἴρω] your pallet"; he carries (αἴρω) the pallet; he goes out (ἐξέρχομαι, *exerchomai*); presence of crowd (2:11–12c)

Narrative conclusion (2:12d)

That this account is more than a narrative of healing is clear: "[W]hat could have been a straightforward account of Jesus' power over physical illness is given a new dimension by his (apparently unsought) declaration of the forgiveness of sins, leading to the scribes' theological objection to his assumption of the divine prerogative."[6] Moreover, the center of the chiasm is not the healing, but rather the offence taken by the scribes at Jesus' pronouncement of forgiveness. In fact, the healing, as the story is told, merely serves to demonstrate publicly the reality of Jesus' authority to forgive

5. From Kuthirakkattel, *Beginning of Jesus' Ministry*, 181.

6. France, *Gospel of Mark*, 121.

sins (2:10).[7] The focus is on the opposition Jesus faces: the adversaries are not pleased with Jesus adopting the divine role of forgiver—"blasphemy" they call it, and later "blasphemy" will be one of the grounds for his execution (14:64).

The scribes collectively exclaim in their hearts: εἷς ὁ θεός (heis ho theos, 2:7; literally, "Yahweh [is] one!" but translated idiomatically as "God alone"). Implicit in this indignant reaction is a defense of the Jewish creed of the uniqueness of Yawheh (Deut 6:4; also see Mark 10:18). "A man who claims to do what only God can do threatens that unique status, and that is blasphemy."[8] Jesus is clearly assuming prerogatives reserved for God, and in doing so he encounters opposition. And those who follow the one who exercises divine authority will also, likewise, face antagonism. The claim to be following one who can forgive sins is not one that will fly well with the world; disciples can expect to be attacked for making such assertions, and for "assuming," in the eyes of the world, that they are, therefore, in some way, better than others.[9]

"Son of Man" in Mark is always a self-designation by Jesus. In light of Daniel 7:13, the primary OT source for that title of Jesus Christ, such a statement in Mark 2:10 is rightly understood by the opposition as an arrogation of the status of God's viceroy and Messiah, indeed of deity itself.[10] Forgiveness, thus far a divine function exercised from heaven, is now being conducted on earth by one who takes upon himself a title of deity.[11] Here is a human being who bears divine authority, even to forgive sins: Daniel 7:13–14 also depicts the Son of Man receiving authority over all the earth from the Ancient of Days. The sense of identification between the Son of Man and the "saints of the Most High" in Daniel 7:13–18 (both entities receive an everlasting kingdom) is also reflected in this pericope (in the episodes involving the disciples; see below). Son and saints are closely involved, in a solidarity that renders them equally susceptible to hostile action from the religious authorities. The implications for those who follow Jesus on the way are obvious: disciples are going to face opposition, for the world will refuse to accept Jesus' deity and his authority to forgive sin.

---

7. While the verb πιστεύω (pisteuō, "to believe") is used in different contexts in Mark, the nouns πίστις (pistis, "faith," ×5) and ἀπιστία (apistia, "unbelief," ×2) are always used with miracle accounts (4:40; 5:34; 6:5–6; 9:22–24; 10:52; 11:22–24), suggesting that the "faith" mentioned is specifically faith in Jesus' ability to heal. That is not surprising, remembering the crowds' adulation of Jesus for just this reason in the previous pericope. In other words, the faith of the companions may not have had anything directly to do with Jesus' forgiveness of the paralytic's sins—a potential problem that has vexed many an interpreter—but rather with his healing.

8. France, Gospel of Mark, 126.

9. As in the previous pericope, here too there is the sense that wholeness is not merely physiological, the removal of pathology. Wholeness involves spiritual integrity as well, and that comes out of a right relationship with God depicted in the forgiveness of sins. Jesus came to bring wholeness, so that it would characterize the citizenry of God's kingdom.

10. "Unlike the Messiah, who is usually pictured as a human ruler and warrior, the son of man comes down from heaven"—there are resonances of deity in the appellation (Placher, Mark, 44). The impact of this self-designation of Jesus is veiled until Mark 13, when connections with Dan 7 are made more explicitly. See Winn, Purpose of Mark's Gospel, 105–7, for a discussion of the Markan "Son of Man" (SM) sayings. "While it is true that not all Mark's SM sayings allude to Dan 7, it seems likely that Mark intends them to be understood in such a light" (ibid., 106).

11. France, Gospel of Mark, 129.

3.2 Mark 2:13–17

THEOLOGICAL FOCUS 3.2

3.2 The call of sinners to join the company of disciples, a message integral to the mission of Jesus to extend the kingdom of God, attracts opposition from self-righteous ones, for it implies they are sinners, as well (2:13–17).

Section Summary 3.2: In asserting that the essence of his mission is to "call" sinners, Jesus implicitly places all mankind in the category of "sinners," needing forgiveness. Such a call, an integral part of the establishment of the kingdom of God, arouses antagonism from a self-righteous world.

TRANSLATION 3.2

2:13 *And He went out again by the sea, and the whole crowd was coming to Him, and He was teaching them.*

2:14 *And passing by, He saw Levi [the son] of Alphaeus sitting in the tax booth, and said to him, "Follow Me!" And he got up and followed Him.*

2:15 *And it came about that He was reclining at the dinner table in his house, and many tax collectors and sinners were dining with Jesus and His disciples; for there were many and they were following Him.*

2:16 *And when the scribes of the Pharisees saw that He was eating with sinners and tax collectors, they said to His disciples, "He is eating with tax collectors and sinners?"*

2:17 *And hearing [this], Jesus said to them, "The healthy have no need of a physician, but the sick do have [need]; I did not to come to call the righteous, but sinners."*

NOTES 3.2

3.2 *The call of sinners to join the company of disciples, a message integral to the mission of Jesus to extend the kingdom of God, attracts opposition from self-righteous ones, for it implies they are sinners as well.*

Here, in a daring move, a tax collector is invited to join Jesus' band.[12] The account of Levi's summons is similar to the call of the four fishermen; common elements integrate the two scenes: "passing by" the seashore (1:16 and 2:13, 14); "He saw" (1:16, 19 and 2:14); "follow" (1:18, 20 and 2:14); also present in both are the same immediate response to Jesus' call by those called, and their prompt abandonment of former stations of life.[13] An unprincipled tax collector (heaven forbid!) is joining the band of

---

12. Usually Jews, these tax collectors were despised by their fellowmen for associating with Gentiles, collecting monies for the Roman oppressor, and charging extra for the "service" so rendered. The *Mishnah* equated them with robbers, murderers, and others of befouled ilk (*b. Ṭehar.* 7; *m. Ned.* 3.4; also see *m. B. Qam.* 10.2), and the NT with sinners (Matt 9:10; 21:31; Mark 2:15; Luke 7:34; 15:1; 18:11) and Gentiles (Matt 5:46–47; 18:17). See Witherington, *Gospel of Mark*, 120; and Donahue and Harrington, *Gospel of Mark*, 101–2.

13. "Levi" is used only here and in Luke 5:27–32. Matthew 9:9–13 has the same story with "Matthew,"

Jesus-followers. A sinner becomes a disciple. With Mark's narrative skill, sinner, in fact, begins to look like disciple (see below).

The blending of disciples, sinners, and tax collectors is embedded in a double chiasm in the Greek in 2:15–16; in each chiasm "disciples" form the center (in bold below), with "tax collectors" (in italics) and "sinners" framing "disciples."

Tax collectors
   Sinners
      Disciples
   Sinners
  Tax collectors
Disciples
  Tax collectors
   Sinners

Such a blurring of what was in those days a very distinct line between tax collectors/sinners and the rest of humanity is a prominent feature of this section. In the telling of the story, what Mark is doing is equivalent to Jesus' calling the former group of disreputables to be part of his company of disciples/followers, just as he did Levi (2:14).[14] In addition, Mark's repetition of "many" in 2:15b may actually be an indication of the number of *disciples* (nearest antecedent), rather than referring to the collective "tax collectors/sinners," as does the first "many" in 2:15a. Reading "many" with "disciples" would balance "many tax collectors/sinners" (2:15a) with "many disciples" (2:15b): "*many tax collectors/sinners* . . . dining with Jesus and His disciples . . . *many disciples*." The groups are literarily being superimposed upon each other.

One notices also that this is the first instance of "disciple" in this Gospel. This is a significant moment to introduce the term, especially when disciple and sinner are made to look quite similar by the way the terms are interwoven. Needless to say, it is the sinner who becomes the disciple; the disciple is but a called sinner. In Jesus' mission, everyone is equal before God—"there are now only sinners on the road of discipleship," in contrast to the Pharisaic program of separation.[15] Disciples are sinners who have responded to the divine call to follow Jesus on the way of discipleship, becoming part of God's kingdom. And that creates problems for the "scribes of the Pharisees." A tax collector called and now a coterie of sinners counted among Jesus' followers, and all of these included in a festive meal? Jesus' response to their conceit is stinging. The mission of the physician is to cure the sick; the mission of the divine healer is to restore sinners to wholeness, inviting them into the divine kingdom. The so-called "righteous," the self-identified healthy ones, are going to miss out on this

---

and Matt 10:1–4 has "Matthew, the tax collector." Both Levi and James are said to be sons of Alphaeus (Mark 2:14; 3:18); these two could very well be brothers, thus paralleling the first call of two sets of siblings, Peter/Andrew and James/John. If Levi is, indeed, Matthew, this connection with Alphaeus might explain why Matt 10:3 and Acts 1:13 juxtapose Matthew and James in those lists of the Twelve. See Witherington, *Gospel of Mark*, 119.

14. Guelich, *Mark*, 105.

15. Myers, *Binding the Strong Man*, 157.

marvelous remission of the disease of sin, not to mention the blessings of the kingdom. According to Jesus, such a calling of the sick and sinful—this is implicitly a labeling of the world as sinful and in need of healing—is at the core of his mission to establish the kingdom of God (2:17).

Jesus' calling the exclusivists and separatists "righteous" (2:17) is probably ironical, "referring to Jesus' critics as those who, in their own view, are δίκαιοι [*dikaioi*, "righteous"] (and therefore do not need his ministry)."[16] Jerome rightly observed: "Since no one is perfectly righteous, Christ has not come to call those who are not there, but the multitudes of sinners who are there, with whom the world is filled, remembering the psalm which says 'Help, O Lord, for there is no longer anyone who is godly'" (*Against the Pelagians* 2.12).[17] Bearing the authority to forgive, and identifying the essence of his ministry as a call to sinners, Jesus is in effect asserting the need of *all* mankind (= "sinners") for forgiveness. But the attitude of his adversaries is that they themselves have no disease that needs a physician's touch. Those who consider themselves already healthy—the self-righteous—will have nothing to do with a physician, and object to anyone labeling them as less than whole. That is the thrust of the episode: the refusal of the self-righteous to see themselves in need of forgiveness from one who had just demonstrated his authority to grant it. Thus, in carrying on the mission of Jesus to extend the kingdom of God, disciples can expect antagonism from the world that resents being described as broken in sin and in need of a Savior.

3.3   Mark 2:18–22

THEOLOGICAL FOCUS 3.3

3.3   The change in the lifestyle of the disciples—their abandonment of old patterns of conduct in light of their new membership in the kingdom of God—raises doubt and opposition (2:18–22).

Section Summary 3.3: The new has come to displace the old. The newness of the values of God's kingdom trumps old patterns of life and religiosity. The two are incompatible. Consequently, the disciple's adoption of new values, as Jesus is followed, will generate accusations of impropriety and non-conformity.

TRANSLATION 3.3

2:18   *And the disciples of John and the Pharisees were fasting. And they came and said to Him, "Why do the disciples of John and the disciples of the Pharisees fast, but Your disciples do not fast?"*

2:19   *And Jesus said to them, "The friends of the bridegroom cannot fast while the bridegroom is with them, can they? As long as they have the bridegroom with them, they cannot fast.*

---

16. France, *Gospel of Mark*, 135.

17. Cited in Oden and Hall, *Mark*, 30.

2:20 *But the days will come when the bridegroom will be taken away from them, and then they will fast in that day.*

2:21 *No one sews a patch of unshrunk cloth on an old garment, otherwise, the patched piece pulls away from it, the new from the old, and a worse tear is produced.*

2:22 *And no one pours new wine into old wineskins, otherwise, the wine will burst the wineskins and the wine is lost, the wineskins also; but new wine [is poured] into new wineskins."*

NOTES 3.3

3.3 *The change in the lifestyle of the disciples—their abandonment of old patterns of conduct in light of their new membership in the kingdom of God—raises doubt and opposition.*

This episode forms the central piece of the entire controversy section of 2:1—3:6 (see structure of this section above). The core issue is "the eschatological newness" represented by Jesus, rightly the focal point of all the disputations in this pericope.[18] The opponents' concern here is not any "unlawful" word or deed of Jesus or of his followers (as in the previous episode and in the following two), but simply a failure on the part of Jesus' disciples to conform to the religious practices of certain Jewish cliques—specifically, the fasting custom of the disciples of John and of those of the Pharisees. Ostensibly, though such abstinence routines are not to be expected of *all* Jews, they are being demanded of Jesus' disciples: a clash of spiritualities—the adversarial challenge is actually "a covert claim to superior religious fervour" from those "more spiritual" factions engaging in such practices. These morally superior ones allege that Jesus and his followers are not taking their religiosity seriously; their piety and spirituality are in question because they do not observe accepted rituals, at least those practiced in certain quarters of Judaism.[19] Jesus, in defense, declares that the newness of his movement supersedes traditional praxis. This episode in the center of the controversy incidents crystallizes the conflict and contrast between the old and the new. "The dispute is not merely about how somber religious people should be, but what time it is on God's redemptive schedule. Jesus and his disciples do not fast in order to encourage God to bring the kingdom, but celebrate in the light of the kingdom that is already dawning."[20] The new, in short, can no longer be combined with the old; the new has obviated any return to the old. The wedding imagery in this section suggests an intimate relationship between God and his people in this age, such as was

18. Boring, *Mark*, 83.

19. France, *Gospel of Mark*, 137–38. The one regular fast prescribed in OT law was that undertaken on the Day of Atonement (Lev 16:29, 31; 23:26–32; Num 29:7–11—the "humbling" described in these texts indicated various forms of self-denial, usually including fasting: see Ps 35:13; Acts 27:9; *m. Yoma* 8.1–2). Perhaps there were more fasts in the postexilic period (see Zech 8:19). In any case, it was essentially the Pharisaical stipulations that expanded the frequency of the biblically prescribed practice (Luke 18:12; *Did.* 8.1; *b. Ta'an.* 10a, 12a).

20. Boring, *Mark*, 85.

only hinted at in the past.[21] And new relationships and times call for new practices. A new kingdom is nigh; forgiveness has come freely to those who will accept it; sinners and tax collectors are becoming disciples, for all are in need of healing at the hands of the divine physician. And celebration is apropos—this is a new era. The resultant change of lifestyle, as disciples follow this new King into God's kingdom, will generate accusations of inadequate piety and spirituality.

Jesus implies that it was the "taking away" of John that led his disciples to fast; one day Jesus' disciples will fast after he too is "taken away."[22] The period of mourning when Jesus is "taken away" could technically be as brief as the two days between his crucifixion and resurrection, or as long as the intervening time between the resurrection and the gifting of the Holy Spirit at Pentecost, through whom Jesus Christ lives in the believer.[23]

In light of the following verses that address the deleterious effects of patching old garments with new cloth, and pouring new wine into old skins, it is obvious that the concern of this episode is not merely fasting, but the discordance between old traditions and the new practices of the Christian life, including, but not necessarily limited to, practices pertaining to spirituality. "What is at stake is not so much the priority of the new over the old as the much more basic question of their compatibility."[24] There can be no reconciliation. The new and radical kingdom message of Jesus is incompatible with existing forms of religious affectations; in fact, the two parables (2:21–22) suggest that compromises can only be counterproductive, even destructive. The newness of lifestyle of the disciple of Christ renders everything connected to the old as anachronistic and inappropriate. It would be out of place—nay, ruinous—to revert to old lifestyles and practices. "Everything has been changed from carnal to spiritual by the new grace of God which, with the coming of the gospel, has wiped out the

---

21. Yahweh had already been depicted as a bridegroom to his people in Isa 54:4–8; 61:10; 62:4–5; Jer 2:2; Ezek 16; Hos 2:19–23. Isaiah 62:5, foreshadowing kingdom relationships, also notes the participation of "sons" (υἱοί, *huioi*) in a wedding in which Yahweh is likened to a bridegroom. So also Christ in the NT: Matt 22:1–14; 25:1–13; John 3:25–30; 2 Cor 11:2; Eph 5:22–32; Rev 19:7–9; 22:17. Jesus' taking on the attribution of Yahweh as the bridegroom is quite a bold move. Disciples, here in Mark 2, are the "sons of the bridegroom" (υἱοὶ τοῦ νυμφῶνος, *huioi tou nymphōnos*, translated "friends of the bridegroom"). Their close association with Jesus, the groom, attests to the picture of corporate solidarity in this pericope between Jesus and his followers. The opposition Jesus faces, they will face; and the opposition they face is opposition to Jesus and his divine mission. See Henderson, *Christology*, 75.

22. The word ἀπαρθῇ (*aparthē*, "be taken away," 2:20) suggests force and points to Jesus' violent death—the first hint in Mark of that eventuality; it may also allude to John's own execution (detailed in Mark 6).

23. Matthew 28:20 is clear about Jesus' constant presence with his disciples post-Easter. It is therefore inaccurate to see the church age as a period in which Jesus is absent. Considering the forceful and violent connotation of "taken away," it is obvious that this condition of Jesus does not pertain in the church age, for after his resurrection Jesus is alive, no longer "taken away." Mark 2:18–22 is therefore not a call for disciples to fast until Jesus comes again.

24. van Iersel, "Concentric Structures," 96. "It would be a mistake, however, to confine the relevance of these parables only to Jesus' confrontations with the scribes and to the specific issues raised in these chapters. The theological issue is a broader one, as applicable to the constricting influence of Christian traditions as it is to the context of first-century Judaism" (Witherington, *Gospel of Mark*, 127).

old completely" (Tertullian, *On Prayer* 1). This episode establishes a new definition of what constitutes spirituality. The world will seek an explanation, objecting to the non-conformity and inadequate piety they observe in the lives of those following Christ. This unit of the controversy pericope thus adds yet another reason to expect opposition when following Jesus: the new practices of the Christian life that characterize the disciple will rile the world.

3.4   Mark 2:23–28

THEOLOGICAL FOCUS 3.4

3.4   The changed lifestyle of the disciples, as they follow Jesus under his authority, critiques the ways of the world, attracting antagonism (2:23–28).

Section Summary 3.4: It is not only the adoption of the new that engenders opposition, but also the disciples' critique (implicit or otherwise) of traditional practices. In this section what is being attacked by opponents is not merely a new lifestyle, but a new life that, by virtue of its distinctiveness, critiques the old and finds it wanting in light of the circumstances of Jesus' kingdom establishment project.

TRANSLATION 3.4

2:23   *And it came about that He was going through the grain fields on the Sabbath, and His disciples began to make their way, plucking the heads of grain.*

2:24   *And the Pharisees were saying to Him, "Look, why are they doing what is not lawful on the Sabbath?"*

2:25   *And He said to them, "Have you never read what David did when he was in need and he was hungry, and those with him;*

2:26   *how he entered into the house of God in the time of Abiathar the high priest, and ate the consecrated bread, which is not lawful to eat except for the priests, and he also gave to those who were with him?"*

2:27   *And He said to them, "The Sabbath was made for man and not man for the Sabbath.*

2:28   *For this reason, He is Lord—the Son of Man—even of the Sabbath."*

NOTES 3.4

3.4   *The changed lifestyle of the disciples, as they follow Jesus under his authority, critiques the ways of world, attracting antagonism.*

While opposition is escalating, so is the "provocation." In the three episodes of Mark 2:13–17, 18–22, and 23–22 (B, C, and B' in the structure of the pericope; see above), food is a critical element: Jesus and his disciples break bread with an "unacceptable" crowd; then they ignore the religiosity of abstaining from food; and now they seemingly break the Sabbath law by harvesting (and eating) grain when hungry. The question at hand is what sort of "work," if at all any, is permissible on the Sabbath. Exodus 34:21 does prohibit harvesting on the Sabbath. Is the disciples' plucking of grain "harvesting," and thus a violation of the sabbatical prohibition of work?[25] Pharisaical circumscriptions of what constitutes "work" were intended to leave nothing to chance or haphazard opinion, "by legislating for every circumstance to protect the faithful from ever breaking the prohibition on Sabbath work." Jesus is not contradicting the Torah, but his dismissal of much of the Pharisees' *halakhic* body of legislation (the oral traditions later codified in the *Mishnah*) sharply counters accepted scribal authority and threatens to overturn the entire process of legal interpretation.[26] The thrust of the pericope, then, points not merely to what appears to be a violation of the Sabbath (which it indeed is not), but to the critique and proactive overriding of the old governances in favor of new kingdom policies, under the authority of Jesus, the Son of Man.

While Jesus agrees that David's action was not "lawful" (2:26), he establishes that the right to supersede traditional conventions and the right to declare what work was acceptable or not on the Sabbath belongs to none other than the "Lord of the Sabbath." This Lord is now claiming an authority even greater than that of David.[27] That the Sabbath could be set aside in emergencies was well accepted, but no human had dared to declare himself "Lord of the Sabbath."[28] The focus here is on Jesus' authority, as it is in the whole pericope (2:1—3:6): he forgives sins, he comes to call sinners who need deliverance (i.e., all of humanity), he introduces new practices fit for the new kingdom, and now he even critiques old traditions. The issue of authority has been escalating all along. Jesus has already been revealed as Lord in his teaching and actions, exorcisms and healings, and in the forgiveness of sins; now he declares himself Lord even over the Sabbath.[29] Not only, then, do Jesus and his followers adopt new practices (2:18–22), but, in the current unit, a further step forward is taken: they are now *critiquing* traditional practices, reckoning them revocable, finding them wanting in light of the newness of the kingdom Jesus is establishing. This is, of course, not to say that Jesus is disregarding the OT law; rather, he is only disagreeing with what ought and ought not to be permitted on the Sabbath as determined by the oral tradition of

---

25. For lists of activities prohibited on the Sabbath, see, e.g., *Jub.* 50.6–13; *m. Šabb.* 7:2.

26. France, *Gospel of Mark*, 143–44. *Halakah* comes from Neh 10:29, לָלֶכֶת בְּתוֹרַת הָאֱלֹהִים, *laleketh betorath ha'elohim*, "to walk in God's Torah."

27. Jesus' replacement of the OT historian's Ahimelech with the latter's father, Abiathar, may be intentional, in order to strengthen the association between priest and house of God in Jerusalem: Abiathar officiated in the house of God in Jerusalem (2 Sam 15:29), and not in Nob, where Ahimelech is said to have offered the showbread to David (1 Sam 21:1–6). See Gundry, *Mark*, 141.

28. See 1 Macc 2:41; *2 Bar.* 14.18; *b. Yoma* 85b. Rabbi Simeon ben Menassia (ca. 180 CE) declared: "The Sabbath is handed over to you and you are not handed over to the Sabbath" (*Mek.* on Exod 31:12–17). Nonetheless, death was the punishment for working on the Sabbath: Exod 31:14; Num 15:32–26; *Jub.* 2.25–27; 50.6–13.

29. This is the first use of "Lord" to refer to Jesus (outside of the introductory section, Mark 1:3, citing Isa 40:3). "Lord of the Sabbath" comes close to an attribution to Jesus of the authority of Yahweh (Exod 16:23, 25; 31:13; 35:2; Lev 19:3, 30; 23:3, 38; 26:2; Deut 5:14; Isa 56:4, 6; Ezek 20:12–14; 22:8, 26; 23:38; 44:24). "Son of Man," in every instance in Mark, refers to the unique authority of Jesus (Boring, *Mark*, 91–92).

the Pharisees. The new practices of those within the kingdom of God will be a critical commentary on the old assumptions and rituals of those without this realm.

The leader's association with the led (οἱ μετ' αὐτοῦ, *hoi met autou*, "those with him," 2:25, i.e., David and his men; and a similar phrase, οἱ σὺν αὐτῷ ὄντες, *hoi syn autō ontes*, "those who were with him," 2:26) is again intended to reflect the disciples' close identification with Jesus: the phrase μετ' αὐτοῦ ("with Him") shows up in 3:14 at the formal commissioning of the disciples; they are called by Jesus to be with him. Such a descriptor, here, provides a precedent for all who would follow Jesus: the disciples' actions are grounded in the authority of their Lord and covered by his dominion (2:27). His mission is theirs, and his authority devolves upon them (as will be evident when disciples are sent out later in the Gospel). Again, one espies the solidarity between Jesus and his disciples. Naturally, it also follows that the antagonism faced by the Jesus will be felt by the disciples as well. When disciples' new lifestyle and practices implicitly begin to critique and cast aspersions upon the ways of the world, antagonism is sure.

3.5 Mark 3:1–6

THEOLOGICAL FOCUS 3.5

3.5   Jesus' boldness and persistence in the fulfillment of his divine call, though he was grieved and angered by his hardhearted antagonists, is the pattern for disciples to follow, not letting opposition deter them from their own divine call to follow Jesus on his mission to establish the kingdom of God (3:1–6).

Section Summary 3.5: In this final episode of the pericope, no new issues are raised for the religious leaders to oppose. This closing unit, instead, depicts the escalation of antagonism in the entire pericope (2:1—3:6) coming to a head with the adversaries' intent to destroy Jesus. The model of Jesus' bold persistence, despite the obviously dangerous situation, is a pattern for his disciples to follow as they walk in his way and under his authority.

TRANSLATION 3.5

3:1   *And He entered again into the synagogue, and there was a man there having a withered hand.*

3:2   *And they were watching Him closely if He would heal him on the Sabbath, in order that they may accuse Him.*

3:3   *And He said to the man having the withered hand, "Rise up [and come] to the middle."*

3:4   *And He said to them, "Is it lawful on the Sabbath to do good or to do evil, to save a life or to kill?" But they were silent.*

3:5   *And looking around at them with anger, grieved at their hardness of heart, He said to the man, "Stretch out your hand." And he stretched [it] out and his hand was restored.*

3:6   *And the Pharisees went out immediately, plotting with the Herodians against Him, how they may destroy Him.*

NOTES 3.5

*3.5   Jesus' boldness and persistence in the fulfillment of his divine call, though he is
grieved and angered by his hardhearted antagonists, is the pattern for disciples to
follow, not letting opposition deter them from their own divine call to follow Jesus
on his mission to establish the kingdom of God.*

The parallels between 2:1–12 and 3:1–6 indicate that these members of the pericope
are functioning as frames, opening and closing, respectively, the larger unit.

MARK 2:1–12		MARK 3:1–6	
2:1	"He entered again into . . ."	3:1	"He entered again into . . ."
2:5, 10	"He said to the paralytic" ×2	3:3, 5	"He said to the man" ×2
2:9	Silent objection; Jesus' question	3:4	Silent objection; Jesus' question
2:11–12	Healing with a word (bodily restoration)	3:5	Healing with a word (bodily restoration)

Mark 3:1–6 functions as an appropriate conclusion to the controversy section: there is
no new subject matter generating opposition; no new pathological condition is being
healed ("paralysis" is reasonably equivalent to "withering"); the sanctity of the Sabbath
is the issue again, as in the previous unit; there is no explicit christological statement
here, unlike in the preceding four (2:10, 17, 20, 27–28); there are hints in these first and
last episodes of the deadly outcome of Jesus' controversy with the religious hierarchies
("blasphemy" in the first, and outright plotting to destroy him in this last); and no one
else speaks aloud in either of these two episodes but Jesus. On the other hand, while
all the controversies are brought to the fore with questions, in the first four incidents
(A, B, C, and B′ above) it is the particular opponents in each episode that raise the
questions, silently or otherwise. However, in this last unit (A′) Jesus himself initiates
the questioning. Also, unlike the previous sections, significant space is allotted here
to describing Jesus' emotions (see below).[30] The escalation of opposition reaches its
zenith in this section. What started off as covert thoughts in the minds of opponents
(2:6) have now become overt plotting to kill Jesus (3:6).

The Sabbath, Jesus claims, is a time for doing good, a permissible goal that re-
defines "work" (as understood by Pharisaical tradition) on the Sabbath.[31] Ironically,
it is on the same Sabbath when Jesus does a good work that his opponents do an evil
one—scheming to kill him (3:6). Apparently one is not allowed to do good, as per the
religious leaders, but one can plot to kill! The forward positions of the words "lawful,"
"good," "evil" and "life" in the Greek ("Lawful is it, good to do or evil to do . . . life to
save or to kill?" 3:4) accentuate the contrast between what the opponents are considering doing (evil) and what Jesus actually does (good).

Leviticus 21:16–24 prohibits those with conditions such as this man's withered
hand from participating in temple worship. Jesus' healing permits him to do so, once
again underscoring Jesus' interest in rendering people whole, physiologically, socio-

---

30. Dewey, *Markan Public Debate*, 119.

31. In fact, even the *Mishnah* gives room for situations that can "override" the Sabbath. See *m. Pesaḥ*
6.1–2.

logically, and cultically: it is an *illness* that he cures, not just a disease. Again, this episode points to Jesus' single-mindedness in his mission to establish God's kingdom that would set all things right. Interestingly, the cure itself gets very little space—a brief command and a response that demonstrably prove the healing. The command is composed of a mere three words (in the Greek). How could the Pharisees label such a brief utterance as "work"?

As with the first unit in the pericope (2:1–12), Jesus clearly takes the initiative right there in the synagogue, by requesting the man to come into the limelight ("to the middle," 3:3). This man, it must be remembered, was a patient who is not said to have requested any healing himself in the first place. The invitation was entirely Jesus'. Such a bold action on his part, despite the obvious malevolence of his opponents throughout the pericope, shows him to be determined to force the issue "to the middle." Myers notes that this is carefully staged political theater—Jesus is being an agent provocateur![32] The point is that Jesus is not in the least bit intimidated by all the opposition he has faced thus far (2:1–28). He continues in his mission to extend the kingdom of God; physical healing is a demonstration of his authority and a means of pushing the boundaries of the kingdom forward. Jesus' divine call takes precedence over his personal safety. He will persist boldly in doing what he has been sent to accomplish, despite opposition.

Jesus' emotions are on display here considerably more than anywhere else in the Gospel: anger at his opponents' mercilessness, and grief at their callousness. Gundry notes ironically that their hardness of heart is worse than the man's withering of hand.[33] Thus, this final episode of the pericope is marked by Jesus' compassion and sorrow, as well as his anger at the hard-hearted opposition. But antagonists do not stop him, and maleficent intentions do not impede the fulfillment of divine mission. Jesus continues unshaken and proceeds to cure the afflicted man forthwith. Despite his anger and grief, despite the virulence of opposition he faces at great risk to his personal well-being, he is not deterred from his determination to do good and to extend the kingdom of God. The one who follows Jesus in discipleship will, likewise, be resolute in fulfilling the call to follow Jesus in his mission, boldly and persistently pressing on against all manner of opposition. After all, it is the disciple's identification with Jesus that brings about the opposition; it is only appropriate that followers of Jesus follow him in his response, identifying with him in that aspect also.

SERMON FOCUS AND OUTLINES

THEOLOGICAL FOCUS OF PERICOPE 3 FOR PREACHING

3 **Following Jesus in discipleship involves facing opposition boldly and persistently, without being deterred from God's calling (2:1—3:6).**

It is probably wiser to deal with the various facets of opposition in a single sermon instead of breaking up the pericope into five sermons; the considerable similarity in

32. Myers, *Binding the Strong Man*, 162; Witherington, *Gospel of Mark*, 135.

33. Gundry, *Mark*, 151–52. This "hardness of heart" will also later characterize the disciples themselves (6:52; 8:17).

subject matter between the episodes is not conducive to a fivefold division of 2:1—3:6 for preaching. The manner in which the first and last episodes bookend the pericope also seems to call for a single and unified approach to its exposition. As well, such a strategy will enable one to lay before the congregation different aspects of opposition disciples are likely to face: to the divine authority of their leader to forgive sins, to the (implicit) labeling of humankind as sinners in need of a Savior, to the newness of the disciples' lifestyle that does not fit the world's definition of spirituality, and to Christians' critique of the ways of the world. Depending on the circumstances of the listeners, the preacher may choose to focus more on one facet of opposition than another (in the outline below, this would be in the "Problem" section); in any case, concluding with 3:1–6, Jesus' *modus operandi* in dealing with such antagonism would be the thrust of the sermon on this pericope.[34]

POSSIBLE PREACHING OUTLINES FOR PERICOPE 3

This outline utilizes the age-old (and effective) rhetorical scheme of problem–solution–application:

I.   PROBLEM: The disciples' changed lives and claims, resulting in opposition

        The facets of life change depicted in each episode (or one particular one) and the opposition so engendered

        Move-to-Relevance: Opposition we might face as a result of life-change in Christ

II.   SOLUTION: The model of Jesus' response: boldness and persistence

        Depict the sequence of commissions: 1:3–8; 1:14–15; 1:17

III.   APPLICATION: *Persist boldly against opposition!*

        Specific application: How can we be boldly persistent against opposition?

Another option:

I.   ACTION: World and culture challenged by disciples' changed lives and claims

        The facets of life change depicted in each episode (or one particular one)

        Move-to-Relevance: How our changed lives and claims challenge our world and culture

II.   REACTION: World and culture counters disciples' changed lives and claims

        The opposition of the world and culture

        Move-to-Relevance: Opposition we might face as a result of life-change in Christ

III.   APPLICATION: Jesus response, our model: *Persist boldly against opposition!*

        The model of Jesus' response to opposition: 3:1–6

        Specific application: How can we be boldly persistent against opposition?

---

34. A subsequent pericope (6:7–32) will also deal with opposition, but there the focus will be on divine provision in times of opposition. Here, on the other hand, the thrust is simply on persisting boldly, following Jesus' model. It must be remembered that this Gospel, dealing with the demands of discipleship, shines its light on the various facets of what it means to follow Jesus; pericopes may deal with similar issues, but invariably each one highlights a unique angle that must be taken to heart.

PERICOPE 4

Who Is the Disciple?

Mark 3:7–35

[Disciples Commissioned; Relatives Seek and Scribes Accuse Jesus]

REVIEW, SUMMARY, PREVIEW

Review of Pericope 3: Mark 2:1—3:6 demonstrates the opposition disciples can expect, and how it may be faced—with boldness and persistence—as Jesus did.

Summary of Pericope 4: This pericope (3:7–35) carries on the story from Pericope 1 (1:21–45). A reminder of the incomprehension of some who seek Jesus only for existential benefits (3:7–12) raises the question of who exactly is *for* Jesus. The rest of the pericope answers that question. Disciples are appointed by the divine authority of Jesus to be with him and then to be sent from him in the extension of his mission in the service of God's kingdom. The subsequent Markan "sandwich" expounds on the identity of the disciple by defining a disciple as an "insider" who, discerning Jesus' person, does the will of God—being with Jesus and then being sent by him to engage in his work in the world for the kingdom of God. This is the one who is *for* Jesus.

Preview of Pericope 5: The next pericope (4:1–34) explains the responsibility of the disciple in the process of bearing fruit in discipleship (being receptive to the word of God), and details, as well, the divine element in such fruit production.

4   Mark 3:7–35

THEOLOGICAL FOCUS OF PERICOPE 4

4   Disciples are those who are "insiders" with Jesus, doing the will of God as authoritatively commissioned by Jesus—remaining with him and being sent by him to extend his mission (3:7–35).

4.1   Disciples—all who follow Jesus on the way—are those who are authoritatively appointed by him, to be with him and also to be sent by him to extend his own mission, unlike those who do not recognize his authority, or seek Jesus for the wrong reasons (3:7–19).

    4.1.1   They are not disciples who follow Jesus for the wrong reasons, not recognizing his authority or understanding his mission.

    4.1.2   The making of disciples in any generation is a momentous and authoritative appointment by Jesus.

    4.1.3   Disciples are appointed to be with Jesus and to be sent by him to extend his mission.

4.2   Disciples—"insiders" with Jesus—are those who do the will of God, not like "outsiders" who fail to discern Jesus' authority (3:20–35).

    4.2.1   Genetic proximity to Jesus, while disregarding his authority, has nothing to do with "insidership."

    4.2.2   Physical or ecclesiastical proximity to Jesus, while disregarding his authority, has nothing to do with "insidership."

    4.2.3   "Insidership" with Jesus, the status of the disciple, has to do with obedience to the will of God.

OVERVIEW

THE PERICOPE OPENS WITH a summary (3:7–12) that recapitulates the story preceding it. It harks back to the popularity of Jesus described in 1:21–45. But this opening summary also looks forward to what follows. The crowds are still following him, looking for what Jesus has to offer in terms of healing of disease and alleviation of affliction: they are following him for the wrong reasons. The demons who actually recognize Jesus are shushed to preclude any misapprehension of Jesus by the populace as a "miracle man" to whom they could come to find redress for grievance and relief from woe. The reader is beginning to wonder: If everyone is after Jesus for ulterior motives, is there anybody at all who is truly *for* Jesus and for his mission, understanding who he is and what he is about? Had no one understood what it means to follow him? This is the question that the pericope answers: What does it mean to be *for* Jesus? Who is *for* him?

4.1   Mark 3:7–19

THEOLOGICAL FOCUS 4.1

4.1   Disciples—all who follow Jesus on the way—are those who are authoritatively appointed by him, to be with him and also to be sent by him to extend his own mission, unlike those who do not recognize his authority, or seek Jesus for the wrong reasons (3:7–19).

    4.1.1   They are not disciples who follow Jesus for the wrong reasons, not recognizing his authority or understanding his mission.

    4.1.2   The making of disciples in any generation is a momentous and authoritative appointment by Jesus.

    4.1.3   Disciples are appointed to be with Jesus and to be sent by him to extend his mission.

Section Summary 4.1: The context is set up in the first few verses of this pericope, recapitulating the earlier adulatory activities of the crowd and the imposition of silence upon the unclean spirits. In the process of defining who the disciple is, the authoritative commissioning of Jesus' followers is described, along with the role of disciples: they are to be with their leader, and they are to be sent by him to extend his own mission.

TRANSLATION 4.1

3:7   *And Jesus withdrew to the sea with His disciples, and a large multitude from Galilee followed, and from Judea,*

3:8   *and from Jerusalem, and from Idumea, and beyond the Jordan, and around Tyre and Sidon—a great multitude, hearing all what He was doing, came to Him.*

3:9   *And He told His disciples that a boat be stood ready for Him because of the crowd, so that they would not crush Him;*

3:10   *for He healed many, so that whoever had afflictions fell upon Him, in order to touch Him.*

3:11   *And the unclean spirits, whenever they saw Him, were falling before Him and crying, saying, "You are the Son of God!"*

3:12   *And He was earnestly warning them so that they would not make Him known.*

3:13   *And He went up on the mountain and summoned those He Himself wanted, and they came away to Him.*

3:14   *And He appointed Twelve, whom He also named apostles, so that they would be with Him, and so that He could send them to preach*

3:15   *and to have authority to cast out demons.*

3:16   *And He appointed the Twelve: to Simon He gave the name Peter,*

3:17   *and James, [the son] of Zebedee, and John the brother of James (and He also gave them the name "Boanerges," which is "Sons of Thunder"),*

3:18   *and Andrew, and Philip, and Bartholomew, and Matthew, and Thomas, and James [the son] of Alphaeus, and Thaddaeus, and Simon the Zealot,*

3:19   *and Judas Iscariot, who also gave Him over.*

NOTES 4.1

4.1.1   *They are not disciples who follow Jesus for the wrong reasons, not recognizing his authority and misunderstanding his mission.*

As before, the crowds come, one and all, seeking only the healing and exorcism Jesus provides; unlike in 1:21–45, in this section Jesus' teaching is not mentioned at all—it is all about the crowd's finding existential satisfaction. Subtle deprecatory tones are struck in this chord: having heard of "all what He was doing" (3:8), the crowd "falls upon" Jesus (or "presses upon," ἐπιπίπτειν, *epipiptein*, 3:10), while the unclean spirits prostrate themselves, "falling before" him (προσέπιπτον, *prosepipton*, 3:11). Both crowds and demons seem to be doing the same thing—falling upon/before Jesus. That is definitely not a positive commentary on the crowd's response to Jesus. Ironically, it is the demons who identify Jesus correctly as "Son of God," while the crowds are never said to do so.[1] With that note, and in this third chapter of the Gospel, it is certainly time for the reader to ask if anyone at all is *for* Jesus. The rest of the pericope endeavors to answer this question. First, the Twelve are selected from among the larger congregation of enthusiasts enchanted by Jesus' supernatural powers, and their commission is formalized (see below, on 3:13–19). Then, in the subsequent "sandwich" episode (3:20–35), the answer is conclusively given as to what constitutes a disciple, an answer that also expands the circle of disciples beyond the Twelve.

4.1.2 The making of disciples in any generation is a momentous and authoritative appointment by Jesus.

The mountaintop calling of the Twelve (3:13) is reminiscent of Moses' trip up Mt. Sinai and the Israelites covenanting with God (Exod 19) in the middle of their wilderness experience—between the exodus event and the Promised Land. Jesus and his disciples, similarly, live "between God's active intervention in the world, specifically in the person of Jesus, and the 'promised land' of God's coming kingdom."[2] All those who follow Jesus in this age are in the season of the already-but-not-yet.

In light of the allusions to Moses and his encounter with God on Mt. Sinai (Exod 19:1–12), the "mountain" here in Mark 3:13 has symbolic connotations of "the place where heaven and earth meet and where a holy man encounters God and the people receive revelation."[3] This event in Mark 3 is the enactment of a "new Sinai covenant" on the mountain, a formal appointment of the disciples to follow the One who is at least as authoritative as Moses, on a journey at least as critical as the one to the Promised Land in Moses' day. However, the analogy breaks down, for in Exodus 19 it is Yahweh who calls Moses to himself, while in Mark 3 it is Jesus who sovereignly calls disciples to himself. This Jesus, hereby equated with Yahweh, is far greater than Moses.

---

1. "Son" as applied to Jesus (excluding "Son of Man") is found in several locations in the Gospel: "beloved [or only] Son" (1:11; 9:7; 12:6), "the Son" (13:32), "Son of God," (3:11; 15:39), "Son of the Most High God" (5:7), and "Son of the Blessed One" (14:61). Discounting this last occurrence, where the title is used skeptically, only one of the other references is found on human lips: 15:39, the centurion's exclamation. The imposition to silence, here in 3:12, reflects the incompleteness of the revelation of Jesus' person; only after his mission of suffering has been revealed (in Act II) will Jesus' identity be allowed to be broadcast, lest he is followed for the wrong reasons.

2. Henderson, *Christology*, 80; also see 79–81.

3. Collins, *Mark*, 215. Also see 9:2 for the Transfiguration, another consequential event taking place upon a mountain. Boring notes that "He went up on the mountain" was a stock phrase occurring twenty-four times in the LXX; eighteen times it is found in the Pentateuch, where it is used mostly of Moses (Boring, *Mark*, 100).

EXODUS 19:3 LXX	MARK 3:13
And Moses went up	And He went up [= *Jesus as Moses*]
on the mountain of God and God called (ἐκάλεσσεν, *ekalesen*) him.	on the mountain and He summoned (προσκαλεῖται, *proskaleitai*) those He wanted. [= *Jesus as God*]

Jesus' appointment of the Twelve in Mark 3:14, 16 employs a verb used for the appointment of priests (ποιέω, *poieō*, 1 Kgs 12:31; 13:33 LXX) and that of Moses and Aaron (1 Sam 12:6 LXX). The verb is also used in Mark 1:17 in Jesus' declaration that he would "make" his disciples fishers of men. This is certainly an authoritative appointment of great moment.

In keeping with the announcement of the fulfillment of time and the nearness of the kingdom of God (1:15), and with the numerous exodus-evocative allusions—the "way" of Jesus that begins in the wilderness, the forty-day motif (1:1–20), and the commissioning of the disciples in this pericope—the number "twelve" (3:14, 16) is surely hinting at the twelve tribes as representing the wholeness of the community of Israel and its eschatological reconstitution (Ezek 47:13; also Sir 36.11, 23). For the Israelite audience, to whom Jesus primarily ministered in his earthly life, this mountaintop event is symbolic of the creation of a new "Israel." In the context of the arrival of God's kingdom, this tribal number indicates the creation afresh of a community of God's people who choose to follow Jesus on the way into that kingdom. Clearly the number is symbolic, for many of the Twelve are known only by their presence on this roster. "Their number and their corporate identity were more important to tradition than any individual profile."[4] The theological thrust, therefore, goes beyond the actual twelve men, and indicates the constitution of a new people of God. Any and all who answer the call of Jesus to follow him on the Trip of Discipleship are, in a sense, included in the "twelve."

Substantiating that conclusion is the fact that the Twelve are themselves included in the larger company of the "disciples"; for instance, in 10:32, the Twelve are part of the disciples—"those who followed Him [Jesus]." In fact, the Twelve do not even appear to be the core of this larger body of Jesus-followers: at the raising of Jairus's daughter (5:37), at the Transfiguration (9:2–8), during the apocalyptic discourse (13:3–4), and in Gethsemane (14:32–42), a smaller group of three or four selected out of the Twelve becomes prominent. "Though the narratives of the call and commissioning of the Twelve are important in the structure of Mark, their main function seems to be to symbolize the nature of discipleship."[5] This call by Jesus is for *all* who would follow him (as the definition of "disciple" later in the pericope, corroborates).

---

4. France, *Gospel of Mark*, 158–59. This, of course, is not to deny that there were twelve men called by Jesus, but it is to suggest that the choice of that number was also likely symbolic on Jesus' part.

5. Donahue and Harrington, *Gospel of Mark*, 126–27. Also see the Preface for a discussion of this issue.

4.1.3   Disciples are appointed to be with Jesus and to be sent by him to extend his mission.

The disciples are appointed to be "with Him" (μετ' αὐτοῦ, *met autou*) and to be sent out by Jesus (3:14). Here is a curious paradox—they are appointed to be with him *and* to be sent out from him.[6] They are to experience Jesus' proximity and exercise Jesus' authority as they are sent away from him to preach and exorcise. Indeed, one might say that only if one is "with" Jesus can one be sent "from/by" him. The first is a prerequisite for the second. Remaining in his presence is essential if one is to participate in the extension of Jesus' mission. In other words, as followers become companions, companions become participants in the mission of Jesus, extending his work, taking on Jesus' own role of preaching and exorcising—they become disciples. Jesus' personal purpose, stated in 1:38 ("Let *us* go . . . so that *I* may preach"—note the singular for the verb of purpose), is now beginning to be shared with the disciples (*they* were now being sent to preach)—the training has begun![7] Indeed, after 1:39, Jesus is not recorded in Mark as preaching. The baton has been passed on. And the baton will be passed on again, to future generations of readers of the Gospel who choose to become disciples.[8]

4.2   Mark 3:20–35

THEOLOGICAL FOCUS 4.2

4.2   Disciples—"insiders" with Jesus—are those who do the will of God, not like "outsiders" who fail to discern Jesus' authority (3:20–35).

   4.2.1   Genetic proximity to Jesus, while disregarding his authority, has nothing to do with "insidership."

   4.2.2   Physical or ecclesiastical proximity to Jesus, while disregarding his authority, has nothing to do with "insidership."

   4.2.3   "Insidership" with Jesus, the status of the disciple, has to do with obedience to the will of God.

Section Summary 4.2: Mark's first "sandwich" story is an eventful one, packed with ironic allusions as to the insider and outsider status of various groups of people. This episode builds upon the previous one where disciples were commissioned by

6. Both these elements of the disciples' commission will show up again, later in the Gospel.

7. For the fulfillment of the commission by the Twelve, see 6:7–13, where they actually go out to perform those duties.

8. What elements of the commissioning of the Twelve are normative for the disciple today will be determined by the interpreter's canonical and systematic theology. Most strands of Christendom would agree with the preaching mandate; not all would unite on the need to conduct exorcisms or exercise healing (as the Twelve did: 3:14, 15; see also 6:12–13). The fact that Jesus engages in both exorcisms and healings subsequent to the disciples' commissioning, in contrast to the fact that he is never said to preach again in Mark, may be a hint as to what, in particular, the "baton" constitutes, and what exactly has been handed over to the responsibility of his followers. Notice those to whom the verb κηρύσσω (*kērussō*, "preach/proclaim") is applied in this Gospel (other than Jesus in 1:14 and 1:38–39): John (1:4, 7), a leper (1:45), an ex-demoniac (5:20), a deaf-mute (7:36), the Twelve (3:14; 6:12), and the early church (13:10; 14:9)—all of whom fall into the category of "disciples" in Mark's reckoning. On the other hand, exorcism and healing powers are not handed out so indiscriminately (in Mark, apart from Jesus and Twelve, only one other is said to have possessed the ability to exorcise, 9:38), suggesting a restriction of those ministries.

Jesus to be "with him" and to be sent by him. Both Jesus' family and the Jerusalem scribes represent "outsiders" who fail to recognize Jesus' person (especially his authority). They are not "with him" and are starkly contrasted with the "insider," the disciple who does the will of God—the one who is "with Jesus."

TRANSLATION 4.2

3:20   *And He came in to the house, and the crowd came together again, so that they were not even able to eat bread.*

3:21   *And when His family heard [of this], they went out to seize Him, for they were saying, "He is out of His mind."*

3:22   *And the scribes who came down from Jerusalem were saying, "He has Beelzebul," and "By the ruler of the demons, He casts out demons."*

3:23   *And summoning them, He was speaking to them in parables, "How is Satan able to cast out Satan?*

3:24   *And if a kingdom is divided against itself, that kingdom is not able to stand.*

3:25   *And if a house is divided against itself, that house will not be able to stand.*

3:26   *And if Satan has risen up against himself and is divided, he is not able to stand, but he has [come to] an end.*

3:27   *But no one is able to enter into the house of the strong man to plunder his property unless he first binds the strong man, and then he will plunder his house.*

3:28   *Truly, I say to you that all sins will be forgiven the sons of men, and whatever blasphemies they may blaspheme;*

3:29   *but whoever blasphemes against the Holy Spirit does not have forgiveness eternally, but is guilty of an eternal sin"—*

3:30   *because they were saying, "He has an unclean spirit."*

3:31   *And His mother and His brothers came, and standing outside, they sent for Him and called Him.*

3:32   *And a crowd was sitting around Him, and they said to Him, "Behold, your mother and Your brothers are seeking You outside."*

3:33   *And answering them, He said, "Who are My mother and My brothers?"*

3:34   *And looking around at those sitting around Him in a circle, He said, "Behold My mother and My brothers.*

3:35   *For whoever does the will of God, he is My brother and sister and mother."*

NOTES 4.2

This unit is the first of six classic, well-accepted "sandwich" stories in Mark—a literary arrangement with one story intercalated into another, giving the narrative the structure of a bipartite outer story and a single inner story.[9] Here 3:20–21 and 3:31–35

---

9. See Edwards, "Markan Sandwiches"; and Shepherd, *Markan Sandwich Stories* for excellent accounts of this literary feature in Mark's Gospel. The other five obvious "sandwiches" in Mark are located in 5:20–43; 6:7–32; 11:12–25; 14:1–11; and 14:53–72. The outer and inner stories are usually "mutually illuminating," as will be seen (France, *Gospel of Mark*, 19).

form the two halves of the outer story, and 3:22–30 the inner story. Both stories are centered on the "house" in relation to which some are inside and others outside; notice also the "house" divided on itself (3:25, 27).[10] As with most of these "sandwiches," the only character common to both stories is Jesus. Indeed, the symmetrical way in which the characters are introduced centers upon (and is bookended at either end by) the protagonist of the story.[11]

A   **Jesus** (3:20a)
   B   Crowd (3:20b)
     C   Relatives (3:21)
       D   Scribes (3:22)
         Jesus (3:23–29)
       D'   Scribes (3:30)
     C'   Relatives (3:31)
   B'   Crowd (3:32)
A'   **Jesus** (3:33–35)

Two discrete groups approach the house: the family of Jesus and the scribes from Jerusalem. Apparently they are on different errands, but with the same goal: to oppose Jesus. The "sandwich" technique in this unit compares the parallel charges brought against Jesus—by his family (accusation of madness, 3:21) and by the scribes (accusation of demonic control, 3:22, 30).[12]

Mark 3:20–35 forms the "sandwich" proper; however a better feel for the theological thrust is obtained if one visualizes the structure of the entire section of 3:7—4:1. Notice the symmetrical layout of the "insiders" and "outsiders" (in bold).[13]

Narrative Summary: Large crowds (πολύς, *polys*); boat (3:7–12)

A   Those "with" Jesus—disciples (3:13–20) [ποιέω, *poieō*,"appoint," 3:14]   **Insiders: Twelve**
Narrative Foil: Crowd (3:20)
   B   Those accusing Jesus of madness—family (3:21)   **Outsiders: Family**
     C   Those accusing Jesus of demonic control—scribes   **Outsiders: Scribes**
       (3:22–30)
   B'   Those sending for and calling Jesus—family (3:31)   **Outsiders: Family**
Narrative Foil: Crowd (3:32)
A'   Those "around" Jesus—"inner circle" (3:33–35) [ποιέω, "do," 3:35]   **Insiders: Anyone**
Narrative Summary: Large crowds (πλεῖστος, *pleistos*, superlative of πολύς); boat (4:1)

10. Perhaps Mark's readers would have been aware of the fragmentation of the kingdom and household of Herod the Great after his demise in 4 BCE. They might also have recalled that the downfall of Herod Antipas began with his defeat at the hands of the stronger army of the Nabatean king Aretas (Josephus, *Ant.* 5.1), not to mention the fractures within the "house" of Roman imperial power with the death of Nero. See Donahue and Harrington, *Gospel of Mark*, 130–31.

11. Shepherd, *Markan Sandwich Stories*, 111–38, discusses 3:20–35 in detail.

12. The family of Jesus is not shown in a good light in this Gospel. They "remain for Mark completely outside the Jesus movement, as at best skeptical onlookers. . . . If it were not for 6:3 [and, perhaps, 15:40, 47; and 16:1] a reader of Mark would not even know the names of any of Jesus' natural family" (France, *Gospel of Mark*, 164).

13. Modified from van Iersel, "Concentric Structures," 94.

Strikingly, there is no description of the responses of the family members (who are "snubbed" by Jesus) or of the Jerusalem scribes (who are condemned by him); they make no replies to Jesus. This episode, therefore, is rather static, and "not so much a narrative as a tableau, enabling us to see graphically the contrast between insiders and outsiders."[14] Also note that those "with" Jesus (3:14) are parallel with those "around" Jesus (3:34)—the insiders (both groups of people are related to the word ποιέω; "to appoint," 3:14; "to do," 3:35). In other words, the insiders "doing" the will of God are disciples who are "appointed" to be with Jesus. Outsiders, on the other hand, are those who are *not* with him; they do not fall into the "disciple" category.

4.2.1 Genetic proximity to Jesus, while disregarding his authority, has nothing to do with "insidership."

The first outer slice of the "sandwich" (3:20–21):

- The disciples come inside the house with Jesus (indicated by the plural: "*they* were not even able to eat," 3:20)—disciples are *physically* inside the house.

- Because they are with Jesus morally (μετ᾽ αὐτου, *met autou*, 3:14), they are *morally* "insiders."

- Jesus' family (οἱ παρ᾽ αὐτοῦ, *hoi par autou*, literally "those of Him," 3:21) go "out" (ἐξῆλθον, *exēlthon*, 3:21; note the prefix ἐξ, *ex*, "out-") to seize him—the family are *physically* outside.

- And their accusation is that Jesus is "out" of his mind (ἐξέστη, *exestē*, 3:21, with the prefix ἐξ again)—Jesus is accused of being *morally* "outside." The family's use of κρατέω (*krateō*, "seize," 3:21) is also significant; it always has negative connotations in Mark (6:17; 12:12; 14:1, 44, 46, 49, 51), except when Jesus is the subject doing the seizing (1:31; 5:41; 9:27). The hostile actions of Jesus' family indicate that they are not on the "inside" with Jesus.[15]

The irony is that the ones *genetically* "inside" (the family Jesus shares genes with) are *physically* outside; and, accusing Jesus of being "outside," it is they themselves who are *morally* "outside" in relation to the Jesus "circle." The second outer slice of the "sandwich" (3:31–35) confirms this diagnosis of the family's moral location:

- Jesus' family are said to be "standing outside" (ἔξω στήκοντες, *exō stēkontes*, 3:31)—they are *physically* outside. The forward position of ἔξω ("outside") further emphasizes the family's "outsider" status—this despite being *genetically* "inside" with Jesus.

- The family is again described as being outside, seeking Jesus (ἔξω, 3:32).[16]

---

14. France, *Gospel of Mark*, 178.

15. Shepherd, *Markan Sandwich Stories*, 122. Interestingly, all of Jesus' actions employing κρατέω are healings.

16. As well, the family's "seeking" has a deprecatory tone (as the verb ζητέω, *zēteō*, almost always does in this Gospel: 8:11, 12; 11:18; 12:12; 14:1, 11, 55), rendering their activities inimical to Jesus' mission (see also under 1:32–39).

- The irony goes further: the family "sends" and "calls" for Jesus—ἀποστέλλω (*apostellō*) and καλέω (*kaleō*) are key words in the commissioning activity of Jesus (1:20; 2:17; 3:14; 6:7). It is he who alone has the authority to send and call; but here we see these "outsiders" daring to send for and call Jesus.

In sum, the family of Jesus, those whom one expects to be inside (and inside they are, *genetically*), turn out to be outside *physically*, but even more important, outside *morally*. They fail to recognize Jesus' person (unlike the demons in 3:11), and thus disregard his authority. They are not "with" Jesus, and they are certainly not disciples.

4.2.2 *Physical or ecclesiastical proximity to Jesus, while disregarding his authority, has nothing to do with "insidership."*

Mark clearly points to the origin of the scribes—they are from Jerusalem (3:22). One would assume that they, coming from this hub of religious activity where the temple was located, would be "insiders." The reader may safely deduce, from the dialogue the scribes have with Jesus in this inner story (3:22–30), that they are physically inside the house. There they are, *physically* inside with Jesus, and presumably, being religious functionaries, *morally* inside as well. However, their openly hostile charge of Jesus being under demonic control gives lie to that presumption.

The scribes lay on Jesus two accusations; he responds to each, in reverse order.[17]

A	Accusation 1 (3:22a)	*His deeds are in the power of Beelzebul!*
	B Accusation 2 (3:22b)	*He casts out demons by ruler of demons!*
	C Jesus' statement on Satan (3:23–26)	
	B′ Response to Accusation 2 (3:27)	*Satan does not cast out Satan!*
A′	Response to Accusation 1 (3:28–30)	*My deeds are in the power of the Holy Spirit!*

The scribes' allegation is that Jesus' exorcisms, rather than being empowered by the Holy Spirit, were being performed under the control of Satan—"a total perversion of the truth and a repudiation of the rule of God," an arrant rejection of the saving grace and power of God. There can be no forgiveness for this outright repudiation—indeed, such an attitude makes forgiveness impossible.[18] That this is the issue is underscored by the narrator's explanatory tag that concludes the section: ". . . because they were saying, 'He has an unclean spirit'" (3:30). It must be remembered that it is the Holy Spirit who had initiated the first confrontation with Satan in 1:12; the same Spirit is implicitly responsible for the ministry of Jesus (3:29), a fact that the scribes refuse to acknowledge, instead attributing Jesus' works to satanic influence.[19] Theirs is an utter denial of the work of God in Jesus. They, too, disregarded Jesus' authority.

17. Harrington, *Mark*, 43.

18. France, *Gospel of Mark*, 177; Witherington, *Gospel of Mark*, 159; Stein, *Mark*, 187. Rabbinic polemical literature continued the accusation of demonic activity in Jesus: *b. Sanh.* 43a, 107b; see Justin Martyr, *Dial.* 69; Origen, *Cels.* 1.6.

19. France, *Gospel of Mark*, 174. The verb δύναμαι (*dynamai*, "is able") occurs five times in rapid succession: "How is Satan *able* to cast out Satan?"; "a kingdom is not *able* to stand"; "a house is not *able* to stand"; "Satan is not *able* to stand"; and "no one is *able* to enter the strong man's house" (3:23–27).

The inner story of the "sandwich" (3:22–30):

- The scribes are ostensibly "insiders" (from Jerusalem)—*ecclesiastically* "inside."[20]

- They are within the house arguing with Jesus—*physically* inside.

- Accusing Jesus of being in league with Satan, and of casting "out" demons by Satan (note the verbal prefix derived from ἐξ [*ex*] in ἐκβάλλω, *ekballō*, "cast out," 3:22, 23), they imply Jesus is *morally* "outside" (just as his relatives accused him of being "out" of his mind, ἐξέστη, *exestē*, 3:21).

- Jesus counters, accusing the scribes of blasphemy, and declaring forgiveness for them impossible—*they* are the ones *morally* cast out eternally.

In sum, Mark's account of the inner piece of the tableau is filled with irony: the ones *ecclesiastically* "inside" and *physically* inside turn out to be *morally* "outside." They too, like Jesus' relatives, disregard his authority, and they too are not "with" Jesus! Disciples they are hardly! Who then, one wonders, is on the "inside" with Jesus? Who is *for* him?

4.2.3   "Insidership" with Jesus, the status of the disciple, has to do with obedience to the will of God.

Finally we get to the *real* "insiders"—those sitting "around Him in a circle" (περὶ αὐτὸν κύκλῳ, *peri auton kuklō*, 3:34).[21] The question of what exactly constitutes "insidership" or "outsidership" is answered here: Jesus' true/new family is made up of those who do the will of God. These are the ones who are *morally* "insiders" with Jesus—the inner circle. These are the ones who are "with" Jesus—his disciples. In contrast are those who not only fail to follow Jesus, but proactively take on an offensive stance of repudiating him, disregarding his authority—the relatives and scribes: those not "with" Jesus.[22]

The location of these insiders (περὶ αὐτὸν κύκλῳ, *peri auton kyklō*, "around Him in a circle," 3:34) is parallel to the station of the disciples (μετ᾽ αὐτου, *met autou*, "with Him," 3:14).[23] Not only does this parallelism again equate "insiders" with those who are appointed to be "with" Jesus (i.e., disciples), it also indicates the broadening of the circle. It is not just the Twelve alone who are in the coterie of insiders, but *anyone* who does the will of God: "insiders" (the new family of Jesus) includes all those who

---

The only one who is "able" is Jesus—his power is great indeed: by binding the ὁ ἰσχυρός (*ho ischyros*, "the strong man"), it is he who is the strong*er* one (ὁ ἰσχυρότερός, *ho ischyroteros*, as John the Baptist described Jesus in 1:7). Satan's kingdom is coming under siege—not by an internal demonic enemy, but by an external divine one, working in the power of the Holy Spirit. See Busch, "Questioning and Conviction," 493.

20. "Ecclesiastically" is, of course, anachronistic here, but conveys the sense of officialdom, indicating those who were professionally and habitually handling the things of God.

21. These, though part of the "crowd," are clearly distinguished from that larger body, which in its anonymous and nondescript character simply serves as a narrative foil in the Gospel.

22. France, *Gospel of Mark*, 164.

23. In fact, 4:10 employs the same wording as does 3:34, including the Twelve in that particular group: οἱ περὶ αὐτὸν σὺν τοῖς δώδεκα (*hoi peri auton syn tois dōdeka*, "those around Him with the Twelve").

are "with" Jesus and who follow him "on the way," doing the will of God—"the wider, and in principle indefinitely extendable, family."[24] That Jesus uses deliberately inclusive language with his addition of "sister" (3:35, the only time in this "sandwich" where "sister" appears) suggests this extendability of "disciple"/"insider" beyond the confines of that historic circle. This addition is pointed, for neither Mark nor the crowd says anything about sisters searching for Jesus or coming for him in 3:31–33.[25] In other words, *anyone* who does the will of God is an "insider"—and such a one, who is "with Jesus," is a disciple!

SERMON FOCUS AND OUTLINES

THEOLOGICAL FOCUS OF PERICOPE 4 FOR PREACHING
4 Disciples—insiders with Jesus—are those who do the will of God (3:7–35).

In contrast to outsiders who fail to recognize Jesus' person and thus disregard his authority (his Lordship), insiders—those who do the will of God—are the true disciples. These are the ones who have authoritatively been appointed by Jesus to be with him and then to be sent by him to extend his mission in the world in the service of God's kingdom (a dramatic and momentous commissioning that is not to be disparaged or disregarded). And to engage in this activity with all of one's life is what it means to do the will of God. The way the story is told (see the chiastic structure of 3:7—4:1 above), there is a clear equation of the following elements:

> those appointed (ποιέω, *poieō*) to be with Jesus (and then to be sent by Jesus) [3:14]
>> = disciples ("insiders"/the new family of Jesus) [3:34]
>>> = those who do (ποιέω) the will of God [3:35].

Or . . .

> to do (ποιέω) the will of God [3:35]
>> = to fulfill the role of the disciple ("insider") [3:34]
>>> = to be with him (and then to be sent by him) as appointed (ποιέω) by Jesus [3:14].

The obedience of "insiders" (i.e., the Twelve and the spiritual family of Jesus) to the will of God and their remaining "with" Jesus is contrasted with the response of "outsiders" (i.e., the physical family of Jesus and the scribes from Jerusalem) who disregard his authority and fail to recognize his Lordship. This is one of first steps in the Trip of Discipleship—the submission to his authority and Lordship. That acknowledgement, evidenced in a life of obedience to the will of God, Mark tells us, is a key element of being a disciple—one who obeys the call to be with Jesus and to be sent out by him.

---

24. France, *Gospel of Mark*, 180.

25. The testosterone-partial *Gos. Thom.* 99, in recounting this pericope, omits "sister" (and also places "brother" before "mother").

POSSIBLE PREACHING OUTLINES FOR PERICOPE 4

I.   OUTSIDERS: Family and scribes

   The outer story depicts the family's disregard for Jesus' authority—outsiders: 3:20–21, 31–32

   The inner story depicts the scribes' disregard for Jesus' authority—outsiders: 3:22–30

   Move-to-Relevance: ways we might wrongly assume we are insiders

II. INSIDERS: Disciples

   The definition of the disciple—insider: one doing the will of God: 3:33–35

   The will of God: obedience to Jesus' commission of 3:14

III. *Be an insider with Jesus: Do the will of God!*

   Specific way(s) we can do the will of God, especially relating to Jesus' commission of 3:14

As with all narratives in Scripture, not every verse in this pericope needs to be attended to in detail in the sermon, neither does every exegetical/theological point raised in the notes above. The constraints of the audience (their circumstances and spirituality), the time available, the occasion of the preaching event, and the preacher's own style should dictate which parts of the text are highlighted. Expediently demonstrating the theology of the pericope (i.e., the authority of the text) and, thence, moving to application (i.e., the relevance of the text) should be the goal of the homiletician when preaching this and every other pericope.

Another way of looking at the pericope is to see the family of Jesus and the scribes from Jerusalem as representing "genes" and "status"—elements that, in the eyes of the world, privilege one before God. A correction to this misconception is made by the inspired text: it is obedience that privileges one, not pedigrees or taxonomies of power attained by virtue of birth, ancestry, vocation, wealth, etc.

I.   WORLD: "Genes and/or status in society/religion privileges one in God's eyes."

   Genes: Jesus' family disregards his authority: 3:20–21, 31–32

   Status: The scribes disregard Jesus' authority: 3:22–30

   Move-to-Relevance: ways we might wrongly assume we are privileged insiders

II. GOD: "Doing my will privileges one in my eyes."

   Obedience to God's will is the mark of a disciple: 3:33–35

   The will of God for the disciple: undertaking Jesus' commission to be with him and be sent: 3:14

III. *Be privileged: Do the will of God!*

   Specific way(s) we can do the will of God, especially relating to Jesus' commission of 3:14

The homiletical imperative in either outline is, admittedly, quite general. One will want to focus on obedience particularly to the elements of Jesus' commission of the disciples—to be with him and to be sent by him. Indeed, the preacher may want to focus primarily on one or the other these two, drawing out its importance in determining closeness to Jesus ("insidership"), as opposed to what the world considers as important in making one "spiritual."

PERICOPE 5

Fruit-Bearing Project

Mark 4:1–34

[Seed Parables and Explanations]

REVIEW, SUMMARY, PREVIEW

Review of Pericope 4: Mark 3:7–35 identifies the disciple, the "insider," as one who does the will of God—being with Jesus and being sent by him.

Summary of Pericope 5: Mark 4:1–34 depicts a variety of responses to the word of God, but the disciple is exhorted to be receptive to the word to obey it (the human element in fruit-bearing discipleship), without allowing satanic or worldly distractions to interfere, in order that fruit may be produced for the cause of the kingdom of God. The negative corollary to fruit-bearing is that a lack of receptiveness to God's word to obey it results in unfruitfulness, judgment of hard-heartedness, and possible loss of God's blessing. Besides the human element in fruit-bearing, the divine element is also stressed in this pericope: it is incomprehensible, it is automatic, and it is momentous—it causes the humblest efforts of the disciple to result in great eschatological significance.

Preview of Pericope 6: The next pericope (4:35—5:20) demonstrates that disciples respond to Jesus by having faith in his power over nature and "super-nature," and fearlessly accepting Jesus' commission to proclaim that power.

5   Mark 4:1–34

THEOLOGICAL FOCUS OF PERICOPE 5

5   **The Christian's responsibility in the process of bearing fruit in discipleship (the human element)—to be receptive to God's word to obey it without being distracted, lest loss of blessing result—works in tandem with the divine element in the process—God's incomprehensible and automatic work, which is momentous, for even the seemingly insignificant human effort of the disciple will result in great eschatological significance for the kingdom of God (4:1–34).**

5.1   While there is a variety of responses to Jesus and his mission, the disciple is called to be receptive to God's word to obey it without being distracted—the human element of fruitfulness in discipleship for the kingdom of God—lest, by rejection, diminution of blessing result (4:1–25).

5.1.1   To the proclamation of Jesus and of his mission, the disciple can expect a variety of responses.

5.1.2   The dynamic category of "outsiders" denotes those who are fruitless.

5.1.3   Receptivity of the disciple to God's word, without being distracted, results in fruitfulness.

5.1.4   One can expect a consequence of gain or loss, depending on one's receptiveness to God's word.

5.2   The divine element in bearing fruit in discipleship for the kingdom of God governs the entire process—God's incomprehensible and automatic work, which is momentous, for it causes even the seemingly insignificant human element in the process of fruitfulness to result in great eschatological significance (4:26–34).

5.2.1   God's work of fructification of the disciple is incomprehensible and automatic.

5.2.2   God's work of fructification of the disciple is an event of great significance and consequence, causing even the seemingly insignificant human elements of the process to produce great yields.

OVERVIEW

THIS EXTENDED DISCOURSE, 4:1–34, in Act I of the Gospel is parallel in placement to the other extended discourse in Act III (Mark 13; see the Introduction). "Each discourse provides an explanatory framework to help the reader gain a true perspective on the narrative which precedes and follows it."[1] There is much emphasis in 4:1–2 on teaching—this is a *didactic* discourse (διδάσκειν/ἐδίδασκεν/διδαχή, *didaskein/edidasken/didachē*, "to teach/He was teaching/teaching"). And in Mark, Jesus is depicted as sitting only on this occasion (4:1) and in 13:3, equating these two blocks of didactic discourse.[2]

Thus far, the throngs and the religious leaders (and on occasion even the disciples), though having observed his miracles and listened to his teaching, have failed to recognize Jesus' person, his authority, and his mission (Mark 1:21–45; 2:1—3:6, 20–35). And, surprisingly, Jesus' own family seems to have gone astray on this matter (3:20–35). However, some are more perspicacious: notice the positive narrative treatment of the disciples/"insiders" (1:1–20; 3:7–19, 20–35) and of Simon's mother-in-law

---

1. France, *Gospel of Mark*, 182.

2. The posture of sitting likely indicates Jesus' authority: Ps 29:10; Rev 3:21.

(1:30–31); in response to Jesus' authority these characters have obeyed and/or served. All of these varied responses—"outsidership" vs. "insidership" (selfish association with Jesus or antagonism towards him vs. obedience or selfless service)—are to the same message of Jesus announcing the good news of the kingdom of God. How could there be such a diversity of responses to the *same* message? This variation in response to Jesus is again depicted in this pericope, in the different degrees of fruitfulness of the seeds/soils. In particular, for the purposes of discipleship, the question 4:1–34 addresses is how one is to respond to Jesus in order to be fruitful. How may fruit-bearing be ensured in the disciple's life?

The "kingdom of God," first announced in 1:14–15, returns in this extended discourse (4:11, 26, 30), indicating that the seed parable early in the pericope, the statements of hiddenness and revelation, and the later seed parables are all dealing with this kingdom—its growth and its development.[3] Of course, the growth of the kingdom parallels the growth of the community of disciples. Thus, in this pericope the fruitfulness of disciples is equated with the increase of the kingdom: to be fruitful unto God is to engage in the extension of the kingdom of God. In addition, this pericope teaches that there is both a human and a divine element to this advancement and development of the kingdom.

The structure of the pericope may be visualized thus[4]:

Narrative Introduction		(4:1–2)	(ἐν παραβολαῖς πολλὰ, *en parabolais polla*, "many things in parables")
Seed Parable		(4:3–9)	Lesson Expressed: **Parable of Growth**
	Mystery	(4:10–13)	
Private Discussion		(4:14–20)	Lesson Explained: **Human Element in Growth**
	Revelation	(4:21–25)	
Seed Parables		(4:26–32)	Lesson Extended: **Divine Element in Growth**
Narrative Conclusion		(4:33–34)	(παραβολαῖς πολλαῖς, *parabolais pollais*, "many parables")

The concept of "parables," already introduced in 3:23, echoes throughout this section (4:2, 10, 11, 13 [×2], 30, 33, 34). The lesson of growth that forms the foundation of the pericope is expressed in the seed parable of 4:3–8. Subsequently, the disciples (followers + Twelve; see 4:10) seek enlightenment on Jesus' figurative language, and Jesus proceeds to explain the parable—the "mystery of the kingdom" (4:10–13)—what exactly the human element is, in the process of a disciple's growth and fruitfulness (4:14–20). This private discussion with his followers is concluded with a statement on the revelation of the "mystery" (4:21–25), reinforcing the truth that to those who accept the word, more will be given—more understanding and, thus, more fruit-bearing (4:25;

---

3. Perhaps not surprisingly, after this pericope, "kingdom of God" does not reappear in Mark; the focus slowly shifts to the suffering and Passion of Jesus, which must come first, before the consummation of the kingdom.

4. From Dowd, *Reading Mark*, 39.

see below). However, for those who do not accept the word, there will be a punitive "subtraction"—they will understand even less and be rendered fruitless (4:25). The return to seed parables at the end of the pericope, in 4:26–32, illustrates the divine element in growth and fruitfulness.

5.1 Mark 4:1–25

THEOLOGICAL FOCUS 5.1

5.1   While there is a variety of responses to Jesus and his mission, the disciple is called to be receptive to God's word to obey it without being distracted—the human element of fruitfulness in discipleship for the kingdom of God—lest, by rejection, diminution of blessing result (4:1–25).

    5.1.1   To the proclamation of Jesus and of his mission, the disciple can expect a variety of responses.

    5.1.2   The dynamic category of "outsiders" denotes those who are fruitless.

    5.1.3   Receptivity of the disciple to God's word, without being distracted, results in fruitfulness.

    5.1.4   One can expect a consequence of gain or loss, depending on one's receptiveness to God's word.

Section Summary 5.1: The context prior to this pericope demonstrated a variety of responses to Jesus and his mission. Parabolically, this diversity is depicted here in the differential responses of the seeds/soils. Jesus explains that the reason for unfruitfulness in a follower is the lack of receptivity to his word, exacerbated by satanic attack, tribulation, and the distractions stemming from the worries and pleasures of the world. On the other hand, receptivity to the word of God, to obey it, yields fruit in the life of the disciple, and the kingdom of God is thereby furthered.

TRANSLATION 5.1

4:1   *And again He began to teach by the sea. And a very large crowd gathered to Him, so that He got into a boat on the sea and sat down, and the whole crowd was beside the sea, upon the land.*

4:2   *And He was teaching them many things in parables, and was saying to them in His teaching,*

4:3   *"Listen! Behold the sower went out to sow.*

4:4   *And it came about that while He was sowing that some [seed] fell by the way, and the birds came and consumed it.*

4:5   *And other [seed] fell upon the rocky ground where it did not have much soil, and immediately it sprang up, not having depth of soil.*

4:6   *And when the sun came up, it was scorched and, not having root, it withered.*

4:7   *And other [seed] fell among the thorns, and the thorns went up and choked it, and it did not yield fruit.*

4:8   *And other [seed] fell into the good soil and were yielding fruit as they went up and grew, and were producing—one thirtyfold, one sixtyfold, and one hundredfold."*

4:9   *And He was saying, "He who has ears to hear, let him hear."*

4:10   *And when He was alone, those around Him, along with the Twelve, were asking Him [about] the parables.*

4:11   *And He was saying to them, "To you the mystery of the kingdom of God has been given, but to those outside everything is in parables,*

4:12   *so that while seeing, they may see and not perceive, and while hearing, they may hear and not comprehend; otherwise they may return and it be forgiven them."*

4:13   *And He said to them, "Do you not understand this parable? And how will you recognize any of the parables?*

4:14   *The sower sows the word.*

4:15   *These are the ones by the way where the word is sown and when they hear, immediately Satan comes and takes away the word which has been sown in them.*

4:16   *And these are the ones sown upon rocky ground who, when they hear the word, immediately receive it with joy,*

4:17   *and do not have root in themselves, but are temporary; then, when trouble or persecution arises because of the word, immediately they fall away.*

4:18   *And others are the ones sown among the thorns; these are the ones who hear the word,*

4:19   *and the worries of the age, and the seduction of wealth, and the desires for other things, coming in, choke the word, and it becomes unfruitful.*

4:20   *And those are the ones sown upon the good soil, who hear the word and accept [it] and bear fruit—one thirtyfold, and one sixtyfold, and one hundredfold."*

4:21   *And He was saying to them, "A lamp does not come to be placed under a grain-measuring basket or under a bed, does it? Is it not to be placed on a lampstand?*

4:22   *For it is not hidden, except to be shown; neither is it concealed, but that it may come into sight.*

4:23   *If anyone has ears to hear, let him hear."*

4:24   *And He was saying to them, "Watch what you hear. By the measure you measure, it will be measured to you and it will be added to you.*

4:25   *For whoever has, to him it will be given; and whoever does not have, from him even what he has will be taken away."*

NOTES 5.1

*5.1.1   To the proclamation of Jesus and of his mission, the disciple can expect a
variety of responses.*

Jesus is clearly identified with the sower in the first seed parable (4:3–8):

- Both sower and Jesus "go out" (ἐξέρχομαι, *exerchomai*, 4:3 and 1:35, 38, 39;
  2:13, 17).

- One sows the word, the other preaches the word (4:14–15, 33 and 1:38–39; 2:2;
  8:32).

- For sower and Jesus, sowing has both negative and positive results: failure of the
  "seeds" to respond to Jesus was depicted in preceding pericopes (the crowds and
  their purely self-interested enthusiasm for Jesus, 1:21–45; scribes, Pharisees, and
  Jesus' family, and their refusal to submit to the authority of Jesus, 2:16, 24; 3:6, 21,
  22, 31–35); success of the "seeds" responding to Jesus was also pictured earlier
  (disciples, a mother-in-law, and "insiders," who obeyed Jesus, 1:16–20, 30–31;
  3:32–35).

The precise, but somewhat redundant, description of the crowd as being on "land"
(γῆ, *gē*, "beside the sea, upon the land," 4:1) prepares the ground for the parable that
deals with different kinds of "soil" (γῆ), both good and bad. The parable dwells on the
utility of the various soils, graded upon their response to the "word" (λόγος, *logos*)
sown (4:15, 16, 18, 20, 33). This is a discourse on hearing the word and responding
to it.[5] And to the degree that one hears and responds to Jesus' word, one bears fruit.
Obviously, there is a variety of responses to the mission of the sower. The failures of the
first three seeds/soils occur at progressively later stages in their growth—the first does
not even begin the process of growth, another withers soon after sprouting,[6] and the
third survives but remains fruitless.[7] None of them turn out to be useful to the sower.

The balance is carefully created—three unsuccessful seeds (soils) and three successful ones. Failure is not necessarily the predominant experience of the sower sowing
the seed of the word. In fact, there might be a focus here upon the latter group of three
productive seeds: while the fate of the first three seeds is described in the aorist, the
second set of fruitful seeds has imperfect verbs (ἐδίδου, *edidou*, "yielding"; and ἔφερεν,
epheren, "producing") and present participles (ἀναβαίνοντα, *anabainonta*, "came up";
and αὐξανόμενα, *auxanomena*, "grew"), all denoting continuous fruitfulness—a hint
that this is to be the uninterrupted and ongoing norm of the disciple's life (4:7–8).

5. Rather than "seed" parables, these may be better labeled "soil/earth" or "growth" parables (Tolbert,
Sowing the Gospel, 149). Nonetheless, even while the soils are contrasted, so also are seeds, three of
which fell into the good soil, but produced different yields.

6. As quickly as the seed "springs up" on rocky places (ἐξανατέλλω, *exanatellō*, 4:5), equally rapidly
the sun "comes up" to scorch it (ἀνατέλλω, *anatellō*, 4:6).

7. Marcus, *Mystery of the Kingdom*, 22. Though a bit incongruous in this parable about grain production, in light of 4:20, I have chosen to translate καρπός (*karpos*) and its cognates as relating to "fruit."

5.1.2   *The dynamic category of "outsiders" denotes those who are fruitless.*

"Mystery" (μυστήριον, *mystērion*, 4:11) is equivalent to the English "secret," in that it is hidden, not that it cannot be understood (4:11). A revealed mystery, as in a divulged secret, is not necessarily incomprehensible. Unlike the esoteric usage of the term in Greco-Roman culture, Mark's employment of "mystery" designates a teaching intended to be revealed and made known.[8] Mark 4:21–22 disabuses one of any thought that "mystery" might indicate a kind of concealment of God's truth/word that is permanent; rather, what is seemingly hidden is invariably brought to sight . . . to those who are receptive (see below).

The parables, Jesus explains, give the mystery of the kingdom of God to those already inside; from those already outside these mysteries are hidden (4:11–12).[9] This equates "outsiders" with those who do not believe in the first place (see 1 Cor 5:12–13; Col 4:5; 1 Thess 4:12; Rev 22:15). "The parables, like Jesus' healing and preaching ministry in general, do not force people outside or pull people inside; they simply reveal the type of ground already present."[10] The fact that to outsiders "everything is in parables" (Mark 4:11) suggests that the "everything" is more than Jesus' parabolic teaching; it includes his entire ministry, his deeds as well as his speech: they are all parables to those unwilling to hear. "[W]hat they are failing to appreciate is not just a sequence of puzzling sayings, but the whole revelation, visible as well as audible," that is manifested in the works and words of Jesus.[11] Everything—all that Jesus has said and done so far—comes in parables to these already blind and deaf people, and remains parabolic to them. They do not grasp the life-changing significance of what they are hearing. And this failure to comprehend is a function of human (ir)responsibility.[12] In other words, Mark 4:12 (= Isa 6:9–10) deals with the *fact* of opposition and obduracy to the message of Jesus, and the resultant inaudibility and opaqueness to already deaf ears and blind eyes, rather than with a divine purpose of preventing listeners and viewers from returning to God.[13]

The citation from Isaiah 6:9–10 in Mark 4:12 reflects a typical prophetic device for warning about the inevitable consequences of rejection of God's word, thereby challenging the remnant to pay attention (also see Jer 5:21 and Ezek 12:2).[14] Here in Mark 4, too, the insiders (disciples) are encouraged to have open ears and eyes to the teachings of Jesus. This Parable of the Sower is bracketed by two commands to

---

8. France, *Gospel of Mark*, 196; Myers, *Binding the Strong Man*, 175.

9. In parallel with 3:20–35, the "inside" vs. "outside" element is prominent here: οἱ περὶ αὐτὸν σὺν τοῖς δώδεκα (*hoi peri auton syn tois dōdeka*, "those around Him, along with the Twelve," 4:10) are contrasted with οἱ ἔξω (*hoi exō*, "those outside," 4:11; and especially 3:32, 34). The numbering beyond "twelve" again indicates that the focus is on the community of Jesus-followers and not just upon the historical Twelve; the term "disciples" is not restricted to that latter number.

10. Tolbert, *Sowing the Gospel*, 160.

11. France, *Gospel of Mark*, 198.

12. This is not to minimize God's sovereign role in the opening of eyes and hardening of hearts. Mark's focus in this section of the pericope is upon human responsibility; divine action is addressed later.

13. Another option would be to see 4:12 as being ironic (see Hollenbach, "Lest They Should Turn"). Again, God's sovereignty in rendering ears dull and eyes dim is not the thrust of the section.

14. Snodgrass, "Hermeneutics of Hearing," 70–71.

"hear," in verses 3 and 9 (ἀκούω, *akouō*). In fact, this verb shows up thirteen times in the space of thirty-four verses (4:3, 9 [×2]; 12 [×2]; 15, 16, 18, 20, 23 [×2], 24, 33). As the explanation section (4:14–20) emphasizes, disciples do well to receive, hear, and accept the word of Jesus (4:16, 18, 20), that they, unlike the bad soil/seeds, may become fruit-bearing. *Why* only some respond with interest is not Mark's concern: his concern is that the reader (hopefully one seeking to be a disciple or who already is) should respond. This is the factor of man's responsibility—the human element—the act of receiving/hearing/accepting God's word and producing fruit.

Of striking interest is that terms from Isaiah 6:9–10 are also applied later to the Twelve in Mark 8:17, 21 (hearts neither seeing nor understanding). Indeed, on several occasions in Mark's Gospel, those not among the Twelve seem to respond with far keener hearing and sight than do Jesus' closest associates (5:34; 7:29; 9:24; 14:3–9; 15:39). Thus the "inside"/"outside" descriptions turn out to be merely "the result of ways of responding to parables on a given occasion"—in other words, it is a "fluctuating" or fungible concept, more "a *character* rather than a fixed *class*." One could place oneself in either dynamic category at different times, as the Twelve seem to do in this Gospel—they are sometimes "in," but more often than not they are depicted as being "out."[15] Every disciple runs the risk of becoming an uncomprehending "outsider" and should guard against this tendency.

In contrast to the group that responds positively and comes "inside" for a private explanation of the parables (4:10), others remain "outside," indifferent to, and unconcerned about any elucidation of the "mystery."[16] The very fact of the entering "inside" of the former is an indication of their desire to receive/hear/accept the word of Jesus. "There is a sense, therefore, in which the terrible verdict of vv. 11b–12 may be regarded as only temporary, leaving hope that those categorized as ἔξω [*exō*, "outside"] need not be permanently written off, that the division between insiders and outsiders is not a gulf without bridges."[17] The bearing of fruit in the life of the disciple is not an all-or-none phenomenon, or a once-for-all event. The follower of Jesus may (and does) oscillate between periods of barrenness and fruitfulness. The exhortation here is to strive for the continuous operation of the latter state.

5.1.3 *Receptivity of the disciple to God's word, without being distracted, results in fruitfulness.*

Jesus' rebuke of the disciples in 4:13 is strange after the implied assertion in 4:11 that they are insiders. Obviously, the giving of the "mystery" from God's part does not produce instantaneous and complete enlightenment in disciples. In some sense, an

---

15. Moule, "Mark 4:1–20," 99 (italics original). Among the Twelve are those who will betray (14:10–11, 43–46), desert (14:50), and deny (14:66–72) Jesus.

16. The imperfects in 4:10–11 (ἠρώτων, *ērōtōn*, "they were asking," and ἔλεγεν, *elegen*, "He was saying") could be iterative, indicating what frequently and customarily happened. So also the imperfects in the summary of 4:33–34. Moule concludes that "the responsible hearer . . . recognizes the parable as a challenge to investigation and . . . asks the teacher for more light, and is *thereby and therewith* 'given' the very heart of the matter" (ibid., 105, italics original).

17. France, *Gospel of Mark*, 201.

appropriate *receiving* is also required—the human element of reception of truth.[18] As the explanation section (4:14–20) emphasizes, there is a requirement for "hearing the word" (4:16, 18, 20), "receiving [the word] with joy" (4:16), and "accepting it" (4:20). It is this receptivity that is demanded of the disciple and it is this receptivity that is the essential human element for the consequential bearing of fruit. Such receptivity is, of course, more than mere cognition, and includes commitment and obedience. In 4:14–20, "word" occurs eight times (λόγος, *logos*, 4:14, 15 [×2], 16, 17, 18, 19, 20), and the verb "hear" four times (ἀκούω, *akouō*, 4:15, 16, 18, 20). Hearing the word (considered synonymous with "receiving"/"accepting") takes special emphasis here. The "insider," by very virtue of location, demonstrates this kind of receptivity, for "any true grasp of the nature of God's kingdom derives not from human speculation but from close affiliation with Jesus," from remaining in his presence, from being "with him," as disciples are called to do (3:14). This is not just for the historical Twelve, but for all who would follow Jesus.[19] Mark's intent (and that of Jesus, not to mention the Holy Spirit's) is to have the readers think of themselves rather than of the characters in the story. "It is not for nothing that the last sentence of the interpretation is about *whoever . . .* hears and accepts the word [4:25]."[20] This is a warning, too, against complacency and smugness, lest one's ears become dull and one's eyes dim. The disciple is to be receptive to God's word, seeking to hear and to obey.

It is only by this kind of receptivity—the human element in the disciple's growth—that fruit-bearing occurs. Such fruit-bearing represents normative discipleship, marked by Christlikeness in conduct (Matt 3:8–10 [Luke 3:8–9]; 7:16–20 [Luke 6:43–44]; 12:33; John 15:1–17; Rom 7:4–5; Gal 5:22–23; Eph 5:9; Phil 1:11, 22; Col 1:10; Jas 3:17–18; also see *Barn.* 11.11). God's kingdom is thus established, at least in its initial and incipient stages, not by military strategies and conquests, but by the followers of Jesus participating in God's rule by being receptive to his word, and thereby bearing fruit.[21]

It is implied here that fruitfulness, at the very least, involves the rejection of the attitudes listed in Mark 4:19, the repudiation of worldly values (which tend to squelch receptivity and fruitfulness), and the adoption of kingdom values. Among the unfruitful are those that are *by* (and not *on*) the "way" of Jesus (παρὰ τὴν ὁδόν, *para*

---

18. Ibid., 204.

19. Henderson, *Christology*, 125.

20. van Iersel, *Mark*, 186–7 (italics added).

21. Gundry, *Mark*, 206–7. The analogy of the character of Peter (Πέτρος, *Petros*) to places that are rocky (πετρώδης, *petrōdēs*) is not fortuitous; the fate of the seeds that fall upon the latter parallel the rocky career of the former—initial enthusiasm (1:16–18) but subsequent failure under pressure (14:66–72). See Donahue and Harrington, *Gospel of Mark*, 142. Mark, until this current parabolic section, labels this disciple consistently "Simon" (1:16 [×2], 29, 30, 36; 3:16 [he adds "Peter" in 3:16 to explain Jesus' naming of the disciple]); but after Mark 4, the Evangelist just as consistently refers to him as "Peter" (except when Jesus directly addresses him in 14:37, but Mark, the narrator, immediately adds "Peter" there). In the other Synoptics, "Peter" first shows up in Matt 4:18 and Luke 5:8, far removed from the rocky ground of this same parable found in Matt 13:5 and Luke 8:6. "Matthew . . . counters Mark's implicit etiology [of Peter's name] with a radically different explicit etiological legend of its own, also founded on paronomasia [Matt 16:18]. . . . Mark's hard-hearted disciple has become in Matthew the sure (hard!) foundation of the church; yet both authors establish their opposite typologies for the leading disciple by exploiting various connotations of Simon's nickname" (Tolbert, *Sowing the Gospel*, 145–46).

tēn hodon, 4:4, 15), whom Satan deceives[22], those who defect in times of tribulation (4:5–6, 16–17), and those who are distracted by the world, its worries and its pleasures (4:7, 18–19). The homiletician may explore, with profit, in the life of the congregation, those agents and circumstances that dull receptivity to God's word.

5.1.4   *One can expect a consequence of gain or loss, depending on one's receptiveness to God's word.*

The "revelation" section (4:21–25) parallels the "mystery" section (4:9–13; also see overall structural scheme of the pericope, above).

MYSTERY: Mark 4:10–13	REVELATION: Mark 4:21–25
4:11b, to you has been given (δίδωμι, *didōmi*)	4:25a, to him it will be given (δίδωμι)
4:11, μυστήριον (*mystērion*, "mystery")	4:22, κρυπτόν, ἀπόκρυφον (*krypton, apokryphon*, "hidden, concealed")
4:11c, everything is (γίνομαι, *ginomai*) in parables	4:22b, neither is (γίνομαι) it hidden
4:12, ἵνα (*hina*; telic/result) clause	4:21–22, four ἵνα clauses
4:12, see–hear (βλέπω–ἀκούω, *blepō–akouō*)	4:24, see–hear (βλέπω–ἀκούω)

Two pairs of two sayings constitute this "revelation" motif (4:21, 22 and 4:24, 25).[23] The emphasis of this "revelation" section is, again, that all are given an opportunity to hear and to heed, to listen and to accept the call to discipleship (the Gospel narrative, one remembers, began with such a broad invitation: 1:4–5, 14–15, 38–39). In other words, there is nothing to keep *anyone* from being receptive to God's word.[24] The lamp is indeed on the lampstand, visible to all who would seek it; it is not hidden. The use of the personal verb ἔρχομαι (*erchomai*, "come") in 4:21, 22 takes the reader by surprise: how can a lamp "come"? But this may simply suggest that it is, indeed, the preaching Jesus in view—the lamp who "came" (1:7, 14, 38–39; 2:13; 4:3; also see Ps 119:105; Prov 6:23, for the word of God as a lamp). Jesus' invitation is an open one to all who will receive his word; the mystery of the kingdom is a secret that has been revealed (and proclaimed). The synonymous parallelism underscores this truism:

κρυπτὸν . . . φανερωθῇ (*krypton . . . phanerōthē*, "hidden . . . shown," 4:22a)

ἀπόκρυφον . . . ἔλθη εἰς φανερόν (*apokryphon . . . elthē eis phaneron*, "concealed . . . come into sight," 4:22b)

But to those who are unreceptive to this revealed and open word—the visible lamp—recompense would be measured out by the same measure they themselves used in

---

22. Demonic elements as birds also occur in Rev 18:2; also see *1 En.* 90.8–13; *Apoc. Ab.* 13.1–14.

23. The first element in each pair begins with καὶ ἔλεγεν αὐτοῖς (*kai elegen autois*, "and He was saying to them"); the second is an explanatory clause introduced by γάρ (*gar*, "for"). Noticeable also is the use of τίθημι (*tithēmi*, "place," 4:21 [×2]) in the first pair, and the use of προστίθημι (*prostithēmi*, "add," 4:24) in the second. Perhaps another connection between the two elements is the use of the "grain-measuring basket" in the first pair (μόδιος, *modios*, 4:21) and the concept of measuring in 4:24.

24. Once again, the human element is in view here, not God's sovereign action.

disparaging the word. The degree of neglect they demonstrated to Jesus and his word would be reciprocated in their direction (4:24–25): the parables would be obscure to such, and even the seed they already had would be confiscated. This is likely to be a punitive *subtraction* of what understanding these "outsiders" already had.[25] On the other hand, those who had been receptive to the word would receive more understanding and, ostensibly, produce more fruit, explaining the differential fruit production in the seed parable. Thus there are serious consequences for those who refuse to heed the word; and there are blessed rewards for those who do. "But the Holy One, blessed be He, is not so; He puts more into a full vessel but not into an empty one. . . . If you have heard, you will continue to hear; if not, you will not hear. . . . If your heart turns away, you will not hear any more" (*b. Ber.* 40a).

The tension is patent between 4:21–23 and 4:24–25: the optimism of the former regarding sureness of revelation is balanced by the realism of the latter—not all will be receptive to this revelation, and these will suffer the consequences.[26] This realism leads to the subsequent section that pictures the sovereign work of God—the divine element—in disciples' growth and fruit-bearing.

5.2   Mark 4:26–34

THEOLOGICAL FOCUS 5.2

5.2   The divine element in bearing fruit in discipleship for the kingdom of God governs the entire process—God's incomprehensible and automatic work, that is momentous, for it causes even the seemingly insignificant human element in the process of fruitfulness to result in great eschatological significance (4:26–34).

   5.2.1   God's work of fructification of the disciple is incomprehensible and automatic.

   5.2.2   God's work of fructification of the disciple is an event of great significance and consequence, causing even the seemingly insignificant human elements of the process to produce great yields.

Section Summary 5.2: The last section of this pericope concentrates on the divine element in the fruit-bearing of the disciple who has been faithful to be receptive to God's word (the human element). In concert with the discharge of human responsibility, the divine element operates incomprehensibly (to the human mind and view) and automatically (without help from human hands). Moreover, such a divine work results in the transformation of the humblest offering from the disciple into something of great eschatological significance for the kingdom of God.

25. That the mystery of the kingdom of God is taken away from outsiders as retribution, and more given to insiders as reward, is stressed in 4:24–25 by: the threefold use of "measure" (4:24); the antithetical parallelism of 4:25 ("whoever has" vs. "whoever does not have"); the triple employment of "has/have" and the emphatic καί (*kai*, "even") before the last ἔχει (*echei*, "has," 4:25); and the assonance of four verbs ending in -θήσεται (*-thēsetai*): μετρηθήσεται (*metrēthēsetai*, "it will be measured"), προστεθήσεται (*prostethēsetai*, "it will be added"), δοθήσεται (*dothēsetai*, "it will be given"), and ἀρθήσεται (*arthēsetai*, "it will be taken away"; 4:24–25). See Gundry, *Mark*, 218. There is a hint here that the "taking away" is, in fact, Satan's work (albeit, divinely permitted): the same verb αἴρω (*airō*) in 4:25 was employed earlier in 4:15 to describe Satan's deception and his "taking away" of the word that had been sown.

26. France, *Gospel of Mark*, 212.

TRANSLATION 5.2

4:26 *And He was saying, "Thus is the kingdom of God—like a man casting seed upon the soil.*

4:27 *And he sleeps and rises, night and day, and the seed sprouts and grows—how, he himself does not know.*

4:28 *By itself, the soil produces fruit, first the stalk, then the head, then the full grain in the head.*

4:29 *When the fruit allows, immediately he sends the sickle, because the harvest has come."*

4:30 *And He was saying, "How shall we compare the kingdom of God, or in what parable shall we present it?*

4:31 *Like a mustard seed, which when sown upon the soil—it is smaller than all the seeds upon the soil—*

4:32 *and when sown, it comes up and becomes larger than all the garden plants and forms large branches, so that under its shade the birds of the air are able to nest."*

4:33 *And with many such parables He was speaking to them the word, to the degree that they were able to hear;*

4:34 *and without a parable He was not speaking to them, and privately to His own disciples He was explaining everything.*

NOTES 5.2

Each of the two parables in this section (4:26–29 and 30–32) begins with καὶ ἔλεγεν (*kai elegen*, "and He was saying," 4:26, 30), parallel to the phrases used in the public discourse of (4:1–9; see 4:2, 9); however, each of the two parables in the previous section (4:21–23 and 24–25) began with καὶ ἔλεγεν αὐτοῖς (*kai elegen autois*, "and He was saying *to them*"). The two sets of two parables are seemingly kept distinct. The current pair in 4:26–32 is thus likely to have been given in public as well, as opposed to the pair in 4:21–25. Also, while the parabolic sayings in 4:21–25 deal with indoor domestic items (lamp, grain-measuring basket, bed, lampstand), those in 4:26–32 deal with outdoor agricultural elements (sower, seed, soil, growth, harvest). The latter section is, therefore, a return to the seed-related parables of the opening section of Mark 4.[27]

5.2.1   God's work of fructification of the disciple is incomprehensible and automatic.

The current section also demonstrates deliberate structuring in 4:26–29.[28]

A   Sowing (4:26)

    B   "sleeps and rises, night and day" (4:27a)   [*activity of man*]

        C   "seed sprouts and grows" (4:27b)   [*activity of seed*]

---

27. Heil, "Reader-Response," 282n28.

28. From Fay, "Introduction to Incomprehension," 74n38.

> D   "how he himself does not know" (4:27c)   [*activity of God*; **incomprehensibility** (four words)*
>
> D'   "by itself, the soil produces fruit" (4:28a)   [*activity of God*; **automaticity** (four words)]]
>
>   C'   "first stalk, then head, then full grain" (4:28b)   [*activity of seed*]
>
>   B'   "he sends the sickle" (4:29a)   [*activity of man*]
>
> A'   Harvesting (4:29b)

* The four words referred to, here and in Mark 4:28a, are in the Greek, of course.

There is a deliberate movement from the activity of man (4:26–27a) to the activity of seed (4:27b), followed by an aside dealing with the implied activity of God (4:27c–28a), and then, in reverse order, back to the activity of seed (4:28b) and the activity of man (4:29a). The incomprehensibility and automaticity of fruit production—the center of the chiastic structure delineating the activity of God (elements D and D' above)—reflect the changes in the day-night cycle and the sprouting and growth of the seed, all without human comprehension and all occurring automatically; this is the inscrutable and sovereign work of God (see Eccl 11:4–6).[29] Whereas the previous public seed parable (Mark 4:3–9) demonstrated the contingency of the human element of receptivity (fruit depended on the receptivity of the soil and on resistance to distractions), this current public seed parable demonstrates automaticity—fruition is inexorable, for the good soil/seed yields fruit under the management, not of man, but of God, a work incomprehensible to man.[30] Outside of the initial sowing and the final harvesting, the sower does nothing but wait. Here, the seed-thrower (4:26), the ignoramus (4:27), and the sickle-sender (4:29) obviously do not depict God or Jesus. In fact, the broadcasting of seed and dispatching of sickle are not emphasized at all; they are, rather, passive activities that only indirectly impinge upon the main work of fruit production—and here, that is entirely the work of God.[31] As Luther wrote: "I simply taught, preached, and wrote God's Word; otherwise I did nothing. And while I slept or drank Wittenberg beer with my friends Philip [Melanchthon] and [Nicolaus

29. Αὐτόματος (*automatos*, "by itself") occurs in 4:28.

30. Also strikingly, the first seed parable earlier in the chapter is mostly narrated using verbs in the past tense; this second seed parable, Collins notes, is a simile, "a comparison made in the present tense" (*Mark*, 254). Of note also is the shift from the neutral σπέρμα/-ατα (*sperma-ata*, "seed[s]"), implied by ἄλλο and ἄλλα (*allo* and *alla*, "other") in 4:3–8, to the masculine σπόρος (*sporos*, "seed") in 4:26–27, likely indicating the special seed—the good seed.

31. The concluding clauses ἀποστέλλει τὸ δρέπανον, ὅτι παρέστημεν ὁ θερισμός (*apostellei to drepanon, hoti parestēmen ho therismos*, "He sends the sickle, because the harvest has come," 4:29) echoes the LXX of Joel 4:13 (3:13, English), which has ἐξαποστείλατε δρέπανα, ὅτι παρέστηκεν τρύγητος (*exaposteilate drepana, hoti parestēken trygētos*, "send the sickle, because the grape harvest has come"; τρύγητος [LXX] pertains to "grape harvest," whereas the Hebrew word קָצִיר, *qatsir* [MT] pertains, as in Mark's parable, to "grain harvest"). Both in Joel and in Mark, the reference is to an eschatological judgment, though the prophet, unlike the Evangelist, describes a negative state of affairs on judgment day (France, *Gospel of Mark*, 214–15).

von] Amsdorf, the Word so greatly weakened the papacy that no prince or emperor ever inflicted such losses on it. I did nothing; the Word did everything."[32]

Thus the disciple is to persist in being receptive to God's word to obey it—the human element. Fruit-bearing by the disciple who is receptive, this section suggests, will be automatic under the superintendence of God. Such fruition is incomprehensible; there is no need to struggle to understand it, for it is the inscrutable work of a sovereign God. One need only concentrate on the responsibility that has devolved upon the disciple—to be receptive, in obedience, without allowing the distractions of 4:14–19 to sabotage one's sensitivity to God's word.[33]

5.2.2 *God's work of fructification of the disciple is an event of great significance and consequence, causing even the seemingly insignificant human elements of the process to produce great yields.*

The second parable (4:30–32) likewise serves as an encouragement to disciples seeking to bear fruit. Well might disciples wonder: "The little we can do, will it ever amount to much?" The human element of growth and the bearing of fruit is, in a broader perspective, as insignificant as a tiny mustard seed. The seed of the black mustard (*Brassica nigra*) was proverbial for something very minute (Matt 17:20; also see *b. Naz.* 8a; *b. Nid.* 13b, 16b, 40a; etc). The thrust of the simile in 4:31–32 is therefore the contrast between an inauspicious onset, almost invisible, and an impressive finale, quite remarkable. Disciples are to take heart; they are assured by Jesus of the ultimate value of their undertaking, as God, in his precise timing and inscrutable sovereignty, consummates his kingdom (incomprehensibly and automatically), as he causes his people to bear fruit. In this terminus of God's sovereign design and purpose, his people will be abundantly fruitful, we are assured.

In fact, one might go so far as to say that it is in the fruitfulness of his people that God's kingdom is gradually being brought about, to reach its *telos* at the establishment of the kingdom of Jesus Christ. That eschatological tone is discernible in the wording of this parable. The nesting birds (4:32) evoke the imagery of Ezekiel 17:23 and 31:6, where God's dominion becomes a refuge for the lost and a locus for the ingathering of nations. It is no small endeavor that the community of Jesus' followers is engaged in— and the future wide scope of God's kingdom is described in no uncertain terms with an OT allusion that "reinforces the 'imperial' pretensions of the kingdom of God."[34] The

---

32. Luther, "Second Sermon," 77.

33. There might be a hint of encouragement to disciples who themselves proclaim the word of God after the manner of their divine leader Jesus. The disciples too "go out" and preach (ἐξέρχομαι, *exer-chomai*, 6:12; just as Jesus "went out": 4:3 and 1:35, 38, 39; 2:13, 17), doing the very things Jesus did, exorcising and healing (6:13)—a "participatory Christology" (Henderson, *Christology*, 109). What Jesus does, the disciples (will) do. The proclamatory endeavors of Jesus' disciples, as they carry on his work, will therefore also meet with the same sort of diversity of reception from their own listeners. They are to be encouraged because, ultimately, fruit-bearing is in the safe hands of God (1 Cor 3:6).

34. France, *Gospel of Mark*, 216–17. Witherington thinks there is something quite subversive about the choice of the mustard tree as the image of God's grand kingdom: a cedar of Lebanon (as in Ezek 17:22–24) would have made for a grander mascot. The mustard bush is a noxious plant that tends to overgrow everything else in the garden—a despicable weed. Moreover, this is being announced as be-

humble work of the disciple, in being receptive to God's word (the human element of the disciple's growth and fruit-bearing) should never be underestimated in its future significance, however imperceptible and inappreciable its current and initial impact might be (and however unfathomable the developmental process might be). What began in Galilee would, one day, be worldwide in scope and breadth; what was now hidden would, then, be spectacularly manifest in its global and universal dimensions. Like the magnificent yield in the first seed parable—thirtyfold, sixtyfold, and a hundredfold of grain—this amazing metamorphosis from diminutive seed to great tree is made possible, in the end, by the power of God alone, as he undertakes a work that is incomprehensible and automatic, and thereby consummates his kingdom. Those who are receptive to God's word *will* yield fruit and *will* be incorporated into the grand scheme of God's kingdom. Stock's words are wise[35]:

> The kind of imagery used in the three parables is significant. Not that of marching armies, heroic deeds, and valorous exploits, but the humble, homely imagery of sowing, tilling, and harvest. The seed is scattered, falls, and lies on the ground, and meets a variety of fates. Instead of striking out, defiant and aggressive, the Kingdom of God appears lowly and vulnerable. The seed is subject to adversity, rejection, delays, and loss. The parables contain no promise of instant and universal triumph. If partial loss is stressed in the first parable, the notion of long delays and slow expansion is conveyed in the others. But a positive trait of the Kingdom is also described—that of irresistible growth. No matter how slowly, and however great the losses may be, the seed produces. Finally, the three parables depict the inevitability of a final success that is out of all proportion to the seemingly insignificant and precarious beginnings of the Kingdom.

The pericope concludes with 4:33–34. The phrase λαλέω τὸν λόγον (*laleō ton logon*, "speak the word," 4:33) occurs frequently in Acts as a idiom for preaching the Christian message (4:29, 31; 8:25; 11:19; 13:46; 14:25; 16:6, 32); moreover seed is identified with λόγος (*logos*, "word") in 4:14.[36] The extensive use of the imperfect tense in this narrative conclusion of 4:33–34 (ἐλάλει, *elalei*, "He was speaking" [×2]; ἐπέλυεν, *epeluen*, "He was explaining") indicates that what was depicted in this entire pericope was, in fact, Jesus' normal practice: he spoke in parables publicly; he explained everything to his disciples privately.[37] For those receptive, further light was always available.

---

coming home to various and unwanted birds (the sinners and tax collectors?). Such a dominion as is being proclaimed by Jesus "was a threat to the existing garden or field of early Judaism. If Jesus' proclamation took root, it stood in danger of subverting existing kingdom visions and power structures in Israel" (Witherington, *Gospel of Mark*, 17).

35. Stock, *Method and Message*, 156.

36. France, *Gospel of Mark*, 217.

37. The "disciples" in 4:34 are likely to be those referred to in 4:10 as "those around Him, along with the Twelve"—the group of "insiders." As Witherington observes, "there was not an impermeable boundary between outsiders and insiders, but rather, the outsiders who heard and heeded the word would become insiders. Indeed, this was the goal, and the purpose of the parables was not obfuscation but revelation" (*Gospel of Mark*, 173).

SERMON FOCUS AND OUTLINES

> **THEOLOGICAL FOCUS OF PERICOPE 5 FOR PREACHING**
>
> **5** God's sovereign action produces results of great significance through a fruit-bearing disciple who is receptive to God's word to obey it (4:1–34).

The preacher would do well to focus on 4:14–20, the section that explains the parable, depicting the human element in the process of fruit-bearing in discipleship, and on 4:26–32, the section that extends the parable, depicting the divine element in fructification. The agencies and circumstances that cause the disciple to be unfruitful are worth considering: Satan, tribulation, distractions of the world, etc., and what they might look like today for one's own listeners.[38] Negative consequences for not being receptive to God's word must also be considered, as well the human element—the responsibility of the Jesus-follower—and what it looks like for the congregation. The magnificent outcome of the disciple's fulfillment of this responsibility is a powerful incentive in the walk with Jesus. Christians are engaged in an incredibly grand project as they walk with their Master on this journey of discipleship, a project with extraordinary ramifications and moment for the eschaton, when the kingdom of God is consummated. Such a heightened sense of the whole will motivate the disciple to be faithful, receptive to the word of God. No humble act of receptive obedience to God's word is insignificant!

POSSIBLE PREACHING OUTLINES FOR PERICOPE 5

I.   WHAT? [The general demand of the text] The human element in fruitfulness

   Receptivity to the word of God: 4:1–9, but focus more on 4:14–20, and, if one has time, 4:21–25

   Negative consequences for not being receptive: 4:11–12

   Move-to-Relevance: What keeps us from receptivity and fruit-bearing? (Hint: the distractions of 4:15–19)

II. WHY? [The consequence of meeting that demand] The divine element in fruitfulness

   God's work, inscrutable and automatic, making fruit-bearing momentous and significant: 4:26–32

   Move-to-Relevance: The significance of our work for God

III. HOW? [The specific application for the current audience] *Be receptive to God's word!* *
   What exactly can we do to fulfill the human element—positive or negative (*not* being "distracted")?

   * This is not simply to repeat the demand of the text; the preacher must provide application that is specific, appropriate for, and directed to the circumstances and situation of the auditors.

Another possibility would be rework the inductive outline above (a what–why–how schema) into an inductive–deductive form that has the homiletical imperative in the

---

38. In this way, the preacher makes a Move-to-Relevance. One will have noticed by now that such Moves-to-Relevance show up with almost every point in every sermon outline provided in this work. Connecting the theological focus of the text to the lives of listeners is absolutely essential in any sermon.

middle of the outline, with the subsequent point explaining or otherwise expanding upon the issue of fruitfulness.

I. The human element in fruitfulness

    Receptivity to the word of God: 4:1–9, but focus more on 4:14–20, and, if one has time, 4:21–25

    Negative consequences for not being receptive: 4:11–12

    Move-to-Relevance: What keeps us from receptivity and fruit-bearing? (Hint: the distractions of 4:15–19)

II. *Be receptive to God's word!*

    What exactly can we do to fulfill the human element—positive or negative (*not* being "distracted")?

III. The divine element in fruitfulness (that gives us confidence even as we engage in our responsibility)

    God's work, inscrutable and automatic, making fruit-bearing momentous and significant: 4:26–32

    Move-to-Relevance: The significance of our work for God

PERICOPE 6

Power Trusted and Proclaimed

Mark 4:35–5:20

[Storm Stilled; Demoniac Healed]

REVIEW, SUMMARY, PREVIEW

Review of Pericope 5: Mark 4:1–34 explains the responsibility of the disciple to be receptive to God's word in order to bear fruit in discipleship (the human element), and also details the divine element in such fruit production and its grand consequences that God brings about.

Summary of Pericope 6: This pericope (4:35—5:20) is a bifocal one, with two episodes paralleling each other in theme. The characters in the second (5:1–20) serve as foils for the Twelve in the first (4:35–41); together the paired accounts explain what is expected of the one following Jesus on the way. Disciples respond to Jesus having faith in his power over natural calamities and supernatural antagonism (unlike the Twelve), and fearlessly proclaim that power (like the ex-demoniac).

Preview of Pericope 7: The next pericope (5:21—6:6) teaches that the follower of Jesus, recognizing his care and concern, and his power and authority over issues of life and death, demonstrates fearless, efficacious faith in him on the journey of discipleship.

6   Mark 4:35–5:20

THEOLOGICAL FOCUS OF PERICOPE 6

6   **Disciples' fearless fulfillment of their commission from Jesus, even in the face of calamities natural and foes supernatural, involves faith in Jesus' power, and proclamation of that power (4:35—5:20).**

6.1   Disciples' faith in Jesus' power enables them to fearlessly face natural calamities (4:35–41).

6.2   Disciples' fearless fulfillment of their commission from Jesus, even against supernatural foes, involves faith in Jesus' power and the proclamation of that power (5:1–20).

6.2.1   Disciples' faith in Jesus' power enables them to fearlessly face supernatural foes.

6.2.2   Disciples' fulfillment of their commission from Jesus involves the proclamation of Jesus' power.

OVERVIEW

THERE ARE A NUMBER of sea crossings in Mark, three of them eventful (4:35–41; 6:45–52; and 8:13–21).[1] Broadly, these voyages to and from Gentile land symbolize the moral boundaries that are crossed, between unclean and clean: 5:1–20 has unclean spirits and pigs, in Gentile land; 5:22–34 has the bleeding and the dead; 7:1–23 has purity and food laws; and 7:24–30 has an unclean spirit and a Gentile woman.

Mark 4:35–41 deals with the first voyage "to the other side," and a storm accompanies the trip. The second voyage that is a subject of the story (6:45–52) is also accompanied by a storm. Both incidents begin a sequence of episodes highlighting the general theme of lack of discernment on the part of the disciples—the major motif of Act I (see the Introduction).

Mark 4:35—5:43 is united by the demonstration of Jesus' power over nature, over demons, over disease, and even over death itself—the gamut of forces that most afflicted and decimated life in ancient days. There is an escalation in power, scale, and range of the miracles wrought in this portion of Mark's narrative. Salvation from *near death* by capsizing in a storm on the lake occurs in 4:35–41 (= Jesus' power over natural calamities). Whereas previous exorcisms were of individual demons, here a whole army of them is expelled (5:9), as a man *living among the dead* is healed (= Jesus' power over supernatural foes). A woman ill with hemorrhage for over a decade—*living dead* (see Lev 17:11)—is restored to wholeness (5:25–26) (= Jesus' power over deathly diseases). A girl, *actually dead*, is revived (5:35) (= Jesus' power over death itself).[2] "There is thus in this section of the gospel a mounting sense of excitement, as the ἐξουσία [*exousia*, "authority"] of Jesus is tested by, and proves victorious over, ever

---

1. There are several other incidental crossings as well (5:21; 6:32, 53; 8:10), the historical details of which are impossible to reconstruct. See van Iersel, *Mark*, 121.

2. These four episodes have been grouped into two pericopes, 4:35—5:20 and 5:21–43. The latter is clearly a single unit, a typical Markan "sandwich" structure. The former could conceivably be split into two, 4:35–41 and 5:1–20, but the similarities in the two episodes (for which, see below) and the closeness of their theological foci render them best dealt with in a single sermon.

more challenging situations of need."[3] In these depictions of Jesus' authority, there are lessons for the disciples: How must they respond to these destructive forces as they continue the Trip of Discipleship?[4]

6.1 Mark 4:35–41

> **THEOLOGICAL IDEA 6.1**
>
> 6.1 Disciples' faith in Jesus' power enables them to fearlessly face natural calamities (4:35–41).

Section Summary 6.1: The negative response of the Twelve in this episode is a prod to disciples of all time who follow Jesus on the way of discipleship. Disciples, having seen and heard the deeds and words of Jesus, are to remember with faith the power of God.[5] Only then will they be able to face future crises created by natural calamities without fear.

TRANSLATION 6.1

4:35 *And on that day, when evening came, He said to them, "Let us go over to the other side."*

4:36 *And leaving the crowd, they took Him along, just as He was, in the boat, and other boats were with Him.*

4:37 *And there came about a great storm of wind and the waves were breaking into the boat, so that the boat was already being filled.*

4:38 *And He was in the stern, sleeping on a cushion. And they roused Him and said to Him, "Teacher, don't You care that we are perishing?"*

4:39 *And He arose and rebuked the wind and said to the sea, "Silence, be quiet!" And the wind ceased and there came about a great calm.*

4:40 *And He said to them, "Why are you cowardly? Do you still not have faith?"*

4:41 *And they were greatly fearful and were saying to one another, "Who then is this, that even the wind and the sea obey Him?"*

NOTES 6.1

6.1 *Disciples' faith in Jesus' person and power enables them to fearlessly face natural calamities.[6]*

---

3. France, *Gospel of Mark*, 220.

4. Were these stories being read by Mark's contemporary audience in a situation of persecution? "Mark's first readers, who had experienced the upsurge of the power of chaos and evil during Nero's persecution and the civil turmoil in Rome following his death in 68 and during (or shortly before) the Jewish War of 66–73 CE, though gifted like the disciples in the gospel with the mystery of the kingdom, may well have cried out: 'Don't you care that we are about to die?!'" (Donahue and Harrington, *Gospel of Mark*, 162). One is reminded of the age-old questions of theodicy: *Is God good?* and *Is God powerful?*

5. This depiction of Jesus' power falls under the theme of Act I—the discernment of Jesus' mission.

6. These theological foci, here and elsewhere, are often positive statements of facets of discipleship that were *negatively* illustrated in the Gospel story by the Twelve.

The episode in Mark 4:35–41 is narrated in the form of an exorcism, as the similarity of details between 1:21–28 (the first exorcism of Jesus in Mark) and 4:35–41 attests.[7]

MARK 4:35–41—"Exorcism" on the Sea	MARK 1:21–28—Exorcism in the Synagogue
Disciples' ask Jesus about perishing (ἀπόλλυμι, *apollymi*) (4:38)	Unclean spirit asks Jesus about destruction (ἀπόλλυμι, 1:24)
Jesus rebukes (ἐπετίμησεν, *epetimēsen*) the wind (4:39)	Jesus rebukes (ἐπετίμησεν) the unclean spirit (1:25)
He commands the sea to be quiet (φιμόω, *phimoō*, 4:39)	He commands the spirit to be quiet (φιμόω, 1:25)
Wind calms greatly (μεγάλη, *megalē*) as it subsides (4:39)	Unclean spirit cries out loudly (μεγάλη) as it exits (1:26)
Disciples are fearfully awed (4:41)	Crowd is amazed (1:27)
Disciples ask one another . . . (4:41)	Bystanders question among themselves . . . (1:27)
"Who then is this?" (τίς ἄρα οὗτός ἐστιν; *tis ara houtos estin?*, 4:41)	"What is this?" (τί ἐστιν τοῦτο; *ti estin touto?*, 1:27)
"Even the wind and sea obey Him?" (ὑπακούω, *hupakouō*, 4:41)	"Even unclean spirits . . . obey Him?" (ὑπακούω, 1:27)

As if the stilling of the storm was in itself not impressive enough, Mark is at pains to equate it with an exorcism to demonstrate that this was a ferocious natural calamity.[8] The demonic anthropomorphism of the tempestuous sea and stormy wind, and their powerful rebuke is noteworthy. This censure of the wind as if it were an animate being is striking, not to mention the specific command to the elements to be silent, as though they were one "unruly heckler."[9] The "great [μεγάλη, *megalē*] storm" of 4:37 becomes, at the rebuke of Jesus, a "great [μεγάλη] calm" in 4:39. The dramatic transition from storm to calm demonstrates the power of Jesus. Even the astounded reaction of the bystanders in the boat (the Twelve) is parallel to that of the onlookers after the exorcism in Mark 1 (see above).

Dowd notes that Mark's Gospel presents the first written evidence for referring to the large freshwater lake in north central Palestine as the "*Sea* of Galilee." Contemporary writers, instead, called it a "lake" (λίμνη, *limnē*).[10] Mark's employment of θάλασσα (*thalassa*, "sea") for this body of water (4:1, 39, 41; 5:1, 13, 21; 6:47, 48, 49; 7:31) is a deliberate reflection of the Hebrew םֹי (*yam*, "sea," translated in the LXX as θάλασσα, Num 34:11; Josh 12:3; 13:27), enabling the evangelist to evoke the Ancient Near Eastern myth of the divine warrior who conquers the forces of chaos represented by the sea, a feat that Yahweh duplicates.[11] The calming of the raging waters and wind is indeed a mighty act of God, a demonstration of his mighty power over nature and creation.

7. From Kuthirakkattel, *Beginning of Jesus' Ministry*, 247.

8. Is there a hint here that some of these natural catastrophes might be demonic in origin?

9. France, *Gospel of Mark*, 223. Rebuking the elements is also performed by Yahweh elsewhere: Ps 18:15; 104:5–7; 106:9.

10. See Josephus, *J.W.* 2.20.6; *Ant.* 5.1.22; *Life* 65; Pliny, *Nat.* 5.15; and also Luke 5:1, 2; 8:22, 23, 33.

11. Gen 1:1–10; 8:1; Job 38:8–11; Ps 65:5–8; 74:12–17; 77:16–20; 89:9–14; 104:1–9; 106:9; 107:23–32; Isa 27:1; 51:9–11; Jer 5:22; 31:35; etc. See Dowd, *Reading Mark*, 52; and Boring, *Mark*, 143. The sea as a quasi-demonic entity is also noted in *1 En.* 60.16; 69.22; and 1QH 6.22–24. Also see Achtemeier,

And so, through the storm, Jesus can sleep. Rather than depicting indifference (or fatigue), Ancient Near Eastern extrabiblical texts utilize the motif of the sleeping deity as a symbol of divine rule, for rest is the prerogative of deity.[12] Biblical authors frequently deploy this theme in the theologizing of Yahweh as the divine regent (Gen 2:2–3; Exod 20:11; 1 Chr 28:2; Ps 132:13–14). Thus this unique depiction of Jesus sleeping is a significant element of the narrative, demonstrating his control over his surroundings. Jesus' sleep (and the detail of his repose, Mark 4:38) is a drastic contrast to the utter panic of the Twelve. The irony of the carpenter who is in slumber while the fishermen are in shock is not lost on the reader. The disciples' interpretation of Jesus' serenity as an indifference to their plight is echoed in the Psalmist's exhortations to Yahweh to rouse himself and render aid (Ps 35:23; 44:23–26; 59:5; 78:65–66).[13] One wonders how the disciples could forget so quickly the compassionate actions and words of Jesus throughout the first four chapters of Mark's Gospel (1:31, 34, 39, 41; 2:5, 17, 27; 3:5, 10). He is not being indifferent to his surroundings or to the plight of his fellow-passengers; rather, his sleep demonstrates his sovereignty.[14] Sleep, on the part of Jesus, also signals his trust in God the Father (Ps 3:5–6; 4:8; Prov 3:24). "Much like the one who sows the seed of the kingdom only to 'sleep and rise night and day' (Mark 4:27), entrusting its care to God, Jesus' slumber implies a simple reliance on God's dominion even over the sea."[15] In either case, whether Jesus' sleep indicates his mastery over the elements or his confidence in God (or both), the need for the disciple to trust in the sovereign power of God, rather than accuse God of negligence, is established subtly by the narrator. That the Twelve in the boat question Jesus with the same verb (ἀπολλύμι, apollymi, "destroy") that the unclean spirit employed in a challenge to Jesus in 1:24 (see above) shows the disciples in a poor light. At least as far as their faith was concerned, they seemed not to be very different from a demon. This Jesus, to them, as to the demon, is out to get them all destroyed!

Myers observes that the elements obey (ὑπακούω, hupakouō) Jesus (4:41). Inanimate nature listens to him, but will the disciples—those who have just been commanded to listen (ἀκούω, akouō, 4:3, 9, 20)?[16] It appears they do not. After being labeled as "insiders" entrusted with the mystery of the kingdom of God (4:11), they

---

"Person and Deed," for the frequent theme of Yahweh's battles against the primeval force of chaos. If the miracle story of Mark was based on Ps 107:23–32, the "other boats" (Mark 4:36, which completely disappear from the remainder of the episode) may be reflecting the plural "ships" in Ps 107:23 (Collins, *Mark*, 258). God's people buffeted by stormy waters is also well represented in the Psalms (69:1–2; 124:4–5), and the community of God's people as a "boat" was a frequent metaphor in the writings of the Fathers (*T. Naph.* 6; Tertullian, *Bapt.* 12; Clement of Alexandria, *Quis. div.* 34.33; Minucius Felix, *Oct.* 29; Justin Martyr, *1 Apol.* 55; Origen, *Comm. Matt.* 11.6; etc.).

12. Batto, "Sleeping God."

13. While extensive verbal similarity is absent, the narrative elements in Mark 4:37–38 parallel those in Jonah 1:4–6: winds, boats in danger of sinking, protagonists asleep, their arousal by their copassengers fearing doom (ἀπόλλυμι, apollymi), and the subsequent calming of the wind.

14. "The ship carried his humanity, but the power of his Godhead carried the ship and all that was in it" (Ephrem the Syrian, *Three Homilies: On Our Lord,* 50).

15. Henderson, *Christology,* 140.

16. Myers, *Binding the Strong Man,* 196.

still lack faith—the ability to respond to a crisis with confidence in the power of God. Jesus' exclamation using οὔπω (*oupō*, "still") expresses his frustration: "Do you *still* not have faith?" (4:40). This query crystallizes the theological thrust of the narrator: the disciples have seen Jesus' power; they have been specifically chosen by him (3:7–12); they have been given the mystery of the kingdom of God (4:10–12) and are privileged to be insiders to Jesus' teaching and explanation (4:34). Jesus is there with them personally, in the boat; earlier he had warned of succumbing in trial (4:16–19); moreover, he has just assured them that God is working even when sowers sleep (4:26–29). Yet they fear and fail in this situation of natural calamity.[17] They have forgotten all they have seen, all they have heard, and all they have learned—theirs is an abysmal lack of faith in his power, as Jesus points out. Even after seeing an amazing miracle of nature wrought before their eyes as the storm is stilled, they remain "afraid with a great fear" (4:41) at the end of this episode. A great (μεγάλη, *megalē*) storm (4:37) is turned into a great (μεγάλη) calm (4:39), but all the disciples can produce is great (μέγαν, *megan*) fear (4:41)! They are not remembering what they had heard or seen of Jesus' power. In fact, the disciples respond to Jesus' question about their faith with a question of their own: "Who is this?" (4:41). Clearly their faith is rudimentary. The disciples "have neither emulated Jesus' secure trust in God's domination of demonic powers of chaos . . . nor anticipated his authoritative quelling of those powers."[18] This is the crux of this episode: the disciples do not remember what Jesus has already done—his power, his authority, his control, his concern. This faithlessness (forgetfulness?) in a time of crisis—here, a natural disaster—renders them fearful. True disciples, then, on the other hand, remember God's power with faith, and are therefore able to respond in times of crises without fear.[19] The crisis in question, while a maritime drama, actually goes beyond the immediate watery peril in its resemblance to an exorcism. All manner of violent natural calamities and raging catastrophes may afflict disciples; but this stilling of an almost demonic storm assures those who follow Jesus that he may be trusted, because of his power, in dire circumstances of natural origin.

6.2 Mark 5:1–20

> **THEOLOGICAL IDEA 6.2**
>
> 6.2 Disciples' fearless fulfillment of their commission from Jesus, even against supernatural foes, involves faith in Jesus' power and the proclamation of that power (5:1–20).
>
> > 6.2.1 Disciples' faith in Jesus' power enables them to fearlessly face supernatural foes.
> >
> > 6.2.2 Disciples' fulfillment of their commission from Jesus involves the proclamation of Jesus' power.

---

17. Marshall, *Faith as a Theme*, 217.

18. Henderson, *Christology*, 140.

19. Boring notes appropriately: "The story calls them to a faith in the God who saves through and beyond death, not necessarily from death" (*Mark*, 146). The lesson here is not that fearless disciples will always escape every crisis they go through, but that their faith ought to be in a God who is able to rescue them—in this case, from the calamities of nature.

Section Summary 6.2: The demons, demoniac, and onlookers are all foils in this section for the Twelve who performed poorly in the previous episode. The demons, ironically, recognize Jesus (unlike the Twelve, who question his identity); the demoniac faithfully departs to proclaim what Jesus did for him in mercy (unlike the Twelve, who faithlessly fail to remember and even accuse Jesus of not having mercy); even the onlookers show less fear than do the Twelve. Disciples, then, faithfully remembering his power over supernatural foes, fearlessly follow Jesus' commission to proclaim that power.

TRANSLATION 6.2

5:1 *And they came to the other side of the sea into the region of the Gerasenes.*

5:2 *And when He came out of the boat immediately a man from the graves with an unclean spirit met Him,*

5:3 *who had [his] dwelling among the tombs, and no one was able to bind him anymore—not even with a chain—*

5:4 *because frequently with shackles and chains he had been bound, and the chains had been torn apart by him, and the shackles had been broken, and no one was strong [enough] to subdue him.*

5:5 *And constantly, night and day, among the tombs and in the mountains, he was crying out and cutting himself with stones.*

5:6 *And seeing Jesus from afar, he ran and bowed down before Him,*

5:7 *and cried out with a loud voice, saying, "What is it with me and You, Jesus, Son of God Most High? I adjure You by God, do not torment me."*

5:8 *For He was saying, "Come out of the man, unclean spirit."*

5:9 *And He was asking him, "What is your name?" And he said to Him, "Legion is my name, for we are many."*

5:10 *And he began to implore Him earnestly that He not send them out of the region.*

5:11 *Now there was by the mountain a large herd of pigs feeding.*

5:12 *And they implored Him, saying, "Send us into the pigs, that we may enter into them."*

5:13 *And He allowed them. And going out, the unclean spirits went into the pigs, and the herd rushed down the steep bank into the sea, about two thousand, and they were drowned in the sea.*

5:14 *And those feeding them fled and reported [it] in the city and in the countryside, and they came to see what it was that had happened.*

5:15 *And they came to Jesus, and observed the one who was demon-possessed sitting, clothed and in [his] right mind—the one who had had the legion—and they were afraid.*

5:16 *And those who had seen [it] related to them how it happened to the one who was demon-possessed, and about the pigs.*

5:17 *And they began to implore Him to go away from their district.*

5:18 *And as He was getting into the boat, the man who had been demon-possessed was imploring Him, that he may be with Him.*

5:19 *And He did not permit him, but said to him, "Go to your home, to your own [people], and report to them how much the Lord has done for you and [how] He had mercy on you."*

5:20 *And he went away and began to preach in Decapolis how much Jesus had done for him, and all were amazed.*

NOTES 6.2

6.2.1   Disciples' faith in Jesus' power enables them to fearlessly face supernatural foes.

Jesus inaugurated his ministry in Jewish territory with an exorcism performed in a synagogue (1:21–27). Now he inaugurates his ministry in Gentile lands with an exorcism in a graveyard (known to be places of pagan worship; see, for example, Isa 65:4, which also mentions swine). Everything about the account has uncleanness writ all over: Gentile country, demons, tombs and graves, and pigs. France notes that this is Mark's most spectacular exorcism account—the longest exorcism in the Synoptics—with its striking depiction of the hopeless condition of the demoniac, multiple possession, naming of demons, and the tangible demonstration of Jesus' success in exorcism by the subsequent demonic possession and destruction of two thousand pigs.[20] Jesus' ἐξουσία (*exousia*, "authority") is unparalleled.

The incredibly horrific state of the demoniac is depicted in the painstakingly detailed description of his habitat, diagnosis, uncontrollability, immense strength, shrieking, and self-mutilation—pathetic situation, indeed (5:2–6).[21]

A   Man meets (confronts?) Jesus (5:2)*

  B   Dwelling among tombs (5:3a)

    C   No one able (οὐδεὶς ἐδύνατο, *oudeis edynato*) to bind him (5:3b)

      D   Bound with shackles and chains (5:4a)

      D′   Destruction of chains and shackles (5:4b)

    C′   No one strong enough (οὐδεὶς ἴσχυεν, *oudeis ischuen*) to subdue him (5:4c)

  B′   Screaming among tombs and mountains (5:5)

A′   Man "reverences" Jesus (5:6)†

* The word ὑπαντάω (*hypantaō*, "to meet") though not always hostile in intent, could possibly be so, as in Matt 8:28; Luke 8:27; 14:31; Acts 16:16; also see Josephus, *J.W.* 1.177; *Ant* 7.128.

† This structure of 5:2–6 is modified from Reid, *Preaching Mark*, 56. The verb depicting the demoniac's prostration before Jesus in 5:6 (προσκυνέω, *proskyneō*) is found only one other time in Mark, in 15:19, describing the parody of homage paid to Jesus by the Roman guards. In all probability, this obeisance in 5:6 performed by a demon-possessed man is also a caricature of true worship.

20. France, *Gospel of Mark*, 226.

21. Geddert, *Mark*, 115. Both episodes, the storm-stilling and this exorcism, portray extremes, respectively, of natural calamity and supernatural (demonic) activity. The proliferation of negatives—οὐκέτι (*ouketi*, "anymore), οὐδεὶς (*oudeis*, "no one"; ×2), οὐδε (*oude*, "not"; 5:3–4)—further focuses upon the direness of the condition of the demon-possessed man. The phrase οὐδεὶς ἴσχυεν αὐτὸν δαμάσαι (*oudeis ischuen auton damasai*, "no one was strong [enough] to subdue him," 5:4) alludes to the ἰσχυρότερός (*ischyroteros*, one "mightier") announced by John the Baptist (1:7), and to the binding of the ἰσχυρός (*ischyros*, "strong man") in 3:27.

The military imagery in the story is also striking, bespeaking forces of considerable power and organization: ἀγέλη (*agelē*, "herd," 5:11), used of bands of military recruits; ἐπιτρέπω (*epitrepō*, "allow," 5:13), used of military commands to dismiss parades; ὁρμάω (*hormaō*, "to rush," 5:13), used of troops rushing into battle; and ἀποστέλλω (*apostellō*, "to send," 5:10), which has also been used of troop movements. The drowning of the pigs in the sea (5:13) evokes the perishing of Pharaoh's army (Exod 15:4). This is truly a mighty act of God against some formidable foes. Of course "legion" is itself a military term. The significance of the name "Legion" is not so much in an actual number, as it is on the character of the host of demonic agents acting in concert to oppose Jesus.[22] The entire cascade of bellicose images emphasizes the dreadfulness of the demonization of the afflicted man and the magnificence of the act of rescue Jesus undertook.

As with the incident with the storm (Mark 4:35–41), this incident too shows considerably similarity to the first exorcism in 1:21–27. Incidentally, the only time Jesus converses with demons in Mark is recorded in these two exorcisms.[23]

	MARK 5:1-20	MARK 1:21-27
Demonic element(s)	Unclean spirits	Unclean spirit
Demoniac's vocalization	"and [he] cried out, saying" (5:7)	"and he cried out, saying" (1:23–24)
Demoniac's challenge	"What is it with me and You, Jesus" (5:7)	"What [is it] with us and You, Jesus" (1:24)
Identification of Jesus	Jesus, Son of God Most High (5:7)	Jesus of Nazareth, the Holy One of God (1:24)
Jesus' command	"Come out" (ἔξελθε, *exelthe*, 5:8)	"Come out" (ἔξελθε, 1:25)
Demons' response	Unclean spirits went out (ἐξέρχομαι, *exerchomai*, 5:13)	Unclean spirit went out (ἐξέρχομαι, 1:26)
Onlookers' reaction	Fear (5:15)	Astonishment (1:27)

The form of the demoniac's challenge, "What have I to do with you?" (5:7), is almost always hostile in intent, and usually employed against someone more powerful than the speaker, in anticipation of, or in response to, an action from the other that adversely affects them.[24] That this incident is more intense than the parallel situation in 1:21–27 is underscored by the recognition of Jesus by demons not as the "Holy One of God" (1:24), but as the "Son of God Most High" (5:7). With that utterance is provided the answer to the disciples' question of 4:41, "Who is He . . . ?" Ironically, it is an unclean spirit that provides the answer! The reader might remember that the only title the Twelve could come up with in the foundering boat, after all their extended time with Jesus, was "Teacher" (4:38). The irony is extended further in the picture of the demoniac "worshiping" (προσκυνέω, *proskyneō*, 5:6) Jesus; Jesus' disciples have done nothing of the sort thus far. They have, for all practical purposes, forgotten who

22. Theoretically, 5,400 troops constituted a Roman legion in the first century CE, but the number of pigs here was only 2,000; see 5:13. See Dowd, *Reading Mark*, 54.

23. Table modified from Myers, *Binding the Strong Man*, 193.

24. E.g., Jdg 11:12; 2 Sam 16:10; 19:22; 1 Kgs 17:18; 2 Kgs 3:13; 2 Chr 35:21; Matt 8:29; Mark 1:24; Luke 4:34; 8:28; John 2:4. See O'Donnell, "Translation and the Exegetical Process," 176–77n50.

Jesus is; they need help to remember—help from demons (!), who clearly recognize Jesus' power and beseech him not to use it against them.

The account of the onlookers' reactions is unusually long (5:14–17), suggesting that Mark is *doing* something significant in that portrayal. The crowd's fear after the exorcism (ἐφοβήθησαν, *ephobēthēsan*, "they were afraid," 5:15) is the same as the disciples' fear after the storm-stilling miracle (ἐφοβήθησαν, 4:41), though, with the addition of the noun form (φόβος, *phobos*) and the adjective "great," the disciples' fear after the storm was stilled is marked as being greater in magnitude than the townspeople's (the disciples were "*greatly* fearful"—literally "fearful with a great fear," 4:41)! Incidentally, with this description of the disciples' fear comes the first occurrence of the verb φοβέω (*phobeō*, "fear") in Mark, and the only occurrence of the noun, φόβος, in the Gospel. Quite telling that the first description of fear is the fear of the *disciples!* At least for the onlookers in Mark 5, one might be able to condone their fear—this is the first they are seeing of Jesus. Not so for the disciples—narratively speaking, they have seen four chapters' worth of him, yet theirs is a fear greater than that of Gentile townsfolk, who, one might grant, do have something to be apprehensive about—this miracle worker has just driven off a sizable portion of their local porcine population into the sea. Earlier, the Twelve could have taken a lesson from the demons on remembering Jesus; now they can learn a thing or two from the *Gentiles*, who are less afraid than they were!

Thus, even in the account of the exorcism of 5:1–20, where the disciples do not find a mention, the Evangelist is highlighting their deficient and inadequate response to Jesus by means of foils—the demons and the onlookers, and later, the ex-demoniac. Thus 5:1–20 is a continuation of the story of 4:35–41, juxtaposed to underscore the failure of the disciples to remember with faith the power of Jesus (earlier over natural calamities; here over supernatural antagonism). Moreover, given that each of these accounts—storm calming and demon exorcising—shows a great deal of similarity with the exorcism of 1:21–27 (see above), it comes as no surprise that there is also considerable thematic correspondence between 4:35–41 and 5:1–20 (see below; the two main differences between the accounts that clue the interpreter to the theological focus of the pericope are emphasized).

	MARK 4:35–41	**MARK 5:1–20**
Participants	Jesus, Jews, violent nature	Jesus, Gentiles, demons
Crisis	Severe storm (4:37)	Severe demonic-possession (5:2–5)
Initiative	Disciples question (4:38–39)	Demoniac/Legion questions (5:6–12)
Addressing Jesus	**"Teacher"** (4:38)	**"Jesus, Son of God Most High"** (5:7)
Jesus' response	"Exorcism" of sea (4:39a)	Exorcism into sea (5:8, 13)
Crisis result	Storm calmed (4:39b)	Demoniac "calmed" (5:15)
Onlookers' response	**Great fear** (4:40–41a)	**Fear** (5:15)

In sum, the disciples are clearly no better than the demons or townsfolk; if anything, in their deficient address of Jesus ("Teacher"), they are worse than the former ("Jesus, Son of God Most High"); and in the "greatness" of their fear, worse than the latter. Having been with Jesus all along (at least until this point of the narrative), the disciples ought to know better; they ought to remember with faith the power of Jesus even against supernatural foes (he has already demonstrated this power to them earlier: 1:21–28, 34, 39; 3:11–12, 27). But, sadly, they "still" do not have the requisite faith—they have forgotten his power (4:40).

6.2.2 Disciples' fulfillment of their commission from Jesus involves the proclamation of Jesus' power.

One significant difference in the two accounts (4:35–41 and 5:1–20) is the *positive* response of the *real* disciple (the ex-demoniac)—he wants to be "with Jesus." While his fellow yeomen are afraid (as were the disciples earlier—"greatly" afraid), the healed man, seemingly fearless, wants to be with Jesus (ἵνα μετ' αὐτοῦ ᾖ, *hina met autou ē*, "that he may be with Him," 5:18). Whereas the crowd wants distance between themselves and Jesus—they "implore" him to go away (5:17)—this one wants to remain in Jesus presence, "imploring" Jesus to permit him to remain in Jesus' presence (5:18). No such positive response from the Twelve is mentioned in this pericope.

The request of the demoniac—and it is initiated by him—is reminiscent of the commissioning and appointment of the Twelve in 3:14, "that they might be with Him" (ἵνα ὦσιν μετ' αὐτοῦ, *hina ōsin met autou*). Notice also the similarities between the disciples' commissioning (3:13–15), the activities of the ex-demoniac (5:1–20), and the later episode dealing with the actual sending out of the disciples (6:7–13).

MARK 3:13–15	MARK 5:1–20	MARK 6:7–13
Be with Jesus (3:14)	Be with Jesus (5:18)	
Preach (3:14)	Preach (5:20)	Preach (6:12)
Exorcism (3:15)	Exorcism (5:8)	Exorcism (6:13)
	Many demons (5:9)	Many demons (6:13)

Thus, even before the Twelve are sent out, this man is dispatched by Jesus. He wants to be "with Jesus," and he begins to preach, *before even the Twelve do so*. Jesus had called the Twelve "that he might send them out to preach" (ἵνα ἀποστέλλῃ αὐτοὺς κηρύσσειν, *hina apostellē autous kēryssein*, 3:14). While no disciple has done anything of the sort yet, this man, the ex-demoniac, proceeds to obey Jesus perfectly: καὶ ἤρξατο κηρύσσειν (*kai ērxato kēryssein*, "and [he] began to preach," 5:20). He is fulfilling Jesus' commission. The content of his preaching as commanded by Jesus is important; twice it is mentioned (5:19, 20): he is to tell how much Jesus has mercifully done for him; in other words, he is to tell of Jesus' power. That is precisely the information that slipped the minds of the Twelve: forgetting what Jesus has already done in their presence and what he is capable of doing—his power—they accused him of being merciless, an uncaring God, insensitive to their travails (4:38). But while the disciples can hardly remember what Jesus had done for/with them in the past, the demoniac proceeds to obey, fulfilling his mission, proclaiming exactly that—Jesus' great power exercised on his behalf (5:20). That his countrymen are hostile to Jesus suggests that his proclamation in the future may also be expected to attract hostility. But this one evinces no hesitation; there is no fear on his part—he is a model disciple!

This is what true disciples have to remember by faith: Jesus' power over natural calamities and even over supernatural opponents. Not only that, disciples are to proclaim that power. The cured demoniac ends up looking more and more like a *real* disciple, while the Twelve, in this pericope at least, acquit themselves less than honorably in this regard. "It would appear, then, as if the nameless man is added as a sort of thirteenth member to the circle of twelve selected by Jesus in 3:13–15."[25] This man demonstrates the true qualities of the disciple—one who has faith in Jesus' power and who proclaims it fearlessly.

SERMON FOCUS AND OUTLINES

THEOLOGICAL FOCUS OF PERICOPE 6 FOR PREACHING

6   **Fearless fulfillment of disciples' commission from Jesus involves faith in, and proclamation of, Jesus' power, even over natural calamities and supernatural foes (4:35—5:20).**

The pericope, comprised of two episodes, can render its preaching a bit complicated. It would therefore be best to encourage congregation members to familiarize themselves with the stories before the sermon is delivered.[26] There is much material presented in the theological sections above; the intent of this commentary is not that every last bit of detail here be regurgitated to an unwary audience. There is neither need nor time for the information dump that would result. Instead, the preacher must exercise discretion as to what is to be presented to listeners. The comparisons between the Twelve, the demons, the demoniac, and the townspeople will be helpful in this regard. Other elements may be mentioned as necessary, all for the goal of enabling the congregation to grasp what Mark is doing with what he was saying (the Theological Focus). The main thrust of the pericope is that faith in Jesus' power over nature and "super-nature" is demanded of the disciple; indeed, so is proclamation of that power. While other pericopes deal with different facets of fearlessness, this one considers fearlessness in dire circumstances of natural calamities and fearlessness when facing opposition from a supernatural quarter.[27] God is powerful enough and caring enough to protect and to save. The responsibility of the believer is to trust in his power and, so trusting, to go forth to proclaim that power. Indeed, in the very proclamation of Jesus' power, the proclaimer's faith in that power will increase!

25. van Iersel, *Mark*, 202.

26. Certainly a reading of the text (dramatic or otherwise) would be appropriate in a worship service in which this pericope is to be preached. Even a Sunday School class the week before, or a pastor's blog, or other medium could be beneficially employed in tandem to expound exegetical details of the text that might be too much for a thirty- to forty-minute sermon. This author believes that a sermon in the context of a worship service of the congregation should be used to motivate life change, in the power of the Holy Spirit, by means of the particular pericope preached. Enough—and this is key: *enough!*—information should be conveyed to move the audience to undertake life change. "Enough" will definitely not include all the exegetical morsels that might be savory for the preacher in the pulpit, but unappetizing (and unnecessary) for the person in the pew.

27. That such antagonism today may come from the supernatural realm may need some establishment in an overwhelmingly naturalistic and reductionistic Western culture; in most other parts of the world no such convincing is necessary.

Below are the characters in the pericope and the main elements to focus on:

- The Twelve: what they have already seen and heard of Jesus; their inadequate address of Jesus; their accusation of him as being uncaring; their question of his identity; their great fear.

    Foil: the demons: their accurate address of Jesus (as opposed to the Twelve's defective address).

    Foil: the townspeople: their fear (as opposed to the Twelve's *great* fear).

- The ex-demoniac: his desire to be with Jesus; his willingness to be sent to preach; his fearless testifying to Jesus' power exercised on his behalf.

POSSIBLE PREACHING OUTLINES FOR PERICOPE 6

I. The power of the Master over nature and "super-nature"

   Move-to-Relevance: natural/supernatural calamities that afflict us

II. The reaction of the Twelve—their faithlessness

   Reactions: the Twelve vs. demons (deficient address of Jesus by the Twelve; 4:38/5:7)

   Reactions: the Twelve vs. townsfolk (*great fear* of the Twelve; 4:40–41a/5:15)

   Move-to-Relevance: our reactions of faithlessness and fear in calamites of nature and "super-nature"

III. The response of the disciple—*Remember and recount!*

   The ex-demoniac, a model disciple who proclaimed Jesus' power with faith: 5:15–20

   How can we faithfully proclaim the power of Jesus over nature and "super-nature"?

A problem–solution–application form might work well, too, with only minor adjustments to the first outline:

I. PROBLEM: Situations of calamity—natural and supernatural—that cause fear

   The ferocity of the storm, almost demonic in character (4:35–41)

   The virulence of the demon possession (5:1–3)

   Move-to-Relevance: Situations of our fearfulness and failure to trust Jesus' power over nature and "super-nature"

II. SOLUTION: Trusting in the power of Jesus over nature and "super-nature"

   Reactions: the Twelve vs. demons (deficient address of Jesus by the Twelve; 4:38/5:7)

   Reaction: the Twelve vs. townsfolk (*great fear* of the Twelve; 4:40–41a/5:15)

III. APPLICATION: *Remember and recount!*

   Model: the ex-demoniac, proclaims Jesus' power with faith (5:18–20)

   How can we faithfully proclaim the power of Jesus over nature and "super-nature"?

The preacher may want to give specifics of how one may remember Jesus' power; journaling, testimony, frequent recollections, etc., are some examples.

PERICOPE 7

Efficacious Faith for Excruciating Times

Mark 5:21–6:6

[Hemorrhaging Woman Healed; Jairus' Daughter Raised; Faithless Hometowners]

REVIEW, SUMMARY, PREVIEW

Review of Pericope 6: Mark 4:35—5:20 teaches that disciples respond to Jesus, having faith in his power over natural calamities and supernatural foes, and fearlessly proclaiming that power.

Summary of Pericope 7: In this pericope (5:21—6:6) one sees paragons of discipleship (the hemorrhaging woman and Jairus) as well as some reproachable examples (the disciples and the bystanders/mourners). The follower of Jesus, recognizing Jesus' care and concern, and his power over disease and death, demonstrates fearless faith in him in the journey of discipleship. A coda with the unbelieving hometowners of Jesus demonstrates the significant impact of such a faith on Jesus' kingdom mission.

Preview of Pericope 8: The next pericope (6:7–32) commissions the disciples to extend the kingdom of God despite dangerous antagonism, trusting in divine provision.

7 Mark 5:21–6:6

THEOLOGICAL FOCUS OF PERICOPE 7

7 The care and concern of Jesus for his disciples, as well as his power over disease and death, inspire fearless, efficacious faith in his disciples, a lack of which can "hinder" Jesus' kingdom mission (5:21—6:6).

> 7.1 The care and concern of Jesus for his disciples, as well as his power over disease and death, inspire fearless, efficacious faith in his disciples (5:21–43).
>
> > 7.1.1 Disciples are involved in the mission of One who demonstrates care and concern for his followers.
> >
> > 7.1.2 Jesus' power over disease inspires fearless, efficacious faith in his disciples.
>
> 7.2 Lack of faith on the part of disciples can "hinder" the kingdom mission of Jesus (6:1–6).

OVERVIEW

As was noted with the previous pericope, there is an intensification of the scale of powerful acts that Jesus performs in the larger section, 4:35—5:43, comprising four episodes. His authority is all-encompassing—over nature, over demonic elements, over disease, and even death. The previous pericope (the first two of these four episodes, 4:35–41 and 5:1–20) dealt with the theme faith in Jesus' power, even over nature and "super-nature," and the fearless proclamation of that power. The last two of these four episodes, in 5:21–43, also deal with the disciple's faith—efficacious faith—this time in the face of the catastrophes of disease and death.[1] The pericope closes out with an incident in Jesus' hometown that demonstrates the impact of such faith on Jesus' kingdom mission.

The first voyage "to the other side" (4:35—5:21) has been completed and Jesus and the disciples are back in Jewish territory (5:21). Jesus continues his confrontation of the unclean, even as he returns to "clean" Jewish territory: in this pericope Jesus is touched by an unclean hemorrhaging woman, and he himself proactively touches an unclean corpse (5:27, 41).

7.1 Mark 5:21–43

THEOLOGICAL FOCUS 7.1

7.1 The care and concern of Jesus for his disciples, as well as his power over disease and death, inspire fearless, efficacious faith in his disciples (5:21–43).

> 7.1.1 Disciples are involved in the mission of One who demonstrates care and concern for his followers.
>
> 7.1.2 Jesus' power over disease inspires fearless, efficacious faith in his disciples.

Section Summary 7.1: In this section, one sees paragons of discipleship (the hemorrhaging woman and Jairus) as well as some reproachable examples (the disciples and the bystanders/mourners). In and through their actions, Mark tells us that the follower of Jesus, recognizing his care and concern, and his power and authority over disease and death, will have fearless, efficacious faith in God.

---

1. By "efficacious" faith is meant faith that results in God's power being manifest in the lives of the faithful (as opposed to faithlessness that "hinders" the work of God; see below)—not that there is any *intrinsic* efficacy to faith.

TRANSLATION 7.1

5:21   *And when Jesus had crossed over again in the boat to the other side, a large crowd gathered before Him, and He was by the sea.*

5:22   *And one of the synagogue officials, named Jairus, came, and seeing Him, fell at His feet*

5:23   *and implored Him earnestly, saying, "My little daughter is at the point of death; come, that You may lay hands on her that she may be healed and live."*

5:24   *And He went away with him. And a large crowd was following Him and pressing upon Him.*

5:25   *And a woman having a flow of blood for twelve years,*

5:26   *and having suffered much under many physicians, and having spent all that she had and was not being helped, but rather was becoming worse,*

5:27   *hearing about Jesus, coming in the crowd behind, touched His garment.*

5:28   *For she was saying, "If I only touch His garments, I will be healed."*

5:29   *And immediately her fountain of blood dried up, and she knew in [her] body that she had been healed from her affliction.*

5:30   *And immediately Jesus, perceiving in Himself that power went out from Him, turned in the crowd [and] said, "Who touched My garments?"*

5:31   *And His disciples said to Him, "You see the crowd pressing upon You, and You say, 'Who touched Me?'"*

5:32   *And He looked around to see the one who had done this.*

5:33   *But the woman, fearing and trembling, knowing what had happened to her, came and fell down before Him and told Him the whole truth.*

5:34   *And He said to her, "Daughter, your faith has healed you; go in peace and be whole from your affliction."*

5:35   *While He was still speaking, they came from [the house of] the synagogue official, saying, "Your daughter has died; why still bother the teacher?"*

5:36   *But Jesus, overhearing the word that was spoken, said to the synagogue official, "Do not be afraid, only believe."*

5:37   *And He did not allow anyone to follow along with Him, except Peter and James and John the brother of James.*

5:38   *And they came into the house of the synagogue official, and He observed commotion and weeping and loud wailing.*

5:39   *And entering, He said to them, "Why create a commotion and weep? The child has not died but sleeps."*

5:40   *And they began ridiculing Him. But putting them all out, He took along the father of the child, and the mother, and those with Him, and entered where the child was.*

5:41   *And grasping the hand of the child, He said to her, "Talitha koum," which is translated, "Little girl, I say to you, rise!"*

5:42   *And immediately the little girl got up and began to walk around; for she was twelve years [old]. And they were astounded with great astonishment.*

5:43   *And He gave strict orders to them that no one should know this, and He said to give her [something] to eat.*

NOTES 7.1

This is the second of the six "sandwich" stories in Mark's Gospel.[2] Mark 5:21–24 and 5:35–43 form the two halves of the outer story; 5:25–34 becomes the inner story. The settings progressively get narrower as one traverses the "sandwich" from one end to the other: the seashore (5:21), on the way to the synagogue official's house (5:24), and within the house (5:38–39). The clock continues to tick as time runs continuously from the outer story to the inner and back to the outer. In the outer story, Jesus breaks the social and cultic border of death: he touches a corpse (5:41); in the inner story, the hemorrhaging woman breaks another social and cultic border by touching Jesus (5:27). The parallels between the two stories and its characters indicate a great deal of intentionality in the patterning. The stories are not only connected; they may, in one sense, be a single tapestry, albeit interwoven with two threads.

Outer Story: MARK 5:21–24, 35–43	Inner Story: MARK 5:25–34
Jairus, male, leader in synagogue, prominent (5:22)*	Anonymous, woman, ritually unclean, penurious (5:26)
Sees Jesus (5:22)	Hears about Jesus (5:27)
Father in a hopeless situation (5:23, 35)	Woman in a hopeless situation (5:25–26)
Face-to-face with Jesus (5:22)	Hiding from Jesus (5:27)
Falls at Jesus' feet (πίπτω, pipto, 5:22)	Falls before Jesus (προσπίπτω, prospipto 5:33)
Fear proscribed (φοβέω, phobeo, 5:36)	Fear exhibited (φοβέω, 5:33)
Faith enjoined (πιστεύω, pisteuo, 5:36)	Faith commended (πίστις, pistis, 5:34)
Daughter of a father (θυγάτριον, θυγάτηρ, thygatrion, thygater, 5:23, 35)	"Daughter" of Jesus (θυγάτηρ, 5:34)
Twelve years old at death (5:42; life began twelve years ago)	Twelve years of suffering (5:25; death began twelve years ago)
Impurity of a corpse (Num 19:11–21)	Impurity of vaginal bleeding (Lev 15:19–30)
Jesus touches the daughter (Mark 5:41)	Woman touches Jesus' clothes (Mark 5:27–28)
Misunderstanding by bystanders (5:31)	Misunderstanding by bystanders (5:40)
Miracle in the seclusion of the house	Miracle in the middle of the crowd
Healing (σῴζω, sozo) sought; life regained (5:23, 42)	Healing (σῴζω) sought; health regained (5:28, 34)

* "Jairus" may transliterate either יאיר (y'yr, "he enlightens") or, more likely, יעיר (y'yr, "he awakens") (Guelich, *Mark*, 295). His naming in this section appears to be deliberate, for it stands out from most other healing stories in the Gospel with anonymous protagonists.

2. The others are 3:20–35; 6:7–32; 11:12–25; 14:1–11; and 14:53–72. See Shepherd, *Markan Sandwich Stories*, 138–72, for details of this particular "sandwich" story. This commentary views these literary structures as significant (as will be evident), *contra* France, who declares: "Here, while the sequence certainly fulfils a valuable literary function in creating narrative suspense, it is not at all obvious what the thematic connection is achieved by this particular 'sandwich,' other than the rather obvious point that both victims are women" (*Gospel of Mark*, 234–35). Again, France notes skeptically: "Some commentators find a further link in the fact that the woman has suffered for twelve years (v. 25), and Jairus' daughter is twelve years old (v. 42); this is surely a counsel of despair" (*Gospel of Mark*, 235n20). Hardly! Not only is the link between woman and child strengthened (death and life being juxtaposed), the recurrence of "twelve" evokes the twelve tribes of Israel, reminding the reader that Jesus is back in Jewish territory. But even more, "twelve" alludes to the reconstitution of the new community of God in the power of One who has authority over life and death.

7.1.1 Disciples are involved in the mission of One who demonstrates care and concern for his followers.

This woman's account is introduced with a sentence that has a cascade of seven participial clauses (one present tense and six aorist tense; 5:25–27) before the main verb (ἥψατο, *hēpsato*, "touched," 5:27): having a flow, having suffered, having spent, not being helped, becoming worse, hearing, coming . . . touched.[3] That relentless progression of participles culminating in the "touch" not only describes her hopeless condition (notice the occurrences of πολλὰ [*polla*, "much"], πολλῶν [*pollōn*, "many"], and πάντα [*panta*, "all"] in 5:26), it also comes as a shock as "unclean" makes contact with the "clean," a breach of ritual protocol (see Lev 12:4 for the prohibition; also see 15:25–30). In attending to this woman on the inferior rungs of the social ladder while on his way to help another at the superior rungs—Jairus, a named man, a prominent synagogue leader—Jesus demonstrates that nobody is beyond the pale of his concern. He cares for his disciples.

Later on, after the woman is healed, Jesus' address to her is unique: the only one to be addressed as "daughter" by him in the entire Gospel is this "unclean" woman who had faith (Mark 5:34).[4] The rest of the "sandwich" has another child becoming (again) a daughter to her father, as she is restored to life (5:35). But in this inner story, the woman becomes a daughter to God. She has literally become part of the new family of Jesus (3:31–35), impurity removed, societal status restored, rendered whole. Needless to say, the contrast between the daughter who has a (powerful) father to work on her behalf to summon Jesus, and this other "daughter" who has wasted time and money and energies on physicians, with no one to speak for her, is stark. She was devoid of champions on her side. But henceforth, Jesus will fight for her, for now she is *his* "daughter." "From the bottom of the honor scale she intrudes upon an important mission on behalf of the daughter of someone on the top of the honor scale—but by the story's conclusion, *she* herself has become the 'daughter' at the center of the story! . . . Not only is her integrity restored, but she receives a grant of status superior to that of Jesus' own male disciples, who are 'without faith' (4:40)!" A "profound reversal of dignity," indeed. Jesus cares, even for the simplest and seemingly most insignificant of his followers.[5]

7.1.2 Jesus' power over disease inspires fearless, efficacious faith in his disciples.

It is also remarkable that the woman comes "behind" (ὄπισθεν, *opisthen*, an adverb; 5:27) Jesus. While it occurs only here in Mark, the spatial location of the woman is symbolic of the follower as indicated by the related preposition ὀπίσω (*opisō*, "behind,"

---

3. France observes that this is unusual in Mark: "This interesting departure from Mark's more usual paratactic style allows the reader (or hearer) to build up a sympathetic mental portrait of the woman's situation before her story begins, and predisposes us in her favour"—there is something special about her (*Gospel of Mark*, 236n24).

4. The paralytic in 2:5 and the disciples in 10:24 are also addressed by Jesus as "child"/"children" (τέκνον/τέκνα; *teknon/tekna*).

5. Myers, *Binding the Strong Man*, 202.

1:17, 20; 8:34). In fact, the rest of this episode makes it abundantly clear that she is indeed a disciple:

- The woman displays praiseworthy faith (5:34; see 1:15 for Jesus' exhortation to believe; and 4:40 for Jesus' expectation that his disciples would).

- The healed woman is called "daughter"; she becomes part of the "family" of Jesus (see 3:34–35 for the "family" of Jesus' disciples).

- The woman suffers "like" Jesus (5:26; 8:31; and 9:12; πάσχω, *paschō*, "suffer," is used only of this woman and of Jesus in all of Mark).

- She is "scourged" like Jesus (5:29, 34 uses the noun μάστιξ, *mastix*, translated "affliction"; 10:34 uniquely utilizes the verb μαστιγόω, *mastigoō*, "scourge," in the last of Jesus' Passion Predictions, the only two occurrences of these related words in the Gospel).

- Only this woman and Jesus are connected with the shedding of blood (5:25, 29; 14:24; again, these are the only occurrences of αἷμα, *haima*, "blood," in Mark's Gospel).[6]

This is one special woman—she is a *true* disciple, and her noteworthy characteristic, faith, is one that is to be emulated by all disciples, as Jesus implicitly enjoins (5:34, 36). Though she was greatly afraid (5:33), Jesus' exhortation to go in peace (5:34) indicates what must also be the accompaniment of the disciple's faith—fearlessness.

The Lukan version of the woman's healing (Luke 8:43–48) emphasizes Jesus' reasoning about his awareness of power going out of himself; there is no description of what the woman is thinking. The woman's subsequent confession is explicitly noted to be public: "in the presence of all the people" (8:47). The Matthean version of this story focuses upon the internal reasoning of the woman; she speaks to herself about touching Jesus' garment (Matt 9:21). In that account, it appears to be Jesus' declaration, and not her touch, that renders the woman whole (9:22); moreover, there is no forced admission from her after the healing. In both Luke and Matthew, therefore, the emphasis is on the ability of Jesus to heal, with added prominence given to the public confession of faith on the part of the woman in Luke. On the other hand, the Markan description details not only the woman's thought processes prior to her healing, but also her own perception of her healing after the fact (γινώσκω, *ginōskō*, Mark 5:28–29); it also describes Jesus' own perception of power leaving him (ἐπιγινώσκω, *epiginōskō*, 5:30). Moreover, the woman is said to fall down before *him* and tell *him* the whole truth—there is no emphasis on this being a public disclosure (unlike in Luke, where a point is made of the openness of the woman's admission; Luke 8:47). The thrust in Mark is thus on what constitutes faith, which renders the woman cured, even when Jesus is

---

6. Miller, *Women in Mark's Gospel*, 65. The similarity between Jesus' suffering and the woman's is only in the physical agony both face; the atoning nature of Jesus' Passion is incomparable and his suffering for the sins of humankind incommensurate with any other kind of suffering any other person has ever undergone, or ever will.

not directly aware of what is transpiring.[7] This faith is a complete trust in the ability of Jesus to handle anything, even a debilitating disease. The trust in Jesus' ability, the actual healing, and the woman's realization of her cure (Mark 5:28a, 29a, and 29b, respectively) are collectively distinguished from Jesus' perception and his question to the crowd (5:30). In other words, the faith of the disciple is a powerful one—an efficacious faith that, in Mark's narrative, appears to operate without the express permission of, and almost unbeknownst to, the healer. Rhetorically, Mark is signifying the vigor and potency of a disciple's faith (see below on 6:1–6 for a reinforcement of this truth).[8]

Jairus, too, comes off as positive in this account, serving as a secondary model of a disciple (see the table above for similarities between him and the woman). Like the woman, he comes to Jesus in the midst of a hopeless situation and falls at his feet. Subsequently, there are three powerful assaults on Jairus's faith: the delay as Jesus pauses to interrogate the woman who is healed, the news of his daughter's death brought by those from his house, and the mourners' certitude of the finality of her death. These attacks are countered, respectively, by Jesus' demonstration of his power to heal those who have faith (the inner story of the woman with the hemorrhage, 5:25–34), Jesus' explicit assurance to Jairus with the exhortation to believe (5:36), and Jesus' verdict that the child is only "asleep" (5:39). Jairus successfully faces these challenges to his faith, for he does not despair despite the delay, and he sets out with Jesus even after he receives news that his daughter has died. He does have faith, for his daughter is ultimately restored as Jesus promised. No matter how dire the situation or how hopeless the circumstance, whether it be the ravages of disease or the rapacity of death, Jesus bids the disciple trust in him faithfully and fearlessly. It must be borne in mind that the thrust of these two episodes is *not* that every instance of disease will be overcome and that every occurrence of death will be overturned by Jesus in the earthly situations of his disciples.[9] The focus of the pericope is simply upon the fearless, efficacious faith of the disciple in Christ's ability to handle every such disastrous contingency of disease and death in this life.

As was noted, the woman perceived (γινώσκω, *ginōskō*) in her body that she was healed (5:29), and Jesus perceived (ἐπιγινώσκω, *epiginōskō*) in himself that power had gone forth (5:30). What she thought was a surreptitious one-way contact proves to be two-way, and she is detected: power has gone out from Jesus.[10] One might have expected that the contagion from the woman would affect Jesus, for Mosaic law declared her condition unclean. But no, contagion from her does nothing to him; instead, his wholeness affected her, rendering her cured . . . and clean. The power of Jesus' own

---

7. Also see Robbins, "Woman Who Touched," 197–99.

8. This is, of course, not to deny Jesus' sovereign willingness to heal or his knowledge of what has transpired (despite the question of 5:30). The narrative is simply a rhetorical stratagem on the part of Mark to accomplish something—to demonstrate the critical importance of efficacious faith in the life of the follower of Jesus.

9. Most certainly they *will* be, on another day, a day of glory, but not necessarily on this side of life.

10. France, *Gospel of Mark*, 237. Other instances of δύναμις (*dynamis*, here "power") indicate "miracle" (6:2, 5, 14; 9:39). It is likely that that sense of the word is being alluded to in 5:30.

purity is hereby demonstrated: "Holiness for Jesus, we might say, was not a negative, defiling force, but a positive, healing force."[11] The direction of the movement of divine power is the same when Jesus contacts another unclean element later in the pericope, this time a corpse, in 5:41–42. He is not contaminated there, either; rather, the dead child he touches is rendered alive . . . and clean.

This simultaneity of Jesus' benediction upon the woman (5:34) and the announcement of the death of Jairus' daughter (5:35) juxtaposes life and death; it is almost as if Mark is attempting to superimpose the two. And in close proximity to Jesus' address to the woman as "daughter" (θυγάτηρ, *thygatēr*, 5:34), Jairus' child, earlier called "little daughter" (θυγάτριον, *thygatrion*, 5:23), now pointedly has become "daughter" (θυγάτηρ, 5:35); the connections are being quite explicitly pointed out by the narrator. As one "daughter" was just healed, so the other daughter is too.[12] The Son of God is powerful over disease and, indeed, even over death. The disciple with faith need have no fear.

On the other hand, faithlessness is deprecated in this pericope. The dialogue between Jesus and the disciples is a comic relief cameo (5:30–31). Jesus, the "comedian," asks amidst a "pressing" crowd (5:24, 31), "Who touched me?" Clearly, Jesus could distinguish the touch of faith from an unbelieving touch.[13] The irony of this account is that though Jesus knew, and though the woman knew, and though the reader knows, the ingenuous disciples do not: "the disciples not only stand with the imperceptive crowds but their protestations sound very much like the mocking crowds at the house of Jairus" (5:40).[14] In fact, the second comic cameo of the seemingly ridiculous occurs when those bystanders/mourners at the little girl's deathbed laugh at Jesus for assuming the girl to be sleeping (5:39–40). The joke, however, is on those who laugh at him: while they weep at death, Jesus laughs at it! Thus Mark is subtly drawing a picture of the disciples—faithless like the bystanders, and unlike the woman or Jairus. The one who follows Jesus is thus being exhorted to be like these faith-filled exemplars, not like the faithless disciples. Whatever the crisis of life may be, whether disease or even death, the disciple is called to demonstrate fearless, efficacious faith in Jesus, the one able to conquer anything!

---

11. Dunn, "Jesus and Purity," 461.

12. One wonders why silence is later imposed on the parents (5:43). Surely the populace is going to see that this corpse has now come back to life. Gundry supposes that all of this, including the girl's feeding, is to buy Jesus time to make a getaway, noting Jesus' constant attempts to separate himself from the crowds (Gundry, *Mark*, 276–77). Be that as it may, Malbon's explanation is more consistent with the thrust of the narrative of Mark: she considers the silence motif here as simply a means to keep Jairus from talking about the power of Jesus the life-giver—an incomplete picture of Jesus that portrays him only as a wonder-worker, carrying no implication or hint of his mission of suffering (Malbon, "Narrative Criticism," 46).

13. "The faith of the few touches it [the body of Christ], the throng of many press it" (Augustine, *Sermon on the Words of the Gospel, Matt 8:8*; Sermon 12.5).

14. Boring, *Mark*, 161.

7.2   Mark 6:1–6

THEOLOGICAL FOCUS 7.2

7.2   Lack of faith on the part of disciples can "hinder" the kingdom mission of Jesus (6:1–6).

Section Summary 7.2: In this episode, a counterpoint is provided to the explicit faith of the woman and the implicit faith of Jairus in the "sandwich" story (5:21–43). Lack of faith on the part of those who follow Jesus "precludes" the power of God working in their lives, in contrast to faith that can be the agent for his mighty work. Disciples are therefore exhorted, in connection with the previous episode, to have faith, for it results in the experience of divine power in their lives, exercised for the kingdom mission of Jesus—thus, *efficacious* faith.[15]

TRANSLATION 7.2

6:1   *And He went out from there and came into His hometown, and His disciples were following Him.*

6:2   *And when the Sabbath came, He began to teach in the synagogue, and many listening were amazed, saying, "From where did this one [get] these things? What is the wisdom given to this one, and such miracles performed by His hands?*

6:3   *Is not this the carpenter, the son of Mary and brother of James and Joses and Judas and Simon? And are not His sisters here with us?" And they took offense at Him.*

6:4   *And Jesus said to them, "A prophet is not dishonored except in his hometown and among his relatives and in his house."*

6:5   *And He was not able to do any miracle there, except to lay hands on a few sick people and heal.*

6:6   *And He wondered because of their unbelief. And He was going around the villages nearby teaching.*

NOTES 7.2

7.2   Lack of faith on the part of disciples can "hinder" the powerful work of Jesus.

The cameo of the unbelieving hometowners (6:1–6) demonstrates the power of faith (or actually the powerlessness of "unfaith").[16] These folks will have nothing to do with him, even after they see his miracles and his wisdom (6:2). The threefold use of οὗτος

---

15. This is not to distinguish between faith that is efficacious and faith that is not; "efficacious faith" merely underscores that faith in the right Person is always efficacious; faithlessness, on the other hand, is effete.

16. "Power," of course, is that which comes from Jesus; it is not inherent in the disciples or their faith, neither is it distinguishing a particularly potent kind of faith. Nevertheless, the caveat of God's sovereignty notwithstanding, disciples' faith *is* crucial for the experience of Jesus' power in their lives, as well as for the extension of God's kingdom through them. The role of faith and God's sovereignty must be held in balance, neither one being negated or diminished.

(*houtos*, "this one/this," 6:2 [×2], 3) is probably somewhat derogatory, tinged with contempt (as in 2:7; equivalent to "this guy").[17] This lack of recognition of who Jesus really is marks these bystanders as being "outsiders" without faith, as 6:6 confirms. Indeed, all uses of σκανδαλίζω (*skandalizō*, "take offense," 6:3) in Mark are negative in connotation, having as their subjects those without faith in Jesus (4:17; 9:42, 43, 45, 47; 14:27, 29). Thus, this verb effectively indicates the opposite of believing in him: σκανδαλίζεσθαι ἐν αὐτῷ (*skandalizesthai en autō*, "took offense at him") vs. πιστεῦσαι εἰς αὐτόν (*pisteusai eis auton*, "believed in him").[18] The striking thing about this brief account is that, as a result of this faithlessness, Jesus is "unable" (οὐκ ἐδύνατο, *ouk edynato*) to perform miracles there in his hometown. After the submission to Jesus' power and authority over wind, waves, demons, disease, and even death (see the preceding pericopes), here, seemingly, the divine One has "met his match" in the unbelief of the people: he is "not able to do any miracle there." Calvin observes that "unbelievers, as far as lies in their power, bind up the hands of God by their obstinacy; not that God is overcome, as if he were an inferior, but because they do not permit him to display his power" (*Harmony of the Evangelists* 2:216).

Faith in Jesus' power has figured prominently in the earlier part of this pericope (explicit faith of the woman, 5:34, 36; and implicit faith of Jairus) as well as in the previous one (see 4:40). "Power"/"miracle" (δύναμις, *dynamis*) shows up in both 5:30 and here in 6:2, 5. "Unfaith," therefore, turns out be, in some way, an obstacle to Jesus' miracle-working power, in stark contrast to all the wondrous deeds performed by him in Mark 5. Rhetorically, however, what Mark is trying to do is show the reader the efficacy of faith by demonstrating that "unfaith" is a serious obstacle to the experience of Jesus' power in the extension of the kingdom mission. So powerful is faith that Jesus himself is caught wondering about its absence in this situation (6:6)—the only time he is said to do so in the Gospel. Not to have faith, it is implied, may even have "grave implications for the 'success' of Jesus' mission."[19] Particularly in light of the previous "sandwich" episode, where the demonstration of faith was concurrent with the performance of the miracles and the display of Jesus' incredible power over disease and even death (5:34, 36), this episode forms a counter to that one—a negative illustration of the efficacious faith of a disciple.[20] The consequences of the disciple's faith are momentous!

---

17. The rest of Jesus' family, it appears, later joins the church (Acts 1:14; 1 Cor 9:5; grandsons of Judas were supposedly still known to the first-century church, according to Eusebius (*Hist. eccl.* 3.20). See France, *Gospel of Mark*, 243. "Son of Mary" itself might be a slur; even if Joseph were deceased, it appears that the practice was to continue to use the patronymic (*b. Yoma* 38b, noting the case of a Doeg ben Joseph). See Collins, *Mark*, 290.

18. Collins, *Mark*, 291.

19. Henderson, *Christology*, 142.

20. Of course, Mark is careful to add a postscript to this strikingly audacious remark of Jesus' "incapacity" to perform miracles (6:5). Lest the reader think that the power of God is limited by the faith of mankind, the narrator mentions that Jesus *is* able to heal some, albeit only a few. Lack of faith on the part of the dead child or of the demoniac in this chapter, for instance, does not prevent Jesus from healing either one. Incidentally, this is the last time Jesus is shown entering a synagogue in Mark; when he is not outdoors, all Jesus' subsequent teaching in this Gospel occurs in homes (7:17; 9:28, 33; 10:10).

SERMON FOCUS AND OUTLINES

THEOLOGICAL FOCUS OF PERICOPE 7 FOR PREACHING

7 **Jesus' care, and his power over disease and death, evokes disciples' fearless, efficacious faith (5:21—6:6).**

In both this pericope and the previous one, the theme of fearless faith is prominent. While 4:35—5:20 focuses on the fearless faith of disciples who remember God's power over nature and "super-nature," the focus here, in 5:21–43, is upon two of the greatest scourges of earthly life—disease and death—and Jesus' astounding power over both. The disciple on the journey with Jesus need have no fear at all in the face of these, life's most traumatic catastrophes. Instead he or she is called to have faith in Jesus, who is powerful over all of life and all of death. Even terminal crises need have no terrorizing hold upon the believer (the sermon on this pericope is best focused upon such extreme situations; later pericopes address the need for fearless faith in other assorted exigencies of life). As has been mentioned, this pericope does not confer a promise that Jesus will revive the diseased and restore the dead.

But one day in the future, for sure, he will annihilate both disease and death. But until that moment of glory, the followers of Jesus are called to fearless faith in him, as they journey onward in discipleship with their Lord. That this faith is efficacious— i.e., it leads to the experience of God's power in their lives, operating for the extension of the kingdom of God—is pointedly made clear in the narrative of 6:1–6 (as well in the way the story of the woman with the hemorrhage is told). While nothing can thwart the sovereign work of God, lack of faith will definitely keep the disciple from experiencing God's magnificent power through him or her, thus "hindering" Jesus' kingdom mission.

POSSIBLE PREACHING OUTLINES FOR PERICOPE 7

I.   PROBLEM: The dire circumstances of disease and death
       Jairus' situation (implied disease, and death): 5:21–24
       Move-to-Relevance: the catastrophes we face in life, and the inevitability thereof

II. SOLUTION: Fearless, efficacious faith
       The woman's powerful faith (vs. the meager faith of the disciples): 5:25–34 (6:1–6)

III. APPLICATION: *Have faith that is fearless and powerful!*[*]
       Jairus' faith (vs. that of the bystanders): 5:35–43
       Specifics of what this faith looks like in real life, in the face disease and death

   [*] As was mentioned in connection with the previous pericope, the homiletician must take care to make these general imperatives more specific for the situation and circumstances of the listening audience.

I have attempted to weave the problem-solution-application around the story in its textual order, respecting the "sandwich" structure: considering, in order, the first half of the outer story (using that to develop the Problem), the inner story (to develop the Solution), and finally the second half of the outer story (to develop the Application). In Point II, the preacher could briefly touch upon the consequences of lack of faith—the precluding of the experience of God's power in one's life (6:1–6). Indeed, this "obstruction" of Jesus' miracle-working powers hints at the hindrance such a lack of faith is, for the extension of the mission of Jesus and the kingdom of God.

Another option:

I. CONTRAST 1: Woman vs. Disciples
    The woman's powerful faith (vs. the meager faith of the disciples): 5:25–34 (6:1–6)
    Move-to-Relevance: the aggression of disease, and our lack of faith

II. CONTRAST 2: Jairus vs. Bystanders
    Jairus' faith (vs. that of the bystanders): 5:21–24, 35–43
    Move-to-Relevance: the assault of death, and our lack of faith

III. APPLICATION: *Have faith that is fearless and powerful!*
    Specifics of what this faith looks like in real life, in the face disease and death

PERICOPE 8

Provision for Persecution

Mark 6:7–32

[Disciples Sent; John the Baptist Beheaded]

REVIEW, SUMMARY, PREVIEW

Review of Pericope 7: Mark 5:21—6:6 demonstrates that the follower of Jesus, recognizing his care and concern, and his power over disease and death, demonstrates fearless, efficacious faith in him on the journey of discipleship.

Summary of Pericope 8: In 6:7–32, a "sandwich" story, the outer story details the commission of the disciples to extend the kingdom of God, with hints of rejection. Those hints become reality in the depiction of the gory execution of another "disciple" who preached, John the Baptist, by an immoral, temporal king. In his death is foreshadowed what will likely be faced by Jesus' disciples—dangerous antagonism from the enemies of the true King, Jesus. Yet divine provision is adequate, and Jesus himself encourages disciples to persist in the fulfillment of their divine commission.

Preview of Pericope 9: The next pericope (6:32–56) depicts Jesus' expectation of his disciples to recognize his incredible power and their own divine empowerment for any circumstance.

8 Mark 6:7–32

THEOLOGICAL FOCUS OF PERICOPE 8

8   **The disciples' authoritative commission from Jesus to extend his mission brings with it vigorous opposition from the enemies of the true King, but it also comes with divine provision for the mission (6:7–32).**

    8.1   The disciples' authoritative commission from Jesus to extend his mission comes with divine provision for all their needs, while also hinting at the opposition they might face (6:7–13).

        8.1.1   Disciples are authoritatively commissioned and provided for by Jesus, to extend his mission to establish the kingdom of God.

        8.1.2   The disciples' commissioning comes with a hint of the opposition they might face from those who reject their message.

    8.2   Even as enemies of the true King, Jesus, vigorously oppose disciples who are engaged in the mission of Jesus, divine encouragement enables them to persist in fulfilling their commission (6:14–32).

        8.2.1   Enemies of the true King vigorously oppose his followers.

        8.2.2   Divine encouragement of disciples enables them to persist in fulfilling their commission.

OVERVIEW

THAT THERE IS NARRATIVE "stitching" is clear from the motifs that trickle through these last few chapters of Mark. Each of chapters 5–7 has a woman and a daughter (5:21–43; 6:7–32; 7:25–30). Each of chapters 6–8 has a "bread motif" linking them (6:32–45; 7:1–24, 25–30; 8:1–12, 13–21); and in these same three chapters, the disciples' incomprehension is the main issue (in two cases this is portrayed in conjunction with a sea story: 6:46–52 and 8:13–21; and in one case it happens on land, 7:17–23).

This pericope—another Markan "sandwich" (outer story: 6:7–13 and 6:30–32; inner story: 6:14–29)—builds on the previous pericope, 5:21—6:6, which made a call for fearless, efficacious faith from the disciple. Mark 6:1–6, with the rejection of Jesus' ministry by those in his own hometown, also adumbrated the rejection of the disciples and of Jesus' message that they proclaim. In other words, what might be expected on the mission is rejection, and even death, as happened to John (and would happen to Jesus).

As with most of the "sandwich" stories, Jesus is the only common character in both the outer and inner stories; in the latter he is present indirectly, referred only to as "he"/"his," and mistakenly identified as somebody else (6:14–16).[1] John and Jesus are being implicitly compared in this unit, as shown below.

---

1. See Shepherd, *Markan Sandwich Stories*, 172–209, for details on this Markan "sandwich." This commentary detects narrative purpose in the intercalation, *pace* Hooker, who sees "no logical connection" between the two stories (*Commentary on the Gospel*, 158). It is unfortunate that such a disregard for the literary structuring of this narrative is not uncommon among scholars.

JOHN	JESUS
Reported by Herod as raised from the dead (6:14)	Reported by young man as raised from the dead (16:6–7)
Sent for (ἀποστέλλω, *apostellō*, by Herod (6:17, 27)	Sends (ἀποστέλλω) the Twelve (6:7)
κρατέω (*krateō*, "arrest") and δέω (*deō*, "bind") used of John (6:17)	κρατέω (14:1, 44, 46, 49) and δέω (15:1) used of Jesus
Suffers under reluctant ruler at feast time (6:21, 26)	Suffers under reluctant ruler at feast time (15:1–15)
Herod considers John holy and righteous (6:20)	Pilate considers Jesus not to have been an evildoer (15:14)
Ruler afraid of John (6:20)	Rulers afraid of Jesus (11:18)
Feast and head of John (6:21, 27)	Last Supper and body and blood of Jesus (14:22–24)
Referred to as Elijah (9:11–13)	Referred to as Elijah/John the Baptist (6:14–16; 8:27–28)
Buried in tomb by disciples (6:29)	Buried in tomb by a "disciple" (15:42–46)

The analogies show that what happens to John will happen to Jesus. Or perhaps one should say: What would happen to Jesus is foreshadowed in John's life. And, in the future, what happens to Jesus, will be, in turn, reflected in his disciples' lives as well. In that regard, it is worthwhile observing the key comparison between John and the disciples.

JOHN	DISCIPLES
Imprisoned	Free
Sent for (ἀποστέλλω, *apostellō*) by an immoral king (6:17, 27)	Sent (ἀποστέλλω) by a moral King (6:7)
Preached repentance (1:4; [6:18])	Preached repentance (6:11, 12)
Others hearing (ἀκούω, *akouō*) John (6:14, 16, 20 [×2])	Others hearing (ἀκούω) the disciples (6:11)
Appears in the wilderness (1:3, 4)	Appear in the wilderness (6:32)
ἡμέρας εὐκαίρου (*hēmeras eukairou*, "opportune day," 6:21)	εὐκαίρουν (*eukairoun*, "opportune moment," 6:31)
Loss of life (6:27)	**[Fate?]**

The linkage of the fates of John and the disciples (and of Jesus, as well) is sharp and poignant, emphasized subtly in the "sandwich" of this story.[2] Not only does the inner story foreshadow Jesus' own violent ending, it bespeaks danger for his followers as well, and this is the primary thrust of this unit. Mark's readers were no doubt aware of what had befallen Jesus. This narrative, therefore, serves as a forewarning to all who would follow their Lord "on the way."[3] Discipleship is costly!

2. Shepherd, *Markan Sandwich Stories*, 185n2. "[D]iscipleship carries a cost even greater than the austere conditions of missionary journeys" (ibid., 194). Violence against the disciples themselves is predicted in 8:34–38; 10:35–40; and 13:9–13.

3. Of course, while John is slain and buried, Jesus is slain, buried, and *raised*.

ACT I: IN GALILEE

8.1 Mark 5:21–43

> **THEOLOGICAL FOCUS 8.1**
>
> 8.1 The disciple's authoritative commission from Jesus to extend his mission comes with divine provision for all their needs, while also hinting at the opposition they might face (6:7–13).
>
> 8.1.1 Disciples are authoritatively commissioned and provided for by Jesus, to extend his mission to establish the kingdom of God.
>
> 8.1.2 The disciples' commissioning comes with a hint of the opposition they might face from those who reject their message.

Section Summary 8.1: In this outer story of the "sandwich," the disciples are officially commissioned and sent. That God would provide for all their needs is evident in the minimal equipment and appurtenances they possess. The allusion to the survival of the Exodus generation is obvious. Yet, with all of the divine provision that accompanies them as they extend Jesus' mission, there are hints of rejection: there would be those who refuse to accept the message of God's coming kingdom.

TRANSLATION 8.1

6:7 *And He summoned the Twelve and began to send them two by two, and He gave them authority over the unclean spirits,*

6:8 *and He instructed them that they should carry nothing on the way, except a staff only—no bread, no bag, no money in belt,*

6:9 *but to put on sandals, and not to wear two tunics.*

6:10 *And He said to them, "Wherever you come into a house, stay there until you go out from there.*

6:11 *And whatever place does not receive you or hear you, as you go out from there shake off the dust beneath your feet as a testimony against them."*

6:12 *And they went out and preached that they should repent.*

6:13 *And they were casting out many demons, and anointing with oil many sick people and healing [them].*

NOTES 8.1

8.1.1 Disciples are authoritatively commissioned and provided for by Jesus, to extend his mission to establish the kingdom of God.

The outer story (Mark 6:7–13, 30–32) is the fulfillment of the appointment and commissioning of the Twelve that had taken place in Mark 3; here they actually depart, to undertake the mission entrusted to them: προσκαλέω (*proskaleō*), ἀποστέλλω (*apostellō*), κηρύσσω (*kēryssō*), and ἐξουσία (*exousia*; over demonic elements)—all occur in both Mark 3 and 6 ("summon," "send," "preach," and "authority," 3:13–15; 6:7, 12).[4] Thus far "they have been extras rather than actors in the proclamation of the kingdom of God"; now they get significant roles, as promise now becomes reality.[5] They

---

4. Προσκαλέω, *proskaleō*, occurs in the present indicative only in 3:13 and 6:7.

5. France, *Gospel of Mark*, 245.

are sent (ἀποστέλλειν, *apostellein*, and sent "on the way," 6:7), and they also return as "the sent ones" (οἱ ἀπόστολοι, *hoi apostoloi*, "the apostles," 6:30).[6] Jesus' call involves "two complementary thrusts: *both* remaining in Jesus' presence *and* being sent out by him as agents of God's coming rule."[7] Both thrusts were evident before in the original appointing and commissioning of the Twelve (3:14), and both are discernible here as well: the disciples are sent (6:7) and the "sent ones" return to be in Jesus' presence (6:31). To be with Jesus *and* to be sent from him is not a contradiction: one must be *with* Jesus in order to be sent *by* Jesus. Even as one is sent, one remains with him, "for apart from Me you can do nothing" (John 15:5); this is particularly evident in the sending of the ex-demoniac—one who wanted to "be with Jesus" (ἵνα μετ' αὐτοῦ ᾖ, *hina met autou ē*, Mark 5:18)—back home and to his people to preach (5:20).[8]

This is an official, authoritative commissioning. The sending "two by two," outside of strength in numbers, may reflect the practice of legal witnessing in the OT (Num 35:30; Deut 17:6; 19:15), as well as subsequent early Christian custom (Paul and Barnabas were sent together, for instance). Jesus, himself, began his ministry by calling two pairs of siblings (Mark 1:16–20; and perhaps a third, Levi/Matthew and James, the sons of Alphaeus). The dress code noted in 6:8–9 was the garb of the exodus generation (Exod 12:11): the footwear symbolizing preparedness, and the staff serving as a symbol of authority and divine calling (Exod 4:2–3; Num 17:1–10; etc.).[9] Also note Deuteronomy 8:4 and 29:5, for the durability of these accoutrements throughout the wanderings of the Israelites in the wilderness—God provides! The one undertaking this Trip of Discipleship can trust God's provision for the journey.

The message of the disciples, calling for repentance (Mark 6:12), is intended to sound like the continuation of Jesus' own proclamation (1:14–15) and, in context, even more like that of John (1:4). Such a similarity between messages is what Herod discerns (6:14, 16), and it is this congruence that leads him to the conclusions he draws. In doing what Jesus did—preaching, exorcising, and healing—the apostles extend the scope of his ministry. Indeed, his powers are "eclipsed" by them: they heal "many" (6:13); Jesus, immediately preceding this pericope, in his own backyard, could heal

---

6. Jesus is doing to them what God has done to him; ἀποστέλλω, *apostellō*, is used of Jesus' being sent by God in 9:37 and 12:6.

7. Henderson, *Christology*, 136.

8. "[T]he Twelve are missionaries of Jesus only insofar as they respond to the initiative of Jesus, remain with him, recognize that their authority to preach conversion, to cast out demons and to heal the sick is from him. They remain at all times 'followers' of Jesus" (Moloney, "Mark 6:6b–30," 656, italics removed).

9. The staff "repeatedly mediates, through authorized leaders, God's demonstrable provision for God's people" (Henderson, *Christology*, 155). Moloney observes that till Jesus arrives in Jerusalem, almost every section commences with a verb of motion (1:12, 14, 16, 19, 21, 29, 35; 2:1, 13, etc.). Adding to this is the frenetic restlessness implied by the Evangelist's prolific use of εὐθύς (*euthys*, "immediately"). The sparse clothing and paraphernalia are symbolic of this peripatetic, almost agitated, lifestyle; and the disciples, here, are being invited to join Jesus on his journey to Jerusalem—the Trip of Discipleship. See Moloney, "Mark 6:6b–30," 652–53. As France wisely notes, "loyalty to the kingdom of God leaves no room for a prior attachment to material security" (*Gospel of Mark*, 249–50). However, one wonders whether the command not to take any money is actually obeyed by the Twelve. In 6:37–38, these men apparently have 200 denarii, and also a number of loaves and fish (also see 8:5–7).

only a "few" (6:5). Thus, it is implied that "the new family of Jesus (cf. 3:34–35) takes over and expands the mission of Jesus beyond the boundaries imposed upon him by those who could not transcend the limitations of his human origins."[10] At the same time, this first part of the outer story ends with a curious gap: Mark has told the reader about the result of the disciples' work (6:13)—success! But what about the rejection they were warned about by Jesus? Did they have to shake the dust off their feet? The inner story provides the answer.

8.1.2   The disciples' commissioning comes with a hint of the opposition they might face from those who reject their message.

Of interest is that each of the "calls" of the disciples is immediately followed by a controversy story or a negative response to the ministry of Jesus: 1:16–20 is followed by 1:21–28, an exorcism; 3:7–19 is followed by 3:20–35, where Jesus is accused of being out of his mind and operating in league with Satan; and 6:7–13 is followed here by 6:14–32, the execution of John the Baptist.[11] Again, the suggestion of persecution and oppression casts its long shadow over the Twelve, as it also does for every new crop of Jesus-followers. But even before the tragic story of John the Baptist is recounted here, there is anticipation that the disciples might meet with less than an enthusiastic welcome, for Jesus instructs them on what to do if they are not received or heard (6:11). Analogous to Nehemiah 5:13 (and perhaps Acts 13:51), this shaking off of dust from the feet serves as a curse. "The idea is that God or a divine agent will punish the people who reject the proclamation and the persons of the missionaries."[12] Such an interpretation fits the "testimony against them" (6:11)—a parabolic act declaring eschatological judgment awaiting those so condemned, for the disciples are Jesus' representatives and ambassadors; when they are rejected, it is actually Jesus who is repudiated.[13]

8.2   Mark 6:14–32

THEOLOGICAL FOCUS 8.2

8.2   Even as enemies of the true King, Jesus, vigorously oppose disciples who are engaged in the mission of Jesus, divine encouragement enables them to persist in fulfilling their commission (6:14–32).

8.2.1   Enemies of the true King vigorously oppose his followers.

8.2.2   Divine encouragement of disciples enables them to persist in fulfilling their commission.

---

10. Moloney, "Mark 6:6b–30," 655. Perhaps the introduction of a new therapeutic modality, "anointing" (6:13), implies the difference between the character of the healings performed by the disciples and that by Jesus: he uses speech (2:11; 3:5), direct touch (1:31, 41; 5:41), and indirect touch (3:10; 5:28–30). The disciples, on the other hand, use oil—they anoint (6:13). Theirs is a deputized authority, their operations simply being extensions of Jesus' unique direct and divine activity.

11. One might also discern a similar pattern after the call of Levi: 2:14 is followed by opposition from the "scribes of the Pharisees" (2:15–17).

12. Collins, *Mark*, 301–2. Such an act is also one of deprecation, performed by a Jew upon returning from pagan lands (*m. Ṭehar.* 4.5; *m. ʾOhal.* 2.3; *b. Šabb.* 15b).

13. Stein, *Mark*, 294. Also see Mark 9:37.

Section Summary 8.2: In the inner story, the gory decapitation of John the Baptist at the hands of Herod is detailed. Two kings are contrasted—Jesus and Herod. Two daughters are contrasted—Jairus' and Herod's. Enemies of the true King bring only danger to disciples and opposition to their mission, in contrast to Jesus who brings life and peace in the kingdom of God. This opposition is countered by the encouragement of Jesus, extended to all who follow him.

TRANSLATION 8.2

6:14   *And King Herod heard [this], for His name had become known, and they were saying, "John the Baptist has been raised from the dead and, because of this, miraculous powers are operating in him."*

6:15   *But others were saying, "He is Elijah." And others were saying, "A prophet, like one of the prophets."*

6:16   *But when Herod heard, he was saying, "John, the one whom I myself beheaded—he has been raised."*

6:17   *For Herod himself had sent, seized John, and bound him in prison because of Herodias—the wife of Philip, his brother—because he [Herod] had married her.*

6:18   *For John had been saying to Herod, "It is not lawful for you to have the wife of your brother."*

6:19   *So Herodias had a grudge against him [John] and she wanted to kill him, and was not able,*

6:20   *for Herod was afraid of John, knowing him [to be] a righteous and holy man, and he protected him. And when he [Herod] heard him, he was much perplexed, but gladly heard him.*

6:21   *And an opportune day came about on his birthday, when Herod gave a banquet for his courtiers and the commanders and prominent men of Galilee.*

6:22   *And when the daughter of Herodias herself[14] came in and danced, she pleased Herod and his dinner guests. The king said to the girl, "Ask me for whatever you want and I will give [it] to you."*

6:23   *And he swore to her, "Whatever you ask of me I will give to you, up to half of my kingdom."*

6:24   *And going out, she said to her mother, "What shall I ask?" And she said, "The head of John the Baptist."*

6:25   *And immediately she came in to the king with haste, [and] asked, saying, "I want you to give me at once, upon a platter, the head of John the Baptist."*

---

14. The majority reading has τῆς θυγατρὸς αὐτῆς Ἡρῳδιάδος (*tēs thygatros autēs Hērōdiados*, "the daughter of Herodias herself"), which is retained here. There is some external attestation for τῆς θυγατρὸς αὐτοῦ Ἡρῳδιάδος (*tēs thygatros autou Hērōdiados*, "her daughter, Herodias"), thus naming the girl "Herodias." It is conceivable that Antipas had a daughter also named Herodias, which name, some have suggested, is even a dynastic one, the feminine equivalent of Herod. In any case, the alternate reading does not make a significant difference to the thrust of the text. See France, *Gospel of Mark*, 258.

6:26   *And though the king became deeply grieved, because of the oaths and the dinner guests, he did not want to refuse her.*

6:27   *And immediately the king sent an executioner [and] commanded [him] to bring his [John's] head. And he went away and beheaded him in the prison,*

6:28   *and brought his head on a platter, and gave it to the girl, and the girl gave it to her mother.*

6:29   *And when his disciples heard, they came and carried his body and laid it in a tomb.*

6:30   *And the apostles gathered together to Jesus and reported to Him all what they had done and what they had taught.*

6:31   *And He said to them, "Come away yourselves privately to a wilderness place and rest a little." For there were many who were coming and who were going, and [there was] not even an opportune moment to eat.*

6:32   *And they went away in the boat to a wilderness place privately.*

NOTES 8.2

8.2.1   Enemies of the true King vigorously oppose his followers.

The label "king" for Herod Antipas (20 BCE–39 CE; ruled 4 BCE–39 CE) is technically imprecise and contrasts with "tetrarch" used by Matthew and Luke (Matt 14:1; Luke 3:19; 9:7), who recognize Herod's rulership over a fourth of the kingdom of his father. The title "king" was explicitly refused to Antipas by the Roman Emperor Augustus.[15] As France notes, "[s]uch constitutional niceties were, however, probably of little significance in Galilee, where Antipas acted, and was recognized, to all intents and purposes as 'king.'"[16] While that argument may give the Evangelist a degree of accuracy, one must not discount his narrative intent to contrast one king with another; that intent, along with the despot's own claim to kingship, would suffice to explain Mark's labeling.[17]

Herod's responsibility as ruler of Galilee and Perea led him to be concerned about any major populist movement; one that made no secret of its nature as a "kingdom" (Mark 1:15) could surely be expected to catch his attention. Rumors, no doubt, were flying; see 1:28, 37, 45; 3:7–12. That Herod hears is duly noted multiple times (ἀκούω, *akouō*, "hear," 6:14, 16, 20 [×2]). That this is also defective hearing is certain, thus fulfilling Jesus' warning in 6:11 regarding those who will not listen (ἀκούω) to the disciples. In any case, this king was a person hostile to the preaching of God's new kingdom. All four references in Mark to Herod or the Herodians are inimical to Jesus and his

15. Indeed, it appears that Herod's desire to be king led to his downfall; he was banished to Gaul for stockpiling weapons, according to Josephus (*Ant.* 18.240–56).

16. France, *Gospel of Mark*, 252.

17. Yet another "theological" reason for Mark's nomenclature, but one less likely, might be to place John's rebuke of the "king" in the tradition of Jewish prophets who thought nothing of admonishing rulers (1 Sam 15:17–29; 2 Sam 12:1–15; 2 Kgs 20:16–18; Jer 38:14–23). See Dowd, *Reading Mark*, 66.

mission (3:6; 6:14–29; 8:15; 12:13). Also strikingly, of the twelve references to βασιλεύς (*basileus*, "king") in Mark, six occur in chapter 15 (during Jesus' Passion), and five in the present chapter (13:9 is the remaining occurrence). These uses of "king" in Mark thus refer almost exclusively to either Jesus or Herod, contrasting the true King, Jesus, and the other so-called "king," the enemy of the real one.

The account of John's execution resembles the story of Ahab and Jezebel, with Elijah (John's *doppelganger*) as the victim. John's condemnation of Herod is as poorly received as was Elijah's of Ahab and Jezebel. Leviticus 18:16 and 20:21 (and *b. Yebam.* 55a) make it clear that Herod's marital adventures are unacceptable to God. With Herodias's husband still alive, this was a scandalous undertaking, indeed. Josephus, who records the death of John, attributes it to political causes (*Ant.*18.116), not necessarily contradicting Mark. "Intermarriage was a matter of politics among rulers, key to building and sustaining dynasties. Relationship between political authority and Jewish law in Palestine was political and volatile. The part-Jewish kings of the Herodian dynasty complied with Jewish law only when expedient."[18]

Occurring in the very next pericope after the one in which Jairus's "girl" is raised, this story of an unprincipled "girl" is a "perverse reversal" of that earlier one, particularly considering that these are the only uses of κοράσιον (*korasion*, "girl") in Mark's Gospel (5:41, 42; and 6:22, 28 [×2]).[19] Notice the comparisons below.

JAIRUS' DAUGHTER (Mark 5)	HERODIAS' DAUGHTER (Mark 6)
κοράσιον (*korasion*, 5:41, 42)	κοράσιον (6:22, 28 [×2])
Unnamed, but has a named parent	Unnamed, but has a named parent
Father with confidence in Jesus	Father with some respect for John
She responds immediately (εὐθύς, *euthys*, 5:42)	She responds immediately (εὐθύς, 6:25)
Gets up and walks about (5:42)	Comes in and dances (6:22)
She is to be given to eat (5:43)	She wants a head on a platter (6:25)
She is brought back to life	She is the agent of a grisly murder

The contrast is between the work of a life-giving King and that of a life-taking king—and the activities of each involve a "daughter." In sum, opposition to Jesus and his kingdom can be, and will be, dangerous for the disciples.

Kaminouchi explains Herod's dilemma. Here he is before his most prominent clients, the base of his power—military commanders and civil administrators—at a privileged occasion for the display of his honor and the reinforcement of patron-client

---

18. Myers, *Binding the Strong Man*, 215. There are some inconsistencies between the family tree arrangements noted by Mark and those listed by Josephus. Given the uncertainty among historians as to who was who after Herod the Great (he had children after ten wives, two of whom had the same name, Mariamne; moreover, many of his sons and grandsons were called Herod), this bewilderment is not altogether surprising. Adding to these complications were the assorted incestuous entanglements between members of that vast family that defied identification: Herodias's daughter, for instance, works out to be Herod Antipas's niece on her father's side, his grandniece on her mother's side, and his own stepdaughter (see Stein, *Mark*, 303)! Also see Donahue and Harrington, *Gospel of Mark*, 197.

19. van Iersel, *Mark*, 222. Matthew also utilizes κοράσιον, *korasion*, in this exclusive fashion in 9:24, 25; and 14:11. The word is absent from Luke and John.

relationships. Herod simply cannot afford to lose face and credibility by breaking an oath, albeit a foolish one, risking the crumbling of his already fragile power. "It is not the king's vice, lust or anything else that leads him to kill John the Baptizer. It is ironically his virtue as a ruler, his commitment to the system of values that sustains his power that causes the king to make the decision to kill. Mark presents a king trapped by the web of power over which he reigns."[20] And therein lies the ironic sacrifice of another King, the most powerful of them all, who is willing to die for the ones he loves.

8.2.2 Divine encouragement of disciples enables them to persist in fulfilling their commission.

The outer story resumes in 6:30–32. The disciples' return is more than just a simple regathering. A distinct posture of proximity is adopted by them—πρὸς τὸν Ἰησοῦν (*pros ton Iesoun*, "to Jesus," 6:30), reminiscent of their being "with Him" (μετ᾽ αὐτοῦ, *met autou*, 3:14). Now they "report" (ἀπαγγέλλω, *apangellō*, 6:30) on their accomplishments, parallel to the instruction they had received earlier (παραγγέλλω, *parangellō*, 6:8) from Jesus.[21] The ones sent earlier (ἀποστέλλω, *apostellō*, 6:7) have now returned as the "sent ones," apostles (ἀπόστολος, *apostolos*, 6:30). The report on the response to their preaching and teaching is still cryptic (6:30). Narratively, however, by portraying the gruesome death of John the Baptist, Mark has presaged the potential response disciples may encounter when on they are on Jesus's mission. The "sandwich" thus serves a rhetorical function, hinting at what the disciples may face—consequences that may even be lethal.

There is a moment of tenderness as Jesus bids his disciples, freshly returned from their recent sending, come away and rest. Remarkably, both halves of the outer story touch upon this aspect of the disciples' commission—that divine provision goes with them (there is also a suggestion of divine presence, here). No, Jesus does not call them to retire from their ostensibly arduous mission when they are burdened with rejection, but, encouraged by Jesus, they are to keep on going, as are all of Jesus' subsequent followers. John preached, was rejected, and has now been killed. Jesus has preached, been rejected (the controversies in 2:1—3:6), and his death is coming, for what had been done to "Elijah" would be done to the Son of Man (9:12–13). The disciples have preached; what might happen to them has now been implicitly pictured. Yet, God's provision is sufficient, and they are to continue in that strength on the journey of discipleship, as are all those who will one day follow them. And so it will be until the kingdom of God is consummated when Jesus returns—disciples persisting in fulfilling their commission despite opposition.

---

20. Kaminouchi, "*But It Is Not So*," 186.

21. Moloney considers the disciples' report a bit arrogant as they announce to Jesus what *they* have done and what *they* have taught ("Mark 6:6b–30," 660). According to him, they have missed the point of their being *sent by Jesus* to do *His* work: "Mark has already portrayed the disciples' inability to understand *who Jesus is* in 4:35–41 (see 4:41); in 6:7–30 he further shows that they have difficulty in grasping *who they are*" (ibid., 661). This might fit well with what Jesus expects his empowered disciples to do in the next pericope, with the feeding of the 5,000 (see there).

SERMON FOCUS AND OUTLINES

THEOLOGICAL FOCUS OF PERICOPE 8 FOR PREACHING

8 **Disciples' commission from Jesus, that attracts the world's opposition, is enabled by God's provision (6:7–32).**

While the first pericope of Mark (1:16–20) adumbrated the fate of the disciples in general, pointing to the dangers of the journey of discipleship as a whole, this pericope (6:7–32) is more specifically geared to address the dangerous consequences of the disciples' commission. The first may be treated as more of a general introduction to the Gospel; the thrust of this pericope is to depict the potential result of the proclamatory activities of Jesus' followers, as they engage in his mission to extend the kingdom of God. And, in contrast to 2:1—3:6, the pericope that details facets of opposition the disciple might face and how one should respond (with boldness and persistence), this pericope focuses on the divine provision that accompanies and enables the disciples' mission that is fraught with danger and beset by hostility. Because God provides for the needs of the disciple even in the face of virulent opposition, the disciple is to trust God's care and concern in the lifelong journey of following Jesus.

The possibility of antagonism—against Jesus himself—has been raised as recently as in 6:1–6; the disciples have also been warned about it by Jesus in 6:11. Mark's construction of the "sandwich" story suggests that such opposition will be a dangerous reality in the future for all who would follow Jesus. "There is a basic conflict of interests, even of ideologies, between the kingdom of God and the norms of human society. An ambassador of the kingdom of God is called not only to a mission of restoration and deliverance, but also to a conflict of which John's fate provides an extreme example."[22] Till death, even in the face of rejection, disciples are to shake the dust off their feet and move on, encouraged by God's provision.

For preaching purposes, the antagonism encountered by the disciples may be considered as being directed towards every aspect of their commission, their call to proclaim being, of course, a particularly important one emphasized in this pericope.[23] It is probably expedient, therefore, to keep a broader focus upon the disciples' trust in God's provision as they encounter opposition to *all* the various facets of the mission of God they undertake, not just to their proclamatory activities (2:1—3:6, likewise, portrayed a diversity of opposing strategies to Jesus' mission).[24]

---

22. France, *Gospel of Mark*, 246.

23. The emphasis on proclamation in this pericope might be intended by Mark to draw together John's ministry and that of the Twelve, as both engaged in proclamation (it is likely that John did not engage in exorcism and healing, as the Twelve did).

24. There it was these various facets of antagonism (and the appropriate response, modeled by Jesus) that were highlighted. Here it is divine provision for harrowing times such as those that is in focus.

POSSIBLE PREACHING OUTLINES FOR PERICOPE 8

I.   COMMISSION

The sending of the disciples: 6:7, 10–13

Move-to-Relevance: our own calling and sending by Jesus

II. OPPOSITION

The hostility John faced: 6:14–29

Move-to-Relevance: dangers we might encounter on the mission

III. PROVISION*

Divine provision for the mission: 6:8–9, 30–32

Move-to-Relevance: how God provides for our mission today

IV. APPLICATION: *Engage God's mission with God's provision!*

Specific application: How we can begin to do this so that it becomes a part of our lives

* What exactly this provision looks like for God's people today will need to be explored by the preacher.

If one combines Points I and II, one could convert this outline into a problem–solution–application format.

I.   PROBLEM: The Opposition to the Commission

The sending of the disciples: 6:7, 10–13

Move-to-Relevance: our own calling and sending by Jesus

The hostility John faced: 6:14–29

Move-to-Relevance: dangers we might encounter on the mission

III. SOLUTION: The Provision

Divine provision for the mission: 6:8–9, 30–32

Move-to-Relevance: how God provides for our mission today

IV. APPLICATION: *Engage God's mission with God's provision!*

Specific application: How we can begin to do this so that it becomes a part of our lives

PERICOPE 9

Empowered to Serve

Mark 6:32–56

[Five Thousand Fed; Jesus Walking on Water; Healings]

REVIEW, SUMMARY, PREVIEW

Review of Pericope 8: Mark 6:7–32 commissions the disciples to extend the kingdom of God despite dangerous antagonism, trusting in divine provision.

Summary of Pericope 9: In Mark 6:32–56 are two episodes—a feeding miracle and a sea miracle. In both, Mark depicts Jesus' expectation of his disciples to recognize his incredible power. However, it is in the deputized exercise of that same power with which they themselves have been enabled that disciples are adequate for any circumstance, as they extend Jesus' mission to establish the kingdom of God.

Preview of Pericope 10: The next pericope (7:1–30) shows the importance of faith that produces obedience, the essential criterion for moral acceptability before God.

9   Mark 6:32–56

THEOLOGICAL FOCUS OF PERICOPE 9

9   Disciples commissioned by Jesus, the divinely powerful One, to extend his mission, are themselves divinely empowered by him, rendering them adequate for any circumstance (6:32–56).

   9.1   Disciples commissioned to extend Jesus' mission are divinely empowered by the abundance of God's provision to meet the needs of others (6:32–44).

      9.1.1   Divine provision is abundantly adequate to meet all needs.

      9.1.2   Disciples commissioned to extend Jesus' mission are divinely empowered to meet the needs of others.

> 9.2 The discernment by the disciples of the divine power of Jesus, and their own empowerment by him, renders them adequate for any crisis as they follow Jesus (6:45–56).
>
> 9.2.1 Divine power, adequate for any crisis, is assured to the disciple.
>
> 9.2.2 Disciples recognize their own divine empowerment, because the One they follow is the divinely powerful Jesus.

OVERVIEW

THE FEEDING MIRACLE OF 6:32–44 is the only such one found in all four Gospels. And, coming right after Herod's macabre banquet, this feast looks very different. While the elements are basic and the settings rustic, the miracle and the allusions to OT events mark out this banquet as one of great ultimate significance—akin to a messianic feast (as, for instance, in Isa 25:6–9). The image of "sheep not having a shepherd" (Mark 6:34) denotes an army without a leader (see 1 Kgs 22:17); this is a significant motif of this pericope. In brief, Mark's emphasis is on the disciples' empowered (leadership) role in the provision of food during Jesus' feeding miracle. The second episode of the pericope (Mark 6:45–56), builds upon this emphasis, concentrating upon the incredible authority of Jesus, which devolves upon his disciples by virtue of their following him, thus empowering them for ministry.

The wilderness frequently attains the significance of being the place where God's kingdom commences (see on Pericope 1). It is the locus where God staged his deliverance of his people (Isa 40:3; 41:18; 42:11; 43:19; 44:26; 51:3), where he fed the Exodus generation (Exod 16:1–35; Num 11:1–10; Ps 78:24; 105:40), where enthusiasts and zealots went to commence God's work (Josephus, *J. W.* 2.258–63), where righteous warriors gathered (1QM 1.2), where a highway would be cleared for God (1QS 8.13–14; 9.18–21), etc.[1] This desolate place has already figured in Mark's account, particularly at its commencement (1:3, 4, 12, 13, 35, 45; also see 6:31, 32, 35). The wilderness area where this pericope is set is likely to be in Jewish territory.[2]

9.1 Mark 6:32–44

THEOLOGICAL FOCUS 9.1

9.1 Disciples commissioned to extend Jesus' mission are divinely empowered by the abundance of God's provision to meet the needs of others (6:32–44).

9.1.1 Divine provision is abundantly adequate to meet all needs.

9.1.2 Disciples commissioned to extend Jesus' mission are divinely empowered to meet the needs of others.

---

1. See Henderson, *Christology*, 183–84.

2. Boring, *Mark*, 180. Also see later in this commentary on Mark 8:1–9 for reasons to claim that the incident described there (the second feeding miracle) was likely occurring in Gentile territory. In any case, the theological thrust is not dependent upon a specific locale.

Section Summary 9.1: This first feeding miracle of Jesus is marked by its emphasis on the needy populace—"sheep not having a shepherd." Equally striking is Jesus expectation that the disciples can meet the needs of these hungry ones. They can—in the power of God and with the provision of God. In seeking to extend Jesus' mission, the disciple meets the needs of others through divine empowerment.

TRANSLATION 9.1

6:32   *And they went away in the boat to a wilderness place privately.*

6:33   *And they [a crowd] saw them going away, and many recognized [them] and ran there together on foot from all the cities, and came ahead of them.*

6:34   *And when He came out [of the boat] He saw a large crowd and had compassion upon them, because they were as sheep not having a shepherd, and He began to teach them many things.*

6:35   *And when it was already a late hour, His disciples came to Him [and] said, "The place is a wilderness, and [it is] already a late hour.*

6:36   *Dismiss them, so that they may go away into the nearby countrysides and villages [and] buy themselves something to eat."*

6:37   *But He answered [and] said to them, "You yourselves give them to eat." And they said to Him, "Shall we go away and buy two hundred denarii of bread and give them to eat?"*

6:38   *But He said to them, "How much bread do you have? Go, look." And finding out, they said, "Five, and two fish."*

6:39   *And He commanded them all to recline in groups on the green grass.*

6:40   *And they sat down in parties of hundred and of fifty.*

6:41   *And taking the five [loaves of] bread and the two fish, looking up to heaven, He blessed and broke the bread and gave to the disciples that they may set before them; and the two fish He divided among all.*

6:42   *And they all ate and were satisfied.*

6:43   *And they picked up twelve baskets full of the fragments and of the fish.*

6:44   *And there were five thousand men who ate the bread.*

NOTES 9.1

9.1.1   Divine provision is abundantly adequate to meet all needs.

Without a doubt, it is the incredible power of Jesus to provide that is in view here, but—as will be seen below—*through the hands of his disciples*. Continuing the theme of divine provision in the previous pericope, there are echoes here of manna in the desert: the parallel in John 6:31 actually cites Exodus 16:3–4; Mark alone of the Gospel writers mentions the wilderness location in this connection (Mark 6:31, 32, 35); linked to the exodus, there is an allusion in the Markan account to Numbers 27:17 and the leaderless people of the exodus generation in the employment of the shepherd/sheep metaphor (Mark 6:34); and the organization of the crowd in hundreds and fifties (6:39–40) harks back to Exodus 18:21 and Numbers 31:14.[3] The use of the verb χορτάζω (*chortazō*, "satisfy," Mark 6:42) indicates that this might be more than just another meal: not only is there an allusion to the eschatological banquet (Isa 25:6–8, as was noted earlier), there is also a subtle recollection of the satisfaction provided by manna in an earlier era (Deut 8:10; Ps 132:15 LXX, in particular, also employs χορτάζω). This surplus at the bountiful hand of the Messiah (eschatological extravagance?), though, far outstrips the precise daily adequacy of the historical manna—no leftovers of that ancient item were permitted. A resonance with Elisha's miracle (2 Kgs 4:42–44) is also audible with Jesus' command to the servant/disciple to feed the crowd, the latter's skeptical response, and the ultimate sating of hunger, with leftovers. Nevertheless, that prophetic miracle too is completely eclipsed by Jesus here: the number of customers Elisha served was only a hundred, and the quantity of loaves available pre-miracle was four times more than in this account in Mark.[4] Jesus' miracle trumps them all; his capacity to provide for his people's needs is inexhaustible.

Whether Mark is deliberately employing Last Supper terminology in 6:41 is un-certain; there are suggestive parallels, however: the late hour in both (6:35; 14:17), the reclining (6:39; 14:18), and the many verbs employed in 6:41 that are traditionally linked with the Lord's Supper: λαμβάνω (*lambanō*, "take"), εὐλογέω (*eulogeō*, "bless"), κατακλάω (*kataklaō*, "break"), and δίδωμι (*didōmi*, "give")—these are used in exactly the same sequence in 14:22 (note also the echoes in 1 Cor 11:23–24). Perhaps the omission of fish as explicitly being the object of Jesus' liturgical expression in Mark 6:41—Jesus is said only to bless and break the bread, not the fish—is a deliberate at-tempt to keep this feeding miracle parallel to the later breaking of bread at the Last Supper.[5] The significance of these analogies may simply be that the power of Jesus is indeed great to provide for his people, both physically and, as would be seen later, salvifically: he is the Provider par excellence.

9.1.2 Disciples commissioned to extend Jesus' mission are divinely empowered to meet the needs of others.

The "wilderness motif" shows up again (ἔρημος, *erēmos*, 6:32, 35): this is going to be a testing ground for the disciples. "Sheep not having a shepherd" (6:34) is a proverbial metaphor in the OT, not only used of Israel in the wilderness after Moses (Num 27:17), but also of Ahab's army after his death (1 Kgs 22:17; 2 Chr 18:16—part of Micaiah's prophecy) and of Israel lacking trustworthy leaders (Ezek 34:5–6). This attention to a

---

3. God is depicted as a shepherd numerous times in Scripture: Gen 48:15; 49:24; Ps 23:1; 28:9; 80:1; Isa 40:11; 49:9–10; Jer 31:10; Ezek 34:8, 15; Micah 5:4; Matt 2:6. Israel's lack of a shepherd is also fre-quently lamented in the OT: Num 27:17; 1 Kgs 22:17; 2 Chr 18:16; Ezek 34:5, 8; Zech 10:2. Mark himself describes Jesus as a shepherd in 14:27. Yahweh's promises of future shepherd(s) for his people are found in Isa 40:11; Jer 23:1–8; and Ezek 34:11–31.

4. The precise annotation of the five thousand here in the wilderness as being "men" (ἄνδρες, *andres*, 6:44) could well mean that there were also women and children in addition to the five thousand men enumerated (as, for instance, in Exod 12:37).

5. There is no fish there. On the other hand, there is no wine here, nor any explication of a body metaphor.

leadership vacuum sets the stage for the role the disciples are directed by Jesus to play. But they have apparently given no thought to providing for the crowd, as their recommendation to Jesus reveals (Mark 6:36). The two adversatives (δε, "but," 6:37, 38) prefacing Jesus' reply to the disciples reflect his disagreement with their assessment of the situation; it also contrasts starkly with the disciples' desire that the crowd may go "buy *themselves* something" (ἐαυτοῖς, *heautois*, 6:36). Jesus counters with an emphatically placed ὑμεῖς (*hymeis*, "you *yourselves*," 6:37)—it was up to the *disciples* to provide. The disciples, though, are unwilling to accept that responsibility and they make a sarcastic response: 200 denarii is, after all, more than half a year's wages (see Matt 20:1–16).[6] "Earlier the crowd had preempted the disciples' holiday (Mark 6:31); now the crowd threatens to devour their treasury as well."[7] The disciples' rather peremptory "Dismiss them" (ἀπολύω, *apoluō*) has the ring of a command directed to Jesus, and it is perhaps a contrast to Jesus' own compassion (6:34).[8] Nonetheless, Jesus does comply, and he does dismiss the crowd (6:45, ἀπολύω)—but *after* meeting their needs.

In light of the proximity of this account to that of Jesus' sending his disciples to minister with minimal provisions and paraphernalia (6:7–9), one has to wonder if the sarcasm of the disciples springs from their memory of that command of Jesus in 6:8 not to take any money. But both that command and this exhortation from Jesus to feed the starving hordes stem from the same foundation—trust in the provision of God for all needs.[9] Jesus is surely aware of his own injunction; of course he is not expecting them to carry bread, or money for bread, to satisfy several thousand. The intent of his exhortation to the disciples in 6:37–38 is clear—he is teaching the disciples a lesson: one must rely not on one's own money (or bread) to meet others' or even one's own needs, but must lean upon the power of God. Successful ministry—what the disciples had ostensibly reported on in 6:30—involves meeting people's needs in the power of God. Thus the focus here is on the disciples: Can they provide, trusting in the provision of the One they followed? The structuring of the first episode is deliberate and underscores this very point[10]:

A   Comes ashore, compassion on crowd (ὄχλος, *ochlos*, 6:34)
    B   Need for food voiced by disciples (6:35–36)
        C   Disciples asked to "give ... to eat" (δίδωμι/ἐσθίω, *didomi/esthio*, [×2]) (6:37)
            D   Five loaves and two fish located (6:38)
                E   Crowd seated in groups on the green grass (6:39–40)

---

6. Tacitus, *Ann.* 1.17, also denotes the denarius as a reasonable daily wage for soldiers.

7. Fowler, *Loaves and Fishes*, 81.

8. The verb σπλαγχνίζομαι (*splanchnizomai*, "have compassion") is only used of Jesus in Mark (1:41; 6:34; 8:2; 9:22), and it appears in both the miracle feedings of the multitudes. However, in this pericope, Jesus' compassion is on account of their leaderless state, not because of their hunger (as it is explicitly stated to be, in the second feeding miracle, 8:2). Jesus' benevolent response to the situation here is to teach them (6:34).

9. In the previous pericope (Mark 6:7–32), it was divine provision in the face of hostility that was the focus; in this section, it is the power to meet others' needs that is provided to the disciple by God.

10. Reid, *Preaching Mark*, 69–70.

> D′   Five loaves and two fish taken, blessed and broken (6:41a)
>
> C′   Jesus gives (δίδωμι) disciples to distribute; crowd eats (ἐσθίω) and is satisfied (6:41b–42)
>
> B′   Remnants picked up by disciples (6:43–44)
>
> A′   Boat to other side, crowd dismissed (ὄχλος) (6:45)

The center of the chiastic structure (E) focuses on the shepherdless sheep seated on the green grass (an allusion to Ps 23[11]), with divine provision being distributed by the disciples taking up all the textual space around that pivot. While the focus is, no doubt, squarely upon the messianic provider of plenty, the details of the disciples being co-opted into Jesus' ministry of provision are striking. This is the story of the transformation of the disciples from helpless and cynical disbelievers, who see the problem but propose an inadequate solution, into those empowered to be God's agents of abundance to meet his people's needs. This is part of what it means to "be with" Jesus—tapping into his divine power to undertake his mission, including the meeting of others' needs.[12] "[T]he focus here is not on Jesus' miracle . . . but on Jesus' challenge to the disciples: 'you give them something to eat.'"[13] The word παρατιθήμι (paratithēmi, "set before," Mark 6:41) is often used to denote the hospitable provision of food to guests by a householder (Gen 18:8; 24:33; 2 Sam 12:20 LXX; Luke 11:6; Acts 16:34). While the disciples were all for dismissing the crowd right away, Jesus welcomes his "dinner guests" as part of his household and "sets before" them a table overflowing.[14] His is the attitude the disciples ought to have had. His is the (deputized) power they possess and ought to have exercised.

In all of these feeding activities, "Jesus remains front and center, actively working alongside his disciples to meet the need before them. The emerging portrait of discipleship is one of vital participation in which Jesus empowers the Twelve to perform the miracle (to be 'sent out') not in his stead but working in concert (being 'with him') with this eschatological shepherd."[15] It is the *disciples'* food that serves as the foundation for this miracle—*they* must provide, as well as serve the food to the people (who are "sheep not having a shepherd") in the power of God. Jesus' provision of food for his people is actually mediated by them, in his name, as his agents, as they set the food before the people (6:41). This episode is well located here, right after the "apprenticeship" of the disciples in 6:7–32. Their training continues: not only has Jesus demonstrated "how the impossible can be made possible," he has also directed disciples to perform

---

11. The description of the shepherd in Ps 23 who gives his flock "rest" is clearly in the author's mind (ἀνάπαυσις, *anapausis*, is used in Ps 23:2, and the verbal form, ἀναπαύω, *anapauō*, was employed earlier in Mark 6:31); the shepherd motif shows up as well (6:34), as also does green grass (6:39), and meal preparation (6:41–42), howbeit employing different words than does the LXX for Ps 23. See Gundry, *Mark*, 328, for links to that psalm in this pericope.

12. Henderson, *Christology*, 175.

13. Boring, *Mark*, 184n133. Fowler, too, thinks "the crux of both feeding stories [in Mark 6 and 8] is the interaction between Jesus and the disciples" (*Loaves and Fishes*, 93).

14. Donahue and Harrington, *Gospel of Mark*, 207.

15. Henderson, *Christology*, 199.

the impossible with what impossibly little they have![16] In his power, Jesus takes what disciples have to offer and enables its adequacy. Earlier he had given them (ἐδίδου, *edidou*, 6:7) authority; now he gives them (ἐδίδου, 6:41) sufficiency of provision and marvelous enablement to meet the needs of others. The role of the disciples is "a collective extension of Jesus' own divinely sanctioned mission."[17] They are learning to lead as he does. The followers of Jesus, then, trust in his empowerment to enable them to meet the needs of God's people.

9.2   Mark 6:45–56

THEOLOGICAL IDEA 9.2

9.2   The discernment by the disciples of the divine power of Jesus, and their own empowerment by him, renders them adequate for any crisis as they follow Jesus (6:45–56).

> 9.2.1   Divine power, adequate for any crisis, is assured to the disciple.
>
> 9.2.2   Disciples recognize their own divine empowerment, because the One they follow is the divinely powerful Jesus.

Section Summary 9.2: This second sea-crossing is notable for Jesus' almost forcing a test of upon the Twelve. Empowered they were by his divine authority but, despite all that they had heard and seen of Jesus, they fail to understand their enablement. Only by discerning God's authority that has been given to them can disciples hope to succeed in any crisis as they follow Jesus..

TRANSLATION 9.2

6:45   *And immediately Jesus compelled His disciples to get into the boat and go ahead to the other side to Bethsaida, while He Himself dismissed the crowd.*

6:46   *And taking leave of them, He went away to the mountain to pray.*

6:47   *And when evening came, the boat was in the middle of the sea, and He was alone on the land.*

6:48   *And seeing them straining to row—for the wind was against them—around the fourth watch of the night He came to them walking on the sea, and He wanted to pass by them.*

6:49   *But when they saw Him on the sea walking, they thought that it was a ghost, and they cried out.*

6:50   *For they all saw Him and were terrified. But immediately He spoke with them, and said to them, "Be courageous, it is I; do not fear."*

6:51   *And He climbed up to them in the boat and the wind ceased, and they were very amazed in themselves.*

6:52   *For they did not understand about the bread, but their heart had been hardened.*

---

16. van Iersel, *Mark*, 230.

17. Henderson, *Christology*, 200.

6:53 *And when they crossed over, they came on the land at Gennesaret and anchored.*

6:54 *And when they came out of the boat, immediately recognizing Him,*

6:55 *they [a crowd] ran about that whole country and began to carry about on pallets those who were ill, to where they heard He was.*

6:56 *And wherever He entered into villages or into cities or into the countrysides, they were laying the sick in the marketplaces, and imploring Him that they may just touch the edge of His garment; and as many as touched it were being healed.*

NOTES 9.2

9.2.1   Divine power, adequate for any crisis, is assured to the disciple.

The striking parallel text to Mark 6:45–52 is Exodus 14, the story of Yahweh's overthrow of the Egyptian army; in both is manifest the visible presence of God in a dramatic and miraculous mid-sea rescue. The parallels are so remarkable that "[t]he only words [in this episode] in the Greek not found in Exodus 14 (LXX) are 'for,' 'immediately' and 'not.'" And in the reverse direction, Exodus 14 (LXX) contributes 32 of the 139 words in Mark 6:45–52![18] This awe-inspiring divine power being manifest in Jesus is sure to remind readers of the exploits of Yahweh during the Exodus.[19]

The verb παρέρχομαι (*parerchomai*, "pass by," Mark 6:48) is also found in Exod 33:22; 34:6; and 1 Kgs 19:11 (LXX), where Yahweh showed himself to Moses and to Elijah, respectively, when both were in a crisis—God performing a "passing by."[20] Incidentally, both these OT characters crossed major water barriers (Moses, the Red Sea; and Elijah, the Jordan, 2 Kgs 2:8). The verb thus turns out to be almost a technical term for a comforting epiphany, not, as it appears on the surface, an attempt by Jesus to avoid the boat in distress.[21] Other clues to the phenomenon of divine manifestation here include:

18. The use of θάλασσα (*thalassa*, "sea," ×15 in Exod 14 LXX; ×3 in Mark 6:45–52) is notable in Mark, instead of the more common λίμνη (*limnē*, "lake") for the Sea of Galilee. No doubt the former is intended to evoke memories of the Exodus. Other words and phrases in Exod 14 LXX shared with Mark 6:45–52 include: ἐπὶ τὴν θάλασσαν (*epi tēn thalassan*, "on the sea," Exod 14:16, 21, 26, 27), μέσος τῆς θαλάσσης (*mesos tēs thalassēs*, "middle of the sea," 14:16, 29), ὁράω (*horaō*, "see," 14:13, 30, 31), "say + tell" (in the present tense, 14:1, 12), φοβέω (*phobeō*, "fear," 14:10), ἐγώ εἰμι (*egō eimi*, "I am," 14:4, 18), θαρσέω (*tharseō*, "be courageous," 14:13), (συν)θαράσσω ([*syn*]*tharassō*, "terrify," 14:24), νύξ (*nyx*, "night," 14:20, 21), καρδία (*kardia*, "heart," 14:4, 5, 8, 17), γῆ (*gē*, "land," 14:3, 11), ἐναντίος (*enantios*, "against," 14:2, 9), ἄνεμος (*anemos*, "wind," 14:21), and φυλακή (*phylakē*, "watch," 14:24). See Stegner, "Jesus' Walking on the Water," 217–20.

19. See Job 9:8; 38:16; Ps 77:19; Isa 43:16; Hab 3:15; and Sir 24.5–6; etc., for descriptions of Yahweh "walking" on water; also see *Mek.* on Exod 15:2 (the Holy One who "revealed Himself at the sea"), and *Pirqe R. El.* on Ps 77:19 ("Holy One . . . walking before them"). Collins shows that "the motif of walking on water had become proverbial for the (humanly) impossible and for the arrogance of the ruler aspiring to empire." It was not unknown in Greek, Roman, biblical, or Jewish tradition, and appears in 2 Macc 5.21 depicting the conceit of Antiochus IV Epiphanes, one who claimed to be divine (*Mark*, 331–32).

20. The verb is also used in Amos 7:8 and 8:2 in the sense of "to save."

21. Jesus' "passing by" clearly is not a ploy to leave the disciples to their own devices—that would not be consistent with Jesus' compassionate attitude towards the needy and suffering: he sees the disciples' adversity and he walks on the water (twice mentioned in 6:48–49) to reach them.

- the accompaniment of the epiphany with a time stamp in Mark 6:47–48, as with other descriptions of numinous appearances (Mark 16:2; Matt 28:1; Luke 1:8, 26; 2:8; etc.);

- the expression of fear, and the divine exhortation not to be afraid, which is frequently associated with epiphanies (Mark 6:49–50; 16:5, 6, 8; Matt 28:4, 5, 10; Luke 1:12–13, 29, 30; 2:9, 10; etc.);

- the self-attestation formula "It is I!," which also often coincides with the manifestation of God.[22]

In other words, "passing by" is a divine act of reassuring self-disclosure that meets God's people at their point of greatest desperation.[23] "[W]hen Jesus 'comes toward them' intending to 'pass them by,' he stages an epiphany designed to fortify them through a reminder of his presence for the leadership for which they have been called and equipped."[24] Unfortunately, this unique thrust of the encounter in 6:45–52 is completely lost on the disciples—their reaction is sheer terror, the opposite of what is intended (6:50). In light of the allusions to the Exodus and epiphanic phenomena, not to mention all that the disciples have already heard and seen of Jesus prior to this event, it is astonishing that the disciples fail to discern who Jesus really is—the divine one with power; instead, they think he is a phantasm, a ghost (6:49).[25]

Henderson notes that, in the context of the power conferred on the disciples in 3:14 and 6:7, "the purpose of this sea voyage may well be for the disciples to exercise that authority over the evil spirits of the sea."[26] And evil, indeed, the stormy powers certainly are, as they are described in this pericope: βασανίζω (*basanizō*, "straining," 6:48) hints at the demonic forces animating the winds against the disciples. The word essentially means "to torture/torment"—the disciples are literally "tormented in the rowing."[27]

The surprisingly strong verb ἠνάγκασεν (*ēnankasen*, "compelled," 6:45) also indicates that Jesus virtually forces the disciples to undertake this journey—by themselves, as he deliberately removes himself from their presence. Perhaps the disciples did not want to go alone, while Jesus, equally strongly, felt they should. This, then, is a purposeful sending of those he has called—"no mere happenstance"—and as deliberate as the initial commissioning and sending of 6:7–13; they are being authorized

22. See Stein, *Mark*, 325. While ἐγώ εἰμι (*ego eimi*) is normal colloquial Greek (as in Matt 26:22, 25; John 9:9; etc.), the parallels with Exod 14, noted above, and the thrust of the episode as pointing to a divine epiphany, suggest that the phrase has the significance of a divine claim (Gen 17:1; 26:24; 31:13; Exod 3:6, 14; 14:4, 18; Deut 32:39; Isa 41:4; 43:11 LXX; John 8:58; 18:5–8; etc.).

23. Notice also the introduction of παρέρχομαι, *parerchomai*, into the LXX of Dan 12:1, even when the corresponding verb is absent in the MT.

24. Henderson, *Christology*, 228–29 (also see 227).

25. Again, here is a failure of discernment of Jesus' person, a key motif of Mark's Act I.

26. Henderson, "'Concerning the Loaves,'" 18.

27. For other relevant uses of βασανίζω, *basanizō*, see 2 Macc 7.13, 17; 4 Macc 6.5, 10, 11; Wis 11.9; Sir 4.17; Matt 8:6, 29; Mark 5:7; 2 Pet 2:8; Rev 9:5; Josephus, *Ant.* 2.105; 16.232; etc.

to demonstrate God's authority over the powers of chaos in that watery domain.[28] That this is the thrust of the text is also evidenced by the previous episode, where the disciples, in the testing ground of the "wilderness," were expected to meet the needs of the crowd by depending on the provisions only their Master could muster. "Especially in the context of Mark as a whole, the implication in 4:40 that the disciples themselves could have stilled the storm and in 6:37 that they could have multiplied the loaves makes it likely that the hidden motivation of Jesus in 6:45–46 is to give the disciples yet another opportunity to exercise and demonstrate the power of their faith."[29] All this suggests this second sea-crossing as being akin to a second "missionary journey" of the disciples as they go out by themselves on Jesus' mission. "In the first [Mark 6:7–13, 30–32], they have laid claim to God's dominion within the human sphere, where they have preached, healed, and cast out demons; now they go forth to assert God's dominion by subduing the adverse spiritual powers associated with the sea."[30] Indeed, they have already been authorized *twice* to act against the powers of evil (3:13–15; 6:7–9). In other words, this sea voyage is a test, yet another opportunity for the disciples to exercise their authority as empowered by Jesus. And disciples of all time, empowered by the incredible power of the divine One they follow, are enabled to pass these tests easily.

9.2.2 Disciples recognize their own divine empowerment, because the One they follow is the divinely powerful Jesus.[31]

The reaction of the disciples (6:51) parallels the amazement of the "crowd," a recurrent response of this collective character foil in Mark (1:22, 27; 2:12; 5:20, 42). That the reactions of both parties—disciples and crowd—are equivalent is a sad commentary on the disciples' discernment of Jesus person/power.[32] In fact, the connections between the feeding miracle and the one of walking on water, link these events to the wonders of the exodus period—the provision of manna and the crossing of the sea. The one providing manna is surely powerful enough to walk on water! And the disciples, just having observed Jesus reenact the former, should have been prepared for the latter. But their ears and eyes, seemingly, are still closed. Worse yet, their hearts, Mark informs us, have been hardened (6:52). This marks an intensification of Mark's "polemic" against the disciples for their lack of discernment; the terms used here are echoed elsewhere: συνίημι (*syniēmi*, "understand," first in 4:12; here in 6:52; and later in 8:17, 21) and καρδία πεπωρωμένη (*kardia pepōrōmenē*, "hardened heart," in 6:52 and also in 8:17)— all marks of "outsiders" and opponents of Jesus (see 3:5).[33] The disciples, sadly, do not discern anything about Jesus' power, not to mention their own divine empowerment.

---

28. Henderson, *Christology*, 213, 219.

29. Collins, *Mark*, 336.

30. Henderson, *Christology*, 219–20.

31. The theological points raised herein are depicted *negatively* in the failure of the Twelve.

32. Hooker, *Commentary on Mark*, 169.

33. The "hardening of heart" is also reminiscent of that of the Pharaoh of the Exodus (see Exod 14:4, 8, 17).

The narrator's rebuke of the disciples, mentioning bread alone (6:52)—without fish—is likely to be significant. The disciples contributed and distributed *both* bread and fish, though even in the feeding miracle itself, the fish are sidelined (6:41). It was observed earlier that this might have been to preserve the eucharistic comparison. But note that what the disciples themselves are explicitly said to have distributed in that feeding miracle was *bread*, not fish (6:41); perhaps 6:52 is the narrator's way of stating that they have forgotten even their *own* role in the foregoing miracle, let alone that of Jesus, the divine provider and purveyor of power supernatural. Henderson concludes: "[T]he disciples fail the test in this passage on more than one level: it is not just Jesus' self-disclosure that they mismanage; at least for the moment, they have also misappropriated the power he has entrusted to them. Even when he comes toward them to renew that authority, they can only cower in fear."[34] This is a discipleship training program, replete with instruction (6:7–32), illustration (6:32–45), test (6:45–52), and failure, as well as Jesus' contingency rescue plan. The disciples' downfall is their neglect to recognize Jesus' power and to exercise the empowerment granted them by virtue of being followers of Jesus. The verdict is harsh; the result of the journey is a defeat—they land back at Gennesaret, instead of Bethsaida, the original destination (6:45, 53). With this pericope, then, the disciples are shown as increasingly unable to understand Jesus' mission.

Mark 6:53–56 forms an ironic summary for the chapter, with a pungent note of disparagement struck: whereas the disciples fail to recognize Jesus' person/power, thinking him a ghost (6:49), the crowd recognizes him "immediately" (6:54). That they had heard of Jesus is hinted at in the mention of the "edge of his cloak"—the news of the healing of the woman with the hemorrhage has probably gotten around (6:56; see 5:27–28). They know all about Jesus' power, and so their response to him is vigorous and enthusiastic: they run, they carry the afflicted here and there to wherever Jesus is, and they lay the sick in public places, seeking at least a peripheral touch from this powerful one, whom the disciples, who have been with him for so long, have failed even to recognize!

"For the disciples in Mark's story, for Mark's community, and for interpreting communities today, this passage stands as a reminder of the empowerment and the high calling that is discipleship."[35] Jesus wants his followers to partake of the authority of his divine person—to do the things he does and the things he has empowered them

34. Henderson, *Christology*, 233.

35. Henderson, "'Concerning the Loaves,'" 25. Intriguingly, Henderson raises the question of whether the "Messianic Secret" motif—Jesus' command to silence of demons and those he healed—is "simply because he saw himself as a means of the inbreaking of God's rule and not the exclusive focus of it." Perhaps Jesus' intent to see his mission as a *shared* one, not one that centers on him exclusively, is what prompted his impositions of silence.

> Does not this convergence of Christology and discipleship in the first half of the Gospel cohere with the collective nature of Jesus' messiahship in the second half, where Jesus decisively aligns the disciples' own calling with the way of the Suffering Servant himself (Mk 8:34; 9:35; 10:44)? Finally, in this light, could not the perplexing 'original' ending of Mk 16:8 be designed to thrust the empty tomb encounter upon the text's community, to shift the Gospel story once again from Jesus himself to those who would carry on his mission? (ibid.)

to do. Disciples, then, are to discern the awesome power of Jesus and their own divine enablement, if they are to be successful in their mission and participate in God's work.

SERMON FOCUS AND OUTLINES

> **THEOLOGICAL FOCUS OF PERICOPE 9 FOR PREACHING**
>
> **9** **Disciples commissioned by the divinely powerful Jesus are themselves divinely empowered by him to meet any need (6:32–56).**

The previous pericope (6:7–32) discussed the necessity for disciples to remember the provision of God when facing hostility, as they undertake the mission of discipleship. This pericope takes off from that theme, but here the focus is on disciples engaging in the extension of Jesus' ministry with his power shared with them. Such engagement occurs successfully only insofar as disciples recognize and respond to their empowerment by God to meet any need. While the first episode of the feeding miracle focuses on the disciples' capacity to meet others' needs, the second episode of the sea-crossing broadens the canvas somewhat: disciples are enabled to be adequate for any crisis. Nevertheless, focusing specifically, in the sermon, on empowerment that enables disciples to meet others' needs is an appropriate homiletical narrowing of a broader theological focus.

A critical facet of discipleship is serving others (see 1:21–45, where that theme already surfaced), and this pericope emphasizes that God provides the wherewithal to accomplish these acts of benevolence. What one has, one offers, and God empowers the disciple to use what has been offered to aid and strengthen many in all kinds of different ways. Thus the disciple demonstrates a recognition of his or her own inadequacy and, even more, an acknowledgment of the total adequacy of God and his power alone, for the undertaking of the mission of discipleship, particularly for the aspect of service towards others.

POSSIBLE PREACHING OUTLINES FOR PERICOPE 9

I.   TESTS: Crowd-feeding and sea-crossing
        The two tests of this pericope: 6:33–37 and 45–48
        Move-to-Relevance: the "impossible" needs/situations in lives of others that disciples encounter today

II.   FAILURES: Lack of discernment of Jesus' empowerment
        The disciples' failure in the two tests of this pericope: 6:38–44 and 49–52
        The crowds as a foil for the disciples: they recognize Jesus' person, 6:53–56
        Move-to-Relevance: reasons for our incapacity and failure to serve successfully

III. LESSON: *Act on the empowerment of God for ministry!*
        What specifically does it mean to act in God's empowerment to meet others' needs?

Another option:

I.   PROBLEM: The crises of hungry crowds and angry seas

    The two crises in this pericope: 6:33–37 and 45–48

    Move-to-Relevance: the "impossible" needs/situations disciples encounter today

II. SOLUTION: The empowerment of God to meet the demands of those crises

    The disciples' failure in the two tests of this pericope: 6:38–44 and 49–52

    The crowds as a foil for the disciples: they recognize Jesus' person, 6:53–56

    Jesus' expectation of the disciples to meet the needs of the moment themselves: 6:37, 41–43

    Move-to-Relevance: reasons for our incapacity and failure to serve successfully

III. APPLICATION: *Act on the empowerment of God for ministry!*

    What specifically does it mean to act in God's empowerment to meet others' needs?

PERICOPE 10

Piety or Purity?

Mark 7:1–30

[Purity Question Answered; Syrophoenician's Daughter Exorcised]

REVIEW, SUMMARY, PREVIEW

Review of Pericope 9: Mark 6:32–56 shows Jesus expecting his disciples to recognize his incredible power and their own divine empowerment to meet any need.

Summary of Pericope 10: In Mark 7:1–30, a bicameral pericope with two episodes, the Pharisees are censured for their adherence to manmade rules of piety and rituality without compliance to divine morality—hypocrisy unacceptable to God. On the other hand, a Syrophoenician woman, a Gentile and the mother of a girl with an unclean spirit, demonstrates acceptability before God by her faith that produces obedience to Jesus.

Preview of Pericope 11: The next pericope (7:31—8:26) calls the disciple to trust in Jesus' person as one who is able to provide for life's daily needs.

10   Mark 7:1–30a

THEOLOGICAL FOCUS OF PERICOPE 10
10   **What renders a disciple morally acceptable before God is faith in him that produces obedience to his word, in contrast to hypocritical adherence to manmade rules of piety or ritual (7:1–30).**
10.1   Disciples' compliance to the word of God, rather than the hypocritical observance of rules of piety or ritual, is the criterion for their purity (7:1–23).

10.1.1	Obedience to God's word is the criterion for purity, not allegiance to manmade rules of piety.
10.1.2	Sinful thoughts and deeds are what render a person morally impure, not the violation of rules of ritual.

10.2	Acceptability before God comes with faith in God that produces obedience to his word (7:24–30).

OVERVIEW

JESUS HAS JUST RECEIVED widespread acclaim on the Jewish west bank (6:53–56). Now after a conflict with the Pharisees (7:1–23), he takes an extensive trip through Gentile regions, exorcising the daughter of a Gentile woman (7:24–30), healing a Gentile man (7:31–37), taking a circuitous route through other Gentile lands (7:31), and then feeding four thousand people in Gentile territory (8:1–10).[1]

The topic of this pericope is purity and acceptability before God. This controversy appropriately becomes the "narrative hinge between the Jewish and Gentile phases of Jesus' ministry."[2] The first episode of the pericope stages the issue and culminates in a list of sinful elements coming from the heart that render one morally unacceptable before God. The second episode, in contrast, shows what is acceptable to God and worthy of commendation by Jesus.

10.1   Mark 7:1–23

THEOLOGICAL FOCUS 10.1

10.1	Disciples' compliance to the word of God, rather than the hypocritical observance of rules of piety or ritual, is the criterion for their purity (7:1–23).
10.1.1	Obedience to God's word is the criterion for purity, not allegiance to manmade rules of piety.
10.1.2	Sinful thoughts and deeds are what render a person morally impure, not the violation of rules of ritual.

Section Summary 10.1: The disciples' eating with unwashed hands galls the Pharisees. Jesus places the controversy in proper perspective: what is important for moral purity is obedience to God's commandments, rather than observance of manmade regulations of piety. Moral impurity comes from disobedience to God's commandments, not from external contact or consumption of what might be ritually impure. Therefore, the hypocritical observance of rules of piety or ritual, without compliance to the commandments of God, renders one morally impure. The vice list enumerates sinful tendencies that ought to be replaced by obedience.

1. Boring, *Mark*, 196.
2. France, *Gospel of Mark*, 277.

TRANSLATION 10.1

7:1   *And the Pharisees and some of the scribes coming from Jerusalem gathered together to Him.*

7:2   *And they saw that some of His disciples were eating bread with defiled hands, that is, unwashed.*

7:3   *(For the Pharisees and all the Jews, unless they ceremonially[3] wash hands, do not eat, holding to the traditions of the elders,*

7:4   *and [when they come] from the marketplace, unless they cleanse, they do not eat, and there are many other things which they have received to hold—cleansing of cups and pitchers and copper pots and couches.)*

7:5   *And the Pharisees and the scribes asked Him, "Why do Your disciples not walk according to the tradition of the elders, but with defiled hands eat bread?"*

7:6   *But He said to them, "Rightly did Isaiah prophecy concerning you hypocrites, as it is written, 'This people honors Me with lips, but their heart is far away from Me.*

7:7   *And in vain they worship Me teaching as doctrines the precepts of men.'*

7:8   *Neglecting the commandment of God, you hold the tradition of men."*

7:9   *And He was saying to them, "Rightly[4] you reject the commandment of God, in order to establish your tradition.*

7:10   *For Moses said, 'Honor your father and your mother,' and 'He who speaks evil of father or mother must surely be put to death.'*

7:11   *But you say, 'If a man says to father or mother, "Whatever you would have benefited from me is Corban"'" (which is "offering"),*

7:12   *"you no longer permit him to do anything for father or mother,*

7:13   *annulling the word of God with your tradition which you passed down. And you do many similar things such as this."*

7:14   *And summoning the crowd again, He began saying to them, "Hear me, all, and understand.*

7:15   *Nothing is outside of man which is able to defile him coming into him, but the things which come out from the man are the things that defile the man."*

[7:16][5]

7:17   *And when He entered into the house away from the crowd, His disciples asked Him [about] the parable.*

7:18   *And He said to them, "Are you also this way, without understanding? Don't you understand that everything from outside going into the man is not able to defile him*

---

3. "Ceremonially" translates πυγμῇ, *pygmē*, literally "with the fist." The specific connotation is uncertain.

4. The word καλῶς, *kalōs*, employed also in 7:6 introducing the Isaiah quotation, is obviously sarcastic here in 7:9.

5. Verse 7:16 is not found in the earliest manuscripts.

7:19 *because it does not go into his heart, but into his belly, and into the la-*
trine it goes out, cleansing all foods?"

7:20 *And He was saying, "The things which come out from man, that defiles*
the man.

7:21 *For from inside, from the heart of men, come out evil ideas, sexual im-*
moralities, thefts, murders,

7:22 *adulteries, greed, evil deeds, deceit, debauchery, envy, slander, arrogance,*
foolishness.

7:23 *All these evil things come out from inside and defile the man."*

NOTES 10.1

10.1.1   *Obedience to God's word is the criterion for purity, not allegiance to*
manmade rules of piety.

This episode primarily deals with an issue of the "heart" (7:6, 19, 21): both purity
and impurity begin "inside" (7:21, 23), not "outside" (7:15, 18). Jesus' concern here is
with moral purity—obedience to God's commands. On the other hand, the Pharisees'
burden is adherence to manmade laws, while sinning against God "from the heart,"
"from inside" (7:21–23)—an artificial piety. Three sets of antitheses expressed by Jesus
bring the argument to the fore:

	ACTION	OBJECT	SOURCE
Antithesis 1	**Neglecting** Holding	**the commandment** the traditions	**of God** of men (7:8)
Antithesis 2	**Rejecting** Establishing	**the commandment** tradition	**of God** your (7:9)
Antithesis 3	**Annulling** Passing down	**the word** tradition	**of God** your (7:13)

The issue, at least initially in this pericope, is not whether the disciples should
obey the OT laws, but rather whether the regulations later developed in Pharisaical
Judaism avail for moral purity. These latter human rules stipulating ritual behavior are
what the Pharisees call the "tradition of *elders*" (7:5). That descriptor is subtly modified
by Jesus to "precepts of *men*," "tradition of *men*," and "*your* tradition" (7:7, 8, 9, 13):
the default assumption of authority in those traditions is being challenged by Jesus
here. The contrast between these (sourced in man) and the "commandment"/"word"
(sourced in God) is stark. Handwashing, the specific concern in the first part of the
pericope, is enjoined only of priests in the OT (Exod 30:17–21; 40:30–32); *m. Parah*
11:5 explicitly notes that washing is required before consumption of sacred, not common, food (so also *m. Ḥag* 2:5–6).[6]

6. France, *Gospel of Mark*, 278n9, 280n7, 280–81. Ritual washings in the context of prayer are mentioned in Jdt 12.7; *m. Yad.* 1.1–2.4; etc. The *Let. Aris.* 305 asserts that the translators of the LXX washed
their hands in the sea in the context of their prayers—"a token that they had done no evil." Josephus's version of that event also notes that such ablutions were equivalent to "purifying themselves" (*Ant.* 12.106).
See Collins, *Mark*, 346. The "traditions of the elders" were supposed to have been delivered to Moses

The fundamental contrast in this episode is thus the one in the last column of the table above, the source of the injunction: "of men"/"your" vs. "of God." The adoption of tradition engenderd first, a benign neglect of God's commands (Mark 7:8), and later, a more proactive nullification and invalidation thereof (7:9 and 7:13)—an escalating degree of abandonment of God's word. The already strong verb ἀθετέω (*atheteō*, "to reject," 7:9) is replaced by an even more forceful forensic term ἀκυρόω (*akyroō*, "to annul," 7:13). "They have actually dared to rule [the word of God] to be unlawful!"[7] The religious leaders would deny such a charge, claiming instead that their developing traditions are only designed to be "a fence around the Torah" (*m. 'Abot* 1.1; 3.13). Jesus' accusation is that, whatever the theory, in practice, the commandments of God have been rendered secondary to tradition.

Jesus provides an illustration in Mark 7:10–11 of the contrast between "Moses said" (God's word) and "you say" (man's word). The stakes are raised considerably with the example of a specific item of law from the Decalogue, the breaking of which would incur the death penalty (Exod 20:12; 21:17; Lev 20:9; Deut 5:16). A son's resources, from which parents may reasonably expect support, is, apparently with Pharisaic approval, being declared "Corban" ("offering" to God as "divine property"), thus making it no longer accessible for such a philanthropic purpose. "This vow is thus a clever way in which a son can prevent his parents from using any of his property." Doubtless, this declaration of "Corban" would be reinforced by the scriptural principle of not violating oaths (Num 30:2; Deut 23:21–23). Thus the son calculatedly (and callously) evades his Mosaic law-mandated responsibility to honor his parents.[8] This is a rejection of God's commandment in the service of selfish gain, while adhering to a manmade regulation.

It is interesting that the Pharisees, while feeling free to abandon (ἀφίημι, *aphiēmi* God's commandment (Mark 7:8), find it necessary not to permit (also ἀφίημι) the son to honor his parents in any fashion (7:12). For them, it is acceptable to reject God's word but not acceptable to support one's parents! The use of the same verb makes the hypocrisy of the Pharisees more vivid. "Thus what is a capital offense in the law (7:10) is not only permitted but even required by the Pharisaic tradition!"[9] This is clearly a case of misplaced priorities.

All of this has become a form of hypocrisy (7:6–7, citing Isa 29:13): the Pharisees have gotten to assuming that their manufactured (from the Latin *manus* [= hand] + *facere* [= to make]) piety is equivalent to moral purity and therefore acceptable before God—honoring God with their lips. It is not: what they should have recognized is that moral purity involves submission to God's word—honoring God with one's heart.

---

from God at Mt. Sinai (*m. 'Abot* 1.1–12), and later codified into the Mishnah in the late second century CE. Together with its Aramaic commentary, the Gemara, it constitutes the Jerusalem and Babylonian Talmud (ca. fifth century CE) (Stein, *Mark*, 339). Mark's statement of "many other things" (7:4; and "many similar things," 7:13) is "a synecdoche for the larger problem of the power of tradition," which, being outside the word of God, did not constitute divine standards for morality (Salyer, "Rhetoric, Purity, and Play," 147). Also see van Iersel, *Mark*, 239.

7. France, *Gospel of Mark*, 285, 288.

8. Collins, *Mark*, 352; France, *Gospel of Mark*, 286.

9. Stein, *Mark*, 342.

"Heart" in this pericope indicates the essence of the person. Moral impurity comes from here, "inside" a person—by disobedience to God's word—and does not come from the "outside," as the Pharisees assume: by eating with unwashed hands, or because one is a Gentile (see the next episode in this pericope), etc. Witherington notes wryly: "One might say that the Jesus movement and the Pharisaic movement were both holiness movements, but they disagreed on the proper approach to creating a holy people of God."[10] For the one, the commandments of God took priority; for the other, traditions of men. One undertook to obey God's word (morality from "inside"); the other followed the imposition of manmade rules (a piety from "outside"). No amount of punctilious keeping of manmade canons finds acceptability before God; what God desires is obedience to his mandates. Ritualism (i.e., following human rules) without righteousness (i.e., following divine commandments), and assuming that the former without the latter constitutes moral purity acceptable to God is the essence of hypocrisy. Likewise, moral impurity is not an issue of what contaminates from the outside, but rather what defiles from the inside: the sinful thoughts and deeds of a person (see below). In the Pharisees' tradition-keeping there was an earnest piety (keeping manmade rules), but a negligence of morality (keeping God's word).

10.1.2 Sinful thoughts and deeds are what render a person impure, not the violation of rules of ritual.

That this is not merely a discussion of food laws is emphasized in 7:4, 13 ("there are many other things" and "[a]nd you do many similar things"). At stake is the idea of what acceptability before God constitutes. In 7:14–15, Jesus proceeds to take a public stand on the fundamental issue of moral purity, a topic reaching farther than the scribal traditions regarding handwashing, which is only a minor facet of the whole concept of defilement by things that enter into the body (detailed in Lev 11 in terms of clean and unclean foods). The debate is thus carried to a higher level, as Jesus here explains the basic principle of moral impurity: defilement is not by external contact ("outside," 7:15, 18), but stems from an internal source ("inside," 7:21, 23). It is not what goes *into* the person that renders one unacceptable to God, but the sin that comes *out from* the person (from the "heart," 7:6. 19, 21).

The seemingly *absolute* negation-contrast construction in 7:15 (οὐδέν . . . ἀλλά; *ouden . . . alla*; "nothing . . . but") can be rendered in a more *relative* sense in Semitic contexts: "not so much . . . as," rather than the absolute "nothing [at all] . . . but [only]."[11]

---

10. Witherington, *Gospel of Mark*, 227.

11. France, *Gospel of Mark*, 289; and Stein, *Mark*, 344. Holmén notes that "[a]s a Semitic idiom, the formula 'not A, but B' (οὐ . . . ἀλλά, *ou . . . alla*) can be rendered 'not so much A, but rather B.'" Thus 7:15 does not intend to abolish food or cultic laws, any more than OT commands seek to nullify the sacrificial cultus (Isa 1:11–17; Jer 7:22–23; Hos 6:6; Amos 5:21–27; etc.). All of these only relativize the ritual aspect, while emphasizing the importance of the moral aspect. It "depreciates rather than abrogates" the issue of rituals dealt with (Holmén, *Jesus and Jewish Covenant*, 240–41; see Holmén's references to standard Hebrew grammars for more details). Note also Jesus' dialogue with the scribe in Mark 12:28–34, where the former assents to the declaration of the latter that keeping the foremost commandments (the moral aspect of the Mosaic Law) is "greater" than all the offerings and sacrifices (the ritual aspect of the

This verse may therefore be paraphrased: "A person is *not so much* defiled by what enters him from outside *as* by what comes from within." Thus, food and cultic laws that provide for *ritual* purity are not necessarily being abrogated by Jesus, but only relativized, in light of the importance of maintaining *moral* purity.[12] This would sustain the distinction between "ritual impurity" and "moral impurity" made in the Torah. The former is not necessarily sinful (unless intentionally violated) or unavoidable, but is, at least to some extent, a reflection of the (sinful) human condition: menstruation, genital discharge, parturition, contact with the dead during burial, skin diseases, etc. (Lev 12:1—15:33; Num 19:11–22). Ritual purity is thus concerned with the status/position of the person with regard to the sacred (the tabernacle and temple, particularly), and not with one's moral standing before God. Jesus, in Mark 7:14–23, while recognizing ritual purity, prioritizes moral purity as what constituted one's acceptability before God.[13] In the translation of 7:19 provided (see above), the last phrase, "cleansing all foods," is considered to be part of Jesus' question, as the punctuation in the Greek indicates[14]: this could be understood as Jesus declaring (reaffirming?) that all foods are morally clean. Things that go in from the outside cannot defile *morally* (7:18; they conceivably could defile *ritually*). And as those foods do not go into man's heart, they, being eliminated, are, for all practical purposes, "clean" morally, even if they are unclean ritually (7:19b).[15] On the other hand, things that come out from the "inside" (or the "heart," i.e., from the person himself or herself and not from an external source) are what morally defile a person (7:20).[16] Thus, the priority of moral purity (allegiance to God's standard) over mere piety (allegiance to human tradition) is sustained.

A list of attitudes and actions that constitute sin (i.e., moral impurity, and thus unacceptable to God) follows in the vice list of 7:21–22.[17] It is these—sourced in the person—that cause moral impurity, not food or anything else from the outside that does

Mosaic Law). Not that one can be neglected for the other, but there are differences in, and gradations of, importance between them. It must be emphasized that Jesus *does* agree with the need for offerings (see 1:44 where he urges the healed leper to make an offering in compliance with Mosaic Law).

12. Marcus, *Mark*, 453; Rudolph, "Jesus and the Food Laws," 298.

13. Rudolph, "Jesus and the Food Laws," 295–97.

14. The Greek text utilized in this commentary is Aland et al., *Greek New Testament*.

15. Physiologically and anatomically, that is reasonable, for the gastrointestinal tract is technically "outside" the body and, for that reason, it is unsterile: puncturing of the intestines by trauma can cause a lethal peritonitis when bacteria invade the body from the *outside* (i.e., from the lumen of the gastrointestinal tract into the abdominal cavity).

16. "Only now [in the text, that is] does it become clear that the inside of people is represented as having two different circuits, namely, the stomach into which the food goes, and the heart from which thoughts and actions arise. What enters people from the outside (v. 15) refers to the food they eat, and what comes out of people refers to their conduct; so the thesis proposed in these sayings is that human defilement is not caused by food but by evil actions" (van Iersel, *Mark*, 244). In other words, the source of impurity is not external to oneself. By that same token, neither is purity. Neither moral purity nor impurity can be "caught" from the outside—they are intrinsic to a person.

17. Twelve evils are noted with headings on either side ("evil ideas," 7:21; and "evil things," 7:23). The dozen elements are divided into six plural items (repeatable actions) and six singular items (character traits) (Boring, *Mark*, 204–5).

not impinge upon the "heart." The vices listed exemplify those thoughts and deeds that evidence a lack of conformity to the standards of God's word. Jesus thus intensifies the demand for moral purity, far beyond what the Pharisees exhorted in terms of cultic or ritual purity and adherence to manmade laws. In other words, defilement results from sin (lack of conformity to God's word) that originates from "inside" a person, not from "outside" (through foods and contact and such). The counter-principle is that what comes from the "inside" of a person that is in conformity to God's word is what makes one morally pure.[18] In sum, the error of observance of human rituals without compliance to divine morals is the thrust of this episode. Unfortunately, it appears that the disciples of Jesus also failed to understand this important principle. Their discernment is rudimentary and sorely lacking, inviting Jesus' rather frustrated questions in 7:18–19.

While the elements of "in-sourced" sin (as opposed to "out-sourced" contamination) are listed in 7:21–23, the next episode of this pericope depicts a true disciple that *does* understand what is required of her. The account involves a Gentile woman, and demonstrates how she is morally acceptable before God and wins Jesus' approval.

10.2 Mark 7:24–30

THEOLOGICAL FOCUS 10.2

10.2 Acceptability before God comes with faith in God that produces obedience to his word (7:24–30).

Section Summary 10.2: The Syrophoenician woman, a Gentile and the mother of a girl with an unclean spirit, is hardly one whom the Pharisees would recognize as acceptable before God: her external qualifications for purity are non-existent. But she, because of her faith that leads to obedience to Jesus, becomes acceptable to God—she is depicted as a disciple!

TRANSLATION 10.2

7:24 *And from there, He rose and went away into the region of Tyre. And when He came into a house, He wanted no one to know, and He was not able to escape notice.*

7:25 *But hearing of Him, a woman, whose little daughter had an unclean spirit, immediately came and fell at His feet.*

7:26 *And the woman was a Gentile, a Syrophoenician by race. And she was asking Him to cast out the demon from her daughter.*

7:27 *And He was saying to her, "First let the children be satisfied, for it is not good to take bread from the children and throw to the dogs."*

---

18. It will be evident by now that the distinction being made in the pericope is not between attitude and action ("internal" and "external" as commonly understood in contemporary culture), but between what comes from within the person (sourced from "inside"/"heart": thoughts and deeds that determine *moral* purity) as opposed to what comes from without the person (sourced from "outside": foods and other external items that deal with *ritual* purity/piety).

7:28   *But she answered and said to Him, "Lord, even the dogs under the table eat from the crumbs of the children."*

7:29   *And He said to her, "Because of this word, go; the demon has gone out from your daughter."*

7:30   *And going away into her home, she found the child lying upon the bed; and the demon had gone out.*

NOTES 10.2

10.2   *Acceptability before God comes with faith in God that produces obedience to his word.*

The question of purity in the previous pericope has great relevance for the remainder of Mark 7. What God calls morally pure is not equivalent to the Pharisees' ritual purity criteria, which would normally exclude Gentiles. Therefore, in demonstration of the declaration that rituality does not render one acceptable to God, and that only morality does, Jesus provides an exhibition of the integration of *unclean* Gentiles into the new community of God's kingdom—the unified fellowship of disciples. A Syrophoenician woman is implicitly canvassed into the company of disciples; she is found to be acceptable before God, thus morally pure, despite her ritual impurity (see below).

The choice of this episode is appropriate, set outside Jewish lands and with the main character a Gentile woman.[19] "Ritual impurity" is writ large all over the incident. Following on the heels of the radical assertions of Jesus in 7:1–23 deprecating the following of rules of piety and ritual without adherence to divine commands, this healing of the Gentile woman's daughter who has an unclean spirit is perfectly positioned to affirm the criteria of moral purity and acceptability before God. In more than one way, this woman, the protagonist of this story, is an unlikely candidate to be the disciple she proves herself to be: she is a woman, a Gentile, and mother of one with a spirit explicitly labeled "unclean."[20] The comparison with another "disciple," the woman with the hemorrhage (7:24–30), shows that Mark's intention is to depict this Gentile woman also as a "disciple."

---

19. That these subsequent episodes occur in Gentile territory is evidenced by several elements. Geographically, 7:24 has Jesus move north into Phoenicia, thence through Sidon to Decapolis (7:31), till he returns to the unidentifiable Dalmanutha in 8:10 (it is probably Jewish, judging by the arrival of the Pharisees in 8:11), and moves on to Bethsaida (8:22), thus concluding the Galilee section (Act I) of the Gospel. Other telltale elements include the ethnicity of the woman in 7:26 and the discussion of Gentile "dogs" (7:27–28). Notice also the reference to "baskets" in 8:8 using the word σπυρίδες, *spyrides*, as opposed to the specifically Jewish term κόφινοι, *kophinoi* (6:43; see below) (France, *Gospel of Mark*, 294–95).

20. Josephus accused the Tyrians of being "most of all" bearing "ill disposition" towards the Jews (*Ag. Ap.* 1.13; *Ant.* 14.313–22; *J. W.* 2.478). The powerful urban center that Tyre was dominated northern Galilee economically. Boring observes that the poor farmers of Galilee saw the product of their labors end up as bread on the table of the wealthier Tyrians. "'Bread' was thus a potent economic symbol as well as having deep theological overtones" (*Mark*, 209).

MARK 7:24–30	MARK 5:21–43
"Unclean" woman (7:25)	Unclean woman (because of her condition)
ἀκούσασα γυνὴ περὶ αὐτοῦ . . . (7:25)	γυνὴ . . . ἀκούσασα περὶ τοῦ Ἰησοῦ (5:25, 27)
(akousasa gynē peri autou)	(gynē . . . akousasa peri tou Iēsou)
("hearing of Him, a woman . . .")	("woman . . . hearing about Jesus")
She falls (προσπίπτω, prospiptō) at Jesus' feet (7:25)	She falls (προσπίπτω) before Jesus (5:33)
Has a daughter (7:26, 29)	Is called "daughter" (5:34)
Has implicit faith and is commended (7:29)	Demonstrates faith and is commended (5:34)
Commanded to go (ὕπαγε, hypage) (7:29)	Commanded to go (ὕπαγε) (5:34)

The challenge to this woman from Jesus (7:27) appears to be a test, akin to Jesus' asking the disciples what resources they have available to feed a multitude (6:37), or to his sending them out on a stormy voyage (6:45–52).[21] Whereas the disciples fail both times, this woman passes the test magnificently—a remarkable contrast between the disciples' incomprehension about "bread" (6:51) and this one's perspicacity in turning the "bread motif" to advantage in her dialogue with Jesus. Her first directly quoted word is "Lord" (7:28). That in itself is striking! Outside of Scripture citations and Jesus' own words, this is the only time a human addresses Jesus as "Lord" in the entire Gospel of Mark. The narrator accentuates this address by introducing it with the formula ἡ δὲ ἀπεκρίθη καὶ λέγει αὐτῷ (hē de apekrithē kai legei autō, "but she answered and said to Him," 7:28). Of the seventeen times that the two verbs "answer" and "say" occur together in Mark to introduce a speaker's statement, this is the only instance where both are in the indicative mood. In every other case, one member of the pair is in the participial form. This is, then, a significant utterance from an unusually insightful woman—she is a disciple! She effectively counters Jesus' claim to Jewish chronological priority for his ministry ("first," 7:27), asserting that dogs eat crumbs *during* the meal for the children; she claims to deserve the leftovers *even now*, even as the children are being fed.[22] Moreover, the relation between bread and the "overflowing" crumbs hints at the loaves and leftovers of the first feeding miracle and, as well, anticipates the next such miracle in the following pericope.[23] All of this is noteworthy, coming from

21. One could see this as being ironic: "It is . . . to be read as a bit of tongue-in-cheek. . . . It is peirastic irony, . . . a form of verbal challenge intended to test the other's response. It may in fact declare the opposite of the speaker's actual intention" (Camery-Hoggatt, *Irony in Mark's Gospel*, 150–51).

22. Dogs in the Ancient Near East were disdained as scavengers eating unclean food, and were not considered beloved pets. Rabbinic literature used "dog" for those unlearned in Scripture, the ungodly, and the Gentiles (as, perhaps, in *m. Ned.* 4.3 and *m. Bek.* 5.6). Also see 1 Sam 17:43; 2 Sam 9:8; 16:9; 1 Kgs 14:11; 16:4; 21:24; 2 Kgs 9:36; Ps 22:16. Yet the diminutive κυνάριον, kynarion, employed by Jesus could refer to house pets common among Greeks and Romans; thus use of the term may not be entirely derogatory. See Collins, *Mark*, 367; Dowd, *Reading Mark*, 77.

23. In the feeding of the 5,000, Jesus "took . . . bread" (6:41); and the crowd "ate" and were "satisfied" (6:42). In this account of the Syrophoenician woman, the same words recur: "satisfied" (7:27); not good to "take . . . bread" (7:27); and the dogs "eat" (7:28). Subsequently, in the feeding of the 4,000, Jesus again "takes" "bread" (8:6), and the crowd "eats" and are "satisfied" (8:4, 8). While in the two feeding miracles, the male, Jewish disciples fail to understand anything about Jesus' ability to provide bread, this female, Gentile mother of a child with an unclean spirit clearly gets it (Rhoads, "Jesus and the Syrophoenician Woman," 363).

a Gentile woman with a family member having an unclean spirit—she is one with all strikes against her! While this woman externally seems utterly reproachable (in the Pharisaic mind, that is), internally, it will be seen, she is quite remarkable—her heart is faith-filled, therefore she is acceptable before God.

Jesus commendation of the woman's faith is significant: "Because of this word [λόγος, logos] . . ." (7:29). One would expect Jesus to say here, to the woman, "Because of your *faith* . . . ." But essentially, that *is* what he says to the woman, for what proceeds from the heart of this Gentile woman is the λόγος of faith. One will also have noticed that in the previous pericope the Pharisees are excoriated for their annulment of τὸν λόγον τοῦ θεοῦ (*ton logon tou theou*, "the word of God," 7:13; and the similar "commandment of God" in 7:8, 9). But here a woman produces an acceptable λόγος. Not only does she demonstrate a response of faith, she also provides a response of obedience to Jesus' command to go: the woman duly goes back home, after the only time Jesus is said to have healed from a distance without any direct word to the afflicted, and without any specific action pertaining to exorcism—"telemedicine"! Furthermore, this is one of those few times that the healing occurs without a witness, and yet, without any confirmation of the healing having taken place, the woman returns home, with faith, in obedience to Jesus' command, "Go!" (7:29). Her obedience is even one grade higher than that of her counterpart, the woman with the hemorrhage. That one obeyed and departed, but *after* evidence of healing was obtained (5:29, 34). This woman, on the other hand, departs as Jesus instructed, without any proof that the healing of her daughter had been accomplished. She, apparently, has no trouble believing the word of Jesus and obeying—simply because it is Jesus's word—unlike most others in the Gospel, and, especially, the Twelve. She has faith; she obeys. And hers, therefore, is a good "word" that demonstrates what is "inside," despite her ritual unacceptability "outside." She, who responds to Jesus with faith and obedience, is acceptable before God—not based upon any quality or criterion externally applied. This woman is a model disciple!

SERMON FOCUS AND OUTLINES

THEOLOGICAL FOCUS OF PERICOPE 10 FOR PREACHING

10   Faith that produces obedience, not hypocritical allegiance to manmade rules, renders the disciple morally acceptable to God (7:1–30).

Mark 6:32–56 introduced the motif of "bread," which is carried forward in this pericope and the next. The issue of bread brings to the fore the Pharisaical concern for ritual purity—especially their adherence to human rules. Jesus' concern, on the other hand, is for moral purity, which is sourced within a person, not from the outside (foods and other items that are the issue of ritual purity). Such a moral purity that Jesus demands is equivalent to faith evidenced in obedience to God's word. The Syrophoenician woman, a most unlikely candidate for being ritually pure, is commended by Jesus and is found acceptable (morally pure) before God because of her faith and her response of obedience.[24]

24. Mark's concern, it must be remembered, is not the faith of soteriology, but the continuing faith of discipleship.

Discipleship is thus to be characterized by a clear grasp of what constitutes acceptability in the eyes of God: morality, not rituality. Legalism is clearly negated here, as well as the cavalier judgment of others based upon superficialities and whether they heed manmade prescriptions and proscriptions. In the new community of God's people, God's approbation is upon those who have faith in him and seek to adhere to his word, not upon those who construct a façade of piety and attempt to burden others with injunctions and decrees that do not come from God and his word.[25]

The sermon on 3:7–35 (Pericope 4) dealt with obedience to the will of God being a criterion for "insidership." This sermon will be different, reflecting the focus of the pericope against legalism. While the pericope does not explicitly expound on it, the causes of legalism—ego, self-sufficiency, a diminution of God's high standard, an improper understanding of depravity, etc.—may be worth exploring.[26]

POSSIBLE PREACHING OUTLINES FOR PERICOPE 10

I. PHARISEE: Misunderstanding that rituality renders one morally acceptable before God*
    The Pharisees and their hypocrisy: 7:1–15, rituality without morality
    The disciples and their incomprehension: 7:17–23, Jesus' explanation of what is morally acceptable to God
    Move-to-Relevance: legalistic hypocrisies engaged in today; misunderstanding of what God finds acceptable

II. WOMAN: Faith in Jesus that produces obedience to him renders her acceptable before God
    The Syrophoenician woman and her acceptability before God: 7:24–30, the foil to the Pharisees

III. DISCIPLE: *Be a loyalist, not a legalist!* [†]
    How we can ward off the dangers of legalism

[†] By "loyalist" is meant the contrary of "legalist." The latter adheres to manmade rules of piety and ritual, and assumes that that is sufficient for moral acceptability before God. The former has allegiance to God—faith in him producing obedience to his word.

25. While "faith" in this pericope is not necessarily salvific faith (neither is "acceptability before God" dealing with salvation), conceivably one could (perhaps one *should*) present the gospel and invite unbelievers to trust Christ in this sermon. I firmly believe that sermons are primarily for those who constitute the community of God, i.e., believers—those who have already placed their trust in Jesus Christ as their Savior. Thus, preaching is one of the divinely ordained and empowered means for growing believers into Christlikeness. That does not preclude presenting the gospel in the gathering of the church, as could/should be done in a sermon on this pericope. Hermeneutically, a gospel presentation might work well with this pericope; however, this must be done respecting the overall trajectory of Mark developing various facets of discipleship. That is to say, while the gospel could be presented, what the particular pericope means for one already walking with Christ must also be exposited.

26. I might remark here that no homiletical imperative can be obeyed without the aid of the Holy Spirit—to assume that it is possible is only to fall into legalism again (rule-keeping). Homiletical imperatives are not intended to be means of self-improvement by one's own power and one's own efforts for one's own glory (= legalism). Rather, they point to the human-responsibility facet of Christian life, without diminishing the sovereign role of God in sanctification or denying the importance of relying on divine power for growth. One obeys God, fully aware of one's fallibility, fully reliant on the power of the Holy Spirit, fully conscious of the ultimate goal—God's glory.

Another option:

I. RITUALITY: Externals—handwashing, keeping manmade rules, Jewishness, etc.

The Pharisees and their standards: 7:1–15

The "unclean" Syrophoenician woman with a daughter possessed by an unclean spirit: 7:24–25

Move-to-Relevance: Our present-day legalistic misunderstandings of what God finds acceptable

II. MORALITY: Faithful obedience

Jesus' explanation of what is acceptable to God: 7:17–23

The Syrophoenician woman's example: 7:24–30

III. *Go for morals, not rituals!*

How we can cultivate an environment that is not legalistic

This sermon could serve as a warning to the blasé disciples that we often become, in any culture. Having been Christians for a while, and having developed in our own local Christian communities what are "acceptable Christian practices," there is often a tendency to coalesce these "acceptable Christian practices" with "acceptability before God"—the equation of rituality with morality, as the Pharisees did. The two are not the same. Legalistic rituality may run the gamut of issues: whether or not to homeschool, kinds of clothing to wear and not wear, the advisability of reading Harry Potter (and/or of seeing the movies), the consumption of alcohol, Republican/Democrat allegiance, stance on the death penalty, attitude to war, and so on and so forth (your legalisms *du jour*). The dangerous trap is that these manmade rulings often become more important criteria of acceptability before God than do the dictates of God's word—the same hole the Pharisees had fallen into. Therefore, the sermon on this pericope may be a good occasion to (re)evaluate church praxis and custom. Are we using our own rules and criteria to gauge the discipleship status of another? How can we get back to the basics of faith that produces obedience—God's criterion for acceptability? A periodic "physical" for the body of Christ to diagnose legalism (and excise it) is good preventive medicine for optimum spiritual health.

PERICOPE 11

Daily Bread

Mark 7:31—8:26

[Deaf-Mute Healed; Four Thousand Fed; Blind Man Healed in Stages]

REVIEW, SUMMARY, PREVIEW

Review of Pericope 10: Mark 7:1–30 demonstrates the importance of faith that produces obedience, the essential criterion for acceptability before God.

Summary of Pericope 11: In 7:31—8:26, the central feeding miracle is surrounded by two miracles of perception—the healing of the deaf and dumb man and the two-stage healing of the blind man. The feeding miracle emphasizes the importance of the disciple's trust in Jesus' person as one who is able to provide for life's daily needs. The two perception miracles stress the importance of the disciple's discernment of Jesus' person (and all that that entails) for the walk of discipleship, and foreshadow the need for the disciple to accept Jesus' mission (the thrust of Act II).

Preview of Pericope 12: The next pericope (8:27—9:13), providing a snapshot of future glory, offers the disciple the encouragement to continue following Jesus in his suffering mission.

11   Mark 7:31–8:26

THEOLOGICAL FOCUS OF PERICOPE 11
11 **Trust in God for the provision of life's daily needs, grounded in a discernment of the person of Jesus, is a critical facet of discipleship (7:31—8:26).**
11.1   God can be trusted for the provision of life's daily needs (8:1–21).
11.1.1   Jesus has the power to provide for disciples' daily needs.

> 11.1.2   Disciples trust Jesus' ability to provide for life's daily needs.
>
> 11.2   A discernment of Jesus' person is essential for the walk of discipleship (7:31–37;
> 8:22–26)

OVERVIEW

THIS FINAL PERICOPE OF Act I (1:1—8:21), the Galilean phase of the Gospel, apparently begins in Gentile land with the healing of a deaf mute. It ends with another feeding miracle that is followed by a boat journey. A coda for the act (or, better, the first half of an *inclusio* that brackets Act II; see the Introduction) describes the healing of a blind man in Bethsaida (8:22–26). Jesus and his cohort are here beginning the decisive move away from Galilee.

The three sections of this pericope demonstrate the continued lack of discernment on the part of Jesus' disciples, a constant theme in Act I: they were shown to be as uncomprehending as the crowds in their approach to Jesus in 1:21–45; they were accused by Jesus of not understanding his parables in 4:1–34; they were fearful and faithless in 4:35–41; they were skeptical in 5:31 and 6:32–44, fearful and faithless again in 6:45–56; they continued to lack understanding in 7:1–23; and are "still" (8:17, 21) lacking discernment here in 8:1–21. This last depiction of the disciples' obtuseness is bracketed between two miracles of perception: a deaf and mute man is healed (7:31–37), and the sight of a blind man is restored (8:22–26). The structure further emphasizes the disciples' "deafness" and "blindness," and the need for disciples to discern the person of Jesus and all that that entails, including his power.

A   Jesus heals deaf ears with saliva (7:31–37)
   B   Second feeding miracle and its explanation (8:1–21)
A'   Jesus heals blind eyes with saliva (8:22–26)

All hope is not lost for the disciples, though. They continue to be subjects of Jesus' attention and education program in Act II, the middle ("on the way") portion of the Gospel (8:27—10:45); in particular, Jesus' suffering mission is outlined. The blindness of the disciples, unlike that of the religious leaders, is potentially curable as this final pericope of Act I depicts.[1]

For the purposes of this commentary, 7:31–37 and 8:22–26 will be considered together as the second part of this pericope (i.e., Pericope 11.2). While literarily, 8:22–26 is one of the outer brackets of Act II, rhetorically and homiletically it is more convenient to deal with it in conjunction with the other miracle of perception in this pericope, 7:31–37.

---

1. France, *Gospel of Mark*, 310.

11.1 Mark 8:1–21

Section Summary 11.1: Coming to the end of Act I, the issue of the discernment of Jesus' person by the disciples takes center stage, especially in 8:13–21. They fail again to demonstrate any understanding, despite the two feeding miracles they have just witnessed. Instead, their sarcastic comments and naïve discussions reveal their incomprehension, and they end up looking more and more like "outsiders," even to the point of having hardened hearts.

TRANSLATION 11.1

8:1   *In those days, when there was again a large crowd, and they did not have anything to eat, He summoned his disciples, [and] said to them,*

8:2   *"I have compassion on the crowd, because they have remained with Me for three days already and do not have anything to eat.*

8:3   *And if I send them away fasting to their houses, they will faint on the way; and some of them have come from afar."*

8:4   *And His disciples answered Him, "From where will anyone be able to satisfy these with bread, here in a wilderness?"*

8:5   *And He asked them, "How much bread do you have?" And they said, "Seven [loaves]."*

8:6   *And He directed the crowd to sit on the ground; and taking the seven [loaves of] bread, He gave thanks, broke, and gave to His disciples to set before [the crowd], and they set [it] before the crowd.*

8:7   *And they had a few fish; and blessing them, He told [the disciples] to set these before [the crowd] as well.*

8:8   *And they ate and they were satisfied, and they picked up seven large baskets of fragments left over.*

8:9   *And there were about four thousand. And He sent them away.*

8:10   *And immediately, getting into the boat with His disciples, He came into the district of Dalmanutha.*

8:11   *And the Pharisees came out and began to argue with Him, seeking from Him a sign from heaven, testing Him.*

8:12   *And sighing deeply in His spirit, He said, "Why does this generation seek a sign? Truly I say to you, no sign will be given to this generation."*

8:13   *And leaving them, He again got into [a boat] and went away to the other side.*

8:14   *And they forgot to take bread and, except for one [loaf of] bread, they did not have [any] with themselves in the boat.*

8:15   And He was ordering them, saying, "See, watch out for the yeast of the Pharisees and the yeast of Herod."

8:16   And they began discussing with one another that they did not have bread.

8:17   And noticing, He said to them, "Why are you discussing that you do not have bread? Do you still not perceive or understand? Do you have your heart hardened?

8:18   Having eyes, do you not see? And having ears, do you not hear? And do you not remember—

8:19   when I broke the five [loaves of] bread for the five thousand, how many baskets full of fragments did you pick up?" They said to Him, "Twelve."

8:20   When I broke the seven for the four thousand, how many large baskets full of fragments did you pick up?" And they said, "Seven."

8:21   And He was saying to them, "Do you still not understand?"

NOTES 11.1

11.1.1   Jesus has the power to provide for disciples' daily needs.

The second feeding miracle is likely to have been performed in Gentile land, unlike the Jewish location of the first (6:32–44), for the following reasons: location in the movement of the narrative, coming after two Gentile healings (7:24, 31); extension of messianic blessings to the Gentiles ("crumbs" to the "dogs," 7:28); 8:8 has a different term for basket (σπυρίς, *spyris*) than what was used in 6:43 (κόφινος, *kophinos*, a more specifically Jewish term)[2]; the seven loaves of bread and seven baskets of leftovers may be a "Gentile" number (Acts 6 describes seven Hellenistic deacons)[3]; attenuation of Exodus and Psalm echoes in Mark 8 (Mark 6 has "sheep without a shepherd"); the use of εὐχαριστήσας (*eucharistēsas*, "he gave thanks") in 8:6[4]; the crowds came ἀπὸ μακρόθεν (*apo makrothen*, "from afar," 8:3), a phrase often referring to Gentile foreigners or lands.[5]

2. This distinction between the two kinds of baskets is also maintained in 8:19, 20. See Donahue and Harrington, *Gospel of Mark*, 245. Juvenal (*Sat.* 3.14; 6.542) apparently recognized this particularity of language.

3. Other non-Jewish significances of seven include the number of Noachic commands binding on all human beings, enumerated as seven (Gen 9:4–7 and Acts 15:19–20; *Jub.* 7.20; *b. 'Abod. Zar.* 2b); the seven Gentile nations of Canaan (Deut 7:1; Acts 13:19); the Septuagint is called "LXX" (= 70), suggesting it was for all nations, for the world was seen to comprise seventy nations (Gen 10; *1 En.* 89:59; 90:22–25; *Tg. Ps.-J.* on Deut 32:8); and Luke has seventy apostles sent to the Gentiles (10:1, 17). As well, "four" (the crowd numbering four thousand) may stand for the four corners of the universe or even for the four laws Gentiles must obey: Lev 17:8, 10–13; and 18:26. On the other hand, the twelve apostles sent to Israel (Luke 9:1–6), and the five loaves (the Pentateuch?) and twelve baskets of leftovers in the first feeding miracle (Mark 6:43) may all, in turn, have Jewish connotations.

4. The use of εὐλογέω (*eulogeō*, "bless") in 6:41 is a more formal pronouncement of Jewish blessing. While Mark does have Jesus use εὐλογέω in 8:7 for the blessing of the fish, it will be noticed that the blessing was *of* the fish, not *for* the fish, as it would have been in Judaism. On the other hand, in the blessing rendered in 6:41, Jesus prefaces the action with a look to heaven: *God* is being blessed in good Jewish fashion, not the *food*.

5. See Deut 28:49; 2 Chr 6:32; Isa 60:4; Jer 4:16; 46:27; Ezek 23:40; Hab 1:8 LXX; Acts 2:39; 22:21; Eph 2:13, 17; etc. To come from the Gentile side of the lake is not literally a passage of enough distance to be

While there are similarities in the two feeding miracles of Mark 6 and 8,[6] there are significant differences, besides the Jew-Gentile distinction. The duration of the crowd's sojourn in the wilderness appears to have been much longer in 8:2 (three days) than in 6:35, where only the lateness of the hour is of concern. The disciples, overall, play a more passive role in Mark 8 (Jesus calls them in 8:1, whereas they approach him, taking the initiative, in 6:35); neither is there any pointed, direct command from Jesus to the disciples in Mark 8 to the effect that *they* give the crowd to eat (as in 6:37). Also of note is that in the first feeding miracle the mention of Jesus' compassion is expressly directed to the crowds' "shepherdlessness" and, in response, he promptly begins teaching them (6:34). Here his compassion, explicitly admitted by Jesus himself (8:2), is for their hunger and lack of food. Thus, while the first feeding miracle focuses on the disciples' ability and empowerment to provide for the "sheep," in the second feeding miracle the thrust is on whether Jesus can provide at all for the daily needs of his people. This episode, linked with the disciples' later consternation regarding the (in)sufficiency of a single loaf for all (twelve) of them in the boat (8:14–16), emphasizes Jesus' provision for the routine demands of life. But do the disciples hear and see, and are their ears (and mouths) and eyes open? Have they learned from the past that Jesus can indeed provide? Unfortunately, the answer appears to be in the negative.

The phrasing of the disciples' question in 8:4 is sarcastic: "From where will *anyone* be able to satisfy these with bread here in a wilderness?" Surely they should know better. Of course Jesus can provide. Had he not already done so once? And he will do so again: he does "satisfy" the crowd of four thousand (8:8), just as he satisfied the earlier crowd of five thousand (6:42). The disciples, in other words, have learned nothing from the previous miracle about Jesus' ability to provide for the needs of his people. Indeed, the disciples' ears have not heard, and their mouths—when they open them—remain "dumb": they are only capable of uttering an impertinent remark and conducting a naïve discussion about the impossibility of feeding a crowd or even a boatful of disciples with a few loaves (see below). Of course, as far as sight goes, they had been quite consistently blind all along! Their discernment of Jesus, however, is now at an abysmal low. And Jesus' reply in 8:1, using the exact wording of the question he had used in 6:38 ("How much bread do you have?"), resounds with a tone of

---

labeled as being "afar." The phrase is more likely idiomatic for Gentiles, the "distanced ones." In addition, several of the words in 8:1–10 occur only once in this Gospel (προσμένω, *prosmenō*, "remain with," 8:2; νῆστις, *nēstis*, "fasting," 8:3; ἐκλύω, *ekluō*, "faint," 8:3; ἐρημία, *erēmia*, "wilderness," 8:4; περισσεύμα, *perisseuma*, "left over," 8:8; σπυρίς, *spyris*, "large basket," 8:8), suggesting the newness of what is being undertaken. Also see Iverson, *Gentiles in the Gospel*, 67–69.

6. The similarities between the two feedings in Mark 6 and 8 are considerable: both occur in wilderness-like areas (ἔρημος, *erēmos*, 6:35; and ἐρημία, *erēmia*, 8:4); in both, the disciples are skeptical (6:37; 8:4); Jesus asks them the identical question on both occasions (πόσους ἔχετε ἄρτους; *posous echete artous?*, "How much bread do you have?," 6:38; 8:5); the crowd is made to sit (6:39; 8:6); bread and fish are on the menu (6:38, 41; 8:7), which the disciples distribute after Jesus gives thanks (6:41; 8:6); the crowd eats and is satisfied (6:42; 8:8); there are leftovers (6:43; 8:9); the crowd is enumerated (6:44; 8:9); and they are dismissed as a boat journey commences (6:45; 8:9–10).

frustration and resignation: "Here we go again!"[7] One can almost hear the weariness in Jesus' voice as he addresses those deaf, dumb, and blind disciples.

In fact, the disciples, it turns out, are no better than the Pharisees. The interrogation by the latter to receive a "sign" from Jesus, Mark informs us in 8:11, is simply to test Jesus, rather than to make any attempt to learn about him (πειράζω, *peirazō*, "test"; in Mark, the term always has Satan or the antagonistic Jewish religious leaders as its agents: 1:13; 8:11; 10:2; 12:15). In response, Jesus flatly refuses to accede to their demand for a sign, effectively terminating his dialogue with the religious hierarchy. This "generation" has had all it would get from Jesus, yet they remain without discernment.[8] Sadly, this undiscerning company included the disciples, too. With the proximity of two immense feeding miracles right behind them, even the positively inclined disciples do not understand. How would the negatively inclined Pharisees benefit from signs? They have already seen signs aplenty (2:1–12; 3:1–6; etc.). There will be no more, Jesus declares; both disciples and Pharisees should have, by now, discerned his person and been convinced of his power.

11.1.2   *Disciples trust Jesus' ability to provide for life's daily needs.*[9]

The juxtaposition of the dialogue with the Pharisees and the conversation with the disciples (just as in 7:1–20, where both parties have sequential discussions with Jesus) portrays the latter in no better—maybe even worse—light than the religious leaders. The two major boat journeys described thus far in Mark have documented their downward spiral: in the first (4:35–41, to "the other side"), their lack of faith and understanding of the person of Jesus (particularly, his power over nature) was reprehensible; in the second (6:45–52, also to "the other side"), their incomprehension and hardness of heart were explicitly condemned; and in this third trip (8:14–21, a return voyage), that accusation is repeated.

The irony of the disciples fretting over the single loaf they are traveling with is pungent (8:13–16). The mathematical ratio of one loaf for twelve is a far more plausible proposition for provision than the equation of five loaves for five thousand or seven for four thousand. Indeed, this "aside" about the one single loaf that they have with them (8:14) might even be a thinly disguised allusion to that *one* bread Jesus, himself, who is with them: the next occurrence of ἄρτος (*artos*) in the Gospel is the announcement

---

7. France, *Gospel of Mark*, 308.

8. The association between tempting God (8:11) and "this generation" (8:12) points to the collocation of these elements in Ps 95:8–11. "Generation" is mostly negative in Mark (8:38; 9:19); rabbinical understanding of "generation" included the evil ones of Noah's day (Gen 7:1; *Gen. Rab.* 31.1), as well as those who experienced the exodus firsthand in the wilderness (Deut 32:5). Both were unworthy to share in the world to come (*m. Sanh.* 11.2–3). See van Iersel, *Mark*, 262; Stein, *Mark*, 376–77.

9. This theological subfocus is a statement in the positive of what is negatively depicted in the text by the Twelve.

that the "bread" is his body (14:22).[10] "[T]hey worry about food even though *the* one bread is with them in the boat."[11]

Jesus then warns them about the yeast of the Pharisees and Herodians. "Yeast" is usually negative in connotation, proscribed as it was in the Torah from the houses of the Israelites during Passover (Exod 12:15; 13:3–7; Deut 16:3–4). Scripture is generally disparaging about this kitchen item, a metaphor for evil human inclinations (see for e.g., Lev 2:11; Luke 12:1; 1 Cor 5:6–8; Gal 5:9). In this case, the "yeast" of the Pharisees and of Herod is a recalcitrant denial of the truth and a hardened unbelief in Jesus, reflected in their response to him throughout Act I, and in the demand for signs here. And sadly, the disciples are devouring that "yeast," as they display their own lack of discernment of Jesus' person (particularly, here, his power to provide).

While no signs are going to be offered to the Pharisees (Mark 8:12), the disciples have recently been shown at least two (the exorcism of the Syrophoenican woman's daughter and the healing of a deaf mute; 7:24–30 and 31–37, respectively), and probably more. Yet they have now come to resemble "outsiders," members of an unbelieving "generation." As in Mark 4:12, Isaiah 6:9–10 is repeated in Mark 8:18 (also see Ps 115:5–6; Jer 5:21; Ezek 12:2). The disciples are no better off than the "outsiders" at whose door Jesus laid the earlier charge of blindness and deafness in Mark 4.

The condemnation of the disciples is embedded within a staccato of questions (8:17–21). "Hardened" is in the emphatic position in 8:17 (literally, "Hardened, do you have your heart?"), an accusation previously directed towards the Pharisees (3:5; and towards the disciples themselves in 6:52). The singular "heart" signifies a unified, collective misunderstanding that extends the scope of the accusation beyond the disciples' own incomprehension, to include the lack of discernment of *all* who do not/will not "see" or "hear" Jesus.[12] The specific note of having eyes and not seeing, and ears and not hearing, links this episode precisely to the miracle in 7:31–37 (the healing of the deaf and dumb man) and to the one that will take place in 8:22–26 (the healing of the blind man). To describe the disciples with terms used to describe the Pharisees and outsiders (4:11–12) is to accuse the disciples of having consumed the Pharisees' yeast and become utterly dense. This section thus summarizes (and intensifies) the motif of the disciples' lack of discernment in Act I, thereby appropriately concluding this act.

It is not that the disciples have forgotten what has happened: they recollect the numbers of loaves and leftovers quite accurately upon being quizzed. It is just that they "remember the details exactly, but miss the significance entirely."[13] They have data, but not the meaning thereof. The irony of Jesus' stinging rebuke ("Do you *still* [οὔπω, *oupō*]

10. Donahue and Harrington, *Gospel of Mark*, 251. This after eighteen references to "bread" in 6:8—8:19.

11. Boring, *Mark*, 227. The bread that Jesus breaks for his disciples in 14:22, which is noted to be ὑπὲρ πολλῶν (*hyper pollōn*, "for many," 14:24), echoes the ἀντὶ πολλῶν (*anti pollōn*, "for many") of 10:45 (van Iersel, *Mark*, 266n140). It suffices for all!

12. Hard-heartedness is a frequent OT diagnosis for contumacious resistance to God's work, especially on the part of the Pharaoh of the Exodus generation (e.g., Exod 10:1, 20, 27; 11:10; 14:8) and of Israel (e.g., Ezek 3:7; 11:19). See Donahue and Harrington, *Gospel of Mark*, 252.

13. Boring, *Mark*, 227.

not [see or] understand?," 8:17, 21) is that it comes at the end of an act that has been characterized throughout by Jesus' public demonstration of his power.[14] The crowds acclaim these deeds and respond positively to them. Individuals amongst the crowd depict the right attitude and perform the right actions, signifying an accurate discernment of Jesus (Jairus, the woman with the hemorrhage, the Syrophoenician woman, etc.). Surely the disciples could not have failed to "see" and "hear" all of this? Surely they, too, could have been one of the *true* disciples?[15] Instead, they are proving to be in the same boat (!) with the Pharisees. And this despite having "been with Jesus" (3:14), having access to the mystery of the kingdom (4:11) and to private instruction from him (4:10–20; 7:17–23), and having authorization to exorcise, heal, and preach (6:7, 12, 13).[16] Yes, the disciples are blind, but yes, there is hope as well, as the next episode signifies. "They have eyes that fail to see and ears that fail to hear; the good news is that their teacher is able to heal deaf ears (7:31–37) and open blind eyes (8:22–26)" and restore the speech of the dumb![17] It is in the Second Act that Jesus' Passion is explained; it is there that the disciples are called to accept the suffering mission of Jesus as their own. The attempted re-education of the disciples in Act II (Mark 8–10) will not be entirely successful, either: the disciples fail to accept Jesus' mission and, in Act III, finally abandon him.

11.2   Mark 7:31–37; 8:22–26

THEOLOGICAL FOCUS 11.2

11.2   A discernment of Jesus' person is essential for the walk of discipleship (7:31–37; 8:22–26)

Section Summary 11.2: The two miracles of perception (hearing and sight) underscore the importance of discernment of Jesus' person for the journey of discipleship with him. While the "local" focus of these accounts is to emphasize that the discernment of Jesus' ability to provide for daily needs is essential for a disciple, in their strategic placement at the end of Act I, particularly of the two-stage healing of the blind man, there is a "global" focus endorsed as well: a discernment of Jesus' person (and all that that entails) is essential in order for the disciple to follow Jesus on his mission.

---

14. It is notable that the only other question from Jesus containing οὔπω (*oupō*, "still," 4:40) also comes when the group is in a boat, on water, and points to the deficient discernment of the disciples. That incident also highlights Jesus' power.

15. Donahue and Harrington, *Gospel of Mark*, 252–53.

16. Collins, *Mark*, 388.

17. Geddert, *Watchwords*, 70. With reference to Jesus' healing of the man who was not only deaf, but also mute (7:35), the disciples, too, are not only deaf, but also unable to speak properly or appropriately (4:38, 41; 6:36–37; 8:32; 9:6, 33–34; 10:35–41). This last deficiency is portrayed in this pericope in the thoughtlessness and faithlessness of their comments (8:4, 16).

TRANSLATION 11.2

7:31   *And again He went out from the region of Tyre and He came through Sidon to the Sea of Galilee, within the region of Decapolis.*

7:32   *And they brought to Him a deaf man and one with impaired speech, and they implored Him to lay a hand on him.*

7:33   *And taking him aside from the crowd privately, He put His fingers into his ears and spitting, He touched his tongue.*

7:34   *And looking up into heaven, He sighed and said to him, "Ephphatha!" that is, "Be opened!"*

7:35   *And his ears were opened, and the impediment of his tongue was released, and he began speaking plainly.*

7:36   *And He ordered them to tell no one, but as much as He ordered them, they were proclaiming all the more.*

7:37   *And they were utterly amazed, saying, "He has done everything well; even the deaf He makes to hear and the dumb to speak."*

[8:1–21][18]

8:22   *And they came to Bethsaida. And they brought a blind man to Him and implored Him to touch him.*

8:23   *And taking the hand of the blind man, He brought him out of the village and after spitting into his eyes and laying hands on him, He asked him, "Do you see anything?"*

8:24   *And looking up, he said, "I see men, for I see them walking, like trees."*

8:25   *Then again He laid hands upon his eyes, and he looked intently and he was restored, and he saw everything clearly.*

8:26   *And He sent him into his house, saying, "Do not even go into the village."*

NOTES 11.2

11.2   *A discernment of Jesus' person is essential for the walk of discipleship.*

The particular healing in 7:31–37 parallels that in 8:22–26, and these two accounts frame the central section of the feeding miracle and its explanation (8:1–21), thus cohering the various episodes of this pericope. The two miracles deal with the physiology of perception ("discernment"), and their placement at the end of Act I underscores the failure of the disciples to discern, while at the same time raising hope: ears and eyes *can* be opened!

---

18. Mark 8:1–21 constitutes Pericope 11.1 (see above).

MARK 7:31-37—Hearing (and Speaking)	MARK 8:22-26—Seeing
Outside Galilee (7:31)	Outside Galilee (8:22)
Patient is likely a Gentile	Patient is likely a Gentile
Crowd implores (παρακαλέω, parakaleō) Jesus for aid (7:32)	Crowd implores (παρακαλέω) Jesus for aid (8:22)
to lay a hand on him (ἐπιθῇ αὐτῷ τὴν χεῖρα, epithē autō tēn cheira, 7:32)	to lay hands on him (ἐπιθεὶς τὰς χεῖρας αὐτῷ, epitheis tas cheiras autō, 8:23)
or to touch (ἅπτω, haptō, 7:33) the person	or to touch (ἅπτω, 8:22) the person
Man is taken away privately (ἀπολαμβάνω, apolambanō, 7:33)	Man is taken away privately (ἐπιλαμβάνομαί, epilambanomai, 8:23)
Saliva utilized (7:33)	Saliva utilized (8:23)
Imposition of silence (direct, 7:36)	Imposition of silence (indirect, 8:26)*

* As has been noted in previous pericopes, this imposition of silence is a restriction of the announcement of Jesus as merely a wonder-worker, without including the element of his suffering mission. See Placher, *Mark*, 108.

It is quite likely that these two healings—of the deaf and dumb and of the blind man—together serve not only as a conclusion to Act I, but also as a transition to Act II. The broader theme of Act I, the disciple's discernment of Jesus' person and all that that entails, is concluded: a negative depiction, the failure of discernment by the Twelve, underscores for readers the importance of the perception of Jesus' person in the journey of discipleship. In addition, a transition into the theme of Act II, the disciple's acceptance of Jesus' mission, is achieved as well with this pericope: the two-stage healing of the blind man in the final episode hints that there is more to the journey of discipleship than just discernment of Jesus' person (and his power); his mission of suffering must also be accepted.[19]

The deafness and dumbness of the man contrasts with the Syrophoenician woman who had heard about Jesus (7:25) and uttered the right word (7:29); she, as was noted earlier, modeled true discipleship. This deaf and mute person, on the other hand, reflects the lack of discernment of the Twelve.

A   Deaf and mute (7:32)
    B   Privacy sought (7:33a)
        C   Ears touched, tongue touched (7:33b)
            D   Jesus commands, "Be opened!" (7:34)
        C'   Ears opened, tongue released (7:35)
    B'   Secrecy enjoined (7:36)
A'   Deaf hear, mute speak (7:37)*

* From Reid, *Preaching Mark*, 81.

The focal point of the narrative is the command to open (see structure above), recorded both in Aramaic and its Greek translation. Interestingly, it is addressed to a

19. Such a reading is, of course, not to play down the historicity of the account. There is no reason why a narrator of considerable artistry like Mark could not, *in*, *through*, and *with* the historical narrative, portray theological truth in symbolic fashion.

man who, being deaf, would hardly be in a position to hear it.[20] Therefore, in the narrative theology of Mark, this command by Jesus is directed to the ears of *all* who care to hear him. Moreover, the placement of this episode towards the end of Act I suggests that Mark is employing the actual, historical incident symbolically in his narrative. This would also explain Jesus' deep emotions (his sighing, 7:34) in this final pericope of the First Act of the Gospel—his disappointment at the deafness of those who follow him: the verb στενάζω (*stenazō*, "sigh") is used only here in the Gospels.[21] The link to the moral failure of the disciples to hear/listen (ἀκούω, *akouō*, 8:18 and also 4:9, 10, 23; 7:25) is provided by Mark's use of the cognate noun of that verb, ἀκοαί (*akoai*, "ears"), in 7:35, where one would normally expect ὦτα (*ōta*, "ears") in parallel to 7:33, which actually has ὦτα.[22]

In the second miracle of perception in this pericope, the blind man's healing (8:22–26), forms of both verbs found in Jesus' warning to the disciples in 8:15—ὁρᾶτε (*horate*, "watch out") and βλέπετε (*blepete*, "beware" or "see")—reappear. Both verbs relate to sight. In fact, *five* different verbs are allotted to report the blind man's restored sight in 8:24–25: ἀναβλέπω (*anablepō*, "look up"), βλέπω (*blepō*, "see"), ὁράω (*horaō*, "see), διαβλέπω (*diablepō*, "look"), and ἐμβλέπω (*emblepō*, "see"). Coupled with the emphatic reminder that this man was blind (mentioned twice, 8:22, 23), the account, while true to fact, is to be understood theologically. These two healings of 7:31–37 and 8:22–26 are strategically placed to provide a contrast with the disciples who have ears but don't hear and have eyes but don't see (8:17–18, 21), signifying the sorry state of the disciples' discernment of the person of Jesus.

The singular characteristic of the healing of the blind man in 8:22–26 is that it is the only healing miracle that is not instantaneous and complete in its result. The chiastic structure of the account focuses the narrative upon the gradualness of the healing.[23]

---

20. It could also be a command to the ears and tongue of the patient; however, the Greek verb is in the second-person singular.

21. The related verb ἀναστενάζω (*anastenazō*, "sigh deeply") is found in 8:12; the circumstances are similar: in both situations, Jesus is expressing his disappointment and frustration at the lack of discernment of his person.

22. The amazement of the crowd, while a standard accompaniment of Jesus' miracles, is described with the unique use of ὑπερπερισσῶς (*hyperperissōs*, "utterly") in 7:37. France notes that "the healing of the deaf and dumb was a matter of particular amazement, for these are two of the elements in Isaiah's vision of the blessing which will result from God's own eschatological coming (Isa 35:5–6)" (*Gospel of Mark*, 304). Interestingly, the word μογιλάλος (*mogilalos*, "one with impaired speech," 7:32) is not used elsewhere in the NT, and is found only in Isa 35:6 in the LXX. The allusion to that passage in the reference to deafness and dumbness in Mark 7:37 makes the "reuse" of the word here likely to be deliberate—another indicator of the symbolic significance of this account. This eschatological allusion may explain the inclusion of the healing of the dumb—not exactly a miracle of perception/discernment. Nonetheless, as was noted, it is symbolic of the "handicapped" speech of the disciples throughout this Gospel.

23. Reid, *Preaching Mark*, 82. What the historical reason was for the two-stage healing of the blind man we might never find out.

A   Came (ἔρχομαι, *erchomai*) to Bethsaida (8:22)

  B   Blind man brought out from village (κώμη, *kōmē*) (8:23a)

    C   Saliva on eyes; hands laid (ἐπιθεὶς τὰς χεῖρας, *epitheis tas cheiras*) upon the person (8:23b)

      D   "Do you see anything?" (βλέπω, *blepō*) (8:23c)

      D'   "I see . . ." (βλέπω) (8:24)

    C'   Hands laid (ἐπέθηκεν τὰς χεῖρας, *epethēken tas cheiras*) upon the person (8:25)

  B'   Healed man sent home, asked not to enter village (κώμη) (8:26)

A'   Went out (ἐξέρχομαι, *exerchomai*) to Caesarea Philippi (8:27a)

In that the recovery of sight is equivalent to understanding, this miracle signifies the lack of discernment of Jesus' person by the disciples (the thrust of Act I), but it also intimates that something more is necessary than just discernment (unclear sight). Act II emphasizes the need for the disciple to accept the suffering mission of Jesus as well (clear sight): there Jesus predicts his passion thrice.[24]

At the conclusion of Act II is found another healing of a blind man (10:46–52; these are the only two healings of the blind in Mark); this time the recovery of sight is instantaneous, and what is more, the healed man promptly leaves all and follows Jesus "on the way"—the mark of discipleship (on the other hand, the healed man in 8:22–26 is sent home).

blindness to sight (two-stage) (8:22–26)

  Act II: *On the way* (8:27—10:45)

blindness to sight (instantaneous) (10:46–52)

These two blind healings effectively form an introduction and conclusion to Act II, respectively, bookending this central Act of Mark, which attempts to cure the disciples of a serious blindness: they need to accept Jesus' mission of suffering. The two-stage healing of the blind man in this pericope in Mark 8 forms an appropriate illustration of this incremental re-education—the gradual discernment of Jesus' person in Act I, and the total acceptance of Jesus' mission in Act II.[25]

---

24. A symbolic reading of this pericope is also supported by the use of blindness as a metaphor in both Greek (pre-Socratic and Platonic works) and biblical traditions (Isa 6:9 and Jer 5:21, both of which Mark cites) (Collins, *Mark*, 395). Witherington agrees: "The placement of this particular miracle here is not accidental, but rather a visible parable of what was, and what was to come in the psyche of the disciples" (*Gospel of Mark*, 238). Also see Collins, *Mark*, 397–98. R. Benjamin b. Levi and R. Jonathan b. Amram: "[A]ll may be presumed to be blind, until the Holy One, blessed be He, enlightens their eyes" (*Gen. Rab.* 53.14).

25. This ideal situation does not come to pass; the disciple fail on all counts and in every act. Writing as Mark is to disciples of all time, future readers are being enjoined to learn through these negative examples, and to learn as quickly as they can. Best is perceptive here (*Following Jesus*, 136–37):

> Theoretically Mark should show the disciples responding to the teaching of Jesus and there-fore gradually losing their blindness and gaining insight into his mission; but had he done this there would have been a serious conflict with the facts. Everyone knew the basic traditions about the disciples: Judas had betrayed Jesus, Peter had denied him and the remainder had fled when he was arrested. Mark cannot then show the disciples as receiving their sight prior to the resurrection, but by giving the relevant teaching which ought to produce sight he can

SERMON FOCUS AND OUTLINES

THEOLOGICAL FOCUS OF PERICOPE 11 FOR PREACHING
11   God can be trusted for the provision of life's daily needs (7:31—8:26).

This pericope, with its central feeding miracle and the two miracles of perception bracketing it, concludes Act I, reinforcing a critical facet of discipleship that has been the thrust of the Act: a discernment of Jesus' person (and all that that entails). In this particular pericope, the central feeding miracle (8:1–21) emphasizes the need to understand Jesus/God as one who can provide for the daily needs of life. The healing of the deaf and dumb man and the two-stage healing (7:31–37 and 8:22–26) symbolize the failure of the disciples to discern the person (and power) of Jesus, as well as foreshadow the next stage in the disciples' development, the acceptance of Jesus' mission. While this latter aspect of this pericope may be touched upon, time in the sermon should be devoted to the specific thrust of the central episode of this pericope—the discernment of Jesus' person as the one who meets life's daily needs.

Pericope 6 (4:35—5:20) considered Jesus' power over natural calamities and supernatural foes; Pericope 7 (5:21—6:6) dealt with Jesus' power over the "big" issues of life—disease and death; and Pericope 8 (6:7–32) handled Jesus' provision for the disciple's mission in the face of virulent opposition. The current pericope (Pericope 11: 7:31—8:26) addresses Jesus' power over and provision for the "small" issues of life: specifically food, but also, implied, everything else necessary for the daily conduct of life. Thus, in these four pericopes (6–8 and 11) Jesus' person is described as one who can meet *all* the needs of the disciple, because of his divine power and authority over calamities both natural and supernatural, catastrophes of life, antagonism from enemies, and life's daily needs. The one following Jesus on the Trip of Discipleship need have no concerns about any of these issues, for he who leads is abundantly capable of taking care of those who follow. Such a discernment of Jesus' person (and all that that entails—especially his illimitable power) is an essential aspect of discipleship.

POSSIBLE PREACHING OUTLINES FOR PERICOPE 11

I.   PROBLEM: The innumerable needs of daily life

The need for food; 8:1–4, 14–16

Move-to-Relevance: the need for food symbolizing the variety of needs we face in life

II.   SOLUTION: Jesus the provider

The miracle of feeding: 8:5–10, 17–21; Jesus the only one who can provide for all our needs

The miracles of perception: 7:31–37; 8:22–26, importance of perceiving Jesus' person rightly—the provider

---

help his own community who, unlike the historical disciples, are in the position of knowing of the resurrection. He preserves the basic accuracy of the tradition in relation to the actual blindness of the disciples and yet at the same time instructs his own people in the nature of Jesus' suffering and the necessity of their own. He can only do this symbolically. Thus the two stage healing of 8:22–26 is a picture of what ought to happen.

III.   APPLICATION: *See God as the provider for daily needs!* *

Specific action to consolidate the right perception of God as our provider

* This homiletical imperative, like all the others this commentary provides, is admittedly non-specific. One must keep asking, "How do I [how does my congregation] do that?" of such general statements until an acceptable level of specificity is arrived at. Being concrete is the essence of sermonic application (in addition to being creative and compelling). The goal is to instill in disciples a practice, that becomes a habit, that creates a disposition, that blooms into Christlike character (all by the power of the Holy Spirit)! It begins with specificity in application.

Another option:

I.   THEY PANIC: The Twelve despair about food

The need for food; 8:1–4, 14–16

Move-to-Relevance: the need for food symbolizing the variety of needs we face in life

II.   HE PROVIDES: Jesus the provider

The miracle of feeding: 8:5–10, 17–21; Jesus the one who provides for all our daily needs

III.   WE PERCEIVE: *See God as the provider for daily needs!*

The miracles of perception: 7:31–37; 8:22–26, importance of perceiving Jesus' person rightly—the provider

Specific action to consolidate the right perception of God as our provider

ACT II: "ON THE WAY"

Acceptance of Jesus' Mission

PERICOPE 12

Glory Is a-Comin'!

Mark 8:27—9:13

[First Passion Prediction; Transfiguration]

REVIEW, SUMMARY, PREVIEW

Review of Pericope 11: Mark 7:31—8:26 calls the disciple to trust in Jesus' person as one who is able to provide for life's daily needs.

Summary of Pericope 12: In 8:27—9:13 the first Passion Prediction of Jesus and the account of his Transfiguration outline the suffering mission of Jesus. It warns of what the disciple ought to expect on the way of discipleship, following Jesus. The snapshot of future glory in this pericope offers the disciple immense encouragement to continue "on the way."

Preview of Pericope 13: The next pericope (9:14–50) exhorts the disciple to humility—prayerfully depending on God's power, by faith, as one serves those who are seemingly insignificant and unimportant.

12   Mark 8:27—9:13

THEOLOGICAL FOCUS OF PERICOPE 12
12   **Disciples are encouraged by the magnificent hope of future glory, as they accept Jesus' divine mission that promises suffering in the present (8:27—9:13).**
12.1   The model of discipleship for followers of Jesus is the pattern of Jesus' own mission: self-denying suffering first, glory later (8:27—9:1).
12.1.1   Disciples of Jesus recognize his mission of suffering.
12.1.2   Jesus' mission of self-denying suffering is to be accepted as their mission by his followers as well.

12.1.3	The proper sequence of events in the mission of Jesus is suffering first, glory later.
12.2	Disciples are encouraged by the magnificent hope of future glory, as they accept Jesus' divinely ordained mission that promises suffering in the present, foreshadowed by the suffering of Elijah/John (9:2–13).
12.2.1	Jesus' Transfiguration provides an encouraging vision of the future glory that he had predicted.
12.2.2	The transfigured Jesus, who promises future glory but predicts present suffering, is the One disciples must listen to, and whose mission they should accept.
12.2.3	The suffering of Elijah/John foreshadows Jesus' own suffering mission, reinforcing Jesus' Passion Prediction.

OVERVIEW

ACT II OF MARK (8:27—10:52) concentrates on the passage of Jesus and his followers from Galilee to Jerusalem, from north to south, from homeland to "foreign" land: ἐν τῇ ὁδῷ (en tē hodō, "on the way") or a similar phrase echoes frequently in this act to reinforce the discipleship motif (8:27; 9:33–34; 10:17, 32, 52; see the Introduction for the "journey" theme of Mark).[1] In Act II, Jesus also speaks openly of the suffering his Messianic mission involves: the three Passion Predictions (8:31; 9:31; and 10:32–34). It is significant that all three occur in Act II, while Jesus and the disciples are "on the way" from Galilee to Jerusalem. "This is but one more indicator that this Gospel is about the way of the cross, both as an expression of Christology and also of discipleship."[2] The details of the three predictions are given below.

Passion Prediction I MARK 8:31	Passion Prediction II MARK 9:31	Passion Prediction III MARK 10:33–34
Son of Man must suffer be rejected by elders/chief priests/scribes	Son of man to be delivered into hands of men	In Jerusalem Son of man will be delivered to chief priests/scribes who will condemn him to death, hand him over to the Gentiles, who will mock, spit upon, scourge,
be killed after three days rise again	they will kill Him after three days rise again	and kill Him after three days rise again
Indirect speech	Direct speech	Direct speech + detail
"follow" (8:34)	"follow" (9:38)	"follow" (10:32)
"whoever wishes" (8:34)	"if anyone wishes" (9:35)	"whoever wishes" (10:43)
save live/lose life	first/last	great/least
Peter rebukes (8:32)	Disciples quarrel (9:33–34)	Brothers petition (10:35–39)

1. Of the sixteen references to ὁδός, hodos, in Mark, seven of them occur in the three chapters of Act II, Mark 8–10.

2. Witherington, Gospel of Mark, 286.

There is an escalation in the intensity of the three predictions as they go from indirect speech, to direct speech, and finally to direct speech with great detail and elaboration. All three have εἴ τις θέλει (*ei tis thelei,* "if anyone wishes") or some variation thereof, and all these "conditional" utterances by Jesus are linked to the theme of what it means to "follow" Jesus on the way: accepting and adopting Jesus' mission of self-sacrifice as one's own is an integral part of following Jesus in discipleship.

Act II is also characterized by its being neatly framed by the healings of two blind men and the confessions of Jesus as the Christ; the only other healing in this act is an exorcism in 9:14–29, unlike the "power"-packed Act I.[3]

A   Healing of a blind man (8:22–26)
  B   Confession of Jesus as the Christ (8:27–30)
    C   Discipleship teaching "on the way" (8:31—10:45)
  B′   Confession of Jesus as the Christ (10:46–48)
A′   Healing of a blind man (10:49–52)*

  * Geddert, *Mark,* 199.

Understood symbolically (see under Pericope 11, 7:31—8:26), this framing by the two healings of the blind denotes the incremental increase in understanding about Jesus that disciples go through (or are *supposed* to go through): Act I dealt mostly with Jesus' person (and all that that entails, particularly his power); Act II deals with his mission of suffering. These accounts, however, are not particularly creditable for the disciples. Unfortunately their growth in understanding, as the blind healings suggest should have happened, does not take place. After each of the three Passion Predictions that anchor this section, they are shown in extremely poor light—their obtuseness is evidenced by their lack of acceptance of Jesus' mission. To fully know Jesus includes accepting his mission—"his destiny of suffering and tragic death. And this acceptance implies the disposition to follow Jesus on his road to the cross."[4] Would disciples of future generations accept Jesus' mission and follow?

In Act II, while the historical disciples retain center stage, the crowd, an integral feature of Act I, for the most part retreats to the background (8:34; 9:14; 10:1, 13, 46). Also, from parabolic speech, Jesus appears to shift into more direct and clear revelation (the Passion Predictions, for instance), with themes of discipleship becoming more prominent and linked inextricably with christological motifs. Throughout this act, Jesus and the disciples are always depicted together. But they abandon him in Act III (see 14:50).[5] No, the disciples do *not* follow Jesus to the end.

---

3. And this latter exorcism is performed by Jesus because the disciples are unable to do so!

4. Stock, *Method and Message,* 230. "Jesus cannot be understood apart from his passion and resurrection. . . . No more can discipleship be understood apart from the passion and resurrection of Jesus" (Best, *Disciples and Discipleship,* 6).

5. Boring, *Mark,* 231–32.

12.1   Mark 8:27–9:1

Section Summary 12.1: Peter's inadequate confession and his subsequent rebuke of Jesus underscores the disciples' failure to accept the suffering mission of Jesus. Jesus, however, sternly rebuking his disciples for this neglect, outlines the pattern of discipleship for all who would follow him: suffering will necessarily come first; glory later.

TRANSLATION 12.1

8:27   *And Jesus went out—and His disciples— into the villages of Caesarea Philippi; and on the way He asked His disciples, saying to them, "Who do people say I am?"*

8:28   *And they told Him, saying, "John the Baptist, and others [say] Elijah; but others, one of the prophets."*

8:29   *And He asked them, "But you—who do you say I am?" Peter, answering, said to Him, "You are the Christ."*

8:30   *And He warned them that they tell no one about Him.*

8:31   *And He began to teach them that it was necessary for the Son of Man to suffer many things and be rejected by the elders and the chief priests and the scribes, and to be killed and rise after three days.*

8:32   *And He was speaking the word plainly. And Peter, taking Him aside, began to rebuke Him.*

8:33   *But turning around and seeing His disciples, He rebuked Peter and said, "Go behind me, Satan, for you are not thinking the things of God but the things of man."*

8:34   *And summoning the crowd with His disciples, He said to them, "If anyone wishes to follow behind Me, let him deny himself and take up his cross and follow Me!*

8:35   *For whoever wishes to save his life will lose it; but whoever will lose his life on account of Me and of the gospel, will save it.*

8:36   *For what does it benefit a man to gain the whole world and forfeit his life?*

8:37   *For what will a man give in exchange for his life?*

8:38   *For whoever is ashamed of Me and of My words in this adulterous and sinful generation, the Son of Man will also be ashamed of him, when He comes in the glory of His father with the holy angels."*

9:1   *And Jesus was saying to them, "Truly I say to you, there are some of those standing here who will not taste death until they see the kingdom of God has come with power."*

NOTES 12.1

12.1.1   *Disciples of Jesus recognize his mission of suffering.*[6]

Allusions to who Jesus is have permeated the Gospel all along thus far (1:1, 24, 34; 4:41; 6:3, 14–16); the crowds have often been amazed at Jesus' words and deeds (1:22, 27; 2:12; 5:20, 42; 6:14–16; 7:37), and they have congregated in large numbers before him (1:45; 2:2, 13; 3:7–8; 4:1; 6:54–56), but all—crowds *and* disciples—have failed to (fully) grasp the person of Jesus and all that that entails. Now Jesus delivers his first Passion Prediction, going beyond a description of his person: his suffering mission is made clear. That Jesus chooses Caesarea Philippi for this first Passion Prediction is significant; it was in these environs that Herod had built a temple dedicated to Augustus Caesar.[7] No doubt, the locus of an imperial cult is an appropriate place to raise the question of the identity of the Jesus, Son of the supreme Deity, the one who is the lawful King. "The effect is to place the Christian reverence for Jesus in competition with pagan religious belief and practice and to co-opt the sacredness of the locality."[8]

Thus far, the only title with which the disciples have addressed Jesus is "Teacher" (4:38), and shortly thereafter, they ask themselves, "Who is this . . . ?" (4:41). All this despite the demons accurately portraying Jesus as the Holy One or Son of God (1:24; 3:11; 5:7), a Gentile woman calling Jesus "Lord" (7:28), and Jesus himself alluding to his status as the Son of Man (2:10, 28). The incomplete grasp of the person of Jesus, as depicted in Act I, explains the accurate but inadequate confession of Peter that Jesus is "the Christ" (8:29). It appears that, in his Passion account, Mark uses the term "Christ" as a royal designation: for instance, in the mocking of Jesus as King of the Jews (15:32, "Christ, the King of Israel"). Thus, "for Mark at least, calling Jesus the Christ/Anointed is tantamount to calling him God's *king*." And the problem with this one-sided identification is the inevitable and understandably unenthusiastic response of his followers to Jesus' suffering mission.[9] "Kings are supposed to wield power, not to fall victim to it."[10]

6. This theological subfocus, too, is a positive representation of what the actual Markan disciples fail to do in the account.

7. The site of the temple was Paneas, so called in honor of the god Pan; it might also have been a place where Baal was worshipped.

8. Collins, *Mark*, 401; Witherington, *Gospel of Mark*, 240. Also see Guttenberger, "Why Caesarea Philippi," 120.

9. "In spite of all its orthodoxy Peter's reply shows that he has no better understanding than the demons in [Mark] 3:11 and 5:7, who give a far better answer" (Schweizer, *Good News*, 174). Winn, rejecting the assertion that Peter's confession is incomplete, states that Peter's statement is identical to 1:1 (*Purpose of Mark's Gospel*, 116–18; so also Stein, *Mark*, 399–400). But it is not: the "Son of God" motif, present in 1:1, is absent in human mouths; *that* will have to wait until it appears on the lips of a Roman centurion in 15:39.

10. Driggers, *Following God*, 65. The hope of at least some branches of Second Temple messianism was congruent with the understanding of the Messiah as the future Davidic king who would restore the

Therefore an exclusively regal designation of Jesus, that does not take into account his suffering, is deficient.[11] The subsequent unfolding of the narrative of Peter's rebuke and the event of, and the discussion following, the Transfiguration (as well as the symbolic import of the prior episode of 8:22–26 in Pericope 11, with its motif of "blindness") indicates that Peter's response, although true, is, at the very least, in need of clarification.[12]

As will be evident, the missing element in Peter's identification is the aspect of Jesus' suffering mission: he (and presumably, the rest of the disciples) does not accept that the way of the Messiah is one of suffering and death. "Somehow Peter comes to know that Jesus is the messiah [Christ]. But his knowledge is only partial because he does not have the proper understanding of the role of the messiah, which Jesus proceeds to teach him and others in v. 31."[13] The command to secrecy after both the healing of the blind man (8:25–26) and after Peter's confession (8:29–30) denotes that neither the blind man (though restored in sight) nor Peter (though producing an accurate confession) has fully grasped the suffering mission of Jesus. Only those with such a complete understanding are permitted to proclaim Jesus, for any other conception of the person and mission of Jesus is insufficient and inadequate for the purposes of discipleship.

12.1.2 Jesus' mission of self-denying suffering is to be accepted as their mission by his followers as well.

What is striking in this ominous portent of Jesus' death in 8:31 is the absence of any fatalistic overtones whatsoever; it is the "necessary" trajectory (δεῖ, dei, 8:31) for the fulfillment of his larger purpose to establish the kingdom of God; it is the means of the substitutionary atonement; it is the prelude to his resurrection.[14] It therefore comes as no surprise that Peter's attempt to thwart this *necessary* aspect of Jesus mission earns him one of the sternest rebukes from Jesus recorded.

Forebodings of Jesus' death have already appeared in Mark's account (2:20; 3:6); however, in this first Passion Prediction is the assurance that "death will come not as the triumph of the opposition but as the fulfillment of the divine purpose, to be welcomed rather than bewailed. . . . The death is the means to the glory, and the outcome will be the powerful coming of the kingdom of God." And it is "on the way" to Jerusalem that the followers of Jesus will learn this "radical new ideology of the kingdom of God."[15] Discipleship is a call to glory . . . by way of suffering.

---

fortunes of God's people (See Evans, *Mark*, 15). This rather militaristic ideal was potentially problematic for the comprehension of Jesus' mission, and was likely to have been one of the reasons that led Jesus to call for silence from those who viewed him in this fashion as a potential political warlord.

11. "The meaning of the title ["Christ"/"Messiah"] first had to be revised by linking it to the Crucified, so that instead of a political liberator, a messianic king, there would be seen a suffering Messiah" (Pannenberg, *Systematic Theology*, 2:312).

12. Collins, *Mark*, 402.

13. Ibid., 394.

14. France, *Gospel of Mark*, 332. Even the resurrection is part of this divine "necessity."

15. Ibid., 333.

Perhaps the switch from Peter's "Christ" (8:29) to Jesus' "Son of Man" (8:31) is a hint that Peter had missed something in his identification and confession. The idea of the suffering of the Son of Man (the title itself is drawn from Dan 7:13–14, describing a conquering and majestic figure with heavenly authority) is incomprehensible to Peter and to his Jewish contemporaries. Yes, glory will indeed come with the Son of Man (Mark 8:38), but not *before* his rejection and suffering.[16] Peter's problem is not incomprehension—after all, Jesus' word is spoken "plainly" (8:32). His problem is accepting that disagreeable mission of suffering. This failure of acceptance is severely rebuked by Jesus (8:33). Not thinking the thoughts of God, but rather those of men (and, therefore, of Satan), Peter is here depicted as an "outsider," not amenable to—indeed, opposing—the necessary will of God, unlike the "insiders" in 3:31–35, who accept God's will.[17]

Ἐπιτιμάω (*epitimaō*, "rebuke," the verb indicating the silencing of demonic elements (1:25; 3:12; 4:39; 8:33; 9:25), echoes in this pericope. Its first use by Peter to rebuke Jesus is shocking (8:32)—does he consider Jesus' explanation of his suffering to be demonic? Then it is Jesus' turn to employ it of Peter (8:33); here Satanic influence upon Peter's thought is expressly stated. "Incompatible ideologies" are clashing here.[18] It is to be noted that Jesus' response in 8:30–31 is addressed to the entire body of disciples (he warns "them," 8:30, also ἐπιτιμάω): the group as a whole is complicit in Peter's unaccepting remonstration of Jesus and his mission. The content of Peter's rebuke is unstated; however 8:32 (Peter's drawing Jesus aside) and 8:38 hint that Peter may have been ashamed of Jesus.[19] Notice that 8:38 has Jesus accuse those who are "ashamed of Me *and my words*" (λόγους, *logous*). In light of the fact that, in 8:32, Jesus is described as stating the "word" (λόγος, *logos*) plainly, upon which Peter rebukes him, this interpretation appears valid: Peter is one who is ashamed of the words of his Master—his mission of suffering. The thrust of these verses is simply this: The disciples

---

16. See Pss 22, 69; Isa 53; Zech 11:4–14; 12:10–14; 13:7–9. Of course, the aspect about the resurrection (repeated in the other two Passion Predictions as well) is completely ignored by Jesus' listeners; they are unable to go beyond the grievous announcement of his suffering and death, and they essentially declare it unacceptable. Connotations of "Son of Mark" terminology vary in Mark: 2:10, 28 = authority and lordship; 8:31; 9:12, 31; 10:33–34, 45; 14:21, 41 = suffering and/or death; 8:31; 9:9, 31 = resurrection; 14:62 = exaltation; 8:38; 13:24–27; 14:62 = future coming. The ones rejecting Jesus will be the elders, chief priests, and scribes—a comprehensive repudiation by the top tier of Israel's representatives, intensifying the paradox of the unrecognized Son of Man suffering as the Messiah (see also 11:27; 14:43, 53; and 15:1, where this triumvirate is again specified). Ἀποδοκιμάζω (*apodokimazō*, "reject," 8:31) will show up again in 12:10, citing Ps 118:22 LXX.

17. Donahue and Harrington, *Gospel of Mark*, 146.

18. France, *Gospel of Mark*, 338. Indeed, Jesus has already used the word ἐπιτιμάω in this pericope (translated "warned" in 8:30) to dissuade his followers from publicizing his identity. Was that imposition of silence also intended to be equivalent to an exorcism of a demonic misconception of Jesus?

19. The prefix προσ- (*pros-*) of the verb describing Peter's action (προσλαμβάνω, *proslambanō*, "take aside," 8:32) indicates Peter almost taking a stand *in front of* Jesus, "in his face" (Boring, *Mark*, 242). Hence the appropriate redirection from Jesus, "Get *behind* Me" (8:33). Peter needs to return to the posture of following Jesus "behind" him, where a disciple ought to be, neither dictating nor deviating from the divine, necessary will.

are unwilling to accept Jesus' mission of suffering rather than glory; in fact, they are ashamed to hear him talk of such an ignominious end.

The introduction of the crowd in this somber pronouncement (8:34) indicates that the demands of discipleship are not restricted to the Twelve alone; all who desire to follow Jesus must acquiesce to the self-denying and cross-bearing that Jesus enjoins. "[T]his is not a special formula for the elite, but an essential element in discipleship."[20] The repetition of ὀπίσω μου (opisō mou, "behind Me," 8:33, 34) underscores the proper position of the disciple in relation to Jesus—the locus of the follower (1:17–18, 20; 2:14); so also the repetition of ἀκολουθέω (akoloutheō, "follow") in 8:34. "Peter has a choice—he can either be a hindrance or an obstacle serving Satan . . . or he can be a follower of Jesus, in which case he gets in line behind Jesus, takes up his own cross, and prepares for suffering as Jesus is doing."[21] Jesus' mission is to be the disciples' mission; they are called to accept it for themselves.

What Jesus calls for is not a denial *to* self of things, but a denial *of* oneself. Best puts it best[22]:

> It is the opposite of self-affirmation, of putting value on one's being, one's life, one's position before man or God, of claiming rights and privileges peculiar to one's special position in life or even of those normally believed to belong to the human being as such (e.g. justice, freedom). Self-denial thus obviously involves the willingness not to affirm any right to life when faced by the persecutor. . . . Self-denial is the inner attitude; cross-bearing is the outward activity which should accompany the inner attitude.

The power of the metaphor of taking up one's own cross is therefore not to be attenuated; this is not merely a call to endure hardship with patience, but to be ready even for death. And, ironically, what Peter, the disciple in focus in this section, accomplishes in the Gospel is not self-denial, but the denial of his Master: ἀπαρνέομαι (aparneomai, "to deny") occurs in Mark only here and with Peter's betrayal (14:30, 31, 72; the related word ἀρνέομαι, arneomai, "to deny," is also found in the account of that same event, 14:68, 70). The verb is in the reflexive middle form in 8:34, connoting a refusal to accede to self-interest: "[W]hat Jesus calls for here is thus a radical abandonment of one's own identity and self-determination, and a call to join the march to the place of execution follows appropriately from this."[23]

---

20. France, *Gospel of Mark*, 339.

21. Witherington, *Gospel of Mark*, 244. The two aorist verbs ("deny" and "take up" in 8:34) are followed by a verb in the present tense ("follow"), indicating an ongoing process for life: deny, take up, and keep on following. Following Jesus on the way is, of course, the theme of this Gospel.

22. Best, *Following Jesus*, 37, 39. Also see idem, *Disciples and Discipleship*, 8. "It requires the denying or saying no to the self as the determiner of one's goals, aspirations, and desires" (Stein, *Mark*, 407).

23. France, *Gospel of Mark*, 340. Plutarch reminded his readers: "Every malefactor who is punished by the infliction of pain on his body bears his own cross" (*Sera* 9). Or as Bonhoeffer put it, "When Christ calls a man, He bids him come and die" (*Cost of Discipleship*, 89). Mark 8:34 has the first instance of "cross" in the Gospel. While the rabbis urged their disciples to take up the yoke of the Torah or the commandments (e.g., *m. 'Abot* 3.5; *m. Ber.* 2.2), no one had suggested taking up the *cross* before, an instrument of execution. This would certainly have sounded bizarre, if not gruesome.

Mark's original, post-Easter Roman readers would have immediately caught on. Tacitus mentions the cruelty of Nero towards Christians, who had them crucified and set on fire (*Ann.* 15.44.4); Christians were also likely to have been (or would soon be—depending on when the Gospel was written) among the many crucified by Vespasian during the war in Palestine. Readers of the Gospel would also, no doubt, have been aware of Jesus' own crucifixion (see confessional formulas in Acts 2:34–36; 4:10; 1 Cor 15:1–3; 2 Cor 13:4; etc.), and grasped the somber implications of this call to discipleship.[24] "Discipleship to Jesus as willingness to take up the cross was not metaphorical to many of Mark's original readers. Nor was it a matter of internal, private devotion—crucifixion was not only slow and agonizing death, it was public and shameful."[25] Jesus himself, in his willingness to undergo such an end, is the exemplar of this mission of suffering.[26] The paradox: you save life by losing it (by self-denial and cross-bearing—the essence of discipleship); you lose life by saving it (by avoiding self-denial and cross-bearing). The "saving" and "losing" here is not dealing with the gain or loss of eternal life; that is not Mark's interest in this passage. Rather, he is dealing with what it means for a disciple to live life truly, abundantly, in accord with the demands of discipleship (including, as well, a fullness of life in eternity marked by rewards). On the other hand, for those who refuse to accept Jesus' mission, rejecting these demands of discipleship, there will only be shame in the future, in the presence of the glory of Christ (8:38; 1 John 2:28)—not the loss of eternal life, but the foregoing of eternal rewards.

12.1.3 *The proper sequence of events in the mission of Jesus is suffering first, glory later.*

In this section, readers are given two reasons for accepting Jesus' invitation to self-denial and cross-bearing: 1) without doing so, one cannot follow Jesus (Mark 8:34); and 2) unless one does so, at Jesus' second coming in glory there will be shame upon the disciple who chose not to follow (8:38). The "coming" (8:38) of the Son of Man likely refers to Daniel 7:13–14, where also the Son of Man is said to be "coming"; the throne of God, and glory, and angelic beings are in attendance in Daniel 7:9–10 as well—all of these emphasize the divine authority and establishment of the Son's governance over the world.[27] Jesus' earthly rejection ("Son of Man" in Mark 8:31) will end in heavenly vindication ("Son of Man" in 8:38); the followers of this Son must expect the same result (or its contrary if they choose not to follow him). Suffering first; glory later!

The focus of the prediction in 9:1 is not on the arrival of the kingdom, but on its visibility. The motifs of sight and power (ἴδωσιν . . . ἐν δυνάμει, *idōsin . . . en dynamei*, "see . . . with power," 9:1), drawn from Daniel 7:13–14, recur in Mark 13:26 (ὄψονται

---

24. van Iersel, *Mark*, 287–88; Boring, *Mark*, 244.

25. Boring, *Mark*, 244–45.

26. Jesus' being an example in no way denies the salvific value of Jesus' death and resurrection. However, the thrust in this pericope, and indeed in most of Mark's Gospel, is on following the example of Jesus.

27. France, *Gospel of Mark*, 342. Also see Zech 14:5.

... μετὰ δυνάμεως πολλῆς, *opsontai* ... *meta dynameōs pollēs*, "they will see ... with great power") and 14:62 (ὄψεσθε ... τῆς δυνάμεως, *opsesthe* ... *tēs dynameōs*, "you will see ... of power").[28] These three sayings (9:1; 13:26; 14:62, utilizing verbs from the same root, ὁράω, *horaō*) all relate to something the contemporary generation of Jesus would see. In the current passage, the best explanation of how those living in the time of Jesus would see the coming of his kingdom is to link it with what follows immediately (9:2–13). The Transfiguration occurs after a precise interval of time (six days), is seen by the disciples, and in it heavenly glory (power?) is apparent.[29] While such a temporary mountaintop experience is not exactly the actual event of the kingdom of God coming in power, it is "a heavenly preview of what was still to be achieved"—the glory promised in 8:38. The Transfiguration, Witherington states, "reveals the kingdom by unveiling the king."[30] As a preview, this snapshot of future glory, howbeit brief and transient, serves as "a needed reassurance to the disciples after the pessimistic projection for their likely fate in 8:34–38."[31] Suffering there might be, but glory is certainly coming, one day!

Mark 8:38 and 9:1 are fitting conclusions for the first Passion Prediction. The first (8:38) outlines the consequence for those who refuse to accept Jesus' mission and follow him, conforming instead to the "adulterous and sinful generation"—for them it will be shame. The second (9:1) depicts the consequence for those who do accept and follow—for these it will be glory. "This prophetic-apocalyptic conclusion provides a powerful incentive to faithful discipleship."[32]

12.2 Mark 9:2–13

THEOLOGICAL FOCUS 12.2

12.2 Disciples are encouraged by the magnificent hope of future glory, as they accept Jesus' divinely ordained mission that promises suffering in the present, foreshadowed by the suffering of Elijah/John (9:2–13).

    12.2.1 Jesus' Transfiguration provides an encouraging vision of the future glory that he had predicted.

    12.2.2 The transfigured Jesus, who promises future glory but predicts present suffering, is the One disciples must listen to, and whose mission they should accept.

    12.2.3 The suffering of Elijah/John foreshadows Jesus' own suffering mission, reinforcing Jesus' Passion Prediction.

---

28. Ibid., 344.

29. Of interest is that while "glory" is mentioned in 8:38 and "power" in 9:1, 13:26 has the Son of Man coming with *both* power and glory. "What is indicated is that the triumphant revelation of the Son of Man invested with the glory of the Father is the manifestation of the sovereignty of God in the full display of its power" (Nardoni, "Redactional Interpretation," 373). Thus the Transfiguration appears to be the event that was predicted by Jesus in 9:1.

30. Witherington, *Gospel of Mark*, 262. Also see France, *Gospel of Mark*, 345. "[W]e may well conclude that Mark understood the event on the mountain to be at least a partial and proleptic fulfillment of Jesus' words, even though the historical reality remained to be made visible" (ibid.).

31. France, *Gospel of Mark*, 346.

32. Collins, *Mark*, 413.

Section Summary 12.2: The Transfiguration of Jesus is the snapshot of future glory promised to disciples. Such a magnificent preview, overshadowing even the glory of the Mt. Sinai event with Moses, sustains disciples as they continue along the journey of discipleship, accepting Jesus' mission that promises suffering. Such suffering is exemplified in the death of Jesus' forerunner, John the Baptist.

TRANSLATION 12.2

9:2   *And after six days, Jesus took along Peter and James and John and led them up on a high mountain by themselves. And He was transfigured before them,*

9:3   *and His garments became radiant, exceedingly white, as no launderer on earth is able so to whiten.*

9:4   *And Elijah appeared to them with Moses, and they were conversing with Jesus.*

9:5   *And Peter, answering, said to Jesus, "Rabbi, it is good for us to be here, and let us make three tabernacles, one for You, and one for Moses, and one for Elijah."*

9:6   *For he did not know what to answer, for they became terrified.*

9:7   *And there came a cloud overshadowing them, and a voice came from the cloud, "This is My beloved Son, listen to Him!"*

9:8   *And suddenly, when they looked around, they no longer saw anyone with them, but Jesus alone.*

9:9   *And as they were coming down from the mountain, He ordered them not to relate to anyone what they had seen, until the Son of Man was risen from the dead.*

9:10 *And they seized upon the word, discussing among themselves what it was "to rise from the dead."*

9:11 *And they asked Him, saying, "Why do the scribes say that it is necessary for Elijah to come first?"*

9:12 *And He said to them, "Elijah does come first and restore all things. And how is it written of the Son of Man that He will suffer many things and be despised?*

9:13 *But I say to you that Elijah has indeed come, and they did to him whatever they wished, just as it is written of him."*

NOTES 12.2

12.2.1   Jesus' Transfiguration provides an encouraging vision of the future glory that he had predicted.

Since it is something the disciples "see" (as was promised in 9:1), the account of the Transfiguration is narrated from the disciples' perspective: Jesus transfigured "before them" (9:2); Elijah's appearance "to them" (9:4); Peter's rather ingenuous response (9:5); the terror felt (9:6); their being overshadowed by the cloud (9:7); the voice addressing them about Jesus (in the third person) and commanding them to listen to him (9:7); and their looking around and seeing no one else but Jesus "with them" (9:8). The disciples, like the historic Moses and Elijah (Exod 24–34; 1 Kgs 19), ascend the mountain at a time of discouragement and receive a preview of what glory will be like, in order to keep them persevering in the discipleship mission that, for now, only involves self-denial and cross-bearing.[33] The parallels with Moses' Mt. Sinai experience are many (see below), and suggest that this miraculous event in Mark is to serve as a shot in the arm for the disciples, almost equivalent to one of the most defining events in the history of God's people—the theophany of Yahweh. The message for Jesus' disciples is clear: While suffering has been foretold, glory is sure to come; they are to take heart.[34]

	MARK	EXODUS
Six days	9:2a	24:16
Jesus/Joshua	9:2–13	24:13
Three named disciples	9:2a	24:1, 9
Ascent of mountain	9:2b	24:9, 12–13, 15–18; 34:3
Transfiguration	9:2b–3	34:29–30, 35
Moses	9:4	24:1–18
συλλαλέω (syllaleō, "converse")	9:4	34:35
Tabernacle	9:5	25:8–9
Fear of onlookers	9:6	34:30
Cloud	9:7b	24:15–18; 34:5
Voice out of cloud	9:7b	24:16*

* See Dowd, *Reading Mark*, 90.

This preternatural incident of Jesus' Transfiguration is a snapshot of the promised glory of God's kingdom; indeed, considering their question to Jesus in 9:11 following the vision of glory, it is obvious the disciples understand what they see as being eschatologically significant.[35] That is, indeed, Mark's intent: this scene of great glory is a precursor to what is sure to happen in the future. The disciples are to persevere through suffering (promised for all who follow Jesus), for glory is coming (also promised to disciples, as opposed to the shame facing those who would not so follow).[36] "Thus the

33. Myers, *Binding the Strong Man*, 250.

34. Apart from the closely sequenced episodes of the Passion (Mark 14–16) and the "sandwich" in Mark 11, 9:2 has one of the most precisely timed transition statements between episodes in this Gospel: "after six days." It links 8:27—9:1 with 9:2–13 tightly, but even more, it may have symbolic significance. Witherington guesses it may allude to Exod 24:16 and the six-day preparation for the Sinai revelation, or that it may reference the time between the Day of Atonement and the Feast of Tabernacles (this might also explain Peter's reaction in 9:5 regarding making tabernacles) (*Gospel of Mark*, 262).

35. The Transfiguration is "an anticipated view of Jesus enthroned with the glory of the Parousia as an accomplished fact," for it serves as "an illustration of what the eschatological life for them is like and provides a basis of assurance for their hope" (Nardoni, "Redactional Interpretation," 384).

36. Unlike Exod 24:10–11, where God shows himself, here in Mark 9 he makes visible the divine, heavenly form of Jesus; μετεμορφώθη (*metemorphōthē*, "He was transfigured," 9:2) suggests a divine passive (also see Rev 1:16). See van Iersel, *Mark*, 294. While the concept of metamorphosis (μεταμορφόω, *metamorphoō*) was known in the Greco-Roman world (see, e.g., Ovid's *Metamorphoses*), Donahue and Harrington (*Gospel of Mark*, 269) suggest that a better analogy is the christological hymn of Phil 2:6–11:

transfiguration scene is . . . a proleptic vision of the exaltation of Jesus as kingly Son of man granted to the disciples as eschatological witnesses."[37]

The presence of Elijah triggers the hope of Jesus' future return (note the tendency to identify Jesus as Elijah, 6:15; 8:28). The appearance of Moses, too, would raise the hopes of the arrival of a "prophet like Moses" (Deut 18:15–19, which, incidentally, also contains a command that this prophet be listened to, just as in Mark 9:7). In other words, "[t]he reappearance of these two great figures of the past thus symbolizes the coming of the long-expected messianic age."[38] Moses and Elijah are the only two to have ever seen a theophany on a mountain (Elijah met with God on the same mountain as did Moses, 1 Kgs 19:8–18); both were faithful servants who suffered because of obedience; neither one saw death (2 Kgs 1:1–12; Josephus, *Ant.* 4.326; but see Deut 34:6 for Moses' death, albeit with an unknown grave). It is appropriate, then, that this duo should be with Jesus at his Transfiguration.[39] "This story has united two expectations which were alive in Judaism: the coming of the prophet of the end-time who is like Moses and the appearing of Elijah at the dawning of the end-time."[40] Both expectations are being met by Jesus. The kingdom of God is nigh! Glory is at hand . . . *after* suffering, as the remainder of the unit makes clear.

12.2.2   The Transfigured Jesus, who promises future glory but predicts present suffering, is the One disciples must listen to, and whose mission they should accept.

Coming right after all the discussion about the identity of Jesus, the vocative "Rabbi" in Mark 9:5 (equivalent to "Teacher," as in 4:38), sounds woefully inadequate, not to mention Peter's complete disregard for the mission that Jesus has just announced in 8:31. The disciple is willing to abandon the entire suffering project for a more sedate mountaintop residence with heavenly beings. Peter apparently thinks the kingdom has *finally* come in power (9:1) and he wants to build tabernacles for the ultimate Feast of Tabernacles celebration.[41] Moreover, he ranks Jesus as merely being one of the prophets, "for the proposal is to build three booths, not one throne."[42] Peter (with his

---

the transfiguration in Mark 9 provides the disciples with a rare glimpse of the μορφή θεοῦ (*morphē theou*, "form of God," Phil 2:6). Brilliance and shining white is the quality of the garb of heavenly beings (Ps 104:1–2; Matt 28:3; Mark 16:5; Luke 24:4; John 20:12; Acts 1:10; as well in apocalyptic texts: Dan 7:9; *1 En.* 14.20; *2 En.* 22.8–9; *3 En.* 12.1); it is also, ominously, the garment of martyrs (Rev 3:5, 18; 4:4; 6:11; 7:9, 14). See Myers, *Binding the Strong Man*, 250. The focus on "white" in this pericope will be found to be significant later in the Passion account.

37. Kee, "Transfiguration in Mark," 150.

38. France, *Gospel of Mark*, 351–52.

39. The feeding of the 5,000 in Mark 6 was already noted to allude to Jesus as a new Moses.

40. Schweizer, *Good News*, 183.

41. Witherington, *Gospel of Mark*, 263–64. The concept of booths itself was understood eschatologically: Ezek 37:27 and Zech 14:9–11 predict Yahweh dwelling in Jerusalem to reign, with Zech 14:16 associating this consummation of victory with the Feast of Tabernacles. See Kee, "Transfiguration in Mark," 147.

42. Myers, *Binding the Strong Man*, 250. "Do not set up tents equally for the Lord and his servants. 'This is my beloved Son; hear him,' my Son, not Moses or Elijah. . . . They, too, indeed are dear to me, but he is my beloved; hear him, therefore. They proclaim and teach him, but you, hear him; he is the Lord

compatriots) has not accepted the nature of the task that lies ahead for their Master or for themselves. Inasmuch as Peter's statement in 9:5 is explicitly said to be inappropriate (9:6), it is notable that the introduction to his artless and naïve suggestion (ἀποκριθεὶς ὁ Πέτρος λέγει τῷ Ἰησοῦ, *apokritheis ho Petros legei tō Iēsou*, "and Peter, answering, said to Jesus") is almost exactly the same as the introduction to his earlier confession of the identity of Jesus (ἀποκριθεὶς ὁ Πέτρος λέγει αὐτῷ, *apokritheis ho Petros legei autō*, "Peter, answering, said to Him," 8:29). Ergo, that earlier utterance, too, was likely to have been equally inadequate.[43] At any event, Peter's suggestion here is not taken seriously—there is much to come before glory, i.e., suffering. The disciples fail to accept that aspect of Jesus' mission (and their own): an incomplete confession of Peter that attempted to bypass the cross is now followed by an incomplete proposal from Peter that attempts to bypass suffering and take a shortcut to glory.

As was noted earlier, God's command here (ἀκούετε αὐτοῦ, *akouete autou*, "listen to Him") also echoes Deuteronomy 18:15 (αὐτοῦ ἀκούσεσθε, *autou akousesthe*, "to him you will listen"), where the sending of a "prophet like Moses" is predicted. "Jesus is this Second Moses, come to guide the New Israel through the new, definitive exodus."[44] "Who do *people* say I am?" (Mark 8:27) was followed by "Who do *you* say I am?" (8:29). Now the disciples get to hear who *God* says Jesus is (9:7). This is God's beloved Son, who must be listened to.[45] In light of the "plain" word of Jesus in 8:38, and the fact that the disciples (led by Peter) did not accept Jesus' mission, this imperative is apropos: they (and all future followers of Jesus) must pay close attention to Jesus and, particularly in the context of 8:34–38, to his call of suffering discipleship.[46] Curiously, Jesus does not speak at all in this episode; perhaps he has already said enough, and "plainly" at that!

As was noted, this account emphasizes all that is *seen*: Jesus' radiance (9:3), Elijah and Moses (9:4), cloud (9:7); etc.—things Jesus promised some would *see* (9:1). So it might have made more sense for the heavenly voice to urge, "See Him" or "Behold Him!" Instead we find, "*Listen* to Him!" Tolbert observes that the divine requirement to *hear* the one who is not speaking, but radiating in brilliance, "turns the whole episode on its head."[47] While the glorious vision of the future serves to bolster disciples' hope and sustain them in days of darkness, the imperative for the present is clear: disciples are to listen to Jesus! What Jesus has said about his mission and that of his followers—the way of suffering discipleship (8:31–38)—is what must be heard and

---

and master, they are companions in servitude. Moses and Elias speak of Christ; they are your fellow servants; he is the Lord; hear him" (Jerome, *Homily* 80).

43. Collins, *Mark*, 424.

44. Stock, *Method and Meaning*, 246.

45. The three "Son of God" announcements in Mark come at three strategic points—1:1; 9:7; and 15:39—juxtaposed to three references to the coming kingdom: 1:15; 9:1; and 14:25. "[F]or the evangelist Mark there was a very close connection between the coming of the kingdom and Jesus' identity as Son of God" (Hooker, "Mark's Parables," 82).

46. Listening is something the disciples have not been doing much of: 4:3, 9, 23, 24; 7:14, 16; 8:18.

47. Tolbert, *Sowing the Gospel*, 206.

accepted now. Glory (and sight) will come later. For the present, the call is to "listen to Him," i.e., to accept the mission Jesus undertakes, denying oneself and taking up one's cross to follow him who goes ahead.[48]

12.2.3 *The suffering of Elijah/John foreshadows Jesus' own suffering mission, reinforcing Jesus' Passion Prediction.*

Just as with the working of miracles and the exhibition of powers, the imposition of silence (9:9) indicates that the Transfiguration also is incomprehensible unless seen in retrospect, from the vantage point of the death and resurrection of Jesus—the completed mission of suffering. Even the disciples who have just been given advance notice of the Passion (8:30) have not grasped the significance of what they have observed on the mountaintop—Peter exemplifies their mystification (9:5–6). How much less, then, the general populace, without any such predictive counsel. Thus the order to keep mum, until such time as Jesus' mission is fully revealed.

Jesus' mention about "rising from the dead" (9:9) puzzles the disciples (9:10), and for good reason: outside of the corporate hope of resurrection for God's people at the eschaton, no clear precedent for an individual's resurrection as a special event had ever been discussed in contemporary Jewish literature.[49] But the disciples have just been warned by Jesus himself of this contingency (8:30–31). Of all the Twelve, these three who accompanied him on to the mountaintop, Peter, James, and John, had the best chance of understanding the scenario: they are the very ones who had witnessed an earlier miracle of this nature (5:37). And if Jesus was associated with the two "death-less" ones, Moses and Elijah, could not Jesus himself die and rise again?

At any rate, not surprisingly at this juncture, the three disciples attempt to clarify their eschatology. They have just heard of judgment (8:38–9:1) and of Jesus rising (8:31)—all intimately associated with the coming of the kingdom—and they just have seen Elijah. These portentous visions trigger a question: Elijah must come before all that happens, as the prophets foretold ("the great and terrible day of the Lord," Mal 4:5–6; Sir 48.1–10; *m. B. Meṣiʿa* 1.8; 2.8; 3.3; *m. ʿEd.* 8.7), but where is he (Mark 9:11)?

Jesus replies in two parts: first, he agrees that Elijah has to come first; second, he asserts that Elijah already has come. As Hooker notes, logically, the reply would make sense if 9:12b followed 9:13, paraphrased thus[50]:

Elijah must come first (9:12a).

But he came and he suffered (9:13).

Therefore the Son of Man (coming after Elijah), is going to suffer as prophesied (9:12b).

---

48. The imperative to listen is no doubt being addressed to all Mark's readers, then and thereafter, for many of these readers will not get the opportunity to see the transfigured Jesus personally.

49. France, *Gospel of Mark*, 357.

50. Hooker, *Son of Man*, 129–31. This explanation of Jesus reuses the phrase πολλὰ παθεῖν (*polla pathein*, "to suffer many things") from 8:31. Whereas ἀποδοκιμάζω (*apodokimazō*, "reject") was used in 8:31 (citing Ps 118:22 LXX), ἐξουδενέω (*exoudeneō*, "despise") is used here in Mark 9:12. Note that this verb is also used in Acts 4:11 to cite the same verse, Ps 118:22 (is Peter employing an alternate Greek version of the psalm?); ἐξουδενέω is also found in Ps 22:6, 24, an important text relating to Jesus' Passion.

In other words, the experience of Elijah foreshadows and anticipates the Passion of the Son of Man.[51] "Elijah has come, and, in fulfillment of scripture, has suffered. The messiah has come, and, in fulfillment of scripture, he will suffer. The placement of the saying about the suffering Son of Man in the center makes this whole speech another prophecy of the passion."[52]

Major premise:	*The forerunner of the Messiah must foreshadow the Messiah's own mission (9:11–12a).*
Minor premise:	*The mission of the Messiah includes suffering and death (8:29–33; 9:12b).*
Conclusion:	*The forerunner, foreshadowing the Messiah's mission, also must undergo suffering and death. He, John, did (9:13).**

* Dowd, *Reading Mark*, 93.

The thrust of this dialogue is Jesus' pointing to Elijah/John and reminding his disciples that, contrary to what they thought, Elijah/John would suffer first, and already has. As the disciples remember the forerunner's fate, they are to reconsider Jesus' own Passion Prediction, the acceptance of which, of course, will have serious ramifications for their own Trip of Discipleship and their role in the extension of Jesus' suffering mission. That suffering will be upon them is what Jesus is warning—just as it had come upon Elijah/John, and just as it will soon be upon himself. This is the core of the pericope: suffering must come before glory. Not surprisingly, this is not a message disciples care to hear. But there can be no shortcut to glory. The path to triumph is one of suffering. In the Transfiguration the disciples have been given assurance of the promised glory, a snapshot to give them hope. With that hope they are to press on, "on the way."

SERMON FOCUS AND OUTLINES

THEOLOGICAL FOCUS OF PERICOPE 12 FOR PREACHING

12   Amidst present suffering while following Jesus, disciples are encouraged by the hope of future glory (8:27—9:13).

This pericope, with Jesus' first Passion Prediction, starkly displays the suffering mission of Jesus, following it up immediately with a demand to the disciples to undertake the same journey, by denying oneself and taking up one's cross to follow Jesus. However bleak and unappetizing this might be, future glory is promised, right at the outset, along with the very first of Jesus' Passion Predictions. "Suffering now; glory later" is the resounding theme. And for those who refuse to walk this suffering mission, the theme might conceivably be "comfort now; shame later." This is an important—albeit, difficult—lesson for disciples to learn; for we are so rooted in this

51. While Mark does not explicitly connect Elijah to John the Baptist, enough clues are present in the narrative that his readers might link the two (see 1:4; 6:7–32; 8:28). France explains that the scriptural basis for Elijah's suffering (γέγραπται, *gegraptai*, "it is written," 9:13) may be a theological reading of 1 Kgs 17–19, 21, which depicts this faithful one as almost a martyr (France, *Gospel of Mark*, 359).

52. Collins, *Mark*, 432.

world and its temporality, that this is not easy to accept: glory seems far away and quite intangible. That is exactly why the magnificent snapshot of glory—the vision of the majesty of Jesus' Transfiguration and of the representatives of God's people, all in a glorified state—is provided in the final episode of this pericope. This is what the disciple can anticipate in the future, no matter how bleak and dire the present journey might be. Mark's intention is clear: keeping one's eyes fixed on future glory makes present suffering bearable. In the sermon, it may be necessary to touch upon what exactly "present" suffering involves (i.e., specifics as regards "denying self" and "bearing the cross"; however, a subsequent pericope, 14:53–72, will provide a better opportunity to expound on this concept; there the non-denial of self will be equated more closely with the exemplary self-denial of Jesus), as well as what exactly future glory and rewards mean for the believer. For this pericope, it would be best to focus on how an eternal perspective of glorious blessing can be proactively and preemptively developed so that God's people may be readied to face temporary banes with fortitude.

POSSIBLE PREACHING OUTLINES FOR PERICOPE 12

I.   PRESENT: The suffering mission of Jesus and his disciples
    The mission of Jesus and disciples clarified: 8:27–38
    Move-to-Relevance: Following Jesus is to go on the way of suffering with him
II. FUTURE: The glorious consummation of the kingdom
    The Transfiguration: 9:1–13, the "sneak preview" of future glory
    Move-to-Relevance: What the disciple can expect in the future
III. *Hang on the future to get through the present!*
    How exactly do we develop this eternal perspective?

Another option that results from minor tweaks to the above outline:

I.   Jesus' EXAMPLE: Suffering first, glory later
    The mission of Jesus involves suffering: 8:27–33; 9:9–13
    Suffering will be followed by glory: 8:38; 9:1–8
II. Disciples' EXPERIENCE: Suffering first, glory later
    Following Jesus in his mission involves suffering: 8:34–37; 9:11–13
    Suffering will be followed by glory: 8:35–38
    Move-to-Relevance: Specifics on suffering for the disciple today and glory tomorrow
III. Our EXHORTATION: *Hang on the future to get through the present!*
    How exactly do we develop this eternal perspective?

PERICOPE 13

Serving with Humility

Mark 9:14–50

[Disciples' Failed Exorcism; Second Passion Prediction; Serving Others]

REVIEW, SUMMARY, PREVIEW

Review of Pericope 12: Mark 8:27—9:13, by providing a snapshot of future glory, offers the disciple encouragement to continue following Jesus in his suffering mission.

> **Summary of Pericope 13:** Mark 9:14–50 exhorts the disciple to humility. The failed exorcism of the disciples reminds the follower of Jesus to depend humbly and prayerfully upon God's power by faith. The second Passion Prediction and the subsequent teaching section by Jesus further urge the disciple to serve with humility those who are seemingly insignificant and unimportant. In fact, the serious consequences of a failure to do so beckons the disciple to be diligent about removing every obstacle that stands in the way of a humble, servant-like attitude.

> > **Preview of Pericope 14:** The next pericope (10:1–12) teaches the importance of undertaking the journey of discipleship with one's spouse, permanently united, as evidence of the disciples' tenderheartedness towards one another and their adherence to the demands of Scripture.

13   Mark 9:14–50

THEOLOGICAL FOCUS OF PERICOPE 13

13   The acceptance of Jesus' suffering mission by disciples involves their maintaining a heart of humility—depending prayerfully upon God's power in faith, and seeking to serve the last and the least—diligently removing any obstacle that keeps them from such an attitude (9:14–50).

13.1   The divine empowerment of disciples is exercised in humility, as they regard themselves as incapable, instead depending prayerfully upon God in faith (9:14–29).

13.2   The acceptance of Jesus' suffering mission by disciples involves their seeking to serve the last, the least, and the insignificant, being diligent to remove any obstacle that keeps them from such humble service, lest negative consequences result in the eschaton (9:30–50).

13.2.1   The acceptance of Jesus' suffering mission involves serving the last and the least.

13.2.2   Disciples following Jesus on the way maintain an attitude of humility that accepts the insignificant.

13.2.3   The removal of every obstacle to a humble, servant-like attitude will prevent negative consequences for the disciple in the eschaton.

OVERVIEW

THIS PERICOPE CONTAINS THE final exorcism account in Mark and the only one in Act II of the Gospel. It is the story of nine disciples failing at the bottom of the mountain while three failed on the top. Other accounts of miracles usually end with the astonishment or fear of witnesses; here, instead, we have corrective instruction from Jesus on how to conduct an exorcism, followed by the second Passion Prediction and a collection of assorted sayings from Jesus on the related theme of being the last and serving the least.

Appropriately for the final exorcism of the Gospel, this account is a "[c]onspectus alluding to at least one element of each of the previous healing/exorcism episodes before Bethsaida," signifying to its symbolic role in Mark's narrative[1]:

Element of Exorcism	Previous Occurrence	Occurrence in MARK 9
Parent–child	5:35–43; 7:24–30	9:14–27
Amazement of crowd	1:27 (θαμβέω, thambeo)	9:15 (ἐκθαμβέω, ekthambeo)
Details of possession	5:3–6	9:18, 20, 22
Faith	5:34, 36	9:19, 23, 25
Convulsions	1:26 (σπαράσσω, sparasso)	9:20, 26 (σπαράσσω)
Compassion	1:41 (σπλαγχνίζομαι, splanchnizomai)	9:22 (σπλαγχνίζομαι)
Unclean spirit	1:26; 5:2; 7:25	9:25
Deaf and mute healing	7:31–37	9:25
Crowd claims death	5:35–43	9:26–27 (apparent death)
Taking by the hand	1:31; 5:41	9:27
Raising and getting up	5:41–42	9:27

1. Myers, *Binding the Strong Man*, 254.

The striking inability of the disciples to accomplish an exorcism contrasts with the commission already given them in 3:15 and 6:7, which they apparently fulfilled quite successfully at an earlier time (6:13). What, then, happened here?

The second section of this pericope (9:30–50) is one of the more difficult portions of the NT to elucidate.[2] Yet, in light of what happens following Jesus' second Passion Prediction, with the disciples' conceited pursuit of greatness (9:31–37), one can make sense of this cryptic section as portraying in vivid terms the importance of disciples' maintaining a heart of humility and being accepting of the seemingly insignificant and unimportant. Indeed, they are to do so with utmost diligence, lest they be guilty of grievous sin (9:43–50).

13.1 Mark 9:14–29

THEOLOGICAL FOCUS 13.1

13.1 The divine empowerment of disciples is exercised in humility, as they regard themselves as incapable, instead depending prayerfully upon God in faith (9:14–29).

Section Summary 13.1: The failure of the "unbelieving" generation, particularly the disciples, was their inability to cast out the demon: this was the consequence of a presumptuous self-confidence in their own abilities and a lack of faith in God's power working through them. Instead, the follower of Jesus must be like the father in the episode, with humility seeking God's power in prayerful dependence, by faith.

TRANSLATION 13.1

9:14 *And when they came to the disciples, they saw a large crowd around them and scribes arguing with them.*

9:15 *And immediately, when the whole crowd saw Him, they were amazed, and running up, they greeted Him.*

9:16 *And He asked them, "What are you arguing with them?"*

9:17 *And one from the crowd answered Him, "Teacher, I brought to You my son having a mute spirit;*

9:18 *and whenever it seizes [him], it throws him down, and he foams at the mouth, and grinds teeth, and becomes stiff. And I told Your disciples to cast it out, and they were not strong [enough]."*

9:19 *And He answered them, saying, "O unbelieving generation, how long must I be with you? How long must I endure you? Bring him to Me!"*

9:20 *And they brought him to Him. And seeing Him, the spirit immediately convulsed him, and falling down, he was rolling on the ground, foaming at the mouth.*

9:21 *And He asked his father, "How long has it been like this with him?" And he said, "From childhood.*

2. Boring rightly declares: "[T]he fact is, here we have one of the New Testament passages that defy interpretation" (*Mark*, 284).

9:22   *And it has often thrown him both into fire and into water to destroy him. But if You are able to do anything, have compassion on us and help us."*

9:23   *And Jesus said to him, "'If You are able'? All things are possible to the one who believes."*

9:24   *Immediately the father of the child, crying out, said, "I believe; help my unbelief."*

9:25   *When Jesus saw a crowd running together, He rebuked the unclean spirit, saying to it, "You mute and deaf spirit, I command you, come out from him and no longer go into him."*

9:26   *And crying out and greatly convulsing [him], it came out; and he became like a corpse, so that many said, "He is dead."*

9:27   *But Jesus grasped his hand and raised him, and he got up.*

9:28   *And when He came into the house, His disciples began asking Him privately, "Why were we not able to cast it out?"*

9:29   *And He said to them, "This kind is not able to come out by anything except by prayer."*

NOTES 13.1

13.1   *The divine empowerment of disciples is exercised in humility, as they regard themselves as incapable, instead depending prayerfully upon God in faith.*[3]

A major theme in this pericope is faith: Jesus laments the lack of faith of this generation (γενεὰ ἄπιστος, *genea apistos*, "unbelieving [or faithless] generation," 9:19); he tells the child's father that all things are possible for the one with faith (τὸν πιστεύων, *ton pisteuōn*, "the one who believes," 9:23); and the father confesses his need for help with his own lack of faith (ἀπιστία, *apistia*, "unbelief," 9:24). Thus the dialogue on faith between Jesus and the father forms the central element of the structure.[4]

A   Disciples' failure reported (9:14–18)
   B   Jesus and the boy (spirit; convulsions) (9:19–20)
      C   Jesus and father: belief (9:21–24)
   B'   Jesus and the boy (unclean spirit; convulsions) (9:25–27)
A'   Disciples' failure explained (9:28–29)

The complaint of the father, using οὐκ ἴσχυσαν (*ouk ischysan*, "not strong [enough]," 9:18), rather than οὐκ ἐδύναντο (*ouk edynato*, "not able") to describe the disciples, intensifies this group's collective incapacity and discomfiture: "they proved too weak, and have been defeated in a power struggle" with a demonic force.[5] The verb ἰσχύω, *ischuō*, and its derivatives have already appeared in Mark, hinting at

---

3. Stating the negative lesson in the positive, of course: the Twelve were quite faithless.

4. Iverson considers this incident to be taking place in Gentile territory (*Gentiles in the Gospel*, 104–8).

5. France, *Gospel of Mark*, 364.

skirmishes with demonic influences (3:27; 5:4; also remember John the Baptist's description of Jesus as the "stronger" one [ἰσχυρότερός, *ischyroteros*], 1:7). As if to reinforce the intensity of the demonic struggle, the affliction of the boy, with its etiology and its symptoms, gets extended coverage in the account (9:17–18, 20, 22, 26). The "unbelieving generation" is likely to refer to the disciples, labeled so because of their faithless inability to perform the exorcism. Because of their faithlessness, they are no better than "outsiders" who opposed the kingdom, already considered a reprehensible "generation" (8:12). As 9:19 indicates, Jesus expects his disciples to be capable of handling even such an advanced degree of demon possession. They, however, have not succeeded, unbelieving as they are (9:19). But the father is different (9:24): there is something creditable about the man's confession of unbelief. Unlike the disciples, he is at least aware of his problem of lack of sufficient faith.

In likening the boy to a corpse (9:26), and in employing two suggestive verbs (ἐγείρω, *egeirō*, "raise" and ἀνίστημι, *anistēmi*, "get up," respectively, 9:27), the narrator alludes to the raising and getting up of Jairus's daughter who had died (ἐγείρω and ἀνίστημι occur in 5:41, 42; and, there also, as here, Jesus grasped the afflicted one's hand). As was mentioned earlier, this current miracle, with elements of many previous ones, is almost a résumé of all the miracles that have been wrought thus far.[6] This "summarizing" miracle is being employed here in Mark's narrative to demonstrate *how* disciples should have used the power they have been granted by virtue of being followers of Christ. Jesus' answer to the disciples' question of why they are not able to perform the exorcisms is illuminating: such actions, Jesus notes, call for prayer (9:28–29). In other words, Jesus-followers must depend on God for his help and for his power to work through them.

It appears that the disciples may be so taken with their own authority and ability that they attempted the exorcism without seeking help from God in prayer (also see 11:23–24). Their problem was a lack of dependence on Jesus' power and, perhaps, a reliance on their own capacities. They should have recognized that theirs was only a delegated authority; intrinsic authority is Jesus' alone and therefore the disciples needed to rely upon him, even when exercising their own divine empowerment. "God's power is not an impersonal force to be manipulated, but a gift to be prayed for."[7] In a way, this exorcism and the lesson it teaches is a summary of how disciples, deputized by Jesus, are to engage in acts of power for the sake of the Gospel. "The focus is not upon the miraculous healing of the boy, for no amazement is reported after 9:27; rather, the concern is 'Why could we not drive it out?' (9:28)."[8] Perhaps in light of their earlier success in this arena (6:13), they have become "acclimatized to miracles and [think] of themselves as now the natural experts in such a case, as capable as Jesus *on their own strength;* they must learn that in spiritual conflict there is no such automatic power inherent in themselves."[9] Their own power, exercised earlier, is no intrinsic or deserved

6. That does not detract from its own historicity or veracity.

7. Dowd, *Reading Mark*, 93–94.

8. Myers, *Binding the Strong Man*, 255.

9. France, *Gospel of Mark*, 370.

possession, but the result of divine commission. Theirs is a deputized authority, to be employed anew on each individual occasion by dependent prayer, in faith. There is no place for presumption and pride in the disciple who follows behind Jesus. The humiliation, here, hopefully teaches them humility. Out of this humility should arise a faithful dependence upon God as evidenced by prayer. Self-confidence must be tossed overboard in favor of God-dependence. And the disciple must engage in prayer, not as a special *mantra* or manipulative technique, but as a humble seeking of God by faith, to fulfill the mighty tasks the disciple is called to undertake. While self-confidence may fool one into thinking that one has faith, such unwarranted optimism is almost a dangerous arrogation of divine power; "it is in fact unbelief, because it disregards the prerequisite of human powerlessness and prayerful dependence on God."[10]

Indeed, the only one whose prayer in this pericope results in the successful casting out of the demon is the father: "I believe; help my unbelief!" (9:24). This is the attitude disciples should have, an attitude of humility and trustful dependence expressed in prayer. The father's exclamatory "prayer" simultaneously confesses confidence in the power of God in Jesus, and a lack of confidence in his own ability, even to maintain faith. "To this attitude the disciples are now summoned, and at the same time reminded that 'all things are possible to one who believes'—and *only* to one who *truly* believes." Even the exorcism of demons of great power (indicated by the sorry state of the child and by the gathering together in this episode of elements from all previous exorcisms) is achievable for the believer. This account, a précis of all earlier healings, emphasizes that the disciples could have—and should have—accomplished what Jesus had to do himself in the end. But they needed an attitude of humility and dependence upon God to do so. The "unbelief" they have demonstrated was not the despair of being in a dire situation (as in 4:35–41, or as in the case of the father in this episode), but "a blasé self-assurance that fails to see the centrality of dependent prayer in deploying Jesus' delegated power, treating it almost as a technique learned from him," a skill that works simply because a formula is expressed and a method followed—*ex opere operato*. This self-confidence is but a species of "unbelief." Instead, disciples must be humble, trusting in God alone as the source of their empowerment.[11]

This pericope thus directs the thrust of Act II in a different, but crucial, direction: the momentum of the act is on the disciples' acceptance of Jesus' mission—the inevitability of suffering and its precedence before glory. A key aspect of suffering discipleship is the concept of humility taught here. In this section, such an attitude of dependent humility upon God is enjoined, as expressed in the prayer of faith, as disciples undertake to do great things for God. In the following episode (9:31–50) humility is further exhorted upon the disciples in their service to God's people.

10. Marshall, *Faith as a Theme*, 222–23.

11. Ibid., 223.

13.2 Mark 9:30–50

Section Summary 13.2: The disciples' complete neglect of Jesus' Passion Prediction is stunning. Instead, they are concerned with who among them is the greatest. Jesus teaches them that the role of the disciple is to serve with humility the last and the least, the insignificant and unimportant. The consequences of not doing so are grievous, and one should be diligent about removing any obstacle that keeps one from serving humbly.

TRANSLATION 13.2

9:30   *From there they went out and began to pass through Galilee, and He did not want anyone to know.*

9:31   *For He was teaching His disciples and saying to them, "The Son of Man is to be given over into the hands of men, and they will kill Him, and when He is killed, He will rise after three days."*

9:32   *But they did not understand the saying, and they were afraid to ask Him.*

9:33   *And they came to Capernaum. And when He was in the house, He asked them, "What were you arguing on the way?"*

9:34   *But they kept silent; for on the way they had argued with each other [about] who was the greatest.*

9:35   *And sitting down, He called the Twelve and said to them, "If anyone wishes to be first, he shall be last of all and servant of all."*

9:36   *And taking a child, He stood him in their midst, and taking him in [His] arms, He said to them,*

9:37   *"Whoever receives one of such children in My name, he receives Me; and whoever receives Me, does not receive Me, but the one who sent Me."*

9:38   *John said to Him, "Teacher, we saw someone casting out demons in Your name and we prevented him, because he was not following us."*

9:39   *But Jesus said, "Do not prevent him, for there is no one who is able to do a miracle in My name and who will be able, soon afterward, to speak evil of Me.*

9:40   *For he who is not against us is for us.*

9:41   *For whoever gives you a cup of water to drink in the name because you are of Christ, truly I say to you that he will never lose his reward.*

9:42   *And whoever causes one of these little ones who believe to stumble, it would be much better for him if, with a large millstone worn around his neck, he had even been cast into the sea.*

9:43   *And if your hand causes you to stumble, cut it off; it would be better for you to go into life crippled than, having two hands, to go away into hell, into the unquenchable fire.*

[9:44][12]

9:45   *And if your foot causes you to stumble, cut it off; it would be better for you to go into life lame than, having two feet, to be cast into hell.*

[9:46][13]

9:47   *And if your eye causes you to stumble, cast it out; it would be better for you to go into the kingdom of God one-eyed than, having two eyes, to be cast into hell,*

9:48   *where their worm does not die and the fire is not quenched.*

9:49   *For everyone will be salted with fire.*

9:50   *Salt is good; but if salt becomes unsalty, with what will you season it? Have salt in yourselves, and be at peace with one another."*

NOTES 13.2

13.2.1   *The acceptance of Jesus' suffering mission involves serving the last and the least.*[14]

The second Passion Prediction (9:31) occurs in this section. As in the first (8:31), the disciples demonstrate their blindness of kingdom values (9:33–34) which Jesus attempts to correct (9:35–37). Here again, the issue is pride, continuing the theme from the previous episode of the failed exorcism. Despite Jesus' admonition, at least one of the disciples, John, still does not get it (9:38), and so Jesus resumes the reeducation program for his followers with a series of brief but explosive sayings connected by catchwords (9:39–50).[15] The entire section unveils a facet of discipleship essential for those who would follow Jesus—what it means to be humble in service to others.[16]

    The irony of the Son of Man being delivered into the hands of men (9:31) must not be lost: the one to whom all authority is given (Dan 7:13–14) is now to be given over to the authority of men. Note also the futuristic present of παραδίδοται (*paradidotai,* literally "is given over," Mark 9:31), indicating the certainty of the event. It is also a divine passive, underscoring God's will in the whole enterprise. That verb (παραδίδωμι, *paradidōmi*) was used to indicate the fate of John the Baptist (1:14), it had anticipated

---

12. 9:44 is not found in the earliest manuscripts.

13. 9:46 is not found in the earliest manuscripts.

14. This is another theological subfocus that spins a negative account into a positive statement.

15. These catchwords are: "one of such children"/"one of these little ones" (9:37, 42); "name" (9:37, 38, 39, 41); "causes . . . to stumble" and "it is better" (9:42, 43, 45, 47; also 9:50); "Gehenna" (9:43, 47); "fire" (9:43, 48, 49); and "salted" (9:49, 50).

16. Myers, *Binding the Strong Man,* 259.

Judas' betrayal (3:19), it will describe Jesus' betrayal in the next Passion Prediction (10:33 [×2]), and will show up frequently in the actual account of his Passion (14:10, 11, 18, 21, 41, 42, 44; 15:1, 10, 15).[17] But the disciples still do not accept Jesus' suffering mission. In fact, suffering is the last thing on their minds (see also 6:52; 7:18; 8:17). Their fear of asking any questions following the second Passion Prediction (9:32) may stem from Jesus' response to Peter's comment after the first Prediction (8:33). They certainly do not want to raise any more queries, especially when these have only produced answers they were loathe to hear. If Jesus were to be handed over and killed, that fate could surely befall them as well (8:34). "They understand enough to be afraid to ask to understand more."[18] Their lack of discernment is now a full-blown failure to accept Jesus' mission: they are unwilling to proceed on this painful pathway of suffering.

Instead, they are looking out for themselves and contending about who is the greatest (9:33–34); they, like all of us, would rather have glory than suffering. France wonders if the question of who is the greatest was spurred by the Jesus' choice of Peter, James, and John to accompany Jesus to the mountaintop to observe the Transfiguration; this perceived slight would probably have been aggravated even more by the weakness and inability of those left below to perform an exorcism, and that in front of a reproachful crowd. Or perhaps they *did* grasp the part about Jesus' death, and were wondering who would get to be leader of the pack after Jesus' departure. Incredibly, the question of status consumes the disciples even as Jesus is anticipating his martyrdom.[19] Clearly the Twelve are refusing to accept the unappetizing aspects of Jesus' mission.

In reply to the disciples' self-engrossment and ambition, Jesus makes a profound statement (9:35–37): the highest status in the kingdom of God is appointed for those who are last of all and who are servants of all. Augustine's observation is apt: "Observe a tree, how it first tends downwards, that it may then shoot forth upwards. It fastens its root low in the ground that it may send forth its top toward heaven. Is it not from humility that it endeavors to rise? But without humility it will not attain to higher things. You are wanting to grow up into the air without a root. Such is not growth, but a collapse" (*The Gospel of John*, Sermon 38).[20]

Lowest on the social scale are children, under the authority and care of others and without the right of self-determination—last and least of all. Yet a disciple is to go one step further by serving those who, like this child, are last and least (9:35). A disciple too is thus to become least of all and, even more, servant of all; he or she is to serve those who are the least—those who are like children in their littleness and "leastness" (9:35, 37).[21] Disciples are to become the lowest of the low, servants to those who are

17. France, *Gospel of Mark*, 371–72. It is likely that Mark's original Roman audience would already have been familiar with the word (Rom 4:25; 8:32; παραδίδωμι, *paradidōmi*, also occurs twice in Isa 53:12 LXX).

18. Best, *Following Jesus*, 73.

19. France, *Gospel of Mark*, 373.

20. Cited in Oden and Hall, *Mark*, 126–27.

21. Fleddermann, "Discipleship Discourse," 63–64. In Aramaic the word טליא (*tly'*) can mean both "servant" and "child"—a deliberate wordplay may be present here.

last and least. This is nothing but a drastic reversal of the conventional scale of values and a complete overturning of the disciples' pursuit of greatness powered by their pride.

Serving and receiving the least is to be performed by the disciple "in My name" (9:37), i.e., as though the child/least represents Jesus. To receive the child, therefore, is to receive Jesus, and 10:45 explicitly shows Jesus as exemplifying this servanthood to the least. And, as Jesus represents God, to receive Jesus is to receive God (9:37).[22] In other words, being servant to the least is perhaps the most significant attitude a disciple can adopt, in stark contrast to the arrogant yearning for prestige and honor. "Jesus . . . is trying to get his disciples to humble themselves, rid themselves of the usual hubris and power struggles for dominant position, and serve, even serve a child, a humiliating task in the minds of some ancients."[23]

13.2.2   Disciples following Jesus on the way maintain an attitude of humility that accepts the insignificant.

The call to disciples to be last and to serve the least is followed by 9:36–41, which bids them be open to those whom they may otherwise reject (the last, the least, the insignificant, the unimportant); in doing so disciples prove themselves to be humble servants. That it is an illustration of what Jesus has just taught, regarding receiving and serving the least, is evident in the catchword link: 9:37, 38, 39, and 41 are connected by "in My/Your/the name."

From his comment in 9:38, it is evident that John has not grasped what Jesus has so carefully been telling them, even after employing an object lesson! Exorcism is a special commission to the disciples (3:14–15; 6:7, 13), and their discovery of others performing such healings stung their egos, particularly when they had just been un-able to perform one successfully in the previous episode. John is unwilling to surrender his "special" status. His use of the first-person plural suggests that the other disciples agree with this breach of protocol (9:38). What is striking also is John's accusation that that unknown exorcist is "not following *us*." One would think he would have caught on by now that disciples are to follow *Jesus*, not the Twelve: ἀκολουθέω (*akoloutheō*, "follow") elsewhere in Mark is always used of following Jesus.[24] "Never was a 'royal we' less appropriate!"[25]

Such a conceited focus on membership in the "elite" band of disciples is exactly what Jesus has been attempting to disabuse them of (it is surely significant that once again Jesus is addressed merely as "Teacher" by this disciple). Instead of being inclu-sive and open to the insignificant (9:37), John advocates the opposite. The issue of hierarchy, status, and position (addressed in 9:33–37) appears to be a deeply ingrained problem for these disciples, and probably for most other disciples after their time. In fact, their non-acceptance of Jesus' suffering mission, and of their own potential suffering discipleship, is a symptom of their underlying egoism and self-interest, evi-

22. France, *Gospel of Mark*, 374–75.

23. Witherington, *Gospel of Mark*, 270.

24. Mark 14:13 is another exception, for obvious reasons.

25. Myers, *Binding the Strong Man*, 261

denced in the episodes of this pericope: lack of dependence, seeking to be great, unwilling to accept the last and the least, etc. John's "we prevented him" (9:38) is expressly countered by Jesus' "Do not prevent him" (9:39). As was exhibited in the first episode of this pericope, the power that God gives is not intrinsic to any individual. Rather, since the source of the ability is Jesus himself, there can be no superiority among Jesus' human agents based on one's own self; there is no inherent ability that confers an elevated status upon any one disciple. What Jesus is advocating here is not just "naïve tolerance, but one which indicates knowledge of where the exorcist's true allegiance and true source of power lies"—in God. For this reason, John ought to have accepted that unnamed exorcist, for he, too, is *for* Jesus (9:40).[26] If the least service done in Jesus' name is reckoned for reward—even the serving of water (9:41)—how much more an exorcism done in his name (9:38–40)! Therefore, both the one who serves water and the exorcist are to be accepted by disciples who are humble and servant-hearted.

13.2.3 *The removal of every obstacle to a humble, servant-like attitude will prevent negative consequences for the disciple in the eschaton.*

The consequences for *not* being humble and servant-hearted are serious. Mark 9:42–50 is a stern passage that adjures disciples to be proactive in the care of the least, the "little ones" (μικροί, *mikroi*, 9:42). In light of the disciples' quarrel about the "greatest" (μείζων, *meizōn*, 9:34), it seems appropriate to employ the antonym μικροί for disciples who are humble and servant-like. Throughout 9:30–50, it is these μικροί that are the focus of attention in Jesus' discourse. In fact, it may not be too farfetched to surmise that Jesus wants all his disciples to consider themselves the least (9:35–37).

Instead of receiving children, if those "little ones" (including all the "insignificant") are led astray or "caused to stumble" (9:42)[27], the punitive ramifications will be considerable. The one who so causes others to stumble is, in effect, disabling another's discipleship; how this is accomplished the reader is not told, but "[t]o be the cause of another's spiritual shipwreck is so serious an offence that a quick drowning would be preferable to the fate it deserves."[28] The disciple is not to be a stumbling block to the last and the least; a refusal to receive these μικροί is nothing less than hubris and conceit—which will also get its appropriate reward.

The remainder of the section (9:43–50) is rather cryptic, but what Mark is doing might simply be exhorting the disciples "to deal rigorously with all temptations to abuse their role and their authority in relations with the Christian community they are in fact called upon to serve."[29] The particular organs Jesus mentions that promote

---

26. Fleddermann, "Discipleship Discourse," 56. Cicero, *Lig.* 11.33, likewise affirmed to Caesar: "We have often heard you assert that, while we held men to be our opponents, save those on our side, you counted all men your adherents who were not against you."

27. The verb σκανδαλίζω (*skandalizō*, "stumble") has been encountered before in 4:17 and will show up again in 14:27, 29—all referring to the falling away of the disciple.

28. France, *Gospel of Mark*, 380. "The danger consists of those who, self-absorbed, fail to have consideration for the weaker and more vulnerable" (Evans, *Mark*, 70).

29. von Wahlde, "Mark 9:33–50," 59.

this unservant-like attitude are the hand, the foot, and the eye. Quite appropriately, these are implicitly recommended by Jesus as the instruments of acceptance of the last and least: Jesus takes a child in his arms (9:36)—the disciples' *hands*, in contrast, are implicated in the rejection of the last and least; the exorcist is, in John's opinion, not following Jesus (9:38–40)—the *foot*, the organ of interest here, is what causes John to call for the exorcist's exclusion; and John's complaint arises from his "seeing" that individual perform exorcisms in Jesus' name (9:38)—it is the *eye* that apparently leads John astray.[30] Thus, Jesus is warning the disciple that anything—*anything!*—that causes one to disparage or reject one of the least (i.e., anything that stands in the way of the disciple's humble, servant-like attitude) better be eliminated, lest negative consequences result in the eschaton.[31] The harshness of punishment stresses the seriousness of offence. This is a call to radical living: nothing is allowed to interfere with the disciple's service toward the insignificant and unimportant, least of all the attitude of arrogance.

Salt, in 9:49–50, evokes the imagery of temple sacrifice (Lev 2:13, like Mark 9:49 has πᾶς, *pas*, "everyone," and ἁλισθήσεται, *halisthēsetai*, "will be salted"). Ezekiel 43:24 notes salt as being added to burnt animal offerings in the restored temple (also see Josephus, *Ant.* 12.140; *m. Mid.* 5.3). Here it is the disciple who is the salted "sacrifice." Rather than being thrown into *eternal* fire, disciples are to be salted sacrifices in fire *now*. Their attitudes of servanthood and their hearts of humility render them as appropriate sacrifices, "salted" and acceptable to God. Of note is the linkage of salt with the covenant of God (Lev 2:13; Num 18:19; 2 Chr 13:5), and with qualities of purity and holiness (Exod 30:35). Thus the salting by fire "speaks of one who follows Jesus as totally dedicated to God's service, and warns that such dedication will inevitably be costly in terms of personal suffering" (Rom 12:1 seems to agree).[32]

As opposed to struggling for priority (9:33–37), disciples are to be at peace with one another (9:50). In sum, being humble and servant-like—the thrust of this pericope—will surely bring suffering in its wake. Disciples must be ready to live a sacrificial

---

30. The three sources of stumbling mentioned are parallel to what is seen in Job 31:1, 5, 7, dealing with purity of eye, foot, and hand. Another way of understanding Jesus' use of the three organs is noted by Marcus: he sees the biblical use of "hand" as the instrument for the commission of sin, the "foot" as the means of transport to the locus of that commission, and the "eye" the portal of entry for the temptation to sin—"injunctions of increasing inwardness": "If your *hand* offends you . . ."—don't *commit* sins! (9:43); "If your *foot* offends you . . ."—don't *go anywhere* where you may commit sins! (9:45); "If your *eye* offends you . . ."—don't *even think about* committing sins! (9:47). See Marcus, *Mark*, 697. This is reasonable, but may not fit as seamlessly into the rest of the section as does seeing the hand, foot, and eye as the very agents of the discrimination that came under rebuke earlier.

31. Mark's image of hell ("Gehenna") is derived from Isa 66:24, with worms and fire and all (also see Jdt 16.17; Sir 7.17). If Jesus has in mind the whole of Isa 66:24 that deals with transgressors, the stumbling envisaged here may be equivalent to rebellion against God, the kind that inevitably results in eternal damnation. However, Mark's account is not intended to be a systematic schema of how eternal life is gained or lost. Jesus' language is graphic hyperbole; both his listeners and Mark's readers would have recognized that. For, needless to say, resurrection would bring about full restoration of body parts earlier lost (*Gen. Rab.* 95.1 [on Gen 46:28]). Thus the reader must simply see Jesus as directing attention to the sinfully heinous nature of snobbery and the rejection of the least (an unservant-like and proud attitude); he is not asserting that the one who so sins will undergo eternal damnation.

32. France, *Gospel of Mark*, 384.

("salted") life. "These enigmatic words, we may reasonably assume from their context, relate to the cost of taking up the cross to follow Jesus"—the theme of suffering now in order to experience glory later.[33] The entire discussion has established a trajectory towards 10:45, soon to be encountered.

SERMON FOCUS AND OUTLINES

> **THEOLOGICAL FOCUS OF PERICOPE 13 FOR PREACHING**
> **13** **The humble disciple, dependent on God's power in prayer by faith, diligently serves the last and least (9:14–50).**

While the first episode of this pericope (9:14–29), and the Passion Prediction and its aftermath (9:30–37), are quite clear in their theological intent, the remainder of the text (9:38–50) poses some challenges for the preacher, because of its exegetical difficulties and the seemingly *ad hoc* nature of the comments of Jesus. Therefore it would be best to focus primarily on 9:14–37, with 9:38–50 as an adjunct, bringing home the main point of the disciple's humble and serving attitude, evidenced in prayerful dependence on God by faith. Mark 9:38–50 may simply be taken as portraying, in strong terms, the negative consequences in the eschaton for failing to have such an attitude. The hyperbolic style in which this is urged should be an incentive to disciples today to take this exhortation very seriously.

Thus, this pericope turns out to be a lesson in humility (patterned after Jesus himself, as will be seen in 10:45). Two parallel thrusts are visible: the humble disciple depends on God's power, without being presumptuous; and the humble disciple serves the least, without being arrogant or assuming oneself to be in a position of greatness. The preacher may see these two thrusts as part of one focus: the vertical thrust depicts the servant's attitude to God; the horizontal thrust depicts the servant's attitude to others. This twofold thrust is reflected in the bifid homiletical proposition: "*Be humble: Depend on God*" and "*Be humble: Serve the least!*" The two are simply facets of the same focus on maintaining humility.

The responsibility of remaining humble and servant-like is one of immense gravity, and the disciple should assiduously and conscientiously cultivate this attitude, removing everything that stands in the way of such servanthood.

POSSIBLE PREACHING OUTLINES FOR PERICOPE 13

I.   HUMILITY: Depending on God

> The failed exorcism: 9:14–29, the disciples' failure to depend on God in prayer, for his power

> *Be humble: Depend on God!*

> Specifics on how one can be humbly dependent in prayer, rather than be proud and presumptuous

II. HUMILITY: Serving the least

---

33. Ibid., 383.

The Passion Prediction and the Lesson: 9:30–50, the disciples' continued failure to be humble and serving

Be humble: Serve the least!

Specifics on how one can be humbly serving the seemingly insignificant and unimportant

Another option:

I. POWERLESS: Disciples have no power of their own

Failure to exorcise: 9:14–27

II. How to gain POWER: *Be humble: Depend on God!*

The means of gaining power: dependence on God in prayer, 9:28–29

Specifics on how one can be humbly dependent in prayer, rather than be proud and presumptuous

III. POSITIONLESS: Disciples have no position of their own

Failure to be the least: 9:33–34, 38

IV. How to gain POSITION: *Be humble: Serve the least!*

The means of gaining power: suffering like Jesus, becoming and serving the least, 9:30–32, 35–37, 39–50

Specifics on how one can be humbly serving the seemingly insignificant and unimportant

PERICOPE 14

"One-Fleshed" Discipleship

Mark 10:1–12

[Marriage and Divorce]

REVIEW, SUMMARY, PREVIEW

Review of Pericope 13: Mark 9:14–50 exhorts the disciple to humility—prayerfully depending on God's power, by faith, as one serves the seemingly insignificant and unimportant.

Summary of Pericope 14: Mark 10:1–12 contains Jesus' teaching on the permanence and "one-fleshed" character of marriage, an institution divinely ordained as such from creation. In its context in a Gospel dealing with discipleship, the importance of undertaking the journey "on the way" with one's spouse is evidence of one's tenderheartedness, as well as one's adherence to the demands of Scripture.

Preview of Pericope 15: The next pericope (10:13–31) pictures another facet of the humility and dependence of disciples, calling upon them to be willing to abandon material possessions, knowing that both present recompense (despite suffering) and eternal rewards await.

14   Mark 10:1–12

THEOLOGICAL FOCUS OF PERICOPE 14

14   Following the radical lifestyle demanded by Jesus, his followers remain tenderheartedly united to their spouses for life, in obedience to Scripture, undertaking the journey of discipleship together (10:1–12).

14.1   Discipleship does not disrupt the one-fleshed nature of the marriage relationship.

14.2   Divorce, a sign of hard-heartedness and of non-adherence to Scripture, is incompatible with discipleship.

OVERVIEW

THE PREVIOUS PERICOPE, IN its latter portions, discussed the importance of disciples humbly serving the last and the least, the seemingly insignificant and unimportant. It concluded with an exhortation to peace: "Be at peace with one another" (Mark 9:50). In this pericope (10:1–12), an important area of this communion of peace, the relationship between spouses, is addressed. But in and through the specifics of this pericope is conveyed the singular importance of "one-fleshed" discipleship—the joint journey undertaken by spouses following Jesus together.

In 3:31–35, Jesus had declared that a new family is being formed that relates to him, follows him, and represents him. Questions would have arisen then regarding the implications of this new unit of relationship for the already-existing unit of the traditional family: What part does marriage and family play in the life of the disciple? Does Jesus' own example of "rejecting" mother and brothers have to be a model for others? If Mark's original readers were living around the time of the Jewish revolt (66–70 CE), then this question would have attained even greater significance, for those were days of distress and difficulty.

Leading up to his second Passion Prediction (10:33–34), Jesus will soon address some of the particular implications of his call to discipleship that relate to the issue of sacrificing everything "for My sake" (10:28–31). But before he does, it is appropriate that the issue of marriage be touched upon. Is that relationship sacrosanct, or is it one that must also be sacrificed for the cause of discipleship? Lest anyone suspect that the sacrifice of "everything" (10:28) includes spouses, Jesus makes an authoritative pronouncement: he is against divorce, for any reason (10:1–12).

In doing so, Jesus radically overturns contemporary societal values regarding marriage. The kingdom of God, at least its operation in this life, calls for a return to the values of marriage promulgated by God, he asserts.[1] But such countercultural viewpoints are not new in Mark's portrayal of the journey of discipleship. France observes[2]:

> A revolutionary perspective has already been emerging since 8:31 as Jesus has called his disciples to accept the paradoxical concept of a messianic mission accomplished through rejection and suffering, to lose their life in order to find it, to choose between the approval of other people and the claims of the Son of Man, to become the least and the servant in order to be the first, to welcome those whom they would naturally reject, and to envisage the possibility of drastic renunciation in this world in order to gain "life."

In the pericopes of Mark 10, those paradoxes are applied to aspects of daily domestic life—marriage in this pericope, earthly values and property in the next, to climax in the third and final Passion Prediction. The cost of discipleship is high, and the nature of kingdom living is radical. Not all will be willing to accept it.

---

1. Mark 10 resounds with "kingdom of God"; it figures prominently in 10:14, 15, 23, 24, and 25.

2. France, *Gospel of Mark*, 386.

14   Mark 10:1–12

THEOLOGICAL FOCUS OF PERICOPE 14

14   Following the radical lifestyle demanded by Jesus, his followers remain tenderheartedly united to their spouses for life, in obedience to Scripture, undertaking the journey of discipleship together (10:1–12).

14.1   Discipleship does not disrupt the one-fleshed nature of the marriage relationship.

14.2   Divorce, a sign of hard-heartedness and of non-adherence to Scripture, is incompatible with discipleship.

Section Summary 14: The Pharisaic demand that divorce be permissible reveals hard-heartedness, as well as a less-than-firm adherence to Scripture. Jesus proscribes such attitudes and actions for the disciple. Disciples, in keeping with the radical lifestyle demanded by their Lord, remain in monogamous, faithful union with their spouses for life, in obedience to Scripture, undertaking the journey of discipleship together.

TRANSLATION 14

10:1   *And rising up, He went from there into the regions of Judea, beyond the Jordan, and crowds came together again to Him, and as was His custom, He again began to teach them.*

10:2   *And Pharisees came to Him, testing Him, [and] asked Him if it was lawful for a man to divorce a wife.*

10:3   *But, answering, He said to them, "What did Moses command you?"*

10:4   *And they said, "Moses permitted [one] to write a certificate of dismissal and to divorce."*

10:5   *But Jesus said to them, "Because of your hard-heartedness he wrote to you this commandment.*

10:6   *But from the beginning of creation, male and female He made them.*

10:7   *For this reason a man shall leave his father and mother,*

10:8   *And the two shall be one flesh; so they are no longer two, but one flesh.*

10:9   *What, therefore, God joined together, man should not separate."*

10:10 *And in the house, the disciples began asking Him about this again.*

10:11 *And He said to them, "Whoever divorces his wife and marries another, commits adultery against her;*

10:12 *and if she herself, divorcing her husband, marries another man, she commits adultery."*

NOTES 14

14.1   Discipleship does not disrupt the one-fleshed nature of the marriage relationship.

The debate on divorce in this pericope is comparable to the *halakhic* debate on handwashing in 7:1–23: both are initiated by questions from the Pharisees (ἐπερωτάω, *eperōtaō*, "ask," in 7:5 and 10:2); in both cases a pronouncement from Jesus is recorded that refers to what Moses said (7:6–13; 10:5–9), followed by further teaching in the privacy of a house, in response to the questioning from his disciples (again ἐπερωτάω, 7:8–23; 10:10–12); in both episodes Jesus seeks to uncover fundamental guidelines established by God that govern the matter in question, and the concerns of the Pharisees and bystanders for mere legalistic injunctions are converted into concerns for core ethical principles: "a more radical obedience to the essential purpose of God" is called for by Jesus.[3] That, of course, is appropriate: radical journeys call for radical measures; new kingdoms call for new constitutions. "The prospective disciple is warned that his present sexual ethic will have to be abandoned and a new and rigorous attitude adopted, an attitude where he will almost certainly have to take his cross and deny himself."[4] Indeed, one might need a rewriting of this principle of 8:34 for married couples: "he+she" (as one flesh) will have to take "his+her" cross and deny "himself+herself" as "he+she" follows Jesus in discipleship. The "one flesh" concept is foundational to marriage, and remains so for discipleship, Mark teaches.

In this connection, it is worth mentioning that neither in 3:33–35 nor in 10:28–30 (both of which touch upon giving up fathers, mothers, brothers, sisters, children . . .) is there any hint of husbands giving up wives or vice versa for Jesus' sake. That relationship, as will be established in this pericope, is one ordained by God and is inviolable. The call to discipleship does not disrupt that unique bond. How could it? For husband and wife have become "one flesh," inseparable (10:8–9). In fact, for married folks, the Trip of Discipleship calls for a "one-fleshed" undertaking—a joint enterprise. There is never any indication in Scripture of it being otherwise. And in this pericope, Jesus makes that principle explicit.

14.2 Divorce, a sign of hard-heartedness and of non-adherence to Scripture, is incompatible with discipleship.

The question of the Pharisees (10:2) is no innocent query, but a ploy to trap Jesus. Considering where John the Baptist had ended (6:17–29), an imprudent reply from Jesus, they must have been hoping, would pitch him against Herod, especially since Jesus was now in the latter's territory and in the locus of John's activity and subsequent murder in Peraea (10:1).[5] Herod's divorce of the daughter of Aretas, king of Nabatea, had created a political crisis that culminated in a war between Galilee and Nabatea; with the help of the Romans, Herod survived, but barely retaining his kingdom. In such a volatile atmosphere, the tetrarch would probably not have been inclined to look kindly upon someone criticizing his marital antics.[6]

The possibility of divorce was not questioned in those days; Deuteronomy 24:1–4 was seen as an authoritative pronouncement "permitting" divorce.[7] However, what

---

3. Ibid., 387.

4. Best, *Following Jesus*, 101.

5. Πέραν τοῦ Ἰορδάνου (*Peran tou Iordanou*, "beyond the Jordan," 10:1) probably refers to Peraea, east of the Jordan and the Dead Sea, and south of Decapolis, a region ruled by Herod Antipas. See France, *Gospel of Mark*, 389–90.

6. Evans, *Mark*, 82.

7. Collins, *Mark*, 459–65.

exactly the grounds were for such a separation—what constituted the "indecency" of Deuternomy 24:1 (עֶרְוַת דָּבָר ['erewath dabar], ἀσχήμων πρᾶγμα [aschēmōn pragma, LXX], "some [matter of] indecency")—was an issue of considerable debate. The school of Rabbi Shammai averred that divorce was permissible only on the basis of sexual immorality; the school of Rabbi Hillel, the majority view, decided that the offending matter allowing for separation could be *anything* that displeased the husband—a spoiled meal, finding a fairer prospect (*m. Giṭ.* 9.10; *b. Giṭ.* 90a–b; *Sipra Deut.* 269; *Num. Rab.* 9.30), a wife's refusal of the husband's control (Sir 25.26), the husband "not liking her behavior" (as Josephus confessed when he divorced his wife, *Life* 426–27), or "for whatever cause" (Josephus, *Ant.* 4.253; also see Philo, *Spec. Laws* 3.30–31).[8] Thus, broadly, there were two camps on the grounds for divorce: the adultery-only camp (following Shammai) and the "any cause" camp (following Hillel). The permissibility of divorce itself was not generally questioned. It is in such a lax cultural milieu that Jesus unleashes his proscriptive decree on divorce.

In Matthew 19:3–9, the similar discussion is focused upon the "any cause" grounds for divorce (championed by the Hillel camp); this is expressly repudiated by Jesus, though allowing for adultery as an exception (agreeing with the Shammai camp). However, in Jesus' statement in Mark 10, there is no explicit mention of any of the Pharisaic grounds for divorce—adultery or "any cause." At stake is the legitimacy and legality of the practice of separation itself, and that practice is unambiguously rejected by Jesus. Such a strong assertion does not rule out exceptions, but this Markan declaration of Jesus clearly shows the latter's fundamental stance of opposition to divorce for *any* reason. What Mark is doing is establishing firmly the crucial importance of "one-fleshedness" in the economy of God and for the purposes of discipleship. That Mark is directing his text to a Roman audience and the early church might explain why he does not describe Jesus addressing the idiosyncratic Jewish grounds for divorce (adultery or "any cause," following Shammai or Hillel, respectively), which would be more appropriate in the context of Palestinian Pharisaism.[9] None of those rabbinical

---

8. At any rate, such divorces—conservative or liberal, following Shammai or Hillel—were permitted only for a man divorcing his wife, never the other way around. See Instone-Brewer, *Divorce and Remarriage*, 110–14.

9. Instone-Brewer offers a different, but intriguing, interpretation of the divorce debate in the Gospels. According to him, both Matthew and Mark portray Jesus being deliberately lured into the Shammai-Hillel debate on this issue; the difference between the accounts is the inclusion in Matthew of the phrases "for any cause" (Matt 19:3) and "except for immorality" (19:9; and also 5:32), phrases that formed the crux of the positions of Hillelites and Shammaites respectively, in their arguments over the precise meaning of עֶרְוַת דָּבָר ('rwth dbr, "some [matter of] indecency") in Deut 24:1. Instone-Brewer asserts that Matthew's "insertions" simply include what was actually present in the original debate, while Mark did not append them in his account "because they were so obvious and well known to the original audience that they were superfluous. They would have been mentally inserted by any Jewish reader whether they were included or not." Thus, for Instone-Brewer, the question of whether it was lawful to divorce a wife is "nonsensical" because it only had an affirmative answer—it *was* lawful. The issue was only whether it was lawful to divorce a wife for "any cause" as the Hillelites assumed, or only for immorality as the Shammaites argued—that would be the test for Jesus, and that was the question that was being put to him *even in Mark*, even where those incriminating phrases are absent. Thus, in Instone-Brewer's understanding, the debates in both Gospels are identical, and Jesus' reply to the Pharisees in

discussions on divorce are being allowed by Jesus to prevail; this is a stunning demand by Jesus for lifelong monogamy and fidelity, and such a call in this section functions as a response to the brokenness of humanity and their self-centeredness and hard-heartedness (10:5), which cause them to disrupt even the most sacred of human relationships, one divinely established—that between spouses. Needless to say, this unit also underscores the demand of discipleship for strict adherence to the commands of Scripture.

Jesus asks about Moses' *command* (10:2) and the Pharisees reply that Moses *permitted* divorce (10:4). However, Deuteronomy 24:1–4, the passage referred to, does not command or even explicitly permit divorce; it *assumes* the situation and attempts to regulate it, preventing spousal abuse *after* a divorce has occurred. Deuteronomy 24:1–3 consists only of conditional clauses (beginning with כִּי [*ki*], ἐὰν δέ [*ean de*, LXX], "if"), setting up the scenario for the Mosaic legislation of 24:4 asserting that a husband who has divorced his wife cannot remarry her.[10] The divorce itself is not a matter of discussion for the purposes of this commandment—it is neither permitted nor proscribed, but simply assumed to have happened. "To interpret this even as a permission for divorce is a matter of inference from the fact that divorce is envisaged without expressed disapproval."[11] Jesus' subsequent labeling of Moses' words as a "commandment" (Mark 10:5) is not a concession to the Pharisees' opinion; he is not agreeing with them that divorce is "commanded." Deuteronomy 24:1–4 *as a whole* is, after all, a commandment, one dealing with remarriage between a divorced couple. This entire "commandment" (i.e., Deut 24:1–4 as a unit), Jesus' states, was given as a result of the "hard-heartedness" of the Israelites (in the NT, σκληροκαρδία, *sklērokardia*, is found only in Mark 10:5 and in Matt 19:8). Deuteronomy 10:16; Psalm 95:7–8; and Jeremiah 4:3–4 indicate that the root of this hard-heartedness (and "stiff-neckedness")

Mark 10:6–9 is merely a "digression on monogamy." See Instone-Brewer, "Jesus' Old Testament Basis," 89–91 (and the entire article); also see his extensive monograph on this issue, *Divorce and Remarriage*. One wonders, though, why Mark (and Luke) has the abbreviated account, when his (and Luke's) primary audience appears to have been Gentiles quite unlikely to be cognizant of the niceties of Pharisaic legal debates. If the arguments in Matthew and Mark are identical, it would have been more appropriate for *Mark* to contain the expanded version than for Matthew to do so, as the latter was writing to a Jewish audience more in tune with theological disputes. Neither does the disciples' response to Jesus' utterance in Matt 19:3 ("it is better not to marry") sound appropriate if all Jesus is doing is arbitrating between two fractious rabbis. Moreover, the absoluteness with which Jesus makes his pronouncement in Mark 10:5–12, as well as the geographical and historical context of the episode (Herod's divorce and John the Baptist's condemnation thereof), seems to direct this discussion as dealing with more than simply grounds for divorce. It makes sense to see Jesus as prohibiting the practice altogether—a foundational ethic, albeit with the possibility of exceptions as Matthew's Gospel notes. Thus, in my reading, the reason for the difference in the accounts of the two Gospels is because Mark is interested in stating for the disciple the utmost significance of "one-fleshedness." Hence, his narrative of Jesus' total proscription of divorce; such a *rhetorical* thrust with a definite agenda (to stress the importance of "one-fleshedness") does not preclude exceptions, but emphasizes the overwhelming seriousness of the issue of marital unity, particularly in the context of discipleship.

10. See Gundry, *Mark*, 539, for reasons why the LXX version of Deut 24:1–3, specifically, does not read as a command—the future indicative verbs, "write," "give," and "send," function more like subjunctives than as imperatives.

11. France, *Gospel of Mark*, 390–91.

is rebelliousness towards God. The Jeremiah passage is particularly pertinent, for it follows Jeremiah 3, which opens with a clear allusion to Deuteronomy 24:1–4 and goes on to describe Israel's divorce from God because of her adulteries and stubbornness (Jer 3:3, 13, 17, 20)—the stubbornness of an unfaithful partner who refuses to repent. This fits aptly with Jesus' teaching that divorce is not necessarily compulsory, but is merely a permission because of hard-heartedness. In other words, Deuteronomy 24:1–2 is not to be seen as offering divorce as a valid option for those on the journey of discipleship.[12]

Jesus then proceeds to show what Moses actually *commanded*—his texts of recourse are Genesis 1:27 and 2:24. The imagery of unified, single flesh "lifts marriage from being a mere contract of mutual convenience to an 'ontological' status. It is not merely that 'one flesh' *should* not be separated; it *cannot*."[13]

Jewish divorce in those days explicitly allowed remarriage; for instance, the certificate of marriage to a divorced woman read, "You are free to marry any man" (*m. Giṭ.* 9.3).[14] But Jesus corrects this misconception, expanding the Mosaic prohibition of a husband remarrying the wife he once divorced: Jesus' proscription of remarriage extends to any divorcé marrying another woman, and any divorcée marrying another man (Mark 10:11–12). Such an understanding implies the original, divine view of marriage as a "one flesh" union that is essentially inseparable. This "two" becoming "one" also presupposes monogamy.

The wife's right to divorce, though not accepted in the Jewish world, was recognized in the Roman milieu of Mark's readers.[15] Adultery in the literature of the Jewish Scriptures as well as in the Greco-Roman world was defined as a man having relations with a woman who is married or engaged to another man, thus violating the marriage of another *man* (Deut 22:22–24; Lev 20:10). "Thus the Markan Jesus innovates significantly in teaching that any man who divorces his wife and marries another commits adultery *against his first wife*. Men are no longer responsible only to respect the rights of other men over their spouses and those they have betrothed. According to v. 11 [Mark 10:11], men are responsible also to their own wives."[16] By redefining divorce as enabling and facilitating adultery, Jesus conclusively condemns divorce as a violation of God's will revealed in Scripture.[17]

Following Jesus is a radical step, and radical steps call for radical measures and radical changes in worldview. This pericope is a call to a corresponding radical lifestyle

---

12. Instone-Brewer, *Divorce and Remarriage*, 145–46.

13. France, *Gospel of Mark*, 392. This is not to deny that it is, indeed, humanly *possible* to separate. Also see Instone-Brewer, *Divorce and Remarriage*, 141.

14. See France, *Gospel of Mark*, 29.

15. Catchpole, "Synoptic Divorce Material," 110–12. See also Josephus, *Ant.* 15.259–60; 18.360–62; *m. Yebam.* 14.1; etc., for prohibitions on women obtaining divorces; however women could on certain occasions sue to obtain a divorce (*m. Yebam.* 14.1; *m. Ketub.* 7.9–10).

16. Collins, *Mark*, 469.

17. Boring, *Mark*, 287. This element of the remarriage being adultery against the first spouse is absent from Matt 5 and 19.

in the divinely ordained institution of marriage, commensurate with the revolutionary call of discipleship.

SERMON FOCUS AND OUTLINES

THEOLOGICAL FOCUS OF PERICOPE 14 FOR PREACHING

14 **Followers of Jesus, in obedience to Scripture, remain united to their spouses for life, in the journey of discipleship (10:1–12).**

This pericope constitutes an important directive to disciples regarding the closest union humanly possible—the institution of marriage. Lest one imagine that discipleship and its call for self-denial and cross-bearing involves the abandonment of this union, Jesus quickly disabuses one of this misconception. Mark places this teaching in the context of a debate with the Pharisees on divorce, and highlights Jesus' declaration on the permanence of marriage, rooted in the divine injunctions of the creation account.

It is obvious that this pericope does not seem to give any ground for divorce, unlike the Matthean account. A comprehensive view of marriage and divorce must surely take into account these canonical parallels and the exceptions cited. However, the homiletician must be careful not to major on those exceptions in a sermon on this pericope; the rule, rather than the exception(s), is Mark's (and Jesus') theological thrust here, and that thrust must be respected. As was noted, the difference in the accounts in the two Gospels is primarily one of *rhetorical intent*: Mark is interested in underlining the seriousness of the marriage covenant and its inviolate nature in the lives of married disciples; for this reason, he does not belabor the issue of Jesus' permission of exceptions in his narrative, as Matthew does.

In light of the likely presence of many in every congregation who may have suffered the devastation of a divorce (for whatever reason), a good dose of tact and grace must be dispensed by the preacher, *without diluting the theological focus* of the pericope, which the Holy Spirit has inscripturated through Mark, that divorce is outside God's foundational scheme for discipleship.[18] Emphasis should be placed on the importance of the walk of discipleship being a joint affair as far as married couples are concerned.

POSSIBLE PREACHING OUTLINES FOR PERICOPE 14

I. WORLD: The world's (mis)conception of marriage
    A matter of convenience and pleasure, easily undone and rapidly remade
    Move-to-Relevance: Illustrations of the world's misconceptions
II. GOD: The divine conception of marriage

---

18. An option would be spend more than a single week dealing with the issue of marriage, remarriage, and divorce, etc., bringing to bear on these issues all that Scripture teaches in a comprehensive coverage of the subject (i.e., in a topical sermon or two). That would be a good excuse for a break from the Mark series. Once again, this detour must not create the impression that marriage (and its ancillary concerns) constitutes the most important issue a disciple must contend with while following Jesus. Marriage is no doubt of immense consequence in the eyes of God, but it should not be forgotten that marriage does not constitute the *summum bonum* of the Christian life.

A matter critical to discipleship: 10:1–12, evidence of tenderheartedness and faithfulness to Scripture

III.   DISCIPLE: *Follow Jesus "one-fleshed"!*

What does it specifically mean to follow Jesus jointly as a couple?[*]

[*] The author of this commentary is a confirmed celibate, unschooled in the ways of marriage, and confesses that he has no idea how to preach this pericope; if he were preaching through Mark, he would probably pass 10:1–12 to a married person to undertake that august task!

A rearrangement of the points provides another option for an outline for this pericope:

I.   God's INJUNCTION: Marriage is permanent
     God's demand of marriage: 10:6–12
     God's demand for faithfulness to Scripture

II.   World's VIOLATION: Marriage is trivial
     World's distortion of marriage: 10:1–5
     Move-to-Relevance: Illustrations of the world's misconceptions

III.   Disciples' CORRECTION: *Follow Jesus "one-fleshed"!*
     What does it specifically mean to follow Jesus jointly as a couple?

PERICOPE 15

Depending on the Dollar

Mark 10:13–31

[Rich Man Walks Away; Jesus Teaches Eternal Perspective]

REVIEW, SUMMARY, PREVIEW

Review of Pericope 14: Mark 10:1–12 teaches the importance of undertaking the journey of discipleship permanently united with one's spouse, evidence of disciples' tenderheartedness towards one another, and their adherence to the demands of Scripture.

Summary of Pericope 15: Mark 10:13–31 pictures the humility and dependence of children, an attitude essential for the acceptance of the radical demands of discipleship. The second episode of this pericope furthers that idea, calling upon disciples to relinquish their dependence upon possessions, being willing to abandon them for the sake of the Gospel, knowing that both present recompense (despite suffering) and eternal rewards await.

Preview of Pericope 16: The next pericope (10:32–52), with the third Passion Prediction of Jesus, demonstrates what true greatness means: to suffer and serve as Jesus did, accepting his mission.

15   Mark 10:13–31

THEOLOGICAL FOCUS OF PERICOPE 15

15   Followers of Jesus accept the radical demands of discipleship with humble dependence upon God, maintaining proper perspective on possessions and being willing to part with them, in expectation of abundant recompense in the present, despite sufferings, and abundant reward in the future (10:13–31).

211

15.1 The demands of discipleship are accepted by followers of Jesus with humble dependence upon God (10:13–16).

15.2 The radical demands of discipleship include the willingness to relinquish the possessions of this life, in the expectation of abundant recompense in the present age, despite its sufferings, and abundant reward in the age to come (10:17–31).

15.2.1 The radical demand of discipleship includes the willingness to relinquish the possessions of this life.

15.2.2 Obedience to the sacrificial demands of discipleship in this life will be abundantly rewarded in the kingdom of God.

15.2.3 Sacrifice in obedience to the demands of discipleship will not only be rewarded by eternal life in the age to come, but will also be abundantly recompensed in the present age, despite its sufferings.

OVERVIEW

THE RADICAL OVERTURNING OF conventional societal values that began in Act II with the Passion Predictions and Jesus' subsequent teaching in each case, continues in Mark 10:

10:13–16   Having the status of a child is necessary for kingdom entry

10:17–31   Antitheses between meekness and pride, service and power, way of this age and way of the kingdom

10:32–34   Jesus' humbling himself: suffering before glory

10:38–39   Necessity for Jesus' disciples to share his suffering

10:42–43   Conventional hierarchies of power in opposition to the values of God's kingdom

10:43–45   Jesus' sacrifice as the model of service*

* From Minear, "Needle's Eye," 159.

Will the disciples accept Jesus' suffering mission and adopt these divine values as they follow Jesus on way of discipleship?

The pronouncement in 10:15 on the reception of God's kingdom focuses the first episode of this pericope upon discipleship, rather than upon the children themselves and their treatment. The double mention of the "kingdom of God" (10:14, 15) emphasizes this point. Whereas in 9:36–37 the issue is the acceptance of children in Jesus' name (the disciple's service to the least—reception *of* children), here the lesson drawn from the disciples' rebuke of children is the manner of children's acceptance of the kingdom of God (reception *by* children). This stands in contrast to the second episode of the pericope, in which the rich man refuses to accept Jesus' mission and its values, thus jeopardizing his entry into the kingdom of God. "A child, in contrast, has virtually no possessions or responsibilities and is thus much more likely to respond positively to the opportunity to enter the kingdom (v. 15)." [1] Children do so simply and unconditionally, exercising their total dependence upon another person. On the other hand, those entangled in the cares of the world, like the rich man, do not find it as

1. Collins, *Mark*, 471. See also Evans, *Mark*, 91.

easy to trust another and relinquish oneself, having much more to be (self-)dependent upon—in this pericope, possessions. This unit about children paves the way for Jesus' interaction with the rich man, linking the two episodes with the themes of entry into God's kingdom.

15.1   Mark 10:13–16

THEOLOGICAL FOCUS 15.1

15.1   The demands of discipleship are accepted by followers of Jesus with humble dependence upon God (10:13–16).

Section Summary 15.1: Jesus' pronouncement on the reception of kingdom demands as a child receives them emphasizes the need for disciples to accept the demands of discipleship with the humility and dependency characteristic of children.

TRANSLATION 15.1

> 10:13 *And they were bringing children to Him so that He might touch them; but the disciples rebuked them.*
>
> 10:14 *But seeing [this], Jesus was indignant and said to them, "Let the children to come to Me; do not prevent them, for of such is the kingdom of God.*
>
> 10:15 *Truly I say to you, whoever does not receive the kingdom of God as a child, will never enter into it."*
>
> 10:16 *And taking them in His arms, He blessed [them], laying His hands on them.*

NOTES 15.1

15.1   *The demands of discipleship are accepted by followers of Jesus with humble dependence upon God.*

Mark 9:36–37 (the previous episode involving children) and 10:13–17 share several terms:

παιδίον (*paidion*, "child") and μὴ κωλύετε (*mē koluete*, "do not prevent") (9:36, 37; 10:13, 14, 15)

τῶν τοιούτων (*tōn toioutōn*, "of such") (9:37; 10:14)

ὃς ἂν ... δέξηται (*hos an ... dexētai*, "whoever ... receives") (9:37; 10:15)

ἐναγκαλισάμενος (*enankalisamenos*, "taking [them] in [His] arms") (9:36; 10:16)

In 10:15 the logic of 9:37 is furthered: the disciple is not only to receive the least, but is to *be like the least*, for these least are the ones who enter into the kingdom of God; i.e., the kingdom is to be received the way children receive it.

The ἀμήν (*amēn*, "truly") sayings in Mark introduce important pronouncements; here, in 10:15, is a strong warning about how one may miss God's dominion. The kingdom of God is the rightful portion of the least—those who share the status of children, the "insignificant" ones. "It is the literal children whom Jesus tells the disciples to allow to come to him, but the reason is that they belong to and represent a wider category of οἱ τοιοῦτοι [*hoi toioutoi*, 'such as these'] who are the ones who matter to God."[2] The characteristic of children that enables them to accept everything as a gift is what one should demonstrate: receiving the kingdom of God without presumption, without the assumption of any deservedness, and with humility acknowledging total dependency on the grantor.[3]

As Best observes, this reception of God's kingdom is more than just a one-time event. The adoption of kingdom values and acceptance of the consequences of participating in Jesus' mission is a lifelong enterprise. "He does not achieve this all at once when he becomes a disciple; it is a gradual process; hence our pericope fits appropriately into a discussion of the nature of discipleship."[4] The "kingdom of God" is possessed, received, and entered into (10:14, 15); all three deal with Markan processes of discipleship, rather than with the initial movement of faith by which one becomes a child of God, a believer in Christ.[5] "Entering into" (or "coming into") the kingdom seems to indicate destiny in the hereafter—specifically, the concept of reaping its benefits and appropriating its rewards. "Possessing" the kingdom has a similar connotation. "'[R]eceiving' it relates more to a person's attitude and response towards God's demands in this life"—the daily demands of discipleship in the here and now. "To 'receive the kingdom of God' means to be God's willing subject, gladly embracing the radical values which Jesus has come to inculcate." In other words, reception of the kingdom involves acceptance of the suffering mission of Christ. "It is such a 'reception' now which is the key to 'entry' hereafter."[6] Reception now leads to entrance/possession (i.e., the rewards of the afterlife) later. Thus, one could envisage two dimensions or characteristics of the kingdom of God: a present suffering (reception), as well as a future glorious reward (entrance/possession). Suffering first, glory later, has, of course, been Mark's theme all along.[7]

This episode with the children thus demonstrates the importance of disciples receiving (now) the demands of discipleship in this life with humility and dependency

2. France, *Gospel of Mark*, 396–97.

3. Stein, *Mark*, 463–64.

4. Best, *Following Jesus*, 108.

5. Mark does not display much interest in the soteriological agency of faith and the point of justification. That is not to say that elements of substitutionary atonement are absent in this Gospel (see especially, within this chapter, on 10:45). Nonetheless, he is more concerned with matters of discipleship post-conversion, than he is with the details of how conversion is effected. Importing theological emphases from Paul, or even the other Gospels, is not recommended, at least for preaching purposes. Such conflations only mute Mark's particular theological foci and thrust.

6. France, *Gospel of Mark*, 397.

7. Witherington, *Gospel of Mark*, 278–79. As will be seen in the next unit, "grown up" values prevent the rich man from "being in tune with God's value scale"; he will fail to "enter" or possess the kingdom and its "treasure" (10:17, 21, 23–25), because he fails to "receive" the values of Jesus' mission, the demands of discipleship in this life: one must "receive" (like a child, i.e., with humility and dependence) in order to "enter" and possess the kingdom of God (France, *Gospel of Mark*, 397–98). Of course, this humility and dependence (= faith/trust) is also applicable to the initial step of accepting Jesus Christ as one's Savior.

like a child, in order to enter into (later) the blessings of the kingdom of God.[8] That principle is illustrated in the second episode of this pericope, the story of the rich man. Thus, the pericope, as a whole, is not dealing with the matter of obtaining eternal life (by faith alone in Christ alone) but—in the broader discipleship context of the Gospel, and the more focused context of the pericope—with the question of what sorts of demands are made upon a disciple, as that one follows Christ and his mission of extending the kingdom of God, in order that the entrance into the kingdom of God might be abundant.

15.2   Mark 10:17–31

THEOLOGICAL FOCUS 15.2

15.2   The radical demands of discipleship include the willingness to relinquish the possessions of this life, in the expectation of abundant recompense in the present age, despite its sufferings, and abundant reward in the age to come (10:17–31).

15.2.1   The radical demand of discipleship includes the willingness to relinquish the possessions of this life.

15.2.2   Obedience to the sacrificial demands of discipleship in this life will be abundantly rewarded in the kingdom of God.

15.2.3   Sacrifice in obedience to the demands of discipleship will not only be rewarded by eternal life in the age to come, but will also be abundantly recompensed in the present age, despite its sufferings.

Section Summary 15.2: This episode of the rich man negatively demonstrates the perspective disciples are to have on possessions. They are to be willing to relinquish them for the journey of discipleship, fully aware and confident of the reception of the disproportionate plenty that will be their reward both in the age to come and in the present, despite the suffering they may face today.

TRANSLATION 15.2

10:17   *And as He was going out in the way, one ran up and, kneeling before Him, asked Him, "Good Teacher, what shall I do to inherit eternal life?"*

10:18   *But Jesus said to him, "Why do you call Me good? No one is good except one—God.*

10:19   *You know the commandments: do not murder, do not commit adultery, do not steal, do not bear false witness, do not defraud, honor your father and mother."*

10:20   *But he said to Him, "Teacher, all these I have kept since my youth."*

10:21   *But looking at him, Jesus loved him, and said to him, "One thing you lack: go, whatever you have, sell, and give to the poor, and you will have treasure in heaven, and come, follow Me."*

8. That is not to say that they would *not* be justified (saved) without meeting Jesus' demands of discipleship, but simply to assert that the blessings and rewards of the kingdom of God in the hereafter are commensurate with one's obedience to Jesus' demands in the life here.

10:22   *But saddened by the word, he went away distressed, for he had many possessions.*

10:23   *And looking around, Jesus said to His disciples, "How hard for those having wealth to enter into the kingdom of God!"*

10:24   *And the disciples were amazed at His words. But Jesus again, answering, said to them, "Children, how hard it is to enter into the kingdom of God.*

10:25   *It is easier for a camel to go through the eye of a needle than for a rich man to enter into the kingdom of God."*

10:26   *And greatly astonished, they said to one another, "Then who can be saved?"*

10:27   *Looking at them, Jesus said, "With people it is impossible, but not with God; for all things are possible with God."*

10:28   *Peter began to say to Him, "Behold we left everything, and we have followed You."*

10:29   *Jesus said, "Truly I say to you, there is no one who has left house or brothers or sisters or mother or father or children or fields for My sake and for the sake of the gospel,*

10:30   *who will not receive hundredfold now in this age—houses and brothers and sisters and mothers and children and fields, with persecutions—and in the age to come, eternal life.*

10:31   *But many first will be last, and last, first."*

NOTES 15.2

15.2.1   The radical demand of discipleship includes the willingness to relinquish the possessions of this life.

This unit, 10:17–31, dealing with Jesus' dialogue with the rich man and, subsequently, with his disciples, is carefully structured, centering upon Jesus' extended explanation about the problems wealth poses.

A   Question regarding eternal life (ζωὴν αἰώνιον, *zōēn aiōnion*) (10:17)
  B   Jesus' command: go, sell, give; and you will have . . . (10:18–21a)
    C   "Follow Me" (ἀκολούθει μοι, *akolouthei moi*): unwillingness to give up property (10:21b–22)
      D   Jesus' explanation; disciples' reaction (10:23–27)
    C'   "We have followed You" (ἠκολουθήκαμέν σοι, *ēkolouthēkamen soi*): willingly left all (10:28)
  B'   Jesus' promise: those who leave . . . will receive . . . (10:29–30a)
A'   Answer regarding eternal life (ζωὴν αἰώνιον) (10:30b–31)

It is significant that this interaction occurs as Jesus was "in the way" (εἰς ὁδὸν, *eis hodon*, 10:17); the command of Jesus to come and "follow" him (the key verb; 10:21) is a call to discipleship. This person is quite serious: he comes running, he kneels, and he addresses Jesus as "good" (10:17)—the adjective is nowhere else used of a person in Mark. Taking the man's "good" in an absolute sense, to mean "perfect," Jesus questions his use of that address for someone he recognizes only as "Teacher" (10:17, 20). The counter question is emphatic in the Greek: "Why *Me* do you call good?" (10:18). In asserting that God alone is good, Jesus is also pointing out that the radical standards of a "good" (i.e., perfect) God are way beyond attainment by mere human effort, anticipating the discussion that would follow.

Despite the man's τί ποιήσω (*ti poiēsō*, "what shall I *do*," 10:17), Mark is not concerned here about any conflict between faith and works. Indeed, Jesus' response also gives the man something to *do* (10:19)—even the corrective to the "one thing you lack" (10:21) is framed as a series of actions: go, sell, give, come, follow. The "inheritance of eternal life" (10:17) is likely to be equivalent to "entering the kingdom of God," the reward element of the afterlife, the possession of its blessings (10:23, 24, 25). In the ОТ, "there can be no doubt that נַחֲלָה [*nakhalah*, 'inheritance'] refers originally and almost exclusively to the possession of land."[9] This would seem to indicate that all of those terms pertaining to the hereafter in Mark 10 primarily indicate future rewards for believers who have accepted ("received") Jesus' radical demands of discipleship in the present. In this pericope, such demands relate to personal property and its use.[10] There will be occasion for glory *then* ("entrance" and inheritance/possession) if suffering *now* is accepted willingly ("received") on the Trip of Discipleship.

Missing from Jesus' list of demands to the rich man (10:19)—taken from the second tablet of the Decalogue—is "You shall not covet" (Exod 20:17). In its place, Jesus puts, "Do not defraud." This is a pointed alteration that would have been obvious to listeners. Jesus is *doing* something with this replacement: he is likely to be drawing attention to what might conceivably be the man's felonious acts of economic exploitation (ἀποστερέω, *apostereō*, "defraud," is used in this sense in Mal 3:5; Sir 4.1; 29.6–7; 34.21–22; 1 Cor 6:7–8; Jas 5:4), the racketeering characteristic of the landed aristocracy of the time.[11] Jesus' rejoinder thus becomes an overt rejection of the then-prevalent idea that riches are a sign of divine favor (Deut 28:1–14; Job 1:10; 42:10; Prov 10:22; etc.). In this case, at least, Jesus seems to assume that wealth has come by fraudulent means.[12]

Despite Jesus' subtle jab, the man persists: he claims to have a clear conscience (Mark 10:20). The dialogue is composed of a question from the man (10:17), a counter question from Jesus (10:18–19, introduced by ὁ δέ, *ho de*, "but he [Jesus]"), a rejoinder from the man (10:20, also introduced by ὁ δέ), and a surrejoinder from Jesus (10:21,

---

9. Foerster and Herrmann, "κλῆρος" [*klēros*], 774. See Gen 47:27; Exod 23:30; Lev 20:24; Num 14:24; Deut 1:8; Josh 1:15; Jdg 1:19; 1 Kgs 21:15; 2 Kgs 17:24; 1 Chr 28:8; Ezra 9:11; Neh 9:15; Ps 25:13; Isa 14:21; Obad 20; etc.

10. Notice the virtually synonymous use of "eternal life" (10:17, 30—only here in Mark), "treasure in heaven" (10:21), "kingdom of God" (10:23, 24, 25), and "saved" (10:26) in this pericope.

11. Marcus, *Mark*, 721–22.

12. Wealth was acquired in Roman Palestine exclusively at the expense of peasant farmers, usually by defrauding them in taxes and tithes, or by lending to them and calling in the loans. See Hellerman, "Wealth and Sacrifice," 155n27. Jesus "lays at least partial responsibility for the highly inequitable distribution of landed wealth in Roman Palestine at the feet of the elite aristocracy"—"a censure of institutionalized greed" (ibid., 155–56).

again introduced by ὁ δέ). The described response of the man's final grieved departure (10:22) is, not surprisingly, also introduced by the narrator with ὁ δέ. Jesus and the man are going different ways, as Mark pointedly portrays with these adversatives: but ... but ... but ... but .... The value systems of the two dialogue partners, in striking contrast, now clash. Jesus disagrees with the man's assertion of perfect obedience: the man's "all" ("All these things I have kept," 10:20) is contrasted with Jesus' accusation of his "one" lack. The verb ὑστερέω (hystereō, "lack," 10:21) is related to ἀποστερέω (apostereō, "defraud," 10:19). Jesus appears to be linking the man's deficiency with his fraudulence; he lacks perfection because he defrauds, amounting, in effect, to the breaking of the commandment not to covet (which Jesus had subtly rephrased earlier). And so, as an appropriate corrective for the man's unconfessed sin, he is asked to sell and give away all he has. The structure of Jesus' statement centers on this demand: "Give to the poor" (10:21; see below). The result would be "treasure in heaven," the bounty of God's riches, i.e., the rewards of the kingdom of God. An exchange is required—what one has now is to be relinquished for what one could have later (10:21; the verb ἔχω, echō, makes the contrast clear):

A Go
  B Whatever you have (ἔχω), sell
    C Give to the poor
  B' You will have (ἔχω) treasure in heaven
A' Come, follow Me

"Jesus is asking not only for renunciation of possessions but also for a total change in his lifestyle: he is to join the itinerant group of Jesus' closest disciples, with their communal resources and dependence on the material support of others." Remarkably, Jesus' demand deals not with the man's excess or even with the actual amounts he had possibly defrauded, but "whatever he had"—the demand is total, and the call of discipleship absolute. This renunciation, a radical demand of discipleship, would be the means to a better end—treasure in heaven, the inheritance the man originally wanted; rewards in the afterlife, abundant entrance into the kingdom of God. Whatever he gives away now will be recompensed manifold then.[13]

15.2.2 Obedience to the sacrificial demands of discipleship in this life will be abundantly rewarded in the kingdom of God.

But the man refuses the offer of Jesus. Κτῆμα (ktēma, "possessions," Mark 10:22) was often used of land (Prov 23:10; 31:16; Hos 2:17; Joel 1:11; Sir 28:24; 36:25; Acts 5:1). The man who has accumulated much (land), ostensibly by fraudulent means, wants an inheritance (land) in eternity. But Jesus puts a crimp in his calculations: for it is only by losing, here, that one can gain rewards in the afterlife, i.e., the entrance into the kingdom of God with the possession/inheritance thereof. This is a difficult lesson

---

13. France, *Gospel of Mark*, 403. Surprisingly, this is the only time in Mark that Jesus is said to love another (10:21), and the object of this love will be the only man to refuse the call to discipleship in this Gospel (even Judas, one must admit, follows for awhile).

for the rich man, as it is for any disciple with an overflow of material goods, even if that overflow is not achieved by fraud. With the abundance of one's chattel comes one's trust and dependence upon that abundance, accompanied by a strong reluctance to relinquish that seemingly secure reservoir of plenty. And upon that very abundance the rich man too has placed his hope. It is nigh impossible for him to depend on anything else, particularly on an intangible promise of "treasure" in the afterlife, let alone the invitation to a discipleship in *this* life with its unpalatable guarantee of persecution (10:30, and all along in Mark). That exchange sounds rather dodgy to the man. How can he give up what he can see for something he cannot see? It does not look like a good investment idea in the least.

Kingdom entrance in the previous episode (10:15) is linked with kingdom entrance in the current episode (10:23–25), pointing to the contrast between children, without any possessions to their name, and those with much (our rich man). While Jesus' address to his disciples with "children" here (τέκνα, *tekna,* 10:24) is not in itself particularly significant, it is likely an allusion to the humility and dependency of children (παιδία, *paidia*) in the earlier incident. The threat there ("[he] will never enter into it," 10:15) finds its partner here in 10:25; both deal with difficult, or even impossible, entry into the kingdom. To receive the kingdom as a child is to receive it and its accompaniments as one not depending on one's own possessions or wealth, but depending rather upon the grace of God, the grantor of all good things, both here and in the hereafter. The problem is not necessarily possession of wealth or property; rather, "[t]he implication is that *attachment* to property is a hindrance in responding properly to the demands of the kingdom."[14] The making of money, the keeping of money, the protection of money, and the generation of even more money—all, if conducted with an attitude of dependence upon it, will turn out to be distraction from the singular focus of discipleship that Jesus demands. Such a tenaciously retentive attitude to possessions will surely interfere with a discipleship that, all along in this Gospel, is characterized by sacrifice and suffering.

On the other hand, acceptance of Jesus' mission of discipleship in this life will guarantee entrance into God's kingdom, with its rewards in the hereafter. The explanatory interchange between the disciples and Jesus (10:24–27) does not permit the interpreter to conclude that this rich man is an exceptional case; the universality and comprehensive nature of Jesus' assertion is severe in its bluntness: it is virtually impossible for the rich to obtain the rewards of the kingdom, the structure of the dialogue seems to affirm.

Disciples amazed (ἐθαμβοῦντο, *ethambounto*) (10:24a)
  It is hard (δύσκολόν ἐστιν, *duskolon estin*) to enter the kingdom of God (10:24b)
    It is easier (εὐκοπώτερόν ἐστιν, *eukopōteron estin*) . . . to enter the kingdom of God (10:25)
Disciples even more astonished (περισσῶς ἐξεπλήσσοντο, *perissōs exeplēssonto*) (10:26)

---

14. Collins, *Mark*, 480 (italics added).

In sum, a wealthy man turns away from "receiving" the kingdom (equated, here, with the radical demands of discipleship) because of the stringent requirements made on him by Jesus—an implicit promise of suffering, made explicit in 10:30.[15] In an age in which wealth was considered a sign of God's favor, it is no wonder the disciples are completely disoriented by Jesus' conception of what is important in the kingdom of God—they are "amazed" and "even more astonished" (10:24, 26). "The threefold repetition of the phrase εἰς τὴν βασιλείαν τοῦ θεοῦ εἰσελθεῖν [eis tēn basileian tou theou eiselthein, 'to enter into the kingdom of God,' 10:23, 24, 25], following hard on the words about sharing, receiving, and entering that same βασιλεία [basileia, 'kingdom'] in vv. 14–15, provides an unmistakable guide to where Mark wishes his readers to find the relevance of the story of the rich man. It is, again, all about the 'upside down' values of God's kingdom."[16]

The disciples have the same question as the rich man (and their question must be interpreted in light of all the synonyms in this passage): How can one be saved/enter, i.e., possess/inherit kingdom rewards?[17] From a human point of view—the conventional wisdom of the original readers' contemporary culture—if a wealthy person does not necessarily have divine favor, guaranteeing a splendid afterlife, who then does? Jesus' answer, again, is that the value system of God's kingdom is very different from that arising from humankind's misdirected expectations. He asserts that while there is a greater degree of difficulty for the rich to be willing to follow Jesus, in the end, such willingness is a matter of the grace of God, for whom nothing is impossible. It would be "hard" (10:24),[18] but not *impossible*, for God's grace is powerful and efficacious. All this being said, the fact that God's grace is the operating factor does not mean one can ignore Jesus' demand to sacrifice possessions.[19] The narrator emphasizes the radical

---

15. It is remarkable that the rich man's reaction of sadness is to Jesus' "word" (λόγος, logos, 10:22). While the word could stand for the neutral "matter" or "thing," the use of λόγος in Mark has a particular nuance: it is the word of Christ (the "radical demand") that is often rejected, and rarely accepted; see 1:45; 2:2; 7:13, 29; 8:32, 38; 9:10; 10:22, 24; 13:31; not to mention the numerous occurrences in Mark 4 (4:14, 15, 16, 17, 18, 19, 20, 33). It is indeed relevant to this pericope that the rich man perfectly fits the response of the seed sown on among thorns: "these are the ones who hear the word, and the worries of the age, and the seduction of wealth, and the desires for other things, coming in, choke the word, and it becomes unfruitful" (4:18–19).

16. France, *Gospel of Mark*, 399.

17. As already noted, Mark's interest is not in the precise exposition of salvific faith and its exercise, as may be found in the Epistles. "Saved," then, is likely a synonym for the abundant life in the age to come, the enjoyment of one's kingdom rewards.

18. Frederick Buechner likened the camel going through the eye of a needle (10:25) to Nelson Rockefeller getting through the night deposit slot of the First National City Bank! See Buechner, *Telling the Truth*, 63.

19. Hellerman's warning is well taken: "[T]he fact that they [current interpretations of this pericope] preserve both our Protestant theological traditions [salvation by faith without works] *and* our opulent Western lifestyle [the assumption that Jesus' demands are only for that rich young ruler, and not to be generalized to trouble anyone else] causes me to suspect that our interpretations of the pericope have been socially constructed by a worldview influenced by popularized Reformation soteriology, radical individualism, and conspicuous consumption, rather than by ancient Palestinian (and early Christian) perspectives on economics" ("Wealth and Sacrifice," 145). It must be reiterated that the thrust of the

demands of discipleship with regard to possessions (10:28). And, subsequently, Jesus expands the context of that individual rich man and his wealth to the plurality of his disciples and their sacrifices: the gospel *does* have economic repercussions in the lives of Jesus' followers in *all* times (note the sacrifices some of the Twelve have already made to follow Jesus: 1:16–20 and 2:14; Peter asserts as much, 10:28).[20] Mark 10:28–31 concludes the section by contrasting the disciples with the rich man: the one goes away clinging to his property, while the others follow Jesus, abandoning everything. The latter, who have left all, will reap rewards both in the present age (which also includes persecution) and in the age to come. God's values are not humankind's: the first will be last and the last first. Discipleship demands are radical, indeed.

15.2.3   *Sacrifice in obedience to the demands of discipleship will not only be rewarded by eternal life in the age to come, but will also be abundantly recompensed in the present age, despite its sufferings.*

What was a discussion of abandoning wealth/possessions is now, in 10:29–30, almost overwhelmed by the leaving of family ("house[s]" and "fields" also show up in 10:29, 30). The litany of deprivations in 10:29 are linked by "or," and the list of gains in 10:30 by "and." Therefore, while "it is overexegesis to conclude that the abandonment of any *one* of the items in the list will be rewarded by the gain of *all* of them," there is no doubt that gains will far outweigh the deprivations—hundredfold! These rewards are attained in the "present age," suggesting that the community of believers is the gain (also intimated in 3:34–35). Lucian of Samosata claimed that Christians "despise all worldly goods alike, regarding them merely as common property" precisely because "it was impressed on them by their original lawgiver that they are all brothers, from the moment that they are converted, and deny the gods of Greece, and worship the crucified sage, and live after his laws" (*Peregr.* 13).[21] The unexpected item in the list of compensations must not be missed, either—persecution (10:30), parallel and consequential to the acceptance of Jesus' mission and the walk of discipleship ("for My sake and the sake of the gospel," 10:29; see below for the parallels). This, no doubt, discourages mercenary interest—the gain of a hundredfold—in joining the family of believers! Nonetheless, the fact remains: there will be recompense now (as well as in the future). What exactly present compensation entails Jesus does not specify, but, in connection with his declaration in 3:35 that the disciple is his "brother and sister and

---

episode is not necessarily upon what it takes for one to be saved; the disciples' question to that effect ("Then who can be saved," 10:26) may simply be understood as an inquiry into how one might win God's favor in this age and his blessings for the age to come (see Jesus' answer, 10:29–30).

20. Incidentally, the question, "Who can be saved?" (τίς δύναται σωθῆναι; *tis dynatai sōthēnai?*, 10:26) is obliquely answered later in 10:52: "Your faith has made you well [σέσωκέν σε, *sesōken se,* 'saved you']." Thus it is that God's grace and sovereignty (addressed in this pericope) work through the agency of man's faith (dealt with in the next pericope).

21. Hellerman, connecting the command in 10:21 (go, sell, give) with 10:29–30, thinks that the former is a charge to the rich man "to make his wealth available to the members of Jesus' alternative community, that is, to his potential new family of fellow believers.... this is how the early Christians in Jerusalem understood Jesus' teaching" ("Wealth and Sacrifice," 159). See Acts 2:44–45; 4:32–37, especially 4:34: "there was not a needy person among them."

mother," one suspects that it is the new community of God, the body of Jesus' disciples, that becomes the source of this recompense: family members occupy a prominent place in Jesus' list in 10:30. The two records in 10:29 and 10:30 differ in the omission of "father" in the second one (the same exclusion occurs in 3:35): "this may reflect the theological scruple that the disciple has only one heavenly Father."[22]

10:29	house	brothers	sisters	mother	**father**	children	fields	for My sake and for the sake of the gospel
10:30	houses	brothers	sisters	mothers		children	fields	with persecutions

This emphasis on "family" matters actually furthers the thesis that Jesus does not command a summary relinquishing of all possessions. If the family that may have been given up "for My sake and for the sake of the Gospel" is now made up of the community of disciples, then the houses and fields (wealth and possessions) also given up by the disciple could very well be recompensed by the houses and fields of others in this community in this age. This arithmetic would certainly not work if every disciple were to completely relinquish every possession, leaving nothing for sharing with one's newly found "brothers," "sisters," "mothers," and "children."[23] Clement of Alexandria's *Quis dives salvetur?* ("Who Is the Rich Man Who Is Saved?") supports such an understanding. Against an unnuanced and literal reading, Clement asks how Christians could feed the needy, cover the naked, and shelter the homeless as commanded, "if each of us were himself already in want of all these things [by having given up all possessions]?" (*Quis div.* 13). Adducing the characteristic of the community of believers as family, Clement expects kinship to trump individuality, sharing to overturn hoarding. A rich person who shares this divine perspective "holds possessions and gold and silver and houses as gifts of God . . . and knows that he possesses them more for his brothers' sakes than his own. . . . . [He is] a ready inheritor of the kingdom of heaven" (*Quis div.* 16).[24] Such a caring community cannot be achieved if each Christian, having given away everything, is himself in need. Clement would argue, then, that there is nothing inherently wrong with riches. It is the clinging on to them, as was the case with the rich man in Mark 10, that is antithetical to Jesus' radical demands of discipleship.

The abandonment and relinquishment by the disciples should not be overstated; after all, Peter and Andrew still retained their home after deciding to follow Jesus (Mark 1:29); the boat employed for ministry purposes in 3:9; 4:1, 36, etc., also likely

22. France, *Gospel of Mark*, 407. As was already noted, no spouses are mentioned, either, in the discussion here or in 3:35. The journey of discipleship for those married is "one-fleshed," jointly undertaken in that permanent union between husband and wife (see 10:1–12, Pericope 14).

23. In light of 10:1–12, which emphasizes the unbreakability of the marriage bond, at least in this life, one notices that spouses are not mentioned in the lists of 10:29–30. The "children" that *are* mentioned must therefore be adult children (possibly part of the extended family residing together, the norm for Ancient Near Eastern households), not the dependent and defenseless ones of young age who, as Jesus had already declared, must be protected and cared for.

24. Translations of Clement's work are from Hellerman, "Wealth and Sacrifice," 161–63. "To interpret the command literally, and then to apply it across the board to all of the faithful, would be to obviate the very social vision Jesus shares with Peter and the eleven in vv. 29–30" (ibid., 163).

belonged to one of the Twelve. "This is not monastic poverty so much as pragmatically sitting light to possessions and family" for the sake of the gospel.[25] Rather, the radical demand of this pericope has embedded within it the understanding that one's material possessions belong to the local body of Christ as whole. The kingdom introduced by Jesus is, therefore, a community "where material needs of all are met and where wealth is utilized in ways that benefit the community as a whole"; a radically different community life is being envisaged in the kingdom of God.[26] And Peter et al. follow that guideline with their boats and nets and houses. Thus, what Jesus inveighs against is greed and covetousness (and the accumulation of wealth by fraudulent means), which are the symptoms of the core disease of depending upon possessions and wealth, rather than upon God, who gives all things, and for whom nothing is impossible. The epigram of 10:30 "functions as a sort of slogan for the revolutionary values of the kingdom of God as Jesus has been presenting them"—an overthrow of conventional wisdom and attitudes: the first will be last, and the last first.[27]

In sum, while the problem of wealth and its hindrance to the following of Jesus is depicted in Mark 10, the mere possession of an abundance of worldly goods is not deprecated here; rather, it is the dependence thereon by the rich man (and his fraudulent accumulation thereof, perhaps), in contrast to the children of the previous episode, who depend not on what they possess, but upon the one who gives. As Chrysostom said[28]:

> Let us not then blame the things, but the corrupt mind. For it is possible to be rich and not to be deceived; and to be in this world and not to be choked with its cares. . . . [T]hey that are in sound health know that it [luxury] pricks sharper than any thorn, and that luxury wastes the soul worse than care. . . . Yea, it brings on premature old age, and dulls the senses, and darkens our reasoning, and blinds the keen-sighted mind, and makes the body tumid [flabby], . . . whence our falls are many and continual, and our shipwrecks frequent.

In closing, a balance is necessary. Those living in a culture and lifestyle of abundance must heed this warning: "The nature and degree of renunciation of wealth which the gospel requires may be something which will be worked out differently in different times and circumstances, but if we lose sight of the principle that affluence is a barrier to the kingdom of God we are parting company from Jesus at a point which seems to have been fundamental to his teaching."[29] There is an intrinsic danger to possessions and wealth; that danger must be feared. The rich of this world (and "richness"

---

25. France, *Gospel of Mark*, 407–8. Other examples include Levi's festive partying, Mark 2:15; the dependence of Jesus and his itinerant group upon the provision of supporters like Mary, Martha, and Lazarus at Bethany (Luke 10:38–42; John 11; 12:2), and the women of Luke 8:2–3. All of this assumes personal resources being made available for community use.

26. Hellerman, "Wealth and Sacrifice," 163–64.

27. France, *Gospel of Mark*, 408. Jesus does not call for justice to be established by "the reformation of the social structure of Roman Palestine as a whole, but rather by establishing an alternative community in which resources would be distributed in such a way as to assure the adequate satisfaction of the needs of every member" (Hellerman, "Wealth and Sacrifice," 156).

28. *Homily* 44.7 in *Comm. Matt.*

29. France, *Gospel of Mark*, 400–401.

is admittedly a matter of degree) must always be cautious, lest Chrysostom's warnings become reality. The rich man of this pericope, simply because of his dependence upon, and allegiance to, riches, rejects the radical demands of discipleship and the call to follow Jesus on the way. He will, as a result, lose out on rewards in the afterlife.

SERMON FOCUS AND OUTLINES

> **THEOLOGICAL FOCUS OF PERICOPE 15 FOR PREACHING**
>
> **15** Confident of the abundance of their present recompense and eternal reward, disciples are able to give freely of their possessions, with humble dependence upon God (10:13–31).

This pericope is not intended by Mark as a screed against wealth and possessions. Neither is it a permission to maintain the plush and pampered status quo that characterizes many "rich Christians in an age of hunger."[30] The balanced words of Clement of Alexandria (*Quis div.* 26) are worth reflecting upon again:

> The Savior by no means has excluded the rich on account of wealth itself, and the possession of property, nor fenced off salvation against them, if they are able and willing to submit their life to God's commandments, and prefer them to transitory things. . . . If one is able in the midst of wealth to turn from its mystique, to entertain moderate desires, to exercise self-control, to seek God alone, and to breathe God and walk with God, such a man submits to the commandments, being free, unsubdued, free of disease, unwounded by wealth.

The two episodes of this pericope thus teach the one acceding to the radical demands of discipleship a significant facet of humble dependence upon God: the proper attitude and disposition toward possessions. This is surely an important issue in the Christian West, where abundance is almost obscene; however, one must remember that the Scriptures were originally inscribed in the East—wealth and possessions are not the exclusive problems of Westerners. In fact, in its silence of what exactly constitutes "abundance" and "richness," this pericope is clear that, despite differing degrees of affluence, *no one* is exempt from this demand of discipleship, whether in the East, West, North, or South. The demonstration of willingness to give up all for the cause of the gospel is required of *all* who would follow Jesus on the way. In a sense, this pericope is a corrective to an exclusively earthly focus, inviting us to look to eternity and its plenty, instead of the temporal (and temporary) abundance of this life.

POSSIBLE PREACHING OUTLINES FOR PERICOPE 15

I. WRONG IDEA: Dependence on possessions
   The rich man's perspective: 10:13–22
   Move-to-Relevance: Our dependence and trust in possessions
II. RIGHT IDEA: Dependence on God
   A child's perspective: 10:13–16; dependence on another, not on self
   Jesus' corrective: 10:22–27; an eternal viewpoint

30. See Sider, *Rich Christians.*

III.   *Give all and get more!* *
> Specifics on developing an eternal perspective and on giving our resources, particularly material possessions

* While this homiletical imperative can sound rather mercenary, that is not the intention, of course. It is dependence upon God's provision, both for this age and for the age to come, that is the emphasis of this pericope.

The preacher could conceivable follow the sequence of the text more closely by employing the episode of the dependent child to raise the question of what the congregation (and the world) depends on for security.

I.   CHILD: Attitude of dependence
> A child's attitude of dependence, 10:13–16
> Move-to-Relevance: What do we depend on?

II.   MAN: Dependence on possessions
> The rich man's attitude of dependence upon goods, 10:13–22
> Move-to-Relevance: Our dependence and trust in possessions

III.   JESUS: Dependence on God
> Jesus' corrective: an eternal viewpoint and dependence on God, 10:22–27

IV.   ME: *Give all and get more!*
> Specifics on developing an eternal perspective and on giving our resources, depending on God

PERICOPE 16

Suffering Service

Mark 10:32–52

[Third Passion Prediction; Blind Bartimaeus Healed]

REVIEW, SUMMARY, PREVIEW

Review of Pericope 15: Mark 10:13–31 teaches the humble dependence of disciples, calling them to be willing to abandon material possessions, with the expectation that both present recompense (despite suffering) and eternal rewards await.

Summary of Pericope 16: Mark 10:32–52, with the third Passion Prediction of Jesus, demonstrates what true greatness means: to suffer and serve like Jesus, accepting his mission. The story of Bartimaeus closes out Act II of Mark, depicting one to whom Jesus grants discernment and who accepts Jesus mission, following him into Jerusalem.

Preview of Pericope 17: The next pericope (11:1–25) exhorts disciples to receive their divine king properly, and to respond to him by functioning as communities of prayer founded upon faith and mutual forgiveness.

16 Mark 10:32–52

THEOLOGICAL FOCUS OF PERICOPE 16

16 The true sign of greatness of disciples, who have been granted discernment by Jesus, is their acceptance of the mission of Jesus, following his model of suffering and service (10:32–52).

16.1 The true sign of greatness of disciples, who have accepted the suffering mission of Jesus, is their willingness to suffer and serve, following his model (10:32–45).

16.1.1	Disciples accept the suffering mission of Jesus.
16.1.2	The suffering mission of Jesus is the model for the serving attitude of discipleship, the true sign of greatness.
16.2	Disciples, granted discernment by Jesus, accept his suffering mission and follow him on the way (10:46–52).

OVERVIEW

NOTABLY, EACH OF THE Passion Predictions (8:31; 9:31; 10:33–34) occurs in Act II, the "On the Way" (ἐν τῇ ὁδω, *en tē hodō*) section of Mark (8:27–10:52; see the Introduction). Those who would follow Jesus are the ones who have been transferred from "by the way" (παρὰ τὴν ὁδόν, *para tēn hodon*) to "on the way" (ἐν τῇ ὁδῷ, 10:46, 52), like the blind man in this pericope. Readers of the Gospel will also remember that among the seeds that did not produce any fruit were those that fell "by the way" (παρὰ τὴν ὁδόν, 4:4, 15).[1] To be "on the way" of discipleship is to follow Jesus, discerning his person (Act I) and accepting his mission (Act II).

Nowhere else is Jesus' mission as explicit as it is in this pericope. The first episode of this pericope contains the most climactic of Jesus' three Passion Predictions—the last and most detailed (10:33–34). The events of his Passion are here divided into two phases—the actions taken by the chief priests and scribes after Jesus is delivered to them (10:33), and the actions taken by the Gentiles, after he is delivered to that group (10:34). The first Passion Prediction mentioned Jesus' death in the passive; the second attributed it to "men"; here it is specifically the chief priests and scribes who condemn him to death, and the Gentile Romans who actually carry it out.[2]

This Passion Prediction is followed by "the most emphatic of all Jesus' reversals of accepted values in the call to serve rather than be served," culminating in 10:45 with a clear pronouncement of the reason for Jesus' own death; its redemptive purpose now finds expression. In between the prediction and Jesus' pronouncement of the purpose of his mission is the misguided aspiration of the sons of Zebedee. These disciples' self-promoting goal is in stark contrast with Jesus'; for him, "the fulfillment of God's redemptive plan will involve leaving behind the world's scale of achievement and accepting that the first will be last and the last first."[3] And, unlike James and John, those who wish to follow Jesus must adopt that value system themselves.

---

1. Boring, "Mark 1:1–15," 69.

2. France, *Gospel of Mark*, 413. Mark 10:33 will be fulfilled in 14:43–44, 64; 15:1; and 10:34 will be fulfilled precisely in 15:20, 31 (mocking); 14:65 (spitting); 15:15, 19 (scourging); 15:15, 24 (killing); and 16:6 (rising).

3. Ibid., 409. The third Passion Prediction stands out for its several unique elements: the first mention of Jerusalem as the final destination (emphatically announced with ἰδού, *idou*, "behold," 10:33); the amazement and fear of Jesus' disciples and followers (10:32); the double use of παραδίδωμι, (*paradidōmi*, "give over", 10:33); the calling aside of the Twelve (10:32); and the details of what will transpire at his Passion. (For a comparison of the three Passion Predictions, see on 8:31 in Pericope 12.) The rhyming qualities of at least nine words ending in -σιν in 10:33–34 make this last prediction "the definitive drumroll for the Passion": ἀρχιερεῦσιν, γραμματεῦσιν, κατακρινοῦσιν, παραδώσουσιν,

16.1   Mark 10:32–45

THEOLOGICAL FOCUS 16.1

16.1   The true sign of greatness of disciples, who have accepted the suffering mission of Jesus, is their willingness to suffer and serve, following his model (10:32–45).

16.1.1   Disciples accept the suffering mission of Jesus.

16.1.2   The suffering mission of Jesus is the model for the serving attitude of discipleship, the true sign of greatness.

Section Summary 16.1: The third Passion Prediction demonstrates Jesus suffering and contains the magnificent pronouncement in 10:45, his model of service for the disciple. Disciples accept Jesus mission and follow his example, suffering and serving—greatness according to God's way—rather than emulating worldly standards of greatness by wielding authority over others.

TRANSLATION 16.1

10:32   *They were on the way going up to Jerusalem, and Jesus was going ahead of them, and they were amazed, and those who followed were afraid. And again taking along the Twelve, He began to tell them what was going to happen to Him,*

10:33   *"Behold, we are going up to Jerusalem, and the Son of Man will be given over to the chief priests and the scribes, and they will condemn Him to death, and will give Him over to the Gentiles.*

10:34   *And they will mock Him and spit on Him and scourge Him and kill [Him], and after three days He will rise."*

10:35   *And coming to Him, James and John, the sons of Zebedee, said to Him, "Teacher, we want You to do for us whatever we ask You."*

10:36   *And He said to them, "What do you want Me to do for you?"*

10:37   *And they said to Him, "Grant to us that we may sit, one on Your right and one on Your left, in Your glory."*

10:38   *But Jesus said to them, "You do not know what you are asking. Are you able to drink the cup that I drink, or to be baptized with the baptism [with] which I am baptized?"*

10:39   *And they said to Him, "We are able." And Jesus said to them, "The cup that I drink, you shall drink, and the baptism [with] which I am baptized, you shall be baptized [with].*

ἔθνεσιν, ἐμπαίξουσιν, ἐμπτύσουσιν, μαστιγώσουσιν, and ἀποκτενοῦσιν (archiereusin, grammateusin, katakrinousin, paradōsousin, ethnesin, empaixousin, emptysousin, mastigōsousin, and apoktenousin; "to the chief priests," "to the scribes," "they will condemn," "they will give over," "to the Gentiles," "they will mock," "they will spit," "they will scourge," and "they will kill," respectively; 10:33–34). See Kaminouchi, "But It Is Not So", 68. The double use of παραδίδωμι for Jesus' betrayal to the chief priests/scribes and his betrayal to the Gentiles intensifies the movement towards the end, anticipating δίδωμι (didōmi, "give"—Jesus' giving his life) in the immediate context (10:45). Other uses of παραδίδωμι for the same idea include Mark 9:31; 10:33; 14:41, 42; also see Matt 10:4; 26:2; Luke 24:7; Acts 3:13; Rom 4:25; 8:32; 1 Cor 11:23; Gal 2:20; Eph 5:2, 25.

10:40 *But to sit on My right or on [My] left is not Mine to grant, but to those [for whom] it has been prepared."*

10:41 *And hearing [this], the ten began to feel indignant with James and John.*

10:42 *And summoning them, Jesus said to them, "You know that those recognized as rulers of the Gentiles lord over them, and their great men exercise authority over them.*

10:43 *But it is not this way among you, but whoever wants to become great among you shall be your servant,*

10:44 *and whoever wants to be first among you shall be slave of all.*

10:45 *For even the Son of Man did not come to be served, but to serve and to give His life a ransom for many."*

NOTES 16.1

16.1.1 Disciples accept the suffering mission of Jesus.[4]

Jesus and the disciples are "on the way." The description of Jesus going ahead of his followers (10:32) continues to express the theme of the literal journey to Jerusalem symbolizing discipleship, with Jesus at the head.[5] The cause of the amazement of Jesus' entourage (10:32) is likely the announcement of his destination, the same reason for the fear of the "followers," who by now probably suspect what is going to transpire in that location. This is a death march, indeed. Why would anyone voluntarily take himself to a place of obvious danger? For Jesus' allies ("those who followed," 10:32), not only is this incomprehensible, it is alarming—his fate and his intrepid attitude towards the whole enterprise are putting their own lives at risk.

The radical nature of the kingdom of God is perhaps most explicitly stated in this episode, with its stark announcement of Jesus' tragic betrayal and death. Therefore, the assumption on the part of the disciples that Jesus is on the way to glory right now (10:37) is quite astonishing, seeing that he has just made the third and most detailed prediction of his sufferings.

Once again, in their conversation with Jesus, the disciples address him as "Teacher" (10:35). Coming soon after an identical address by the rich man who failed to make the discipleship cut because of his attachment and dependence on possessions, it reminds readers that the disciples are not that far ahead themselves, despite Peter's assertion that they had abandoned all for the cause of Jesus (10:28). The subsequent dialogue in this pericope proves this thesis.

James and John already have had a fairly higher standing around Jesus than the rest: they have been individually called (1:19); they have accompanied Jesus to the house of Simon and Andrew (1:29); they have been given a special surname (3:17); and they, with Peter, were the only ones to witness the raising of the little girl (5:37) and the Transfiguration (9:2). Perhaps it is that latter event (δόξα, *doxa*, "glory," is found both in

---

4. This theological subfocus converts a negative picture of the Twelve in the text to a positive lesson for all disciples.

5. Collins, *Mark*, 398. Also see the Introduction for an excursus addressing "on the way" (ἐν τῇ ὁδῷ, *en tē hodō*) in Mark.

8:38 and here in 10:37) and the approach to the "royal" city of Jerusalem that precipitates their itch for glory, which they mistakenly suppose is coming soon.[6] The brothers apparently have heard only the part of the Passion Prediction that deals with the resurrection—now they want to share in that glory. (Peter, in 8:31, on the other hand, had heard only the part about the crucifixion, and wanted no part of that ignominy.) Here the two siblings seek to be elevated to positions adjacent to Jesus' own glorified locus. A more likely explanation of this bizarre behavior is that, while "those who followed" (10:32) recognize the danger into which they are headed, the Twelve, intentionally taken aside by Jesus as a separate group (10:32), simply do not realize the seriousness of what is going to happen in Jerusalem.[7] The desire to be "great" in the kingdom is ample evidence that the sons of Zebedee (and, likely, the rest of the Twelve, 10:41, who were indignant with the brothers) have not gotten it yet; one would have thought that 9:35, with its lesson on being servant-like and "last of all," would have clarified the issue for them. But, alas, not only have they failed to accept Jesus' mission of death, they have effectively refused to accept his suffering as a model for their own discipleship.[8] The way Mark structures the dialogue shows the contrast between Jesus' conception of his mission and that of the disciples. Like Jesus' exchange with the rich man in 10:17–22, this one, too, describes the contributions of each of the parties in the conversation as beginning with ὁ δέ (*ho de*, "*but* he/they," 10:36, 37, 38, 39 [×2], 40)—but . . . but . . . but . . . but . . . but . . . Jesus and the sons of Zebedee are on two opposing tracks: the two disciples have not accepted Jesus' suffering mission.

The route to glory for Jesus, as well as for all who would follow him, will be suffering, symbolized by the "cup" (10:38–39).[9] While the disciples make an imprudent declaration of their ability to share in Jesus' suffering (10:39), the reader who remembers the details of the Passion will no doubt recollect that the ones subsequently positioned at Jesus' right and left are not these glory-seeking disciples, but thieves, with "the setting not a throne but a gibbet (15:27)."[10] In other words, "the specific

6. The kingship of Jesus is alluded to by the employment of "Son of Man" (10:33) borrowed from Dan 7:14, not to mention the numerous mentions of a "kingdom" in the previous pericope (10:13–31). Collins thinks that this current attempt at exaltation on the part of James and John is to achieve a rank higher than that of Peter, the *de facto* leader of the Twelve (ibid., 495). Kaminouchi wonders if they are asking to replace Elijah and Moses who accompanied Jesus at the Transfiguration (*"But It Is Not So"*, 100). In any case, the motive of the sons of Zebedee is self-aggrandizement, pure and simple!

7. Mark makes it a point to distinguish here between "those who followed" and "the Twelve" in 10:32. The former are "frightened," while the latter, it turns out, are naïvely optimistic at best, or abysmally dense at worst.

8. "He [Jesus] intends loftiness to be preceded by humility, and to prepare the way to elevation itself through humility. For those disciples, were of course seeking glory . . . ; they thought only of the goal, and saw not by what way it must be reached; the Lord recalled them to the way, that they might come to their homeland in due order. For the homeland is on high, the way there lies low . . . , the way is Christ's death . . . , Christ's suffering. He that refuses the way, why seeks he the homeland?" (Augustine, *Tract. Ev. Jo.* 28.5.2).

9. The cup as an image of Jesus' Passion is clarified in 14:23, 36. It alludes to the cup of God's wrath poured upon sin: Ps 75:8; Isa 51:17, 22; Jer 25:15–29; 49:12; Hab 2:16; *Pss. Sol.* 8.14–15; *Mart. Ascen. Isa.* 5.13; Mark 14:36; John 18:11; Rev 14:10; 16:19. Baptism as symbolic of suffering is mentioned in Josephus, *J.W.* 4.137; Job 9:31 (Aquila); and Ps 68:3 (Aquila and Symmachus).

10. France, *Gospel of Mark*, 418. See below, under Mark 15 in Pericope 24, for the significance of this observation.

and inescapable requirement and constraint of τὸ βάπτισμα ὅ ἐγὼ βαπτίζομαι" (*to baptisma ho egō baptizomai*, "the baptism with which I'm baptized," 10:38) is the way of suffering. That is the way Jesus is going, and that is what it means for disciples to follow him "on the way."[11]

Kaminouchi makes the astute observation that James and John, whenever they are mentioned together, are the only disciples repeatedly named with a patronymic: 1:19 at their call; 3:18 at their appointment; and here in 10:35. At their introduction in 1:19, their higher social status as children of Zebedee (the one with "hired men") is subtly established. They are already part of a select group from among the Twelve (see above). Considering, as well, their "privileged position in the patriarchal structure," it is no wonder that the brothers' petition threatens the other disciples.[12] The indignant reaction of those ten demonstrates that they are not much better informed than the sons of Zebedee (10:41): they are irked also, perhaps, because they did not get the chance to put in their requests for those upgrades to better seats.

16.1.2   The suffering mission of Jesus is the model for the serving attitude of discipleship, the true sign of greatness.

Jesus deplores the contemporary cultural model of rulers lording (κατακυριεύω, *katakyrieuō*) and great men exercising authority (κατεξουσιάζω, *katexousiazō*, 10:42). Interestingly, all the occurrences in Mark of the noun form κύριος (*kyrios*, "lord") refer either to Jesus or to God (1:3; 2:28; 5:19; 7:28; 11:3, 9; 12:11, 29, 30, 36, 37; 13:20, 35). "This exclusive usage is . . . intentional and makes κύριος a word charged with a connotation of power and sacredness"; thus the cognate verb form κατακυριεύω ("to lord," 10:42) is all the more strikingly discordant in Jesus' accusation of the power-pursuing disciples.[13] The modus operandi of the world is contrary to the revolutionary practices of the kingdom of God. Leadership, Jesus avers, is equivalent to service, and sacrificial service at that.

A	Rulers of the Gentiles lord over them (10:42a)		[*to rule = to lord*]
	B	Their great men (μεγάλοι, *megaloi*) exercise authority over them (10:42b)	[*to be great = to exercise authority*]
		C But it is not this way among you (10:43a)	[**a different way**: *instead . . .*]
	B'	Whoever wants to become great (μέγας, *megas*) . . . shall be your servant (10:43b)	[*to be great = to serve others*]
A'	Whoever wants to be first among you shall be slave of all (10:44)		[*to be first = to be a slave*]

11. Gibson, "Jesus' Wilderness Temptation," 29.

12. Kaminouchi, *"But It Is Not So"*, 94.

13. Ibid., 125. If the Zebedee boys are alluding to Ps 110:1 (κάθου ἐκ δεξιῶν μου, *kathou ek dexiōn mou*, "sit at My right hand") in their demand in Mark 10:37 (σου ἐκ δεξιῶν . . . καθίσωμεν, *sou ek dexiōn . . . kathisōmen*, "on Your right . . . we may sit"), Jesus is probably, in turn, alluding to Ps 110:2 in his reply (κατακυριεύω, *katakyrieuō*, "to lord," is used there, and here in 10:42). See Donahue and Harrington, *Gospel of Mark*, 312.

The subtle repetition of θέλω (*thelō*, "want," 10:43) surely alludes to the brothers' demand ("want") in 10:35 (θέλω forms a refrain, occurring at 10:35, 36, 43, 44, 51; it had also shown up, in a similar discussion, in 9:35). The other terms used here have also been encountered before in Pericope 13: μέγας (*megas*, "great," 10:43) recalls μείζων (*meizōn*, "greatest") in 9:34, and πρῶτος (*prōtos*, "first," 10:44) reflects the same word 9:35 and 10:31. While πάντων διάκονος (*pantōn diakonos*, "servant of all") was found in 9:35, the intensification with πάντων δοῦλος (*pantōn doulos*, "slave of all," 10:44) "renders this the most powerful statement yet of the alternative value scale of the kingdom of God. The sequel in v. 45 renders it unforgettable."[14]

Mark 10:45 contains one of three uses of λύτρον (*lytron*, "ransom") in the NT, apart from the parallel in Matthew 20:28 and 1 Timothy 2:6; cognates, especially ἀπολύτρωσις (*apolytrōsis*, "redemption") occur more frequently. In the Roman context of slavery, the word would evoke thoughts of ransom money paid to release a slave (Rom 6:16–23 and 8:14–24 could have come to the minds of Roman Christians familiar with Paul's letters). "The verb λυτρόω (*lytroō*) occurs frequently in the LXX for God's 'redemption' of his people, not only from slavery in Egypt but also from spiritual oppression, and λύτρον (normally in the plural) is used for payments to preserve a life which is legally forfeit (including the firstborn) or subject to divine punishment. . . . The essential meaning is deliverance by the payment of an 'equivalent.'"[15] At any rate, even with its powerful and unique redemptive connotations, this verse (Mark 10:45) sets a pattern for the followers of Jesus—not to give their lives as a ransom, of course, but to be willing to sacrifice themselves for Jesus' mission and for the sake of the Gospel. The thrust of the episode is that disciples, like Jesus, must also serve rather than be served; they too must be ready to lay down their lives (as in 1 John 3:16). This, Jesus implies, is no time for disputes on greatness, completely antithetical to the ways of God and the principles of his kingdom.

16.2   Mark 10:46–52

THEOLOGICAL FOCUS 16.2

16.2   Disciples, granted discernment by Jesus, accept his suffering mission and follow him on the way (10:46–52).

Section Summary 16.2: Bartimaeus turns out to be a picture of the true disciple, conscious of his own frailty, discerning of Jesus' person, and ready to follow him to Jerusalem. Coming at the end of Act II, and just prior to Jesus' entrance into Jerusalem in Act III, this symbolizes the disciple's acceptance of Jesus' mission and willingness to follow him on the way of suffering.

14. France, *Gospel of Mark*, 419.

15. Ibid., 420. Also see idem, *Jesus and the Old Testament*, 110–32; and Witherington, *Gospel of Mark*, 288–90, for evidence that Mark 10:45 is closely linked to Isa 53. While the terms are different there, the giving over, condemning, mocking, spitting, scourging, and killing are all part of the sufferings of the Isaianic servant as well (Isa 50:6; 53:3–6, 8–9, 12); so also the concept of his giving his life (53:10, 12); in addition, "many" (here in Mark 10:45, and also in 14:24) recalls Isa 53:11, 12; etc.

TRANSLATION 16.2

10:46   *And they came to Jericho. And as He was going out away from Jericho even with His disciples and a large crowd, a blind beggar, the son of Timaeus, Bartimaeus, was sitting by the way.*

10:47   *And hearing that it was Jesus the Nazarene, he began to cry out and say, "Son of David, Jesus, have mercy on me!"*

10:48   *And many were rebuking him to be quiet, but he kept crying out all the more, "Son of David, have mercy on me!"*

10:49   *And stopping, Jesus said, "Call him." And they called the blind man, saying to him, "Take courage, rise up, He is calling you."*

10:50   *And throwing away his cloak, he jumped up and came to Jesus.*

10:51   *And answering him, Jesus said, "What do you want Me to do for you?" And the blind man said to Him, "Rabboni, that I may see again."*

10:52   *And Jesus said to him, "Go, your faith has healed you." And immediately he saw again and began following Him on the way.*

NOTES 16.2

16.2   Disciples, granted discernment by Jesus, accept his suffering mission and follow him on the way.

This is the last healing miracle in Mark; it is also the only one in which the one healed is named. On the other hand, the explanation for the naming may be straightforward: this is a call to discipleship, and in such summons in Mark, all the characters are carefully named (1:16, 19; 2:14; 3:13–19). Only the subject of a "failed" call in 10:17–22 remains anonymous. This last explicitly noted potential recruit was on top of the social scale—a wealthy man unwilling to give up his possessions. The recruit in this pericope (10:46–52) is at the other end of the spectrum—Bartimaeus, a blind beggar (10:46–52).[16] Both meet Jesus in some relation to the "way" (εἰς ὁδὸν, *eis hodon*, "on the way," 10:17; παρὰ τὴν ὁδόν, *para tēn hodon*, "by the way," 10:46). One rejected Jesus' direct call; the other, without even waiting for a summons, gives up all to follow Jesus "on the way" (ἐν τῇ ὁδῷ, *en tē hodō*, 10:52, the precise phrase symbolizing the discipleship journey in Mark), sight restored and rendered whole. This healed man is therefore an appropriate illustration of the revolutionary values of, and appropriate response to, the kingdom of God.

The significance of the framing of Act II (8:22—10:52) by two blind healings on either end was noted earlier. The verbal similarities add to the effect.

16. The recording of his name (and that of his father) may also suggest he was well known to Mark's readership (he is not named in the Matthean or Lukan parallel).

MARK 8:22–26—Two-Stage Healing	MARK 10:46–52—Instantaneous Healing
Jesus and disciples come (καὶ ἔρχονται εἰς, *kai erchontai eis*, "and they came to," 8:22) Blindness healed (ἀναβλέπω, *anablepō*, "look," 8:24)	Jesus and disciples come (καὶ ἔρχονται εἰς, "and they came to," 10:46) Blindness healed (ἀναβλέπω, "see again," 10:51, 52)

The importance of these bookends on either side of Act II—one a two-stage healing and the other an instantaneous one—is that they symbolize what happened (or what should have happened) between the two episodes, "on the way." The disciples have been taught clearly ("plainly," 8:32) what the mission of Jesus is all about, and acceptance of Jesus' mission now has become a possibility for all who follow him. This, of course, is not to say that the disciples, at the end of Act II, accept that mission: the sad truth is that the Twelve do not, nor do they remain faithful to him in Act III (see 14:29, 37, 50, 66–72). Mark does not tamper with those sobering facts to accommodate his story; he is not giving us exemplary followers in the disciples. That, of course, would have been an ideal situation, but real life is rarely so precise. Had Mark provided a sanitized account of the Twelve, it would have conflicted with the facts that his contemporary readers would have been well aware of: the disciples' cowardice, Judas' betrayal, Peter's denial, etc. Instead, Mark "preserves the basic accuracy of the tradition in relation to the actual blindness of the disciples and yet at the same time instructs his own people in the nature of Jesus' suffering and the necessity of their own. He can only do this symbolically. Thus the two-stage healing of 8:22–26 is a picture of what ought to happen."[17] Divine inspiration and narrative artistry combine to make that same lesson discernible, even through the less-than-perfect story of the Twelve.

The son of Timaeus, Bartimaeus, calls upon the Son of David, Jesus (the word order in the Greek in 10:47 maintains this parallel structure of the naming of patient and healer).[18] While the blind man's cry, "Son of David," would be functionally equivalent to "Messiah" (10:47, 48), it also loads the address with royal and nationalistic ideology, making this Gentile "confession" all the more remarkable. "No other onlooker has interpreted Jesus in messianic (as opposed to merely prophetic) terms in this gospel"; only here is Jesus called the Son of David by a human voice, and that regal term, appropriately enough, occurs as the king prepares to visit his capital and enter his palace (see 11:9).[19] This man has accepted the mission of Jesus; he has become a disciple. That

---

17. Best, *Following Jesus*, 136–37. This argument is a convincing one for Mark's veracity. Even as he recasts events symbolically in his narrative for the purposes of his theological agenda, he faithfully maintains verisimilitude to history.

18. Of interest is that earlier in the Gospel, the same verb (ἐπιτιμάω, *epitimaō*, "rebuke," 10:48) used to describe the crowd's reaction to Bartimaeus is twice used with Jesus as its subject, as he himself engages in rebuke to impose silence upon others (3:12; 8:30). Here, Jesus prevents people from rebuking one confessing the Messiah. The "silence motif" is gradually giving way to the public acclamation of Jesus' identity, in parallel with the progressive unveiling of the suffering aspect of his mission.

19. France, *Gospel of Mark*, 423–24. "It was no accident that Mark portrays a blind man as the first person to perceive that Jesus was the son of David. His persistent (double) confession of Jesus as such (10:47, 48) is the first use of the title in the Gospel, preparing the way for the interpretation of this title

he has done so is reinforced by the threefold use of the word "call" (φωνέω, *phōneō*), employed by Jesus, Mark, and by the crowd (10:49 [×3]). As was suggested above, this episode is virtually a "call story," symbolic of Jesus' summons to discipleship. And the blind man responds unhesitatingly, leaving behind his (only?) possession—thus doing what the rich man had failed to do earlier.[20] The abandonment of the cloak may itself be a motif of symbolic value: all who are called to follow in this Gospel have to leave things behind, whether they be nets, boats, fathers, or livelihoods (1:18, 20; 2:14; 10:28). Indeed, the failed call in 10:17–22 is a case in particular of the *refusal to give up possessions* to follow Jesus in discipleship (10:21–22).[21]

That Jesus addresses the man with the exact words that he (Jesus) had just addressed James and John is significant: "What do you want Me to do for you?" (τί θέλετέ ποιήσω ὑμῖν; *ti thelete poiēsō hymin?*, 10:36; and τί σοι θέλεις ποιήσω; *ti soi theleis poiēsō?*, 10:51). The brothers make an illegitimate request; the blind man a legitimate one. The two disciples are blithely confident in their own abilities to share the Passion of Jesus ("we are able," 10:39); the blind man simply asks for mercy (10:37), acutely conscious of his own frailty. The sons of Zebedee do not discern or accept Jesus' mission—they view it merely in terms of worldly rankings of power that they might appropriate; symbolically, in his address, in the regaining of his sight, and in his following Jesus, the son of Timaeus discerns Jesus' person and accepts Jesus' mission. Those with eyes do not see; the blind man, in stark contrast, does. The disciples, who have thus far not discerned or accepted the mission of Jesus, are fearful as Jesus moves towards Jerusalem (10:32 is the most recent occurrence of "follow" before the blind man's initiative to do so); Bartimaeus, on the other hand, follows Jesus into Jerusalem with enthusiasm.[22] The account begins with Bartimaeus seated παρὰ τὴν ὁδόν (*para tēn hodon*, "by the way," 10:46) and ends with him following Jesus ἐν τῇ ὁδῷ (*en tē hodō*, "on the way," 10:52). "He began following Him on the way" is clearly more than just a transitional phrase. At the end of this pericope and, thus, at the end of Act II, it has a symbolic role to play. Both "follow" and "the way" are significant terms in the lexicon of discipleship. Bartimaeus represents those disciples who discern Jesus'

---

in the next incident (11.9–10)" (Painter, *Mark's Gospel*, 153). In the context of the journey to Jerusalem, and from his very name, the blind son of Timaeus was likely to have been a Gentile, thus furthering Mark's emphasis on healing and helping those "from afar" (8:3), including the Gerasene demoniac, the Syrophoenician woman's daughter, and the 4,000 making up the Gentile crowd in 8:1–9.

20. Williams, *Other Followers*, 157.

21. Collins, *Mark*, 511. Boring carries the symbolism of the garment further: "Throughout Mark, clothing is often symbolic of the significance of the person, and, like the name, partakes of the reality of the person himself or herself (cf. 1:6; 5:27; 6:9; 9:3; 11:7; 14:51). Already in Paul's time, becoming a Christian meant receiving a new identity, symbolized by putting on new garments" (Rom 13:12; Gal 3:27–28; Eph 4:22–24; 6:11–17; Col 3:12–14; 1 Thess 5:8). There might even be an allusion to the baptismal ritual, already present in nascent form in the pericope (Mark 10:14, 38–39). By the second century, the practice of taking off old garments to be baptized and putting on new garments to symbolize the new life had become part of the baptismal rite. See Boring, *Mark*, 306. Incidentally, the parallels in Matthew and Luke say nothing about a garment being cast aside (Matt 20:29–34; Luke 18:35–43).

22. Marshall, *Faith as a Theme*, 140. Both episodes in this pericope, contrasting the sons of Zebedee and the son of Timaeus, also use the verb κάθημαι (*kathēmai*, "sit," 10:37, 46).

person and accept his mission, and who follow Jesus on the Trip of Discipleship.[23] The blind man is called, and he responds, following Jesus "on the way"—he has become a disciple![24]

SERMON FOCUS AND OUTLINES

THEOLOGICAL FOCUS OF PERICOPE 16 FOR PREACHING

16   **The true sign of greatness of disciples is their acceptance of Jesus' mission, to follow his model of suffering and service (10:32–52).**

This pericope concludes Act II of Mark's Gospel. Bartimaeus's story (10:46–52) is the last before the curtain falls on this act, just as the earlier healing of another blind man (8:22–26) announced the curtain's rise. The theological thrust of the pericope is in the first episode—the third and final Passion Prediction by Jesus, along with the disciples' complete indifference and ignorance about Jesus' suffering mission: they are only interested in power and position for themselves.[25] The incisive pronouncement of Jesus' mission follows in 10:45. Disciples are thereby called to accept this mission, following Jesus in suffering and service—the true mark of greatness. In a culture that is focused in so blinkered a fashion upon the self and its creaturely comforts, this sermon ought to be a perfectly positioned to portray the divine model of greatness through sacrifice.[26] (Pericope 23, 14:53–72, will deal in more detail with self-denial, and how the failure to deny oneself is equivalent to a denial of Jesus.)

POSSIBLE PREACHING OUTLINES FOR PERICOPE 16

I.   OMISSION: Disciples' hunger for power

       Response to Jesus' Passion Prediction: 10:32–41

       Move-to-Relevance: Our acquiescence to cultural models of "greatness"

II.   MISSION: Jesus' suffering to serve

       The true model of greatness: 10:33–34, suffering; 10:42–45, service

III. SUBMISSION: *Suffer and serve to greatness!*

       Specifics on how one may achieve greatness, God's way

---

23. France, *Gospel of Mark*, 425.

24. Interestingly, this is the only call story to have the key phrase "on the way." Had the others (especially the Twelve), when they were called, not yet begun to follow Jesus "on the way"?

25. Therefore the final episode of Bartimaeus's healing and his following need not necessarily play a major role in a sermon on this pericope. That account simply bookends Act II and serves also as a transition into Act III, exemplifying the proper response of a disciple—discernment of Jesus and acceptance of his mission.

26. For an interesting and informative read on this modern cultural preoccupation with the self (and for great illustrations and statistics, as well), see Twenge and Campbell, *Narcissism Epidemic*. Poking a bit of fun at this epidemic in the sermon might be quite appropriate. Creative preachers will consult with their worship leaders and drama teams for how this might be best achieved. Also see Kuruvilla, review of *Narcissism Epidemic*, 877–80.

A second option:

I.   Suffering—integral to Jesus' mission
        The third Passion Prediction, 10:32–34
II. Glory—antithetical to Jesus' current mission
        The disciples' desire for glory, rather than suffering, 10:35–41
        Move-to-Relevance: Our acquiescence to cultural models of "greatness"
III. Service through suffering—the biblical model
        The true model of greatness: serving through suffering, 10:42–45
IV. *Suffer and serve to greatness!*
        Specifics on how one may achieve greatness, God's way

ACT III: IN JERUSALEM

Faithfulness to Jesus

PERICOPE 17

Community of Faithful, Forgiving Prayer

Mark 11:1–25

[Jesus' Entry into Jerusalem; Cleansing of the Temple; Fig Tree Cursed]

REVIEW, SUMMARY, PREVIEW

Review of Pericope 16: Mark 10:32–52, with the third Passion Prediction of Jesus, demonstrates what true greatness means: to suffer and serve like Jesus, accepting his mission.

> **Summary of Pericope 17:** Mark 11:1–25 teaches that disciples appropriately receive their divine king, and respond by functioning as communities of prayer built upon faith and forgiveness. The adumbration of destruction of the nonfunctioning temple also warns disciples of dire consequences for their own dysfunctionality.

> > **Preview of Pericope 18:** The next pericope (11:27—12:12), centers on the question of Jesus' authority and God's ownership, the response to which is fruit-bearing on part of the disciples—the solemn responsibility of stewardship.

17 Mark 11:1–25

THEOLOGICAL FOCUS OF PERICOPE 17

17 Disciples' appropriate reception of their divine king, Jesus, is characterized by their becoming communities functioning properly, dedicated to prayer built upon faith and forgiveness, as they replace the dysfunctional temple, the destruction of which warns disciples of the consequences of dysfunctionality (11:1–25).

17.1 The appropriate reception of their divine king characterizes disciples faithful to Jesus (11:1–11).

241

> 17.2 The proper function of Jesus' disciples is corporate engagement in prayer built upon faith and forgiveness, as the new community of believers takes over the role of the dysfunctional temple, the destruction of which warns disciples of the consequences of dysfunctionality (11:12–25).
>
> 17.2.1 Dysfunctional communities of disciples may face severe judgment from God, just as the dysfunctional temple did.
>
> 17.2.2 The proper function of the communities of disciples involves prayer built upon faith and forgiveness.

OVERVIEW

JERUSALEM GOT SCANT MENTION in the first two acts of Mark's Gospel, and all of the references related either to hostile leaders from that city (3:22; 7:1) or to the violence that Jesus predicted would be inflicted on him there (10:32, 33). In this final act of Mark's Gospel, he enters Jerusalem to die. In a sense, Act III (11:1—16:8) is less spectacular, without any of the miracles that characterized his earlier public presence.[1] In addition, the mostly closed-door instruction to disciples in Act II is now replaced by public confrontations in Act III—particularly in Mark 11–12, a section that is framed by references to the Mount of Olives (11:1 and 13:3) and to Jesus' entering and leaving the temple (11:11 and 13:1).[2] This confrontation section is followed by the Passion proper in Mark 14–16 (framed by episodes relating to women: 14:1–9 and 15:40—16:8). Between these two phases, Mark 11–12 and 14–16, is an extended apocalyptic discourse (Mark 13), parallel to Mark 4, which is another extended discourse in the middle of Act I (see the Introduction). In that earlier lengthy discourse, the reader was able to pull back and see the whole schema of Jesus' mission and its fruit-bearing potential with the human and divine elements involved. Mark 13, likewise, affords the reader an opportunity to reflect on the long-term strategy of Jesus' mission and God's kingdom, and, importantly for Act III, it expands on the overarching theme of the faithfulness of the disciple (depicted negatively in the unfaithfulness of the disciples, primarily the Twelve).

As is visible from the structure below, the entry into Jerusalem and into the temple precincts is an important part of 11:1—13:1; it happens three times, separated by the cursing and withering of the fig tree. The centerpiece (B, A', and B') comprises the temple cleansing episode, bounded on either side by the story of the fig tree (11:12–14 and 11:20–25); together they create another classic Markan "sandwich."

---

1. There is a privately seen cursing of the fig tree in 11:12–13, 20–21 and, of course, the resurrection—a different dimension of miracle altogether, but even that is more implied than described.

2. It is possible to divide the confrontation section of 11:12—12:40 into five controversy narratives, parallel in number to the five conflicts in Galilee (2:1–3:6): 11:12–25 (temple cleansing); 11:27—12:12 (with chief priests and scribes and elders); 12:13–17 (with Pharisees and Herodians); 12:18–27 (with Sadducees); 12:28–40 (with scribes).

A	Jerusalem entry I ("came into," "Jerusalem," "temple," 11:11; "went out," 11:11)	(11:1–11)
	B Fig tree cursed	(11:12–14)
A'	Jerusalem entry II ("came," "Jerusalem," "temple," 11:15; "went out," 11:19)	(11:15–19)
	B' Fig tree withered	(11:20–25)
A''	Jerusalem entry III ("came," "Jerusalem," "temple," 11:27; "going out," 13:1)	(11:27–13:1)

After the final exit from the temple (13:1), Jesus engages in the discourse of Mark 13 and clearly establishes the parameters of faithfulness in discipleship—what he had not observed from the custodians of the temple in the previous chapters.

17.1   Mark 11:1–11

THEOLOGICAL FOCUS 17.1

17.1   The appropriate reception of their divine king characterizes disciples faithful to Jesus (11:1–11).

Section Summary 17.1: The entry of Jesus into Jerusalem and the temple is marked by irony: it has all the trappings of a royal arrival, but nobody in Jerusalem or in the temple appears to have noticed. Those who wish to follow Jesus are expected to be faithful to him, receiving this divine king appropriately.

TRANSLATION 17.1

11:1   *And when they came near to Jerusalem, to Bethphage and Bethany, towards the Mount of Olives, He sent two of His disciples,*

11:2   *and said to them, "Go into the village before you, and immediately as you enter into it, you will find a colt tied, upon which no man has yet sat; untie it and bring [it here].*

11:3   *And if anyone says to you, 'Why are you doing this?' you say, 'The Lord has need of it,' and immediately he will send it back here."*

11:4   *And they went away and found a colt tied at a door, outside in the street, and they untied it.*

11:5   *And some of those standing there were saying to them, "What are you doing, untying the colt?"*

11:6   *And they spoke to them just as Jesus had said, and they permitted them.*

11:7   *And they brought the colt to Jesus and threw their cloaks on it, and He sat on it.*

11:8   *And many spread their cloaks in the way, and others, leafy branches they had cut from the fields.*

11:9   *And those going ahead and those following were crying, "Hosanna! Blessed is the One who comes in the name of the Lord!*

11:10 *Blessed is the coming kingdom of our father David! Hosanna in the highest!"*

11:11 *And He came into Jerusalem, into the temple and after looking around at everything, He went out to Bethany with the twelve, since the hour was already late.*

NOTES 17.1

17.1 *The appropriate reception of their divine king characterizes disciples faithful to Jesus.*[3]

While Jesus' movements during the Passover festival, with its vast throngs in Jerusalem, could have been relatively inconspicuous had he so desired it, the procession into the city and the almost deliberate arrival and later actions at the temple ensure that he is noticed.[4] Catchpole denotes the elements of a triumphal entry of a victorious Roman general or imperator; the correspondences with Mark 11 are noted below in parentheses[5]:

- A victory already achieved and a status already recognized for the protagonist (the three Passion Predictions in Mark 8–10; the authority symbols of the garments on colt and on the road, 11:7–8)

- Formal and ceremonial entry (leafy branches signifying nationalistic interest and Sukkoth, ancient Israel's entrance ceremony, 11:1–11)

- Greetings and/or acclamations together with invocations of God (the crowd's exclamations, 11:9–10)

- Entry to the city climaxed by entry into the temple (Jesus' temple entry, 11:11)

- Cultic activity, either positive, e.g., offering of sacrifice, or negative, e.g., expulsion of objectionable persons and removal of uncleanness (temple cleansing, 11:15–18).

From both Greco-Roman backgrounds and from Zechariah 14, one would have expected Jesus to enter Jerusalem and take up his abode there (city and temple corresponding to capital and palace of the King), inaugurating the new age of blessedness. Instead, there is an abrupt and anticlimactic end to this arrival—it takes only one verse (11:11): Jesus comes into the temple, and then leaves both temple and city. His Jerusalem entry II (11:15) and Jerusalem entry III (11:27; see above) are equally

---

3. The theological subfocus here is again describing what ought to have been, not what was.

4. *m. Ḥag.* 1.1 exempts from the OT requirement for festival pilgrimage one "who is unable to go up [to Jerusalem] on foot." This one occasion when Jesus chose to ride into town, he was surely aware of the impression that mode of transportation would make. Collins notes that after Bartimaeus' address of Jesus as "Son of David," the entry into the city riding on a colt, rather than walking, was "a nonverbal way of making a messianic claim" (*Mark*, 518–19).

5. Catchpole, "The 'Triumphal' Entry," 321. He cites the parallel examples of entrances into Jerusalem—those of Alexander, Apollonius, Simon Maccabeus, Marcus Agrippa, Archelaus, etc. (ibid., 319–21). Also see Duff, "March of the Divine Warrior," 59–64.

jejune; no one in his "capital" or his "palace" appears to pay him any attention. The altercation in 11:27–33 appears to originate *after* Jesus has already entered the temple. In other words, Jesus' entries are the essence of irony! His rejection has begun: rather than being appropriately received, he is completely ignored.

In his call for a colt (11:2–4), it is likely that Jesus is exercising a royal prerogative to requisition an animal for his own use (the system was called *angaria/angariare* in medieval Latin: compulsory requisition into service).[6] The fact that the colt has never been ridden—the disciples also "brought" the colt to Jesus, without riding it themselves—reflects the uniqueness of the king's mount (*m. Sanh.* 2.5; *b. Ber.* 56b; also see Num 19:2; Deut 21:3; 1 Sam 6:7; note νέος, *neos*, "new," in Zech 9:9 LXX, but not in the MT). These elements of royalty subtly shade the narrative: the king has arrived!

The "they" who come near Jerusalem (Mark 11:1) must include the "large crowd" of 10:46—probably of Galilean origin—the band of pilgrims in whose company Jesus and his disciples were heading for Jerusalem. After Bartimaeus's healing, they appear to be disposed favorably towards him, and subscribe to that healed man's estimation of Jesus by crying out (κράζω, *krazo*, 12:9), just as Bartimaeus did (κράζω, 10:47, 48). They too see Jesus' connection with King David.

The balanced (antiphonal?) structure of the crowd's acclamation in 11:9–10 ("Hosanna / Blessed . . . // Blessed . . . / Hosanna") is based on Ps 118:25–26, the last of the Hallel psalms recited in major festivals.[7] France notes that 118:26 may well have been addressed to a king celebrating a victory, and thus would be appropriate for use at the royal entry of Jesus; it also points to the Galilean preacher as contending for the title "King of the Jews" (see Mark 15:2, 9, 12, 18, 26, 32).[8] But this acknowledgement comes from the crowd from Galilee, not from the throngs in Jerusalem. The latter, apparently, could not care less for this king.[9]

In sum, the remarkable thing upon Jesus' entry into Jerusalem and into the temple is that *nothing* happens! For a king entering his "capital" and "palace," this is the ultimate insult! The failure, in antiquity, of cities to extend the customary greeting to dignitaries and military victors would have had dire consequences.[10] "It seems that the evangelist himself . . . has carefully choreographed this 'street theater' in order that the decisively nontriumphal 'triumphal entry' provoke the reader to reconsider his/

---

6. See Derrett, "Law in the New Testament," 243; also see 1 Sam 8:16–18. Royal imagery may also have dictated the use of καθίζω, *kathizo*, "sit," in Mark 11:7, instead of the usual ἐπιβαίνω, *epibainō*, "mount," as in Zech 9:9 (also Num 22:30; 1 Sam 25:20).

7. Ὡσαννά (*Hōsanna*, "Hosanna") is from הוֹשִׁיעָה נָּא (*hoshiʿah naʾ*, "save now," or "save us, we pray"; Ps 118:25), which, of course, is connected with יְהוֹשֻׁעַ (*Yehoshuaʿ*, "Joshua" or "Jesus").

8. France, *Gospel of Mark*, 434–35.

9. It must also be noted that this crowd from Galilee that shouted "Hosanna" is not identical to the crowd from Jerusalem that shouted, "Crucify" a few days later. Jesus' kingdom ideology with messianic overtones, at the core of his confrontations with religious leaders, and now adopted by the crowds, raises the level of suspense on this Passion Week, especially as some Jewish traditions anticipated a purging of Jerusalem by the Davidic Messiah (*Pss. Sol.* 17.22). See Hatina, *In Search*, 308–9; see ibid., 317–19, for other expectations of the Jewish Messiah.

10. Kinman, "Parousia," 283–84.

her presuppositions about such topics as messiahship, discipleship, and the role of the kingdom of God."[11] What will be the disciple's response to the king? Will Jesus be appropriately received? The next episode, thus, deals with the result of such an adequate response to the king in the life of Jesus-followers: appropriate reception leads—or should lead—to appropriate function.

17.2   Mark 11:12–25

THEOLOGICAL FOCUS 17.2

17.2   The proper function of Jesus' disciples is corporate engagement in prayer built upon faith and forgiveness, as the new community of believers takes over the role of the dysfunctional temple, the destruction of which warns disciples of the consequences of dysfunctionality (11:12–25).

17.2.1   Dysfunctional communities of disciples may face severe judgment from God, just as the dysfunctional temple did.

17.2.2   The proper function of the communities of disciples involves prayer built upon faith and forgiveness.

Section Summary 17.2: The fig tree "sandwich" portrays the severity of punishment upon non-functional/dysfunctional communities of God's people. The replacement of such a sterile temple by the new community of Jesus' disciples mandated the proper functioning of the latter by their engagement in prayer founded on faith and mutual forgiveness.

TRANSLATION 17.2

11:11   *And He entered into Jerusalem, into the temple, and after looking around at everything, He went out to Bethany with the twelve, since the hour was already late.*

11:12   *And on the next day, when they were going out from Bethany, He was hungry.*

11:13   *And seeing, from afar, a fig tree having leaves, He went [to see] if perhaps He could find anything on it, and when He came to it, He found nothing but leaves, for it was not the season for figs.*

11:14   *And answering, He said to it, "May no one eat fruit from you ever again." And His disciples heard [Him].*

11:15   *And they came into Jerusalem. And going into the temple, He began to cast out those who were buying and those who were selling in the temple, and He overturned the tables of the money changers and the seats of those who were selling doves,*

11:16   *and He would not allow anyone to carry merchandise through the temple.*

---

11. Duff, "March of the Divine Warrior," 55–56.

11:17   And He began to teach and say to them, "Is it not written, 'My house shall be called a house of prayer for all nations'? But you have made it 'a den of robbers.'"

11:18   And the chief priests and the scribes heard [Him] and were seeking how to destroy Him; for they were afraid of Him, for the whole crowd was amazed at His teaching.

11:19   And when evening came, they went out of the city.

11:20   And as they were going by in the morning, they saw the fig tree withered from the roots.

11:21   And being reminded, Peter said to Him, "Rabbi, look, the fig tree which You cursed has withered."

11:22   And Jesus answering, said to them, "Have faith in God.

11:23   Truly I say to you, whoever says to this mountain, 'Be taken up and be cast into the sea,' and does not doubt in his heart but believes that what he says is going to happen, it will be [so] for him.

11:24   For this reason I say to you, all things for which you pray and ask, believe that you receive, and it will be [so] for you.

11:25   And when you stand praying, if you have anything against anyone, forgive, so that your Father who is in heaven will also forgive you your sins."

[11:26]¹²

NOTES 17.2

7.2.1   *Dysfunctional communities of disciples may face severe judgment from God, just as the dysfunctional temple did.*

This section forms the fourth of Mark's "sandwich" stories (outer story: 11:12–14; 11:20–25; inner story: 11:15–19).¹³ Again Jesus is the only character to be actively present in both stories; in both he rebukes that which does not function properly and meet his expectations.¹⁴ While the eschatological meaning of Jesus' actions appears obvious, one must note that the thrust of this "sandwich" is the repudiation of the institutional body of God's people that does not function as it ought to in God's economy. The cleansing of the temple (11:15–19) denotes its disqualification and warns of inevitable replacement—the moving of the mountain (11:23) conceivably standing for the destruction of the temple mount, and the laying of the cornerstone (12:10–11) representing the foundation for the new temple.¹⁵ Dysfunctional institutions will be

---

12. 11:26 is not found in the earliest manuscripts.

13. See Shepherd, *Markan Sandwich Stories*, 209–41, for details on this Markan "sandwich."

14. Indeed, in its position within the "sandwich," between the cursing and withering of the fig tree, the temple "cleansing" is the beginning of the temple "closing," and Mark intends, by his narrative art, that it be seen in this light. The allusions to the ancient writings implicit in Jesus' actions affirm this trajectory; the messianic triumphal entry would be followed by purification of the temple (Zech 14:21; Mal 3:1–4; *Pss. Sol.* 17.30—"He [Messiah] will purge Jerusalem making it holy as it was even from the beginning"), or even its replacement (Zech 6:12–13; Tob 14.5).

15. Geddert, *Watchwords*, 123.

replaced with a new community. Would that new community function according to Jesus' expectations? If not, it too can expect judgment.[16]

Jesus' "looking around" (11:11) links this temple inspection with the inspection of the fig tree for fruit (11:12). Both temple and tree are faulty and functioning inappropriately. The story of the fig tree has created interpretive agonies throughout the millennia of church history. Augustine (*Sermons on New Testament Lessons* 48.3) puts this problem passage right in focus:

> Did not Christ know what any peasant knew? What the dresser of the tree knew, did not the tree's Creator know? So then when being hungry he sought fruit on the tree, . . . and he found that tree without fruit, but full of leaves, he cursed it, and it withered away. What had the tree done in not bearing fruit? What fault of the tree was its fruitlessness? No; but there are those who through their own will are not able to yield fruit. And barrenness is "their" fault, whose fruitfulness is their will. . . . Our Lord Jesus Christ performed miracles with this view, that by those miracles he might signify something further, that besides that they were wonderful and great, and divine in themselves, we might learn also something from them.

On the other hand, Bertrand Russell claimed this incident to be one of the reasons he was not a Christian: "This is a very curious story, because it was not the right time of year for figs, and you really could not blame the tree. I cannot myself feel that either in the matter of wisdom or in the matter of virtue Christ stands quite as high as some other people known to history. I think I should put Buddha and Socrates above Him in those respects."[17]

Perhaps the best solution to that conundrum comes from Jesus' contemporary, Pliny the Elder (23–79 CE), the Roman naturalist, philosopher, and military officer. In his monumental *Historia naturalis* (written ca. 77–79 CE), he observes: "The fig tree is also the only tree whose leaf forms later than its fruit" (16.49; also see *EncJud* 6.1273). In other words, to see leaves meant the possibility of at least some fruit. Jesus is hopeful, but his hopes are dashed.[18] In Mark 11:14, one finds Jesus "answering" a tree that has not spoken! Perhaps he is "replying" to the tree's failure to provide what it was promising by the presence of its leaves. Fruit was being promised, but it was a promise not being kept. A glorious outside, but without fruit inside, characterizes this fig tree; it also characterizes the temple (the inner story of the "sandwich"). The fig tree has the status of a tree, with leaves promising fruit, but it has borne none. The temple has the status of being the house of prayer, promising much in its physical grandeur, but it is a haven of robbers.[19] Alas, both tree and temple are dysfunctional, and both would be

---

16. Mark is silent about what such punishment may look like, though replacement appears to be a safe guess. Perhaps such replacement might be equivalent to Christ's taking away of the lampstand (= church) as in Rev 1:20; 2:5.

17. Russell, *Why I Am Not a Christian*, 19, from a lecture delivered on March 6, 1927, to the National Secular Society, South London Branch.

18. France, *Gospel of Mark*, 443.

19. Shepherd, *Markan Sandwich Stories*, 219. Mark 11:15 and 16 have εἰς τὸ ἱερὸν, ἐν τῷ ἱερῷ, and διὰ τοῦ ἱεροῦ (*eis to hieron, en tō hierō,* and *dia tou hierou;* "into/in/through the temple"). The

severely punished. Destruction "from the roots" (11:20) is an idiom Mark's audiences would have understood as loss of potency and vitality (Job 18:16; 28:9; 31:12; Ezek 17:9 LXX). Rootlessness was warned of in Mark 4:6 (ξηραίνω, *xērainō*, "wither" and ῥίζα, *rhiza*, "root" occur there as well); such an end can befall anyone. Thus, it is not just the religious hierarchy that is being cautioned here: any community of disciples may end up rootless and functionless, and thus will be castigated, if they are not careful to be functioning properly.[20]

Bracketing the incident in the temple, the cursing of the fig tree becomes an enacted parable of God's judgment on the dysfunctional activities of the cultic system as a whole, and upon effete and sterile institutions in particular—those that do not meet Jesus' expectations as a body of God's people. Fig trees and their fruit are biblical archetypes for the people of God and their service of obedience to him (Jer 8:13; 24:1–10; Hos 9:10–17; Micah 7:1; the fig tree also reappears in Mark in 13:28).[21] The similarities between this account and the oracle in Hosea 9:10–17 are considerable: both have fig trees, Jesus/Yahweh seeing and finding, fruit, casting out, "my house," and roots that are withered. The context of that OT parallel is also significant: Hosea 9 mentions "Baal-Peor" (9:10), referring to Israel's first apostasy in the Canaanite fertility cult (Num 25), and "Gilgal" (Hos 9:15), referring to another cult center (Josh 4:19–20; Jdg 3:19; etc.). In other words, "the divine and prophetic response to Israel's cultic malpractice is one of unmitigated judgment."[22] While the specificities of this judgment upon the temple cultus is clear, the lesson that God will take punitive action when the community of his people do not function appropriately is part of the theological focus of this section, and one that is valid for God's people of all time. In fact the use of ἐκβάλλω (*ekballō*, "cast out," Mark 11:15) to describe Jesus' action in the temple even suggests an exorcism (1:12, 34, 39; 3:15, 22, 23; 6:13; 7:26; 9:18, 28, 38).[23] Judgment will be severe for inappropriately functioning communities of God's people.

Evans notes the comparable features of Jeremiah 7 and Isaiah 56 (the passages Jesus cites in this Markan episode: 11:17) and 1 Kings 8:41–43 (part of Solomon's prayer at the dedication of the temple)[24]:

---

focus is sharply upon this central institution of Israel's cult, and hints at the narrator's deprecation of what was going on within it.

20. There is a hint here that the disciples are—at last!—learning something: they heard (11:14), they saw (11:20), and they remembered (11:21), all three being actions in which they have been sorely deficient in the past (8:17, 18).

21. Telford, *Barren Temple*, 161, examining five tree passages (Isa 28:3–4; Jer 8:13; Hos 9:10, 16; Joel 1:7, 12; Mic 7:1), concludes that the OT "on the whole knows very little of nonsymbolical trees."

22. Krause, "Narrated Prophecy," 241 (see 241–45).

23. Of particular note is the use of ἐκβάλλω, *ekballō*, in 1:34, where it is used with ἀφίημι (*aphiēmi*, "to permit"), also found here in 11:16 (translated "allow") and 11:25 (translated "forgive").

24. Evans, *Mark*, 178.

JEREMIAH 7	ISAIAH 56	1 KINGS 8
alien (7:6)	foreigners (56:6)	a foreigner (8:41)
this house (7:11)	my house (56:7)	this house (8:43)
called by my name (7:11)	shall be called (56:7)	called by thy name (8:43)
	house of prayer (56:7)	prays toward this house (8:42)
	for all peoples (56:7)	all the peoples of the earth (8:43)
	offerings will be accepted (56:7)	prayers will be heard (8:43)

The parallels imply that Jesus' indictment in Mark 11:17, with the employment of Jeremiah 7 and Isaiah 56, is not simply prophetic, but driven by a Solomonic understanding of the original purpose of the temple, and in line with Jesus seeing himself as the Son of David. The mandate of the temple is not being fulfilled; it is dysfunctional—splendid façade, but sterile in function. And improper functioning will meet implacable chastening in any community of the people of God, even one made up of disciples.[25]

17.2.2 The proper function of the communities of disciples involves prayer built upon faith and forgiveness.

That it is prayer, and not sacrifice, that is the issue addressed (11:17) is significant for post-resurrection readers: the temple sacrifices have been superseded and need not be repeated in this dispensation. Also notable is the thrust of Isaiah 56:6–7 cited in Mark 11:17—the entry of Gentiles into the community of God. "Mark's community here sees the destruction of the Jerusalem temple as [the consequence of its] having failed to be a house of prayer for all peoples, a destruction that made way for the true temple of the end time in which 'all peoples'—the church of Jews and Gentiles of Mark's own time—will offer up authentic prayers to God." Jesus goes on, in 11:20–25, to provide instruction on the proper functioning of this new temple/community of disciples, particularly its prayer.[26] This section illustrates what Jesus means by "house of prayer" (11:17)—one that extended beyond the physical confines of the temple, foreshadowing the new institution of the body of believers.

The temple's destruction is looming; its end is nigh. Therefore, Jesus takes on the task of convincing his disciples that, despite contemporary thought closely associating a temple with its deity's existence, repudiation of the temple does not disturb Yahweh's presence and activity in the world. Abandoning faith in the temple, in other words, is not the same as abandoning faith in God (11:22).[27] Neither will the loss

---

25. Jesus' condemnation of the temple serves to unite the opposition that was seeking to dispatch him (11:18–19). The irony is that his death, the consummation of their plot, seals the condemnation of the temple (15:38), and initiates its substitution by a new temple, one "not made with hands" (11:22–25; 14:58; 15:29). See Marshall, *Faith as a Theme*, 163.

26. Boring, *Mark*, 323. Eschatological expectations dictated the restoration of the temple and the assemblage of all peoples for worship: Isa 2:2–4; 66:18–23; Ezek 40–48; Zech 14:14–21; Mal 3:1–4; *T. Levi* 18.9; *1 En.* 90.28–29 (see Shepherd, *Markan Sandwich Stories*, 211–12, n2).

27. Myers, *Binding the Strong Man*, 304–5. Prayer and the temple were yoked together in Jewish thought: 1 Sam 1:1–29; 1 Kgs 8:14–61; 2 Kgs 19:14–37; Jonah 2:8; also see Jdt 4.9–15; 2 Macc 3.15; 10.25–26; 3 Macc 1.20–24. The temple was seen as the gate of heaven, and prayer in its direction was encouraged (*b. Ber.* 30a, 32b).

of the temple mean loss of the tradition of prayer; a new "house of prayer" (11:17) will be formed. "Jesus' authoritative command that the disciples pray (προσεύχεσθε, *proseuchesthe*) with faith in the unlimited power of God to provide all that they ask (11:24) enables them to fulfill God's promise for a house of prayer (οἶκος προσευχῆς, *oikos proseuchēs*) by becoming themselves the communal household of authentic and effective prayer that the temple with its prayer based on the commercial business of sacrifice failed to become (11:17)."[28] Note also the importance of prayer in Mark as an activity frequently associated with Jesus and his disciples (1:35; 6:46; 9:29; 11:24–26; 14:38). "House" (οἶκος, *oikos*) also serves an important motif in Mark's story (1:29–31; 2:1–12; 3:20–35; 7:17; 9:28, 33; 10:10). Instead of gathering at the synagogue (συναγωγή, *synagōgē*), Jesus and those who follow him are constantly gathering (συνάγω, *synagō*) at an οἶκος (e.g., 2:1–2; 1:33; 3:20). This may be a hint that the appropriately functioning place of prayer is none other than the Christian community, the true οἶκος of Jesus.[29] Faith-filled prayer will be one aspect of the proper functioning of this new "house," the community of God's people.

As was noted, "this mountain" of 11:23 is likely referring to the temple mount itself (see Isa 2:2; Mic 4:1; Zech 4:6–10; *b. Pesaḥ.* 87b; *b. Giṭ.* 56b).[30] The verbs describing its taking up and being cast are divine passives—God will be the one to take action. The command of faith to the temple to be cast into the sea resembles, in its outcome, the watery end of the pigs in Mark 5. Both demonic hosts and the temple mount would meet the same fate.[31] Jesus' exhortation that his disciples have faith, even when the temple stands in danger of destruction, corresponds to Habakkuk's assertion that, despite the sacking of Jerusalem and the loss of the temple to the Babylonians, "the righteous will live by his faith" (Hab 2:4). Disciples are to be characterized as a community of God's people praying in faith.[32] This is part of what it means to function properly, in accordance with Jesus' expectations.

The parallels between Mark 11:22–23 and 11:24 indicate the close relationship between prayer and faith—faithful prayer is a crucial function of the new community of Christians:

---

28. Heil, "Narrative Strategy," 80.

29. Marshall, *Faith as a Theme*, 163; Gray, *Temple*, 32–33.

30. Ibid., 50–53.

31. Myers, *Binding the Strong Man*, 305. One must also not forget the punishment meted out in 9:42 to the one who causes others to sin: καὶ βέβληται εἰς τὴν θάλασσαν (*kai beblētai eis tēn thalassan*, "and he had been cast into the sea"), equivalent to καὶ βλήθητι εἰς τὴν θάλασσαν (*kai blētheti eis tēn thalassan*, "and be cast into the sea") here in 11:23.

32. That the verbs in 11:22–25 are in plural indicates the communal nature of the replacement for the temple. France observes that though 11:23 is singular in form, that singularity derives from the structure of the sentence that begins with ὃς ἄν (*hos an*, "whoever"), and not from necessity. Indeed the ὃς ἄν actually generalizes the statement into an activity undertaken by the new community of disciples. The singular in 11:23 is soon overtaken by the plurals in 11:24, 25 (France, *Gospel of Mark*, 448).

MARK 11:22-23	MARK 11:24

"I say to you"
"says to this mountain"
"have faith . . . believes"
    (πίστις, πιστεύω, pistis, pisteuō)
"it will be [so] for him"
	"I say to you"
	"for which you pray and ask"
	"believe"
	    (πιστεύω)
	"for you it will be [so]"

The OT makes it clear that the moving of mountains is God's business alone (Exod 19:18; Job 9:5; Ps 68:8; 97:5; 114:4–7; 144:5; Jer 4:24; Nah 1:5). "By ascribing to faith what is a prerogative of Yahweh alone, it opens up the awe-inspiring proportions of the injunction to have faith in God (v 22 [Mark 11:22]). It is not an invitation to a state of placid reliance on God but to active participation in his kingly dominion. For whoever moves mountains is, *ipso facto,* wielding the creative and judging word of God himself."[33] The new praying-in-faith community will be a fitting replacement for the dysfunctional temple.

Jesus continues his theme of the supplanting of the condemned temple: the disciples must also forgive—yet another condition for answered prayer, besides faith (11:25). "Rather than seeking Gods' forgiveness through the sacrificial system in the temple that has become a 'den of robbers' who take advantage of others instead of forgiving them (11:15–17), the disciples are to forgive anyone against whom they have anything, so as to assure God's forgiveness of their own offenses against him." Such a community is for all peoples of the world (11:17): the prayer of faith encouraged is for all anywhere, and the forgiveness practiced realizes an inclusive community dwelling in peace—the temple replaced by the priesthood of believers.[34]

In sum, the displacement of the nonfunctional temple will result in its replacement by the new community of Jesus' disciples—such a "temple" must be characterized by prayer that is founded upon faith and mutual forgiveness.

SERMON FOCUS AND OUTLINES

THEOLOGICAL FOCUS OF PERICOPE 17 FOR PREACHING
17 The community of disciples is characterized by prayer founded on faith and forgiveness (11:1–25).

This pericope, commencing Act III, has as its first episode Jesus' entry into Jerusalem and the temple—totally and unexpectedly uneventful. This is an inappropriate reception of Jesus, the divine king, who is entering his "capital" and his "palace." Quite naturally, inappropriate reception of the divine king leads to inappropriateness of

---

33. Marshall, *Faith as a Theme,* 166–76.

34. Heil, "Narrative Strategy," 80. Indeed, prayer is not actually enjoined, but assumed as a given; two conditions, however, are given for such prayers to be answered: faith and forgiveness (Marshall, *Faith as a Theme,* 170). Mutual forgiveness is the condition for the community's receiving forgiveness from God. And receiving forgiveness and mercy from God is a condition for its prayers to be heard (Sir 28.1–5; *b. Šabb.* 151b). Also see Dowd, *Prayer,* 126. For sin as an obstacle to prayer, see Ps 66:18; Prov 15:8, 29; Isa 1:15; Jer 7:16–17; 11:14–15; 14:11–12; Mic 3:4; Zech 7:13; John 9:31.

function—dysfunctionality of the temple. Such failure is castigated in the second episode of the pericope with the fig tree "sandwich," which shows the temple as functioning below Jesus' expectations. Its destruction is foreshadowed, as well as the creation of a new community of God's people—Jesus' disciples—who will take over the function of prayer, a role that the temple has failed at. This new "temple" will be characterized by faith and forgiveness—the two conditions for answered prayer. The sermon on this pericope may, therefore, focus more on the corporate activity of prayer, with the individual conditions (faith and forgiveness) being met. Corporate prayer with these appropriate attitudes of heart—faith and forgiveness—is certainly something most congregations could use more of. As a specific communal application, perhaps the church could commence a program of congregational prayer (if there is not one already), as a whole, in small groups, or in other gatherings.

POSSIBLE PREACHING OUTLINES FOR PERICOPE 17

I. Lack of response to Jesus, the divine king
    The unexpected non-eventfulness of Jesus' entry: 11:1–11
    Move-to-Relevance: Dangerous drift—a lack of response to Jesus' divine/royal authority

II. Lack of function as the house of prayer
    The fig tree "sandwich": 11:12–21, lack of function and divine chastening for dysfunctionality
    Move-to-relevance: Punishment and replacement for dysfunctionality today (Rev 1:20; 2:5)

III. *Pray faithfully and forgivingly!*
    The function of the new community of God's people: 11:22–25
    Specifics on how the body of disciples can be a house of prayer—faithful and forgiving

Another option:

I. FUNCTION: Proper function is expected of the community of Jesus' disciples
    The function of the new community of God's people—praying faithfully and forgiving: 11:22–25

II. FAILURE: Lack of function comes under a threat of divine chastening
    No response to Jesus: 11:1–11
    No function as the house of God: 11:15–19
    Danger of punishment—removal, replacement: 11:12–13, 20–21
    Move-to-relevance: Punishment and replacement for dysfunctionality today (Rev 1:20 and 2:5)

III. FAITH and FORGIVENESS: *Pray faithfully and forgivingly!*
    Specifics on how the body of disciples can be a house of prayer—faithful and forgiving

PERICOPE 18

Responsible Stewardship

Mark 11:27–12:12

[Jesus' Authority Questioned; Vineyard Parable]

REVIEW, SUMMARY, PREVIEW

Review of Pericope 17: Mark 11:1–25 teaches that disciples properly receive their divine king, and respond by functioning appropriately as communities of prayer founded upon faith and mutual forgiveness.

Summary of Pericope 18: Mark 11:27—12:12 centers on the question of Jesus' authority. His is an authority from heaven, the authority of the "beloved son" sent to receive fruit from the stewards of God's property. Producing fruit with what God has entrusted disciples is their solemn responsibility owed to God, and the consequences for failure are serious.

Preview of Pericope 19: The next pericope (12:13–44) focuses on the demands made on disciples as a result of God's absolute ownership and authority. As God's image-bearers belonging to him, they owe God the sacrifice of themselves, prompted by utmost love for God and neighbor.

18   Mark 11:27–12:12

THEOLOGICAL FOCUS OF PERICOPE 18

18   Accepting the divine authority of Jesus, disciples have the solemn responsibility of fruit-bearing stewardship towards God, the owner of all things, lest they suffer the consequences (11:27—12:12).

    18.1   Disciples accept the divine authority of Jesus, the one they follow in discipleship.

18.2   Bearing fruit for God is a duty that followers of Jesus on the way of discipleship have to fulfill.

18.3   The consequences of fruitlessness of disciples can be disastrous.

OVERVIEW

AS WAS NOTED WITH the previous pericope, almost all the activities in 11:1—13:1 occur within the holy space of the temple. In that arena, which Jesus has just declared to be in the process of judgment and condemnation (11:12–25), a series of vigorous controversies ensues, focused upon Jesus' authority (and what the response to that authority should look like).[1] All of this ties in with the theme of Act III, the acceptance of Jesus' mission. The conflict reaches its climax in 13:1–2 as Jesus exits the temple for the last time, never to return, explicitly prophesying, even as he departs, about the fate of the temple—its destruction. The narrative is suspended at that point for an extended discourse from Jesus on the implications of what he had just stated (13:3–37).[2]

The larger section, 11:1—12:44, of which the current pericope (11:27—12:12) shares a part, is grounded on the theme of loyalty to God. The link between this and the previous section (11:1–25) is the debate on the authority of Jesus (11:27–33), which necessarily and smoothly moves into the issue of why God can demand loyalty, and what this loyalty ought to look like in the life of the disciple. Acceptance of the mission of Jesus involves demonstrating such loyalty to God.

The structure of Mark 11:27—12:44 is as follows:

Transition: Debate on authority (11:27–33)

A   Illustration: Tenants' disloyalty to God and the parabolic judgment of religious leaders (12:1–9; see 12:12)

   B   Psalm citation (Ps 118:22) re: Christology and ultimate vindication; audience reaction (Mark 12:10–12)

      C   Question/response from Pharisees/Herodians; "Teacher"; "in truth"; audience reaction (12:13–17)

         D   Question from Sadducees; "Teacher" (12:18–27)

      C'   Question/response from scribe; "Teacher"; "in truth"; audience reaction (12:28–34)

   B'   Psalm citation (Ps 110:1) re: Christology and ultimate vindication; audience reaction (Mark 12:35–37)

A'   Illustration: Judgment of religious leaders and a widow's loyalty to God (12:38–44)

The three central episodes (C, D, and C') on the coin of taxation (12:13–17), the possibility of resurrection (12:18–27), and the primacy of the commandments (12:28–34), respectively, establish basic truths about God that call for a response of total loyalty

---

1. As was mentioned earlier, five controversies are found in 11:12—12:40; 11:12–25 (conflict with those in the temple—the buyers and sellers, money changers, and those carrying merchandise); 11:27—12:12 (conflict with chief priests and scribes and elders); 12:13–17 (conflict with Pharisees and Herodians); 12:18–27 (conflict with Sadducees); and 12:28–40 (conflict with scribes).

2. France, *Gospel of Mark*, 451–52.

to him. These are illustrated negatively by the tenants in the parable (A, 12:1–9), and positively by the widow in the temple (A', 12:38–44). The corollary of disloyalty is judgment—that on the religious leaders is stated in both of these units (12:1–9 and 38–44; see below). Two christological sections, with Psalm citations, demonstrate that God's authority and ownership are mediated through Jesus Christ who, though suffering now, will be ultimately vindicated as the Messiah (12:10–12 and 35–37). An explicit declaration of Jesus' Messiahship appears only later, in the formal setting of a trial, when Jesus affirms his status to the high priest in 14:62. Nonetheless, the events and dialogues in 11:27—12:44, while not being a *verbal* claim, constitute an overall *parabolic* assertion of his authority, as well as illustrations of the responses expected by the recognition of this divine authority.

One might summarize the constituent units of Mark 12 thus[3]:

12:1–9   **Negative illustration**: God's ownership demands fruit-bearing by the disciple

12:10–12   *Christology*: God's ownership reinstated through Jesus Christ

12:13–17   God's ownership includes the entirety of the disciple's life

12:18–27   God's faithful ownership extends to eternity

12:28–34   God's ownership demands utmost love from the disciple

12:35–37   *Christology*: God's ownership is manifest through, and mediated by, the Son of God, Jesus Christ

12:38–44   **Positive illustration**: God's ownership demands the disciple's all

The current pericope, 11:27—12:12, contains two reports of the religious hierarchy being "afraid of the people" (11:32; 12:12), thus connecting the unit containing Jesus' dialogue with the religious leaders (11:27–33) with his parable of the tenant farmers (12:1–9) and the Psalm citation and christological statement (12:10–12). Moreover, the addressees in 12:1 are the same as the host of opponents that accosted Jesus in 11:27 (also see 12:12), and the religious leaders' plot "to destroy" (ἀπόλλυμι, *apollymi*) Jesus in 11:18 is echoed in the reuse of the same verb in 12:9, where God is said to "destroy" the disobedient and unfruitful ones.[4] For these reasons, 11:27—12:12 will be considered as one pericope. Mark 12:1–12 also answers the question of the religious leaders in 11:27–33 regarding the source of Jesus' authority. The rest of Mark 12 goes on to demarcate the extent of God's authority/ownership, as well as indicating what the response ought to be towards such a total authority: total loyalty!

18   Mark 11:27–12:12

THEOLOGICAL FOCUS 18

18   Accepting the divine authority of Jesus, disciples have the solemn responsibility of fruit-bearing stewardship towards God, the owner of all things, lest they suffer the consequences (11:27—12:12).

3. "Ownership" here is equivalent to "authority," but the former creates a more compelling image.

4. The citation of Ps 118:22–23 in Mark 12:10–12 also recalls the allusion to the same psalm (118:25–26) in Mark 11:9–10, the acclamation of Jesus as he rode into Jerusalem.

18.1	Disciples accept the divine authority of Jesus, the one they follow in discipleship.
18.2	Bearing fruit for God is a duty that followers of Jesus on the way of discipleship have to fulfill.
18.3	The consequences of fruitlessness of disciples can be disastrous.

Section Summary 18: The debate with the religious leaders in this pericope centers upon the question of Jesus' authority. He answers them somewhat obliquely, first by referring to John the Baptist, and then with a parable. God's ownership and his disciples' stewardship are in view here. Producing fruit with what God has entrusted them is a solemn responsibility owed to God by disciples. The consequences for failure are serious.

TRANSLATION 18

11:27   *And they came again into Jerusalem. And as He was walking in the temple, the chief priests and the scribes and the elders came to Him,*

11:28   *and said to Him, "By what authority are You doing these things, or who gave You this authority to do these things?"*

11:29   *And Jesus said to them, "I will ask you one word, and you answer Me and I will tell you by what authority I do these things.*

11:30   *The baptism of John—was it from heaven or from men? Answer Me."*

11:31   *And they began discussing among themselves, saying, "If we say, 'From heaven,' He will say, 'Then why did you not believe him?'*

11:32   *But shall we say, 'From men'?"—[because] they were afraid of the crowd, for everyone held that John truly was a prophet.*

11:33   *And answering Jesus, they said, "We do not know." And Jesus said to them, "Neither do I tell you by what authority I do these things."*

12:1   *And He began to speak to them in parables: "A man planted a vineyard, and put a fence around [it], and dug a vat [for its winepress], and built a tower, and leased it to tenant farmers, and went away on a journey.*

12:2   *And he sent a slave to the tenant farmers at the [right] time, in order to receive of the fruits of the vineyard from the tenant farmers.*

12:3   *And receiving him, they beat and sent [him back] empty-handed.*

12:4   *And again he sent them another slave; that one they struck on the head and treated shamefully.*

12:5   *And he sent another; that one they killed; and many others, some of whom were beaten, others killed.*

12:6   *He had one more, a beloved son; he sent him last to them, saying, 'They will respect my son.'*

12:7   *But those tenant farmers said to one another, 'This is the heir; come, let us kill him, and the inheritance will be ours.'*

12:8   *And taking [him], they killed him, and cast him out of the vineyard.*

12:9   *What will the lord of the vineyard do? He will come and destroy the tenant farmers and give the vineyard to others.*

12:10   *Have you not read this Scripture? 'The stone which the builders rejected, this became the cornerstone.*

12:11   *From the Lord this came about, and it is marvelous in our eyes'?"*

12:12   *And they were seeking to seize Him, and they were afraid of the crowd, for they knew that He spoke the parable against them. And they left Him and went away.*

NOTES 18

18.1   Disciples accept the divine authority of Jesus, the one they follow in discipleship.[5]

This is the first instance of the appearance together of all three factions of the Sanhedrin—chief priests, scribes, and elders (11:27)—denoting a critical juncture in the ministry of Jesus. They will later serve as his prosecution team (8:31; 11:18; 14:43, 55; 15:1). The two questions they ask Jesus are not for information, but rather for incrimination. Their accusation is simply this: "*We* did not give this authority to you!" They alone have the right to authorize actions in the temple precincts, so this inquisition is an attempt to publicly humiliate Jesus, who obviously has not obtained any prior authorization from the religious hierarchy to conduct his cleansing operations in the temple. On the other hand, if Jesus chooses to claim authority from God, politically he would be liable to get into trouble with the Roman rulers for his messianic pretensions (14:61–64; 15:2–5).[6] The attitude of these religious leaders is obstreperous unbelief, a stubborn and willful refusal to discern Jesus' person and accept the facts of Jesus' mission that are staring them in the face—the two themes of Acts I and II: discernment and acceptance of Jesus and his mission.

The pericope begins with on an accusatory note from the religious leaders regarding Jesus' authority to do "these things" (11:28). While "these things" points to all of Jesus' activities in the temple thus far, there might also be a broader sense in which the phrase refers to his ministry as a whole, particularly to the authority demonstrated in his teaching (1:21–22, 27), exercised in his exorcisms, healing, and forgiveness of sins (1:23–27; 2:1–12; 3:22–30), and granted to his disciples (3:13; 6:7). Daniel 7:13–14, the focal locus of the Son of Man sayings, also depicts the messianic figure obtaining his everlasting authority from heaven. All that Jesus does ("these things"), "he may do *on earth*, because as 'son of man' he has received authority to do so *from heaven.*"[7] Jesus implies as much, responding to the question of the religious leaders, as he links the source of his authority with the ultimate source of the authority of John's baptism—heaven (Mark 11:30). This link with John the Baptist is not adventitious; in making the connection, Jesus implicitly claims authority from heaven and asserts his importance as equal to, and even greater than, that of the prophet. One is reminded of Malachi 3:1–2, which introduces the Gospel (Mark 1:2); that quote also includes, in the prophet, a statement about the Lord suddenly coming into his temple:

5. This theological subfocus states the idea of 11:27–33 in the positive.

6. Evans, *Mark*, 209.

7. Ibid., 202–3 (italics original).

indeed, the Lord has just done so in Mark 11:11, 15, and 27, and had acted within it with heavenly authority.

To be sure, Jesus does not exactly answer the challenge posed to him by the religious hierarchy in 11:28; in fact, he refuses to do so. However, 11:30 is actually an answer—a veiled one, but nonetheless an answer—alluding to Jesus' baptism, reception of the Spirit, and the affirming voice from heaven (1:9–11). "The one who walks imperiously around the temple, who claims the authority to 'cleanse' it, who announced the foundation of a new community of faith, and whom the ruling establishment seeks to destroy, is none other than the Son of God."[8] Not only has Jesus already demonstrated his authority and its source in 11:1–25, he proceeds to do so again in the following parable (12:1–9) and the christological affirmation that concludes it (12:10–12). His authority is from God, indeed. Immediately after the altercation of 11:27–33, Jesus is effectively saying, in the parable of the tenant farmers, "I won't tell you where I got my authority, but here's a story; you decide for yourselves." The rest of Mark 12 is concerned with the ramifications of that claim of authority for all those who would follow Jesus.

18.2   *Bearing fruit for God is a duty that followers of Jesus on the way of discipleship have to fulfill.*

While the parable of 12:1–9 is explicitly addressed to the contentious religious leaders,[9] from the various incidents depicted in Mark 12 "[i]t becomes clear that neither the 'cleansing' episode nor the Vineyard parable is concerned strictly with what goes on in the temple. Robbing God can take place anywhere . . . in the streets, in the marketplace, in synagogues, at banquets, in financial dealings, at prayer times, and the list goes on."[10] And every disciple, not just religious leaders, must grapple with the issue of how to respond appropriately to the ownership and authority of God. In particular, this pericope asks the question of whether disciples are giving to God the fruit that is owed to him—a question of stewardship.

The vine or vineyard often served as an image for the nation of Israel in the OT (Ps 80:8–19; Isa 5:1–7; 27:2–6; Jer 2:21; 12:10; Ezek 19:10–14; Hos 10:1; etc.). Boring notes that in the contemporary Judaism of Mark's time, the parabolic song of Isaiah 5, in particular, had already been allegorized: the tower stands for the temple, and the winepress, for the altar.[11] The parable of Mark 12:1–9 bears much resemblance to the OT text[12]:

---

8. Marshall, *Faith as a Theme*, 200.

9. The "them" in 12:1 and the "they" in 12:12 refer to the religious hierarchy listed in 11:27–28.

10. Geddert, *Watchwords*, 122.

11. Boring, *Mark*, 329. Also see *1 En.* 89.56, 66–67, 73; *Barn.* 16.1–2, 4–5.

12. Modified from Evans, *Mark*, 225.

	MARK 12:1–12	ISAIAH 5:1–7 LXX
"vineyard"	ἀμπελῶμα (ampelōma, 12:1:2, 8, 9 [×2])	ἀμπελῶμα (5:1, 3, 5, 7)
"planted"	ἐφύτευσεν (ephyteusen, 12:1)	ἐφύτευσα (ephyteusa, 5:2)
"and put a fence"	καὶ περιέθημεν φραγμόν (kai periethēmen phragmon, 12:1)	καὶ φραγμὸν περιέθηκα (kai phragmon periethēka, 5:2)
"and dug a vat"	καὶ ὤρυξεν ὑπολήνιον (kai ōryxen hypolēnion, 12:1)	καὶ προλήνιον ὤρυξα (kai prolēnion ōryxa, 5:2)
"and built a tower"	καὶ ᾠκοδόμησεν πύργον (kai ōkodomēsen pyrgon, 12:1)	καὶ ᾠκοδόμησα πύργον (kai ōkodomēsa pyrgon, 5:2)
violence	violence (12:3, 4, 5, 8)	bloodshed (5:7)
"what will the lord do"	τί ποιήσει ὁ κύριος (ti poiēsei ho kyrios, 12:9)	τί ποιήσω (ti poiēsō, 5:4); κύριος (kyrios, 5:7)
destruction	12:9	5:5–6

In Isaiah, it is the vineyard that fails and all hope appears lost; in Mark 12, the tenants fail, the vineyard is transferred to others, and hope is kindled for a fresh start. Judgment, however, is meted out in both cases upon the failing (i.e., non-fruit-bearing) entities that refuse to give God his due—flora in one case, humankind in the other. To them, the leaders of God's people symbolized, the vineyard had been entrusted; having failed to be fruitful (also see, for fruitlessness, 4:7; 11:14), they face dispossession of their trust and resulting punishment.[13] Parallel to Isaiah 5:3–4, the readers/listeners are called by Jesus to arbitrate the lawsuit (Mark 12:9). Both there and here, the rhetorical questions are addressed to the audience: it is, Jesus seems to be saying, self-evident as to the blame of the tenant farmers, and they will get their recompense.

The parallels *within* the parable of 12:1–9 also must not be lost on the reader: the owner "sends" (ἀποστέλλω, apostellō) a slave to "receive" (λαμβάνω, lambanō) fruit. The tenant farmers "receive" (λαμβάνω) him and "send" (ἀποστέλλω) him back empty-handed (fruitless, 12:2–3). That these slaves stand for the prophets is clear from Jeremiah 7:25, which has God claiming he "sent" (ἀποστέλλω) all his bondslaves, the prophets (δοῦλος, doulos, both here and in Mark 12:2, 4; also see Jer 25:4, which has the same set of words, ἀποστέλλω and δοῦλος). In Jesus' parable, the abuse of these slaves by the tenant farmers increased in intensity with each successive incident: from beating (Mark 12:3), to striking on the head (12:4), and finally to killing (12:5).[14] The maltreatment also progressively narrows down in focus: the first is received, beaten, and sent away (three verbs); the second is struck on the head and treated shamefully (two verbs); the third is simply killed (one verb). The lethality and intentionality are heightened by this narrowing, yet escalating, pattern.[15] This is complete disregard for the owner, his wishes, and his representatives. Not giving God, the owner, his due of the fruit is tantamount to rebellion. Fruitfulness is not just a matter of productivity; in fact, towards God it is a responsibility, a duty. Fruit is *owed* God, the owner of all things! And that is not just the duty of the leaders of Israel; all of God's people (in

13. France, *Gospel of Mark*, 456, 458.

14. The unusual verb κεφαλιόω (kephalioō, "strike on the head") that occurs nowhere else in NT could very well be an allusion to the beheading (ἀποκεφαλίζω, apokephalizō, 6:16) of John the Baptist.

15. Gundry, *Mark*, 660.

Mark, particularly the followers of Jesus—disciples) are responsible for fruit-bearing and diligent stewardship of what God has entrusted to them.

18.3   *The consequences of fruitlessness of disciples can be disastrous.*

The "beloved son" (12:6) has already been encountered in Mark, personally affirmed by the voice of God in 1:11 and 9:7; the reader is therefore in no doubt as to who is being referred to here in Mark 12. The description adds emphasis to the finality of this attempt by the owner to obtain his due; it also underscores the uniqueness of the son over the many slaves sent previously.[16] Yet the tenant farmers give him scant regard. Perhaps they assume that the coming of the son himself means that the owner had died. If they kill the remaining righteous claimant, by squatters' rights, they can—they reckon—appropriate the vineyard for themselves.[17] At any rate, whatever their motive, they kill the son. Earlier, Jesus had cast out those in the temple (ἐκβάλλω, *ekballo*, 11:15); now he, the beloved son, is himself cast out (also ἐκβάλλω, 12:8). That, however, is the ultimate insult—the cavalier disposal of a corpse without the decency of a proper burial. Again, the authority, indeed the personal authority of the owner in his son, has been rebuffed and rejected. This is rebellion!

The "destruction" (ἀπόλλυμι, *apollymi*) of the malefactors, rather than their "killing," parallels 3:6 and 11:18, where the religious authorities are reported to be undertaking to do the same thing to Jesus (ἀπόλλυμι is used there too). He, however, has the last word.[18] The authority issue is now answered: Jesus' authority comes from God, and the rejection of Jesus (not giving God his due in fruitfulness) will result in punishment. This is a lesson for disciples as well: fruitlessness is a serious matter.[19]

In the subsequent christological statement, citing Psalm 118:22–23, Jesus firmly asserts the source of his authority, answering the question of the religious leaders. The one the builders (Acts 4:11 labels the religious leaders as the "builders" of Ps 118) have rejected, the same one the tenant farmers also murdered, is the beloved Son of God, in whom is vested the authority/ownership of God. This rejected Son becomes the cornerstone for a renewed "temple" not made with hands, God's new community.[20] Jesus, as the cornerstone (Mark 12:10–11; 14:58) is therefore the "rebuilder" of the temple—the new temple that is the praying community of 11:23–25.[21] The irony

---

16. France, *Gospel of Mark*, 460–61.

17. Boring, *Mark*, 330.

18. France, *Gospel of Mark*, 461.

19. While 12:12 shows that Jesus' parable was against the religious leaders—that was what *Jesus* was doing with what he was saying—one must also consider what *Mark/the Holy Spirit* was doing with what was being narrated herein. Therefore this parable is not simply an excoriation of the fruitless *ancien régime* of an older dispensation, but a warning to disciples in the newer one as well.

20. "The stone described as the head of the corner is probably not a cornerstone in the foundation of a building (the use of 'head' does not fit well a stone that would be buried), but either a capstone at the top of a building marking its completion or a capital that sits on top of a column" (Stein, *Mark*, 538).

21. The handing over of the vineyard to "others" (12:9) was the culmination of the temple "cleansing" episode, where the dysfunctional institution of the temple was replaced and its functions handed over to the new community of disciples engaging in prayer—faithfully and forgivingly (11:22–25; see Pericope 17).

of employing Psalm 118 should not be missed. "The rhetoric of Psalm 118 has been turned back upon itself. Whereas the Psalm celebrates the destruction of the Gentile enemies who have scorned and rejected Israel, the Markan interpretation predicts the vindication by God of the one rejected by Israel's leaders and the replacement of the temple with the multiethnic community of Isaiah's eschatological vision."[22] This is the one facet of divine history that is not addressed in the parable—there is no mention within this story of the rejected son being vindicated. Therefore, the psalm citation tagged on to the parable does exactly that, bringing the curtain down on the vignette with the ultimate victory of the Son.

12:1–9	**Negative illustration**: God's ownership demands fruit-bearing by the disciple*
12:10–12	*Christology*: God's ownership reinstated through Jesus Christ
12:13–17	God's ownership includes the entirety of the disciple's life
12:18–27	God's faithful ownership extends to eternity
12:28–34	God's ownership demands utmost love from the disciple
12:35–37	*Christology*: God's ownership is manifest through, and mediated by, the Son of God, Jesus Christ
12:38–44	**Positive illustration**: God's ownership demands the disciple's all

* The shaded elements show the sections under discussion.

In sum, those who would follow Jesus, the Son, must accept his divine authority and render God his due as good stewards—i.e., they must be fruitful. Otherwise, the consequences can be disastrous. What exactly these disastrous results might be for the disciple is not detailed in this pericope. While the parabolic destruction of the tenant farmers must not be carried too far, the removal of the vineyard from them and its being handed over to others should be a strong warning to disciples to treat their trust and stewardship with diligence and care, before God, the owner.

SERMON FOCUS AND OUTLINES

THEOLOGICAL FOCUS OF PERICOPE 18 FOR PREACHING
18   Fruit-bearing by disciples is their solemn responsibility of stewardship towards God (11:27—12:12).

This pericope begins the series of episodes in Mark 12 reinforcing God's ownership over all things and explicating the disciples' response to such authority. Fruit-bearing takes the front stage again. Mark 4:1–34 (Pericope 5) dealt with this productive endeavor, but from a different angle. There, fruitfulness was emphasized as the result of receptivity to God's word (the human element) and the inscrutable and automatic work of God (the divine element). Here, in Mark 12, fruit-bearing is a solemn duty, an act of responsibility towards God. Fruit is *owed* God in response to the stewardship entrusted to the disciple by God. And not to bear fruit (a deliberate, conscious fruit-lessness) is an act of outright rebellion. The seriousness of this business is underscored

22. Dowd, *Reading Mark*, 129.

by the drastic punishment of the unfruitful tenant farmers.[23] Pointedly, the quantity of fruit is not mentioned at all; after all there is a spectrum of degrees of fertility anyway—thirtyfold, sixtyfold, hundredfold (4:8, 20). It is not necessarily a particular quantum of produce that is enjoined, but the importance of *being fruit-bearing*. In this connection, perhaps the focus in the sermon could be upon spiritual gifts, also a valuable stewardship entrusted to believers.[24]

While the subsequent sections of Mark 12 (see Pericope 19) elucidate the extent of what exactly is owed God (i.e., *everything!*), this pericope might be fruitfully employed for a sermon that emphasizes that fruit-bearing is not an option; it is a mandated duty towards God. Living under the ownership of God, walking in discipleship with the authoritative Son, the follower of Jesus is expected to bear fruit with what has been entrusted to him or her. To accept Jesus' mission, recognizing his authority, implies nothing less than a life of fruitfulness unto God.

This might also be a good point in the Markan sermon series to congratulate the congregation for their fruitfulness. Rather than swat the listeners on their heads with disapproval (*à la* 12:4), or lay on their backs onerous demands, putting them on guilt trips, the preacher must periodically see that the good deeds of many in the church (and surely there are plenty of these) are commended and lauded. Congregations always need encouragement in a positive vein from their leaders. A public venue, such as a pulpit, is an especially fine place to deliver such complimentary remarks, and to remind the saints of God that he is pleased with their service to him.[25]

POSSIBLE PREACHING OUTLINES FOR PERICOPE 18

I. AUTHORITY: God's ownership is recognized

    Jesus reply to the religious leaders: 11:27–33; the setup for the parable: 12:1

    Move-to-Relevance: What God owns

II. RESPONSIBILITY: Fruit-production is a duty

    The rebellion and punishment of the tenant farmers—poor stewards of God's property: 12:2–12

    Move-to-Relevance: What God owns, he gives us to steward, for e.g., spiritual gifts

III. PRODUCTIVITY: *Continue bearing fruit (using your spiritual gifts)!*

    Specifics on how the congregation can further the responsible stewardship of their spiritual gifts

---

23. Note also the link with the thrust of the previous pericope (11:1–25); there proper functioning was the emphasis—prayer founded on faith and forgiveness. Here fruit-bearing, appropriate stewardship of what God has entrusted the disciple with, takes prominence.

24. In fact, if a hiatus from the series of sermons on Mark is needed (besides special events on the church calendar or other holidays, pastoral vacations, etc.), a mini-series on spiritual gifts may be a welcome break at this point (perhaps dealing with some or all of these texts: Rom 12; 1 Cor 12; Eph 4; and 1 Pet 4). Considering that pneumatology is not a prominent theological subject in this Gospel, such a focus on the ministry of the Holy Spirit may also be expedient and apropos. While "stewardship" could very well deal with property and finances, seeing that the pericope regarding the rich man (10:17–31; Pericope 15) has already considered those issues, it might be best to move in a different direction for this sermon; spiritual gifts will work well, though other options are, of course, possible: stewardship of time, children, health, resources, etc.

25. Testimonies might work in this regard as well, perhaps even in the middle of a sermon.

ACT III: IN JERUSALEM

A more "topically" oriented outline:

I. What God gives: (spiritual gifts / talents / resources / time)
    Move-to-Relevance: What God has given disciples
II. What God expects: Fruitful utilization of his gifts for the kingdom
    God's authority/ownership: 11:27—12:1
    God's right to demand fruit of his stewards: 12:2–8
    Consequences of improper stewardship: 12:9–12
III. What disciples render: *Bear fruit (using your spiritual gifts / talents / resources / time)!*
    Specifics on how the congregation can further the responsible stewardship of their gifts . . .

PERICOPE 19

Responsible Stewardship

Mark 12:13–44

[Coin with Caesar's Image; Resurrection;
Greatest Commandments; a Giving Widow]

REVIEW, SUMMARY, PREVIEW

Review of Pericope 18: Mark 11:27—12:12 centers on the question of Jesus' authority and God's ownership, the response to which is fruit-bearing on part of the disciples—the solemn responsibility of stewardship.

Summary of Pericope 19: Mark 12:13–44 focuses on the demands made on disciples as a result of God's absolute ownership and authority. The various episodes in this pericope demonstrate that the disciple, God's image-bearer, belongs to God and owes him utmost love—for God and for neighbor, as demonstrated by the widow who gave her all. The debate with the Sadducees, the centerpiece of the controversies in Mark 12, affirms God as the one in control of life and death and the one who keeps his word. And that forms the basis for the disciple's sacrificial love and giving of oneself, for the God who owns one's life is a trustworthy God who takes care of his people.

Preview of Pericope 20: The next pericope (Mark 13:1–37) calls upon the disciple to persevere faithfully in times of calamity, because of the assurances of God's providence, the Holy Spirit's power, and the promise of the Son's ultimate return to gather believers to himself.

19 Mark 12:13–44

19 **The absolute and illimitable ownership and authority of a faithful God, encompassing the entirety of the disciple's life and extending even to eternity, manifested and mediated through Jesus Christ, demands the disciple's sacrifice of all, prompted by utmost love for God and for neighbor (12:13–44).**

19.1　The extent of the ownership and authority of God includes the entirety of the life of the disciple, made in the image of God (12:13–17).

19.2　The extension of the faithful ownership and authority of God through eternity calls for the disciple's allegiance to this God (12:18–27).

19.3　God's ownership and authority over all, mediated through Jesus Christ, demands utmost love from the disciple—for God and for neighbor (12:28–37).

19.3.1　God's ownership and authority over all demands utmost love from the disciple—for God and for neighbor.

19.3.2　God's ownership and authority over all is mediated through Jesus Christ.

19.4　God's absolute ownership and authority demands the disciple's sacrifice of all, prompted by love of God and of neighbor (12:38–44).

OVERVIEW

AS WAS NOTED WITH the last pericope, Mark 12:1–44 focuses on the theme of loyalty to God, with a structural layout as shown below.

Transition: Debate on authority (11:27–33)

A　Illustration: Tenants' disloyalty to God and the parabolic judgment of religious leaders (12:1–9; see 12:12)

　　B　Psalm citation (Ps 118:22) re: Christology and ultimate vindication; audience reaction (Mark 12:10–12)

　　　　C　Question/response from Pharisees/Herodians; "Teacher;" "in truth;" audience reaction (12:13–17)

　　　　　　D　Question from Sadducees; "Teacher" (12:18–27)

　　　　C'　Question/response from scribe; "Teacher;" "in truth;" audience reaction (12:28–34)

　　B'　Psalm citation (Ps 110:1) re: Christology and ultimate vindication; audience reaction (Mark 12:35–37)

A'　Illustration: Judgment of religious leaders and a widow's loyalty to God (12:38–44)

The episodes in the center of the structure (C, coin of taxation, 12:13–17; D, possibility of resurrection, 12:18–27; and C', primacy of the commandments, 12:28–34) establish why one should be totally loyal to God. Two illustrations bookend these central motifs: a negative illustration (A, the tenants in the vineyard parable, 12:1–12), and a positive one (A', the widow in the temple, 12:38–44). In both these boundary units, the consequences of disloyalty is expressed clearly—judgment on the religious leaders (12:1–9 and 38–44). Two additional sections (B, 12:10–12, and B', 12:35–37) contain christological affirmations from the Psalms that demonstrate the authority of God as being mediated through Jesus.

The thematic summary of these units is as follows:

12:1–9	**Negative illustration**:	God's ownership demands fruit-bearing by the disciple
12:10–12	*Christology:*	God's ownership reinstated through Jesus Christ
12:13–17		God's ownership includes the entirety of the disciple's life
12:18–27		God's faithful ownership extends to eternity
12:28–34		God's ownership demands utmost love from the disciple
12:35–37	*Christology:*	God's ownership is manifest through, and mediated by, the Son of God, Jesus Christ
12:38–44	**Positive illustration**:	God's ownership demands the disciple's all

This pericope, 12:13–44, will primarily deal with the grounds of God's divine ownership and the response the disciple must make to that overarching and all-superseding authority.

19.1   Mark 12:13–17

THEOLOGICAL FOCUS 19.1

19.1 The extent of the ownership and authority of God includes the entirety of the life of the disciple, made in the image of God (12:13–17).

Section Summary 19.1: The coin controversy is a masterful piece of argumentation by Jesus asserting that all things that bear the image of someone belong to that someone—a statement of proprietary rights. Thus humans, who bear the image of God, rightfully belong to God. His authority and ownership extend to encompass the lives of those who follow Jesus (and all other humans, too, of course).[1]

TRANSLATION 19.1

12:13 *And they sent to Him some of the Pharisees and the Herodians in order to trap Him in a word.*

12:14 *And coming, they said to Him, "Teacher, we know that You are truthful and no one['s opinion] is a concern to You, for You do not show partiality to men,[2] but in truth teach the way of God. Is it lawful to give poll tax to Caesar, or not? Should we give or should we not give?"*

12:15 *But He, knowing their hypocrisy, said to them, "Why are you testing Me? Bring Me a denarius to see."*

---

1. However, the thrust of the Gospel is on disciples, hence the narrowing of the focus of God's ownership upon these individuals, despite God's proprietary rights over every human by virtue of the *imago Dei* they bear.

2. Literally, "You do not see the face of men." The translation here is idiomatic. Nonetheless, the literal idiom is striking, for on the coin in 12:16 one actually does see a face—a face that, seemingly, Jesus does not recognize or care to be seen as recognizing. Instead, he pointedly asks his interlocutors to make the identification (12:16).

12:16   And they brought [one]. And He said to them, "Whose is this image and inscription?" And they said to Him, "Caesar's."

12:17   And Jesus said to them, "The things of Caesar, give back to Caesar, and the things of God, to God." And they were amazed at Him.

NOTES 19.1

19.1   *The extent of the ownership and authority of God includes the entirety of the life of the disciple, made in the image of God.*

Of all the Roman taxes, this poll tax or census was especially distasteful to the Jews of Palestine and a constant source of irritation and frustration (Josephus, *Ant.* 17.308). First imposed in 6 CE, it immediately provoked a (failed) revolt under Judas of Galilee (Josephus, *J.W.* 2.118; *Ant.* 18.1–10, 23–25), and later gave rise to the Zealot movement that culminated in their revolt of 66 CE and the catastrophic destruction of Jerusalem four years later. For these revolutionaries, the census was a litmus test of loyalty to God. While, as a Galilean, Jesus was not expected to pay the poll tax, the religious leaders ask his opinion anyway; whatever he says will land him in trouble, either with the Jewish patriots or with the Roman authorities.[3] This is a blatant attempt to catch Jesus in his words, by an official delegation sent by "them" (12:13—likely the same gang of chief priests, scribes, and elders, of 11:27, the same "them" of 12:1 and "they" of 12:12). A "trap" is laid: ἀγρεύω (*agreuō*, 12:13; used of hunting and catching animals for food) is a word of clear hostile intent; the controversial dialogue here is also marked by each participant's words being introduced by the narrator with ὁ δὲ (*ho de*, as in 10:18–22 and 10:36–39, but idiomatically translated as "and" in 12:16a, 16c, 17a), indicating their opposing tendencies.

Jesus' use of εἰκών (*eikōn*, "image," 12:16) is deliberate. It is likely listeners would have thought of the "image" of God in which human beings have been created (Gen 1:26–27; 5:1; 9:6; all use εἰκών in the LXX), and of images of false gods that Israel had been forbidden to worship (Deut 4:16; 2 Kgs 11:18: Isa 40:19 LXX; also using εἰκών).[4] The inscription on such Roman coins as the denarius bordered on blasphemy. On a typical specimen, around the wreath-crowned head of Tiberius were the words: TI[BERIUS] CAESAR DIVI AUG[USTI] F[ILIUS] AUGUSTUS ("Tiberius Caesar Augustus, Son of the Divine Augustus"). That would have been offensive on its own, but on the obverse of the coin was: PONTIF[EX] MAXIM[US] ("High Priest"), further aggravating Jewish sensibilities.[5]

The opponents' question has been about "giving" (δίδωμι, *didōmi*, Mark 12:14) to Caesar; Jesus, however, talks about "giving back" (ἀποδίδωμι, *apodidōmi*, 12:17)—the

---

3. France, *Gospel of Mark*, 464–65; Boring, *Mark*, 334.

4. Boring, *Mark*, 333.

5. France, *Gospel of Mark*, 468. The letters within brackets do not usually appear on the coins, the words being in an abbreviated, but recognizable, form. Incidentally, the only other use of ἐπιγραφή (*epigraphē*, "inscription," 12:16) in Mark's Gospel is found in 15:26—an "inscription" for another king, the *true* King.

return of an item to its owner, the one whose image it bears. In other words, Jesus is exhorting his listeners to return Caesar's property to Caesar and, in parallel, God's property to God. What exactly constitutes God's property is well described by Augustine: "The image of the Emperor appears differently in his son and in a piece of coin. The coin has no knowledge of its bearing the image of the prince. But you are the coin of God, and so far highly superior, as possessing mind and even life, so as to know the One whose image you bear" (Augustine, *Sermons on New Testament Lessons* 43).[6] And elsewhere (*Tract. Ev. Jo.* 40.9), he writes:

> We are God's money. But we are like coins that have wandered away from the treasury. What was once stamped upon us has been worn down by our wandering. The One who restamps his image upon us is the One who first formed us. He himself seeks his own coin, as Caesar sought his coin. It is in this sense he says, "Render to Caesar the things that are Caesar's, and to God the things that are God's," to Caesar his coins, to God your very selves.

Thus, Jesus' argumentation in 12:17 may be unpacked as follows (items in the bold are expressly stated in the text):

Unstated Major premise I: *Ownership of anything is established by the image and inscription on it.*
Minor premise I: The denarius bears Caesar's image and inscription.
Unstated Conclusion I: *The denarius belongs to Caesar.*

Unstated Major premise II: *Ownership of anything is established by the image and inscription on it.*
Unstated Minor premise II: *Humans bear God's image* (Gen 1:26–27).
Unstated Conclusion II: *Humans belong to God.*

Enthymematic Argument: Give Caesar his; give God his—that which bears the *imago Dei*. [*]

* Dowd, *Reading Mark*, 130. Generally, an enthymeme is defined as a syllogism with unstated premises or assumptions that must be supplied by the hearer/reader.

The earlier parable of the vineyard (12:1–9) depicted those who were not prepared to render unto God, the vineyard owner, the fruit that was rightly due him by virtue of his ownership. Here Jesus builds on the concept of God's ownership and authority over the disciple, for he/she is made in the image of God and thus is owned by God. One is to render "the image of Caesar, which is on the coin, to Caesar, and the image of God, which is on man, to God; so as to render to Caesar only money, but to God, yourself" (Tertullian, *Idol.* 15). In short, God's ownership includes the entirety of the disciple's life!

12:1–9	**Negative illustration**: God's ownership demands fruit-bearing by the disciple
12:10–12	*Christology*: God's ownership reinstated through Jesus Christ
12:13–17	God's ownership includes the entirety of the disciple's life [*]
12:18–27	God's faithful ownership extends to eternity

6. Cited in Oden and Hall, *Mark*, 167, 168.

12:28–34	God's ownership demands utmost love from the disciple
12:35–37	*Christology*: God's ownership is manifest through, and mediated by, the Son of God, Jesus Christ
12:38–44	**Positive illustration**: God's ownership demands the disciple's all

* The shaded element indicates the section under discussion.

19.2   MARK 12:18–27

THEOLOGICAL FOCUS 19.2

19.2   The extension of the faithful ownership and authority of God through eternity calls for the disciple's allegiance to this God (12:18–27).

Section Summary 19.2: The Sadducees' mockery of resurrection brings another closely argued response from Jesus. In citing Exodus 3:6, Jesus proceeds to affirm that God's actions proved the ongoing life of the patriarchs. His promise of land as an everlasting possession further reinforces the reality of resurrection. Thus, God's control extends through eternity, a control to which the disciple must submit, and in which the disciple can find comfort. This is a faithful God who keeps his word.

TRANSLATION 19.2

12:18   *And Sadducees, who say there is no resurrection, came to Him, and asked Him, saying,*

12:19   *"Teacher, Moses wrote for us, 'If a man's brother dies and leaves behind a wife, and does not leave a child, his brother should take the wife and raise up descendants for his brother.'*

12:20   *There were seven brothers, and the first took a wife and, dying, he did not leave a descendant.*

12:21   *The second took her, and he died without leaving behind a descendant; and the third likewise;*

12:22   *and the seven did not leave a descendant. Last of all, the wife also died.*

12:23   *In the resurrection, of whom will she be the wife? For the seven had her as wife."*

12:24   *Jesus said to them, "Is it not for this reason you are mistaken, not knowing the Scriptures or the power of God?*

12:25   *For when they rise from the dead, they neither marry nor are given in marriage, but are like the angels in the heavens.*

12:26   *But concerning the dead—that they are raised up—have you not read in the book of Moses, how God spoke to him, on the bush, saying, 'I am the God of Abraham and the God of Isaac and the God of Jacob'?*

12:27   *He is not God of the dead, but of the living. You are greatly mistaken."*

NOTES 19.2

19.2 *The extension of the faithful ownership and authority of God through eternity calls for the disciple's allegiance to this God.*

This is the only section in which the term "Sadducee" is found in Mark. That category of prominent families among the temple priesthood dominated the Sanhedrin until the fall of Jerusalem in 70 CE. They were characterized by a conservative view of the written Scriptures that gave absolute prominence to the Torah and rejected the oral tradition popular with the Pharisees. This meant that they dismissed "the relatively recently developed belief in an afterlife" (Isa 26:19; Dan 12:2); for them, Sheol was the final resting place of the dead, and "continuity of life" simply was the legacy one left behind, and not the actual survival of the person after death.[7] The utilization of a case study in levirate law (Deut 25:5–6[8]) in this section of Mark 12 is an appropriate stratagem for the Sadducees: the legacy of posterity, the "raising up" (ἐξανίστημι, *exanistēmi*, Mark 12:19) of descendants, is the only sort of "raising" that they believe in (ἀνίστημι, *anistēmi*, "raise" and the noun, ἀνάστασις, *anastasis*, "resurrection" are found in 12:17, 23, 25). Jesus, in this instance, appears to be unambiguously on the side of the Pharisees.

The episode is carefully structured by Mark[9]:

A	Sadducees' questioning (12:18)				["resurrection," 12:18]
	B	Moses' teaching (12:19)			
		C	Hypothetical relationships (12:20–22)		
			D	Sadducees' question (12:23)	["resurrection," 12:23]
			D′	Jesus' question (12:24)	["mistaken," 12:24]
		C′	Resurrection relationships (12:25)		
	B′	Moses' teaching (12:26)			
A′	Jesus' pronouncement (12:27)				["mistaken," 12:27]

The Sadducees' conundrum is bracketed by "resurrection" (12:18, 23), and Jesus' response, by "mistaken" (12:24, 27). Their conception of resurrection was both a misconception of Scripture, as well as a misunderstanding of the power of God (12:24).

Jesus attacks the Sadducees' assumption (at least their assumption of the Pharisaic interpretation of the levirate law) that the marital relationship would continue unchanged into the resurrected state. The marriage covenant, as with all covenants, is terminated at death (Rom 7:1–3; 1 Cor 7:39). In fact the very levirate law that the Sadducees cite assumes this; otherwise, the brother who marries his sister-in-law would be guilty of adultery if his brother's marriage did not cease upon the latter's demise. Thus, for anyone to be married in heaven, Jesus asserts in Mark 12:25, they would have to *remarry* in heaven—but, of course, there is no such event happening in that phase

---

7. France, *Gospel of Mark*, 470–71. Also see Acts 23:8; Josephus, *Ant.* 18.16.

8. *Levir* is Latin for "brother-in-law." This member of the family was supposed to raise up descendants for the childless widow of his brother, his sister-in-law.

9. Modified from Reid, *Preaching Mark*, 126.

of life. In other words, the Sadducees have misunderstood the nature of the marriage covenant implied in Scripture: death puts an end to that institution.[10] Theirs is, firstly, a misconception of Scripture (12:24).

But the Sadducees have also misunderstood the power of God, and Jesus repudiates their error on the same principle: death abolishes covenantal obligations. The mention of "on the bush" (i.e., "[in the passage] on the [burning] bush," 12:26) is a clue to the theme of covenant keeping in Exodus. Exodus 3:6, cited in Mark 12:26, is preceded by God hearing his people's groaning and remembering his covenant with Abraham, Isaac, and Jacob (Exod 2:24). The repetition of these three names again in Exodus 3:6 indicates that the exodus of the Israelites from Egypt was foundationally based upon God's faithfulness to his covenantal obligations to these patriarchs. But are they not dead? And does not death abolish covenantal obligations? Yes, death *does* abolish covenantal obligations. But the fact that God decided to act based upon such covenantal obligations must, therefore, surely mean that those patriarchs, with whom God had established his covenant, are, in some sense, alive, and the covenant God made with them ongoing. If not, then the death of the patriarchs would have annulled their covenant with God, and he would not have been obliged to act covenantally to rescue his people. Indeed, it is the patriarchs' continuing life beyond death that preserves the covenant. As far as God is concerned, human life extends beyond physical death, and *therefore,* he upholds his covenants with the patriarchs.[11] This is a dependable God who keeps his word, a faithful God whose authority and ownership extend throughout eternity, past and future.

Thus in correcting the Sadducees' misconception of Scripture and their misunderstanding of the power of God, Jesus establishes one basic fact: God is one whose authority and ownership goes beyond what is visible, audible, and tangible. His authority is from eternity to eternity, for his power knows no bounds; death can do nothing to thwart his plans. And this authoritative One's word in Scripture can be trusted, for he is faithful to his people. The authority God exercises is, therefore, not an idiosyncratic and capricious power-grab. Rather, his is a sovereignty that operates both for his own

---

10. Trick, "Death, Covenants," 242–44.

11. Ibid., 250–51. Granted, this argument only establishes an afterlife, not necessarily a resurrection. But the fact that, right after revealing himself as the God of the patriarchs, Yahweh goes on to identify the fulfillment of the unconditional promise of land as a key goal of the exodus (Exod 3:8, 17; also see Gen 15:13–16), would presumably require the patriarchs' eventual physical resurrection someday to experience the everlasting possession of that land (also promised in Gen 17:8; Exod 6:4; Num 14:23; Deut 11:21; see Trick, "Death, Covenants," 252). The rabbinical proofs of the resurrection in *b. Sanh.* 90b appear to substantiate this logic; e.g., "It has been taught: Rabbi Simai said: Whence do we learn resurrection from the Torah?—From the verse, *And I also have established my covenant with them* [the patriarchs], *to give them the land of Canaan* [Exod 6:4]: 'you' is not said, but 'them'; thus resurrection is proved from the Torah." In addition, the first of the Eighteen Benedictions, which was becoming the standard Jewish prayer by the end of the first century, invoked the God of Abraham, Isaac, and Jacob; the second benediction described him as the God who "revives the dead" (Marcus, *Mark*, 829). Of note: the present-tense verb "am" (in Mark 12:26, English) does not appear in Exod 3:6 (MT; it does in the LXX) or in the Greek citation of that verse in Mark; Matt 22:32 does add the verb. Jesus is unlikely to be creating an argument out of that single (missing) word and its tense, at least in Mark's conception.

glory as well as for the edification, betterment, and fulfillment of his people; the two purposes are transacted conterminously. Therefore the disciple owes total allegiance to this powerful and trustworthy God whose reach spans not only the here and now, but also the hereafter: God's faithful ownership extends to eternity.

12:1–9	**Negative illustration**: God's ownership demands fruit-bearing by the disciple
12:10–12	*Christology:* God's ownership reinstated through Jesus Christ
12:13–17	God's ownership includes the entirety of the disciple's life
12:18–27	God's faithful ownership extends to eternity*
12:28–34	God's ownership demands utmost love from the disciple
12:35–37	*Christology:* God's ownership is manifest through, and mediated by, the Son of God, Jesus Christ
12:38–44	**Positive illustration**: God's ownership demands the disciple's all

* The shaded element indicates the section under discussion.

19.3   Mark 12:28–37

THEOLOGICAL FOCUS 19.3

19.3   God's ownership and authority over all, mediated through Jesus Christ, demands utmost love from the disciple—for God and for neighbor (12:28–37).

    19.3.1   God's ownership and authority over all demands utmost love from the disciple—for God and for neighbor.

    19.3.2   God's ownership and authority over all is mediated through Jesus Christ.

Section Summary 19.3: The surprisingly amicable dialogue between Jesus and a scribe plainly affirms the importance of total allegiance to God, the one who owns all and is the authority over all. Utmost love of God is demanded of the disciple, a love that is also manifest in the love of neighbor. The closing episode of this section reinforces the christological assertion earlier in the chapter: Jesus is the one who mediates God's ownership and authority.

TRANSLATION 19.3

12:28   *And one of the scribes came to [them], and hearing them arguing, seeing that He answered them well, asked Him, "Which is the foremost commandment of all?"*

12:29   *And Jesus answered, "The foremost is, 'Hear, Israel, the Lord our God is one Lord,*

12:30   *and you shall love the Lord your God with all your heart and with all your soul, and with all your mind, and with all your strength.'*

12:31   *The second is this, 'You shall love your neighbor as yourself.' Greater than these, there is no other commandment."*

12:32   *And the scribe said to Him, "Well [said], Teacher. You have said, in truth, that He is one and there is no other besides Him;*

12:33   and to love Him with all the heart, and with all the understanding, and
        with all the strength, and to love the neighbor as oneself, is greater than
        all burnt offerings and sacrifices."

12:34   And when Jesus saw that he had answered wisely, He said to him, "You
        are not far from the kingdom of God." And no one any longer dared to
        ask Him [questions].

12:35   And answering, Jesus said, as He taught in the temple, "How do the
        scribes say that the Christ is the son of David?

12:36   David himself said in the Holy Spirit, 'The Lord said to my Lord, "Sit at
        My right, until I put Your enemies under Your feet."'

12:37   David himself calls Him 'Lord,' and in what way is He his son?" And the
        large crowd heard Him gladly.

NOTES 19.3

*19.3.1   God's ownership and authority over all demands utmost love from the
        disciple—for God and for neighbor.*

The structure of the interaction between scribe and Jesus (12:28–34) shows the emphasis on the foremost commandments—they are repeated (B/B').

A   Question for Jesus (scribe) (12:28)
  B   Love God and neighbor (Jesus) (12:29–31)
  B'   Love God and neighbor (scribe) (12:32–33)
A'   Commendation for scribe (Jesus) (12:34)

What kind of a response the disciple must make, in light of God's expansive, extensive,
and exhaustive ownership, is the crux of this episode. The answer is clear: the two
greatest commandments—the first, the essence of the first table of the Decalogue; the
second, the essence of the second table.[12]

It is surprising that Jesus responds to the scribe's question for *the* foremost commandment with *two* commandments. The first and second (foremost and secondary)
commandments are clearly distinguished. But the two are lumped together in "these"
(12:31), for there is no commandment greater than "these" two—they are, thus, inte-
grally related. "[L]ove of other people finds its true place only on the basis of a prior
love of God." It might mean that the first cannot be adequately obeyed without the second (1 John 4:8, 20–21).[13] "Though they remain two commands, they are inseparable:

---

12. The attempt to locate the foremost commandment of the 613 in the Torah was not unique to
this dialogue: Rabbi Hillel's "silver" rule, the negative of Jesus' "golden" rule (Matt 7:12), stated: "What
is hateful to you, do not do to your neighbor: that is the whole Torah, while the rest is the commentary
thereof" (*b. Šabb.* 31a; also Tob 4.15); *b. Mak.* 24a reduced the law to the eleven principles of Ps 15, the
six of Isa 33:15–16, the three of Mic 6:8, the two of Isa 56:1, and the one in Amos 5:4 (and Hab 2:4); *b.
Ber.* 63a asserted that the basis for all the essential principles of the Torah was found in Prov 3:6; etc. See
Stein, *Mark*, 560.

13. France, *Gospel of Mark*, 480; see also van Iersel, *Mark*, 379. Leviticus 19:18 is combined with Deut
6:4 in *T. Iss.* 5.2; 7.6; *T. Dan.* 5.3; *Jub.* 36.7–8; Philo, *Decalogue* 109–10.

love of God cannot exist without love for all fellow human beings as its content."[14] In light of the *imago Dei* upon humans—implied in the earlier episode, 12:13–17—it might be reasonable to affirm that to love one's neighbor, who also bears the image of God, is an integral part of loving God.

This is the only time in Mark that a religious leader agrees with Jesus (12:32).[15] It is indeed remarkable that this scribe demotes all of the burnt offerings and sacrifices in one sweep; after all, much of the scribes' concerns centered on these cultic activities. Is he implicitly endorsing Jesus' cleansing activities in the temple?[16] However, such a negatory attitude to hypocritical worship is not uncommon in the OT: see 1 Sam 15:22; Ps 40:6; 51:17–19; Prov 21:3; Isa 1:10–17; Jer 7:22–23; Hos 6:6; Amos 5:22. One must also remember the discussion in Mark 7:1–23 (see Pericope 10), where Jesus prioritized moral purity over ritual purity. In light of the phenomenon of the new temple constituted by the new community (11:22–25) and founded upon the new cornerstone (12:10–11), this reworking of moral priorities over cultic ones makes sense.

For the disciple, however, the message is clear: this God with illimitable ownership demands utmost love from the disciple—to God himself, and to one's neighbor. The fact that God's authority is exercised in a faithful manner (12:18–27) makes the act of loving God not one that is forced or grudging, but a perfectly natural response to a perfectly trustworthy God.

12:1–9	**Negative illustration**: God's ownership demands fruit-bearing by the disciple
12:10–12	*Christology*: God's ownership reinstated through Jesus Christ
12:13–17	God's ownership includes the entirety of the disciple's life
12:18–27	God's faithful ownership extends to eternity
12:28–34	God's ownership demands utmost love from the disciple*
12:35–37	*Christology*: God's ownership is manifest through, and mediated by, the Son of God, Jesus Christ
12:38–44	**Positive illustration**: God's ownership demands the disciple's all

* The shaded element indicates the section under discussion.

19.3.2   *God's ownership and authority over all is mediated through Jesus Christ.*

The thrust of the episode in 12:35–37 is related to the corresponding one in 12:10–11, which also contains a Psalm citation. Both are christological assertions, affirming the authority of Jesus as being equivalent to the authority of God. In this section, the Messiah is seen as David's "lord" rather than as his "son." The argument Jesus uses

14. Boring, *Mark*, 345.

15. And how he agrees! The word play must be noted: loving God ἐξ ὅλης . . . (*ex holēs* . . . , "with all . . . ," 12:30, 33) and loving neighbor is greater than all the ὁλοκαυτώματα (*holokautōmata*, "[whole] burnt offerings," 12:33; the ὁλο-, *holo-*, suffix is related to ὅλος, *holos*, "whole").

16. "[S]ubordinating the temple's entire sacrificial worship, designated by a generalizing reference to 'all' of its various sacrifices, to Jesus' double commandment of love, the scribe has in effect called into question the worth and adequacy of worship in the temple of Jerusalem" (Heil, "Narrative Strategy," 85)—and this while listening to Jesus within the temple (11:27)!

depends on a particular view of Psalm 110:1 and of who there is speaking to whom. In Jesus' mouth here, David speaks, asserting that Yahweh invites the Messiah to sit at his right. "Given the way Jesus and his contemporaries read Ps 110, the argument is convincing enough: David the author, referred to the Messiah, the addressee, as κύριος [kyrios, "Lord"], and thus as his superior rather than his son."[17] The argument of Mark 12:35–37 is as follows[18]:

Unstated Major premise: One who addresses another as "Lord" is the inferior of the one so addressed.

Minor premise: David addresses the Messiah as "Lord" in Ps 110.

Conclusion: David is the inferior of the Messiah, who is "Son" and not "son" (Mark 12:35— Jesus disagreeing with scribes)

The motif of "lordship" authority is being carried over from the beginning of Act III: Bartimaeus called Jesus "Son of David" (10:47, 48); that his faith (10:52) was commended confirms the accuracy of his designation of Jesus. Right afterwards, Jesus entered Jerusalem as "Lord" (11:3), and the crowds affirmed that designation explicitly (11:9). However, the lack of acclaim from the king's "capital" (Jerusalem) or his "palace" (the temple) reminded the reader that the leaders of the religious establishment were unwilling to accept Jesus as the Son of David.

Not only did Bartimaeus affirm his Lordship, Jesus also condemned the temple as Lord over his house (11:15–19); he was questioned about his authority (11:27–12:12; "lord" in 12:9, 11); utmost love to the Lord was commanded of the disciple (12:29–30); and here, in 12:36–37, this "Lord" is identified as the Messiah, the Son of God.[19] Jesus goes even further than merely appropriating the title "Son of David"; he essentially stakes a claim to be called something *more* appropriate—"Son of God" (1:11; 1:24; 3:11; 5:7; 9:7; 14:61–62; 15:39).[20] And as Son of the authoritative God, Mark is asserting that God's ownership is manifest through, and mediated by, the Son of God, Jesus Christ!

12:1–9	**Negative illustration**: God's ownership demands fruit-bearing by the disciple	
12:10–12	*Christology*: God's ownership reinstated through Jesus Christ	
12:13–17	God's ownership includes the entirety of the disciple's life	
12:18–27	God's faithful ownership extends to eternity	
12:28–34	God's ownership demands utmost love from the disciple	
12:35–37	*Christology*: God's ownership is manifest through, and mediated by, the Son of God, Jesus Christ*	
12:38–44	**Positive illustration**: God's ownership demands the disciple's all	

* The shaded element indicates the section under discussion.

---

17. France, *Gospel of Mark*, 483–84, 486–87; Collins, *Mark*, 579.

18. Dowd, *Reading Mark*, 132.

19. Heil, "Narrative Strategy," 85.

20. France, *Gospel of Mark*, 484; Stein, *Mark*, 569–70.

19.4 Mark 12:38–44

19.4 God's absolute ownership and authority demands the disciple's sacrifice of all, prompted by love of God and of neighbor (12:38–44).

Section Summary 19.4: This two-part closing section is a powerful positive illustration of a disciple who—in contrast to those only interested in self-aggrandizement instead of loving God, and who oppress, instead of loving, their neighbor—obeys both commandments: her devotion to God is evidenced in her giving of her life, and her love of neighbor is implied in her giving to the temple fund.

TRANSLATION 19.4

12:38 *And in His teaching He said, "Beware of the scribes who want to walk around in long robes, and [want] greetings in the marketplaces,*

12:39 *and foremost seats in synagogues, and foremost places at banquets,*

12:40 *who devour the houses of widows, and in pretense pray long; these will receive greater judgment."*

12:41 *And sitting down opposite the treasury, He observed how the crowd was putting money into the treasury. And many rich people were putting in much.*

12:42 *And one poor widow came and put in two small copper coins, which is [equivalent to] a penny.*

12:43 *And summoning His disciples, He said to them, "Truly I say to you that this poor widow put in more than all those who put in [money] into the treasury;*

12:44 *for they all put in from their surplus, but she from her lack, all whatever she had she put in, all her life."*

NOTES 19.4

19.4 God's absolute ownership and authority demands the disciple's sacrifice of all, prompted by love of God and of neighbor.

Mark 12 closes with the account of the widow, a paragon of loyalty to God. The two sections of this episode, 12:38–40 and 41–44, are linked to each other by the mention of widow(s) (12:40, 42) and of those who practice self-inflating ostentation (12:38–39, 41). Widows are victims in the first, and one of them is a model of loyalty in the second. While the wealthy ones in 12:41 are not identified as scribes (who are labeled the exploiters in 12:38–40), the mention of widow in both sections suggests a less than flattering description of the scribes in the combined unit.[21] The attitude of these pompous ones is deplorable (12:38–39): it violates the foremost commandment to love God and to give him alone the kind of adoration they seek for themselves; 12:40 then

---

21. France, *Gospel of Mark*, 488–89.

proceeds to depict their transgression of the secondary commandment to love one's neighbor.[22] The condemnation of these "disloyal" ones is clear: greater (περισσότερον, *perissoteron*) condemnation is due to such scribes (12:40) for their failure to practice the greater (περισσότερον) commandments (12:33).[23]

The sequence of controversies that began in 11:27 is brought to a close with the final episode in this chapter, 12:41–44. The setting evidently is in the Court of the Women, the closest to the temple that women could approach. In this court stood thirteen "trumpet/shofar chests" (שופרות, *shofaroth*; *m. Šeqal.* 2.1; 6.1, 5; etc.) for the half-shekel temple tax and "freewill" offerings.[24] All of the donations being made could easily be noticed by the curious, as Jesus and his disciples obviously are (12:41). France suspects it was "a recognized tourist attraction."[25]

The analogy between the pretentious rich in 12:41 and the vainglorious and avaricious scribes in 12:38–40 is obvious; both stand as contrasts to that one poor widow (μία χήρα πτωχή, *mia chēra ptōchē*) whose poverty is mentioned twice (12:42, 43). She is selflessly generous, the epitome of loyalty to God, and the keeper of the greatest commandments in both her devotion to God and in her generosity to the temple.[26] The wording draws attention to the antitheses[27]:

	adjective	subject	verb	object
Mark 12:41 [link = καὶ, *kai*]	many	rich people	were putting in	much
Mark 12:42	one	poor widow	put in	two small coins

	subject	source	pronoun	aorist verb
Mark 12:44a [link = δὲ, *de*]	they all	from surplus	their	put in
Mark 12:44b	she	from poverty	her	put

The key words προσκαλεσάμενος (*proskalesamenos*, "summoning") and the introductory formula ἀμὴν λέγω ὑμῖν (*amēn legō hymin*, "truly I say to you," 12:43) underscore the importance of what Jesus has said. "It both commends the widow's self-sacrificing generosity as an example for all God's people . . . and . . . turns upside

---

22. Stein, *Mark*, 574. The "long robes" or stoles are festive, celebratory robes used by priests (Josephus, *Ant.* 3.158; Exod 28:2 LXX) or royalty (2 Chr 18:9; Esth 6:8 LXX).

23. God's concern for widows has always been oft noted in the OT: Deut 14:29; Ps 68:5; 146:9; Isa 1:17, 23; Jer 7:6; 49:11; Ezek 22:7; Zech 7:10; Mal 3:5.

24. Alternatively, the "treasury" (γαζοφυλάκιον, *gazophylakion*) could also be a building in the Court of Women where offerings were stored (Neh 12:44; 1 Macc 14.49; 2 Macc 3.6) (Stein, *Mark*, 579).

25. France, *Gospel of Mark*, 489.

26. The penny (λεπτόν, *lepton*) was the smallest denomination in use, a copper coin of about a centimeter in diameter; two of these made a quadrans, which was a sixty-fourth of a denarius (the latter was the wage of a day laborer) (France, *Gospel of Mark*, 493). Essentially, all this woman has in her possession is less than 2 percent of an average daily wage, and she gives it all!

27. Smith, "Closer Look," 30–31.

down the normal human valuation of people. What matters in God's sight is not what a person has (and therefore is able to give without pain) but the devotion which causes her to give even at great personal cost."[28] This is a devotion that exemplifies the two greatest commandments. She gives *all* she has—both coins, not just one! And it is "all her life" (ὅλος ὁ βίος αὐτῆς, *holos ho bios autēs*) that goes clinking down the coffers. This widow obeys the greatest commandments, loving God with all (ἐξ ὅλης, *ex holēs*, 12:30, 33) her heart, soul, mind, and strength. Her sacrifice, despite its meager absolute valuation, is in God's eyes worth more than all other contributions[29]: as the scribe has affirmed, obedience to the foremost commandments is greater than all sacrifices (12:33).[30] The scribe *knows* the commandments; the widow *obeys* them.[31] She is a disciple!

12:1–9	**Negative illustration**: God's ownership demands fruit-bearing by the disciple
12:10–12	*Christology*: God's ownership reinstated through Jesus Christ
12:13–17	God's ownership includes the entirety of the disciple's life
12:18–27	God's faithful ownership extends to eternity
12:28–34	God's ownership demands utmost love from the disciple
12:35–37	*Christology*: God's ownership is manifest through, and mediated by, the Son of God, Jesus Christ
12:38–44	**Positive illustration**: God's ownership demands the disciple's all*

* The shaded element indicates the section under discussion.

This story is not a deprecation of wealth or of the wealthy, but an appreciation of the loyalty of the poor widow; that kind of devotion is the standard by which sacrifice for God is evaluated. Such sacrificial loyalty is part of the new perspective of the coming kingdom of God. In contrast to the tenant farmers (the negative illustration of the religious hierarchy, 12:1–9) who refused to give God his due, this woman gives her life, in keeping with Jesus' exhortations and the greatest commandments (12:13–17, 28–34). To this God, whose scope of authority and faithful ownership extends eternally (12:18–27), one's allegiance is owed to the utmost. God's ownership demands the

28. France, *Gospel of Mark*, 493.

29. Notice that while the rich put in "much" (12:41; from πολύς), the woman gave "more" (12:43; πλεῖον, also from πολύς) than all of the others.

30. There may be also a subtle allusion to the rich man who refused the call to discipleship (10:17–31; see Pericope 15). Where 12:44 has the woman giving πάντα ὅσα εἶχεν (*panta hosa eichen*, "all whatever she had"), the wealthy man was asked by Jesus to give ὅσα ἔχεις (*hosa echeis*, "whatever you have," 10:21). The widow gives out of her lack (ὑστερήσεως, *hysterēseōs*, 12:44), while the rich man lacked (ὑστερεῖ, *hysterei*, 10:21) one thing, the willingness to give all and follow Jesus. Also, Peter acknowledges that they, the disciples, have left πάντα (*panta*, "all") to follow Jesus (10:28); here the woman gives πάντα ("all") she has (12:44) to the service of God.

31. In Mark 12:30 and 33, loving God with one's whole "strength" is enjoined; ἰσχύς, *ischys*, translates מְאֹד, *meod*, from Deut 6:5 ("might"/"power"/"strength"). Collins notes that in the Dead Sea Scrolls, מְאֹד is interpreted as "wealth/property" (1QS 1.11–15; 3.2–3; etc.). To those familiar with this interpretation of Deut 6:5, the widow's sacrifice of "all her life" would be proof that she loves God with all her "strength," i.e., with all her "wealth"/"property," for she gives everything she has (*Mark*, 590).

disciple's all, given sacrificially, particularly in obedience to the greatest command-ments. And only this unnamed, destitute widow successfully accomplishes that.

With this episode, Jesus' public teaching comes to an end; the remaining teaching sessions are conducted privately with the disciples. The negative pictures of the temple, its activities, and its leaders and their attitudes, that have been depicted so far in Act III, all anticipate the prophetic discourse in Mark 13 on the destruction of the temple.

SERMON FOCUS AND OUTLINES

THEOLOGICAL FOCUS OF PERICOPE 19 FOR PREACHING

19   God's absolute ownership demands the disciple's sacrifice of all, in utmost love for God and neighbor (12:13–44).

This pericope hammers home its theological focus in many ways: the coin story dem-onstrates God's authority over the ones who bear his image (the disciple owes all); the resurrection controversy demonstrates God's faithful authority extending even into eternity (the disciple can confidently give everything up for God); the discussion of the greatest commandment demonstrates what God's authority demands (the disciple is to love God with all of one's being, as well as one's neighbor); and the widow's story por-trays this sacrificial giving of all to God (the disciple sacrifices all to God). Embedded between these episodes are two christological statements: lest anyone have doubts about the one to whom this total allegiance and loyalty is owed, those affirmations point to the divine Son of God, the Messiah, one greater than King David, and the chief cornerstone—Jesus Christ. The disciple owes him all.

That this giving of all makes the giver vulnerable and even, perhaps, uncom-fortable, is not surprising, given humankind's urge for self-preservation and selfish comfort-seeking. But there is a note of assurance in Mark 12. This God, who is in con-trol of life and death and everything beyond death (12:18–27), can surely be trusted confidently and completely; surely he will take care of the sacrificing disciple in this life, not to mention in the hereafter, for this is a dependable God who exercises his ownership faithfully. Perhaps this is why that controversy with the Sadducees is made the central element in the structural arrangement of the various episodes of Mark 12.

A   Illustration of tenant-farmers: God is owed fruit (12:1–9)
  B   Christological affirmation (12:10–12)
    C   Tax debate: giving of all to God (12:13–17)
      D   Resurrection controversy: the *faithful* God of life and death (12:18–27)
    C′   Commandment discussion: loving God with all (12:28–34)
  B′   Christological affirmation (12:35–37)
A′   Illustration of widow: God is given all (12:38–44)

The earlier pericope dealing with the rich man (10:13–31; Pericope 15), consid-ered the importance of giving of one's possessions (and the getting of even more in the hereafter). This pericope, on the other hand, deals more with sacrificial giving as an expression of love of God and man; it also explains why the disciple can give confidently—because God is a caring God.

Closing as this pericope does with a social evil—the depredation of the helpless—this sermon might be a good opportunity to address the issue of care and concern for the needy, a means of sacrificial love toward God and neighbor.

POSSIBLE PREACHING OUTLINE FOR PERICOPE 19

I.   WHO are we? The identity of the disciple—bearer of the image of God
     Tax debate: 12:13–17, God's ownership over our persons—everything we are and have
     Move-to-Relevance: Our faulty perspective—*our* ownership
II. WHAT must we do? The duty of the image-bearer—*Sacrifice all in utmost love!*
     The widow illustration: 12:38–44
     The basis for her action, the greatest commandments: 12:35–37, echoing "all"
     How can we specifically give our all to God in utmost love for him and for neighbor?
III. WHY we are confident? The dependability of God—He can be trusted, so we can sacrifice ourselves in love
     The resurrection controversy: the God of life and death, who keeps his word: 12:18–27
     Move-to-Relevance: Our hesitation/fear to love to the utmost
     God's dependability overcomes that hesitation/fear

Or, focus it more upon God:

I.   God's ownership: Over all that bears his image
     Tax debate: 12:13–17, God's ownership over our persons—everything we are and have
     Move-to-Relevance: Our faulty perspective—*our* ownership
II. God's demand: *Sacrifice all in utmost love!*
     The widow illustration: 12:38–44
     The basis for her action, the greatest commandments: 12:35–37, echoing "all"
     How can we specifically give our all to God in utmost love for him and for neighbor?
III. God's character: He can be trusted, so we can sacrifice ourselves in love
     The resurrection controversy: the God of life and death, who keeps his word: 12:18–27
     Move-to-Relevance: Our hesitation/fear to love to the utmost
     God's dependability overcomes that hesitation/fear

PERICOPE 20

Tenacity in Calamity

Mark 13:1–37

[Eschatological Discourse; Fig Tree and Doorkeeper Parables]

REVIEW, SUMMARY, PREVIEW

Review of Pericope 19: Mark 12:13–44 focuses on the demands made on disciples as a result of God's absolute ownership and authority. As God's image-bearers belonging to a faithful God, they owe him the sacrifice of themselves, prompted by utmost love for God and neighbor.

Summary of Pericope 20: Mark 13:1–37 is an extended answer by Jesus to the disciples' question about the timing of future events. Refraining from giving a precise answer, Jesus instead focuses upon what a disciple is called to do, particularly in times of calamity, distress, and turmoil. A tenacious faithfulness is the demand Jesus makes of his disciples, and such endurance is possible because of the assurances of God's providence, the Holy Spirit's power, and the promise of the Son's ultimate return with the gathering of believers to himself.

Preview of Pericope 21: The next pericope (14:1–11) addresses the necessity of comprehending and accepting Jesus' suffering mission, and responding with extravagant sacrifice.

20   Mark 13:1–37

THEOLOGICAL FOCUS OF PERICOPE 20

20   Dependence on God's providence, the Spirit's power, and the Son's promise of the disciple being gathered to himself at his second coming enables the disciple to remain faithful to Jesus, rather than an institution, even through the most trying circumstances, until such time as Jesus returns—the precise moment of which is unknown to all but the Father (13:1–37).

20.1   Dependence on the providence of God, the power of the Spirit, and the promise of being gathered to Jesus at his coming enables the disciple to remain faithful to him—not to an institution—despite the most trying circumstances (13:1–27).

20.1.1   Disciples remain faithful to Jesus, not to an institution, without being misled from the way of God.

20.1.2   Disciples remain faithful to their mission amidst the most trying circumstances, in the power of the Holy Spirit.

20.1.3   Disciples faithful to Jesus are kept by God's providential and sovereign protection even in the worst of times, ultimately to be gathered to Jesus at his coming, as he promises.

20.2   Alertness and faithfulness in discipleship is the call of the follower of Jesus—not to watch for his return, the precise moment of which is unknown to all but the Father (13:28–37).

OVERVIEW

MARK 13 IN ACT III parallels Mark 4 in Act I of the Gospel drama: each is an extended "apocalyptic" discourse, located in the middle of the respective act, and each follows upon hectic activity by Jesus and hostile confrontations with opponents.[1] These longer pericopes give the reader a respite, enabling one to assess the significance and implications of what has been narrated in the Gospel thus far. However, France reflects the general feeling of Markan scholarship when he declares that Mark 13 "remains the most disputed area in the study of Mark's gospel."[2]

The theme of this chapter continues Jesus' anti-temple stance that began with his entry into Jerusalem in Mark 11 and was carried on into Mark 12. "The failure of Israel, especially of its leadership, to fulfill its mission; its lack of fruit (11:12–26; 12:38–40); and its hostility toward God's anointed (11:1–11, 27–33; 12:13–17, 18–27) all lead to the inevitable judgment resulting in the destruction of the temple and Jerusalem."[3] Mark 13, thus, is an account of the fulfillment of Jesus' prophecy that the old temple will be destroyed and replaced with the new "temple," the community of disciples, founded on Jesus, the cornerstone. In giving this report, Mark warns disciples to be

1. It is probably not accurate to label these blocks of teaching "apocalyptic," for they do not contain key elements of that genre, such as: significant amounts of appropriate verbiage, images, or notions; date setting; details of resurrection, judgment, or punishment and reward; etc. (see Witherington, *Gospel of Mark*, 336; Hooker, *Commentary*, 299). The presence of over a dozen second-person imperatives addressed to disciples (and a few third-person imperatives in 13:14–16) also makes this particular chapter difficult to pigeonhole as "apocalyptic."

2. France, *Gospel of Mark*, 497–98.

3. Stein, *Mark*, 582. Prophecies of the destruction of Jerusalem/temple are found in 1 Kgs 9:6–8; Jer 7:12–15; 12:7; 22:5; 26:6, 18; Mic 3:12; etc.

faithful themselves. Mark 13, interestingly, is bookended by the accounts of two un-named women who are the epitomes of faithfulness, demonstrating incredible loyalty and devotion to God, while the men in each of the two stories practice hypocrisy and deception (12:38–44 and 14:1–11). Not a treatise on eschatology, this chapter, then, is a call to faithfulness to Jesus on the basis of the foreboding events he has predicted. "Faithfulness" subsequently becomes the central theme of Act III. Mark 13 may be outlined as follows[4]:

- Jesus' prediction and the disciples' question (13:1–4)
- Jesus' response (13:5–37), divided into three parts:
  » The time before the coming of the Son of Man (13:5–23)

    A   "watch out" (13:5); false claims of messiahship will mislead (πλανάω, planaō, 13:5, 6) (13:5–6)

       B   *when you hear*: news of wars and natural disasters; **do not be alarmed** (13:7–8)

          C   "watch out" (13:9); *when they arrest you*: persecution; **do not be concerned** (13:9–13)

       B'   *when you see*: desecration of the holy place and tribulation; **flee** (13:14–20)

    A'   "watch out" (13:23); false messiahs will mislead (ἀποπλανάω, apoplanaō, 13:22) (13:21–23)

  » The coming of the Son of Man (13:24–27)

    Cosmological catastrophes ("in those days," 13:24) (13:24–25)
    Coming of the Son of Man ("and then," 13:26) (13:26)
    Gathering of the elect ("and then," 13:27) (13:27)

  » Response to the imminent coming of the Son of Man (13:28–37)

    A   Parable of the fig tree (13:28–29)
       B   Saying relating to time (13:30)
          C   The authority of Jesus' word (13:31)
       B'   Saying relating to time (13:32)
    A'   Parable of the door-keeper (13:33–37)

When exactly and in what circumstances Mark 13 (and indeed the whole Gospel) was written is a matter that has vexed scholars (see Introduction). The issue comes to a head in this chapter; several permutations and combinations have been proposed, with various parts of Mark 13 representing either the destruction of temple and city (66–70 CE) or the Parousia (the Second Advent of Jesus), or both.[5] This author sees 13:5–23 as one integral unit, with the elements therein not finding convincing cor-respondences in the events leading up to the historical destruction of the city and the

---

4. Modified from van Iersel, *Reading Mark*, 159–60; and Dowd, *Reading Mark*, 135.

5. See Cashmore, "'In This Generation,'" for a summary of the options, harmonizing the Gospel accounts; also see Stein, *Mark*, 583; and Gundry, *Mark*, 755.

temple. Thus, the entire chapter appears to be addressing events of the future.[6] Such an understanding would also see the account as being written before the fall of Jerusalem (pre-70 CE), for lacking in Mark's account are discussions of: the fire in Jerusalem's destruction (Josephus, *J.W.* 6.249–87); intramural fighting among various Jewish groups during the siege; the many Jews (thousands) who were crucified by Rome; and what exactly "the abomination of desolation" was, if it did occur during the destruction of the temple by the Romans. Moreover, the destruction of city and temple actually occurred in the summer of 70 CE, not in the winter, as 13:18 appears to be anticipating.[7] In any case, whatever option the interpreter chooses, it probably does not make much difference for preaching the theological thrust of this pericope, as will become evident.

In the First Act of the Gospel (1:1—8:21), the disciples' main problem was their lack of discernment of the person of Jesus ("person" includes his power as well, of course). The Second Act (8:22—10:52) focused upon their lack of acceptance of the mission of Jesus. The Third Act (11:1—16:8), with the Passion account, no longer calls for discernment or acceptance: the concern here is disciples' faithfulness to Jesus—i.e., faithfulness to what they (ought to) have already discerned and accepted. Thus, Act III, in this trajectory, hones in on the disciples' response to all that Jesus has revealed to them, particularly from Mark 13 onwards. Prior to this, the watchword was βλέπω (*blepō*, "watch out")—disciples were to discern and accept the person and mission of Jesus[8]—but βλέπω does not occur after Mark 13. Subsequent to this point, however, the watchword is γρηγορέω (*grēgoreō*, "be alert")—disciples are to respond in faithfulness to Jesus—and γρηγορέω does not occur before Mark 13.[9] While the themes of discernment and acceptance come prior to the Passion, the theme of faithfulness (implied by γρηγορέω) accompanies this culminating event of the Gospel. Geddert advances the convincing thesis that in reporting this discourse of Jesus, opening with βλέπω (13:5) and closing with γρηγορέω (13:37), Mark deliberately selects both verbs as technical terms, controlling their usages and contrasting their meanings.[10] Mark 13 essentially becomes the hinge, the point at which the motifs shift. Much of Mark's intentionality in this regard will be dealt with in the account of the Passion, especially Mark 14–15; the connection between those passages and 13:33–37 will be drawn in the respective chapters (Pericopes 22–24). For the purposes of preaching and applying Mark 13, it will suffice to see (ahem!) that βλέπω focuses upon the discernment and acceptance of Jesus' person and mission by the disciple (the themes of the previous acts), and γρηγορέω focuses upon the disciple's response to such discernment and acceptance—i.e., faithfulness to Jesus (the theme of the last act).

---

6. Whatever the stance of the interpreter, a degree of "expository humility" in clinging to one's own conclusions regarding these less-than-clear issues is certainly called for.

7. Stein, *Mark*, 583; also see Gundry, *Mark*, 755. That is not to deny that sense can be made of the chapter even if written after 70 CE.

8. Βλέπω is found in 4:12, 24; 8:15, 18, 23, 24; 12:38; 13:5, 9, 23, 33, in the sense of "watch out."

9. Γρηγορέω is found in 13:34, 35, 37; 14:34, 37, 38.

10. Geddert, *Watchwords*, 90, 104. Indeed both βλέπω and γρηγορέω occur three times each in this chapter (13:5, 9, 23 and 13:34, 35, 37, respectively).

ACT III: IN JERUSALEM

20.1 Mark 13:1–27

THEOLOGICAL FOCUS 20.1

20.1 Dependence on the providence of God, the power of the Spirit, and the promise of being gathered to Jesus at his coming enables the disciple to remain faithful to him—not to an institution—despite the most trying circumstances (13:1–27).

    20.1.1 Disciples remain faithful to Jesus, not to an institution, without being misled from the way of God.

    20.1.2 Disciples remain faithful to their mission amidst the most trying circumstances, in the power of the Holy Spirit.

    20.1.3 Disciples faithful to Jesus are kept by God's providential and sovereign protection even in the worst of times, ultimately to be gathered to Jesus at his coming, as he promises.

Section Summary 20.1: A rather cryptic, albeit lengthy, response of Jesus to his disciples' question describes a sequence of dreadful events of grave universal and personal consequence. The disciples should be prepared for all of this, including the most severe tribulation of all, accompanied by manifestations of the Antichrist. God's providence and the Holy Spirit's help are assured the disciple even in these most dire situations. The disciple's responsibility, knowing what might happen in the future, is to remain faithful to Jesus on the way of discipleship. Hope is extended as well: at the coming of the Son of Man, Jesus will gather the disciples to himself.

TRANSLATION 20.1

13:1   *And as He was going out from the temple, one of His disciples said to Him, "Teacher, behold what glorious stones and what glorious buildings!"*

13:2   *And Jesus said to him, "Do you see these great buildings? Not one stone will be left upon stone here which will not be thrown down."*

13:3   *And as He was sitting on the Mount of Olives opposite the temple, Peter and James and John and Andrew were questioning Him privately,*

13:4   *"Tell us, when will these things be, and what the sign when all these things are about to be accomplished?"*

13:5   *And Jesus began to say to them, "Watch out, lest anyone mislead you.*

13:6   *Many will come in My name saying, 'I am!' and they will mislead many.*

13:7   *When you hear of wars and rumors of wars, do not be alarmed. It is necessary [for these] to happen, but the end is not yet.*

13:8   *For nation will rise up against nation, and kingdom against kingdom; there will be earthquakes in various places, there will be famines. These are the beginning of birth pains.*

13:9   *But you watch out for yourselves; they will give you over to the councils, and in the synagogues you will be beaten, and you will stand before governors and kings for My sake, as a testimony against them.*

13:10 *And it is necessary for the Gospel to be preached first, unto all the nations.*

13:11   *And when they lead you [to trial] and give you over, do not be concerned beforehand what you will say, but whatever is given to you in that hour, this you say, for it is not you who are speaking, but the Holy Spirit.*

13:12   *And brother will give over brother to death, and father, child; and children will rise up against parents and have them put to death.*

13:13   *And you will be hated by all because of My name. But the one who endures to the end, this one will be saved.*

13:14   *But when you see the abomination of desolation standing where it should not—let the one reading understand—then those in Judea should flee to the mountains.*

13:15   *The one upon the roof must not come down, nor go in to take anything from his house;*

13:16   *and the one in the field must not turn back to take his cloak.*

13:17   *But woe to those who are pregnant and to those nursing in those days.*

13:18   *But pray that it may not happen in winter.*

13:19   *For those days will be [a time of] tribulation such as has not happened from the beginning of creation which God created, until now, and will never happen.*

13:20   *And unless the Lord had shortened the days, no flesh would have been saved; but for the sake of the elect whom He elected, He shortened the days.*

13:21   *And then if anyone says to you, 'Behold, here is the Christ,' 'Behold, there,' do not believe,*

13:22   *for false Christs and false prophets will rise, and will provide signs and wonders, to lead astray, if possible, the elect.*

13:23   *But you watch out; I have told you everything in advance.*

13:24   *But in those days, after that tribulation, the sun will be darkened, and the moon will not give its light,*

13:25   *and the stars will fall from heaven, and the powers that are in the heavens will be shaken.*

13:26   *And then they will see the Son of Man coming in clouds with much power and glory.*

13:27   *And then He will send angels and will gather together the elect from the four winds, from the end of earth to the end of heaven."*

NOTES 20.1

20.1.1   Disciples remain faithful to Jesus, not to an institution, without being misled away from the way of God.

The temple cultus has just been devalued by a scribe (12:33), and Jesus himself has deprecated all the ostentatious contributions to the temple treasury (12:42), not to mention his declaration of the bankruptcy of the entire apparatus earlier (11:12—12:12). It is ironic then that a disciple is enthralled by the magnificent stones and grand buildings (13:1)![11] The followers of Jesus have apparently not yet grasped the newness of the coming kingdom, with its radically different criteria of worth, status, and priority. Appropriately, when the disciples begin the section exhorting Jesus to "behold" (from ὁράω, *horaō*; 13:1), Jesus' response, too, is peppered with verbs of vision: βλέπω (*blepō*, "watch," 13:5, 9, 23, 33) and ὁράω ("see," 13:14, 21[× 2], 26, 29). Vision is something *disciples* ought to have, not Jesus! What Jesus is going to say, *they* must see and understand. And that is not a directive just to the Twelve, but to disciples of all time: notice the parenthetical comment to the reader in 13:14, and Jesus' concluding statement that is addressed "to all" (13:37). What Mark, under the Holy Spirit's inspiration, has chosen to include here (and elsewhere) is directed to everyone everywhere who chooses to follow Jesus on the Trip of Discipleship.

This final exit of Jesus from the temple (13:1) prompts a decisive statement about that institution's fate.[12] The two aorist passive subjunctives ("will be left" and "will . . . be thrown down"), and the double negation in the sentence, make Jesus' denial of the longevity of the buildings extremely emphatic (13:2).[13] "Stone upon stone" (13:2) reflects Haggai 2:15–16, but in reversal; there the temple is being *built* "stone upon stone"; here it is being *destroyed* "stone upon stone"! While Jesus' prophecy appears to have been fulfilled in Titus's devastation of Jerusalem in 70 CE, Jesus does not deign to answer the disciples' question of when exactly this predicted destruction is to occur (Mark 13:4). Rather than seeking a precise chronology, the disciples' call—in that and in every generation—is to be faithful *all the time* (see on 13:33–37, below).

One is also reminded of Mark 12:10, which depicts Jesus as the cornerstone of a newer structure. Thus, in a sense, all the temple's stones are going to be "replaced and exceeded by the metaphorical stone, Jesus, whom God will establish as the cornerstone of a new temple building," the community of those who pray with faith and with a forgiving attitude (11:12–25), and who render to God his due, in light of his ownership and authority (12:1–44).[14]

The ταῦτα συντελεῖσθαι πάντα (*tauta synteleisthai panta*, "all these things are to be accomplished") of 13:4 has its parallel in Daniel 12:7 (LXX: συντελεσθήσεται πάντα ταῦτα (*syntelesthēsetai panta tauta*, "all these things will be accomplished"). While the disciples may be more concerned about the fall of the grand building, from the narrator's point of view the allusion to Daniel 12 and "all these things" are intended to refer to the series of events in Daniel 11:36—12:1 (the arrival of the Antichrist and the great

---

11. Heil, "Narrative Strategy," 89. Josephus describes the massive size of the stones, with dimensions ranging 40–60 × 6–12 × 9–18 feet, and the grandeur of the temple (*J.W.* 5.189, 222–24; *Ant.* 15.392); *b. Sukkah* 51b agrees: "Our rabbis taught . . . he who has not seen the temple in its full construction has never seen a glorious building in his life."

12. The purposeful exodus from the temple in 13:1 is followed in 13:3 by a deliberate posture in opposition to the temple: the preposition is κατέναντι (*katenanti*, "opposite"); a cognate noun, ἐναντίος, *enantios*, means "opponent."

13. Josephus reports the burning of the temple and its leveling to the ground (*J.W.* 6.249–66 and 7.1–3). The "Western Wall" that remains to this day is technically only a portion of the retaining structure for renovations that Herod the Great carried out on the temple in 19 BCE.

14. Heil, "Narrative Strategy," 90.

tribulation). That shows Jesus' intent to answer not just his immediate questioners, but to address disciples of all ages in the future, some of whom would live through the perilous last days he was prophesying about. In any case, whatever the interpreter's eschatology, the mandate to all disciples of all time is to remain faithful, as the rest of the discourse demonstrates.

The dramatic events of the last days take center stage in Jesus' reply in 13:5–37.[15] Within this section, 13:5–23 is set apart by structural idiosyncrasies, as shown earlier. There is also an intensification of oppressive action: from birth pains (13:5–8)[16] to personal suffering and persecution (13:9–13) to tribulation (13:14–23; see 13:19). This section, 13:5–23, is also bookended by warnings against being misled (πλανάω, *planaō*, 13:5, 6 and 13:22). The disciple, amidst the dire circumstances of future tribulation, is to remain faithful to Jesus, and not be lead astray by the pseudo-Christs, prophets, and teachers—those who would mislead the people of God away from the way of God.[17]

20.1.2 *Disciples remain faithful to their mission amidst the most trying circumstances, in the power of the Holy Spirit.*

What is international in scope in 13:5–8 becomes intensely personal in 13:9–13—this persecution is because of Jesus' sake, because disciples follow Jesus. Followers will not be mere spectators, but will themselves bear the brunt of persecution and oppression; they can expect that what happens to their Lord will happen to them also (6:11; 8:34–38; 10:30).[18] Geddert suggests that this is a "new lap" in the future, with the disciples taking over the baton from Jesus who, in this scenario, has already departed. The disciples themselves will be "handed over" (παραδίδωμι, *paradidōmi*, occurs thrice in 13:9–13), and presumably someone else will take over the next lap, for the gospel *must* be proclaimed to all nations (δεῖ, *dei*, "it is necessary," 13:10).[19]

The juxtaposition of the disciples' subjection to persecution (13:9) and the statement about the spread of the gospel (13:10) suggests an integral connection between

---

15. "These things" in both of its instances is plural; it is quite possible that there is more than the destruction of the temple being considered, even by the disciples who ask the question (13:4).

16. "Birth pains" frequently describe Israel's judgment and suffering, particularly as the prelude to the arrival of the Messiah: Isa 13:8–9; 26:17–18; 66:7–9; Mic 4:9–10; also see 2 Esd 4.40–43; *1 En.* 99.1—100.6; *Jub.* 23.11–25; *2 Bar.* 27.1–15; and in the NT, John 16:20–22; Rom 8:21–23; 1 Thess 5:3; Rev 12:1–6. Clearly the birth pains are an extended process, for these travails in Mark 13:5–8 are only the "beginning" (13:8).

17. Boring, *Mark*, 362. See Deut 4:19; 13:5; Isa 28:7; Hos 4:12; Mic 3:5; and 2 Thess 2:11; 2 Tim 3:13; Rev 13:14–15 (all use πλανάω, "lead astray"). The irony of false Christs asserting ἐγώ εἰμι (*egō eimi*, "I am," Mark 13:6) must not be lost; these very words, rightly employed by Jesus, the true Messiah, to assert his identity (14:62), will get *him* rejected as a false prophet.

18. As is Jesus, the disciples, too, will be "handed over" (παραδίδωμι, *paradidōmi*, 3:19; 13:9, 11, 12; 14:10, 11) to councils (13:9; 14:55; 15:1); they will be beaten (12:3, 5; 13:9; 14:65; 15:15) and required to testify before rulers (13:9, 11; 14:53–65; 15:1–5). See Driggers, *Following God*, 75–76.

19. The universal scope of Jesus' ministry—already adumbrated in his movements into, and deeds within, Gentile territory (5:1–20; 7:24—8:10; and in the statement of 11:17)—is explicitly indicated here and in 13:27. Later, the confession of Jesus as the Son of God will be made by a *Roman* centurion (15:39); at that point, when the gospel will have reached a Gentile who makes an accurate confession of Jesus, the first iteration of the Trip of Discipleship in Mark's narrative will have effectively concluded.

the two events. Opposition will not to stand in the way of the gospel. Indeed, its very proclamation will be "a testimony against them," the antagonists and foes (13:9). Generation after generation of faithful disciples will carry on this august responsibility of living and suffering for Jesus, and proclaiming him with their words and their deeds. "Mark's theology of the advancing kingdom is much more like a relay race in which persecution for the sake of the Gospel is the baton passed on from each runner to the next as they take their round on the track . . . or (to stick closer to Mark's imagery), it is the cross passed on from shoulder to shoulder as new recruits travel the 'way' from Galilee to Jerusalem."[20] So, in the interim period until the Parousia, the relay race will continue; it is "not to be a time of passive waiting but of proclamation, of the experience of persecution, and of faithful endurance εἰς τέλος [eis telos, 'to the end']."[21] Such an encouraging note of ongoing progress of the gospel assures even the persecuted disciple that God's kingdom will never fail to advance, no matter how adverse the circumstances.[22] Faithfulness to the task of discipleship is enjoined. A powerful promise to the disciple is extended in 13:11—that of the Holy Spirit's guidance. No calamity can disturb the disciple with this divine comforter and helper alongside. That is why Jesus exhorts: "do not be concerned" (13:11).

20.1.3   *Disciples faithful to Jesus are kept by God's providential and sovereign protection even in the worst of times, ultimately to be gathered to Jesus at his coming, as he promises.*

Finally, in 13:14–23, the "sign" the disciples have asked for is provided—a single event (as opposed to an assemblage of events in the previous section: false teachers, wars, earthquakes, famines, persecutions, etc.; 13:5–13). The phrase βδέλυγμα ἐρημώσεως, *bdelygma erēmōseōs*, literally indicates "an abomination of [i.e., that results in] desolation" (13:14). While "abomination" is in the neuter gender, the description of the abomination as "standing" is a masculine perfect participle, suggesting it has something to do with a person, rather than a thing—perhaps the one who is the agent of the desecration/desolation. Indeed, an event like this did actually occur, in the context of the temple.[23] The "abomination of desolation" (also βδέλυγμα ἐρημώσεως) prophesied in Daniel was part of the sacrilege committed in the temple by the Seleucid king Antiochus IV Epiphanes in 157 BCE (Dan 9:27; 11:31; 12:11 LXX; see also 1 Macc 1.54).

20. Geddert, *Watchwords*, 150, 158, 175–76.

21. France, *Gospel of Mark*, 513. The "end" here, unlike in 13:7 where it indicates the Parousia, probably means the "end" of their lives; i.e., endurance even to the point of martyrdom demonstrates authenticity as a child of God. And the "salvation" promised here (13:13) is more in the nature of vindication, rather than denoting eternal life, as in Job 13:16; Phil 1:19, 28; etc.

22. These adverse circumstances include betrayal by one's own. While what exactly that might be is unclear, it certainly encompasses the martyrdoms of Stephen (Acts 6–7) and James (Acts 12:1–3; Josephus, *Ant.* 20.200), which happened within a Jewish context ("brother" betraying "brother") and not at the hands of Gentile authorities. The history of the church has been punctuated with such tragedies all along. The degree of oppression described here in Mark 13 is unmatched by the evidence of persecution in the first century, once again suggesting that 13:5–37 deals with events not directly related to the destruction of Jerusalem or the temple (France, *Gospel of Mark*, 518).

23. Witherington, *Gospel of Mark*, 345.

"Since the specific events of the Maccabean period were now far in the past, its use in the first century could be understood only of an event or object which in some recognizable way corresponded to what Antiochus had done."[24] The hypothesis that this sacrilege refers to an idol installed in the temple may be justifiable (for such "abominations" referring to false worship, see Deut 7:25–26; 17:4; 18:12; 27:14–15; 29:16–17; Isa 2:20; 44:19; Jer 2:7; 7:30; Ezek 8:10; 20:30; Mal 2:11; 1 Macc 6.7; Wis 14.11; etc.); indeed, the desecration by Antiochus also included the installation of an idol of Zeus in the temple (2 Macc 6.2). However, it is not clear if any such statue was installed in the temple during the Jewish Wars of 66–70 CE.[25] Therefore, it might make more sense to see this passage as linked with 2 Thessalonians 2:3–4, where the ἄνθρωπος τῆς ἀνομίας (*anthrōpos tēs anomias*, "man of lawlessness"—likely the Antichrist) "takes his seat in the temple of God, displaying himself as being God." The motif of "misleading" ([ἀπο]πλανάω, [*apo*]*planaō*) that shows up in Mark 13:5, 6, 22 could conceivably be tied to 2 Thessalonians 2:9–12 as well (πλάνη, *planē*, "delusion," occurs in 2:11). In any case, some sort of repetition of Antiochus's desecration of the sanctuary and the resultant cessation of sacrifice, implicit in the almost technical phrase "abomination of desolation," would be a recognizable signal for fleeing, and escape would be possible only if one acted immediately.[26] What is being advised here by Jesus is quite the opposite of the normal practice of seeking refuge within city walls from violence and depredation (Mark 13:14). That is precisely the issue: the theological point is that the temple is not inviolable; neither will it any longer protect anyone, for God will allow his temple to be destroyed.[27] Instead, the call is to flee, to dissociate oneself from the condemned city and its temple. Yet, during the great tribulation, God's people will be saved (13:20). Daniel 12:1 refers to an eschatological time of tribulation with words similar to those in Mark 13:19–20, and also with a promise of deliverance for "everyone who is found written in the book" (Theodotion uses σῴζω, *sōzō*, "save," there, as also does Mark 13:20, while the LXX of Dan 12:1 has ὑψόω, *hypsoō*, "exalt," and the MT has מלט, *mlt*, "deliver"). This "salvation" of Daniel 12 may well be what is reflected here in Mark 13:20–21—the saving (σῴζω) of the elect by the hand of God. Clearly God's sovereignty and providence in the protection of his people is in view.

There is still no mention of Jerusalem or the temple as the arrival of the Son of Man is described (13:24–27). The descriptions of events here sound more like the cosmic upheaval of the eschatological end; in fact, Matthew 24:3, 27, 37, 39 appear to view the same events described here as referring to the Parousia. Cosmic portents, indicating the last days, are echoed in Isaiah 13:9–11; 34:4–5; Ezekiel 32:7–8; Joel 2:10, 31;

---

24. France, *Gospel of Mark*, 520.

25. The Roman Emperor Caligula's unsuccessful attempt to do so in 40 CE cannot count (see Josephus, *Ant.* 18.261). Other less likely possibilities include: Pilate's attempt to carry Roman standards into Jerusalem (Josephus, *J.W.* 2.169–74; *Ant.* 18.55–59); the installation of Phanni, the high priest appointed by the Zealots in 67–68 CE (*J.W.* 4.147–57); Titus's entry into the temple in 70 CE (*J.W.* 6.260); etc. (see Evans, *Mark*, 318–19). None of these events appear to be comparable in gravity and consequence to what is described here. Therefore, the incident in Mark 13:14 seems to be dealing with an event yet to happen.

26. Winn, *Purpose of Mark's Gospel*, 73–74.

27. Geddert, *Watchwords*, 218–19; Witherington, *Gospel of Mark*, 346.

3:15; Amos 8:9; Micah 3:6; and Haggai 2:6, 21. Jewish pseudepigraphical literature also indicates such imagery as eschatological (2 Esd 5.4–5; *As. Mos.* 10.1–10; *1 En.* 80.4–7; 102.2; also see Rev 6:12–13). "In the first century context, heavenly bodies were often thought of in personal terms, identified with or associated with the gods, influencing or controlling events on earth. Their 'fall' would indeed indicate a change in the rulership of the universe."[28] That is now happening here: the Son of Man is coming to reign.

The strong adversative in Mark 13:24 (ἀλλά, *alla*, "but") signals a decisive shift in the battle; the consummation of the end has arrived, and the coming of the Son of Man is described in 13:24–27. That these events occur "after that tribulation" (13:24; referring to the tribulation first mentioned in 13:19) suggests a temporal and sequential linkage. In this passage on final vindication, the disciples find reward for their faithfulness. Despite all the chaos mentioned thus far (13:5–23), if they remained faithful till the end (13:13) recompense would be nigh. In the day of the coming of the Son of Man they, the elect, will be gathered from all over.[29] Mark 13:24–27 is, in fact, a word of comfort for Mark's readers: Jesus' followers, whether they go through tribulation or not, await the Parousia with eager anticipation.

The "they" and the shift into the third person in 13:26–27 (from the second person employed previously) is probably another indication that that event is to occur well into the future; like the rest of Jesus' response, this too is not particularly directed to the historic disciples of Jesus or the Twelve. While 13:26 deals with the imagery of judgment at the Parousia (see 14:62; also see Isa 64:1–2; Rev 11:12; *1 En.* 62.3–5; etc., for adversaries "seeing" the ultimate victory of God), Mark 13:27 concerns the gathering of the elect, as prophesied in the OT, a gathering not just of the Jewish exiles and diaspora, but all nations from every corner of the globe—the result of the worldwide proclamation of the gospel (13:10).[30]

In sum, disciples are to hear (13:7), see, and understand (13:14). "Mark hammers out the last note to complete his chord. . . . The hearing-seeing-understanding cluster (parallel to Isa 6:9) is complete."[31] Now they must be faithful to Jesus, to the gospel, amidst incredibly trying circumstances, in dependence upon the providence of God, the help of the Holy Spirit, and the hope of the Son's promise: one day, with the arrival of the Son of Man, disciples will be gathered to Jesus. Disciples of all generations must be thus prepared for whatever is to come, whenever it may come (see below on the parables of Mark 13:28–32 and 33–37). Thus, even while the reader is deliberately kept

---

28. Boring, *Mark*, 372. Cosmic language with verb "shaken" (as in Mark 13:25) indicating a theophany or the Parousia is found in Jdg 5:5; 2 Sam 22:8–20; Job 9:6; Ps 18:7; 97:2–5; Sir 16.18–19; *T. Levi* 4.1; etc.; clouds as God's vehicle appear in Exod 19:9; 34:5; Num 11:25; 12:5; 2 Sam 22:12; Ps 18:11–12; 97:2; Isa 19:1; Nah 1:3; the angelic entourage of God shows up in Zech 14:5; also see Deut 33:2; Ps 68:17; *1 En.* 1.9.

29. While it may be puzzling to see the "saved" as being those who "endure to the end" (13:13), their identification as "the elect" puts matters in perspective. God's elect are those who are both saved and who will endure to the end.

30. See Deut 30:4; Ps 147:2; Isa 11:11; 27:12; 43:5–6; Jer 23:3; 29:14; 31:8; 32:37; Ezek 11:17; 34:13; 36:24; 39:27; Zech 10:6–11; also 2 Macc 2.7; *Pss. Sol.* 17.26.

31. Gray, *Temple*, 132.

in the dark about calendars and clocks, the theological thrust of the section is clear: be faithful, until the end, no matter what; and take heart—God is in control.

20.2   Mark 13:28–37

THEOLOGICAL FOCUS 20.2

20.2   Alertness and faithfulness in discipleship is the call of the follower of Jesus—not to watch for his return, the precise moment of which is unknown to all but the Father (13:28–37).

Section Summary 20.2: Two parabolic depictions, that of the fig tree and of the doorkeeper, demonstrate that while the disciple may be cognizant of the general season of Christ's return, no one—not even the Son—knows the day or the hour of this momentous event. In other words, timekeeping is not in the disciple's portfolio. Instead, as the second parable emphasizes, the disciple's call is to be alert, faithful in discipleship.

TRANSLATION 20.2

13:28   *"But from the fig tree learn the parable: when its branch has already become tender, and puts forth leaves, you know that summer is near.*

13:29   *So also you, when you see these things happening, know that He is near at the door.*

13:30   *Truly I say to you, this generation will not pass away until all these things happen.*

13:31   *Heaven and earth will pass away, but My words will never pass away.*

13:32   *But about that day or the hour no one knows, neither the angels in heaven, nor the Son—except the Father.*

13:33   *Watch out, keep awake, for you do not know when the time is.*

13:34   *[It is] like a man away on a journey, leaving his house and giving to his slaves authority, each for his work; and the doorkeeper, he commanded to be alert.*

13:35   *Therefore, be alert, for you do not know when the lord of the house is coming—whether in the evening or midnight or at cockcrow or early in the morning—*

13:36   *lest coming unexpectedly he find you sleeping.*

13:37   *And what I say to you, to all I say, 'Be alert!'"*

NOTES 20.2

20.2   *Alertness and faithfulness in discipleship is the call of the follower of Jesus—not to watch for his return, the precise moment of which is unknown to all but the Father.*

Elements of 13:28–32 lead one to believe that this parable deals with specificities of the disciples' questions at the beginning of the chapter: the wording and sequence of "these things" (13:29) and "all these things" (13:30) are precisely the same as those in the disciples' question in 13:4a ("these things") and 13:4b ("all these things"). However, while the disciples' questions relate, in all likelihood, to the destruction of the city and temple, Jesus' answer moves far away from that historical event to an eschatological one, particularly relating to the arrival of the Son of Man—the one who is "near" (13:29). The nearness of this season of summer (13:28, γινώσκετε ὅτι ἐγγὺς τὸ θέρος ἐστίν, *ginōskete hoti engys to theros estin*, "know that summer is near") is echoed in the nearness of the Son of Man (13:29, γινώσκετε ὅτι ἐγγύς ἐστιν ἐπὶ θύραις, *ginōskete hoti engys estin epi thurais*, "know that He is near at the door"). Summer (θέρος, *theros*) is conceptually and linguistically related to harvest time (θερισμός, *therismos*, "harvest"; the verb is θερίζω, *therizō*), which was just described in 13:27 as the gathering—a harvest of sorts—of God's people. These signs of the *season*, believers must "learn" and "know" (13:28, 29). However, as 13:32 depicts, the *day* and *hour* of the Parousia are known to no one (13:32), not even the Son.[32] While the general "season" of the coming of the Son of Man may be figured out from the signs, no more specificity is given, nor is such specificity to be sought by disciples. The phrase "this generation" (13:30) is likely to be a literal generation and, in light of the mention of the nearness of summer and of the coming of the Son of Man (13:28–29), "generation" could be taken to mean the "generation that sees the signs of fig tree and these things happening" (13:26, 28–29).[33] In other words, the generation that sees the signs will also see the arrival of the Son of Man. In addition, "when you see" in 13:29 likely links with the "when you see" of 13:14, and probably refers to the sacrilege of the (eschatological?) temple—*the* sign that the end is nigh. Thus, all these events—desolation, astronomical turmoil, etc.—are signs of the *season*, not necessarily of the exact *day* or *hour*. Nonetheless, it is possible that all occur relatively close to each other, perhaps within the span of a single generation.

Οὐκ οἴδατε γὰρ πότε ὁ καιρός (*ouk oidate gar pote ho kairos*, "for you do not know when the time," 13:33) is parallel to, and has a degree of assonance with, οὐκ οἴδατε γὰρ πότε ὁ κύριος (*ouk oidate gar pote ho kyrios*, "for you do not know when the lord," 13:35). The "time" is, of course, the moment of the return of the "lord." While the moment of the return is not stated, the hours in question (13:35) are the commonly assigned watches of nighttime. But travelers, especially in those days, would hardly be likely to return at night from a long travel (as assumed by ἀπόδημος, *apodēmos*, "away on a journey," 13:34). These hours of darkness therefore appear to

---

32. The singular use of "day" (13:32) is new; the plural was found in 13:17, 19, 20 (×2), 24. Moreover, here the even more specific "hour" is added. These terms dealing with spans of time must be referring to the singular event of the Parousia, not to the extended period of days that precede it (or the prolonged process of the tribulations of Jerusalem). The ignorance of that day or hour on the part of the Son should not be surprising. "To the extent that Mark is making a christological point, this datum would, like Jesus' identification with sinners, fall on the 'truly human' side of the Chalcedonian ledger, just as placing his own words in the same category as God's in the preceding statement [13:31; see Isa 40:8] places him on the divine side" (Boring, *Mark*, 376–77). As Stein notes: "These passages, and others like them, are better understood along the lines of Phil 2:6–11 as being due to the 'self-emptying'" of Jesus Christ (*Mark*, 623n4).

33. While "generation" in 8:12, 38; and 9:19 has negative connotations, the word in 13:30 is not explicitly noted to be evil. "Generation" could also encompass several lifetimes, as in 1QpHab 2.7; 7.2; etc.

have symbolic intent, especially in light of the recurrence of those very same hours in Mark 14–15. The four watches mentioned here (13:35, the Roman division of the night into four quarters: evening, midnight, cockcrow, and early morning) are directly or indirectly incorporated into the account of the Passion.[34] "[I]t signifies this age of evil, the age in which the Christian lives and which presents him with the perils that would lure him from watchfulness in respect of the way of the cross."[35] The threefold command to "be alert" (γρηγορέω, *grēgoreō*, 13:34, 35, 37) parallels the threefold command in Gethsemane (also γρηγορέω, 14:34, 37, 38). Both here and there the dangers of sleeping are underscored (καθεύδω, *katheudō*, "sleep," 13:36; 14:37, 40, 41).[36] Thus, this parable of the doorkeeper foreshadows the events of the succeeding two chapters of the Gospel.

What is striking in this section is the absence of any injunction to watch for the Lord's return (unlike in Luke 12:36). Geddert observes[37]:

> The Markan parable seems to speak its message most clearly if the primary call is to be a faithful watchman *on the master's behalf* because he is away, rather than to be a faithful watchman *for his appearance* because he is returning. . . . The point at issue is not whether or not a disciple will be found faithfully at his post at the single and precise instant of the master's return. The point at issue is whether or not he has been faithful *right through* the long night of waiting. To be asleep at any point along the way is to become an unfaithful servant, and to fall prey to the enemy. Even a moment's sleep might permit the intruder access.

The issue is not about being ready to receive the returning master. Instead, the key in this pericope is 13:13, "the one who endures to the end, this one will be saved."[38] That is to say, faithfulness at all times is the critical command. The cascade of imperatives in this chapter emphasizes that point and conveys that thrust: "watch out" (13:5); "do not be alarmed" (13:7); "watch out" (13:9); "do not be concerned" (13:11); "pray" (13:18); "watch out" (13:23); "watch out" (13:33); "keep awake" (13:33); "be alert" (13:35); "be alert" (13:37). The final two imperatives exhorting alertness will become the theme of Mark 14–15. As was mentioned earlier, after Mark 13 the specific call to the disciple is to be alert. To do so is to model oneself after Jesus, who himself perfectly accomplishes what he asked his disciples to do in the four watches (as seen in Mark 14–15). In the Passion, Jesus is the faithful servant, the doorkeeper who watches through the night. He models servanthood. "He came as 'servant' the first time; they [disciples] must serve him thereafter. He stood as a faithful doorkeeper the first time; he would return

---

34. Ὀψέ, *opse*, "evening" (14:17, Last Supper; 15:42, after crucifixion); μεσονύκτιον, *mesonyktion*, "midnight" (14:30, Judas' betrayal and the abandonment of Jesus by the disciples); ἀλεκτοροφωνία, *alektorophōnia*, "cockcrow" (14:30, 72, Peter's denial); and πρωΐ, *prōi*, "early in the morning" (15:1, Jesus handed over to the Romans). See below on Mark 14 and 15 (Pericopes 22–24).

35. Best, *Following Jesus*, 153; also see France, *Gospel of Mark*, 545–46.

36. For "sleeping" as a metaphor for spiritual insensitivity, see Eph 5:14 and 1 Thess 5:6–7.

37. Geddert, *Watchwords*, 105 (italics original).

38. van Iersel, *Mark*, 412.

as the master of the house."[39] This last parable of Jesus in the Gospel is a clarion call to faithfulness in discipleship. What those facets of faithfulness are will be the theological foci of the remaining pericopes of Mark.

SERMON FOCUS AND OUTLINES

THEOLOGICAL FOCUS OF PERICOPE 20 FOR PREACHING

20 Dependence on God's providence, the Spirit's power, and the Son's promise to return enables the disciple to be faithful to Jesus in times of trial (13:1–37).

The burden of the preacher here is to delineate what this "faithfulness to Jesus" looks like. Some of the elements of faithfulness obtained directly from the text may be gainfully employed for specific application in the sermon: being courageous despite turmoil in the world (13:7–8) and natural disasters (13:8), standing firm amidst persecution (13:9), continuing in the proclamation of the Gospel (13:10), being unshaken despite betrayal from close quarters (13:12), refusing to be misled (13:6, 21–22), etc.[40] Perhaps if one belongs to the appropriate "generation" (13:30), one might even see *the* sign—the temple (likely a new one that is reconstructed) being desecrated. No matter what the era the disciple may be living in, no matter how virulent the opposition, or what the intensity of turbulence all around, the call to the disciple in this pericope is clear: be alert, faithful to Jesus. Such faithfulness can only be achieved by dependence upon the providence of God, the power of the Spirit, and the promise of the Son's return. This is a powerful lesson for the disciple to learn. It is in times of calamity that the instability of the disciple becomes most manifest—the tendency to drift, whether it be in doctrine, faith, or praxis. Thus, a point in the first sermon outline deals with the *wrong* responses we tend to make during times of calamity ("instability"; see outline below). Clearly, timekeeping—speculating on the precise moment of Jesus' return—is *not* a facet of faithfulness, for that is one thing this pericope asserts is not the call of a disciple.

While other pericopes have dealt with faithfulness in personal situations, whether it be in matters of life and death, or for all of life's daily needs, or for engaging in God's mission, etc., this pericope deals with particular reasons to remain tenacious in nationally/internationally turbulent times (the magnitude of the catastrophes have reached worldwide scope here): the Father's providence, the Spirit's power, and the Son's promise. The focus of the sermon might profitably be upon these reasons, effectively a Trinitarian program of aid for the disciple.

---

39. Geddert, *Watchwords*, 106.

40. Keep an eye, though, on the pericopes ahead: the faithfulness modeled by Jesus in Mark 14–15 will serve as the paradigm for the disciple; one would not want to duplicate any of those specific facets of faithfulness in the exposition of this pericope. Those aspects of faithfulness can be addressed when one encounters them later.

POSSIBLE PREACHING OUTLINES FOR PERICOPE 20[41]

I. CALAMITY: Always facing the disciple

　　The tumults of the world: 13:5–13, 21–22

　　Perhaps even *the* last sign: 13:14–20

　　Move-to-Relevance: The tumults we might face, nationally or internationally

II. INSTABILITY (wrong response to calamity): Swayed by every rough wind

　　Move-to-Relevance: Our "normal" reactions to these tumults

III. TENACITY (right response to calamity): *Be Steadfast in Faithfulness!*

　　Specifics on how this may be put into practice in life today

IV. SECURITY: Why the disciple can be tenacious in faithfulness

　　The providence of God: 13:19–20

　　The power of the Spirit: 13:11

　　The promise of the Son's return and the disciple's gathering to him: 13:27

　　Move-to-Relevance: God's providence, the Spirit's power, and Son's promise to return for us

The outline above may be adapted for a problem–solution–application approach:

I. PROBLEM: Disciples always encounter difficulties and dangers as they follow Jesus

　　The tumults of the world: 13:5–13, 21–22

　　Perhaps even *the* last sign: 13:14–20

　　Move-to-Relevance: The tumults we might face, nationally or internationally

II. SOLUTION: God's providence, power, and promise help the disciple face those tough times

　　The providence of God: 13:19–20

　　The power of the Spirit: 13:11

　　The promise of the Son's return and the disciple's gathering to him: 13:27

　　Move-to-Relevance: God's providence, the Spirit's power, and the Son's promise to return for us

III. APPLICATION: *Be Steadfast in Faithfulness!*

　　The wrong application: swayed, deceived, shipwrecked

　　Specifics on how this may be put into practice; how to depend upon God's providence, power, and promise

41. As has oft been mentioned, the outlines provided in this commentary are merely suggestions. Modifications are certainly possible. For instance, I and II in the first outline may be combined into a single point; the ordering of points may be shifted, perhaps with "Security" showing up ahead of the homiletical imperative ("Tenacity"); etc. Outlines and arrangements (not to mention style and support material and other rhetorical stratagems) are matters for the preacher to work out, depending upon the Spirit, being keenly aware of the audience, and being sensitive to the text and the preaching event.

PERICOPE 21

Extravagant Sacrifice

Mark 14:1–11

[Anointing of Jesus]

REVIEW, SUMMARY, PREVIEW

Review of Pericope 20: Mark 13:1–37 calls upon the disciple to persevere faithfully in times of calamity, because of the assurances of God's providence, the Holy Spirit's power, and the promise of the Son's ultimate return and the gathering of believers to him.

Summary of Pericope 21: Mark 14:1–11 contrasts an unnamed woman playing a cameo role, with male disciples grumbling, and another male (and named) disciple betraying Jesus. Jesus commendation of the woman's profuse, pure, and precious sacrifice makes it praiseworthy, and renders her a paragon of discipleship. The theological focus is on the necessity for disciples to comprehend and accept Jesus' suffering mission—something the woman apparently did—and for them to respond to it with extravagant sacrifice.

Preview of Pericope 22: The next pericope (14:12–52) teaches that the disciple's faithfulness—following Jesus' model—involves confidence in God's sovereignty and submission to his will, and prayerful dependence upon the Holy Spirit, rather than the flesh.

21   Mark 14:1–11

THEOLOGICAL FOCUS OF PERICOPE 21

21   Disciples, accepting the suffering mission of Jesus, are willing to give their all to him, a sacrifice that is profuse, pure, precious, and praiseworthy (14:1–11).

21.1	Disciples are willing to give their all to him, a sacrifice that is profuse, pure, and precious.
21.2	Disciples accept the suffering mission of Jesus.
21.3	Disciples make sacrifices for Jesus that are praiseworthy.

OVERVIEW

MARK 12:41–44 AND 14:1–11 form inclusios for the extended Mark 13 didactic discourse. Both these bookends deal with women, money, and the "poor." Both the unnamed and utterly silent female protagonists in each episode sacrifice lavishly, in contrast to those who gave out of their abundance, or to those who complained foolishly and gave not at all. One of the two women gives her "whole life," the other anoints Jesus for burial. Both accounts contain the phrase ἀμὴν λέγω ὑμῖν (*amēn legō hymin*, "truly I say to you," 12:43; 14:9), and both women, with their "wasted" gifts of devotion, are paradigms of true disciples. Mark is *doing* something with these narratives: he wants readers to follow the examples of those two worthy women.

21   Mark 14:1–11

THEOLOGICAL FOCUS 21

21 Disciples, accepting the suffering mission of Jesus, are willing to give their all to him, a sacrifice that is profuse, pure, precious, and praiseworthy (14:1–11).

21.1	Disciples are willing to give their all to him, a sacrifice that is profuse, pure, and precious.
21.2	Disciples accept the suffering mission of Jesus.
21.3	Disciples make sacrifices for Jesus that are praiseworthy.

Section Summary 21: This fifth Markan "sandwich" story contrasts an unnamed woman, playing a cameo role in the inner story, with male disciples grumbling (inner story) and another male (and named) disciple betraying Jesus in the outer story. Jesus' commendation of her profuse, pure, and precious sacrifice makes it praiseworthy, and renders her a paragon of discipleship. The theological point is the necessity for disciples to comprehend and accept Jesus' suffering mission—something the woman did—and to respond to it with extravagant sacrifice.

TRANSLATION 21

14:1   *Now the Passover and the Feast of Unleavened Bread were after two [more] days. And the chief priests and the scribes were seeking how to arrest Him by cunning, and kill Him,*

14:2   *for they were saying, "Not during the Feast, lest there be a riot of the people."*

14:3   *And He was in Bethany in the house of Simon the leper. While He was reclining [at the table], a woman came, having an alabaster jar of very expensive ointment of pure nard. Breaking the alabaster jar, she poured [it] over His head.*

14:4   *But some were indignantly [saying] among themselves, "Why has this waste of ointment taken place?*

14:5   *For this ointment could have been be sold for over three hundred denarii, and given to the poor." And they were scolding her.*

14:6   *But Jesus said, "Leave her. Why are you causing her trouble? A good deed she has done to Me.*

14:7   *For you always have the poor with you, and whenever you wish you can do good to them; but you do not have Me always.*

14:8   *What she had, she did. She anointed My body beforehand for the burial.*

14:9   *Truly I say to you, wherever the gospel is preached in the whole world, what she has done will also be spoken of in memory of her."*

14:10   *And Judas Iscariot, who was one of the Twelve, went away to the chief priests in order to give Him over to them.*

14:11   *When they heard, they were glad, and promised to give him money. And he was seeking how to give Him over at an opportune moment.*

NOTES 21

This pericope is the fifth of the classic Markan "sandwich" stories (outer story: 14:1–2 and 14:10–11; inner story: 14:3–9).[1] As with most of these literary structures, Jesus is the only character common to both stories. The whole pericope is bounded by ζητέω (*zēteō*, "seek") in 14:1, 11, which frequently carries in Mark a negative connotation (see 3:32 with 21; also 8:11, 12; 11:18; 12:12; 14:55; and perhaps 16:6, as well).

The contrasts between the two stories, inner and outer, are as follows:

MARK 14:1–2, 10–11	MARK 14:3–9
Judas, a named man, one of the Twelve	An unnamed woman
In Jerusalem; temple precincts	In Bethany; home of Simon, a leper
Money: unspecified sum promised	Money: worth more than 300 denarii
Priests rejoice and reward Judas	Some indignant and censorious
Judas gives up Jesus for money	Woman gives up "money" for Jesus
Betrayed unto death	Anointed unto burial
Remembered as betrayer	Remembered with the gospel

21.1   Disciples are willing to give their all to him, a sacrifice that is profuse, pure, and precious.[2]

The confrontation between Jesus and the religious leaders is now coming to a zenith as Act III progresses towards the Passion account. In the wake of Jesus' wildly popular and loudly acclaimed entry into Jerusalem, and considering the enthusiastic support he had been generating (11:18, 32; 12:12, 37), a riot is a distinct possibility if repressive

---

1. See Shepherd, *Markan Sandwich Stories*, 241–66, for details on this Markan "sandwich." This story is found in all the four Gospels, howbeit with variations that further the discrete theological thrusts of the individual narrators.

2. The "disciple" in the story is, of course, the woman. All who follow Jesus "on the way" are urged to be like her.

action is taken against this reputable rabbi. The religious leadership, probably somewhere in the temple precincts, are therefore shrewdly cautious (14:1–2).

Jesus, on the other hand, is still based in Bethany, emphasizing his separation from the city and its doomed temple apparatus. Indeed, he seems to have deliberately made his way to the house of one banned from the temple—a leper (1:40–44).[3] The rejected "stone" goes to the house of another rejected one. Perhaps this is indicative of the new community being created; the cornerstone has been put into place, and the new temple is coming into being.

Suddenly, the cozy meal is interrupted (14:3). It appears the woman is not an invitee: she arrives as the guests are already well into the meal. And she proceeds to do something unexpected and unconventional toward someone who is not her guest, in a place that is not her house—this is no ordinary gesture. It is no ordinary gift either, and Mark takes pains to describe its character with four genitives—jar of ointment, of nard, of purity, of value (14:3)—an eloquent and emphatic assertion of its substantiality and the incredible magnitude of its value. Later (14:5) one finds it is worth more than 300 denarii. Matthew 20:1–15 informs us that a denarius is the daily wage of the average laborer; by that standard, this woman's ointment was worth a year's wages—an astounding sacrifice. In Mark 6:37, 200 denarii was seen to be adequate to feed five thousand. No wonder the onlookers here in Mark 14 call this anointing ἀπώλεια (*apōleia*, "destruction/ruin/annihilation"). Considering that for a woman this might have been her entire nest egg for the future, her act is all the more striking. The absolute irrevocability of her donation is stressed in the shattering of the alabaster jar (14:3), a detail only Mark notes among the four evangelists.[4] Again the immensity of the woman's sacrifice and devotion is underscored: this is a gift that is profuse (the entire jar), pure (of high quality nard), and precious (worth a year's income).

21.2   Disciples accept the suffering mission of Jesus.

"Some," however, find the woman's act objectionable and protest indignantly (14:4)—including, in all likelihood, Jesus' disciples, who have been accompanying him on his journey to Jerusalem. The mention of Judas, "one of the Twelve," slipping off to the chief priests (14:10) after Jesus' rebuke (14:6–9) seems to bear out this possibility.

The statement from Jesus about the poor (14:7) is not permission to neglect the needs of this group, but rather an expression of priority. It is not a question of compassion but of opportunity, which came with the comprehension of Jesus' soon-approaching death (see below). Jesus himself has amply demonstrated his concern for the poor in this Gospel: in 10:21 he advised the rich man to give all he had to the poor; and in 12:44 he made a poor widow a model of discipleship. There can be no doubt about Jesus' own concern for the penurious.

---

3. Heil, "Narrative Strategy," 93.

4. Gundry, *Mark*, 802, 813, believes that by breaking the flask and rendering it henceforth unusable, she demonstrated the totality of her sacrifice. Hooker, *Commentary on the Gospel*, 329, suggests a further symbolism: ointment jars used in burial anointings were often broken and left in the tomb.

On the other hand, in rabbinical literature, good deeds, as performed by the woman and labeled as such by Jesus, were considered more praiseworthy than almsgiving: while the former demanded immediate action and required personal engagement and concern, the latter could be delayed and accomplished at any other time (*t. Peʾah* 4.19; *b. Sukkah* 49b; also see Deut 15:11).[5]

Danker notes that in the Psalms πτωχός (*ptōchos*, "poor," Mark 14:5, 7) frequently denoted the helpless, righteous sufferer (Ps 22:24; 35:10; 41:1; 69:29, 32; 109:21 LXX). Interestingly, Psalm 22:1, 18 would be cited later in Mark 15:24, 34, and perhaps Psalm 69:29 in Mark 15:36. "Since the poor sufferer of the psalms is clearly associated with Jesus, who is also the object of repeated plots, it is not improbable that Mark, or the tradition he incorporates, would see a connection between the πτωχός of Ps 41 and Jesus." The woman's deed is therefore, in a sense, actually rendered to the "poor," i.e., the suffering Jesus. Psalm 41:8–10 reports the ultimate triumph of the "poor" sufferer using ἀνίστημι (*anistēmi*, "rise," 41:10 LXX). That verb echoes Jesus own "rising" (Mark 8:31; 9:9, 10, 31; 10:34). "The praise of the woman . . . is a statement of blessing for her response to the one poor man, par excellence, who is about to suffer."[6]

In any case, the essence of Jesus' response to the objections of the bystanders is that the woman has done a good deed, based on the fact that "you do not have Me always" (14:7). That comment strongly hints that that is something disciples need to be aware of: the suffering mission of Jesus and its imminent consummation. This point is clearly underscored in 14:8, for the woman had anointed Jesus' body ahead of time, *for his burial* (see below).

Surprising is the recognition by Jesus that the woman has done "what she had" (14:8). One would have expected him to give her kudos to her for doing "what she could," not for doing "what she had." While the phrase "what she had" may well be an idiomatic expression denoting "what she could," nevertheless, the use of "had" instead of "could do" is significant. The allusion here is to the last unnamed woman Mark reported on (12:41–44), who performed the same kind of action: that woman used no expensive ointment, but merely two copper coins; hers was not the magnificent gesture of a libation over the Messiah's head, but a tossing of coins into the greedy coffers of the temple. But remarkably, the phrase used of both is identical: each one gave "what(ever) she had" (ὅσα εἶχεν, *hosa eichen*, 12:44; ὃ ἔσχεν, *ho eschen*, 14:8). One poured, the other cast, but in either situation it was their life that was being poured or cast out—*whatever they had*. Theirs were both complete sacrifices—both had become disciples! Myers asks rhetorically:

> [W]hy should we consider the woman's action a paradigmatic discipleship story, given the absence of any "following" motif? The justification lies in the fact that *this* messianic anointing is preparation not for the inauguration of a triumphal reign, but burial (14:8). The woman, unlike the disciples, is not avoiding but rather "anticipating" [προέλαβεν, *proelaben*, "beforehand"] Jesus' "preparation for

---

5. Miller, "Woman Who Anoints," 226.

6. Danker, "Literary Unity," 468, 470.

death." . . . In this she has done "all she could," and demonstrated her ideological solidarity with the way of the cross.[7]

This woman, of all those gathered there, had understood Jesus' suffering mission and given "what she had" for it.[8] In Jesus' mind, this woman had grasped that "you do not always have Me" (14:7). In fact, he explicitly commends her for anointing his body for the *burial* (14:8).[9] His death is front and center in her mind; she understands more about the suffering mission of Jesus than anyone else. The religious leaders in the outer story are plotting to kill, and even those following Jesus apparently never come to grasp the next phase of Jesus' mission—his death. That his disciples never get it is clear from their bemused and self-enamored responses to Jesus' three Passion Predictions (8:31; 9:31; 10:33–34), not to mention their reaction to this woman's praiseworthy deed. Despite Jesus' explicit utterances, none of these male followers, who have been with Jesus for a considerable while, seem to have arrived at the conclusion or expressed the devotion that this woman has. She, on the other hand, understands exactly what Jesus is about. "It is not the self-righteous charity of the (presumably male) onlookers which will be remembered, but the rash extravagance of an unnamed woman whose devotion to Jesus leaves no room for pious calculation."[10] In fact, her anonymity, in contrast to her being named in John's Gospel, is deliberate in this narrative. A named male disciple betrays ("gives over," 14:10–11) Jesus to death, getting money in exchange. This unnamed female "disciple" anoints Jesus for death, giving up "money." The contrast could not be more vivid between disciple and non-disciple. "[T]he woman, who appears in just one sentence of the story, contrasts sharply with the twelve. Not first of all because she is a woman and alone, but mainly because she understands Jesus and acts accordingly while the twelve men remain obstinately unaware of what is going to happen to him. She is similar to the blind seer Bartimaeus, who also saw what remained hidden to the others."[11]

21.3   *Disciples make sacrifices for Jesus that are praiseworthy.*

The formula "truly I say to you" (14:9) heralds a serious declaration of praiseworthiness —a great commendation, indeed, from Jesus, of an unnamed woman who comes and goes in the space of one verse, without even once opening her mouth! No other action or word in the Gospel achieves this much credit. Chrysostom put it well: "[A]like Persians and Indians, Scythians and Thracians, Sarmatians and the race of the Moors,

---

7. Myers, *Binding the Strong Man*, 359.

8. Collins observes that another reason to support the woman's gesture as an anointing of Jesus as king or messiah is that, following the pericope of the anointing, two disciples are sent to find a room for the Passover celebration (14:12–16). The episode evokes 1 Sam 10:1–8, with the anointing of Saul, and the presence of two disciples who help him (Collins, *Mark*, 642n202).

9. It is worth noting that her action of anointing may be related to Jesus being the anointed One, Christ (though the Greek word describing her action in 14:8 is not related to Χριστός, *Christos*); her recognition of Jesus' burial (also 14:8) signifies that she comprehended the mission of this anointed One, Christ.

10. France, *Gospel of Mark*, 549–50.

11. van Iersel, *Mark*, 417.

and they that dwell in the British Isles, celebrate that which was done secretly in a house by a woman that had been a sinner" (*Hom. Matt.* 80.2).[12] She would be spoken of, but strikingly, she says not a word in this story. Rather, the woman opens her heart in a wordlessly eloquent gesture of extravagant sacrifice. And, anonymous and silent, it is her good deed that would be part of the universal good news, for this is what the gospel, in its larger sense means: to discern, accept, and be faithful to Jesus' mission, and to give one's all for it. She had understood, she had responded, she had given her all.

Judas' membership in the Twelve, emphasized here by Mark (14:10), underlines the magnitude of his betrayal, giving even more brilliance to the action of the one-scene, one-verse, no-word woman. The mention of money brings into stark contrast the woman's willingness to pour out a year's worth of wages with Judas' bartering the life of his Master for a paltry sum. That the latter act of treachery is committed by a named disciple who has followed Jesus "on the way" is shocking. The Twelve, in 3:13, had been summoned on a mountain top and ἀπῆλθον πρὸς αὐτόν (*apelthon pros auton*, "they came away to Him"). Here, in 14:10, one of these Twelve treacherously defects and ἀπῆλθεν πρὸς τοὺς ἀρχιερεῖς (*apelthen pros tous archiereis*, "went away to the chief priests") to betray the One who had called him.[13]

SERMON FOCUS AND OUTLINES

THEOLOGICAL FOCUS OF PERICOPE 21 FOR PREACHING

21 Accepting the suffering mission of Jesus, disciples make sacrifices that are profuse, pure, precious, and praiseworthy (14:1–11).

The four elements of the woman's incredible sacrifice, as emphasized by Mark, together make the centerpiece of a sermon on this pericope. Once again, it is important to underscore the basis for this sacrifice: the acceptance of Jesus' suffering mission. The woman in this account understands what Jesus is about and responds with a remarkable act of devotion. Those who seek to follow Jesus must do so too, emulating this paragon of discipleship. It will be up to the preacher to determine what acts of sacrifice might be called for: drastic changes in life, a sizeable financial sacrifice (after all that is what the woman gives—an "outrageous" sum of money) . . .[14] In any case, this is a call for *extravagant* sacrifice—nothing less!

Since the contrast between the woman and her male counterparts is a significant part of the story, the preacher might consider making one of the points in the sermon

---

12. Ephrem the Syrian (ca. 306–373) and Gregory the Great (ca. 540–604) were among the first church leaders to identify the woman of 14:1–11 as Mary Magdalene. It is her anonymity in Mark, however, that makes her a greater contrast to the nefarious characters (one of them named: Judas) in the outer story.

13. Judas had sought an opportune time to betray (14:11); the woman, too, found an opportune time, but to do good (14:7; notice πάντοτε, *pantote*, "always," and οὐ πάντοτε, *ou pantote*, "not always"; i.e., there is an opportune moment to serve Jesus).

14. In a sermon preached on this pericope in Dallas Theological Seminary's Chafer Chapel, this author, a celibate, challenged young seminarians to consider whether remaining single for life, sacrificing unto Christ, might be a gift God had given them.

a recap of the failure of the Twelve to accept Jesus suffering mission, focusing upon their ridiculous and vainglorious responses to his three Passion Predictions (8:31; 9:31; 10:33–34).

POSSIBLE PREACHING OUTLINES FOR PERICOPE 21

I.   WOMAN: What she did and understood
    The woman's sacrifice: profuse, pure, precious (14:1–5)
    The woman's comprehension of Jesus' suffering mission (14:6–8)

II. DISCIPLES: What they did
    The disciples' response to the Passion Predictions: 8:31–34; 9:31–34; 10:32–40
    The disciples' incomprehension of Jesus' suffering mission

III. WE: What we must do: *Sacrifice extravagantly: profuse, pure, precious, praiseworthy!*
    Jesus' commendation: 14:9
    Specific ideas for the congregation on how this might be put into practice

An alternate suggestion:

I.   WHAT? The woman's extravagant sacrifice
    The woman's sacrifice: profuse, pure, precious (14:1–5)
    Contrast with the betrayal by a male disciple: 14:1–2, 10–11

II. WHY? The reason for her extravagant sacrifice
    The woman's comprehension of Jesus' suffering mission (14:6–8)
    Contrast: the disciples' incomprehension even after the Passion Predictions: 8:31–34; 9:31–34; 10:32–40

III. HOW? Our response: *Sacrifice extravagantly: profuse, pure, precious, praiseworthy!*
    Jesus' commendation: 14:9
    Specific ideas for the congregation on how this might be put into practice

PERICOPE 22

Faithfulness or Fleshiness?

Mark 14:12–52

[Last Supper; Gethsemane; Jesus' Arrest; Naked Young Man]

REVIEW, SUMMARY, PREVIEW

Review of Pericope 21: Mark 14:1–11 addresses the necessity of comprehending and accepting Jesus' suffering mission, and responding with extravagant sacrifice.

Summary of Pericope 22: Mark 14:12–52 deals with the disciple's faithfulness in the "evening" and "midnight" watches. Faithfulness in discipleship involves submission to God's sovereignty and his will, and prayerful dependence upon the Holy Spirit (rather than the flesh) to survive the critical periods of testing/temptation. Such faithfulness is modeled after the example of Jesus himself. Also depicted is the consequence of failure to be faithful.

Preview of Pericope 23: The next pericope (14:53–72) contrasts the self-denial of Jesus and the denial of Jesus by Peter in their respective trials, instructing the disciple that faithfulness involves self-denial without concern for self-preservation, even in times of danger, even at risk to life and limb.

22   Mark 14:12–52

THEOLOGICAL FOCUS OF PERICOPE 22

22   Faithfulness in discipleship involves confidence in God's sovereign will and prayerful dependence upon the Holy Spirit (not the flesh), as the disciple emulates Jesus, the Son, lest he or she be shamefully disqualified from God's service (14:12–52).

22.1 The faithfulness of the disciple is grounded in God's sovereign control of all that transpires, rather than in misplaced confidence in oneself (14:12–31).

22.2 Faithfulness in discipleship involves submission to the Father's will and prayerful dependence upon the Holy Spirit (instead of the flesh), emulating the model of Jesus, the Son (14:32–42).

22.3 Faithlessness in discipleship is shameful (14:43–52).

OVERVIEW

THE LAST PARABLE OF Mark 13 (in Pericope 20) is critical to the understanding of the Evangelist's account of Jesus' Passion. The parallels between 13:33–37 and 14:32–42 are remarkable enough to convince one of their narrative intentionality.

- Both have the themes of "being alert-coming-finding-sleeping" (13:33–37; and 14:34, 37, 38, 39, 40, 41).

- Both contain mentions of "hour" (13:32; and 14:34, 37, 41).

- Time stamps are found in both (see below).

- The threefold injunction to be alert (γρηγορέω, *grēgoreō*, in 13:34, 35, 37 is paralleled by the threefold failure of the disciples to be alert (14:37, 40, 41); the verb is found in the Gospel only in these two sets of texts.

Indeed, Geddert asserts that "no other texts in Mark can be paralleled so closely with either of these texts as these can with each other."[1] As will be shown, the narrator of this Gospel employs the Passion account to portray negative and positive examples of "being alert"—i.e., being faithful to Jesus' mission.

Act I of Mark's Gospel (1:1—8:21) dealt with *discernment* of Jesus' person, and Act II (8:22—10:52) dealt with *acceptance* of Jesus' fateful mission—suffering before glory. Unfortunately, the disciples have been anything but discerning or accepting—the key word has been βλέπω (*blepō*, "to watch"); instead, they have been dull and hardhearted. However, with the commencement of the Passion accounts in Act III, the concern is no longer for discernment or acceptance, but for *faithfulness*, going through Jesus' mission with him, willing to suffer: the key word now is γρηγορέω (*grēgoreō*, "to be alert," i.e., to be steadfast and faithful). Faithful discipleship is what Jesus-followers are called to undertake. The Twelve fail in this final act as well, with only the positive model of Jesus to exemplify what this faithfulness looks like. The downfall of the disciples is also given a root cause in this pericope—the weakness of the flesh (14:38).

As was noted under Mark 13, the parable of the doorkeeper is not a call to wait or watch for the master's arrival; rather, it is an exhortation to be alert on the master's behalf as long as he is away. Faithfulness, the parable asserts, is not a one-time event, but a long-term undertaking of obedience, until the master returns.[2] In 13:35, Jesus declared, "Therefore, be on the alert, for you do not know when the lord of the house is

---

1. Geddert, *Watchwords*, 91.

2. Ibid., 104–5.

coming—whether in the evening or midnight or at cockcrow or early in the morning." Those time stamps—evening, midnight, cockcrow, and early morning—are significant, for the same four-watch schema shows up in the Passion account[3]:

- *Evening:* 14:17 (Lord's Supper)

- *Midnight:* 14:37–41 (Gethsemane and Jesus' arrest)[4]

- *Cockcrow:* 14:68, 72 (Jesus' trial and Peter's denial)

- *Early morning:* 15:1 (the crucifixion complex)[5]

While Mark in the rest of the Gospel has shown hardly any interest in time sequences, quite suddenly, after 14:17, the stopwatch is turned on and he keeps it running all the way until Jesus is buried. The narrator's goal is to portray, in each of the four watches, Jesus as the positive example of faithfulness to counter the disciples' negative ones. Jesus succeeds where the disciples fail, and thus "the overall teaching on discipleship which emerges provides a well-rounded definition of what it means to respond appropriately to the temptations and persecutions that post-resurrection believers . . . would face as they awaited their absent master."[6] But the Twelve fail: the predictions of betrayal by Judas (14:18–21), of desertion by the Twelve (14:26–28), and of denial by Peter (14:29–31) are fulfilled precisely in 14:43–49; 14:50–52; and 14:66–72, respectively. Throughout, Jesus is the "foil," the positive model for the negative portrayal of the disciples. Thus, two themes thus are emphasized in parallel: the failure of the disciples and the faithfulness of Jesus.

22.1 Mark 14:12–31

THEOLOGICAL FOCUS 22.1

22.1 The faithfulness of the disciple is grounded in God's sovereign control of all that transpires, rather than in misplaced confidence in oneself (14:12–31).

---

3. See Shepherd, *Markan Sandwich Stories*, 270–71.

4. While there is no explicit mention of "midnight," Jesus refers to "one hour" having passed in 14:37. He "comes" back three times to the disciples (14:37, 40, 41), implying the passage of three hours, and this after the evening watch (ending at 9:00 pm) noted in 14:17. That effectively depicts Jesus' arrest as occurring at midnight. (Interestingly, the specific word "hour" also occurs three times in this section: 14:35, 37, and 41—not all with the same connotation, of course.) At the end of those three hours would be the unmentioned *midnight* at which time the betrayal occurs (14:41, the hour "comes;" and 14:45 where Judas "comes"). The omission of an explicit label of "midnight" might be deliberate, so that the reader realizes that the whole sequence of events from Gethsemane to the abandonment of the disciples (14:32–52) is included in that "hour" (see Geddert, *Watchwords*, 133).

5. Remarkably, the motif of "coming" (ἔρχομαι, *erchomai*; borrowed from 13:35, 36) is located suggestively in each of the four watches: *evening*, 14:17; *midnight*, 14:37, 40, 41, 45; *cockcrow*, 14:66; the *early* watch has no mention of "coming," but the only other use of the verb in Mark 14 occurs in 14:62—that could conceivably be Jesus' victorious arrival on another, more glorious "morning." This would also make sense in light of the prediction of the Parousia (Jesus' Second Advent) in 13:35–37, where the ἔρχομαι motif is introduced.

6. Geddert, *Watchwords*, 95.

Section Summary 22.1: The Last Supper episode marks out what constitutes the faithfulness of the disciple in the "evening" watch: trust in God's sovereign control to determine how events transpire. There is nothing that is outside of his divine plan and purpose. Rather than misplaced confidence in themselves, disciples in dire circumstances place their complete trust in God's governance of all that happens.

TRANSLATION 22.1

14:12   *And on the first day of the Feast of Unleavened Bread, when the Passover lamb was sacrificed, His disciples said to Him, "Where do you want [us] to go away and prepare, that You may eat the Passover lamb?"*

14:13   *And He sent two of His disciples and said to them, "Go into the city, and a man carrying a jar of water will meet you. Follow him,*

14:14   *and wherever he goes in, tell the owner of the house, 'The Teacher says, "Where is My guest room where I may eat the Passover lamb with My disciples?"'*

14:15   *And he himself will show you a large room upstairs, furnished, prepared; and there prepare for us."*

14:16   *And the disciples went out and came to the city and found [it] just as He had told them, and they prepared the Passover lamb.*

14:17   *And when it was evening, He came with the Twelve.*

14:18   *And as they were reclining [at the table] and eating, Jesus said, "Truly I say to you that one of you will betray Me—one who is eating with Me."*

14:19   *They began to be distressed and to say to Him one by one, "Surely not I?"*

14:20   *And He said to them, "One of the Twelve, one who dips with Me in the bowl.*

14:21   *For the Son of Man goes just as it is written about Him, but woe to that man through whom the Son of Man is betrayed! [It would have been] good for him, if that man had not been born."*

14:22   *And while they were eating, He took bread, blessed, broke, and gave them, and said, "Take, this is My body."*

14:23   *And taking the cup [and] giving thanks, He gave them, and they all drank from it.*

14:24   *And He said to them, "This is My blood of the covenant, which is poured out for many.*

14:25   *Truly I say to you, never again will I drink of the fruit of the vine until that day when I drink it new in the kingdom of God."*

14:26   *And after singing a hymn, they went out to the Mount of Olives.*

14:27   *And Jesus said to them, "You will all fall away, for it is written, 'I will strike the shepherd, and the sheep will be scattered.'*

14:28   *But after I have been raised, I will go ahead of you to Galilee."*

14:29   *But Peter said to Him, "Even if they all fall away, yet I [will] not."*

14:30   *And Jesus said to him, "Truly I say to you that today—this very night—before a cock crows twice, you will deny Me thrice."*

> 14:31 *But he kept saying emphatically, "Even if I must die together with You, I will never deny You!" And they were all also saying the same thing.*

NOTES 22.1

22.1   The faithfulness of the disciple is grounded in God's sovereign control of all that transpires, rather than in misplaced confidence in oneself.

That it was women who usually carried water in a pitcher or jar (men usually used skins) makes this rendezvous with a man carrying a jar remarkable (14:13), not to mention the absence of even a murmur of protest from that vessel-bearing individual about the strange goings-on. The text informs us that it is the man who will meet the disciples (14:13), not vice versa; apparently he would be on the lookout for them. Neither does the owner of the house demur at the odd request from the disciples and their "Teacher." He even recognizes that title, and immediately accedes to the demand for "My guest room" (14:14–16). There is a distinct sense in which all of this seems scripted!

The Last Supper dialogue begins and ends with ἀμὴν (*amēn*, "amen," "truly") sayings (14:18, 25).[7] Both of these make a confident assertion about the future; Jesus seems to know exactly what is going to happen and how—God's control over the events is almost tangible. The first statement anticipates the betrayal that will lead to the culmination of Jesus' suffering mission. The second looks forward to the eschaton, to a time when all things are "new" in the consummated kingdom of God. "When Jesus drinks wine again it will be in a situation where God's kingship is more fully realized than was yet in evidence at that Passover meal before Jesus' death"—a contrast between the "cup of death" (14:24) and the "cup of glory" (14:25), a contrast that has permeated this Gospel throughout. The former will come first. Discipleship, as this Gospel has been wont to emphasize, is the way to glory . . . through suffering.[8]

While the circumstances are dire, and the end seems nigh, Mark's account, permeated with these assertions of divine control, points disciples to the source of their

---

7. Discussions addressing the dating of the Passover meal are plentiful in other commentaries (for instance, France, *Gospel of Mark*, 548–49, 559–64; Stein, *Mark*, 642–44; etc.). In any case, the precise fixation of the day of the Last Supper does not particularly contribute to the theological focus of the pericope for preaching purposes. This author would lean towards Stein's understanding of this meal as a Passover meal, for the following reasons: it is eaten within Jerusalem (without returning to Bethany); the posture of reclining, appropriate for the Passover banquet meal (*m. Pesah.* 10.1); the celebration of the meal at night (Mark 14:17; Exod 12:8; *Jub.* 49.1–2, 12); the mention of the "fruit of the vine" as in the Passover liturgy; the presence of the customary interpretation of the significance of the various elements of the meal; the consumption of wine, part of Passover celebration (*m. Pesah.* 10.1); its conclusion with a hymn, standard procedure for the Passover meal that ended with the Hallel Psalms (Pss 113–18); the rest of the night spent in "greater" Jerusalem (in Gethsemane); etc. The account in Mark 14 also reads like a clandestine operation with a safehouse setting—the congregants celebrating "as those in flight" (Exod 12:11) (Myers, *Binding the Strong Man*, 364). Striking, however, is the omission of traditional elements of the Passover meal—the anamnesis of the exodus from Egypt and the divine provision of a lamb as a substitute. Instead, rather odd pronouncements on the significance of the meal are made. Something very new is happening here.

8. France, *Gospel of Mark*, 571–72. The Messianic banquet is in view in Isa 25:6–9; Luke 13:28–30; Rev 19:9; see also *1 En.* 62.13–14; *2 Bar.* 29.5–8; 1QSa 2.11–22.

confidence and trust. Just as Jesus' trust in the Father is evident in the narrative, so also must the followers of Jesus rely upon the Father. Later, this sense of inevitability under God's sovereign hand becomes even more palpable. The Son of Man will "go" (i.e., go to the Father/die) "just as it is written" (14:21); and the disciples will all fall away, also "as it is written" (14:27; also see 14:49). The employment of the preposition διά (*dia*, "through," 14:21), rather than ὑπό (*hypo*, "by"), to denote the agency of Judas indicates that a divine plan is operating "through" him.[9] Therefore, undergirding the entire account is a deep conviction of God's control: all things happen as they have been written or prophesied about; everything is happening according to script(ure) (14:21, 27, 49). Despite the somber tone of the evening and the approach of ominous, dark clouds on the horizon, the disciple must remain confident in God's sovereignty—an important basis for the disciple's faithfulness to Jesus in the "evening" watch.

In response to Jesus' prediction of 14:18 that one of the Twelve will betray him,[10] the disciples are bold in their declarations; one notes a tone of (over)confident assertion in the disciples' response, "Surely not I?" (14:19). Alas, this braggadocio is just that—a façade; they will *all* fall away soon. Little do they realize that their self-confidence will amount to nothing. The faithful disciple in the "evening," on the other hand, places confidence in the only one worthy of that trust—God who is in sovereign control. Indeed, even in Jesus' assurance of the restoration of these failing disciples (14:27–28) there is on display the sovereign work of God.

After Jesus predicts the falling away of all of the disciples (14:27), Peter emits a flash of swaggering bluster—he, of all the others, will never fall away, he declares (14:29)![11] Jesus puts him in his place: instead of denying *themselves*, as he has exhorted them to do (8:34), they (Peter, in particular) will deny *Jesus* (14:30). Brady's interpretive paraphrase makes good sense: "This very night, before a cock has raised its voice twice to witness its wakefulness to approaching dawn, you Peter will raise your voice not merely twice but three times, and not to witness to your wakefulness, but to witness to the wakelessness of your allegiance to me."[12] This is a failure of alertness (γρηγορέω, "be alert," resounds in 13:34, 35, 37 and 14:37, 40, 41): Peter will prove unfaithful. Of course, the disciple still does not believe it, responding with a vigorous denial, which is echoed by his pretentious compatriots (14:31). Their trust is not in God, but in their own selves and in their own ability to remain faithful; that trust will prove to be grossly misplaced. In the next

---

9. France, *Gospel of Mark*, 567.

10. The formality of Jesus' prophecy of betrayal, prefaced by "truly I say to you" (14:18), underlines the dreadfulness of this act of treachery. In addition, the phrase ὁ ἐσθίων μετ᾽ἐμοῦ (*ho esthiōn met emou*, "one who is eating with Me") reflects Ps 41:9 (ὁ ἐσθίων ἄρτους μου, *ho esthiōn artous mou*, "one who is eating My bread"), while the repeated μετ᾽ἐμοῦ (*met emou*, "with Me") of Mark 14:18, 20 would remind the reader of 3:14, where Jesus had appointed the disciples to be μετ᾽ αὐτοῦ (*met autou*, "with Him").

11. The verb σκανδαλίζω (*skandalizō*, "fall away") is appropriately used here in 14:27: earlier, in 4:17, Jesus had warned the disciples about falling away in the face of affliction and persecution. That warning, unfortunately, was not heeded then, neither is its reiteration taken seriously now by the disciples. In a matter of a few hours, they would all fall away (14:50).

12. Brady, "Alarm to Peter," 55.

episode, Jesus teaches his disciples that this source of self-confidence, the flesh, has to be negated; instead, they ought to rely on the Spirit.

Jesus' words of institution of the Last Supper (14:22–25) continue to reverberate with a sense of inevitability regarding what is about to transpire. In a sense, embedded in the context of the Passover meal, his utterances almost constitute another Passion Prediction, albeit one that is more symbolic. There is an overt messianic claim in Jesus' declaration in 14:22 that the bread is his body.[13] And "the blood of the covenant" (14:24) alludes to Exodus 24:8, Moses' institution of the original covenant at Mt. Sinai that formalized the creation of a people of God.[14] Bread and cup are partaken of by the Twelve; as these words of institution depict, the disciples are to participate in the death of Jesus. The result of the messianic work of substitutionary atonement and the new covenant established by Jesus is that a new community of disciples is inaugurated. Of all this Jesus is well aware before it happens. Indeed, that under the Messiah a *new* covenant will consummate the formation of a *new* people of God has already been written about (Jer 31:31–34). God is completely in charge here, even in the face of approaching perfidy by Judas, and the falling away and denial by the remaining disciples.

22.2   Mark 14:32–42

> **THEOLOGICAL FOCUS 22.2**
>
> 22.2   Faithfulness in discipleship involves submission to the Father's will and a prayerful dependence upon the Holy Spirit (instead of the flesh), emulating the model of Jesus, the Son (14:32–42).

Section Summary 22.2: The events in Gethsemane mark out what it means to be faithful in the "midnight" watch. Emulating Jesus' model of faithfulness is critical:

---

13. In true Passover meal fashion, Jesus breaks the unleavened bread; the broken piece is the *afikoman* (אֲפִיקוֹמָן; from ἀφικόμενος, *afikomenos*, "he who comes"). While the antecedents of this particular ritual are unclear, the *afikoman* in Jewish tradition possibly represented the Messiah himself—still true of Sephardic and Ashkenazi Seder rituals. See Nybroten, "Possible Vestiges," 106, 126n6. As Jesus distributed this symbolic element of the Messiah, he also identified it with his "body"—thus Jesus *is* the Messiah. Such an understanding of Jesus and what he was doing at the Last Supper was prevalent in the early church. Melito, the second-century bishop of Sardis, in his paschal homily, specifically called Jesus the ἀφικόμενος (*Peri Pascha* 66, 86). This messianic significance of bread-breaking might also have been what prompted the instant recognition of Jesus by the disciples at Emmaus at the precise moment he is said to have given them the broken bread (Luke 24:30–31): perhaps he said the same words "This is my body" (= "This is I"). That might also explain why early Christian communal meals were described as the "breaking of bread" (Acts 2:42, 46; 20:7), and why Paul adds the phrase "until he comes" to his recapitulation of the Lord's Supper (1 Cor 11:24, 26). Also see Carmichael, "David Daube," 59–60; and Evans, *Mark*, 390–91.

14. The "pouring out" and "for many" (ὑπὲρ πολλῶν, *hyper pollōn*) reflects Isa 53:11–12 (with πολλοῖς, πολλούς, πολλῶν [*pollois, pollous, pollōn*] occurring in the LXX). Note, as well, "poured out his life to death" in Isa 53:12 MT; also see Mark 10:45. For the use of "pour out" (ἐκχέω, *encheō*) pertaining to blood and sacrifices, see Lev 4:7, 18, 25, 30, 34; etc. The irony of "blood" as the binder for covenanted people is poignant: blood, "the ultimate pollution [in the Jewish scheme of cleanness], serves as the very source of purity for Jesus' followers" (Neyrey, "Idea of Purity," 115).

submission to the Father's will and prayerful dependence upon the Holy Spirit, instead of upon oneself (one's flesh), as Jesus instructs the disciples.

TRANSLATION 22.2

14:32   *And they came to a place named Gethsemane, and He said to His disciples, "Sit here while I pray."*

14:33   *And He took along Peter and James and John with Him, and began to be distressed and anxious.*

14:34   *And He said to them, "My soul is deeply grieved to [the point of] death; remain here and be alert."*

14:35   *And going beyond a little, He fell to the ground and was praying that if it were possible, the hour may pass away from Him.*

14:36   *And He was saying, "Abba! Father! All things are possible for You. Remove this cup from Me; but not what I will, but what You [will]."*

14:37   *And He came and found them sleeping, and He said to Peter, "Simon, are you sleeping? Are you not strong enough to be alert for one hour?*

14:38   *Be alert and pray that you may not come into temptation; the Spirit is willing, but the flesh is weak."*

14:39   *And again He went away and prayed, saying the same word.*

14:40   *And again He came and found them sleeping, for their eyes were heavy. And they did not know what to answer Him.*

14:41   *And He came the third time and said to them, "Are you still sleeping and resting? It is enough; the hour has come. Behold, the Son of Man is betrayed into the hands of sinners.*

14:42   *Rise, let us go! Behold, the one who betrays Me is near."*

NOTES 22.2

22.2   *Faithfulness in discipleship involves submission to the Father's will and prayerful dependence upon the Holy Spirit (instead of the flesh), emulating the model of Jesus, the Son.*

Jesus' three sessions of prayer in this episode are balanced by his three disciples' falling asleep three times, despite his explicit exhortation to them to be alert (γρηγορέω, *grēgoreō*, 14:37, 40, 41).[15] Jesus, then, is the faithful counterpart of the failing disciples, as he remains alert and engaged in prayer in this time of grave crisis. His faithfulness to his Father remains unabated, and his submission to divine will and purpose, unquestioned.

The three disciples (Peter, James, and John) who are taken along with Jesus (14:33) are the ones who have been witnesses to Jesus' unique relationship to God: they have observed his power over death (5:37) and his Transfiguration (9:2); they have already, with more swagger than courage, asserted their willingness to suffer with him (10:38–39; 14:29, 31); and, with Andrew, they have listened to Jesus' eschatological instructions that

---

15. Later, there would be a threefold denial by a disciple, as well.

concluded with the injunction to be alert (γρηγορέω, 13:34, 35, 37). This is their chance to prove themselves faithful, for Jesus again commands them to be alert (14:34). Once more, Jesus expects much from them; they are to follow his model, as he takes them along μετ' αὐτοῦ (*met autou*, "with Him," 14:33; see 3:14 for Jesus' original commission to his disciples to that effect).

That Jesus is being taxed to his human limit, and thrown into great distress, there is no doubt. His is "the depth of suffering of a human being who shudders on the threshold of torture and death, but also the numinous terror of the eschatological, transcendent nature of what is about to transpire, a sorrow and anguish so intense it already threatens his life."[16] More agonizing than the physical torment will be the abandonment of him by the Father, as he faces the judgment of God upon sin, being made sin for mankind (2 Cor 5:21) and becoming a curse for humans (Gal 3:13) that they might escape the wrath of God that he is about to face on Calvary.[17] This account again expresses vividly the sovereignty of God—it is God's to give the cup and, were he to will it so, it would be God's to remove it as well. Yet what emerges as remarkable is Jesus' acquiescence to the will of the Father (Mark 14:36). The assent to the sovereign will of God is a positive model for the disciples; this is noted again in Jesus' affirmation that the Scriptures be fulfilled (14:49). Jesus "rejects his own will, that is, he 'denies himself' as he advocated in 8:34, and chooses the will of God."[18] He is faithful, doing what the disciples ought to be doing too.

The rebuke addressed specifically to Peter (14:37) reminds him (and the readers) of his very recent dissent with Jesus and his own assertions of his loyalty (14:29–31). The threefold proof of the weakness of Peter (and the others) in his inability to remain awake hints at his threefold denial down the line. Observing the duplex meaning of πειρασμός (*peirasmos*, "testing" or "temptation"), France notes that "[w]hat confronts the disciples at this point is both 'testing' in the sense of an ordeal which they will prove unable to cope with and 'temptation' in that the urge to run away will put their own safety before loyalty to God and his Son."[19]

Immediately thereafter, the verbs shift from the singular (referring to Peter) in 14:37 to the plural (all disciples) in 14:38. This is the way they can be faithful in the midnight watch—by mistrusting the flesh, relying on the Spirit, and committing to prayer. "We do well to watch heedfully and pray earnestly 'lest we enter into temptation.' For if Christ does not grant us grace, then the Judas in us betrays. If he departs a little way from us, the

---

16. Boring, *Mark*, 397; Stein, *Mark*, 662–63.

17. Witherington, *Gospel of Mark*, 379. The "cup" (14:36) indicates the judgment of God (Ps 11:6; 75:8; Isa 51:17, 22; Jer 25:15; 49:12; Lam 4:21–22; Ezek 23:31–34; Hab 2:15–16; Zech 12:2; Rev 14:10; 16:19; 17:4 with 18:6; *Pss. Sol.* 8.13–14; 1QpHab 11.14–15). The "hour" (Mark 14:35), like the eschatological "day," indicates the moment both of God's judgment and salvation (13:32; 14:25, 30, 35; Rev 9:15).

18. Dowd, *Prayer*, 157. Yet "[t]he prayer of submission does not replace the prayer for divine intervention; it accompanies it" (ibid.). "Prayer . . . consists not in changing God's mind but in finding our own alignment with God's will" (France, *Gospel of Mark*, 585). "Abba" (14:36) is a respectful word used to address the father in intimacy, not only by children, but also adults, and occasionally by students addressing a venerable rabbi (also Rom 8:15; Gal 4:16). See Boring, *Mark*, 399.

19. France, *Gospel of Mark*, 587.

Peter in us sleeps" (Jerome, *The Homilies of St. Jerome*, Homily 84).[20] And, indeed, they sleep. After the account of the heavy eyes of the disciples (14:40), the double occurrence of "Behold!" in Jesus' remonstrance (14:41, 42) is striking. No, the disciples are still not seeing. In any case, here again, the model of faithful Jesus, remaining in prayer through the "midnight" watch, is what the disciples ought to be emulating. This, Jesus tells us, can only be accomplished in the power of the Holy Spirit, negating the pull of the flesh.

"Mark has been at pains to make clear throughout his Gospel that the disciples, had they been faithful, would have stayed with Jesus through his passion" (8:34–38; 14:27). But they are not; they fail to be alert for even an hour, and fall asleep (14:37, 40). Jesus, on the other hand, is the faithful one, who exemplifies the alertness they fail to engage in, as he prays through the long watch (14:34, 38). He watches; they sleep. He trusts God; they, the flesh. He remains; they flee. He is faithful; they are not. What will the reader be—faithful or faithless? To obey the command to be alert is to pray in crisis, to be wary of overconfidence (10:39; 14:19, 29, 31), instead trusting in God and his sovereignty, and to resist fleshly temptation, anticipating suffering according to God's will. To be on the alert—to be faithful—is "*not* a discernment process; *it is to act in obedience*," following the model of the faithful one, Jesus, in submission to the Father's sovereign will.[21]

22.3   Mark 14:43–52

THEOLOGICAL FOCUS 22.3
22.3   Faithlessness in discipleship is shameful (14:43–52).

Section Summary 22.3: Two cameo appearances—one by a bystander who dares to draw and use his sword, the other by a young man who flees naked—follow the treacherous act of betrayal by Judas, who does so with a kiss, no less! Both brief accounts serve to symbolize the potential disqualification from God's service and the utter shame the disciple may suffer if he or she is unfaithful to Jesus in this "midnight" watch.

TRANSLATION 22.3

14:43   *And immediately while He was yet speaking, Judas, one of the Twelve, arrived, and with him a crowd with swords and clubs, from the chief priests and the scribes and the elders.*

14:44   *Now the one betraying Him had given them a signal, saying, "Whomever I kiss, it is He. Seize Him and lead [Him] away under guard."*

14:45   *And coming, he immediately went to Him, saying, "Rabbi!" And he kissed Him.*

14:46   *And they laid hands on Him and seized Him.*

14:47   *But one of those who stood by, drawing a sword, struck the slave of the high priest and cut off his ear.*

20. Cited in Oden and Hall, *Mark*, 212–13.
21. Geddert, *Watchwords*, 99, 104 (italics original).

14:48   *And Jesus answering, said to them, "Have you come out with swords and clubs to arrest Me as against a robber?*

14:49   *Every day I was with you in the temple teaching, and you did not seize Me. But [this has happened] in order that the Scriptures may be fulfilled."*

14:50   *And leaving Him, they all fled.*

14:51   *And a certain young man was following Him, wearing a linen cloth upon [his] nakedness, and they seized him.*

14:52   *But he abandoned the linen cloth and fled naked.*

NOTES 22.3

22.3   *Faithlessness in discipleship risks shameful disqualification from God's service.*

Thus far in the Gospel, Jesus and disciples have been together. From this point onwards, following his arrest, the ones Jesus has chosen to be "with Him" (3:14) are no longer around; they abandon him totally. One of them, in this episode, betrays him. The description of Judas as "one of the Twelve" (14:43) appears redundant, but it serves to reinforce the magnitude of his treason. Notable is the recurrence of μετ᾿αὐτου (*met autou*, 14:43); this time it is Judas who is the subject, and "with him" there is an armed mob. The irony continues: Judas' kiss (14:45), a normal Eastern social greeting (Luke 7:45; Acts 20:37; Rom 16:16; etc.), is the only greeting exchanged between Jesus and his disciples in any of the Gospels—an intimate gesture, but here one of treachery!

Not only is this disciple's action treacherous, so are the operations of the delegation from the temple ("a crowd with swords and clubs, from the chief priests and the scribes and the elders," 14:43). Mark makes this latter point in a roundabout way, with the odd cameo of an earlobe excision in 14:47. With no identification of the assailant, no apparent consequence of the aggression, and no comment by Jesus about it, this violent action seems rather meaningless and out of place. Surprisingly, the identity of the one assaulted is clearly stated: "slave of the high priest" (14:47). Viviano notes that this is no lowly domestic, but a prefect, the chief assistant or deputy of the high priest (*m. Yoma* 4:1; *m. Soṭah* 7:7–8)—thus a representative symbol of the temple administration.[22] Of note also is that it is the tip of the ear, the lobe (the diminutive ὠτάριον, *ōtarion*, 14:47), that is removed, making this unlikely to be an accident caused by a random sword stroke; it had to have been deliberately executed. Viviano explains that this mutilation is symbolic, disqualifying the one so afflicted from any priestly service (see Lev 21:18). Purposeful mutilation of ears to achieve such disbarment from cultic engagement is reported by Josephus (*Ant.* 14.365): the elimination of Hyrcanus II from candidacy for highpriesthood in ca. 37 BCE, an event momentous enough to have been remembered decades later. It is likely, then, that the action in Mark 14:47 is making a powerful statement: "You, and the one you represent, are gravely unworthy to stand as mediator between God and men. You have proven your unworthiness by coming here to lay violent hands upon the anointed holy one of God. I hereby make visible

---

22. Viviano, "High Priest's Servant's Ear," 71–80; also see Evans, *Mark*, 425

your unworthiness and disqualify you further from exercising your high office."[23] The temple authorities, who ought to have been accepting of Jesus, the Son of God, are, by their egregious actions, disqualified from serving God.

In other words, in this episode (including the betrayal by Judas and the fleeing of the disciples) all of the Twelve and all of the religious authorities are shown to be equally unworthy of their offices and designations.[24] All of this depicts for readers the seriousness of unfaithfulness to Jesus in the "midnight" watch. Such actions of infidelity are potentially disqualifying, and can remove one from the journey of discipleship. Indeed the entire gang of disciples disenfranchises itself as they all flee (14:50). Van Iersel wryly notes the conjunction of this statement with Jesus' assertion that all this has happened "in order that the Scriptures may be fulfilled" (14:49). Immediately after that, the disciples decamp. "It looks for a moment as if they had waited for the mention of the Scriptures as the signal to take flight."[25]

Another cameo follows, this time one symbolizing the shameful failure of these disciples and their unfaithfulness (14:51–52).[26] "Rather than representing Jesus, the paradigmatic disciple or the Christian initiate, the young man is best interpreted as one whose flight and abandonment of his linen cloth contrast dramatically with Jesus' obedience in submitting to being arrested, stripped, and crucified."[27] There is irony here as well: the young man literally leaves everything, not to follow Jesus, but to escape arrest, and thus becomes symbolic of the total abandonment of Jesus by the band of disciples who flee to escape the baleful consequences of association with Jesus. "The first disciples to be called left nets and family (1:18, 20), indeed everything (10:28), to follow him; but this last disciple, who at first sought to follow Jesus, ultimately left everything to get away from him."[28] Whereas the temple authorities' actions lead to potential disqualification, the fleeing of the disciples is pointedly an act of great shamefulness. The shame of nudity is sharply thrown into focus by the repetition of γυμνός (*gymnos*, "naked[ness]," 14:51, 52). The symbolic nature of this cryptic account, albeit true, is signaled by the elements within, which are echoes of many of the events of the Passion: κρατέω (*krateō*, "arrest") in 14:51 and 14:1, 44, 46, 49; σινδών (*sindōn*, "linen cloth") in 14:51–52 and 15:46; νεανίσκος (*neaniskos*, "young man") in 14:51 and 16:5; περιβάλλω (*periballō*, "wear") in 14:51 and 16:5; and φεύγω (*pheugō*, "flee") in 14:52 and 14:27; 16:8. The section on the disciples (14:12–50) and that on the mysterious "young man" (14:51–52) both conclude

---

23. Viviano, "High Priest's Servant's Ear," 78.

24. It is possible that Mark's failure to identify Peter as the one performing the partial auriculectomy (John 18:10 tells us it was Peter) stems from an unwillingness to show the incongruity of Jesus' betrayer being the agent of this symbolic enactment of disqualifying the temple authorities from God's service. Not naming Malchus, the slave of the high priest (as John again does, 18:10) keeps the account focused on the entire religious hierarchy rather than upon any particular individual. Clearly, John's agenda in his Gospel is different: he seeks to make a point about employing violence in the service of Jesus—notice Jesus' reproof of Peter's hot-blooded deed (John 18:11).

25. van Iersel, *Mark*, 440.

26. See Kuruvilla, "Naked Runaway."

27. Collins, *Mark*, 695.

28. Brown, "Passion," 118; also see Heil, "Mark 14,1–52," 330; and van Iersel, *Mark*, 441n63.

with this verb of abandonment and escape (φεύγω).[29] "The anonymity . . . could free the figure to become a 'cipher,' a literary device re-emphasizing the flight of the twelve and complete failure on their part to respond faithfully to the call of discipleship."[30] In other words, it is "a dramatization of the universal flight of the disciples," the reversal, indeed, of the Trip of Discipleship, and a complete contrast to Jesus' own act of submissive acceptance of the Father's will.[31] The motif of "leaving everything" to become a disciple has now become the disgrace of "leaving everything" to become a non-disciple![32] All the more glaringly shameful, then, does the disciples' flight appear. It also marks the utter aloneness of Jesus as he enters the final hours of his earthly life. Unlike the failing and faithless disciples, Jesus, the faithful one, is ready to drink the cup assigned to him by the Father.[33]

SERMON FOCUS AND OUTLINES

THEOLOGICAL FOCUS OF PERICOPE 22 FOR PREACHING

22 Faithfulness in discipleship, the emulation of Jesus, the Son, involves confidence in God's sovereignty and prayerful dependence upon the Holy Spirit, rather than upon the flesh (14:12–52).

This pericope covers the "evening" and "midnight" watches of discipleship. The account, except for the faithfulness of Jesus, is entirely negative. The contrast between the one who is faithful and the many who are not is powerful. Multiple elements of faithfulness in discipleship are outlined here: faithfulness involves total confidence in God's sovereign will and control; God's is the power that enables faithfulness; faithfulness is contingent upon prayerful dependence upon the Holy Spirit (rather than the flesh with misplaced self-confidence).[34] Such faithfulness is expected of disciples, in order that they may survive the critical periods of testing/temptation. While it is indeed true that God restores those fallen away (Peter will be the prime example in

29. See Fleddermann, "Flight," 413–14. The significance of these strikingly repeated elements will be brought out in the last pericope, 15:40—16:8.

30. Hester, "Dramatic Inconclusion," 75.

31. Fleddermann, "Flight," 415. The goal of the narrator here is to impress upon the reader, as graphically as possible, "the throes of . . . extreme emotion—sudden, desperate panic at seizure and the hot adrenal instinct to flee" (Jackson, "Why the Youth," 285). This "dramatization" corresponds to that of the ultimate betrayal in the kiss by Judas (14:44–45), and that of disqualification from God's service in the ear lobotomy by "one of those who stood by" (14:47).

32. Boring, *Mark*, 404.

33. Needless to say, the preacher must balance these negative consequences of failure with grace; the positive portrayal of God's restorative power is hinted at in 14:27–28 but detailed in 15:40—16:8 (Pericope 25).

34. It might be worthwhile at this point in this series on Mark to address (perhaps in a separate sermon or two) this important facet of the spiritual life of the Christian—the battle between the flesh and the Spirit; Rom 6–8 would be an appropriate text to base these sermons on. It is particularly important that the congregation understand this concept, lest the preacher's giving of imperatives in each sermon be misconstrued as facilitating legalism, the obeying of commands by the strength of one's own flesh, by one's own resources, for one's own glory. Instead, it is the indwelling Spirit that enables and empowers the believer to obey (Rom 8:9; Gal 2:20; etc.), and all for the glory of God.

the Passion account of Mark), failure of faithfulness can potentially lead to shameful disqualification—removal from God's service.

Not all of these elements need to be highlighted in the sermon, of course. The preacher must exercise pastoral discretion and wisdom in understanding where the congregation is and in deciding where they ought to be, or where they ought to be moving toward. (Since this pericope also contains the Last Supper, celebrating Communion/Eucharist right after the sermon would be a powerful close to the worship service of the faithful.)

As with all pericopes in Mark, the lesson herein is worth taking to heart by those who would be disciples. Trusting God's sovereign control is foundational to faithfulness, as exemplified by Jesus. Being faithful is not easy; it demands much of the disciple, and requires prayerful dependence on the Spirit and overcoming the flesh and its evil proclivities.

POSSIBLE PREACHING OUTLINE FOR PERICOPE 22

I. God's sovereignty: Jesus' confidence in God, disciples' confidence in themselves
   God's sovereign control and scripting of events (14:12–31, 49)
   Jesus' positive model, trusting in God's sovereignty and submitting to his will (14:36)
   Disciples' negative model, relying upon their own capacity (14:19, 29–31)

II. Human responsibility: Jesus' prayerfulness, disciples' sleepiness
   Disciples' negative model, their failure to "be alert" (14:32–42)
   The consequence of failure—shame (14:43–52)
   Jesus' positive model, remaining in prayer (14:32–42)

III. Be faithful—trust God's control in prayerful dependence!
   Specifics on trusting God's power and his will
   Specifics on refusing the flesh and depending on the Spirit

Another way of outlining a sermon on this pericope:

I. JESUS: Confident in God, prayerful, faithful
   Jesus' positive model, trusting in God's sovereignty (14:12–31, 49)
   Jesus' positive model, remaining in prayer (14:32–42)

II. DISCIPLES: Self-confident, fleshly, unfaithful
   Disciples' negative model, relying upon their own capacity (14:19, 29–31)
   Disciples' negative model, their fleshly failure to "be alert" (14:32–42)
   Disciples' negative model, the consequence of failure—shame (14:43–52)

III. Be faithful—trust God's control in prayerful dependence!
   Specifics on trusting God's power, submitting to his will, in prayerful dependence on the Spirit, not the flesh

PERICOPE 23

Self-Defense or Self-Denial?

Mark 14:53–72

[Jewish Trial of Jesus; Denial of Peter]

REVIEW, SUMMARY, PREVIEW

Review of Pericope 22: Mark 14:12–52 teaches that the disciple's faithfulness —following Jesus' model—involves submission to God's sovereignty and his will, and prayerful dependence upon the Holy Spirit, rather than the flesh.

Summary of Pericope 23: Mark 14:53–72 continues the theme of faithfulness, this time in the "cockcrow" hour. The pericope juxtaposes the Jewish trial of Jesus and the "trial" of Peter. These paired trials contrast the self-denial of Jesus with the self-defense of Peter. Positive and negative models, the depictions of Jesus and Peter instruct the disciple that faithfulness involves self-denial without concern for self-preservation, even in times of danger.

Preview of Pericope 24: The next pericope (15:1–39), while encouraging disciples with hints of Jesus' victorious kingship, reminds them that submitting to Jesus' reign involves sacrifice and suffering ridicule in this world. Faithfulness to Jesus till the very end is called for from those who have discerned his person and accepted his mission.

23   Mark 14:53–72

THEOLOGICAL FOCUS OF PERICOPE 23

23   **Disciples' faithfulness, in the fulfillment of their calling to be with Jesus, involves self-denial for his cause, even in dangerous circumstances, without concern for self-preservation, following Jesus' own example (14:53–72).**

23.1	Disciples are called to follow fully and faithfully, denying themselves, emulating Jesus, despite the danger of the situation.
23.2	Disciples' fulfillment of their calling to be with Jesus involves self-denial for his cause, without thought of self-preservation.

OVERVIEW

THERE IS QUITE A bit of camera movement to and fro in this section as it follows the action: 14:53, before the high priest; 14:54 in the courtyard; 14:55–65 before high priest again; and 14:66–72 back in the courtyard.[1] The effective "sandwich" that this recounting creates puts Jesus and Peter in sharp contrast to each other: the former, in the face of false witnesses, is open about his identity, and that gives his opponents ground to condemn him; the latter, refuting his own accurate identification by others (true witnesses), completely denies any connection with Jesus, and thus escapes condemnation. With the strong connection between this section and 8:34, in the use of the key verb ἀπαρνέομαι (*aparneomai*, "to deny," found in 8:34 and repeated here in 14:72, as well as in Jesus' prophecy of Peter's denial, and Peter's own rebuttal of that prophecy: 14:30, 31),[2] this pericope is a depiction of how to deny oneself. Self-denial is positively depicted by Jesus, and negatively by Peter. While this pericope explicates what it means to deny oneself, the next pericope (15:1–39) concerns what it means to take up one's cross. In other words, these two pericopes of the Gospel appear to reflect the core demand made by Jesus of his disciples in 8:33–34: following Jesus means to deny themselves and to take up their crosses.

This pericope forms the sixth and last of the classic Markan "sandwich" stories (outer story: 14:53–54; 14:66–72; inner story: 14:55–65).[3] Here, too, Jesus is the main character either present or referred to in both outer and inner stories. The two stories are compared below[4]:

	Outer Story: MARK 14:53–54, 66–72	Inner Story: MARK 14:55–65
Protagonist	Peter	Jesus
Status	Free	Captive
Location	Outside (down)	Inside (up)
Accusers	Slave girl, bystanders	False witnesses, high priest
3 Accusations	Issues of identity	Issues of identity*
3 Responses	Deny, deny, curse and swear	Silence, silence, affirmation and explanation
Result	Falsehood uttered; saved	Truth told; condemned to die
Titles of Jesus	Jesus, Nazarene; "this man" (14:67, 71)	Christological titles (14:61–62)
Role	Failing disciple fulfills prophecy	Blindfolded prophet's prophecy fulfilled

1. That Peter is somewhere other than where Jesus is located is noted in 14:66; the use of ἕως (*heōs*, "right into") as a spatial marker in 14:54 (as also in 13:27; 15:38) indicates that Jesus went farther than did the disciple (see Shepherd, *Markan Sandwich Stories*, 269).

2. A related verb, ἀρνέομαι (*arneomai*, also "to deny"), is employed in 14:68, 70.

3. See Shepherd, *Markan Sandwich Stories*, 267–310, for details on this Markan "sandwich."

4. From ibid., 285. See the Notes for further details.

* The accusations against Jesus: He is a temple-destroyer/rebuilder; a question reiterating the accusation and challenging his silence; a query as to whether he is the Christ (14:58, 60, 61). "The threefold form itself may reflect courtroom procedure in which the accused are given three opportunities to deny their membership in the suspect group (cf. Pliny, *Letters* 10.96.3; *Mart. Pol.* 9–10)" (Boring, *Mark*, 415).

France summarizes the significance of the structure[5]:

> The effect of this way of telling the story (in contrast to Luke, who records Peter's denial before Jesus' hearing) is to throw Jesus and Peter into sharp contrast. Each will be under pressure, but whereas Jesus both in his silence and in his final dramatic utterance will stand firm, Peter will crumble. Jesus will go to his death, but with his witness to his mission undimmed; Peter will escape, but at the cost of his integrity as a disciple of Jesus. . . . As such, it could be expected to offer serious food for thought to Mark's readers as they assessed their own faithfulness and built up their strength for witness in a potentially hostile world.

As will be seen, this "sandwich" is a double trial—Jesus' (the inner story) *and* Peter's (the outer story).[6] The inner story of this pericope, unlike any other section of the Gospel, has a concentration of christological titles for Jesus: Christ, Son of the Blessed One, and Son of Man; the outer story, too, refers to Jesus, but as Jesus, Nazarene, and "this man."[7] This suggests that the inner story is where truth is announced; the outer story, seemingly, depicts a concealment of the truth, in more ways than one. These motifs of truth and falsehood punctuate the entire pericope: "false testimony" occurs twice (14:56, 57); the inconsistency of the witnesses is also noted twice (14:56, 59); and, of course, the truth and forthrightness of Jesus' confession are prominently displayed.[8] One cannot but notice also the nod to truthfulness from even the bystanders in 14:70 (their accusation of Peter begins with "truly," and they accurately identify the disciple), to which Peter responds with lies, curses, and swearing. Thus the inner story of truthfulness and faithfulness (Jesus' self-denial) is strongly contrasted with the outer story of untruthfulness and unfaithfulness (Peter's denial, not of self, but of Jesus).

23 Mark 14:53–72

THEOLOGICAL FOCUS 23

23 Disciples' faithfulness, in the fulfillment of their calling to be with Jesus, involves self-denial for his cause, even in dangerous circumstances, without concern for self-preservation, following Jesus' own example (14:53–72).

5. France, *Gospel of Mark*, 598. Matthew has a similar structure at this juncture: 26:57–75.

6. Since the interest of this commentary is upon what the author is *doing* with what he is *saying*, it will not remark upon the (il)legality of the trial or other factors relating to first-century Jewish jurisprudence. Another reason for not pursuing this issue is that Mark seems to be interested in maintaining a semblance of forensic propriety, in that inconsistent testimonies are not pursued any further. Thus the nature of the trial per se is not a key issue for Mark as far as his theological agenda is concerned.

7. Shepherd, *Markan Sandwich Stories*, 281–82.

8. Borrell, *Good News*, 129.

23.1	Disciples are called to follow fully and faithfully, denying themselves, emulating Jesus, despite the danger of the situation.
23.2	Disciples' fulfillment of their calling to be with Jesus involves self-denial for his cause, without thought of self-preservation.

Section Summary 23: The parallel trials of Jesus and Peter, artfully presented by the narrator, contrast the faithfulness of the one with the unfaithfulness of the other. One denies himself; the other defends himself and denies his Master. Positive and negative models, the depictions of Jesus and Peter instruct the disciple that faithfulness in the fulfillment of the calling to be "with Jesus" involves self-denial without concern for self-preservation, even in times of danger.

TRANSLATION 23

14:53   *And they led Jesus away to the high priest, and all the chief priests and the elders and the scribes came together.*

14:54   *And Peter followed Him from a distance, as far as within the courtyard of the high priest, and he was sitting together with the officers and keeping warm at the fire.*

14:55   *Now the chief priests and the whole Sanhedrin were seeking testimony against Jesus to put Him to death, and they could not find [any],*

14:56   *for many were giving false testimony against Him, and the testimonies were not consistent.*

14:57   *And some, rising up, gave false testimony against Him, saying,*

14:58   *"We heard Him saying, 'I will destroy this temple made with hands and, in three days, I will build another, made without hands.'"*

14:59   *Not even in this way was their testimony consistent.*

14:60   *And the high priest, rising up in [their] midst, questioned Jesus, saying, "Do You not answer anything—what these men are testifying against You?"*

14:61   *But He kept silent and did not answer anything. Again the high priest questioned Him and said to Him, "Are you the Christ, the Son of the Blessed One?"*

14:62   *And Jesus said, "I am, and you will see the Son of Man sitting at the right hand of power and coming with the clouds of heaven."*

14:63   *And the high priest, tearing his clothes, said, "What further need do we have of witnesses?*

14:64   *You heard the blasphemy. How does it appear to you?" And they all condemned Him to be deserving of death.*

14:65   *And some began to spit at Him, and to cover His face, and to strike Him with their fists, and to say to Him, "Prophesy!" And the officers took Him with blows.*

14:66   *And as Peter was below in the courtyard, one of the servant-girls of the high priest came,*

14:67 *and seeing Peter keeping warm, she said, looking at him, "You also were with the Nazarene, Jesus."*

14:68 *But he denied [it], saying, "I neither know nor understand what you are saying." And he went outside onto the forecourt, and a cock crowed.*[9]

14:69 *And the servant-girl, seeing him, again began to say to the bystanders, "He is [one] of them."*

14:70 *But again he denied [it]. And after a short time, again the bystanders were saying to Peter, "Truly, you are [one] of them, for you, too, are a Galilean."*

14:71 *But he began to curse and swear, "I do not know this man whom you are talking [about]."*

14:72 *And immediately, a second time, a cock crowed. And Peter remembered the statement as Jesus had said to him, "Before a cock crows twice, thrice you will deny Me." And breaking down, he wept.*

NOTES 23

23.1   Disciples are called to follow fully and faithfully, denying themselves, emulating Jesus, despite the danger of the situation.[10]

Thus far in the Gospel, Jesus and the disciples have been in proximity all along. From this point forth, in the last hours of his earthly life as he goes to the cross, Jesus is utterly alone: the disciples have failed to be faithful to Jesus, they have failed to follow fully. Jesus is not in the company of his unreliable disciples, but in the hands of unfriendly adversaries (14:50, 53). Theirs is a solemn and formal gathering, as evidenced in the description of Jesus' accusers: "*all* the chief priests and the elders and the scribes"; "all" serves to contrast the solitary Jesus with the assemblage of opponents (the plurality of the latter is also contrasted with the paucity of Peter's accusers).

That Peter "followed" (14:54) reminds the reader that this is a *disciple*, one who had been called to follow (1:18; 2:14). Yet this following here is tainted, for Peter follows "from a distance."[11] Moreover, he is not μετ' αὐτοῦ (*met autou*, "with Him [Jesus]," 3:14), as disciples were appointed to be, but μετὰ τῶν ὑπηρετῶν (*meta tōn hypēretōn*, "with the officers," 14:54). Indeed, Peter's is an incomplete following—only "as far as" the courtyard, not further. This disciple is unwilling to share the sufferings of his Master. Self-denial is not on his agenda.

The whole legal procedure of the Sanhedrin appears to be governed by a predetermined goal—to kill Jesus (announced earlier in 14:1). The affair begins with accusations against Jesus who, the witnesses claimed, had threatened to destroy the temple, a charge remembered by mockers even at the foot of the cross (15:29). This is, no doubt,

---

9. This last phrase is absent in some of the older manuscripts. Internally, however, the phrase is consistent with Mark's narrative, in view of 14:30 and 14:72 mentioning the cock crowing twice.

10. Again, this is a positive statement of the lesson negatively portrayed in the narrative.

11. Ἀπὸ μακρόθεν (*apo makrothen*, "from a distance"), here and in 15:40, likely implies a criticism, and is possibly an allusion to Ps 38:11, where the Psalmist's allies remain unsympathetically ἀπὸ μακρόθεν from his sufferings. Like Jesus, the Psalmist remains silent (38:13–14) (Marcus, *Mark*, 1013).

a serious indictment: Jeremiah, predicting the destruction of the same edifice, barely escaped death; Uriah, his fellow-prophet, did not (Jer 26:7–24).[12] That God would destroy the temple seems to have already been foreshadowed in the OT (Jer 7:12–15; 26:4–6, 9; etc.), as well as in *1 En.* 90.28–29. It is possible, then, to view the accusation here simply as Jesus arrogating to himself what is the prerogative of Yahweh alone.[13] Moreover, things "made with hands" (χειροποίητος, *cheiropoiētos,* Mark 14:58) often denoted idols in the OT (Lev 26:1; Isa 2:18; 10:11; 16:12; 19:1; 31:7; 46:6 LXX; also see Ps 115:4), and such an attribution to the temple would be immediately offensive to the religious leaders (Acts 17:24).[14] Whether Jesus actually claims to destroy the temple himself is doubtful. He employs two "divine" passives in his prophecy in Mark 13:2 ("Not one stone will *be left* upon stone which will not *be destroyed*"), suggesting God's role in this action. Nor does he make any explicit assertion regarding a subsequent re-building of the temple, though it seems to have been widely accepted in those days that the Messiah would personally undertake that task.[15] In short, the charges are flimsy. Twice Mark notes that the witnesses are bearing false testimony (14:56, 57); twice he asserts the inconsistency of their evidence (14:56, 59). That the high priest and his false witnesses are in collusion is evident. Both "rise" (ἀνίστημι, *anistēmi,* 14:57, 60) against Jesus, while he sits in a vision of a session of the heavenly court (14:62). Ironically, the high priest appears to be observing theological niceties in not pronouncing the name of God (14:61), instead employing a euphemism—all this, while condemning the Son of God to death![16] Whatever the state of legality of this late-night forum, one thing is clear: the accusations are false and unfair, and the judge, jury, and witnesses are biased; they are out to get the defendant.

After not responding to two sets of accusations (14:56–59 and 60–61, from the false witnesses and the high priest, respectively), finally, the third time around, Jesus replies to the high priest (14:62). Impositions of silence (the "secrecy motif") have permeated the Gospel (1:34; 3:11–12; 8:30; 9:9; 9:30–31), but now the time for procla-mation has arrived—*after* the Passion Predictions and the development of the Son of Man sayings.[17] Jesus now declares himself to be the Son of God: ἐγώ εἰμι (*egō eimi,*

12. France, *Gospel of Mark,* 605.

13. A similar appropriation of divine authority may also have precipitated the execution in 62 CE of Jesus ben Ananias, who made threats against the temple (Josephus, *J.W.* 6.300–309).

14. Interestingly, all along, Jesus has been shown by Mark to be in precincts of the ἱερόν, *hieron,* the whole temple complex (11:1, 15 [×2], 16, 27; 12:35; 13:1; 13:3; Jesus himself confirms this setting of his activities in 14:49). But from this point onwards, that word is replaced by ναός, *naos,* the sanctuary proper (14:58; 15:29, 38). It is likely that this change does not indicate a different locus, but reflects Mark's narrative weaving in of what is, by his time, a significant Christian theme—that of the new sanc-tuary, made without hands: Jesus' own resurrection body and the body of Christ, the community of believers united in fellowship with him. See France, *Gospel of Mark,* 606–7; and Witherington, *Gospel of Mark,* 384.

15. *Tg. Neb.* on Zech 6:12: "Behold, the man whose name is Messiah will be revealed, and he shall be raised up, and shall build the temple of the Lord" (also see *1 En.* 90.28–29; *Jub.* 1.17; 11QTemple 29.8–10; 4QFlor 1.3, 6).

16. Stein, *Mark,* 683.

17. "Son of Man" in Act I of Mark's Gospel (2:10, 28) conveys the sense of divine power, relating as

"I am," 14:62). Proclamation is always appropriate when the person and suffering mission of Jesus are been completely revealed (5:19; 10:47–49).

Jesus' switching of terms, from the high priest's "Christ" and "Son of God [the Blessed One]" to "Son of Man," is significant, not to mention the coda, which shows this Son of Man sitting at the right hand of God, and coming with heavenly clouds. The allusion to clouds, the vehicle of Yahweh in the OT, is a clear indication that a theophany is the subject here. Possessing a divine station of authority and a divine mode of transportation, there can be no doubt as to who Jesus is asserting himself to be. It is a bold claim that he is even higher in status than what the high priest alleges Jesus had claimed.[18] "He *is* the Messiah (ἐγώ εἰμι), but his messianic vision is on a different level altogether from what the high priest might have been implying. Any concept of the Messiah as a nationalistic deliverer at a political level has been left far behind: Jesus' 'triumph' is to be at the right hand of God."[19] To Jews, this elevation of himself to be equal to God—sitting at his right hand and sharing his ethereal vehicle—would be close to, if not equivalent to, blasphemy.[20] The high priest's response demonstrated that he takes Jesus' declaration exactly that way (14:62–63). Now Jesus' fate is sealed by his own truthful admission. No doubt he knows full well what his assertion will lead to. Equally damaging, the claim to be the "Christ" would be equivalent to political treason for the Roman rulers. Surely Jesus is aware that neither the Jewish establishment nor the Roman authorities will let him remain unpunished for claiming to be both divine as well as messianic. Yet there is no faltering, no hesitation, no holding back. Jesus does not defend himself at all, neither arguing against the false witnesses nor clarifying what exactly he meant in his earlier statements in the temple or what he means now in his current declaration. Upon being asked an explicit and direct question, Jesus gives an explicit and direct answer, without regard for consequences, without an eye for his own safety and self-preservation (14:61–62). Jesus is modeling faithfulness (at the "cockcrow" watch), denying himself, in contrast to Peter, who, almost at the very instant, as will be seen, is busy defending himself and denying another!

---

it does to the authority to forgive sins and authority over the Sabbath. For most of the remainder of the Gospel (Acts II and III), "Son of Man" has strong connotations of sacrificial suffering (8:31; 9:12, 31; 10:33, 45; 14:21, 41). While, for sure, 8:38 shows the Son of Man coming in glory, even in that episode the theological thrust is on the suffering (8:31) that precedes glory (8:38); the exaltation of the Son of Man is clearly proleptic (as also in 13:26 and 14:62, depicting the glory of the Son of Man). Thus in the latter half of the Gospel, the earthly ministry of the Son of Man is marked by sacrificial suffering.

18. Witherington, *Gospel of Mark*, 385.

19. France, *Gospel of Mark*, 613.

20. Gundry, *Mark*, 916–17. See *b. Sanh.* 38b, where Rabbi Akiba's interpretation of the thrones of Dan 7:9 as including one for David was alleged by Rabbi Jose to be blasphemy ("profanation of the *Shekinah*") for his audacious equation of an earthly regent with the divine one.

23.2   Disciples' fulfillment of their calling to be with Jesus involves self-denial for his cause, without thought of self-preservation.[21]

The Passion accounts of Matthew and Luke inform readers of the intention of the mockers as they blindfold Jesus and strike him with their fists: they taunt him to identify the one who has hit him (Matt 26:68; Luke 22:64). Mark, on the other hand, is silent about the purpose to lampoon Jesus (14:65); for him the mockery will show up in the next pericope, 15:1–39. This Evangelist, without giving the reader the explanatory gloss that the other Synoptic Gospels do about what the assailants were asking him to prophesy, cleverly shifts the camera angle to focus on an actual prophecy by Jesus being fulfilled—the denial by Peter, before the third cockcrow (14:66–72).[22] With Mark's "sandwich" strategy—two stories interwoven—Jesus' prophecy of 14:30 is fulfilled precisely by Peter as he denies the Master. Then, to cap it off, the backsliding disciple later remembers that very prophecy, we are told in 14:72. By Peter's lying denial of Jesus, thus fulfilling Jesus' prophecy, he proved the truthfulness of Jesus' christological claims.[23]

The "sandwich" structure is a masterpiece of a literary creation, especially in this pericope: Mark attempts to parallel these two protagonists in two separate trials, for Peter too is in a "trial" here (see parallels between outer and inner stories, above). The multiplicity of Jesus' accusers (and the resulting emphasis on his abandonment by his disciples)—signified by ὅλον (*holon*, "all," 14:53), πάντες (*pantes*, "whole," 14:55), and πολλοί (*polloi*, "many," 14:56)—is in contrast to the solitary accuser facing Peter, at least initially (explicitly noted as μία, *mia*, "one," 14:66). The disciple is unable to deny himself even before so meager a host of prosecutors. Peter quails before this lone servant girl, while Jesus stands strong before the whole Sanhedrin and a gang of accusers and false witnesses (14:55). Nevertheless, the danger to Peter must not be minimized; Mark is careful to note in 14:64 that Jesus' accusers "condemned Him to be deserving of death." If labeled a co-conspirator, Peter could conceivably join Jesus among the ranks of those convicted and sentenced.

21. This, of course, is *not* what Peter did.

22. Matthew's account (26:57–75) is quite similar to that of Mark, except that there is no blindfold for Jesus (perhaps those who hit him were behind him?), and the explicit taunt of the mockers was that he, "Christ," prophesy who hit him. "Christ" immediately connects with the high priest's question to Jesus, asking if he were the Christ (26:63). This is a mocking of his messianic status and his "blasphemous" prophecy equating himself with Yahweh. Thus Matthew's "Prophesy to us" (26:68) looks *back* to the trial. Mark's "Prophesy" (14:65) looks *forward* to a fulfillment of prophecy (that of Peter's denial). Obviously, harmonization of the Gospel accounts would disrupt Mark's carefully constructed narrative and alter the (pericopal) theological thrust of his account, at least for preaching purposes. Mark is more interested here in contrasting Jesus and Peter and how the prophecy of the former came true in the denial of the latter, rather than in the defamation and scorn heaped on Jesus; that will come in Mark 15. Homileticians must be aware, therefore, of the difference between "what actually happened" (*behind* the text) and "what the A/author recounts as having happened." While such an acknowledgement in no way diminishes the accuracy of what is recorded, it must be remembered that the recorded material is selective, and that it is the selected material that is inspired, not the event *behind* the text. As such, it is the inspired text of Scripture that bears and projects the theology (*in front of* the text, so to speak), which in turn guides preachers to valid application, both authoritative and relevant. The interpreter must take care to privilege the text, and not event over text. See Kuruvilla, "Pericopal Theology"; and idem, *Text to Praxis*.

23. Shepherd, *Markan Sandwich Stories*, 291.

Jesus' faithfulness and forthrightness, despite the risk of condemnation and execution, is in stark contrast to Peter's unfaithfulness and deceit in an attempt to escape risk and danger—an unwillingness on part of the disciple to deny himself. Moreover, Peter negates his call from Jesus to be μετ' αὐτοῦ (*met autou*, "with Him," 3:14), an appointment the servant-girl accurately gauges: "You also were with the Nazarene, Jesus" (μετὰ τοῦ Ναζαρηνοῦ ἦσθα τοῦ Ἰησοῦ; *meta tou Nazarēnou ēstha tou Iesou*, 14:67). Unwittingly, she has stumbled upon what Peter is actually supposed to be doing and upon what precisely his commission is. Servant girls may guess correctly, but the disciple does not care: "I neither know nor understand what you are saying" (14:68). He is lying, of course; so also with his last words in this Gospel: "I do not know this man" (14:71). He is denying Jesus, not denying himself as he had been called to do (8:33–34). In another sense, the reader, accompanying the disciples and Jesus on this literary Trip of Discipleship of Mark's Gospel, might suspect that this bumbling disciple is, in fact, being perfectly truthful: Peter neither knows nor understands who Jesus is and what Jesus is about. He never has. In fact, none of the Twelve fully understood Jesus' person and suffering mission.[24] One of them betrays him. The rest flee.

Twice more, Peter is identified as having been a member of the Jesus party (14:69–70). At that, Peter expostulates that he does not know "this man" ("fellow"/"guy")—a strikingly cavalier dismissal of the one he had once confessed as the Christ (8:29). And he attempts to establish his claim of ignorance with cursing and swearing. The verb ἀναθεματίζω (*anathematizō*, "curse," 14:71) is transitive, without the reflexive ἑαυτούς (*heautous*, "himself") as in Acts 23:12, 14, 21 (the only other uses of this verb in the NT): it is doubtful that Peter is uttering an oath to bind himself (as in "Cursed be me, if I ever knew this man rather, the verb used this way without the self-direction raises the significant possibility that the object of the disciple's vituperation is Jesus himself![25] If so, Peter is doing what Pliny the Younger (61–112 CE) would later assert "those who are really Christians cannot be made to do"—curse Jesus (*Ep.* 10.96.5).[26] Of course, in this case, Mark's failure to clarify Jesus as the object of Peter's cursing is understandable: it is unspeakably shocking!

Such an interpretation also fits with the pattern of Peter's denial becoming progressively more severe as the accusations mount:

- a generic negation in the aorist (ἠρνήσατο, *ērnēsato*, "denied," 14:68) to a single servant girl;

---

24. Myers, *Binding the Strong Man*, 377.

25. Several English translations of 14:71 add in the object "himself" to the verb for purposes of clarification. Notwithstanding this gloss—absent in the Greek—it is more in line with the development of the narrative to see Jesus as the object of Peter's curse. Note that in Matt 26:74, the verb is καταθεματίζω, *katathematizo*, the prefix κατα- (*kata-*) immediately evoking the calling "down" of curses, likely upon himself (this verb occurs only once in the NT, and not at all in the LXX).

26. Lampe, "St. Peter's Denial," 354. Also see Merkel, "Peter's Curse," 67–68: "[N]either LXX, Aquila, Symmachus, Theodotion, nor the extra-biblical literature, use ἀναθεματίζειν (*anathematizein*) as a description of self-cursing." Also see Justin Martyr, *1 Apol.* 31.6, for Bar Kokhba's ultimatum to Christians to curse Jesus (in 132–136 CE), and also *Mart. Pol.* 9–10 for the refusal of bishop Polycarp of Smyrna (ca. 70–156 CE) to do so under Roman pressure.

- a denial in the imperfect (ἠρνεῖτο, *ērneito*, "denied," 14:70) to the servant-girl + bystanders; and finally,

- an imprecatory renunciation of Jesus before the bystanders (14:71).

Notice, then, the comparison between Jesus' responses to his three sets of accusations and that of Peter to his.

	JESUS' RESPONSES	PETER'S RESPONSES
First Accusation	Silence (14:56–59)	Denial (14:68)
Second Accusation	Silence (14:60–61a)	Denial (14:70)
Third Accusation	"**I am!**" (14:61b–62)	**Cursing and swearing** (14:71)

The vividness of the contrast achieved by the juxtaposition of Jesus' powerful and truthful self-declaration and Peter's shameful and vile cursing could not be more poignant, crushing, and tragic.[27] In the end, Peter has utterly violated Jesus' command in 8:34 to deny (ἀπαρνέομαι, *aparneomai*) oneself; instead he has denied Jesus (the same verb is employed in 14:72, and a related verb, ἀρνέομαι, *arneomai*, in 14:68, 70).[28] The one who ought to have voiced the truth—the first one Jesus called (1:16–17), the leader of the band of Twelve (3:16) and their spokesman (1:36; 8:29, 32; 9:5; 10:28; 11:21), the one who made a christological confession earlier (8:29)—now opens his mouth . . . to lie, curse, and swear! The last of the disciples to appear in the Gospel, Peter too has failed; he has been unfaithful at cockcrow. The "rock" has cracked![29]

The theological focus of this section is that disciples are to be like Jesus: self-denying even at the threat of death, uninterested in self-preservation for its own sake, and always truthful, always faithful. They are to be unlike Peter, who, to save his own skin, violates his commission to be "with Jesus" and transgresses his calling to deny himself, being untruthful and unfaithful to his Lord. In and through this "sandwich" structure, Mark declares that not to deny oneself is, in essence, a denial of Jesus.

Lest the reader despair that the account ends in defeat and hopelessness for the denying Peter, Mark provides us with the latter's agonizing and penitent reaction to the cockcrow (14:71). The repentance of Peter recorded in the Gospel is the vital difference between this disciple and Judas. Later, Peter is singled out for specific mention in the message of the resurrection and regathering in 16:7. "His remorse, contrasted with Judas's apparently settled disloyalty, points to failure under pressure rather than a

---

27. Comparing the two "trials," one almost gets the impression that in this "sandwich" Mark is attempting, to the best of his ability, to provide readers with a "picture-in-picture" depiction of Jesus' trial and Peter's—almost a superimposition in time, one over the other. A *tour de force*, indeed, and powerful in its theological thrust and emotional effect. It might be worthwhile to explore the possibility of having these simultaneous trials acted out in the worship service, prior to the sermon, in a picture-in-picture format. Matthew's arrangement (26:57–75) is similar, though the theological focus may not be exactly the same as Mark's, concentrating as the former does on the Messiahship of Jesus.

28. As well, he broke his own word never to deny Jesus (14:31, also using ἀπαρνέομαι).

29. Peter's trifold failure to watch with Jesus in Gethsemane (13:34, 35, 37) parallels the trifold betrayal of his Master (14:68, 70, 71). Even his going out (14:68) stands as a symbol of his further distancing from Jesus (see 14:54). What Peter does is true to his nature as one who is "rocky" (4:5–6, 16–17).

deliberate change of allegiance, and for that, Mark's readers will have noted with relief, there remains the prospect of forgiveness and rehabilitation."[30]

In sum, another night watch is clocked as the cock crows and Jesus' prophecy is fulfilled. Mark's "sandwich" account places Jesus' trial and witness in striking contrast with Peter's: one denies himself, the other denies his Master; one is faithful, the other is not; one stands in confidence before the highest authorities, while the other cowers in fear before those who are humble bystanders and laborers; one makes his confession boldly and truthfully, while the other curses, almost at the very instant of Jesus' forthright declaration. Ironically, the charge of blasphemy is laid on Jesus, not on Peter, the one who actually deserves it.[31] "Peter had indeed been 'caught napping', but God sent a cock to awaken him and lead him towards repentance and restitution. . . . Peter who deserves to lose his life because he is trying so hard to save it, will have it bought back by the one who will save his life precisely because he is willing to lose it."[32] The events at cockcrow are an exhortation to the disciple to deny oneself without thought of self-preservation, by being truthful and faithful.

SERMON FOCUS AND OUTLINES

THEOLOGICAL FOCUS OF PERICOPE 23 FOR PREACHING

23 **Faithfulness in discipleship involves self-denial for the cause of Jesus, without concern for self-preservation (14:53–72).**

The pericope dealing with the joint "trials" of Jesus and Peter, the last of Mark's "sandwich" stories, is a literary pearl, with these two episodes juxtaposed and intertwined together. The contrast between the one who denies himself and one who, instead, denies his Master is thereby made stark and sharp. Jesus, the faithful self-denying one, gives a boldly truthful testimony before a large and formal gathering of officials, in the face of false accusations, injustices, and despicable treatment at the hands of his captors. Despite being fully aware of where this confession would take him, Jesus does not hesitate or falter. There is absolutely no hint of interest in self-preservation. This is what it means to deny oneself: Jesus is ready for the cross.

On the other hand we have Peter, who recoils in fright before a lone servant girl. He denies, and denies again, lying, but inadvertently uttering the truth—"I do not know this man." If Peter had remained at the denial phase, it might have looked better for him, but, no, Peter proceeds to curse (Jesus?) and to swear (almost at the very instant at which Jesus affirms his identity, "I am!"). This disciple is unfaithful at the "cockcrow" watch. Peter's interest, it appears, is only to preserve his skin; he therefore, instead of denying himself, proceeds to deny Jesus. He and his compatriots have not

---

30. France, *Gospel of Mark*, 619.

31. Geddert, *Watchwords*, 100–101. Then again, is not Jesus the one who "bore our sins in His body on the cross, so that we might die to sin and live to righteousness" (1 Pet 2:24)? Jesus takes upon himself Peter's sin of blasphemy as well.

32. Ibid., 101.

discerned Jesus' person or accepted his mission; and now they have all become un-faithful to him.

Since the interweaving of the two stories is such an integral part of what Mark is *doing* with what he is *saying*, it might be better to keep the number of points of the sermon at a minimum (probably two, as one of the outlines below has), and attempt to go back and forth between the elements of each trial, contrasting the two protagonists —the faithful one and the unfaithful one. This pericope on self-denial is implicitly teaching disciples that failure to deny oneself is, in effect, a denial of Jesus—serious indictment indeed, particularly in the pampered situations of many Christians today. At least in a Western culture, where oppression may not be particularly malevolent, this might call for some careful and prayerful thought as to the circumstances in which the imperative could be faithfully applied (Liberal educational institutions? Foreign mission settings? Inimical work situations?). However, there is no doubt that God intends for the disciple to practice self-denial, even in the absence of oppression or persecution.

The issue of self-denial without self-defense is, doubtless, a hard pill to swallow, let alone apply. It does not mean that self-defense is proscribed for the disciple, but only that self-defense should not stand in the way of self-denial. Self-denial is our mandate, not self-preservation. Anything that excludes self-denial is a denial of Jesus! Again, not denying oneself is to deny Jesus.

A way to apply the self-denial motif may be to suggest that the congregation *practice* self-denial, even before persecution hits. Such a practice is surely within the stream of historical Christianity that has always undertaken the spiritual disciplines. This sermon might be a place to introduce these disciplines to a congregation that might be unfamiliar with these powerful modes of living that bring God's order into life. This is what Eugene Peterson calls *askesis* (from ἀσκέω, *askeō*, "toil," "labor," "exert"; the root of "asceticism" but without its negative connotations): "*Askesis* is to spirituality what a training regimen is to an athlete."[33] Rehearsing *askesis* before the actual trial or persecution hits is surely a profitable enterprise. Indeed, if the series on Mark is timed to conclude on or around Easter Sunday, a sermon on this pericope that deals with spiritual disciplines would be quite appropriate in the season of Lent.

POSSIBLE PREACHING OUTLINES FOR PERICOPE 23

I. JESUS vs. PETER: Self-denial vs. self-defensiveness
    Contrasts: accusers, accusations, responses (see contrast outer vs. inner story)
    Denying oneself without any concern for self-preservation or self-defense

II. DISCIPLE: *Be faithful in trial: self-denial without self-defense!*
    What specifically can the congregation do to deny themselves?

Focusing separately upon Peter and Jesus, gives us another possibility:

33. Peterson, *Under the Unpredictable Plant*, 74. Also helpful in this regard is Willard, *Spirit of the Disciplines*, who divides the spiritual disciples usefully into those of abstinence and those of engagement.

ACT III: IN JERUSALEM

I. PETER: Self-defensiveness

Peter's response of untruthfulness and unfaithfulness, 14:54, 66–72

Defending oneself with concern only for self-preservation

Move-to-Relevance: How we respond in trials seeking self-preservation, self-defense

II. JESUS: Self-denial

Jesus' response in trial of truthfulness and faithfulness, 14:53, 55–65

Denying oneself without any concern for self-preservation or self-comfort

III. DISCIPLE: *Be faithful in trial: self-denial without self-defense!*

What specifically can the congregation do to deny themselves?

PERICOPE 24

Suffering Servant

Mark 15:1–39

[Roman Trial of Jesus; Humiliation; Crucifixion]

REVIEW, SUMMARY, PREVIEW

Review of Pericope 23: Mark 14:53–72 contrasts the self-denial of Jesus and the denial of Jesus by Peter in their respective trials, instructing the disciple that faithfulness involves self-denial without concern for self-preservation, even in times of danger.

Summary of Pericope 24: Mark 15:1–39 carries on the theme of faithfulness to Jesus, portraying the dreadful suffering he undergoes in his Passion, all alone. This pericope, while encouraging disciples with hints of Jesus' victorious kingship, reminds them that following Jesus involves sacrifice and suffering. Faithfulness to Jesus till the very end is called for, from those who have "seen"—i.e., discerned his person and accepted his mission.

Preview of Pericope 25: The next pericope (15:40—16:8) focuses again on the importance of faithfulness to Jesus, particularly on disciples' failure to demonstrate such faithfulness. God's gracious restoration to his service of those who may have fallen on the way is patently laid out in the narrative.

24   Mark 15:1–39

THEOLOGICAL FOCUS OF PERICOPE 24

24   **Faithfulness to the ultimately victorious King, Jesus—remaining with him all the way, as disciples who have discerned his person and accepted his mission—involves suffering and sacrifice (15:1–39).**

> 24.1 Faithfulness in discipleship acknowledges the ultimately victorious kingship of Jesus as suffering and sacrificial (15:1–20).
>
> > 24.1.1 The true King, who is ultimately victorious, is Jesus, the Son of God, whom disciples follow faithfully.
> >
> > 24.1.2 A kingship that is suffering and sacrificial marks the regency of Jesus.
>
> 24.2 Faithfulness in discipleship involves remaining with Jesus all the way, from beginning to end, participating in his suffering, as those who have discerned his person and accepted his mission (15:21–39).
>
> > 24.2.1 Faithfulness to the mission of Jesus is to be willing to suffer persecution with him.
> >
> > 24.2.2 Faithful discipleship is undertaken by those who have discerned Jesus' person and accepted his mission.
> >
> > 24.2.3 Faithfulness to Jesus involves remaining with him all the way, from the beginning to the end of his mission of suffering.

OVERVIEW

THIS IS THE LAST pericope that deals with the time slots from the parable of the doorkeeper in Mark 13—the "morning" watch is in focus here, broadly encompassing all of the daylight hours on the day Jesus was crucified.

It was noted earlier that the previous pericope (14:53–72) and the present one (15:1–39) deal with what it means to deny oneself, and what it means to take up one's cross, respectively. Thus Pericopes 23 and 24 expand on the essential demand of discipleship made by Jesus in 8:33–34. Pericope 24 is structured quite intentionally:

A   Roman procurator questions Jesus, the King of the Jews (15:1–5)
> B   Crowd calls for the death of the King of the Jews; release of Barabbas (substitution) (15:6–15)
> > C   Soldiers mock (ἐμπαίζω, empaizō) the King of the Jews (15:16–20)
> > > *Suffering with Jesus: Simon, "pseudo-disciple" (15:21)*
> > > > D   Jesus crucified as the King of the Jews (15:21–26)
> > > > > *Suffering with Jesus: Two robbers, "pseudo-disciples" (15:27)*
> > C'   Passersby, religious leaders, and robbers mock (ἐμπαίζω) Christ, the King of Israel (15:29–32)
> B'   Death of Jesus; cosmic signs; temple veil rent; forsaken by God (implied substitution for sin?) (15:33–38)
A'   Roman centurion acknowledges Jesus, the Son of God (15:39)

The significance of these elements will be noted below.

24.1 Mark 15:1–20

THEOLOGICAL FOCUS 24.1

> 24.1 Faithfulness in discipleship acknowledges the ultimately victorious kingship of Jesus as suffering and sacrificial (15:1–20).
>
> > 24.1.1 The true King, who is ultimately victorious, is Jesus, the Son of God, whom disciples follow faithfully.
> >
> > 24.1.2 A kingship that is suffering and sacrificial marks the regency of Jesus.

Section Summary 24.1: The persecution and ultimate execution of the true King, Jesus, is the focus of this section. This is a kingship that is sacrificial: Jesus, in a supreme act of self-denial, takes up his cross, being the atoning substitute. Yet, paradoxically, there are hints that this kingship is ultimately victorious, greater than all the regencies that even Rome, in all its glory, could muster. It is to such a kingship that disciples are called to be faithful.

TRANSLATION 24.1

15:1   *And immediately, early in the morning, the chief priests, with the elders and scribes and the whole Sanhedrin, after holding a consultation, bound Jesus and, leading [Him] away, delivered [Him] to Pilate.*

15:2   *And Pilate questioned Him, "Are You the King of the Jews?" And answering him, He said, "You say [so]."*

15:3   *And the chief priests began to accuse Him of many things.*

15:4   *And Pilate again questioned Him, saying, "Do You not answer anything? See how much they are accusing You."*

15:5   *But Jesus no longer answered anything, so Pilate was amazed.*

15:6   *Now during the Feast he used to release to them one prisoner whom they asked for.*

15:7   *There was one named Barabbas, imprisoned with the insurrectionists, who had committed murder in the insurrection.*

15:8   *And the crowd went up and began to ask [him to do] just as he was usually doing for them.*

15:9   *And Pilate answered them, saying, "Do you want me to release to you the King of the Jews?"*

15:10   *For he knew that the chief priests had given Him over because of envy.*

15:11   *But the chief priests incited the crowd [to ask him] to release Barabbas to them instead.*

15:12   *And Pilate again answering, said to them, "Then what do you want me to do with the one you call the King of the Jews?"[1]*

15:13   *And they again cried out, "Crucify Him!"*

15:14   *But Pilate said to them, "Why—what evil has He done?" But they cried out even more, "Crucify Him!"*

15:15   *Then Pilate, wishing to satisfy the crowd, released to them Barabbas and, after flogging Jesus, gave Him over to be crucified.*

15:16   *And the soldiers led Him away into the palace—that is, the Praetorium—and summoned the whole [Roman] cohort.*

15:17   *And they dressed Him in purple and, braiding a crown of thorns, they put it on Him,*

15:18   *and they began to salute Him, "Hail, King of the Jews!"*

---

1. While some of the important manuscripts lack θέλετε (*thelete*, "you want"), for reasons discussed in other critical commentaries, this longer version has a bit more weight. In either case, the theological thrust of the pericope remains the same.

15:19   *And they kept striking His head with a staff, and spitting on Him, and kneeling and prostrating themselves before Him.*

15:20   *And when they had mocked Him, they stripped Him of the purple and dressed Him in His garments. And they led Him out to crucify Him.*

NOTES 24.1

24.1.1   The true King, who is ultimately victorious, is Jesus, the Son of God, whom disciples follow faithfully.

From a historical point of view, the arrogation to himself of the titles "Christ," "Son of God," and "Son of Man" provided enough grist to accuse Jesus of claiming royal authority. This would explain the peppering of this account with the sardonic application of "kingship" to Jesus. From a theological point of view however, Mark is casting an ironic eye at the way Jesus is so labeled; he is, after all, rightly the King, but no one recognizes him as such, even if they address him that way.[2] As France observes, "King of the Jews" is an appropriate rendition of Jesus' messianic claim in language that Rome would have recognized as tantamount to sedition and rebellious treason. But from Mark's inkwell, Jesus' kingship becomes a powerful truth—sarcastically affirmed by the scoffers but true nonetheless—that holds the pericope together: it occurs six times (15:2, 9, 12, 18, 26, 32), not to mention the implicit basis it forms for all the mockery and insults heaped on Jesus in this section. Despite the incongruities and indignities of the entire gruesome episode, "[t]he reader is expected to recognize that . . . Jesus does enter into his true kingship, paradoxically enthroned on the cross."[3] The way to glory, as this Gospel has often reminded the reader, is through suffering.

The parallels between the Jewish and Gentile trials are illustrative of the fact that there is no distinction in the way Jesus is treated by the two factions. All are equally culpable. Nobody recognizes him for who he is, despite the labels they attach to him.

---

2. Witherington notes that in the days of the early church there was a whole cottage industry engaged in spinning out the ironies of the Passion (*Gospel of Mark*, 393n142). So Cyprian: "He received the spittle of revilers, who, a short time before, with his spittle had cured the eyes of a blind man. . . . He was stripped of his earthly garment, who clothes others in the vestment of immortality. . . . He was given vinegar to drink, who offered the cup of salvation. He, the innocent and just—indeed, innocence and justice itself—is counted among transgressors, and truth concealed by false witnesses. He who will judge is judged, and the Word of God is silently led to the slaughter" (*Good of Patience* 7). And Gregory Nazianzen: "As a sheep, he is led to the slaughter, but he is the shepherd of Israel, and now of the whole world also. As a lamb, he is silent, yet he is the Word. . . . He is bruised and wounded, but he heals every disease and infirmity. He is lifted up and nailed to the tree, but by the tree of life he restores us. . . . He is given vinegar to drink mixed with gall. Who is he? He who turned water into wine and destroyed the taste of bitterness, who is sweetness himself. . . . He dies, but he gives life, and by his death destroys death" (*Oration* 29, "On the Son," 20).

3. France, *Gospel of Mark*, 628.

MARK 14:60–62, 63–65 (Jewish Trial)	MARK 15:4, 2, 8–20 (Gentile Trial)
And the high priest . . .	*Then Pilate again*
questioned Jesus saying,	*questioned Him saying,*
"Do you not answer anything—	*"Do you not answer anything?*
what these men	*See how much they*
are testifying against You?"	*are accusing You."*
But He kept silent	*But Jesus no longer*
and did not answer anything.	*answered anything, . . .*
Again the high priest	*And Pilate*
questioned Him	*questioned Him,*
and said to Him,	
"Are you the Christ	*"Are you the King*
the Son of the Blessed One?"	*of the Jews?"*
And Jesus said,	*And He answered him, saying,*
"I am, . . ."	*"You say [so]."*
Consultation with Sanhedrin (14:63–64a)	Consultation with crowd (15:8–14a)
Condemnation to death (14:63b)	Condemnation to death (15:14b–15)
Mocking and torture (14:65)	Mocking and torture (15:16–20)*

* From Myers, *Binding the Strong Man*, 370; and Witherington, *Gospel of Mark*, 388.

Schmidt has demonstrated the notable parallels between the triumphal procession of a Roman military victor and the sequence of events in 15:16–21.[4] He observes that the details in this pericope are carefully chosen to evoke the picture of the triumphal march of a victorious general: commencement at the Praetorium (15:16); attendance of the whole cohort (15:16); clothing of purple (outlawed for lower ranks) (15:17); crown (15:17); formulaic accolades from soldiers (15:18–19); the procession (15:20); etc. Even the requisition of Simon, the passerby (15:21), appears to be deliberately utilized: monuments depicting Roman triumphs show an official bearing a double-bladed axe accompanying a sacrificial bull dressed and crowned to be identified with the triumphator (the triumphant warrior); the weapon borne is, of course, the instrument of the victim's death (Simon bears Jesus' cross, 15:21). Moreover, the terminus of every such procession in Rome was also a "place of the head" or the Capitoline Hill (from *caput*, "head"), at the Temple of Jupiter (an obvious parallel with Golgotha, the "place of the skull," 15:22). Wine was routinely offered to the triumphator at the sacrifice of the bull; refused, it was poured on the altar or on the bull (akin to Jesus' refusal, 15:23). "The wine obviously signifies the precious blood of the victim, and the links between sacrificant [the sacrificial victim], wine, and victim signify their identity."[5] It was also common in a triumphal procession for lictors to bear placards announcing the identity of the peoples conquered by the victor (an inscription stated the kingship of Jesus over the Jews, 15:26). Frequently at the culmination of the procession a threesome (the triumphator and his two closest advisors, generals, or vice-regents) was elevated

4. Schmidt, "Mark 15.16–32."
5. Ibid., 11.

above the adoring throngs (two robbers were crucified with Jesus, 15:27). This account of Jesus' procession is thus an "anti-triumph." "For Mark, it is the mocked Jesus, not the gaudy Roman emperor, who is the true epiphanic triumphator."[6] Emphasizing the "irreconcilable hostility" between the kingdom of God and the kingdom of man, between Jesus and the Roman *imperium*, Mark's Gospel portrays the victorious kingship of Jesus, even in the account of his sufferings.[7] This is perhaps the main reason why disciples who follow the suffering and sacrificing Jesus can take heart—the king they follow will ultimately triumph over every adversary.

Jesus' reply to Pilate's question about his kingship is non-committal (15:2), as the procurator himself seems to take it (15:4, 12). Yes, Jesus is the Messiah alright, but not in the sense that Pilate assumes—the regent of a supposedly earthly kingdom in competition with the temporal authority of Rome.[8] While these instances are the only times "King of the Jews/Israel" is found in Mark, the broader and more comprehensive understanding of Jesus' kingship has been implicit throughout: the Transfiguration (9:1–9), the seating of his disciples at his right and left (10:37), the salutation by Bartimaeus and later by the adoring crowds on Palm Sunday (10:47–48; 11:10), the allusions to Zechariah 9:9 (Mark 11:1–7), Jesus own acknowledgement of his messiahship (12:35–37), and the general exercise of his authority demonstrated in all his actions and words throughout the Gospel. In a roundabout way in this pericope, with the concept of the ultimate victory of this king—*the* King—Mark is encouraging the followers of Jesus to remain faithful "on the way" with Jesus.

24.1.2   A kingship that is suffering and sacrificial marks the regency of Jesus.[9]

Jesus' silence in Mark 15:5 alludes to Isaiah 53:7; so also Pilate's amazement (θαυμάζω, *thaumazō*)—Isaiah 52:15 notes that the nations are amazed (θαυμάζω) at the Suffering Servant. Such a stoic acceptance of his faith would also, in the Greco-Roman context of Mark's Gospel, endear Jesus to readers; the ethical tradition of that contemporary culture highly valued such noble qualities.[10]

The substitute for Jesus has an ironic name: "Bar-abbas" (= "son of the father"; one remembers that just a few verses back, in 14:36, Mark had translated "Abba" as "father" for his readers). This "son of the father," guilty of rebellion and sentenced to death, goes free (15:6–15); the real "Son of the Father," innocent and falsely accused, will die in the other's place. The "imprisoned" one (δέω, *deō*, 15:7), who killed someone (15:7), is released, and another becomes "bound" (δέω, 15:1) in his place, one who has brought another back to life (5:41–42).[11] In the chiastic structure of 15:1–39 (see

---

6. Idem, "Jesus' Triumphal March," 30–37.

7. Myers, *Binding the Strong Man*, 380.

8. Witherington, *Gospel of Mark*, 390.

9. That is, in the present age.

10. See Plutarch, *Mor.* 498d–e; Plato, *Resp.* 2.361e: "the just man who is thought unjust will be scourged, racked, bound, will have his eyes burnt out, and, at last after suffering every kind of evil, he will be impaled."

11. That such a practice of releasing prisoners was in vogue is hinted at in *b. Pesah.* 91a; also see Livy, *Epon.* 5.13.8; and Josephus, *Ant.* 17.200–205; 20.215.

above), this substitution of Barabbas finds its counterpart in the forsaking of Jesus by God (15:33–38; elements B and B'). However, there is a "gap" in the narrative—the reason for God forsaking his Son is not explicitly noted. In light of the parallels between Barabbas and Jesus, and the replacement of one with the other, not to mention the declaration of Mark 10:45 and its allusions to Isaiah 53, a not-so-subtle hint of the substitutionary atonement may be recognized here.[12] The kingship of Jesus is a suffering and sacrificial one, and ought to prompt disciples to follow Jesus, being willing to suffer and sacrifice as Jesus has explicitly taught (Mark 8:34; 10:45; etc.).[13]

Crucifixion, while being the normal Roman punishment for political rebels in the province, was, nonetheless, deplored by most notable Romans. Cicero writes on the shamefulness of this execution: "Even if we are threatened with death, we may die free men. But the executioner, the veiling of the head, and the very word 'cross' should be far removed not only from the person of a Roman citizen but his thoughts, his eyes, and his ears. For it is not only the actual occurrence of these things but . . . the very mention of them that is unworthy of a Roman citizen and a free man" (*Rab. Perd.* 16).[14] It is even more "disconcerting to find it requested by a Jewish crowd (the approved Jewish methods of execution being stoning, burning, beheading, or strangling, *m. Sanh.* 7.1)," not to mention the fact that it is the crowd, not the procurator, who passes sentence—almost like the culmination of Roman gladiator games where the spectators voted on the fate of the vanquished![15]

The entire scene of mockery is revolting (15:16–20); again, it is carefully structured to emphasize the degradation.[16]

A   Soldiers led him away into the palace (ἀπήγαγον . . . ἔσω, *apēgagon . . . esō*) (15:16)

    B   Disrobed: Purple cloak and crown of thorns placed (ἐνδιδύσκω, *endidyskō*) (15:17)

        C   Homage: "King of the Jews" (15:18)

            D   Struck head, spat (15:19a)

12. Nonetheless, Mark does not seek to expound on a theory of the atonement; he has a different agenda—how disciples of Jesus should follow him. For preaching purposes, at least, that agenda must be respected.

13. From a symbolic narrative sense, Jesus' refusal of the offer of myrrh-admixed wine (Mark 15:23) corresponds to the refusal of the Roman triumphator to drink (see above). Historically, however, Jesus' denial may have had to do with his determination not to alleviate any part of his suffering and to "drink the cup" allotted to him without mitigating the agonies thereof. Citing Prov 31:6, *b. Sanh.* 43a exhorts: "When one is led out to execution, he is given a goblet of wine containing a grain of frankincense, in order to benumb his senses." Perhaps Jesus' pledge at the Passover meal not to drink wine again until the eschaton (Mark 14:25) was also in his mind. He is determined to suffer according to the will of the Father.

14. Crucifixion was the "most cruel and disgusting penalty" and "the extreme and ultimate penalty for a slave" (Cicero, *Verr.* 2.5.168)—"a most miserable death" (Josephus, *J.W.* 7.203).

15. France, *Gospel of Mark*, 634. It must be noted that this "crowd" is highly unlikely to be the same laudatory "crowd" of Passover celebrants who accompanied Jesus in his entry into Jerusalem, and that was feared by the Sanhedrin (11:32; 12:12). Those Galilean pilgrims cried out (κράζω, *krazō*, 11:9; the last time Mark uses this verb before 15:13–14) "Hosanna!," but these hordes cry out (also κράζω, 15:13–14) for his death: "Crucify Him!"

16. Reid, *Preaching Mark*, 155–56.

C′   Homage: prostrated (15:19b)

B′   Disrobed again: Purple cloak removed (ἐκδύω, ekduō) (15:20a)

A′   Soldiers led him out (ἐξάγουσιν, exagousin) (15:20b)

While the size of a Roman cohort varied, it was technically a tenth of a legion, therefore comprising about 600 soldiers. Jesus is humiliated before a huge crowd (the "whole" cohort, 15:16), and likely not a genteel one at that. Their action of dressing him (15:17) employs the verb ἐνδιδύσκω (endidyskō, instead of the usual ἐνδύω, enduō; it occurs elsewhere in the NT only in Luke 16:19, also connected with the donning of "purple." The verb thus connotes a more elaborate "dressing up" and caparisoning in regal wear. Notice that in all the robing and disrobing, Jesus is actually stripped naked twice, an obvious shaming device. And "Hail, King of the Jews" (Mark 15:18) is clearly a parody of "Hail, Caesar!" The mocking takes center place in this part of the narrative (see above: B, C, D, C′, B′); later, his fellow crucifixion victims mock him too (15:32). The crucifixion, on the other hand, takes a mere three words in the Greek (καὶ σταυροῦσιν αὐτὸν, kai staurousin auton, "and they crucified Him," 15:24). Mark's focus is not so much on the atoning death of Jesus as it is on the suffering this King goes through. The king that disciples follow suffers sacrificially. Can they, in turn, expect to do less?[17]

24.2   Mark 15:21–39

THEOLOGICAL FOCUS 24.2

24.2   Faithfulness in discipleship involves remaining with Jesus all the way, from beginning to end, participating in his suffering, as those who have discerned his person and accepted his mission (15:21–39).

24.2.1   Faithfulness to the mission of Jesus is to be willing to suffer persecution with him.

24.2.2   Faithful discipleship is undertaken by those who have discerned Jesus' person and accepted his mission.

24.2.3   Faithfulness to Jesus involves remaining with him all the way, from the beginning to the end of his mission of suffering.

Section Summary 24.2: The stories of Simon the Cyrenian and that of the two robbers articulate poignantly the abandonment of Jesus by the disciples. In the demonstration of faith by a Roman centurion, disciples are reminded that those who have "seen" must believe—i.e., remain faithful even to the end of the suffering mission.

---

17. Despite the opprobrium of mockery and insults, there is implicit—even in this narrative that focuses on Jesus' suffering—a sense of divine ordination in these events: God's purpose *is* being fulfilled. Mark interweaves allusions to Scripture throughout, reminding the reader that all these things happened "as it is written" (14:21); for instance: division of garments (Mark 15:24; Ps 22:18); mockery, wagging of heads (Mark 15:29; Ps 22:7); "save yourself!" (Mark 15:30–31; Ps 22:8); reviling (Mark 15:32; Ps 22:6); cry of dereliction (Mark 15:34; Ps 22:1); vinegar given to drink (Mark 15:36; Ps 69:21); and bystanders looking on at a distance (Mark 15:40; Ps 38:11). See Evans, *Mark*, 498.

TRANSLATION 24.2

15:21 *And they pressed into service a certain passerby to take up His cross— Simon the Cyrenian, coming from the country, the father of Alexander and Rufus.*

15:22 *And they brought Him to the place Golgotha, which is translated, "Place of the Skull."*

15:23 *And they gave Him wine mixed with myrrh, but He did not take [it].*

15:24 *And they crucified Him, and divided His garments, casting lots for them, [to see] who might take what.*

15:25 *And it was the third hour, and they crucified Him.*

15:26 *And there was an inscription of His charges which had been inscribed: "The King of the Jews."*

15:27 *And with Him they crucified two robbers, one on His right and one on His left.*

[15:28][18]

15:29 *And those going by were reviling Him, shaking their heads and saying, "Ha! The one going to destroy the temple and build [it] in three days—*

15:30 *save Yourself, coming down from the cross."*

15:31 *In the same way, the chief priests also were mocking [Him] among themselves with the scribes, saying, "Others He saved; Himself He cannot save!*

15:32 *Let Christ, the King of Israel, come down now from the cross, that we may see and believe." Those who were crucified with Him also were insulting Him.*

15:33 *And when the sixth hour came, darkness came upon the whole land until the ninth hour.*

15:34 *And at the ninth hour, Jesus called out with a loud voice, "Eloi, Eloi, lema sabachthani?" which is translated, "My God, My God, why have You forsaken Me?"*

15:35 *And some of the bystanders hearing [this], said, "Behold, He is calling Elijah."*

15:36 *And someone ran and filling a sponge with sour wine, put it on a staff, [and] gave Him to drink, saying, "Let us see if Elijah is coming to take Him down."*

15:37 *And Jesus let out a loud cry and gave up the spirit.*

15:38 *And the veil of the temple was rent in two from top to bottom.*

15:39 *Then the centurion, who was standing by in front of Him, seeing that He gave up the spirit in this manner, said, "Truly this man was the Son of God!"*

---

18. The best manuscripts do not contain 15:28.

NOTES 24.2

24.2.1   Faithfulness to the mission of Jesus is to be willing to suffer persecution with him.[19]

An intriguing structure develops in 15:21–27, framing the crucifixion of Jesus. There is Simon the Cyrenian on one side, and two robbers on the other. Both, playing the part of "disciples," suffer *with* Jesus.

> *Suffering with Jesus: Simon, "pseudo-disciple"* (15:21)
> > Jesus crucified as the King of the Jews (15:21–26)
> *Suffering with Jesus: Two robbers, "pseudo-disciples"* (15:27)

Simon is a disciple figure, as seen in the parallels between this account and the calling of the disciples in Mark 1, and the cross-bearing in Mark 8 that the disciples were supposed to be undertaking. Simon is thus a "pseudo-disciple"—a stark contrast to the real ones who are missing.

Simon Co-opted (MARK 15:21)	Disciples Co-opted (MARK 1:16–20)
παράγοντα (*paragonta*, "passerby," 15:21) Simon the Cyrenian (15:21) Gentile (from the names of his sons) father (15:21) Two brothers (15:21) ἄρῃ τὸν σταυρὸν αὐτοῦ (*arē ton stauron autou*, "to take up His cross," 15:21)	παράγων (*paragōn*, "passing by," 1:16; 2:13)[*] Simon (twice, 1:16) Jewish disciples father (1:20) Two brothers (twice, 1:16, 19)[†] ἀράτω τὸν σταυρὸν αὐτοῦ (*aratō ton stauron autou*, "take up your cross," 8:34)[‡]

[*] These are the only three occurrences of παράγω, *paragō*, in this Gospel.

[†] It is quite possible that the naming of Simon's two sons in 15:21 indicates knowledge of this family by Mark's Roman Christian audience; Rom 16:13 mentions a Rufus too.

[‡] The σταυρός (*stauros*, "cross") which was borne to the scene of the execution was probably the horizontal beam (the *patibulum*) that would be slotted into a vertical beam (the *staticulum*) that was left in a public, prominent place, like gallows.

The robbers, too, are "pseudo-disciples" (15:27), stand-ins (if one may put it that way) for the real disciples, James and John, who had boldly declared their intention to be on Jesus' right and left, and had asserted their capacity to share in Jesus' "cup" and "baptism" (10:35–40).[20] Again, irony penetrates and sears: the real disciples of Jesus are nowhere to be found in this "morning" watch; it is only these "pseudo-disciples" who remain "with him" (as the actual disciples had been called to do, 3:14). Now it is these robbers who are to be "baptized" with the baptism Jesus undergoes; the Twelve have already fled, refusing to be "numbered with the transgressors" (Isa 53:12).

In keeping with his theological thrust, Mark completely overlooks the details of the crucifixion and its theological significance. As was noted, with just three words in

19. This is something the Twelve do not demonstrate!

20. The "cup" as a metaphor of Jesus' Passion was explicitly clarified in Mark 14:23, 36. For "baptism" as symbolic of suffering, see Josephus, *J. W.* 4.137; Job 9:31 (Aquila); and Ps 68:3 (Aquila and Symmachus).

the Greek (15:24) Mark is done with the description of one of the most momentous events since creation.[21] The Evangelist's focus, here, is on the abandonment of the suffering, sacrificing Jesus by one and all—particularly the unfaithfulness of the disciples in the "morning" watch. Only pseudo-disciples keep Jesus company in this dark hour. In the barren loneliness of abandonment, "the cross becomes the throne of a king without a country, without subjects, and without power."[22] The total aloneness that Jesus experiences with the fleeing of the disciples is now made more shocking: darkness descends (15:33) as even light flees. And soon God will forsake him, too (15:34). Jesus' abandonment will be total.[23]

The exhortation of the mockers that Jesus "come down from the cross" (15:29–30) is diametrically opposed to Jesus' own command to those who would follow him that they take up their cross and not attempt to save their own lives (8:34–36). Ironically, the disparaging remarks here show that these scorners clearly have understood Jesus' claim to be able to "save." They even understand the response Jesus wanted from them —to "believe" (15:32)—but that, however, they are unwilling to do. "Their unbelief then lies not in a failure or inability to discern Jesus' potential significance, but in a conscious repudiation of him and of his works. For this reason the narrator describes their invective as 'blasphemy' (15:29) [ἐβλασφήμουν, *eblasphēmoun*, "reviling"]. . . . Ironically, they are thus doing the very thing for which they condemned Jesus (2:7; 14:64), and so bring condemnation on themselves."[24]

But the mockers are right; Jesus *has* saved others: 3:4; 5:23, 28, 34; 6:56; and 10:52 all use the same verb, σῴζω (*sōzō*, "save" or "heal") for the relief of those sufferers' afflictions. And yes, Jesus refuses to save himself, choosing instead to sacrifice himself for "many" (10:45). That is the model disciples should emulate (8:34–35)—not in the salvific sense of atonement, of course, but in the Markan theological sense of following Jesus in his suffering mission, being faithful to him in the "morning" watch. Particularly, in this pericope, the suffering is the bearing up of the cruel and despicable ridicule and persecution, perhaps even to death, that will confront them.

24.2.2 *Faithful discipleship is undertaken by those who have discerned Jesus' person and accepted his mission.*

Mark 15:32–39 is also carefully crafted: the motif of "sight" is constantly repeated in the unit.

---

21. The resurrection, too, is more implied than demonstrated in Mark's Gospel, without Jesus ever reappearing on the scene after his crucifixion.

22. van Iersel, *Mark*, 469.

23. That this is a scene of desolation is verbally depicted in the many words in the passage prefixed with κατα- (*kata-*): καταλύων (*kataluōn*, "destroy," 15:29); καταβάς (*katabas*, "coming down," 15:30); καταβάτω (*katabatō*, "come down," 15:32); ἐγκατέλιπές (*enkatelipes*, "You have forsaken," 15:34); καθελεῖν (*kathelein*, "to take down," 15:36); καταπέτασμα (*katapetasma*, "veil," 15:38); and κάτω (*katō*, "bottom," 15:38). This is analogous to the way "down-" is prefixed with other English words ("downcast," "downturn," "downfall," etc.) to generate a negative tone.

24. Marshall, *Faith as a Theme*, 204–5.

A   Mockers: "… that we may see [ὁράω, horaō] and believe" (15:32)

    B   First judgment: darkness for three hours (15:33)

        C   Cry in a great voice (φωνή μεγάλη, phōnē megalē); forsaken by the Father (15:34)

            D   Bystanders: "Behold [ὁράω] He is calling Elijah" (15:35)

            D′   Man giving wine: "Let us see [ὁράω] if Elijah is coming . . ." (15:36)

        C′   Cry in a loud voice (φωνή μεγάλη): the departure of the spirit (ἐξέπνευσεν, exepneusen) (15:37)

    B′   Second judgment: rending of the sanctuary curtain (15:38)

A′   Centurion sees (ὁράω) and, apparently, believes (15:39)*

* Myers, *Binding the Strong Man*, 389.

The Jewish religious leaders want to see Jesus escape death in order for them to believe (15:32).[25] On the other hand, the Roman centurion sees Jesus undergo death and believes (15:39). This soldier's acclamation of Jesus as "Son of God" is the first time the label is applied with conviction by a human voice in the Gospel (as opposed to the incredulous query by the high priest in 14:61). "The identity of that witness, a pagan soldier without the benefit either of Jewish theological education or of having been a disciple of Jesus, fits well with Mark's persistent theme of the inability of either the Jewish leadership or even Jesus' own disciples to recognize who he is."[26] Chronis asserts that "υἱὸς θεοῦ [huios theou, "Son of God"] functions in Mark as a designation for Jesus' divinity." Mark's narrative, it would appear, has been moving towards this all along, even balking at the applicability of "Son of David" where it did not carry the notion of Jesus' divine Sonship (12:35–37).[27] Yet, in this utterance of the centurion, 15:39 creates a humanly irreconcilable paradox with 15:34—the abandonment of the Son of God by God![28]

25. He did. But they did not. In a final irony, even Jesus' last words are misunderstood (15:34–35)!

26. France, *Gospel of Mark*, 650.

27. Chronis, "Torn Veil," 105–6. In this Gospel, the acclamation of Jesus as "Son of God" comes from Mark, the narrator (1:1); God, to those around (1:11); demons, to Jesus (3:11; 5:7); God, to Peter, James, and John (9:7); in the high priest's skeptical question to Jesus (14:61–62); and, finally, from the centurion as an exclamation (15:39).

28. As if abandonment by disciples was not enough! One might, however, concede, that it is *because* of the abandonment of the disciples (i.e., their sin) that God abandons his Son (that the latter may pay for their sins, and the sins of everyone else). Bearing this out, the abandonment by God is accompanied by an unnatural darkness, a mark of God's judgment, as well as the rending of the temple veil—this, likely, a sign of the sufficiency of Jesus' atonement, symbolized in the unveiling of access into God's presence. (It could also indicate the departure of God from the temple, in which case the rending of the veil also would indicate judgment.) For darkness as a token of divine judgment, see Deut 28:29; Isa 13:9–10; 24:23; Jer 4:28; 13:16; 15:9; Ezek 32:7–8; Joel 2:10, 31; 3:15; Amos 8:9 (mourning for an only son); Zeph 1:15; Mark 13:24–25; Acts 2:20; Rev 6:12; etc. Of course, the penultimate plague before the slaying of the firstborn during the paradigmatic event of redemption in the OT was also darkness (Exod 10:21–23). Mark does echo the language of this phenomenon. Exodus 10:22 LXX has ἐγένετο σκότος . . . ἐπὶ πᾶσαν γῆν Αἰγύπτου (egeneto skotos . . . epi pasan gēn Aigyptou, "there came darkness . . . upon the whole land of Egypt"). Mark 15:33 uses a strikingly similar phrase: σκότος ἐγένετο ἐφ' ὅλην τὴν γῆν (skotos egeneto eph holēn tēn gēn, "darkness came upon the whole land"). This is judgment, indeed; and God's Son is slain for the sins of humanity.

The centurion, probably in charge of the execution squad, and the same one later to be summoned before Pilate (15:44–45), could see the entire process of Jesus' demise from his vantage point "in front of Him" (15:39). From a purely topological aspect, from where Golgotha was located and where the centurion was stationed, it would be unlikely that he could have seen the outer curtain of the temple being rent (15:38), but Mark does not claim he does. Thus the reader is left in the dark about what exactly it is that convinced the centurion of the divine Sonship of Jesus—the cryptic statement "seeing that He breathed His last in this manner" is not particularly illuminating. However, from a narrative standpoint, Mark is contrasting the unbelief of the others who "saw" with the belief of the centurion who also "saw" (15:32, 39; see the structure of 15:32–39 above). The Roman officer's acclamation, following right after the statement that he *sees* how Jesus dies, suggests he believes from seeing how Jesus dies. That sets him apart from those who want to *see* Jesus escape death in order for them to believe. Even more, the Roman soldier's location, "standing by in front of Him" ("with" Jesus? 15:39), is in dramatic contrast to the disciples, who are nowhere in the vicinity.

No particular sign causes the centurion's insight; his is the acclamation that comes from "seeing" with the eyes of faith (15:39). That "sight" plays an important role in this pericope is not surprising, considering Mark's emphasis on this aspect of sensation all along (4:24–25; 8:29, 35, and especially on the two stories of healing the blind 8:22–26 and 10:46–52). "Now at the climax of the story, one who has seen no miracles, but sees only the crucified Jesus *sees* who he really is . . . [ἀληθῶς, *alēthōs*, 'truly,' introduces the centurion's declaration in 15:39]. This seeing is not a human attainment, but the gift of God, and in this respect the centurion is a model for all later believers."[29] Those who have seen—i.e., every disciple, past, present, and future—must believe: they must be faithful in the "morning" watch, remaining with Jesus in his suffering mission, suffering with him, denying themselves as he does himself. This is discipleship—to be faithful to Jesus, having discerned his person and accepted his mission.

24.2.3   Faithfulness to Jesus involves remaining with him all the way, from the beginning to the end of his mission of suffering.

The declaration of 15:39 also tightly links the appellation "Son of God" with the death of Jesus. This is the label that no one has comprehended until now—least of all the disciples. (This is also why the designation "Christ," as acknowledged by Peter, without the notion of Jesus' death, was considered inadequate [8:27—9:1].) But now the story has been completed; the titles of the incipit ("Jesus Christ" and "Son of God") have now been fulfilled.

MARK 1:1	MARK 8:29	MARK 15:39
Jesus Christ Son of God	Christ	
		Son of God

29. Boring, *Mark*, 433–34. It is surely significant that the only other time Jesus is described as οὗτος ὁ ἄνθρωπος (*houtos ho anthrōpos*, "this man," 15:39) was in Peter's final cursing and swearing denial of his Master (14:71). What a contrast!

The tearing of the veil (15:38), humanly impossible (the outer curtain was about seventy-five feet in height), is accomplished with a divine passive, ἐσχίσθη (*eschisthē*). Geddert observes that there are thirty-five different interpretations for the twelve-word verse of 15:38.[30] The question of which of the two veils of the temple—outer or inner—has obsessed scholars innumerable. The rending of the outer curtain would be more public; that of the inner would be more theologically appropriate, since it led into the very presence of God in the temple. Mark's phrasing, τὸ καταπέτασμα τοῦ ναοῦ (*to katapetasma tou naou*) leans neither way, and perhaps with good reason. The curtains, *both* inner and outer, may have represented the boundary of heaven. Josephus, describing the wilderness tabernacle, says that the Holy of Holies was an imitation of heaven (*Ant.* 3.122–133, 181). Thus the tearing of the *inner* curtain could be considered a rending of the heavens. On the other hand, the same historian also describes the outer veil as having colors that represented the four elements: fire, earth, air, and water. On this was portrayed a "panorama of the heavens" (*J.W.* 5.207–221). Thus the tearing of the *outer* curtain could also be symbolic of the rending of the heavens.[31] This idea of a "heavenly" veil fits Jewish cosmology, which saw the cultic articles of the temple as representing parts of the universe. The temple itself was considered a gateway between earth and heaven, and the metaphor of heaven as a curtain was widely understood (Isa 40:22).[32]

But even more interesting is that the verb σχίζω (*schizō*, "rend") occurs only twice in the entire Gospel; the other instance is an actual rending of the heavens (Mark 1:10). There is a striking similarity in the agencies operating in the events at the beginning and end of Jesus' earthly ministry: God's Spirit descends into him as his ministry commences, this entrance rending the heavens; and Jesus ministry concludes with an ascent of that "spirit" out of him in his dying breath, which also rends the curtain (symbolically heaven?) in its departure.[33]

---

30. Geddert, *Watchwords*, 140–43.

31. There are reports of astonishing events in the temple about four decades before its destruction, perhaps coinciding with the occasion of Jesus' death. The tractate *b. Yoma* 39b mentions that "during the last forty years before the destruction of the temple, the lot for the Lord did not come up in the right hand [lots for the Lord and one for the scapegoat were drawn on the Day of Atonement—Lev 16:8]; nor did the crimson-colored thread become white [as should have happened on the Day of Atonement—Isa 1:18]; nor did the westernmost light shine [sign of departure of God's presence?]; and the doors of the Temple would open by themselves." Josephus (*J.W.* 6.297–300) mentions an earthquake in the temple precincts and a loud sound of many voices. In *J.W.* 6.293, he notes that the massive eastern gate of the inner court of the temple opened on its own, at about the sixth hour of the night. See Plummer, "Something Awry," 306–7.

32. Gurtner, "Rending of the Veil," 300. Considerable correspondence was discerned between the heavens and the temple: Ps 78:69 (see Ps 148:1); 150:1; Heb 8:1–5; Rev 11:19; 14:17; 15:5; *T. Levi* 3.4; 5.1; 18.6–7; Philo, *On the Creation* 18.55; *Gen. Rab.* 4.2 (on Gen 1:6); etc.

33. Jackson, "Death of Jesus," 27.

BAPTISM	CRUCIFIXION
Heavens rent (σχίζω, *schizō*, 1:10)*	Temple veil rent (σχίζω, 15:38)
Holy Spirit (πνεῦμα, *pneuma*, 1:10)	Gave up the spirit (ἐκπνέω, *ekpneō*, 15:37)†
God present (1:11)	God forsakes Jesus (15:34)
John the Baptist as Elijah (1:4–9)	Elijah absent (15:35–36)
Voice from heaven (1:11)	Silence from heaven; darkness falls (15:33)
"You are my beloved Son" (1:11)	"Truly, this man was the Son of God" (15:39)
Jesus' baptism	Jesus' Passion as a "baptism" (10:38–39)‡

* Matthew 3:16 and Luke 3:21 have ἀνοίγω ("open") instead. However, all three Synoptics use σχίζω for the rending of the temple veil.

† Jackson, "Death of Jesus," 26, notes that ἐκπνεῖν (*ekpnein*, "to give up the spirit") was a common euphemism for dying in classical Greek idiom (with or without an object), but not in Koine Greek.

‡ Mark is the only Synoptic writer to carry this analogy between the Passion and "baptism."

With that marvelously fashioned frame of the rending of the heavens, the "*beginning of the gospel of Jesus Christ, Son of God*" (1:1) comes to a close; what remains is an epilogue (15:40—16:8) that deals with the plans for the (re)commencement of the Trip of Discipleship, including the restoration of those who failed in the initial expedition, and recruiting disciples of generations to come.

In sum, the "morning" watch has exhibited Jesus all alone, completely abandoned. He had called followers to be *with* him (3:14; 14:14, 17, 18, 20, 33, 67), yet at this time of crisis they have fled. Jesus is the only one who remains, the only one who stays faithful. This victorious kingship of Jesus is a suffering and sacrificial one, but those who have seen (i.e., those who have discerned Jesus' person and accepted his mission) will be faithful to this King in the "morning" watch.

SERMON FOCUS AND OUTLINES

THEOLOGICAL FOCUS OF PERICOPE 24 FOR PREACHING

24   Faithfulness to the ultimately victorious King, Jesus, involves sacrifice and suffering as part of following him in discipleship (15:1–39).

The culmination of Mark's Passion account, this pericope sets the spotlight unwaveringly upon the sacrificial suffering Jesus undergoes. The kingship of Jesus is ironically established by mockers—procurator, chief priests, elders, scribes, crowds, thieves. . . . That it is a victorious kingship is hinted at in the irony of the narrative and in the resemblance of the events in this pericope to those of a Roman triumphator's celebratory parade. Nonetheless, the focus is on the suffering and sacrifice of the King, and for the disciple seeking to be with Jesus to the end this is the way things will be. There is suffering and sacrifice in following Jesus on the way of discipleship. No matter what century or millennium the disciple is situated in, or what hemisphere of the world, this is a reality that will, and must, be gone through. That is part of what it means to take up one's cross, the theme of this pericope.

The motif of sacrifice and suffering is evident, with Jesus willingly taking up his cross and demonstrating faithfulness even in the face of persecution. Thus, those who have "seen"—i.e., those who have discerned Jesus' person (Act I) and accepted his mission (Act II)—must believe, remaining faithful to this King to the end, facing suffering from the world and its kings.

In contrast to the previous pericope (14:53–72), which focused upon what it meant to deny oneself (not denying oneself is equivalent to denying Jesus), this one deals with the taking up of the cross (going through sacrifice and suffering), and is intended to prepare disciples for all that must be faced if they intend to undertake the Trip of Discipleship following Jesus. An important reason for courage and persistence, even in the face of cruel opposition and abject humiliation, is given in this pericope—the ultimately victorious kingship of the one disciples follow.[34] That should be their sustaining force, their stabilizing factor, in the midst of the tumult and turmoil of the present.[35]

POSSIBLE PREACHING OUTLINES FOR PERICOPE 24

I. WHAT? Reality of ridicule

    The ridicule Jesus faced, abandoned and alone: 15:1–10, 16–32

    Move-to-Relevance: Ridicule we might be called to face

II. HOW? *Share the suffering!*

    Sharing Jesus' scorn is to part of denying oneself sacrificially: 15:11–15, 31, 38–39)

    Specifics on how disciples can (be willing to) suffer for Christ

III. WHY? Victory is waiting

    Jesus' kingship is ultimately victorious: the kingship motif throughout the pericope

    Move-to-Relevance: Our eternal perspective of Jesus' victory

A second option:

I. Everyone ridicules the King

    The ridicule Jesus faced: 15:1–10, 16–20, 29–32

    Move-to-Relevance: Ridicule we might be called to face

II. [and] Disciples renounce the Master

    The abandonment of Jesus: 15:21–28

    Move-to-Relevance: We might be all alone in our trials

34. Pericope 20 (13:1–37) also dealt with persecution but focused on a different set of reasons the disciple could successfully go through oppression: the Father's providence, the Spirit's presence, and the Son's promise of return and regathering.

35. The preacher will remember that 8:27—9:13 (Pericope 12) was a "flash-forward" of Jesus' victory—his future glory seen in his Transfiguration. Unlike that pericope, which calls upon disciples to develop an eternal perspective, this pericope—though there are similarities with the other—urges disciples to share Jesus' suffering and sacrifice, remembering that his Kingship, now ironical, is ultimately triumphant. Coming towards the end of the Gospel, almost as a recapitulation of the theme of suffering which has pervaded the Gospel, 15:1–39 exhorts disciples to bear the suffering that might be heaped upon them, because the one they follow is himself a suffering King. The focus here is not so much on future glory as it is on present suffering.

III.　[but] Centurion recognizes the Son

　　　The recognition of the Jesus: 15:38–39

　　　This recognized Son is ultimately victorious: the kingship motif throughout the pericope

IV.　[so we] *Share the suffering!*

　　　Sharing Jesus' scorn is to part of denying oneself sacrificially: 15:11–15, 31, 38–39

　　　Specifics on how disciples can (be willing to) suffer for Christ

The homiletical focus on willingness to suffer with Jesus is appropriate in this sermon, one of the closing sermons on the Gospel of Mark. Since several of the pericopes of the Gospel have already handled the theme of persecution and its various nuances, here the homiletical proposition might be more general: *Pray daily for strength to suffer persecution!* Such an emphasis may treat persecution more broadly, and may serve as an appropriate way to arrive at the conclusion of Mark. No doubt, in circumstances where suffering for Jesus is not particularly common, this might be a difficult text to apply and a tough sermon to preach. Nonetheless, readying the people of God to face persecution in the future is apropos. Persecution is not far away!

PERICOPE 25

Hope for Restoration

Mark 15:40–16:8

[Burial of Jesus; the Empty Tomb]

REVIEW, SUMMARY[1]

Review of Pericope 24: Mark 15:1–39, while encouraging disciples with hints of Jesus' victorious kingship, reminds them that submitting to Jesus' regency involves sacrifice and suffering. Faithfulness to Jesus till the very end is called for, from those who have discerned his person and accepted his mission.

Summary of Pericope 25: Mark 15:40—16:8, the final pericope of the Gospel of Mark, focuses once more on the importance of faithfulness to Jesus. Disciples fearlessly and faithfully resume the journey of discipleship, even if they have failed in the past, because God's grace restores them to service. There is hope for all disciples who fail and falter along the way.

25   Mark 15:40–16:8

THEOLOGICAL FOCUS OF PERICOPE 25

25 Despite disciples' potential failure, because of God's restoration of them into his service, disciples' can return to the journey of discipleship with Jesus (15:40—16:8).

25.1 Disciples following Jesus on the way remain courageously faithful at all times.

25.2 God extends hope for restoration to the disciple who has failed to be faithful on the journey with Jesus.

---

1. This chapter, dealing with the last pericope of the Gospel, will of course have no Preview of an upcoming pericope.

OVERVIEW

THIS FINAL PERICOPE ALSO functions as the epilogue for the entire Gospel. Of the rather unusual ending of 16:8, with its depiction of the frightened silence of the women at the empty tomb, Tolbert writes: "In attempting imaginatively to enter the ranks of Mark's authorial audience, we need to ask, not what this ending *means*, but what it *does*. . . ."[2] While geared to recruiting potential followers to undertake the journey of discipleship, there is a sharp focus on those who have failed in this venture—those who have not discerned or accepted Jesus' mission and, in the end, failed to be faithful to Jesus. Since there is no one who has followed perfectly, every disciple will want to know what the consequences are for such failure. The answer is clear: *resume the journey!* Will the disciple do so?

The opening and the closing of the Gospel almost mirror each other[3]:

- setting outside the normal, inhabited world: wilderness (1:3, 4, 12, 13), and cemetery (16:2)

- messenger: John the Baptist in prophet's clothing (1:6), and young man in white robe (16:5)

- call: to follow (1:17, 20; and 16:7)

- message: good news of the kingdom of God (1:1, 14–15), and news of Jesus' resurrection (16:6)

The *literary* journey of discipleship that the reader has undertaken from Galilee to Jerusalem concludes with this pericope. Mark, however, does not wish the *literal* journey of discipleship to end at that point; in fact, he would like to see it begin again—the second iteration—with readers committing to undertake that Trip of Discipleship, in particular those who have failed to be faithful to Jesus. In fact, Jesus himself is ready to resume the journey: he assures his followers that he awaits them in "Galilee," the port of embarkation and the point of (re-)entry into this voyage with Jesus, on the way of suffering to glory.

---

2. Tolbert, *Sowing the Gospel*, 295–96. *Contra* France (*Gospel of Mark*, 683), for whom the conclusion 16:8 appears to be "bizarre" and a "*faux pas*" on the part of Mark, I consider this ending as making good sense! This section of Mark, like any other, is an instrument of action, designed to do something based on the agenda of its narrator, rather than merely a recitation of historical facts. At any event, this commentary will not seek to rehash the innumerable discussions on the potential endings of the Gospel (that can be found in any of the standard works on Mark; also see Introduction), choosing rather to accept what is generally recognized by the majority of scholars as the conclusion of the Gospel. Examples of Greek literature that have sentences, chapters, or sections that end with γάρ as does Mark 16:8 (ἐφοβοῦντο γάρ, *ephobounto gar*, "for they were afraid") include: Gen 45:3; Isa 29:11 LXX; John 13:13; Plato, *Prot.* 328d (sentence ends with νέοι γάρ, *neoi gar*); Plotinus, *Enn.* V.5 (29th treatise; ends with τελειότερον γάρ, *teleioteron gar*); Justin Martyr, *Dial.* 32 (first section ends with ἐσταυρώθη γάρ, *estaurōthē gar*); etc. See Iverson, "Further Word."

3. van Iersel, *Mark*, 485.

ACT III: IN JERUSALEM

25   Mark 15:40–16:8

THEOLOGICAL FOCUS 25

25   Despite disciples' potential failure, because of God's restoration of them into his service, disciples' can return to the journey of discipleship with Jesus (15:40—16:8).

25.1   Disciples following Jesus on the way remain courageously faithful at all times.

25.2   God extends hope for restoration to the disciple who has failed to be faithful on the journey with Jesus.

Section Summary 25: The final pericope of the Gospel of Mark focuses once more on the importance of faithfulness to Jesus. It also emphasizes the restoration of those who have failed to be faithful to Jesus on the Trip of Discipleship. The openness of the ending emphasizes the human contingency of this journey, requiring potential disciples to take the initiative to follow Jesus. There is hope for disciples who fail and falter along the way—God's gracious restoration to his service is patently laid out in the narrative.

TRANSLATION 25

15:40   *And there were also women looking on from a distance, among whom also [were] Mary Magdalene, and Mary the mother of James the Less and Joses, and Salome—*

15:41   *who, when He was in Galilee, used to follow Him and minister to Him— and many other women who came up with Him to Jerusalem.*

15:42   *And when evening had already come, since it was the day of preparation, that is, the day before the Sabbath,*

15:43   *Joseph of Arimathea came, a prominent member of the Sanhedrin, who was himself also waiting for the kingdom of God; being courageous, he went in before Pilate and asked for the body of Jesus.*

15:44   *But Pilate wondered if He had died by this time and, summoning the centurion, he questioned him if He was already dead.*

15:45   *And ascertaining [this] from the centurion, he granted the dead body to Joseph.*

15:46   *And he bought a linen cloth, took Him down, wrapped [Him] in the linen cloth, and laid Him in the tomb which had been hewn out of the rock, and he rolled up a stone across the entrance of the tomb.*

15:47   *And Mary Magdalene and Mary [the mother] of Joses were observing where He had been laid.*

16:1   *And when the Sabbath passed, Mary Magdalene, and Mary [the mother] of James, and Salome bought spices in order to come and anoint Him.*

16:2   *And very early on the first [day] of the week, they came to the tomb, when the sun had risen.*

16:3   *And they were saying to themselves, "Who will roll away the stone for us from the entrance of the tomb?"*

16:4   And looking up, they observed that the stone had been rolled away—for it was very large.

16:5   And going into the tomb, they saw a young man sitting on the right, wearing a white robe, and they were alarmed.

16:6   But he said to them, "Do not be alarmed. You are seeking Jesus the Nazarene who was crucified. He has risen; He is not here. Behold, the place where they laid Him.

16:7   But go, tell His disciples and Peter, 'He is going ahead of you to Galilee; there you will see Him, just as He told you.'"

16:8   And going out, they fled from the tomb, for trembling and terror had seized them; and they said nothing to anyone, for they were afraid.

NOTES 25

25.1   Disciples following Jesus on the way remain courageously faithful at all times.

The account holds together with the motif of the women watching all the happenings (θεωρέω, "look," "observe," 15:40, 47; 16:4): Jesus' death and the centurion's confession, Joseph of Arimathea's request for the body and its burial, the young man and the empty tomb. All of the closing elements of Jesus' Passion, his death, burial, and resurrection, are observed by the women.

In 16:1–8, not only θεωρέω (*theōreō,* 16:4), but also ἀναβλέπω (*anablepō,* "look," 16:4) and ὁράω (*horaō,* "see," 16:5, 6, 7) appear several times. The metaphor of vision has been a prominent motif in Mark to denote discernment and understanding. The women in this pericope have obviously "seen" (discerned), and as the ones who alone have remained with Jesus till the end, they have accepted his suffering mission. Will they continue to be faithful?

Thus far, it has all been a male enterprise, without any explicit mention of women supporting the movement, as in Luke 8:2–3, or of specific named women associated with Jesus (like Mary and Martha in Luke 10:38–42). There have been a number of minor characters who were women, all exemplars of faith (Simon's mother-in-law, the woman with the hemorrhage, the Syrophoenician woman, the widow with her two coins, and the woman with the expensive ointment), but all were anonymous and appeared only in their respective pericopes. But now, when their male colleagues have unfaithfully abandoned Jesus, the female section of the entourage is ready to pick up the slack.[4] It is three *women* this time (15:40; 16:1); previously, in the inner circle of Jesus were three *men*—Peter, James, and John. Like them (and the other disciples), these (and "many other women," 15:41) have followed Jesus and, what is more, have been ministering to him (15:41). The paralleling of the numbers of the inner core is probably suggestive: the men have abandoned Jesus in the "morning" watch; the women, on the other hand, are still there, even after the Sabbath.

Everyone in the formal category of "disciples" has fled; and none of them come to claim Jesus' body (see below). These women are the only remaining hope; perhaps

4. France, *Gospel of Mark,* 661–62.

353

they will not be like those others. Even in the description of their "following" and "ministering to" Jesus (15:41), their discipleship is almost palpable; Mark's intent is hardly ambiguous. They *are* disciples.[5] How would they do in continuing the mission of Jesus? They have seen Jesus' death, burial, and the evidence of his resurrection; they have seen the centurion's confession, Joseph's courage, and the young man's corroboration (15:39; 15:43; 16:6). They have enough evidence and incentive to carry on the mission of Jesus on the discipleship journey. Will they be faithful? Or will they fail like their male counterparts?

The use of ζητέω (*zēteō*, "seek," 16:6; the women's efforts to locate Jesus) is uniformly negative in tone in Mark (3:32–35; 8:11–12; 11:18; 12:12 [11:27]; 14:1; 14:11; 14:55; see under 1:37 for comments on the disparaging tone there). So the final occurrence of the verb here in the Gospel does not project the women in a good light, and adumbrates their failure in 16:8.[6] Another indication of their potential failure is the description of their location: like Peter in 14:54 (ἀπὸ μακρόθεν, *apo makrothen*, "from a distance"), these women, too, are watching ἀπὸ μακρόθεν (15:40), raising in the mind of the reader the question of whether they too will be like that other disciple who failed miserably and denied his Master.

In his Gospel, Mark has taken care to point out one scribe (12:34) and one Roman soldier (15:39) favorable to Jesus; here now is one Sanhedrin member, Joseph, also positively inclined (15:43). The courage of this leading figure in Jerusalem cannot be underestimated—it is explicitly pointed out by the narrator (15:43). His is a risky endeavor, seeking the body of this "seditious" Galilean prophet whom Joseph's own Sanhedrin had indicted as a blasphemer and condemned to death. As with the description of the women in 15:40, here too one wonders why the explicit language of discipleship is not employed. Yet, in light of the fact that the coming of the kingdom was Jesus' primary message (1:15), the description of Joseph as one "waiting for the kingdom of God" (15:43) is a powerful, albeit implicit, testimony of this man's "discipleship." Again, Joseph's presence and activities emphasize the woeful absence of those officially labeled "disciples."

---

5. "Mary the mother of James and Joses" (15:40) is likely Jesus' mother. It is strange, however, that Mark does not mention this fact; indeed in the two other instances of her name in this pericope, he identifies her once with one son and once with the other son (15:47; 16:1). There is no mention of Jesus, her most famous offspring, at any time in connection with her name. Is this because Jesus has just been identified as the "Son of God" (15:39) and Mark does not want the mundaneness of a human relationship shortchanging his theological thrust? Or is it because of the less than laudatory activities of this family in 3:20–35? In any case, Mark's readers would have been fully aware of the identity of this Mary. The Evangelist's intention must be to portray her as "everywoman" without affording her any pride of place: any woman (or man, for that matter) could be in her shoes/sandals, or in those of the other Mary or Salome. The narrator, with such a depiction, is seeking to have readers identify with these characters and not with their notable lineage or high connections. After all, this Gospel is a manual of discipleship, and discipleship is for all those who choose to do the will of God (3:35), irrespective of the viscosity of blood or water relationships. For Mark's purpose to be effectively accomplished, a deliberate restraint is exercised by him with regards to the description of the physical family of Jesus, an effort that is perhaps even intended to be recognized as such.

6. Danove, *Rhetoric of the Characterization*, 4.

The contrast in this pericope between the disposition of the body of John the Baptist and that of Jesus does not add to the credit of the latter's disciples: John's disciples took charge of his body (πτῶμα, *ptōma*, 6:29) upon his murder; Jesus' body is handled not by his "official" disciples, but by an unofficial one (15:42–46; here too πτῶμα is used; these are the only two times the word is found in Mark).[7] The Evangelist is clearly pointing a finger at the faithlessness of the disciples, particularly their lack of courage, in comparison to the Sanhedrin member who dared to approach Pilate, the one who had sentenced Jesus to death.[8]

Another jab at the absent male disciples occurs in 16:3. The comment of the women as they wonder who will roll the "very large" stone away (16:3–4) appears, on the surface, to be a rather unnecessary aside. Mark could as well have had the women arrive at the tomb to see the stone already rolled away, without discussing their turmoil and apprehension. But considering the number of contrasts between the unexpected disciples in this pericope (a Sanhedrin member and three women) and the expected male disciples of Jesus, it appears that Mark's insertion of the comment of the women about the discouraging size of the stone is there to remind the audience, once again, of the absence of those men who could have helped them roll that rock away.

25.2   *God extends hope for restoration to the disciple who has failed to be faithful on the journey with Jesus.*

Hester suggests that the inclusion of the detail of the "linen cloth" in the story (16:5) is to serve as a "cipher," a literary device that causes the reader to reflect upon its previous (and only other) presence in 14:51–52 and its implications there: the faithlessness of the disciples and the loneliness of Jesus (see Pericope 22). In fact, that episode and this current pericope contain an unusual collocation of words unique to these sections of the Gospel: not only does σινδών (*sindōn*, "linen cloth") occur only in 14:51–52 and 15:46, but so also do νεανίσκος (*neaniskos*, "young man," 14:51; 16:5) and περιβάλλω (*periballō*, "wear," 14:51; 16:5).[9] Moreover, λευκός (*leukos*, "white") is found only in 9:3 (the white garments of the transfigured Jesus) and here in 16:5, thus linking all of those events together, with an unusual interest being displayed by Mark regarding who is wearing what. It appears that garments have been "exchanged" (in a literary

---

7. However, in the first case, the burial was final. Not so in the second!

8. The verb τολμάω, *tolmaō*, translated "gather courage" (Mark 15:43), also has the sense of "dare" (see Esth 7:5; 2 Macc. 4.2; Matt 22:46; Mark 12:34; Acts 5:13; 1 Cor 6:1; Jude 9; etc.).

9. Hester, "Dramatic Inconclusion," 76–77. Why does Mark go to such lengths to connect one young man with another? He could certainly have called the reporter of 16:5 an "angel"—until now he has shown no reluctance to label heavenly messengers as such (1:13; 8:38; 12:25; 13:27, 32). In light of the fact that the messenger at the empty tomb was, in fact, an angel (as attested by Matt 28:2, 5; indeed, there was more than one—Luke 24:23; John 20:12), Mark must have some purpose in being cagey and discreet. Not that labeling an angel νεανίσκος, *neaniskos*, was being meretricious and deceptive. Angels are so called in 2 Macc 3.26, 33; 5.2; Josephus, *Ant.* 5.8.2 and 5.8.3 (here the Angel of the Lord of Jdg 13 is described both as ἄγγελος τοῦ θεοῦ, *angelos tou theou*, and as νεανίας, *neanias*, "young man"]); Tob 5.5, 7, 10 (where Rafael is also referred to as ἄγγελος, *angelos*, and νεανίσκος, *neaniskos*); *Herm. Vis.* 3.1.6; 3.4.1; etc. The only reason for Mark's unique appellation, calling the angel νεανίσκος in 16:5, then, must be to create an overt link to the other (and only) νεανίσκος in the Gospel, in 14:51–52.

sense, of course): the linen cloth the young man wore, which was stripped from him rendering him naked (14:51–52), covers Jesus' body in the tomb (15:46). In exchange, the white garment Jesus wore at his Transfiguration (9:3) now covers the young man at the empty tomb (16:5).[10]

Young man's (νεανίσκος) linen cloth (σινδών, 14:51–52) shed in shame during the abandonment of Jesus by disciples

→ Jesus linen cloth (σινδών, 15:46) in death.

Jesus' white garment (λευκός, 9:3) worn in glory at the Transfiguration

→ Young man's (νεανίσκος) white clothing (λευκός, 16:5) at the empty tomb.

This not-so-subtle literary prestidigitation represents the rehabilitation of the disciple —the naked and shamed one is clothed, and this with the brilliance of the clothing of Jesus (while the latter takes on the clothing of shame from the former). In other words, the garment of shame of the disciple is transferred to Jesus and, in return, the garment of glory of Jesus is passed on to the disciple. This "white/linen-clad-young-man" motif points to the restoration of the failed disciple(s). One could go even further with the "exchange" theme: the position of the young man now clothed in white is "on the right" (16:5), the rightful position of the Son of God (Ps 110:1).[11] That it is a restoration is clear from this location of the young man: none of the other Gospel writers give us this right-sided location of the angel at the empty tomb.[12]

In sum, the art of the narrator paints a remarkable picture: the fleeing young man, symbolic of the disciples who abandoned Jesus and themselves fled (as was discussed in Pericope 22), escapes shamefully naked, leaving behind a linen cloth used to bury Jesus. That is what the Master is given by the disciple—a *garment of shame*. But at the resurrection, there is a young man, sitting on the "right," no less, and clothed gloriously in a white robe that Jesus wore at his Transfiguration. That is what the disciple is given by the Master—a *garment of glory*. This artistic portrayal of the "exchange" of garments (quite unlikely to be a literal exchange, of course, but rather a literary and theological one) bears an implicit promise: there is hope for disciples who have failed to discern, accept, and be faithful to the mission of Jesus. There is hope for all who will follow Jesus on this Markan Trip of Discipleship, albeit stumbling and failing, clumsy and hesitant. Because of what Christ has done, their shame is exchanged for his glory. Yes, there is hope indeed![13]

10. See Kuruvilla, "Naked Runaway." Interestingly, on both occasions where "white" garments show up—at the Transfiguration and at the scene of the resurrection—there is "astonishment" on the part of beholders: at the former, the crowds are said to have been "astonished" (ἐκθαμβέω, *ekthambeō*, 9:15); at the latter, the women are duly noted to have been "astonished" (ἐκθαμβέω, 16:5, 6). Outside of these two uses, there is only one other use of the verb in the Gospel, in 14:33, where it functions as a homonym meaning "distressed." Indeed, in the entire NT, Mark's Gospel is the only text where this word is found. Neither does the LXX employ ἐκθαμβέω in the canonical books (however, it is found in Sir 30.9).

11. See van Iersel, *Mark*, 504.

12. John orients the angels one at the foot and the other at the head where the body of Jesus had been lying (John 20:12). It is conceivable that Mark was choosing to call one of these two positions "right," in order to promote his unique theological goal.

13. One is reminded of 2 Cor 5:21: "He made Him who know no sin to be sin on our behalf, so that

The specific, and seemingly redundant, mention of Peter ("tell His disciples *and/even* [καὶ, *kai*] Peter," 16:7), in the command of the young man to the women at the empty tomb is to remind that disciple (and the rest of Mark's readers) that failure is not a dead end. There would be forgiveness, there would be restoration—there is hope for those who have failed in their discipleship. Those who have shamefully abandoned Jesus (and equally disgracefully denied him) are now being offered the hope of restoration. There would be a new beginning, for a new iteration of the Trip of Discipleship has just been announced. The promise of a new start, by means of a return to the point of origin, Galilee, had been offered by Jesus in 14:28; here in 16:7 that promise is affirmed once again: Jesus would be waiting for them in Galilee to resume the discipleship journey. Who will join Jesus as he leads his followers, once again, "on the way," on a renewed journey of discipleship? "To be a faithful disciple is to take up the cross and follow Jesus on the road to the passion. It is to walk from 'Galilee' to 'Jerusalem.'"[14]

Anyone can get back "on the way" to following Jesus, and even the cryptic end of the Gospel at 16:8 turns out to be a beginning—a renewed call to discipleship.[15] "The Lord who from the opening words had 'a way' (1:2–3) is the Jesus who has been constantly under way during the narrative. This Jesus does not now rest in peace, but is still under way, going ahead of the fearful disciples."[16] The invitation is open: Will you follow?

Matthew mitigates the fear of these female witnesses by admixing it with "great joy" (Matt 28:8); here in Mark, though, their terror is unrelieved.[17] With a double

---

we might become the righteousness of God in Him." See also Myers, *Binding the Strong Man*, 369. Such an interpretation is not an attempt to belittle the historicity of the events. The fidelity of the narrator to fact is not in question at all. The events did happen as they did; Mark simply chose what events to narrate and what not to—all in the service of his theological purpose of depicting what it meant to be on the Trip of Discipleship with Jesus. In service of this goal, he organizes actual events into a theologically powerful narrative. For instance, there can be no doubt that the young man by the empty tomb was an angel (Matt 28:2–5; Luke 24:4, 23; John 20:12); the women's reaction of terror and the reassuring words of the "young man" (Mark 16:5–8) also indicate a numinous occurrence (see Gen 15:1; Jdg 6:23; Dan 10:12; Luke 1:13, 30; 2:10). However, Mark is not so much interested in the precise identification of this "young man" as much as he is interested in propagating his theological thrust—the restoration of the failing and faltering followers. And to do so, he chooses to connect one "young man" with the other, one garment with the other, one whiteness with the other, all for the sake of the rehabilitative "exchange" he wishes to portray. The reader's appreciation of the narrator's art (also inspired by the Holy Spirit) will determine whether that theological thrust is discerned and accepted, and whether believers will change their lives in order to be faithful to what they are called to be and do.

14. Geddert, *Watchwords*, 167.

15. As had already been mentioned, this author accepts the Gospel as ending at 16:8 (the "shorter" ending); the majority of scholars appear to hold this view. For comprehensive summaries on Markan endings see, in addition to standard commentaries, Wallace, "Mark 16:8"; Magness, *Sense and Absence*; Holmes, "To Be Continued"; Spencer, "Denial of the Good News"; and Stein, "Ending of Mark."

16. Boring, *Mark*, 446.

17. France, *Gospel of Mark*, 682. The cause of their fear is not addressed by Mark; perhaps it is the fear of the numinous, the fear of the unknown (a dead man coming back to life!), fear of inadequacy (4:3–4; coupled with the absence of the remainder of Jesus' disciples), etc. In any case, the fear is negative and subtly disparaged in that they remain silent when commanded to proclaim, and in that they flee—that ignominious verb φεύγω (*pheugō*, "flee," 16:8) shows up again; see below.

negative (literally, "they said nothing to no one," 16:8), the narrator affirms the women's silence. It is indeed ironic that the "secrecy motif" had imposed silence on those prone to tell (1:34, 44; 3:12; 5:43; 7:36; 8:26, 30; 9:9); that injunction had always failed. Now here is a command to go and tell, and the recipients decide to keep it a secret. To add insult to injury, they "flee" (φεύγω, *pheugō*, 16:8), painfully recalling the fleeing of the disciples and that of the young man (also φεύγω, 14:50, 52). The reader may have hoped for better things from the women after the dismal display by the men, but to no avail. These too have failed. Family, friends, and disciples—both men and women— have all fallen "off the way." Who will continue the task? Who remains?

> Is there anyone else who might after all be a faithful disciple? Throughout the story, there has been a nonparticipant observer who has been with Jesus in every scene. The narrator has permitted the reader to be "with Jesus" the whole time, from beginning to end. The reader heard the voice of God declaring Jesus to be his Son, when no one else heard; the reader was present with Jesus in the wilderness, tested by Satan, when no one else was there. When family rejected him, the reader persisted. When religious leaders, crowds, and disciples misunderstood and abandoned Jesus, the reader stood by him. When the inner circle went to sleep in Gethsemane, oblivious to Jesus' plea to watch with him one hour, the reader stayed awake and heard Jesus; anguished prayer. When the disciples fled and were absent at the cross, the reader was present. When Jesus cried out to God in abandonment, the reader was still there. Now, the readers stand at the brink of the incomplete narrative in which all have failed, and, with terrible restraint, the narrator breaks off the story and leaves the readers, who may have thought the story was about somebody else, with a decision to make. . . .[18]

At the end of the Gospel, this striking and open challenge to the reader/disciple assumes critical importance: Will the baton be faithfully carried by the next generation of disciples?

Of course, at the historical level, the women of this pericope *did* pass the message; of course, the disciples were told and they did hear and regather with their risen Lord; and, of course, Christianity did not die out—the second, third, fourth, fifth . . . rounds of discipleship did take place and further iterations continue to be undertaken today.[19] But at the literary level, as Mark leaves us hanging, the direct address to the reader is unavoidable: Will you fulfill your responsibility to undertake the Trip of Discipleship by carrying on the mission of Jesus, even if you have failed in the past?[20] To fulfill this solemn responsibility, the reader is left with a choice: to join Jesus on his

---

18. Boring, *Mark*, 449; also see Rhoads et al., *Mark as Story*, 143.

19. The key verbs in 16:8 are in the aorist tense (ἔφυγον, *ephygon*, "they fled"; and εἶπαν, *eipan*, "they said"); combined with two γαρ clauses, they likely indicate "a particular and punctiliar action motivated in each case by fear. The text implies that fleeing and silence went on only for a specific period of time, namely, for the period while the women were afraid." Such a reading expects a point of time when the women get over their fear; perhaps that was the time when they actually conveyed the good news to others. Witherington, *Gospel of Mark*, 45–46.

20. "Mark was evidently more concerned about his readers' discipleship than their history education" (Geddert, *Watchwords*, 171). Attending to the literary act—what the author is *doing* with what he is saying—is more important for life-changing purposes than merely discerning what the author is saying.

mission (despite past failure), or to flee in terror. "It is perhaps too much to propose that an altar call is needed at the end of Mark, but something similar is implied."[21] This is a serious task for, in the narrator's conception, the next round of following Jesus and the rehabilitation of failed followers are contingent upon disciples' going to Galilee to (re)join Jesus.[22]

The Gospel story, despite its seemingly disappointing and abrupt ending, is not hopeless. On the contrary! The ending signals that the way of Jesus continues; it announces that Jesus is ready to start another iteration of the Trip of Discipleship. And, most importantly, it invites disciples to join him "on the way," even those who have failed in the past. The grave, normally a place of despair, has been transformed into a gateway, an entry point into the next round. The journey is about to begin . . . again!

SERMON FOCUS AND OUTLINES

THEOLOGICAL FOCUS OF PERICOPE 25 FOR PREACHING
25 Disciples restored by God's grace continue to be courageous and faithful to Jesus on the way of discipleship (15:40—16:8).

This pericope functions as the epilogue to the whole Gospel, urging readers to join Jesus "on the way," even those who have failed in the past—there is hope! God's grace enables disciples to be restored in times of failure and such disciples respond in faithfulness, extending the mission of Jesus, by resuming the Trip of Discipleship. This is a crucial aspect of following Jesus, for failure will happen; it is inevitable—everyone is fallible. Disciples need to know that all is not ended if they do fail. Instead, restoration to God's service is powerfully depicted in the exchange of clothing between Jesus and the "young man" (drawing from Mark 9, 14, 15, and 16). Indeed, the story does not end with Mark 16; the journey does not conclude: it only begins again, going back to the start (Galilee), where disciples get back on, or join anew, the journey with Jesus. Keep following, Mark exhorts.

It might be productive for the homiletician to utilize this last pericope of a Gospel so concerned with discipleship to exhort believers to return to following Jesus on the way, even if they have failed in the past. And, for those already "on the way," it is an exhortation to remain faithful. All along in Mark's Gospel the Twelve have been shown failing. It comes as a relief to know that the narrator concludes with a chapter of restoration and restitution. God's grace alone makes a renewed walk with Jesus possible. And so the trip continues . . .

---

21. Meyer, "Taking Up the Cross," 238. "By pointing back to the 'beginning' of the gospel in Galilee (1:1), the end of the narrative invites the audience to continue the task of proclaiming the gospel of Jesus Christ, Son of God (1:1), not just to Galilee but beyond it to all peoples of the world (13:10; 14:9), with the risen Jesus always 'going before' them and leading the way" (Heil, "Narrative Strategy," 99).

22. In the larger scheme of things, God's sovereignty is not at all constrained by human responsibility, of course. But Mark's theological thrust must not therefore be diluted: the responsibility for the next round of the journey is a solemn one that the disciple *must* fulfill.

ACT III: IN JERUSALEM

POSSIBLE PREACHING OUTLINES FOR PERICOPE 25

I.   FAILURE of discipleship of the Twelve

The women remain after the men have abandoned Jesus, following and ministering: 15:41

Joseph shows courage after the men have fled in fear: 15:42–46

But even the women fail in their fear to proclaim, jeopardizing the second round: 16:8

Move-to-Relevance: Our failure to be faithful on the Trip of Discipleship

II. FORGIVENESS of failure of the Twelve

The "white/linen-clad-young-man" motif: 15:46; 16:5–6

The reinstatement of the disciples and the second round: 16:7

Move-to-Relevance: Forgiveness available for our failures

III. FAITHFULNESS: *Get back on the road!*

Specifics on how the congregation can return to the path of faithful discipleship

Another option:

I.   WOMEN: Faithfully remaining

Faithful women remain after the men have abandoned Jesus, following and ministering: 15:41

Contrast the absence of the Twelve

Move-to-Relevance: Our failure, like that of the Twelve, to be faithful on the Trip of Discipleship

II. JOSEPH: Fearlessly requesting

Fearless Joseph requests the body of Jesus: 15:42–46

Contrast the fear of the Twelve

Move-to-Relevance: Our failure, like that of the Twelve, to be fearless on the Trip of Discipleship

III. JESUS: Freely restoring

The "white/linen-clad-young-man" motif: 15:46; 16:5–6

The reinstatement of the disciples and the second round: 16:7

Move-to-Relevance: Forgiveness available for our failure to be faithful and fearless

IV. *Get back on the road, faithfully and fearlessly!*

Specifics on how the congregation can return to the path of faithful, fearless discipleship

CONCLUSION

"He has risen. . . . He is going ahead of you to Galilee;
there you will see Him, just as He told you."

Mark 16:6–7

THOSE WHO LABOR IN pulpits on a weekly basis deal with the "the astonishing supposition that texts which are between possibly 3,000 and almost 2,000 years old can offer orientation for the discovery of truth in the third millennium."[1] It is, indeed, a remarkable predication that from these ancient texts may be discerned and preached, not just truth that informs, but truth that transforms—that is applicable and that changes lives for the glory of God. Yet the lot of the homiletician is not easy, nor is the responsibility minimal: each week the preacher has to negotiate this formidable passage from ancient text to modern audience to expound, with authority and relevance, a specific biblical pericope for the faithful. Thus this intrepid soul, aided by the Holy Spirit, becomes the communicative pastoral agent of the life-transforming truths of Scripture. This book is one small attempt in a larger endeavor to help the preacher move safely, accurately, and effectively across the gulf between text and application.

Karl Barth's indictment must be carefully heeded:

> My complaint is that recent commentators confine themselves to an interpretation of the text which seems to me to be no commentary at all, but merely the first step toward a commentary. Recent commentaries contain no more than a reconstruction of the text, a rendering of the Greek words and phrases by their precise equivalents, a number of additional notes in which archaeological and philological material is gathered together, and a more or less plausible arrangement of the subject matter in such a manner that it may be made historically and psychologically intelligible from the standpoint of pure pragmatism.[2]

This author has taken Barth to heart, and attempted to go beyond the "first step toward a commentary," to deliver not so much what the author was *saying* in comprehensible fashion, but what the author was *doing* with what he was saying. This commentary agrees that "[t]he storyteller is not merely conveying the contents of a story but is trying to do something to the audience in the process of telling the story." Mark's Gospel

---

1. Schwöbel, "Preacher's Art," 7.
2. Barth, *Epistle to the Romans*, 6.

361

is designed to "seduce" its readers to change their lives in thought, in feeling, and in action to comply with the precepts, priorities, and practices of God's world (i.e., the theology of the pericope), which is displayed in, with, and through the inspired story written by the Evangelist. To that end, this particular narrative account of Jesus and his disciples (and, for that matter, every other biblical narrative, as well) "works predominantly along the rhetorical axis of language to affect the reader rather than predominantly along the referential axis of language to convey information."[3] In other words, Mark is *doing* something with what he is saying. The theological agenda of the writer mandates that interpreters, particularly those who interpret for preaching purposes, attend not only to what Mark is *saying,* but also to what he is *doing* with what he is saying. In aiding the preacher, this commentary has approached the Gospel in a unique fashion, undertaking a form of exegesis geared towards discerning the theology of the pericope—the theological focus of each pericope of Mark, his *doing-with-his-saying.*[4]

It is a foundational conviction of this work that valid application of a pericope of Scripture may be arrived at only via this critical intermediary between text and praxis, pericopal theology.[5] The hermeneutical philosophy behind this commentary also holds that such valid application to change lives for the glory of God is the appropriate goal of every sermon. Interpretation of the text is, after all, ultimately a "rewriting the text of the work within the text of our lives."[6] And the task of the preacher with a pastoral heart ought to include the proffering of specific ways in which the theological focus of the pericope may be translated into the real life of real people.

In his Gospel, Mark, inspired by the Holy Spirit, seeks to guide his readers in the "way" of discipleship. In three acts, the narrative seeks to explain what it means for a disciple to discern Jesus' person (1:1—8:21), to accept his mission (8:22—10:52), and to be faithful to him (11:1—16:8). This theme (and scheme) of discipleship is fleshed out in a journey from Galilee to Jerusalem, in which one follows Jesus on the way to glory, but through suffering. The broader theological focus for the entire narrative may therefore be summarized thus: *The disciple is one who follows Jesus, discerning his person* [Act I], *accepting his mission* [Act II], *and being faithful to him* [Act III], *on the way to glory . . . through suffering.*

Every pericope of the Gospel contributes a slice or a quantum of theology to this broad and plenary theological focus of the whole book. A different facet of this multifaceted jewel is highlighted in each pericope, and the goal of this commentary has been primarily to explicate that quantum of theology for each pericope.[7] In preaching

3. Fowler, *Let the Reader Understand,* 10, 222.

4. See Preface. Also see Kuruvilla, *Text to Praxis,* 142–90; and idem, "Pericopal Theology," for details on this hermeneutical entity, pericopal theology, and its value for the homiletical process.

5. In the commentary, this is called the "Theological Focus." Such a theological thrust, I have proposed elsewhere (see references above), is what the author is *doing* with what he is *saying.*

6. Barthes, "Day by Day," 101.

7. After coming across Morna Hooker's incisive remark, I hesitate to compare pericopes within a larger narrative to pearls on a necklace. "It will not, I hope, be regarded as a sexist remark if I suggest that only a man could have used the phrase 'like pearls on a string' to suggest a haphazard arrangement of material. Any woman would have spotted at once the flaw in the analogy: pearls need to be carefully

the book of Mark, then, week by week and pericope by pericope, preachers are called to fulfill the august responsibility, with divine aid from the Holy Spirit, to move themselves and their listeners closer to that model of discipleship espoused in the Gospel. Inasmuch as the application propounded by homileticians in sermons is faithfully assimilated into listeners' lives, creating Christian dispositions and forming Christlike character, the people of God will have aligned themselves to the will of God for the glory of God—the goal of preaching.[8] Text will have become praxis, disciples will have been recruited for Jesus, Christlikeness will have been inculcated in God's children. Then one can say, not that the kingdom of God is near, but that it is *here*!

Who will follow Jesus on the way, discerning his person, accepting his mission, and being faithful to him till the end? Who will be a disciple, extending Jesus' mission for the kingdom of God? Mark, through the Holy Spirit, beckons the listener; the Gospel concludes with an open invitation: Jesus goes ahead, and the next round of the Trip of Discipleship begins. Let's get ready to follow! Will you sign up?

---

selected and graded. And gradually it has dawned on New Testament scholars that this is precisely what the evangelists have done with their material" (*Message of Mark*, 3). But if I had dared to use that phrase, I would never have suggested anything like "haphazard" in the arrangement. *Au contraire!* I completely agree with Hooker: pericopes of narratives are carefully selected and graded, organized and fitted, planned and strategized, into the bigger scheme of things, just as Mark has done.

8. It bears repeating that the commentary is only a "theological" commentary, not a "preaching" commentary. It takes the preacher only part of the way to a sermon, from text to theology (the hermeneutical step). It remains the preacher's burden to complete the crossing by moving now from theology to application, i.e., making concrete application from the theology of the passage that is specific for the particular audience, and presenting all of this in sermon that is powerful and persuasive (the rhetorical step).

BIBLIOGRAPHY

(modern texts only)

Achtemeier, P. J. "Person and Deed." *Int* 16 (1962) 169–76.

Aland, Barbara, Kurt Aland, Johannes Karavidopoulos, Carlo M. Martini, and Bruce M. Metzger. *The Greek New Testament*. 4th rev. ed. Stuttgart: Deutsche Bibelgesellschaft, United Bible Societies, 1996.

Bailey, Kenneth E. "The Fall of Jerusalem and Mark's Account of the Cross." *ExpTim* 102 (1991) 102–5.

Barthes, Roland. "Day by Day with Roland Barthes." In *On Signs*, by Roland Barthes, edited by Marshall Blonsky, 98–117. Baltimore: Johns Hopkins University Press, 1985.

Batto, Bernard F. "The Sleeping God: An Ancient Near Eastern Motif of Divine Sovereignty." *Bib* 68 (1987) 153–77.

Bauckham, Richard. "For Whom Were Gospels Written?" In *The Gospels for All Christians: Rethinking the Gospel Audiences*, edited by Richard Bauckham, 9–48. Grand Rapids: Eerdmans, 1998.

Best, Ernest. *Disciples and Discipleship: Studies in the Gospel According to Mark*. Edinburgh: T. & T. Clark, 1986.

———. *Following Jesus: Discipleship in the Gospel of Mark*. JSNTSup 4. Sheffield: Sheffield Academic, 1981.

———. "Mark's Narrative Technique." *JSNT* 37 (1989) 43–58.

Black, C. Clifton. "Rhetorical Criticism." In *Hearing the New Testament: Strategies for Interpretation*, edited by Joel B. Green, 256–77. Grand Rapids: Eerdmans, 1995.

Bonhoeffer, Dietrich. *The Cost of Discipleship*. Translated by R. H. Fuller. Revised by Irmgard Booth. New York: Simon and Schuster, 1995.

Booth, Wayne C. *The Company We Keep: An Ethics of Fiction*. Berkeley: University of California Press, 1988.

Boring, M. Eugene. *Mark: A Commentary*. NTL. Louisville: Westminster John Knox, 2006.

———. "Mark 1:1–15 and the Beginning of the Gospel." *Semeia* 52 (1991) 43–81.

Borrell, Agustí. *The Good News of Peter's Denial: A Narrative and Rhetorical Reading of Mark 14:54.66–72*. Translated by Sean Conlon. Atlanta: Scholars, 1998.

Brady, David. "The Alarm to Peter in Mark's Gospel." *JSNT* 4 (1979) 42–57.

Breck, John. *The Shape of Biblical Language: Chiasmus in the Scriptures and Beyond*. Crestwood, NY: St. Vladimir's Seminary Press, 1994.

Brown, Raymond E. "The Passion According to Mark." *Worship* 59 (1985) 116–26.

Buechner, Frederick. *Telling the Truth: The Gospel as Tragedy, Comedy, and Fairy Tale*. San Francisco: Harper & Row, 1977.

Busch, Austin. "Questioning and Conviction: Double-Voiced Discourse in Mark 3:22–30." *JBL* 125 (2006) 477–505.

Buttrick, David. *Homiletic: Moves and Structures*. Philadelphia: Fortress, 1987.

Byrne, Brendan. *A Costly Freedom: A Theological Reading of Mark's Gospel*. Collegeville, MN: Liturgical, 2008.

Camery-Hoggatt, Jerry. *Irony in Mark's Gospel: Text and Subtext*. SNTSMS 72. Cambridge: Cambridge University Press, 1992.

Carmichael, Deborah Bleicher. "David Daube on the Eucharist and the Passover Seder." *JSNT* 42 (1991) 45–67.

Cashmore, David. "'In This Generation': The Comings and Goings of the Son of Man." *Stimulus* 12 (2004) 13–19.

Catchpole, D. R. "The Synoptic Divorce Material as a Traditio-Historical Problem." *BJRL* 57 (1974) 97–127.

———. "The 'Triumphal' Entry." In *Jesus and the Politics of His Day*, edited by Ernst Bammel and C. F. D. Moule, 319–34. Cambridge: Cambridge University Press, 1984.

Chronis, Harry L. "The Torn Veil: Cultus and Christology in Mark 15:37–39." *JBL* 101 (1982) 97–114.

Collins, Adela Yarbro. *Mark: A Commentary*. Hermeneia. Minneapolis: Fortress, 2007.

Craddock, Fred B. *As One without Authority*. St. Louis: Chalice, 2001.

———. *Preaching*. Nashville: Abingdon, 1985.

Danker, Frederick W. "The Literary Unity of Mark 14 1–25." *JBL* 85 (1966) 467–72.

Danove, Paul L. *The Rhetoric of the Characterization of God, Jesus, and Jesus' Disciples in the Gospel of Mark*. JSNTSup 290. London: T. & T. Clark, 2005.

Dart, John. "Scriptural Schemes: The ABCBAs of Biblical Writing." *ChrCent* 121/14 (2004) 22–25.

Derrett, J. Duncan M. "Law in the New Testament: The Palm Sunday Colt." *NovT* 13 (1971) 241–58.

Dewey, Joanna. "The Literary Structure of the Controversy Stories in Mark 2:1—3:6." *JBL* 92 (1973) 394–401.

———. *Markan Public Debate: Literary Technique, Concentric Structure, and Theology in Mark 2:1–3:6*. SBLDS 48. Atlanta: Scholars, 1980.

———. "Oral Methods of Structuring Narrative in Mark." In *Intersections: Post-Critical Studies in Preaching*, edited by Richard L. Eslinger, 23–41. Grand Rapids: Eerdmans, 2004.

Donahue, John R., and Daniel J. Harrington. *The Gospel of Mark*. SP 2. Collegeville, MN: Liturgical, 2002.

Dowd, Sharyn Echols. *Reading Mark: A Literary and Theological Commentary on the Second Gospel*. Macon, GA: Smith & Helwys, 2000.

———. *Prayer, Power, and the Problem of Suffering: Mark 11:22–25 in the Context of Markan Theology*. SBLDS 105. Atlanta: Scholars, 1988.

Driggers, Ira Brent. *Following God through Mark: Theological Tension in the Second Gospel*. Louisville: Westminster John Knox, 2007.

Drury, John. "Mark 1:1–15: An Interpretation." In *Alternative Approaches to New Testament Study*, edited by A. E. Harvey, 25–36. London: SPCK, 1985.

Duff, Paul Brooks. "The March of the Divine Warrior and the Advent of the Greco-Roman King: Mark's Account of Jesus' Entry into Jerusalem." *JBL* 111 (1992) 55–71.

Dunn, James D. G. "Jesus and Purity: An Ongoing Debate." *NTS* 48 (2002) 449–67.

Edwards, James R. "Markan Sandwiches: The Significance of Interpolations in Markan Narratives." *NovT* 31 (1989) 193–216.

Eslinger, Richard. *The Web of Preaching: New Options in Homiletical Method*. Nashville: Abingdon, 2002.

Evans, Craig A. "Mark's Incipit and the Priene Calendar Inscription: From Jewish Gospel to Greco-Roman Gospel." *Journal of Greco-Roman Christianity and Judaism* 1 (2000) 67–81.

———. *Mark 8:27–16:20*. WBC 34B. Nashville: T. Nelson, 2001.

Fackre, Gabriel. "Narrative Theology: An Overview." *Int* 37 (1983) 340–52.

Fay, Greg. "Introduction to Incomprehension: The Literary Structure of Mark 4:1–34." *CBQ* 51 (1989) 65–81.

Fleddermann, Harry. "The Discipleship Discourse (Mark 9:33–50)." *CBQ* 43 (1981) 57–75.

———. "The Flight of a Naked Young Man (Mark 14:51–52)." *CBQ* 41 (1979) 412–18.

Foerster, Werner, and Johannes Herrmann, "κλῆρος." In *TDNT* 3:774.

Fowler, Robert M. *Let the Reader Understand: Reader-Response Criticism and the Gospel of Mark*. Minneapolis: Fortress, 1991.

———. *Loaves and Fishes: The Function of the Feeding Stories in the Gospel of Mark*. SBLDS 54. Atlanta: Scholars, 1981.

France, R. T. *The Gospel of Mark: A Commentary on the Greek Text*. NIGTC. Grand Rapids: Eerdmans, 2002.

———. *Jesus and the Old Testament: His Application of Old Testament Passages to Himself and His Mission*. Grand Rapids: Baker, 1982.

Geddert, Timothy J. *Mark*. Believers Church Bible Commentary. Scottdale, PA: Herald, 2001.

———. *Watchwords: Mark 13 in Markan Eschatology*. JSNTSup 26. Sheffield: Sheffield Academic, 1989.

Gibson, Jeffrey B. "Jesus' Wilderness Temptation according to Mark." *JSNT* 53 (1994) 3–34.

Gray, Timothy C. *The Temple in the Gospel of Mark: A Study in Its Narrative Role*. WUNT 2/242. Tübingen: Mohr/Siebeck, 2008.

Greidanus, Sidney. *The Modern Preacher and the Ancient Text: Interpreting and Preaching Biblical Literature*. Grand Rapids: Eerdmans, 1988.

Guelich, Robert A. *Mark 1–8:26*. WBC 34A. Dallas: Word, 1989.

Gundry, Robert H. *Mark: A Commentary on His Apology for the Cross*. Grand Rapids: Eerdmans, 1993.

Gurtner, Daniel M. "The Rending of the Veil and Markan Christology: 'Unveiling' the ΥΙΟΣ ΘΕΟΥ' (Mark 15:38–39)." *BibInt* 15 (2008) 292–306.

Guttenberger, Gudrun. "Why Caesarea Philippi of All Sites? Some Reflections on the Political Background and Implications of Mark 8:27–30 for the Christology of Mark." In *Zwischen den Reichen: Neues Testament und Römische Herrschaft*, edited by Michael Labahn and Jürgen Zangenberg, 119–31. Tübingen: A. Francke, 2002.

Harrington, W. *Mark*. Wilmington, DE: M. Glazier, 1979.

Hatina, Thomas R. *In Search of a Context: The Function of Scripture in Mark's Narrative*. JSNTSup 232. Studies in Scripture in Early Judaism and Christianity 8. London: Sheffield Academic, 2002.

Healy, Mary. *The Gospel of Mark*. Grand Rapids: Baker, 2008.

Heil, John Paul. "Jesus with the Wild Animals in Mark 1:13." *CBQ* (2006) 63–78.

———. "Mark 14,1–52: Narrative Structure and Reader-Response." *Bib* 71 (1990) 305–32.

———. "The Narrative Strategy and Pragmatics of the Temple Theme in Mark." *CBQ* 59 (1997) 76–100.

———. "Reader-Response and the Narrative Context of the Parables about Growing Seed in Mark 4:1–34." *CBQ* 54 (1992) 271–86.

Hellerman, Joseph H. "Wealth and Sacrifice in Early Christianity: Revisiting Mark's Presentation of Jesus' Encounter with the Rich Young Ruler." *TrinJ*, n.s., 21 (2000) 143–64.

Henderson, Suzanne Watts. *Christology and Discipleship in the Gospel of Mark*. SNTSMS 135. Cambridge: Cambridge University Press, 2006.

———. "'Concerning the Loaves': Comprehending Incomprehension in Mark 6:45–52." *JSNT* 83 (2001) 3–26.

Hester, J. David "Dramatic Inconclusion: Irony and the Narrative Rhetoric of the Ending of Mark." *JSNT* 57 (1995) 61–86.

Hollenbach, B. "Lest They Should Turn and Be Forgiven." *BT* 34 (1983) 312–21.

Holmén, Tom. *Jesus and Jewish Covenant Thinking*. Leiden: Brill, 2001.

Holmes, Michael W. "To Be Continued . . . : The Many Endings of the Gospel of Mark." *BRev* 17.4 (2001) 12–23, 48–49.

Hooker, Morna D. *A Commentary on the Gospel according to St. Mark*. London: A. & C. Black, 1991.

———. "Mark's Parables of the Kingdom (Mark 4:1–34)." In *The Challenge of Jesus' Parables*, edited by Richard N. Longenecker, 79–101. Grand Rapids: Eerdmans, 2000.

———. *The Message of Mark*. London: Epworth, 1983.

———. *The Son of Man in Mark: A Study of the Background of the Term "Son of Man" and Its Use in St. Mark's Gospel*. Montreal: McGill University Press, 1967.

Iersel, Bas M. F. van. "Concentric Structures in Mark 1:14–3:35 (4:1) With Some Observations on Method." *BibInt* 3 (1995) 75–98.

———. "Locality, Structure, and Meaning in Mark." *LB* 53 (1983) 45–54.

———. *Mark: A Reader-Response Commentary*. Translated by W. H. Bisscheroux. London: T. & T. Clark, 1998.

———. *Reading Mark*. Translated by W. H. Bisscheroux. Collegeville, MN: Liturgical, 1988.

Instone-Brewer, David. *Divorce and Remarriage in the Bible: The Social and Literary Context*. Grand Rapids: Eerdmans, 2002.

———. "Jesus' Old Testament Basis for Monogamy." In *The Old Testament in the New Testament: Essays in Honour of J. L. North*, edited by Steve Moyise, 74–105. JSNTSup 189. Sheffield: Sheffield Academic, 2000.

Iverson, Kelly R. *Gentiles in the Gospel of Mark: 'Even the Dogs under the Table Eat the Children's Crumbs.'* LNTS 339. London: T. & T. Clark, 2007.

———. "A Further Word on Final ΓΑΡ (Mark 16:8)." *CBQ* 68 (2006) 79–94.

Jackson, Howard M. "The Death of Jesus in Mark and the Miracle from the Cross." *NTS* 33 (1987) 16–37.

———. "Why the Youth Shed His Cloak and Fled Naked: The Meaning and Purpose of Mark 14:51–52." *JBL* 116 (1997) 273–89.

Kaminouchi, Alberto de Mingo. *"But It Is Not So among You": Echoes of Power in Mark 10.32–45.* JSNTSup 249. Sheffield: Sheffield Academic, 2003.

Kee, Howard Clark. "The Transfiguration in Mark: Epiphany or Apocalyptic Vision?" In *Understanding the Sacred Text: Essays in Honor of Morton S. Enslin on the Hebrew Bible and Christian Beginnings*, edited by John Reumann, 137–52. Valley Forge, PA: Judson, 1972.

Kelsey, David H. "The Bible and Christian Theology." *JAAR* 48 (1980) 385–402.

Kinman, Brent. "Parousia, Jesus' 'A-Triumphal' Entry, and the Fate of Jerusalem (Luke 19:28–44)." *JBL* 118 (1999) 279–94.

Krause, Deborah. "Narrated Prophecy in Mark 11.12–21: The Divine Authorization of Judgment." In *The Gospels and the Scriptures of Israel*, edited by Craig A. Evans and W. Richard Stegner, 235–48. JSNTSup 104. Sheffield: Sheffield Academic, 1994.

Kuruvilla, Abraham. "The Naked Runaway and the Enrobed Reporter of Mark 14 and 16: What Is the Author *Doing* with What He Is *Saying*?" *JETS* 54 (2011): 527–45.

———. Review of *The Narcissism Epidemic: Living in the Age of Entitlement*, by Jean M. Twenge and W. Keith Campbell. *JETS* 52 (2010) 877–80.

———. "Pericopal Theology: The Intermediary between Text and Application." *TrinJ*, n.s., 31 (2010) 265–83.

———. *Text to Praxis: Hermeneutics and Homiletics in Dialogue.* LNTS 393. London: T. & T. Clark, 2009.

Kuthirakkattel, Scaria. *The Beginning of Jesus' Ministry according to Mark's Gospel (1,14—3,6): A Redaction Critical Study.* Rome: Editrice Pontificia Instituto Biblico, 1990.

Lampe, G. W. H. "St. Peter's Denial." *BJRL* 55 (1973) 346–68.

Lowry, Eugene L. *The Homiletical Plot: The Sermon as Narrative Art Form.* Rev. ed. Louisville: Westminster John Knox, 2001.

Lund, Nils Wilhelm. *Chiasmus in the New Testament: A Study in the Form and Function of Chiastic Structures.* Boston: Hendrickson, 1992.

Luther, Martin. "The Second Sermon, March 10, 1522, Monday after Invocavit." In *Luther's Works*, translated by John W. Doberstein, 51:75–78. Philadelphia: Muhlenberg, 1959.

Magness, J. Lee. *Sense and Absence: Structure and Suspension in the Ending of Mark's Gospel.* SBL Semeia Studies. Atlanta: Scholars, 1986.

Malbon, Elizabeth Struthers. "Narrative Criticism: How Does the Story Mean?" In *Mark & Method: New Approaches in Biblical Studies*, edited by Janice Capel Anderson and Stephen D. Moore, 29–57. 2nd ed. Minneapolis: Fortress, 2008.

Marcus, Joel. *Mark: A New Translation with Introduction and Commentary.* Anchor Yale Bible Commentary 27. New Haven, CT: Yale University Press, 2002.

———. *Mark 8–16.* Anchor Yale Bible 27A. New Haven, CT: Yale University Press, 2009.

———. *The Mystery of the Kingdom of God.* SBLDS 90. Atlanta: Scholars.

Marshall, Christopher D. *Faith as a Theme in Mark's Narrative.* SNTSMS 64. Cambridge: Cambridge University Press, 1989.

Merkel, Helmut. "Peter's Curse." In *The Trial of Jesus: Cambridge Studies in Honor of C. F. D. Moule*, edited by Ernst Bammel, 66–71. London: SCM, 1970.

Meyer, Marvin. "Taking Up the Cross and Following Jesus: Discipleship in the Gospel of Mark." *Concordia Theological Journal* 37 (2002) 230–38.

Miller, Susan. "The Woman Who Anoints Jesus (Mk 14.3–9): A Prophetic Sign of the New Creation." *Feminist Theology* 14 (2006) 221–36.

———. *Women in Mark's Gospel.* JSNTSup 259. London: T. & T. Clark, 2004.

Minear, Paul S. "The Needle's Eye: A Study in Form Criticism." *JBL* 61 (1942) 157–69.

Moloney, Francis J. "Mark 6:6b–30: Mission, the Baptist, and Failure." *CBQ* 63 (2001) 647–63.

Moule, C. F. D. "Mark 4:1–20 Yet Once More." In *Neotestamentica et Semitica: Studies in Honor of Matthew Black*, edited by E. E. Ellis and M. Wilcox, 95–113. Edinburgh: T. &T. Clark, 1969.

Moyise, Steve. "The Wilderness Quotation in Mark 1:2–3." In *Wilderness: Essays in Honour of Frances Young*, edited by R. S. Sugirtharajah, 78–87. London: T. & T. Clark, 2005.

Myers, Ched. *Binding the Strong Man: A Political Reading of Mark's Story of Jesus.* Maryknoll, NY: Orbis, 1988.

Nardoni, Enrique. "A Redactional Interpretation of Mark 9:1." *CBQ* 43 (1981) 365–84.

Neyrey, Jerome H. "The Idea of Purity in Mark's Gospel." *Semeia* 35 (1986) 91–128.

Nybroten, Arvid. "Possible Vestiges of the *Afikoman* in the Elevation of the *Panagia*." *GOTR* 43 (1998) 105–27.

Oden, Thomas C., and Christopher A. Hall, editors. *Mark*. Vol. 2 of *Ancient Christian Commentary on Scripture, New Testament*. Downers Grove, IL: InterVarsity, 1998.

O'Donnell, Matthew Brook. "Translation and the Exegetical Process: Using Mark 5.1–10, 'The Binding of the Strongman', as a Test Case." In *Translating the Bible: Problems and Prospects*, edited by Stanley E. Porter and Richard S. Hess, 162–88. JSNTSup 173. Sheffield: Sheffield Academic, 1999.

Osborne, Grant R. "Structure and Christology in Mark 1:21–45." In *Jesus of Nazareth: Lord and Christ: Essays on the Historical Jesus and New Testament Christology*, edited by Joel B. Green and Max Turner, 147–63. Grand Rapids: Eerdmans, 1994.

Painter, John. *Mark's Gospel: Worlds in Conflict*. London: Routledge, 1997.

Pannenberg, Wolfhart. *Systematic Theology*. Translated by Geoffrey W. Bromiley. 3 vols. Grand Rapids: Eerdmans, 1988–1998.

Parrott, Rod. "Conflict and Rhetoric in Mark 2:23–28." *Semeia* 64 (1993) 117–37.

Parunak, H. Van Dyke. "Oral Typesetting: Some Uses of Biblical Structure." *Bib* 62 (1981) 153–68.

Peterson, Eugene H. *Under the Unpredictable Plant: An Exploration in Vocational Holiness*. Grand Rapids: Eerdmans, 1992.

Placher, William C. *Mark*. Belief: A Theological Commentary on the Bible. Louisville: Westminster John Knox, 2010.

Plummer, Robert L. "Something Awry in the Temple? The Rending of the Temple Veil and Early Jewish Sources That Report Unusual Phenomena in the Temple around AD 30." *JETS* 48 (2005) 301–16.

Ratner, Sidney. "Presupposition and Objectivity in History." *Philosophy of Science* 7 (1940) 499–505.

Reid, Robert Stephen. *Preaching Mark*. St. Louis: Chalice, 1999.

Rhoads, David. "Jesus and the Syrophoenician Woman in Mark: A Narrative-Critical Study." *JAAR* 62 (1994) 343–76.

Rhoads, David, Joanna Dewey, and Donald Michie. *Mark as Story: An Introduction to the Narrative of a Gospel*. 2nd ed. Minneapolis: Fortress, 1999.

Robbins, Vernon K. "The Woman Who Touched Jesus' Garment: A Socio-Rhetorical Analysis of the Synoptic Accounts." In *New Boundaries in Old Territory: Form and Social Rhetoric in Mark*, by Vernon K. Robbins, edited by David B. Gowler, 185–200. Emory Studies in Early Christianity 3. New York: P. Lang, 1994.

Rudolph, David J. "Jesus and the Food Laws: A Reassessment of Mark 7:19b." *EvQ* 74 (2002) 291–311.

Russell, Bertrand. *Why I Am Not a Christian, and Other Essays on Religion and Related Subjects*. New York: Simon and Schuster, 1957.

Salyer, Gregory. "Rhetoric, Purity, and Play: Aspects of Mark 7:1–23." *Semeia* 64 (1993) 139–69.

Sandmel, Samuel. "Prolegomena to a Commentary on Mark." *JBR* 31 (1963) 294–300.

Schmidt, Thomas E. "Jesus' Triumphal March to Crucifixion: The Sacred Way as Roman Procession." *BRev* 13 (1997) 30–37.

———. "Mark 15.16–32: The Crucifixion Narrative and the Roman Triumphal Procession." *NTS* 41 (1995) 1–18.

Schweizer, Eduard. *The Good News according to Mark*. Translated by Donald H. Madvig. Atlanta: John Knox, 1970.

Schwöbel, Christoph. "The Preacher's Art: Preaching Theologically." In *Theology through Preaching: Sermons for Brentwood*, by Colin E. Gunton, 1–20. Edinburgh: T. & T. Clark, 2001.

Shepherd, Tom. *Markan Sandwich Stories: Narration, Definition, and Function*. Andrews University Seminary Doctoral Dissertation Series 18. Berrien Springs, MI.: Andrews University Press, 1993.

Sider, Ronald J. *Rich Christians in an Age of Hunger: Moving from Affluence to Generosity*. 5th ed. Nashville: T. Nelson, 2005.

Smith, Geoffrey. "A Closer Look at the Widow's Offering: Mark 12:41–44." *JETS* 40 (1997) 27–36.

Snodgrass, Klyne. "A Hermeneutics of Hearing Informed by the Parables with Special Reference to Mark 4." *BBR* 14 (2004) 59–79.

Spencer, Aída Besançon. "The Denial of the Good News and the Ending of Mark." *BBR* 17 (2007) 269–83.

Stanton, Graham N. "The Fourfold Gospel." *NTS* 43 (1997) 317–46.

Stegner, William Richard. "Jesus' Walking on the Water: Mark 6.45–52." In *The Gospels and the Scriptures of Israel*, edited by Craig A. Evans and William Richard Stegner, 212–34. JSNTSup 104. Sheffield: Sheffield Academic, 1994.

Stein, Robert H. "The Ending of Mark." *BBR* 18 (2008) 79–98.

———. *Mark*. BECNT. Grand Rapids: Baker, 2008.

Sternberg, Meir. *The Poetics of Biblical Narrative: Ideological Literature and the Drama of Reading*. Bloomington, IN: Indiana University Press, 1987.

Stock, Augustine. "Chiastic Awareness and Education in Antiquity." *BTB* 14 (1984) 23–27.

———. *The Method and Message of Mark*. Wilmington, DE: M. Glazier, 1989.

Telford, William R. *The Barren Temple and the Withered Tree*. JSNTSup 1. Sheffield: JSOT Press, 1980.

Todorov, Tzvetan. *The Poetics of Prose*, translated by Richard Howard. Ithaca, NY: Cornell University, 1977.

Tolbert, Mary Ann. "How the Gospel of Mark Builds Character." *Int* 47 (1993) 347–57.

———. *Sowing the Gospel: Mark's World in Literary-Historical Perspective*. Minneapolis: Fortress, 1989.

Trick, Bradley R. "Death, Covenants, and the Proof of the Resurrection in Mark 12:18–27." *NovT* 49 (2007) 232–65.

Twenge, Jean M., and W. Keith Campbell. *The Narcissism Epidemic: Living in the Age of Entitlement*. New York: Free Press, 2009.

Viviano, Benedict T. "The High Priest's Servant's Ear: Mark 14:47." *RB* 96 (1989) 71–80.

Von Wahlde, Urban C. "Mark 9:33–50: Discipleship: The Authority That Serves." *BZ* 29 (1985) 49–67.

Wallace, Daniel B. *Greek Grammar beyond the Basics*. Grand Rapids: Zondervan, 1996.

———. "Mark 16:8 as the Conclusion to the Second Gospel." In *Perspectives on the Ending of Mark: 4 Views*, by David Alan Black, Darrell Bock, Keith Elliott, Maurice Robinson, and Daniel B. Wallace, 1–39. Nashville: Broadman and Holman, 2008.

Watson, Francis B. *Text, Church, and World: Biblical Interpretation in Theological Perspective*. Grand Rapids: Eerdmans, 1994.

Weaver, Richard M. *Language Is Sermonic: Richard M. Weaver on the Nature of Rhetoric*, edited by Richard L. Johannesen, Rennard Strickland, and Ralph T. Eubanks. Baton Rouge: Louisiana State University Press, 1970.

Weeden, Theodore J. *Mark—Traditions in Conflict*. Philadelphia: Fortress, 1971.

Welch, John W. *Chiasmus in Antiquity: Structures, Analyses, Exegesis*. Provo, UT: Research Press, 1999.

Willard, Dallas. *The Spirit of the Disciplines: Understanding How God Changes Lives*. San Francisco: Harper, 1988.

Williams, J. F. *Other Followers of Jesus: Minor Characters as Major Figures in Mark's Gospel*. JSNTSup 102. Sheffield: JSOT Press, 1994.

Winn, Adam. *The Purpose of Mark's Gospel: An Early Christian Response to Roman Imperial Propaganda*. WUNT 2/245. Tübingen: Mohr/Siebeck, 2008.

Witherington, Ben. *The Gospel of Mark: A Socio-Rhetorical Commentary*. Grand Rapids: Eerdmans, 2001.

Wright, John. "Spirit and Wilderness: The Interplay of Two Motifs within the Hebrew Bible as a Background to Mark 1:2–13." In *Perspectives on Language and Text: Essays and Poems in Honor of Francis I. Andersen's Sixtieth Birthday July 28, 1985*, edited by Edgar W. Conrad and Edward G. Newing, 268–98. Winona Lake, IN: Eisenbrauns, 1987.

INDEX OF ANCIENT SOURCES

DEAD SEA SCROLLS

Index of Ancient Sources

INDEX OF MODERN AUTHORS

INDEX OF SCRIPTURE

⌇

NEW TESTAMENT

Made in the USA
Columbia, SC
14 January 2021